FIELDS OF CONFLICT
_____

Also by Douglas Scott

*They Died With Custer:
Soldiers' Bones from the Battle of the Little Bighorn*

Also by Lawrence Babits

A Devil of a Whipping: The Battle of Cowpens

Also by Charles Haecker

*On the Prairie of Palo Alto: Historical Archaeology
of the U.S.–Mexican War Battlefield*

Fields of Conflict

Battlefield Archaeology from the Roman Empire to the Korean War

Edited by **DOUGLAS SCOTT, LAWRENCE BABITS, AND CHARLES HAECKER**

Potomac Books, Inc.
WASHINGTON, D.C.

Copyright © 2009 by Douglas Scott, Lawrence Babits, and Charles Haecker.

This paperback edition published in the United States by Potomac Books, Inc.

Fields of Conflict: Battlefield Archaeology from the Roman Empire to the Korean War, 2 volumes, edited by Douglas Scott, Lawrence Babits, and Charles Haecker, was originally published in hardcover by Praeger Publishers, http://www.greenwood.com/praeger, an imprint of Greenwood Publishing Group, Inc., Westport, CT. Copyright © 2007 by Douglas Scott, Lawrence Babits, and Charles Haecker. This paperback edition by arrangement with Greenwood Publishing Group, Inc. All rights reserved.

No part of this book may be reproduced or transmitted in any form or by any means electronic or mechanical, including photocopying, reprinting, or on any information storage or retrieval system, without permission in writing from Greenwood Publishing Group, Inc.

Library of Congress Cataloging-in-Publication Data
Fields of conflict : battlefield archaeology from the Roman Empire to the
    Korean War / edited by Douglas Scott, Lawrence Babits, and Charles
    Haecker. — 1st ed.
      p. cm.
    Originally published in hardcover in 2 v. by Praeger Publishers, 2007.
    Includes bibliographical references and index.
    ISBN 978-1-59797-276-5 (pbk. : acid-free paper)
    1. Battlefields—History. 2. Excavations (Archaeology) 3. Military history.
4. Archaeology and history. I. Scott, Douglas D. II. Babits, Lawrence Edward.
III. Haecker, Charles M.
      D25.5.F53 2008
      930.1—dc22
                                                            2008049466

Printed in the United States of America on acid-free paper that meets the American National Standards Institute Z39-48 Standard.

Potomac Books, Inc.
22841 Quicksilver Drive
Dulles, Virginia 20166

First Edition

10 9 8 7 6 5 4 3 2 1

CONTENTS

Acknowledgments ix

Introduction 1

How Do You Know It's a Battlefield? 5
G. Michael Pratt

Mustering Landscapes: What Historic Battlefields
Share in Common 39
John and Patricia Carman

Characteristics of Ancient Battlefields: Battle of Varus (9 AD) 50
Achim Rost

Finding Battery Positions at Wilson's Creek, Missouri 58
Carl G. Carlson-Drexler

Battlefield Viewsheds, or What the General Saw: Lookout Mountain
Battlefield, Chattanooga, Tennessee 75
Elsa Heckman

What the Musket Ball Can Tell: Monmouth Battlefield State Park,
New Jersey 84
Daniel M. Sivilich

"Listen to the Minié Balls": Identifying Firearms in Battlefield
Archaeology 102
Douglas Scott and Lucien Haag

Total Roman Defeat at the Battle of Varus (9 AD) 121
Susanne Wilbers-Rost

English Battlefields 991–1685: A Review of Problems
and Potentials 133
Glenn Foard

Arrows Point to Mass Graves: Finding the Dead from the
Battle of Towton, 1461 AD 160
Tim Sutherland and Simon Richardson

Indian Resistance in New Spain: The 1541 AD Battlefield of
Peñol de Nochistlán, an Exemplar of Indigenous Resistance 174
*Charles Haecker, Elizabeth A. Oster, Angélica Medrano Enríquez,
and Michael L. Elliott*

Tatars, Cossacks, and the Polish Army: The Battle of Zboriv 193
Adrian Mandzy

Camden: Salvaging Data from a Heavily Collected Battlefield 208
James B. Legg and Steven D. Smith

Apache Victory against the U.S. Dragoons, the Battle of
Cieneguilla, New Mexico 235
David M. Johnson

The Confederate Cantonment at Evansport, Virginia 255
Joseph Balicki

Fort Davidson Battlefield, Missouri 278
Steve Dasovich and Walter Busch

The Confederate Forward Line, Battle of Nashville, Tennessee 294
Carl Kuttruff

Seven Eventful Days in Paraguay: Reconnoitering the
Archaeology of the War of the Triple Alliance 314
Tony Pollard

Buffalo Soldiers versus the Apache: The Battle in Hembrillo Basin, New Mexico *Karl W. Laumbach*	336
Scars of The Great War (Western Flanders, Belgium) *Mathieu de Meyer and Pedro Pype*	359
Pointe-du-Hoc Battlefield, Normandy, France *Richard Burt, James Bradford, Bruce Dickson, Mark E. Everett, Robert Warden, and David Woodcock*	383
"For You the War Is Over": Finding the Great Escape Tunnel at Stalag Luft III *Peter Doyle, Lawrence Babits, and Jamie Pringle*	398
Hill 209: The Last Stand of Operation Manchu, Korea *Jay Silverstein, John Byrd, and Lyle Otineru*	417
Conclusions: Toward a Unified View of the Archaeology of Fields of Conflict	429
Index	439
About the Contributors	443

Acknowledgments

THESE VOLUMES grew out of a series of papers presented at the third Fields of Conflict conference held in conjunction with the American Battlefield Protection Conference in April 2004 at Nashville, Tennessee. The ideas expressed in these volumes are an outgrowth of over 20 years of serious archaeological study of battlefield and conflict sites around the world. The Nashville conference brought many fresh ideas of how to view, study, and interpret archaeological evidence of conflict to the forefront. The editors, who also served as conference organizers, and the presenters all agreed that the works had a wider appeal than to just the researchers who were present. Thus the idea for these volumes was hatched.

We gratefully acknowledge Paul Hawke of the American Battlefield Protection Program, National Park Service, for allowing the Fields of Conflict conference to be held in conjunction with the ABPP conference. We owe a debt of gratitude to Paul, Kristen Stevens, and the ABPP staff for their very generous support, and for making the conference such a wonderful success and memorable event for all.

Elizabeth Demers of Praeger has been our friend and supporter from the inception of this project. We owe her a great deal. Elizabeth and the Praeger staff made this work happen, and to them a sincere thank you.

Introduction

> The history of technology is part and parcel of social history in general. The same is equally true of military history, far too long regarded as a simple matter of tactics and technical differentials. Military history too can only be understood against the wider social background. For as soon as one begins to discuss war and military organization without due regard to the whole social process one is in danger of coming to regard it as a constant, an inevitable feature of international behavior. In other words, if one is unable to regard war as a function of particular forms of social and political organization and particular stages of historical development, one will not be able to conceive of even the possibility of a world without war.[1]

MILITARY SITES HAVE long held the interest of archaeologists, and in the last two and a half decades there has been a growing interest in the archaeological investigation of battlefields or, as Freeman and Pollard[2] aptly named them, fields of conflict. Today there are a plethora of archaeological reports in the literature detailing the results of investigations at military forts, camps, prisons, and battlefields. These investigations have often been conducted as ancillary studies to the preservation, restoration, reconstruction, or interpretation of some military-related site. Many of the investigations have had little or no theoretical orientation or explanatory goal above that set by an architect or interpreter. This statement is not made as a negative criticism of the many fine reports that have resulted; it is a statement of fact made with the knowledge that, until recently, the archaeological study of military sites in general has had a limited research orientation.

That has begun to change, and dramatically so, over the last several years. The archaeology of conflict sites, battlefields, is still in its infancy, although growing at an exponential rate. The first Fields of Conflict conference that addressed international archaeological studies of battlefields was held in Glasgow, Scotland, in 2000, the second in Aland, Sweden, in 2002, and the third was held in association with the American Battlefield Protection

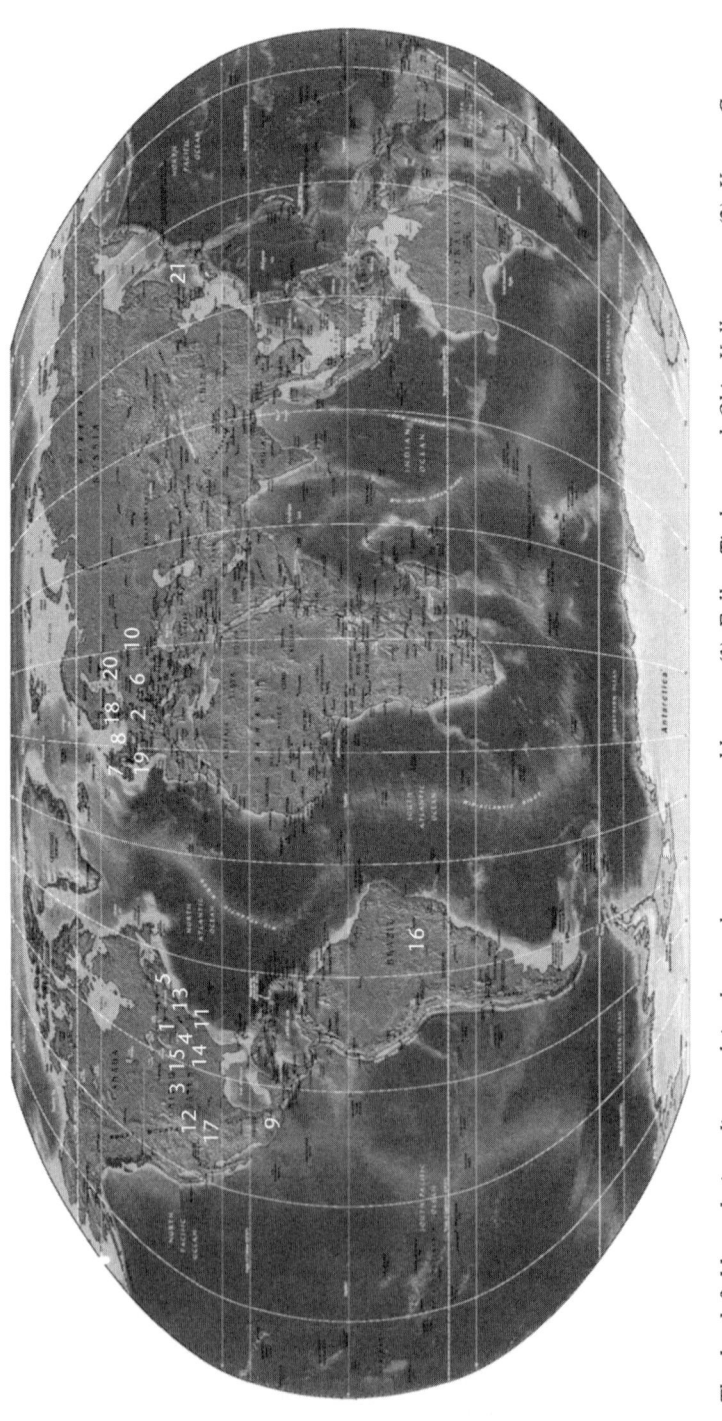

The battlefields and sites discussed in these volumes, on a world map: (1) Fallen Timbers and Ohio Valley area, (2) Varus, Germany, (3) Wilson's Creek, Missouri, (4) Lookout Mountain, Tennessee, (5) Monmouth, New Jersey, (6) Varus, Germany, (7) Edgehill, Nasbey, and English sites, (8) Towton, England, (9) Peñol de Nochistlán, Mexico, (10) Zboriv, Urkraine, (11) Camden, South Carolina, (12) Cieneguilla, New Mexico, (13) Evansport, Virginia, (14) Fort Davidson, Missouri, (15) Nashville, Tennessee, (16) Triple Alliance War, Paraguay, (17) Hembrillo Basin, New Mexico, (18) Iper, Belgium, (19) Pointe-du-Hoc, France, (20) Stalag Luft III, Poland, (21) Operation Manchu, South Korea.

conference in Nashville, Tennessee, in 2004. The continued interest in and growth of the archaeological study of battlefields are exemplified in this volume.

The works presented here build on endeavors of the two previous battlefield archaeological conferences as well as a variety of growing research interest in the area of conflict archaeology. We have chosen to organize these volumes in an essentially chronological fashion with literally 2,000 years of warfare from around the globe being covered in the various chapters. The initial chapters present the latest methods, techniques, and theoretical implications for the archaeological study of battlefields and other fields of conflict. These first chapters are rich in diversity of both time and space, ranging from Roman Germany in the first century AD to the late nineteenth century United States. They also range from presenting arguments of viewing battlefields as part of landscapes to using the powerful analytical capabilities of geographic information systems (GIS) to find new means to look at battlefields from a terrain analysis point of view, as well as the analytical potential of musket balls and firearms residue.

The succeeding chapters present contributions that range again from the first century, in Roman Germany, to the Korean conflict, and nearly everything in between in both time and space. While the chapters on the archaeological studies of battlefields in England, Europe, and the United States predominate, other chapters also present results of work in Mexico, South America, and the Ukraine. What we believe is impressive among the contributions in this volume is not the time depth nor even the global nature of archaeological studies of battlefields, but the fact that the studies are being done using variations of the same basic methods and theoretical models. What is also exciting in reading the various chapters is how each author has adapted, modified, and advanced both the basic methods and the theoretical underpinnings to meet the goals of a specific study. The methodological and theoretical advances presented in these chapters truly reflect the growth of battlefield archaeology in the last few years, and the wide-ranging interest in the definition of archaeological signatures of conflict and warfare.

NOTES

1. Ellis 1986.
2. Phil Freeman and Tony Pollard published the results of the first battlefield archaeology conference in 2001. They coined the term "fields of conflict" as part of the title for the conference and the resulting publication. The title has caught on and has been used as part of the title for each of the two succeeding conferences.

REFERENCES CITED

Ellis, John. 1986. *The Social History of the Machine Gun.* John Hopkins University Press, Baltimore (reprint of 1975 edition).

Freeman, P. W. M., and A. Pollard. 2001. *Fields of Conflict: Progress and Prospect in Battlefield Archaeology.* BAR International Series, 958.

How Do You Know It's a Battlefield?

G. Michael Pratt

BETWEEN 1995 AND 2002 the Center for Historic and Military Archaeology at Heidelberg College conducted multifaceted remote sensing, artifact recovery, and mapping projects at three eighteenth- and nineteenth-century battlefield sites in the Ohio Valley–Great Lakes region. The survey areas included portions of the sites of the Battle of Fallen Timbers (1794), a pivotal battle for control of the Old Northwest Territory; the Battle for Mackinac Island (1814), an unsuccessful U.S. attempt to recover the island after its loss to the British in 1812; and the Battle of Buffington Island (1863), the U.S. defeat of Confederate General John Hunt Morgan's attempt to escape across the Ohio River following his heretofore successful raid through Ohio and Indiana. All three battles were of short duration (less than one day), involved movement across the battlefield, and produced no significant earthworks or other modifications of the natural terrain. At the time of survey, all three sites were relatively undisturbed except for agricultural activities. Finally, all three were subjected to the same survey methods utilizing, for the most part, the same equipment and personnel. The survey method, presented here, provides an effective and efficient manner to assess the condition, content, and extent of a battlefield.

Archaeological surveys of all three sites produced lead shot as the most numerous battlefield artifact type. At the Buffington Island battlefield, recognizable carbine, pistol, and "Minié ball" shot could be identified by shape and size[1]; while spherical lead shot was recovered from all three sites. The recovery, identification, and mapping of shot types representing weaponry utilized by the combatants provided information that sometimes reinforced existing interpretations and sometimes forced a reinterpretation of the course of battle at each site. At each site the results of the survey provided previously unknown details, and at all sites the survey provided ground truth information for the location of battlefield events.

DETECTING THE BATTLEFIELD

Beginning in 1995, in conjunction with a developing battlefield survey program at Heidelberg College's Archaeological Survey (now Center for Historic and Military Archaeology), Richard Green of Historic Archaeological Research (HAR), West Lafayette, Indiana, developed metal detection methods for efficient and effective survey and mapping of battlefields. Under the direction of G. Michael Pratt, Heidelberg and HAR applied a combination of metal detection techniques and utilized Global Positioning System (GPS) mapping to identify the previously unrecognized site of the Battle of Fallen Timbers. The success of this project and national interest generated by efforts to preserve the battlefield provided CHMA and HAR access to several other eighteenth- and nineteenth-century battlefield sites. Over the next five years, Green refined his method and added techniques in an effort to perform a more balanced and intensive approach to remote and electronic investigations of historical battlefield sites. By 2000, CHMA and HAR had developed the specific approach described in this chapter. The sites discussed here were subjected to most or all of the following survey methods, usually in an ordered approach designed to recover an increasingly detailed dataset. All were subjected to metal detection and GPS mapping aspects.

ELECTROMAGNETIC CONDUCTIVITY SURVEY

Electromagnetic conductivity survey has long been utilized on both prehistorical and historical archaeological sites and has the capability to detect subsurface features as well as other types of conductive anomalies. On battlefield sites, an EM 38 ground conductivity meter and DL 600 Polycorder manufactured by Geonics, LTD, Mississauga, Ontario, Canada, are utilized to record conductivity measurements in the predetermined sample units where graves, trenches, or other features may occur. The EM 38 is configured to measure in the vertical dipole orientation and programmed to record data automatically in a 0.5-m resolution survey strategy. In this mode of operation, the technician scans the instrument over the surface along parallel survey lines at a 0.5-m/s pace. Survey lines are positioned at 0.5-m intervals. This technique results in an average of one data point per 0.5 m over the entire survey grid. The operator triggers fiduciary markers at 10-m intervals, permitting data coordinate adjustment between start and stop stations along each transect. The automatic mode is preferable for expeditious survey at the expense of coordinate resolution. Accuracy of the EM 38 thus configured is approximately +/− 0.5 m.

Variations in the measurements may be caused by differences in soil composition, buried features, disturbed areas, and by metal artifacts. These variations appear as anomalies in the data and may be graphically depicted following post-processing of the database. Recorded data is subsequently interpolated with contouring software and converted to color gradient image maps permitting investigators to filter, enhance, and analyze subsurface anomalies.

Following field survey, recorded data is downloaded from the DL 600 Polycorder and Geonics, LTD proprietary DAT38RT software is used to adjust survey line data and export the database to a contouring software package. Golden Software's Surfer 8 is utilized by HAR to create color image maps for analysis of the conductivity survey data.

Highly conductive metallic objects within the survey area tend to skew a dataset by introducing points well outside the normal range of ambient soil conditions. The signature of a metallic surface feature is observed to increase proportionally as it is approached. Buried metal anomalies may appear as both a large positive transition and a sharp negative spike. The buried metal object occurs as an increase in amplitude until the instrument passes directly over the object. At this point the EM 38 can reach a saturation level and a large negative transition takes place, followed by the high conductive reading tapering off as the operator moves out of the vicinity. In order to resolve smaller variations in the data during software manipulation, it is necessary to filter wide swings caused by metal features. The entities causing the sharp increase or decrease are not eliminated, but rather the data is filtered to permit upper and lower limits in a range essential for viewing anomalies of lesser magnitude. By significantly reducing the biasing factors, it may be possible to enhance minute variations inherent to disturbances with no associated metal artifacts.

METAL DETECTION SURVEY

Metal detection surveys have been performed successfully using a wide variety of instruments available on the open market.[2] Richard Green of Historic Archaeological Research (HAR) has refined detection methodology in an effort to develop a standardized, intensive approach which permits comparisons among diverse areas of a battlefield or between battlefields. The HAR approach, described below, was employed in the CHMA surveys of all three battlefield sites.

Three distinct types of metal detecting instruments exhibiting complementary performance characteristics are utilized both to optimize coverage and to reduce procedural variables. These instruments are generically specified as VLF motion, full range, discriminating detectors and are electronically designed with a critically fast response to accepted targets particularly when rejected items are in close proximity. The three kinds of metal detector will be referred to as Types I, II, and III for the purpose of this discussion.

The Type I instrument has an operating frequency at the low end of the VLF band typically in the 5–6 kHz range. The Type I detector has an affinity for ferrous items and is extremely sensitive to artifacts manufactured with materials found on the higher end of the conductivity spectrum (i.e., brass, copper, and silver.) The Type II detector operates at a somewhat higher frequency, generally 10–12 kHz. The high frequency detector is intrinsically sensitive to metal targets in the low to mid conductivity range such as lead, nickel, gold, and small irregularly shaped artifacts. The Type II detector is less sensitive to small iron items, making this instrument a better choice for working in concentrations of modern ferrous debris (i.e., fence wire, nails, etc.). The Type III detector operates on a frequency which overlaps that of both Type I and II.

By utilizing instruments that, when operated in tandem, offer high performance across the entire metal conductivity spectrum, a strategy for comprehensive metal artifact recovery is created. By virtue of the distinctly different operating frequency of each device, Type I and II detectors may be operated in relatively close proximity without cross-talk or spurious interference, while the Type III detector may be utilized in tandem with either of the other types. Thus, fieldwork is designed specifically to take advantage of metal detection attributes while minimizing inherent flaws of both the Type I and II instruments.

Sweep Metal Detection Survey

In the first stage of metal detection survey, the "sweep" method is conducted by alternating Type I and Type II or III metal detection technicians at 5-m intervals. Reconnaissance is carried out over transects established within the overall survey area. The sweep survey is carried out in the attempt to locate a battlefield and/or delineate areas of battlefield activity that merit further, intensive survey. After completion of this stage of the survey, decisions are made to determine the location and extent of additional, intensive metal detection operations.

2-2-90 Metal Detection Survey

Green designed this method of metal detection survey for recovery of a standardized sample of artifacts within a survey area. The method utilizes the propensities of both the detection instruments and the operators, and is referred to as the 2-2-90 method.[3] A grid of 15 × 15 m survey squares is established over the areas producing concentrations of artifacts in the sweep survey. Each grid unit is surveyed methodically in overlapping transects, resulting in 100 percent coverage. Following completion of a grid square, a second technician with an opposite Type I/II/III detector re-surveys the unit at a 90-degree axis with respect to the first operator's sweep. This methodology results in coverage by two operators using two different detectors and at a 90-degree angle of approach (2-2-90). Coverage is improved exponentially and typically either results in a drastic increase of collected artifacts or more thoroughly substantiates the lack of metal remains within a given survey unit.

In both types of survey, all metal artifacts detected are excavated and identified. Artifacts believed to be associated with the battlefield or other significant components are assigned a field specimen number and collected for cataloging and laboratory analysis. Fiberglass shaft flags bearing the field specimen number mark the artifact locations for subsequent GPS survey. All artifacts that are not to be identified in the field are treated the same as those slated for collection, permitting further analysis at a later date. Artifacts not attributed to the battlefield, but of potential significance to the other components are collected and recorded by the survey square. Metal objects deemed of no archaeological significance (such as aluminum foil, aluminum pull tabs, modern cartridges) are counted, recorded, and discarded off site.

GPS Survey and GIS Map Preparation

In all the CHMA battlefield surveys Historic Archaeological Research was retained for GPS/GIS work. HAR utilizes a state-of-the art Trimble Pathfinder Pro XRS GPS System with differential correction (DGPS) service provided by Omnistar, Inc. The Pro XRS is capable of real-time submeter horizontal coordinate accuracy in this configuration. In instances where Omnistar DGPS service is interrupted, raw pseudo-range data is collected for correction by means of post-processing following completion of field data collection. All field specimen locations are surveyed by GPS to meet or exceed +/− 1-m coordinate accuracy. Coordinate data is supplied to CHMA in the UTM system NAD 1927. Project delineation maps and maps indicating the distribution of artifact types are constructed using both CAD and ArcView GIS software. The post-analysis data from the CHMA laboratory and the GPS data files are exported to ArcView and plotted on the georeferenced USGS 7.5-minute quadrangle. HAR also prepares graphic presentation maps for illustrations and provides all geographic software materials for each project.

CASE STUDY 1: THE BATTLE OF FALLEN TIMBERS

On August 20, 1794, Major General Anthony Wayne led his Legion of the United States and two brigades of mounted Kentucky militia against a confederation of Native American tribes consisting of the Miami, Shawnee, Delaware, Ottawa, Wyandot, Mingo, Ojibwa, and Pottawatomie. The Legion approached the battlefield in five parallel columns, each spaced approximately 200 yards apart. Behind the Legion rode some 1,500 Kentucky militia. The battle area was characterized by a mature, open forest. To Wayne's right lay the steep valley of the Maumee River; to his left the forest became increasingly choked with underbrush.[4]

A screen of 150 mounted Kentucky volunteers rode some 400 yards ahead of two companies of regulars, who formed the front guard. These companies marched about 200 yards in front of the main columns. After advancing about five miles the mounted volunteers stumbled into the center of an ambuscade line containing as many as 1,100 Indian warriors and a company of Canadian Queen's Rangers. As gunfire erupted from the ambush, the militia screen collapsed and fled around the front guard of regulars. The front guard attempted to retreat while returning fire, but eventually was overwhelmed and fled the field. A large force of warriors, intent on assaulting the main columns, closely pursued the retreating soldiers of the front guard. A hastily formed skirmish line of light infantry and rifle companies forced the attacking warriors to seek shelter in an area of tornado-felled timber and stemmed the momentum of the initial Indian attack. A sustained firefight developed along this skirmish line and the Legionnaires were slowly forced back some 80 yards under the weight of superior fire.[5]

During this skirmish, the remainder of the Legion deployed from its columns into a battle line. The maneuver required each company to undouble its files, and advance obliquely to the left, forming on the right of the preceding company. On the right wing, the 1st and 3rd Sub Legions formed a single line, while on the left, the 4th Sub Legion formed on the battle line with the 2nd Sub Legion formed as a reserve. During the 30 minutes or so that it took the Legion to form, only the light infantry and artillery companies in the center column joined the battle.[6]

As the firefight spread along the length of the U.S. line, the Legion dragoons were ordered to ride to the river and flank the Indian line. Instead, Capt. Robert MisCampbell led his dragoons from behind the U.S. right wing and charged into the fallen timbers. MisCampbell was killed almost immediately and the cavalry charge quickly faltered when the troopers encountered heavy fire from concealed warriors. On the left side of the line the reserve (2nd Sub Legion) was ordered forward to extend the line and protect the left flank. Before this move was completed the entire Legion began a charge.[7]

The charge was little contested except on the left of the U.S. line where a party of Wyandot and Queen's Rangers attempted to fight a delaying action. The Wyandot and their allies suffered heavy losses before being driven from the field. As the charge developed the Kentucky militia was ordered forward to extend the U.S. flank further to the left; however, thick woods slowed their progress and prevented a major extension of the U.S. front. Nevertheless, hundreds of mounted men did move forward on the left flank of the Legion's line and participated in driving the warriors from the field.

Wayne's charge carried the army one to two miles downstream and was halted when the resistance dissipated and the charge became disorganized. The Legion was brought to a halt, then reformed its line, and remained in a defensive posture for several hours. No Indian counterattack developed. After selection of a campsite, the army moved to the high ground overlooking the foot of the rapids and within sight of Fort Miamis and its garrison, bringing the Battle of Fallen Timbers to an end.[8]

Two U.S. officers killed in the engagement were buried immediately after the battle. Wounded continued to straggle into Wayne's camp for two days and then a burial party found and interred 16 dead. The remainder of the approximately 50 battlefield dead were left unburied, a fact reported by both U.S. and British sources.[9]

A topographic feature mentioned in accounts of the battle and depicted on a contemporary map was a "steep ravine" behind the right wing of the Legion's position.[10] Only a single ravine system (some 600 m downstream from the Fallen Timbers National Historic Landmark property) matched the primary source descriptions. Contemporary accounts also place the battle in the forested and ravine dissected uplands, rather than in the prairies of the Maumee floodplain, where the battle was said to have occurred. Information from more than 20 contemporary accounts was developed into a detailed account of the battle which predicted a new location for the actual battlefield, based on the location of the ravine described above.[11]

Unfortunately, the proposed location was one of the most desirable parcels of undeveloped, agricultural land in the Toledo metropolitan area. After some discussion with the owner (City of Toledo) and the municipality in which the site lay (City of Maumee), an archaeological survey was conducted in 1995. The survey convincingly demonstrated the battle occurred in the predicted area and documented the location of several battlefield events as well as several battlefield casualties. Subsequent surveys were carried out on adjacent private lands in 1996 and 1997.[12] By 2000 the battlefield site had been designated as part of the new Fallen Timbers Battlefield and Fort Miamis National Historic Site, and in 2001 an additional survey was carried out in anticipation of an NPS General Management Plan for development of the NHS as an affiliated NPS unit.[13]

Fallen Timbers Archaeological Survey

The goal of the 1995 Fallen Timbers Archaeology Project was to assess the likelihood, based on contemporary accounts,[14] that the specific project area contained archaeological remains of the Battle of Fallen Timbers. Therefore, a metal detection reconnaissance survey designed to locate and map battlefield artifacts was carried out on a 20 percent sample that consisted of three 50-m-wide corridors spaced at intervals along the longest axis of the 160-acre project area. Corridors were oriented perpendicular to the suspected battle lines and divided into 25 × 25 m survey units.

The 1995 volunteer survey crew was assembled using a core of experienced metal detector operators, experienced members of the Toledo Area Aboriginal Research Society, an amateur archaeology group, and interested members of the general public. The project was directed by G. Michael Pratt, Heidelberg College, and volunteer detector operators were supervised by Richard Green and Larry Hamilton of HAR. Survey and mapping were carried out over

15 consecutive (12-hr) days and involved over 200 volunteers. Within transects, the 25 × 25 m units were surveyed by the 2-2-90 method. A sweep survey was developed to assess the area between high-density areas of two transects. The figure indicates artifact locations within the three transects and in the sweep area east of the forest. The figure also depicts the approximate locations of the original ambush line (right), the U.S. battle formation (left), and the skirmish that occurred in-between these positions.

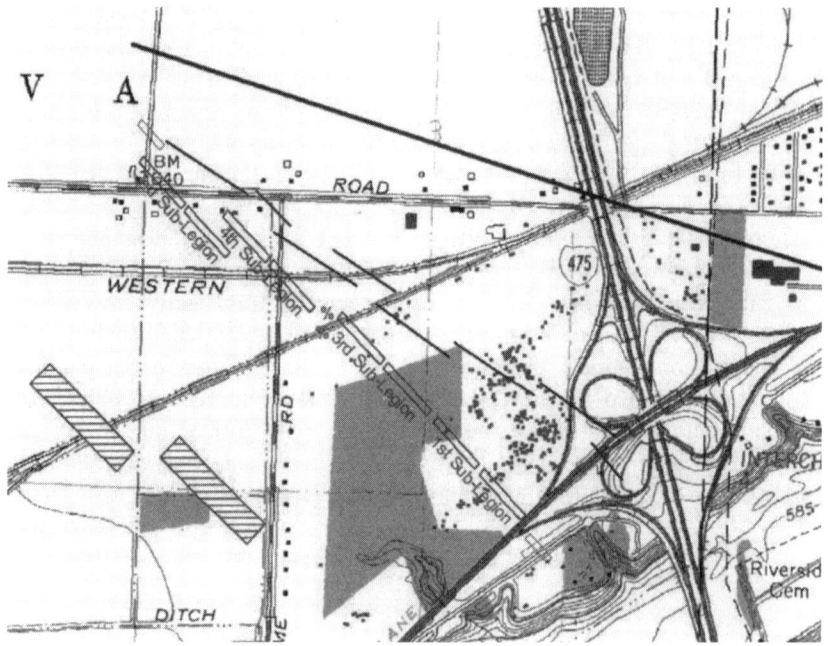

The 1995 and 1997 Fallen Timbers surveys: Results and interpretation. (Heidelberg College)

The 1995 Fallen Timbers Archaeological Project revealed the location of part of the battlefield site. Within the project limits, the area exhibiting the greatest artifact density appears as a 200-m by at least 350-m zone oriented parallel to and 300 m east of the ravine mentioned in a contemporary account. This area contained over 80 percent of the spent musket shot, nearly two-thirds of the spent rifle balls, and all of the buttons recovered from the site.[15] It appears to represent part of the skirmish in the fallen timbers, probably that in front of the 3rd Sub Legion's position. The buttons tend to occur in discrete clusters that often include both coat and vest size insignia buttons and plain buttons. These are interpreted as the remains of battlefield casualties who were left on the field unburied or interred in shallow graves subsequently disturbed by farming.

The 1995 survey successfully located the Fallen Timbers battlefield site, and provided information sufficient for designation of the property as a National Historic Site and an affiliate of the National Park System. As part of this effort, a 1998 ABPP grant to the Fallen Timbers Battlefield Preservation Commission supported the development of a locally produced videotape, *The Battle of Fallen Timbers—The Battle for Fallen Timbers*.

The 1995 survey was not adequate as a resource for the General Management Planning Process mandated by NPS for park planning purposes.[16] (1) The 1995 project addressed an area smaller than the present NHS property and therefore did not consider the northern area of the proposed park. (2) The survey focused on areas most likely to contain archaeological remains of the battlefield and did not attempt to assess the actual distribution of battlefield remains throughout the property. (3) No consideration was given to public use or interpretation of the site, so the potential impacts of such use were not considered. (4) Summer vegetation in the forest area precluded efficient survey, leaving this area under-represented in the sample. (5) Since no subsurface testing was carried out in the 1995 survey, the potential for disturbed or intact burials was not assessed, nor did the survey address the property's potential to contain earlier (e.g., prehistoric) or later (e.g., Canal-era) archaeological/historical components.[17]

The 2001 survey was a four-stage field survey designed to build baseline information necessary to the initial GMP process. The survey was designed to address many of the issues raised but not addressed by the initial survey of the Fallen Timbers Battlefield. By 2001 permanent survey data monuments had been placed to reference all future work at the site and a 15 × 15 m grid was developed over the NHS property. The project was carried out in separate stages in the spring, summer, and fall of 2001 by a crew of up to 14 and with the assistance of over 500 volunteers.

Stage I: Remote Sensing of Button Cluster Areas

The 1995 survey identified five clusters of five or more buttons representing Legion of the United States insignia and plain buttons. Two other button groups (of three and two buttons) and two isolated buttons were also recovered in the survey. The groups of buttons were interpreted as the remains of battle casualties.[18] Primary source accounts indicate the Legion's dead were treated in at least three different ways. The two dead officers (Capt. MisCampbell and Lt. Towles) were buried immediately after the battle, some 19 bodies were buried on the field two days later, and many were left unburied.[19]

Stage I of the 2001 survey gathered additional information on the distribution of buttons and their interpretation by an electromagnetic conductivity (EM) survey. Sample areas of 30 × 30 m were developed for each of seven multiple button locations and one single button find. The EM sample areas, designated EM 1–8, were established on the existing site grid. Heavy rains during March and April of 2001 left portions of the survey areas in standing water throughout the spring. As a result, three of the eight proposed 30 × 30 m areas (EM 3, 4, and 5) could not be explored with the EM 38.[20]

Anomalies in EM 1 (see figure), EM 2, and EM 6 that appeared to represent subsurface disturbances of greater than 1 m in length were selected for subsurface testing in Stage II. No such anomalies were identified in EM 7 or 8. The EM 38 survey also recorded the presence of two groundhog burrows, one each in EM 6 and 7. Openings for both were visible on the surface; however, the subsurface tunnels are identifiable in the image maps for these units.

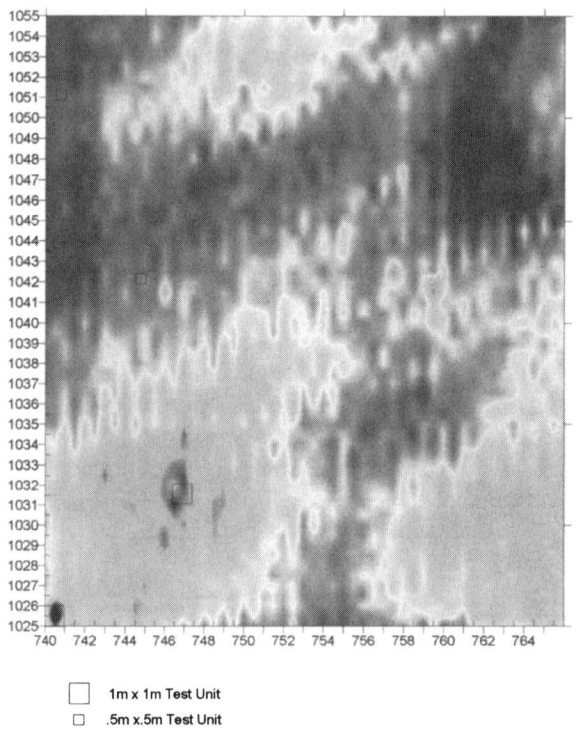

EM 38 results: EM-1, Fallen Timbers. (Heidelberg College)

Stage II: Subsurface Investigation of the "Button Cluster" Areas

Three 1 × 1 m excavation units were placed to encounter the large conductive anomalies recorded in the EM survey. In each case, soil moisture or texture differences were noted within the excavations and these, rather than graves or other features, appear to be the source of the anomalies. All of the survey areas were subjected to 2-2-90 detection efforts that produced an additional 66 buttons and 105 shot, many of which were visible as small conductive spikes in the EM 38 data.[21] The following figure below depicts the distribution of buttons recovered in the 1995 and 2001 (Stage II) metal detection surveys.

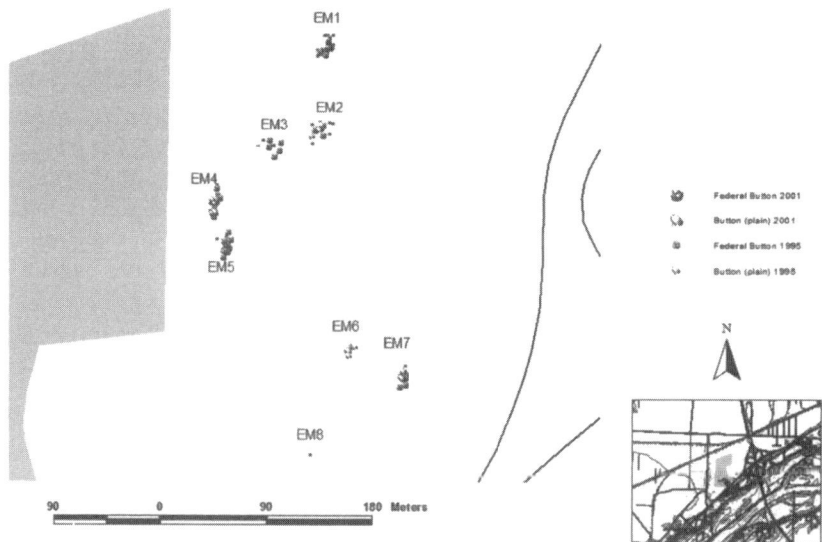

Fallen Timbers: Distribution of buttons 1995–2001. (Heidelberg College)

Stage III: Assessment of Potential NHS Access Area

Stage III activities involved 2-2-90 metal detection and artifact recovery within 15 × 15 m grid units, followed by hand excavation and screening of a 0.5 × 0.5 m test unit in the SW corner of each grid square. This stage of the survey was designed to sample portions of the NHS deemed most likely for selection for park access and facility development; 323 metal detection units were surveyed and 233 test units were excavated along the western edge of the battlefield portion of the NHS. A total of 183 battlefield artifacts, including 138 shot of various caliber, a federal button, a small axe head, and at least 14 pieces of a flintlock rifle were recovered by metal detection. Tool fragments, unidentified metal fragments, and lead waste fragments may also relate to the battlefield, but are equivocal. Two Civil War federal uniform buttons and two prehistoric flakes are clearly not associated with the Fallen Timbers Battlefield component. No battlefield-related artifacts and no significant prehistoric or other historic artifacts were recovered during excavation of the 233 test units. Nor was archaeological evidence of subsurface historic or prehistoric features encountered.[22]

Stage IV: Forested Area Survey

Intensive metal detection in the forest was designed to develop additional information on the location, artifact density, and condition of the archaeological remains of the "fallen timbers" area of the Battle of Fallen Timbers while testing the effectiveness of survey in this area under conditions of minimum vegetation cover. Due to the potential for encountering button clusters similar to those found just east of this section of the forest, EM 38 survey and sampling of subsurface anomalies were planned as contingent upon the recovery of buttons. These operations were not required; however, the stand-by excavation crew completed sixteen 0.5 × 0.5 m test units, arranged at 30-m intervals along four transects. These units documented the lack of a significant plow zone in this portion of the forest. Three musket balls, 19 rifle balls, five buckshot, an axe, and three fragments of unidentified ferrous metal were recovered from the forested area. No buttons or button clusters were encountered in this portion of the battlefield. No archaeological materials or features were encountered in these test units.[23]

CASE STUDY 2: THE BATTLE FOR MACKINAC ISLAND

In the summer of 1814 an invasion force of five companies of U.S. regulars drawn from the 17th, 19th, and 24th Infantry Regiments, Col. William Cotgreave's Ohio Volunteer Regiment, a detachment of the Corps of Artillery, and U.S. Marines were dispatched by ship to retake Mackinac Island, which had been lost in 1812 to a successful British invasion. On August 4, 1814, the ships of the invasion force sailed to the northern shore of the island and anchored in line of battle. Under the command of Lt. Col. George Croghan and Major Holmes, the invasion force was loaded in small boats; the ships opened fire and "cleared the shore"; and Croghan's force landed, uncontested.[24] Croghan's infantry and two artillery pieces set off upon a road which ran through Michael Dousman's farm and across the island to Fort Mackinac.[25]

Lt. Col. McDouall, the British commandant, responded to the invasion by rushing all available forces toward the center of the island to meet Croghan's forces as far from Fort Mackinac as possible.[26] McDouall's military force consisted of about 140 regulars; 50 militia under Lewis Crawford; and two pieces of light artillery. About 350 Indian warriors accompanied McDouall's force. When the British reached Dousman's farm, McDouall posted his line and his artillery just north of the Dousman home along a prominent ridge (known as battlefield beach ridge); a commanding position overlooking the open farm fields. McDouall placed his Indian allies in the woods on his flanks.

As the first U.S. troops emerged from the forest at the north edge of the Dousman fields, the British opened fire with both artillery pieces forcing Croghan to withdraw into the woods. Lt. Col. Croghan re-deployed his troops into two lines of battle (Ohio Volunteers in the advance and the regulars in reserve) and again advanced into the clearing. This advance was covered by ineffective U.S. artillery fire and may have utilized several large isolated hills and other features of the natural terrain as cover.[27]

As the U.S. forces crossed the open farm fields, Croghan determined to change his position "by advancing Major Holmes' battalion on the right of the militia" to outflank the British position.[28] This maneuver extended Croghan's formation into a single line of battle that overlapped McDouall's regulars. McDouall reported that his enemy advanced "slowly and cautiously," gradually gaining his left flank. The warriors on McDouall's left, who had yet to open fire, did not oppose these movements. As Holmes's line of U.S. Infantry approached their position, "a fire was opened by Indians in the thick woods near our right." McDouall reports that Chief Thomas led "Fallovine" (Menominee) warriors in an attack on the enemy.[29] It is unclear whether the Indians fired in response or prior to the charge by Holmes's regulars, but it seems clear that Holmes and several other officers were killed or put out of action by the initial blast of gunfire from the previously concealed warriors. The death of these officers "threw the line into confusion" from which they could not recover; but the charge continued forward, driving the enemy back into the woods.[30]

In the meantime, McDouall had withdrawn his regulars and militia in response to a rumored "second landing" to his rear. Apprised that this report was false, McDouall then reversed course and, leaving his regulars behind, led his militia and the bulk of the warriors back to the battlefield. The arrival of this force may have created the "untenable" situation reported by Croghan who ordered his troops to withdraw. McDouall stated that the Indians pursued the Americans until "under the broadsides" of the ships. Heavy firing continued for another 15 minutes but soon firing ceased and the troops were withdrawn to the ships. The battle for Mackinac Island ended in an American defeat.[31]

McDouall reported that the Americans left 17 dead on the field as well as some wounded. Parsons, the U.S. surgeon, reported Holmes and 12 infantry killed, 3 infantry missing, and 39 infantry and 1 Marine wounded.[32] McDouall claims to have "personally superintended the decent interment of the dead, previous to my quitting the field"; however, it is also clear that Holmes went unrecognized as an officer because he had been stripped by the Indians prior to interment.[33] Although Holmes's body was "unmolested"[34] when returned to the American fleet prior to its departure, others, including Elizabeth Davenport, claimed that the dead were scalped and/or dismembered, that cannibalism occurred, and that scalps or body parts were exhibited within the fort following the battle.[35] Decades later, oral tradition claimed the bodies were "gathered up and buried" at the southeast end of Holmes hill, and Van Fleet produced a map indicating the location of a mass grave.[36] In this battle the British forces lost a single Indian chief who was buried with "great military pomp and ceremony."[37]

Mackinac Island's 57 acre Wawashkamo Golf Course lies upon portions of the 1814 Battle for Mackinac Island battlefield. Dousman and others continued to farm the area until development of the golf course began in 1899. This included construction of the greens and tees, collection and re-deposition of boulders to create hazards, and modification of the sand pit. A "road roller" was also utilized to smooth the entire course area, but no widespread grading occurred. Subsequent to the original construction, cast-iron water lines were added in 1907–1908, and additional property was acquired about 1902 and in 1911.[38] The property continues to be operated as the Wawashkamo Golf Course.

The Wawashkamo Golf Club Archaeological Survey

The Heidelberg College CHMA survey of the Wawashkamo Golf Club portion of the Battle for Mackinac Island battlefield was carried out May 15–22, 2002, as part of a larger project designed to develop interpretive signage for battlefield events in the golf course area. The project was funded by the Wawashkamo Preservation and Restoration Fund which had received ABPP support. G. Michael Pratt directed the project, with the assistance of Richard Green and Ernie Humberger of Historic Archaeological Research. The crew included three field assistants and four metal detection specialists. Four volunteers from the Toledo Area Aboriginal Research Society joined the crew for the majority of the survey. The survey was coordinated with an independently organized cadaver dog search that was carried out prior to, but overlapped with, the beginning of the CHMA survey project.[39]

Sandra Anderson and her cadaver dog were contracted to conduct a search of the area prior to the start of the CHMA survey. Ms. Anderson and her crew placed flags at sites where the cadaver dog indicated an interest (presumably decayed human scent). They also placed flags at the site of surface indications of bone, whether or not the dog indicated the presence of decayed human scent. At the completion of her survey, Ms. Anderson indicated that her dog had encountered no areas that were indicative of a grave or a "body." She indicated that the dog "showed interest" in three areas of the golf course, an area including the southeast end of Holmes Hill (Fairway 5 and adjacent rough areas), near the crest of Battlefield Beach Ridge on Fairway 9, and in the edge of the woods east of the 18th tee. Concentrations of marker flags in these three areas showed the dog's apparent interest, and Ms. Anderson interpreted from the dog's behavior that the area southeast of Holmes Hill was the area of greatest interest for the likelihood of former grave sites.

Electromagnetic conductivity survey was carried out in the area southeast of Holmes Hill. The area was selected for its historic reputation as the site of a mass grave of the battlefield dead and Ms. Anderson's assertion that the area was of greatest interest to her cadaver dog. Anderson's survey team placed a number of flags where the dog indicated the possibility of human remains. The 23 × 38 m survey grid was positioned to encompass as many of these flagged locations (21 flags) as was permissible within the scope and budget of this project. The conductivity survey detected no significant anomalies. Several surfacing boulders and small conductive objects were indicated, but no apparent grave feature was noted. Following completion of the EM 38 operations, the survey grid was metal detected using the 2-2-90 method. Pewter fragments, a harmonica reed, a miniature bell, metal can fragments, several machine cut nails, and a rein or line guide from a horse harness were recovered. No battle-related artifacts were encountered.[40]

Sweep surveys were carried out on the nine golf course fairways, exclusive of tees and greens. Sighting poles (the cup flags) were placed at 5-m intervals at the end of each fairway and each detector operator was assigned to a sighting pole. This helped the detector operators to maintain 5-m intervals over the length of each fairway. The sweep survey recovered a total of 136 field specimens.

Four areas of artifact concentrations became apparent during the sweep survey, and at each a series of contiguous 15 × 15 m survey units was established. Subsequently, an additional eight-unit survey area was established at the west end of the golf course (Fairway 3) at the traditional location of the ambush of Holmes's regulars. A 2-2-90 detection was carried out in all five survey areas (totaling 10,350 m²). An additional 126 field specimens were recovered in this aspect of the survey. The distribution of metal-detected artifacts and the intensive survey areas are depicted in the next figure.

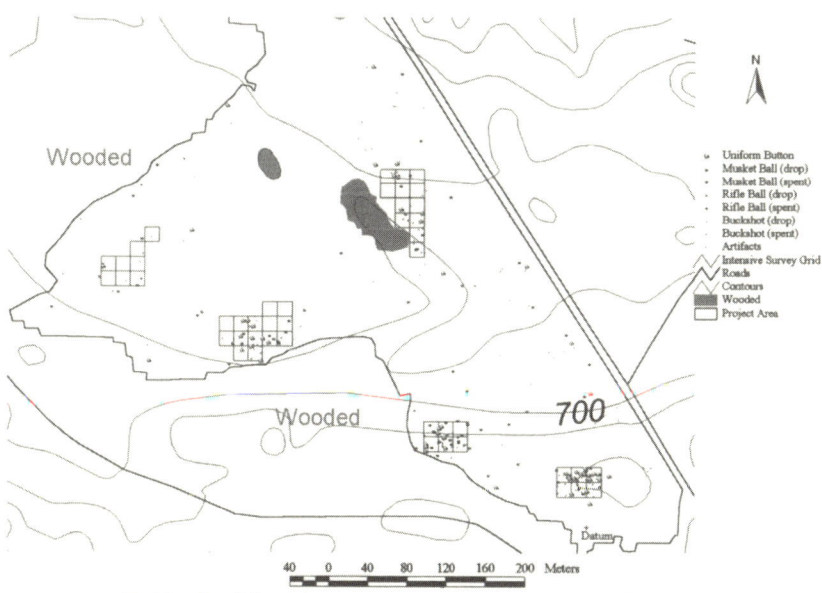

Battle for Mackinac Island Archaeological Survey
Distribution of Artifacts

Wawashkamo survey results. (Heidelberg College)

CASE STUDY 3: THE BATTLE OF BUFFINGTON ISLAND

In the summer of 1863, Confederate General John Hunt Morgan began his "Great Raid" into Northern territory. Morgan, with about 2,000 cavalry and light artillery, crossed Union lines in Kentucky, crossed the Ohio River, and swung eastward through southern Indiana and southern Ohio stealing horses, plundering farms, and creating panic. In Ohio, more than 50,000 militia troops were mustered to defend the state and to impede Morgan's route while over 8,000 Federal soldiers, including cavalry, artillery, infantry, and U.S. Navy gunboats were ordered in pursuit. As Morgan sought to re-cross the Ohio River and escape south, the ford at Buffington Island (Portland, Ohio) became the focus of attention on all sides. General Morgan and most of his 2,000 raiders reached the Portland Bottom late in the evening of July 18 and found the ford guarded by entrenched Ohio militia of unknown strength. The general chose to wait until daylight to attempt a crossing.[41] It was a fatal mistake.

Morgan's second brigade, under the direct command of Col. Basil Duke, appear to have positioned themselves opposite the head of Buffington Island in preparation for an early morning assault on a small Ohio militia earthen fortification placed to guard the approach to the Buffington Island ford. After discovering the Ohio militia position abandoned, elements of Duke's brigade moved south along the river and encountered an advance party of Federals under Gen. Henry Judah. Judah, his staff, and an escort that included a field piece collided unexpectedly with the raiders. A short skirmish ensued in which the Federals were routed with the loss of the artillery piece and a number of prisoners, the loss of several staff officers killed or wounded, and the near capture of Judah himself.[42]

In anticipation of attack by Judah's main force, Duke withdrew and formed a line across the Portland Bottom near the approach to the ford. About this time the Confederates began receiving artillery fire from "Tinclad" gunboats in the river and from Judah's main forces to their south. Shortly thereafter, Duke was attacked by Judah's Federal cavalry and forced from this position with the loss of his two artillery pieces. Duke's account makes reference to his raiders sheltering behind "Indian mounds" during this phase of the battle. The Buffington Island State Memorial Park, which features a mound, is thought to be near the location of Duke's original line of defense.[43]

Further north, near the center of the Portland Bottom, General Morgan anticipated an attack by Federal forces on his first brigade, encamped north of Duke's position. Federal General Hobson, whose cavalry had pursued the Confederates via Chester, was known to be approaching Morgan from the west. Morgan placed a field piece (perhaps the one captured from Judah) south of the Middleswart farmhouse (near the center of the Portland Bottom) and ordered the family to seek shelter from expected Federal artillery fire.[44] Morgan ordered his first brigade, the baggage train, and his remaining artillery to retreat northward along parallel roads on the upper and lower terraces of the bottom. At the northern end of Portland Bottom these roads converged and ran into the deeply entrenched valley of Lauck's Run where the road disappeared into a series of bridal trails climbing the steep, forested hillside across the creek. In attempting to negotiate this road, Morgan's artillery and part of his wagon train fell into the valley of Lauck's Run, while others were abandoned in the road. The stalled wagons also created an impediment to retreating raiders of Duke's and Johnson's brigades.

Col. August Kautz and a "flying column" of about 200 Federal cavalry were the first of Hobson's forces to reach the area. They struck a picket guard in the hills west of the Portland Bottom and drove them through the woods. Strengthened by the arrival of an artillery section and additional troopers under Col. William Sanders, Kautz pushed into the Portland Bottom from the west and confronted regiments of Duke's second brigade under Col. Johnson in a skirmish line along a roughly north-south axis. Fortuitously, Kautz's and Sanders's forces deployed near the apex of an angle formed by the east-west defensive position of Duke's retreating regiments and Johnson's line. Sanders's two Michigan regiments were armed with repeating, seven-shot Spencer carbines, creating an impression of greater numbers of Federals than were actually present. In addition to carbine and artillery fire from the south and west, the raiders also came under naval artillery fire from the Tinclads on the river to the east.[45]

Under attack from three directions, the Confederate defense collapsed into a precipitous retreat. Kautz's and Sanders's forces pressed after them with a combination of dismounted and mounted charges that turned retreat into rout. Fleeing horsemen became blocked by the stalled wagons and lost their mounts trying to negotiate the steep valley of Lauck's Run. Col. Duke and many of his officers and men were forced to surrender, ending the action in the Portland Bottom.[46] Morgan and about two-thirds of his original force escaped the battlefield and fled north along the Ohio River in search of another crossing; but the capture of over 750 officers and men as well as the expedition's entire baggage and artillery train left the Confederates as fugitives. Within a week, Morgan and those with him were prisoners-of-war.[47]

The Buffington Island battlefield area lies within a large alluvial bottomland along a north-south trending portion of the Ohio River, at Portland, Meigs County, Ohio. The once-important ford has been flooded by the modern Ohio River lock and dam system. The town of Portland was ravaged by the 1913 flood and never recovered. Today the area is less populated than in 1863. At the time of survey, and during the Battle of Buffington Island, the bottomland was mostly cleared of forest and was primarily agricultural in nature.[48] Although efforts to preserve the battlefield continue, much of the battlefield is owned by a gravel operation which plans extensive mining of their battlefield lands.

Buffington Island ABPP and "Bloody Ground" Archaeological Surveys

Unlike Fallen Timbers, the general location of the Buffington Island battlefield was well documented; however, the size and limits of the battlefield were unknown. In the 1990s Shelly Materials, Inc. developed plans to mine gravel on properties in the Portland Bottom and applied for a U.S. Corps of Engineers (USCOE) permit to develop a barge-loading facility on the bank of the Ohio River. The proposed mining area lay within the battlefield and public aspects of the permit process generated widespread interest by regional and local historical societies, Civil War interest groups, and descendants of participants in "saving" the Battle of Buffington Island battlefield.

In a draft Memorandum of Agreement circulated in late 1997, Shelly Materials, Inc. proposed mitigation of adverse effects by temporary burial (for approximately 30 years) of approximately 40 acres of property identified in local oral tradition as the "Bloody Ground" area of the battlefield. The draft MOA excluded the remainder of the Shelly Materials property, some 600 acres, from further survey or mitigation of the archaeological remains of the battlefield.

In an effort to provide information on the location and nature of the actual Buffington Island battlefield site, Heidelberg's CHMA proposed an archaeological reconnaissance survey of the entire Portland Bottom, exclusive of the lands owned by Shelly Materials, Inc. The survey was designed to assess the overall battlefield area without becoming embroiled in the controversy over mitigation issues in the Shelly Materials holdings. By conducting survey on a sample of the overall battlefield area, the project expected to predict the nature and extent of battlefield areas within the Portland Bottom, including the proposed mine area. The project, The Battle of Buffington Island: The End of Morgan's Trail was awarded an ABPP grant, GA 2255-99-013.[49]

Archaeological survey of Buffington Island battlefield was carried out over 16 consecutive days, May 29–June 13, 1999. G. Michael Pratt directed the field crew consisting of Richard Green and Larry Hamilton, metal detection supervisors/operators from HAR; four metal detector technicians; a supervisor of volunteers; a field supervisor; and three undergraduate field assistants. Sixty-five volunteers contributed a total of 1000.37 hours of effort to the field survey aspects of this project, while 18 volunteers contributed a total of 67.25 hours in public participation laboratory sessions on June 24, 1999.[50]

The field survey was carried out on properties belonging to 14 different owners and sampled areas throughout the three-mile length of the Portland Bottom area. Initial sweep surveys were carried out on all properties, followed by the development of grid squares for 2-2-90 survey, where appropriate. About

797,628 square meters (ca. 200 acres) of the battlefield area was investigated out of a total of about 406.5 ha (ca. 1,000 acres) of the Portland Bottom, representing a 19.6 percent sample. Several of the survey areas were located among parcels owned by Shelly Materials, Inc., and these provided an opportunity to sample the battlefield within the area proposed for mining.[51]

In the southern portion of the Portland Bottom, over 100,000 square meters were sampled. Survey efforts were designed to determine the location of the initial contact between Judah and Duke, variously placed south[52] and north[53] of the S-curve in S.R. 124 at its intersection with Dry Run. Survey was conducted in lawn, pasture, fallow, and cultivated fields belonging to six different owners.[54]

The central portion of the Portland Bottom is regarded as the area in which most of the battle events took place: Duke's initial defensive position, Hobson's attack from the west, and the site of Morgan's headquarters. This area also contains the Shelly Materials' properties that were excluded from the ABPP–CHMA survey. Over 287,000 square meters of mostly agricultural lands were sampled in the central portion of the valley. A total of six property owners permitted survey on their lands. One of the survey parcels is adjacent to the southernmost limit of the Shelly Materials property, and seven of the survey areas were located on privately owned property within the outline perimeter of the area proposed for mining. Survey in this area was designed to demonstrate the likelihood that battlefield activities occurred within the proposed mining area as well as to define areas associated with key events of the battle.[55]

The northern portion of the Portland Bottom is associated with the collapse and precipitate retreat of Col. Duke's command, the Federal pursuit of Duke, the abandoned baggage train, and the ultimate surrender of Duke. Shelly Materials, Inc. owns much of this area; however, several parcels of private land lie within and north of their holdings. The results of the survey within 11 areas belonging to two property owners clearly demonstrate that the archaeological remains of the battle, and therefore the battle itself, likely occurred on lands presently scheduled for gravel mining. The archaeological survey was also able to identify traces of the Civil War–era road in and east of the Lauck's Run valley. Archaeological survey along the course of this road yielded concentrations of battlefield materials in densities greater than any of the other sample areas.[56] The figure depicts the artifact distribution within the sweep survey areas and the grid system of 2-2-90 survey squares.

A total of 252 unequivocal battlefield artifacts were recovered by the CHMA–ABPP survey. Of those, 224, or 88 percent, consisted of shot or cartridges dropped or expended in the battle.

Following this survey, CHMA was retained by Shelly Materials, Inc. to conduct a survey on the "Bloody Ground," an area of about 343,000 m^2 planned for "preservation" by burial under the MOA. This area comprised the lower terrace and floodplain of the central area of the Portland Bottom

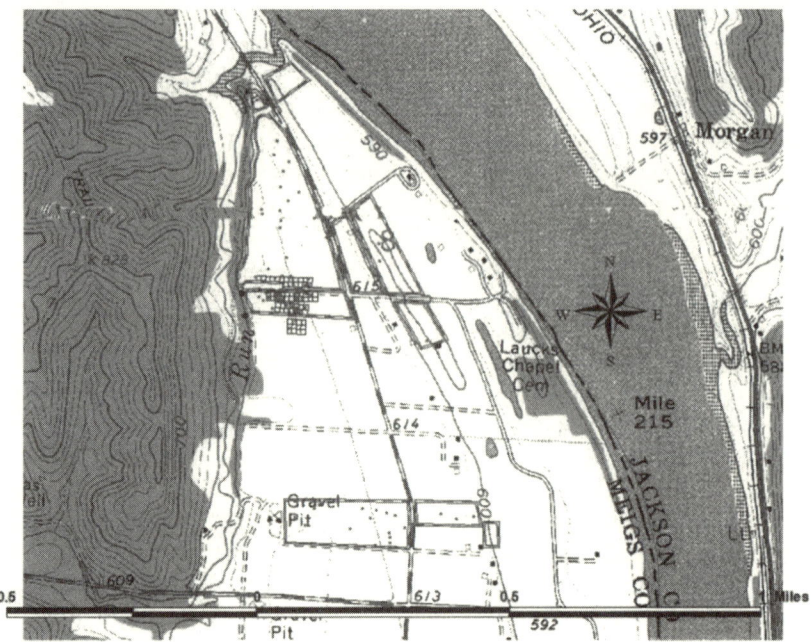

Buffington Island: Survey areas and artifact distribution, northernmost survey areas. (Heidelberg College)

and included the site of the former Tunis Middleswart house, Morgan's headquarters prior to the battle, and subsequently the Federal HQ. Field survey was carried out during December 10–17, 1999.[57]

Six agricultural field areas were identified, numbered, and subjected to the "sweep" methodology, in order to determine the nature and distribution of battlefield remains within the project area. Survey was facilitated by orienting the survey transect parallel to the most recent furrow or crop row pattern. Survey began in the upland fields which yielded battlefield artifacts and debris associated with the two (Tunis and Franklin) Middleswart residential complexes. Survey was then carried out in the lower terrace area. The lower fields included the area where several Civil War–era shot had been recovered in the early twentieth century and near where two bayonets were reportedly found in a fencerow. Recovery of these materials led to the identification of this area by locals as the "Bloody Ground" and to its "preservation" by the MOA. A total of 116 field specimens were recovered during this aspect of the survey.[58]

First, 2-2-90 survey grids were established utilizing a handheld Brunton compass and tape. These grids were designed to delineate a series of 15 × 15 meter survey areas for the metal detection operators, not as a mapping tool. Then, a 2-2-90 survey was carried out primarily in areas of apparent artifact concentration in order to determine the nature and density of the artifact distribution. Also, a 2-2-90 survey was carried out in areas identified as significant by oral tradition regardless of the results of initial stage survey.

Eight areas of survey units were established; three in the upland portion of the project and five on the lower terrace area. The largest of these, totaling 8,100 square meters (36 grid squares), was located immediately west of the Tunis Middleswart residential complex and was also the location of the largest concentration of Civil War–era military artifacts. Two other survey areas in the upper terrace sampled an additional 4,950 square meters (22 grid squares) and were located based on artifact concentrations. In the lower terrace a total of 8,100 square meters (36 grid squares) were surveyed. Initial stage operations encountered fewer battlefield remains on the lower terrace, but since this area has been declared significant through the Memorandum of Agreement, the majority (61 percent) of the 2-2-90 survey of this part of the project area was devoted to the area identified as the Bloody Ground. A total of 101 additional field specimens were recovered during the second stage survey.[59]

Together, the Buffington Island battlefield surveys explored samples of the battlefield along the entire course of the Portland Bottom. Unfortunately, much of the battlefield remains subject to future gravel mining.

INTERPRETING ARCHAEOLOGICAL BATTLEFIELD REMAINS

Surveys of these three battlefields produced significant numbers of archaeological remains which were accurately mapped by GPS and resulted in the creation of distribution maps that can demonstrate the location and relative density of battlefield artifacts, which in turn define the limits of the site and indicate levels of activity. Identification of artifact types, particularly ammunition, presents the further opportunity to assign artifacts to units or groups of combatants and thereby identify and interpret events or actions that occurred within the larger engagement. The following section provides a means to analyze and classify round shot, the dominant artifact on eighteenth- and early nineteenth-century U.S. battlefields and demonstrates the utility of this artifact in interpreting battlefield action.

ANALYSIS AND DISTRIBUTION OF LEAD SHOT: FALLEN TIMBERS AND MACKINAC ISLAND

The surveys at the Fallen Timbers and Mackinac Island battlefields exemplify interpretations based on analysis and distribution of shot, the predominant battlefield artifact. A total of 535 shot were recovered during two surveys at Fallen Timbers, and 122 were recovered from the Mackinac Island battlefield.[60]

The spherical lead shot were analyzed in terms of the caliber (diameter) of the original ball and by its functional category (dropped or unfired, spent or fired, chewed, or carved) at the time of deposition. Caliber was determined utilizing the following formula derived by Sivilich but modified to include the density of lead, rather than lead oxide:[61]

$$D = (V/6)^{1/3} = 1.2407(W/d)^{1/3}$$
$$D = \text{shot diameter in mm}$$
$$V = \text{volume in mm}^3$$
$$W = \text{weight in grams}$$
$$d = \text{density in grams/mm}^3$$
$$d_{pb} = 0.011337 \text{ g/mm}^3$$

All "dropped" or undeformed shot were also measured in inches at 45°, 90°, and 135° to the mold seam. The average of the three diameters was assigned as the caliber to these balls. As expected on a battlefield site, the majority of the spherical lead shot consist of spent or fired rounds: 81 percent at Fallen Timbers and 73 percent at Mackinac Island. These are indicated by visible deformities to the lead sphere including flattening of the shot, fragmentation, and the presence of cloth patch impressions, bore marks, and other damage to the surface. Dropped (unfired) shot at both sites were indicated by the presence of mold seams and/or sprue scars on undeformed shot and a general lack of damage to the shot.

At Fallen Timbers and Mackinac Island, spherical lead shot were arbitrarily grouped as "buckshot" (.25–.36 cal.), rifle or trade gun shot (37–58 cal.), and musket shot (59–75 cal.). These two battles involved U.S. regulars and militia as well as Indian warriors armed with weapons supplied by the British and the fur trade.

In 1777 American armies received orders that "buckshot are to be put into all cartridges which shall be hereafter made." Termed "buck and ball" loads, a musket ball and buckshot cartridge remained in use in American armies for over 50 years. General Wayne specified "One ball & three heavy buckshot" as the general cartridge for his troops.[62] In the 1995 and 2001 Fallen Timbers surveys, the overall buckshot to musket ball ratio was 2.9:1 and 3.3:1, respectively.[63]

The Legion infantry was armed with French muskets obtained during the American Revolution and with muskets of the same pattern assembled from parts made by American contractors. U.S. production of muskets identical to the French pattern began in 1795, and by 1814 production reached 30,000 per year. The French and American muskets were produced in .69 and .70 caliber. Musket ammunition was issued in the form of paper tubes containing the powder charge, ball, and/or buckshot. Although the size of individual bullets varies, "service loads" issued by the French and Americans for these muskets called for balls sized "19-to-the-pound" (about .64 cal.).[64] At the Fallen Timbers Battlefield site, only three .63–.64 caliber musket shot were recovered in 2001 and only a single ball of this size was found in 1995. The presence of numerous .60–.62 caliber musket shot (n=13 for 2001 and n=17 for 1995) strongly suggests the Legion reduced the weight (and size) of the ball in order to accommodate the added buckshot.[65] However, at the Mackinac Island battlefield, twenty .63 or .64 caliber shot and seventeen .60–.62 caliber shot were recovered (representing 57 percent of the identified musket shot).[66] If, as at Fallen Timbers, the 20 smaller balls represent buck and ball loads and the larger shot are single ball rounds, then the buckshot to ball ratio for this site could be 2.75:1.

The standard British muskets of the era were the second and third pattern Land Muskets, versions of the .75 cal. "Brown Bess." Unlike U.S. troops, British forces fired a single .69–.70 caliber ball. No lead shot of these calibers were recovered at either site.[67]

Calibers between .37 and .58 were designated "rifle," although many appear to have been fired from smooth bore weapons. Rifles and small bore trade guns were commonly supplied to the Native Americans by the British; however, the musket was apparently not a common weapon among the warriors. Both Hamilton and Caldwell agree that the smooth bore fusil or fusee (light musket) was the most popular firearm among Native Americans of the late eighteenth and early nineteenth century.[68] The most well known was the Northwest Gun, which conformed to a specific and identifiable lock, serpent side plate, and trigger guard pattern. Initially produced by the Hudson's Bay Company, the pattern was widely copied and by the late eighteenth century, most trade firearms were called Northwest Guns.[69] The standard Northwest Gun was produced in 24 gauge (about .58 cal.) for single balls or for shot. However, smaller shot is repeatedly found in association with trade gun barrels and these may represent the practice of patching a smaller ball to achieve accuracy at a longer range.[70]

Rifles were apparently less desirable trade weapons. The smooth bore fusil was lighter and more versatile as a hunting weapon; nevertheless, U.S. "factories" distributed "treaty rifles" and private commercial ventures also distributed rifles in the fur trade. These appear to be "Kentucky" or "Pennsylvania" pattern rifles. They were produced in a variety of calibers from .35–.60.[71] Legion rifle companies were issued contract-built rifles. Many of the prominent Pennsylvania gunsmiths built rifles for the army, and therefore contract guns may not have differed significantly from civilian versions.

In addition to "rifle/trade gun" shot from both Fallen Timbers and Mackinac Island, parts of such weapons were also found. The Mackinac Island survey recovered two brass, serpentine side-plates typical of late eighteenth-/early nineteenth-century manufacture, and the 2001 survey at Fallen Timbers recovered 14 metal fragments (representing all but the barrel) from a "Kentucky" style rifle.[72]

THE BATTLE FOR MACKINAC ISLAND: AN ARCHAEOLOGICAL PERSPECTIVE

The archaeological survey of the Wawashkamo Golf Club portion of the Battle for Mackinac Island battlefield was designed to provide additional primary source information by identifying the general area of combat and, perhaps, the location of specific maneuvers or actions. Unfortunately, the discovery of significant numbers of post-battle military artifacts on the 1814 battlefield and therefore the lack of unequivocal association of unidentified or undated buttons and military equipment with the 1814 battle must reduce the confidence level of archaeological interpretations.

In general, the recovery of 1814-era U.S. buttons in association with spent musket, rifle, and buckshot confirm that the Wawashkamo golf course represents part of the battle fought on Mackinac Island. Furthermore, the recovery of infantry and artillery buttons as well as general service "U.S." buttons indicates the presence of Croghan's regulars on this part of the battlefield. Finally, the single iron canister shot found east of Holmes Hill indicates that the artillery fire heard by Parsons throughout the early phase of the battle was indeed ineffectual.[73]

The general distribution of shot and occasional buttons, a U.S. neck stock clasp, and perhaps the compass divider in Fairways 1 and 5 indicate that U.S. forces advanced along the route of present British Landing Road, perhaps supported by at least one of the field pieces. The musket shot from this area consists mostly of military shot (.63–.64 cal.) and trade gun shot (.50–.56 cal.). Only three spent rifle shot and 11 buckshot were recovered from the intensive survey grid in this part of the field. The overall shot density in this area was calculated at $0.004/m^2$.

The Fairway 1 and 5 portions of the Wawashkamo golf course appear to represent part of Croghan's slow and cautious approach toward the British position on the ridge.[74] It is likely that the U.S. musket shot in this area represent rounds fired from skirmishers in advance of Croghan's main force that then advanced over their own spent shot. The light return fire from rifles and trade guns may represent harassing fire directed at Croghan's withdrawal by the Indians and militia that followed the retreat "until under the Broadsides of the ships,"[75] rather than in resistance to the American advance. This interpretation is strengthened by McDouall's statement that the Indians permitted the Americans to gain his left flank "without firing a shot."[76]

As the battle developed, Croghan changed his position by "...advancing Maj. Holmes battalion on the right of the militia, thus to out flank..." the British.[77] Tactical maneuvers of the day indicate that such a move is carried out in line, rather than in a column advance. Previous accounts describe Holmes as making a wide swing around the north end of Holmes Hill and being ambushed near the 8th tee – 7th green and Fairway 3 area[78]; however, there is little evidence of fighting in this part of the field. Rather, the archaeological evidence suggests the westward (right) extension of the line occurred south of Holmes Hill.

Here, relatively high density U.S. military musket shot and buckshot recovered from the base and slope of Battlefield Beach Ridge is intermingled with small musket and rifle shot. Overall shot density in the intensive survey grids in this area was calculated at $0.01/m^2$ in Fairway 8, $0.02/m^2$ at the crest of the ridge in Fairway 9, and $0.008/m^2$ behind the ridge and near the clubhouse. The first two areas lie about 300 m apart and suggest that fighting took place over a wide front. Croghan describes Holmes's death "while beginning the charge" and states his "failure to move left ... led to [a] charge by the regulars towards the front."[79] Croghan also states the death of officers "threw the line into confusion"; as a result, he ordered the regulars to charge to the front. Croghan's use of the terms "line" and "charge" support the archaeological evidence that the attack by the "Fallovine Indians" was made on the front and flank of a U.S. battle line rather than on a column of troops (see figure).[80]

In the confusion following the initial "ambush," the regulars were ordered to charge toward the front. Croghan claims to have driven the enemy into the woods in spite of "annoying fire from Indians" and ordered Lt. Morgan to advance an artillery piece, bringing the "enemy to fire at a longer distance." He then determined his position untenable and ordered his forces to retreat back to the beach.[81] Archaeologically, it is unclear how far the Americans advanced, but U.S. general service, infantry, and artillery buttons were recovered at the crest of the ridge. Since 1815 rifle and infantry buttons also occur in this area, the interpretation of these pre-1815 buttons as the high point of Croghan's attack is equivocal.

Although Croghan does not mention it, his position may have become untenable due to the arrival of McDouall with "the greater part of the Indians and 50 militia."[82] McDouall claims his forces followed the retreating Americans to within the range of their naval guns. Parsons recorded that the direction of gunfire changed at 4:30, but continued until 5:00. Most of the troops had returned to the shore when the gunfire ceased.[83] Together, these statements suggest that warriors and militia kept up a harassing fire while following Croghan's retreat. It is likely that this action generated the small musket shot and rifle balls found opposite Holmes Hill in Fairways 1 and 5, as well as the low density small musket shot from Fairways 2 and 3. Fairway 3 also produced a dropped .63 cal. ball, infantry button, and the silver trade brooch fragment (see figure).

Archaeologically, the British regular forces are almost invisible in this battle. No "ounce"(.69–.70 cal.) balls, the standard musket load of the British Army, were recovered during the survey. McDouall claimed, "a natural breastwork" [crest of Battlefield Beach Ridge] "protected my men from every shot"[84]; but the archaeological evidence indicates that these troops made little or no effort to return the fire. It appears likely that the British regulars withdrew from the ridge before Croghan's forces came within effective musket range.

Archaeologically, the ratio of buckshot to musket shot at this site (0.67:1) does not fit the pattern noted at Fallen Timbers where U.S. forces engaged with "buck and ball." Furthermore, this site produced significant numbers of .63–.64 cal. shot in addition to the .61–.62 cal. shot attributed to the buck and ball load.[85] It is possible that buckshot was under-represented in this survey; however, the same recovery techniques, equipment, and some of the same metal detector operators were used in both surveys.[86] It is also possible, but unlikely, that the American regulars deviated from their standard ammunition in this battle. However, in 1980, Dunnigan proposed that the British militia in this battle were armed and accoutered with U.S. equipment captured in the 1812 invasion of Mackinac Island.[87] Fifty of the militia returned to the field in the late stages of the battle and participated in the fighting. Their use of the 1795 pattern U.S. Musket firing (in the British style) a single ball cartridge could explain the low buckshot to musket ball ratio and account for the presence of the larger caliber shot at this battle. If the .63–.64 shot (n=20) are removed from the equation, the ratio of buckshot to .61–.62 cal. musket shot is 2.75:1.

As the battle came to an end, the warriors turned to the dead. In his letter to Croghan, McDouall states that he "personally superintended the decent interment of the dead previous to my quitting field"; however, the body of Holmes was not recognized as an officer due to "being previously stripped by the Indians."[88] The relative lack of U.S. infantry buttons at a site where 17 regulars were left dead on the field suggests that victorious warriors stripped the dead and carried the uniforms away.

Although given a "decent" burial within hours of their deaths, the bodies may have been disinterred shortly after. Elizabeth Davenport remained on Mackinac Island throughout the British occupation, but was under suspicion as the wife of a "Yankee Rebel." She was detained in the fort's blockhouse from the arrival of the American fleet until after the battle. Mrs. Davenport reports when British and Indians returned to the fort, the Indians carried scalps and other body parts. She claims that hands, hearts, and other pieces of the American dead were cooked and consumed while the scalps were hung on the railings near McDouall's quarters.[89] Van Fleet repeats this story and claims that these remains were later buried in an Indian cemetery. Ground conductivity survey of the "mass grave" reported by Van Fleet and assumed to lie at the foot of Holmes Hill found no evidence of subsurface features. If such a feature ever existed, it is likely to have been destroyed by subsequent agriculture or development of the golf course.

THE BATTLE OF FALLEN TIMBERS: AN ARCHAEOLOGICAL PERSPECTIVE

Two archaeological surveys revealed varying levels of shot and button density (indicative of varying levels of combat) in four distinct areas of the battlefield: (1) east of the forest where the highest concentration of artifacts and virtually all of the uniform buttons were recovered (7200 m^2); (2) the northern portion of the NHS property; a field bounded by railroad tracks (2.5 ha);

(3) portions of the northeast section of the forest (1.2 ha); (4) portions of NHS property located between the western edge of the forest and the private homes along the east side of Jerome Road (4.8 ha). Artifact densities from the 2001 survey were calculated for all areas in terms of artifacts/metal detection survey unit (225 m^2) as follows:

1. East field Button Clusters	5.19 artifacts/225 m^2
3. North field	0.75 artifacts/225 m^2
4. Forest	0.57 artifacts/225 m^2
2. Forest to Jerome Road	0.50 artifacts/225 m^2

The relative distribution of battlefield artifacts is consistent with results from the 1995 survey, which identified a much larger area surrounding the button clusters as the area of greatest artifact density (1.12/225 m^2). The 1995 survey interpreted this area as the location of the "fallen timbers" and as the site of the historically documented skirmish between Legion troops and advancing warriors. In the 2001 survey this area produced a greater artifact density than the forest and areas further west, areas interpreted both archaeologically and historically as lying behind the U.S. battle line. To the east of this area, the 1995 survey encountered a drop in artifact density (.47 artifacts/225 m^2). Historically, gunfire dropped precipitously as the U.S. regulars launched a bayonet charge through the fallen timbers area, resulting in the collapse of the Indian position.[90]

All but one of the survey areas that produced multiple (5–23) buttons exhibited buttons from at least two and often three items (coat, vest, or breeches/trousers) of the federal Legion uniform. The single exception yielded "spun back" buttons elsewhere associated with breeches/trousers and a single silver non-military button. The button groups lie within the highest density artifact area and also exhibit high densities of impacted rifle shot within the 2001 survey areas.

Historically, casualties who could not make it off the battlefield on their own or without help from friends were left on the field for two days. When a federal burial party was dispatched, they reported burial of only 19 bodies, well below the most conservative death estimates.[91] The clusters of buttons and lack of grave features in the EM-38 conductivity survey suggest that the casualties interpreted archaeologically were among those "... left to ferment upon the surface, the prey of Vultures..."[92]

THE BATTLE OF BUFFINGTON ISLAND: AN ARCHAEOLOGICAL PERSPECTIVE

The ABPP–CHMA archaeological survey demonstrates convincingly that remains of the July 19, 1863, Battle of Buffington Island are present and recoverable in the Portland Bottom. The survey of nearly 797,628 square meters (ca. 200 acres) throughout the Portland Bottom produced a total of 252 battlefield artifacts, primarily spent munitions. An analysis of the distribution pattern of these remains provides new and significant information on the actual location of key events in the Battle of Buffington Island.

The initial engagement of the battle appears to have occurred east of Dry Run and south of the present McCook monument. The former James Williamsen home, which probably received wounded Federals (including Major McCook and Lieut. F. G. Price), has been altered, but remains as a visible battlefield structure.

The first defensive skirmish line established by the 5th and 6th Kentucky Cavalry of Duke's Brigade was not clearly apparent, but likely lies within the mobile home/construction trailer wrecking yard located between the McCook monument and the Buffington Island State Memorial Park. The position of Duke's two Parrot guns may lie in the uplands west of the wrecking yard. The ABPP–CHMA survey did not have permission to work on that property, nor is the land conducive to metal detection survey. The upland areas associated with that property exhibit visible signs of grading and were impacted by early twentieth-century oil production activity. The archaeological potential of this significant part of the battlefield has not been assessed.

The large fields immediately north of the wrecking yard produced scattered remains of pistol fire, artillery shell fragments, and a few carbine rounds. This area may represent Duke's attempt to rally and recover a defensive position after being driven from his first position and losing his artillery or (as Federal officers claim) the beginning of his retreat north. The area of the Buffington Island State Memorial Park and the fields immediately north of it produced only scattered evidence of the battle. It appears that within this portion of the battlefield, Duke's brigades were in the process of repositioning and were producing and receiving little small-arms fire. North and east of the Ohio Historical Society Park, the Portland School and the modern village of Portland have obliterated parts of the battle site. However, the majority of this area of the battlefield is impacted only by agriculture.

The central portion of the battlefield is threatened by impending gravel mining, slated to occur during 2000–2036, which will destroy the archaeological record as well as the viewscape of this part of the Buffington Island battlefield. Recovery of battlefield remains from parcels within the perimeter of the proposed mine area indicate Federal fire, probably resulting from Kautz's skirmishers and Sanders's artillery, was directed into the present Shelly Materials, Inc. properties. This survey, however, was not able to determine which of several possible routes Kautz's forces traveled to the battlefield, nor the location and movements of Duke's and Johnson's regiments once they were engaged by the Federal cavalry regiments and artillery under Kautz and Sanders.

In late 1999 Shelly Materials, Inc. undertook archaeological survey of their holdings east of the intersection of C.R. 31 and S.R. 124, the reputed

"Bloody Ground" area of the battlefield. Survey of this area supported Confederate participant Curtice Burke's description of the area as General Morgan's headquarters of July 19–20 and as the post-battle prisoner-of-war compound. The high proportion of dropped to spent shot in this area indicates relatively little combat occurred in the "Bloody Ground"[93] area slated for preservation by the MOA.

The flanking attack by Hobson's column and the Confederate response to it is the turning point where Duke's measured withdrawal became a rout. Archaeological investigation of this area of the battlefield has the potential to determine the shape and location of Confederate positions, the relative strength of firepower of each, and their response to Kautz's skirmishers and the artillery and cavalry attack by Sanders. Spencer carbine shot and cartridges have the potential to indicate the movements of the 8th and 9th Michigan in their rout of the Confederate forces. The ABPP–CHMA survey and the 1999 survey of the "Bloody Ground" area both indicate relatively little fighting occurred on the T-2 terrace east of S.R. 124 in the central Portland Bottom area. By process of elimination, Duke's and Johnson's formations, the ground over which they retreated, and the route of the Michigan cavalry charge all lie along the crest of the T-3 terrace within the Shelly Materials, Inc. holdings. Thus, though the archaeological record of the central Portland Bottom has the potential to provide information key to understanding the critical moments of the Battle of Buffington Island, under the current MOA, this portion of the battlefield remains under the threat of destruction without mitigation. The Tunis Middleswart house, which stood in the central part of the Portland Bottom, was demolished in the 1970s. The archaeological site (33Ms88) is presently owned by Shelly Materials, Inc. Structural remains and artifacts are visible on the surface; however, the MOA does not include the site in its mitigation measures.

The final events of the Battle of Buffington Island occurred when the fleeing Confederates of Duke's brigade encountered the abandoned wagons and artillery that choked their only road of escape. Federal and Confederate accounts agree that military organization disintegrated and individuals and small parties were left to escape, fight, or surrender under the pressure of Federal cavalry armed with the rapid fire Spencer carbine. The archaeological remains recovered along the visible traces of the 1863 Portland Road west of S.R. 124 document the close-range combat that ended in the death of some and the surrender of most of General Morgan's rear guard regiments. The rapidly shifting stream bottom and the dense vegetation of the Lauck's Run valley have re-deposited and obscured the archaeological record of the valley floor. The upland fields remain agricultural and the trace of the Portland Road represents a battlefield resource little changed since the Civil War. The old roadbed (see figure) remains a visible representation of where the 1863 Portland Road and Morgan's Great Raid came to an end.[94]

CONCLUSIONS

The remote sensing survey methods presented above have proven effective as a means to recover battlefield remains and to interpret battlefield events. At the Fallen Timbers, Mackinac Island, and Buffington Island battlefields, this method demonstrated archaeologically the areas where various battlefield activities occurred. The distribution, density, and type of lead shot recovered identified areas of relatively heavy or light gunfire which, when considered in light of historical and other archaeological information, help to identify troop positions, attacks, and the weaponry utilized at each site. Electromagnetic conductivity survey at the Mackinac Island and Fallen Timbers sites confirmed the treatment of battlefield casualties at the latter site and refuted claims of a mass grave at the former. All three surveys provided "ground truth" information in support of preservation efforts at these sites and all provided local citizens with the opportunity to play a role in uncovering new information about a significant historic event. Finally, all three surveys involved sites which had or would receive support from the American Battlefield Protection Program.

NOTES

1. McKee and Mason 1994.
2. Fox 1993, Scott & Connor 1997, Scott & Fox 1989.
3. Pratt 2000a, b.
4. Pratt 1995a.
5. Pratt 1995a:11–12.
6. Pratt 1995a:15–17.
7. Pratt 1995a:19–21.
8. Pratt 1995a:22–28.
9. Pratt 1995a:28.
10. Smith 1952, *New York Magazine* 1794.
11. Pratt 1995a.
12. Pratt 1997a, b.
13. Pratt 2002.
14. Pratt 1995b.
15. Pratt 1995b.
16. DOrder 2:4.
17. Pratt 2002.
18. Pratt 1995a:25–26.
19. McGrane 1914:30, Lin 1873:339, Smith 1965:8, McKee 1794.
20. Pratt 2002:46.
21. Pratt 2002:46–49.
22. Pratt 2002:49–50.
23. Pratt 2002:50–51.
24. Fredricksen 2000:87.

25. Dunnigan 1980:22.
26. Dunnigan 1980:22.
27. Dunnigan 1980:24.
28. Wood 1918:307.
29. Fredricksen 2000:87, Wood 1918:306–307, MPHC 1894:592.
30. Wood 1918:307.
31. Fredricksen 2000:87–88, Wood 1918:307, MPHC 1894:593.
32. McDouall 1814, MPHC 1894:592, Dunnigan 1980:26, Fredricksen 2000:90.
33. McDouall 1814.
34. Fredricksen 2000:90.
35. Otsego 1845, Van Fleet 1870:118.
36. Van Fleet 1870:142.
37. Otsego 1845.
38. Straus and Dunnigan 2000:31, 40–41.
39. Pratt 2002.
40. Pratt 2002.
41. Miller et al. 1997, Bennett 1998, Horwitz 1999.
42. Miller et al. 1997, Bennett 1998.
43. Duke 1906, Miller et al. 1997, Bennett 1998.
44. Bush n.d., Middleswart n.d.
45. Allen 1903:223–242, Duke 1906:451, Miller et al. 1997, Bennett 1998.
46. Miller et al. 1997, Bennett 1998.
47. Bennett 1998.
48. Hayes 1877.
49. Pratt 2000a.
50. Pratt 2000a:24.
51. Pratt 2000a:29.
52. Horwitz 1999.
53. Miller et al. 1994, Bennett 1998.
54. Pratt 2000a:29.
55. Pratt 2000a:29.
56. Pratt 2000a:29.
57. Pratt 2000b.
58. Pratt 2000b:25.
59. Pratt 2000b:25.
60. Pratt 1995b:17, 2002:54, 2002:35.
61. Sivilich 1995.
62. Lewis 1956:108–110, Knopf 1960:185.
63. Pratt 1995b:23, 2002:57.
64. Lewis 1956:108–110.
65. Pratt 2002:58.
66. Pratt 2002:51.
67. Neumann 2001:49.
68. Caldwell et al. 1982, Hamilton 1980.
69. Caldwell et al. 1982:7.
70. Caldwell et al. 1982:85.
71. Kauffman 1960:19.
72. Pratt 2001:55, 2002:37.

73. Fredricksen 2000:87, MPHC 1894:591.
74. MPHC 1894:591, Wood 1918:306.
75. MPHC 1894:593.
76. MPHC 1894:592.
77. Wood 1918:307.
78. Dunnigan 1980:25.
79. Van Fleet 1870:117.
80. Wood 1918:307.
81. Wood 1918:307.
82. MPHC 1894:592.
83. Fredricksen 2000:88.
84. MPHC 1894:592.
85. Pratt 2002:57.
86. Pratt 2002.
87. Dunnigan 1980:44.
88. McDouall 1814.
89. Otsego 1845.
90. Pratt 1995a, 1995b:26–27, 2002a.
91. Pratt 1995a:26.
92. Quaife 1929:86–87, Smith 1952:302.
93. Burke n.d., Pratt 2000b.
94. Pratt 2000a:46–48.

REFERENCES CITED

Allen, Theodore F. 1903. Pursuit of John Morgan. In *Sketches of War History*, 223–242. Robert Clarke, Cincinnati.
Bennett, B. Kevin. 1998. The Battle of Buffington Island. *Blue & Gray Magazine*, April 1998:7–58.
Burke, Curtice. n.d. Civil War Journal. Photocopy of unpublished manuscript. Archives, US Army Military History Institute, Carlisle Barracks, PA.
Bush, Susann. n.d. Notebook of information and photographs relating to the Tunis Middleswart Homestead. Prepared by Susan Bush, January 24, 2000. Copy in possession of the author.
Caldwell, W. W., Gooding, J. S., Hamilton, T. M., Hanson, C. E. Jr., Huntington, R. T., Russell, C. P., Smith, C. S., Woodward, A., and J. Barsott. 1982. *Indian Trade Guns*. Pioneer Press, Union City, TN.
DOrder 2. 1998. Director's Order #2: Park Planning. National Park Service. Available at http://www.nps.gov/refdesk/Dorders/DOrder2.html.
Duke, Basil. 1906. *Morgan's Cavalry*. Neale Publishing Co., New York.
Dunnigan, Brian Leigh. 1980. *The British Army at Mackinac 1812–1815*. Reports in Mackinac History and Archaeology Number 7. Mackinac Island State Park Commission.
Fox, Richard A. Jr. 1993. *Archaeology, History, and Custer's Last Battle*. University of Oklahoma Press, Norman.
Fredricksen, John C. (ed.). 2000. *Surgeon of the Lakes: The Diary of Dr. Usher Parsons 1812–1814*. Erie County Historical Society, Erie, PA.
Hamilton, T. M. 1980. *Colonial Frontier Guns*. The Fur Press, Chadron, NE.

Hayes, E. L. 1877. *Illustrated Atlas of the Upper Ohio Valley*. On file, Hamilton County Public Library, Cincinnati.

Horwitz, Lester V. 1999. *Longest Raid of the Civil War: Little-Known & Untold Stories of Morgan's Raid into Kentucky, Indiana & Ohio*. James A. Ramage, Publisher.

Kauffman, Henry J. 1960. *The Pennsylvania-Kentucky Rifle*. Stackpole Co., Harrisburg, PA.

Knopf, Richard. 1960. *Anthony Wayne: A Name in Arms*. University of Pittsburgh Press, Pittsburgh.

Lewis, Berkeley R. 1956. *Small Arms and Ammunition in the United States Service 1776–1865*. Smithsonian Miscellaneous Collections Vol. 129. Smithsonian Institution Press, Washington, D.C.

Lin, John B. 1873. General Wayne's Campaign in 1794 & 1795: Captain John Cooke's Journal. *American Historical Record* II (311–316, 339–345).

McDouall, Robert. 1814. McDouall, Robert ALS to George Croghan. Michilimackinac August 5, 1814. (Original letter) Michigan Papers, William Clements Library, Ann Arbor.

McGrane, R C. 1914. A Journal of Major-General Anthony Wayne's Campaign Against the Shawnee Indians in Ohio in 1794–1795. *Mississippi Valley Historical Review* I:419–444.

McKee, Alexander. 1794. Letter to Joseph Chew, 27 August, 1794. RG 8 I "C" Series 247:222–224.

McKee, W. Reid, and M. E. Mason Jr. 1994. *Civil War Projectiles II: Small Arms & Field Artillery with Supplement*. Publisher's Press, Orange, VA (reprint).

Miller, Orloff G., Ruth G. Meyers, Krystyna Puc, Rita Walsh, E. Jeanne Harris, Christopher J. Baltz, Mathew E. Bechner, and Kevin Paper. 1997. Phase I Cultural Resources Investigations Above Buffington Island, For Richard & Sons, Inc., Meigs County, OH. Manuscript in possession of Paul Rice, Shelly Materials, Inc.

MPHC (Michigan Pioneer and Historical Collections). 1894. Lt. Col. Robert McDouall to Sir George Prevost, 14 August 1814. *Michigan Pioneer and Historical Collections* 25:591. Robert Smith & Co., Lansing.

Neumann, George C. 2001. The Redcoat's Brown Bess. *American Rifleman Magazine* (April 2001):49.

New York Magazine. 1794. Sketch of the Ground at the Rapids of the Miami of the Lake, showing the Position of General Wayne's Army previous to and after the Action of the 20th of August, 1794. *New York Magazine; or Literary Repository: for October, 1794*. Number X.-Vol.V. Printed and Published by T. and J. Swords, No. 167, William St., New York. (Between 642–643).

Otsego. 1845. Untitled article signed "Otsego" based on personal interview with Ambrose R. and Elizabeth Davenport. *Cleveland Daily Advertiser*, Sept. 27, 1845. Transcribed at http://bailiwick.lib.uiowa.edu/woodrow/Davenport.html.

Pratt, G. Michael. 1995a. The Battle of Fallen Timbers: An Eyewitness Perspective. *Northwest Ohio Quarterly* 67(1):4–34.

Pratt, G. Michael. 1995b. The Archaeology of the Fallen Timbers Battlefield: A Report of the 1995 Field Survey. Ms. on file, The Maumee Valley Heritage Corridor, Inc. and http://www.heidelberg.edu/FallenTimbers/.

Pratt, G. Michael. 1997a. A Report to the Property Owners on Fallen Timbers Lane. Unpublished letter 4/5/97, Center for Historic and Military Archaeology, Heidelberg College, Tiffin, OH.

Pratt, G. Michael. 1997b. A Report to the Director of St Luke's Hospital. Unpublished letter 4/16/97, Center for Historic and Military Archaeology, Heidelberg College, Tiffin, OH.
Pratt, G. Michael. 2000a. The Battle of Buffington Island: The End of Morgan's Trail. A Report on the Archaeological Survey American Battlefield Protection Program Grant No. GA-2255-99-013. Ms. on file, American Battlefield Protection Program, National Park Service, Washington, D.C.
Pratt, G. Michael. 2000b. Assessing the "Bloody Ground": The Archaeological Survey of a Portion of the Buffington Island Battlefield. Prepared for Shelly Materials, Inc. Ms. on file, US Army Corps of Engineers, Huntington District, 502 Eighth Street, Huntington, WV.
Pratt, G. Michael. 2001. The General Management Planning Baseline Archaeological Survey: Fallen Timbers Battlefield NHS. Ms. on file, the Metroparks of the Toledo Area, Toledo, OH.
Pratt, G. Michael. 2002. The Battle for Mackinac Island: The Archaeological Survey of the Wawashkamo Golf Course, Mackinac Island, Michigan. Ms. on file, the Mackinac Island State Park Commission and the Wawashkamo Restoration and Preservation Fund, Mackinac Island.
Quaife, Milo, M. (ed.). 1929. General James Wilkinson's Narrative of the Fallen Timbers Campaign. *Mississippi Valley Historical Review* 14:81–90.
Scott, Douglas D., and Melissa A. Connor. 1997. *Metal Detector Use in Archaeology: An Introduction*. Midwest Archaeological Center, National Park Service. Lincoln, NE.
Scott, D. D., and R. Fox. 1989. *Archaeological Insights into the Custer Battle: An Assessment of the 1984 Field Season*. University of Oklahoma Press, Norman.
Sivilich, Daniel M. 1995. Approximation of Musket Ball Caliber Using Weight Measurements. Unpublished paper presented to the Society for Historical Archaeology Annual Meeting.
Smith, Dwight L. (ed.). 1952. *From Greene Ville to Fallen Timbers: A Journal of the Wayne Campaign July 28–September 14, 1794*. Indiana Historical Society, Indianapolis.
Smith, Dwight L. 1965. *With Captain Edward Miller in the Wayne Campaign of 1794*. The William Clements Library, Ann Arbor.
Straus, Frank, and Brian Leigh Dunnigan. 2000. *Walk a Crooked Trail: A Centennial History of Wawashkamo Golf Club*. Wawashkamo Golf Club, Mackinac Island, Michigan.
Van Fleet, Reverend J. A. 1870. *Old and New Mackinac*. Courier Steam Printing House, Ann Arbor.
Wood, Edwin O. 1918. *Historic Mackinac*. The Macmillan Co., New York.

Mustering Landscapes: What Historic Battlefields Share in Common

John & Patricia Carman

THE BLOODY MEADOWS Project[1] has as one of its goals to develop an understanding of changes in warfare practice and ideology over the long term. In operation, it is an exercise in the comparative study of known battlefields from all periods of history and in all parts of the world: this means the earliest site to be examined would be Megiddo in Syria, from around 1469 BC, and we impose our own limit at 1900 AD, since so many others are engaged in studying the warfare of the twentieth century and beyond.[2] The Bloody Meadows Project is distinctive among battlefield archaeology projects in that it takes an overtly *comparative* approach to such places. The project is interested primarily in the *kinds* of places where people have come together to commit mutual slaughter and how one in this time and region differs from that in another time and region. Over the past five years or so, we have looked at 30 sites, all but two in Europe, from classical Greece, through the medieval period, and into the early nineteenth century. Collectively, the battlefields give insights into the kinds of places where people chose to fight in the past.

APPROACH AND METHODS

As a contribution to archaeology more generally, the project is an attempt to apply some recently developed approaches to landscapes to gain insights into how landscapes, especially particular kinds of landscapes, were *perceived* in the past. For us, the key element is the landscape of the battle itself, which we approach by drawing upon ideas from phenomenology as applied in archaeology. The British archaeologist Christopher Tilley has perhaps given the clearest justification for such a phenomenological approach to studying landscapes:

> The landscape [he writes] is continually being encultured, bringing things into meaning as part of a symbolic process by which human consciousness makes the

physical reality of the natural environment into an intelligible and socialised form.... It [is accordingly] evident...that the significance of landscape for different populations cannot be simply read off from the local "ecological" characteristics of a "natural" environment.[3]

Cultural markers [such as monuments are used] to create a new sense of place.... An already encultured landscape becomes refashioned, its meanings now controlled by the imposition of [a new] cultural form.

These comments by Tilley specifically refer to the relationship of prehistoric monuments to mostly empty rural landscapes in Britain. Following his lead, and that of others, a phenomenological approach to the study of landscapes as taken by archaeologists has generally been limited to the monumental "ritual" landscapes of later European prehistory. The approach is, however, also of more general relevance to any encultured space, especially any marked as a particular kind of space. The typical interpretive device in battlefield research is the battlefield plan, an objective view from above, divorced from the action. But as Tilley also emphasizes, place is not something that can be understood "objectively":

Looking at the two-dimensional plane of the modern topographic map with sites [or artifact scatters] plotted on it, it is quite impossible to envisage the landscape in which these places are embedded. The representation fails, and cannot substitute for being there, being *in place*. [The] process of observation requires time and a feeling for the place.[4]

The primary data source used in the Bloody Meadows Project is the physical landscape of the place where warfare was practiced. Drawing upon the work of previous scholars who have identified the locations of many battlefields from the past, we focus upon the landscape itself to ask specific questions, including:

- How clearly bounded is the battlefield space (does it have clear boundaries, such as impassable ground or a water obstacle)?
- Is it high or low ground relative to the surrounding space?
- What kind of use (other than for war) was the site put to, if any?
- Is it near or distant from settlement?
- Is it visible from settlement?
- Does the ground contain particular types of landscape features—natural or built—which play a part in the battlefield action?
- What features present in the landscape (if any) played no part in the battlefield action?
- Was the battlefield subsequently marked by a monument or memorial in any way?

The answers to these questions can be conveniently set out for each battlefield as follows.

An early medieval site: Assandun 1016 AD. Low open ground by a river.

Parameters for Studying Battlefields

Rules of war	Battlefield architecture
Agreement to fight: Y/N	Features present
Mutual recognition as "legitimate" enemies: Y/N	Type of feature used
Level of violence: High, medium, Low	Type of feature not used
Marking of battle-site:	Use of terrain:
	as cover;
	to impede visibility;
	to impede movement
Participants	Structured formations: Y/N
Functional aspects	
Dysfunctional aspects	

Here, the *rules of war* cover such things as the degree of mutual agreement needed before fighting could commence, whether the two sides were required to see each other as "legitimate" enemies or whether anyone could participate in a battle, some assessment of the level of violence employed, and how (if at all) the battle site was remembered immediately afterward.

These are a measure of how "formal" a battle was regarded and how distinctive it was from other forms of conflict at that time.

The characteristics of the battlefield landscape are addressed in order to identify features present in the battle space and how they were used by combatants. This gives some insight into attitudes to the battlefield as a place. The query as to whether structured formations were present (such as ordered columns or lines of troops) gives a clue to how participants moved through the battlefield space: if the landscape is seen as architecture, so too can the forces engaged be seen as a kind of "mobile architecture." The point is not merely to note those features present and used by combatants, as military historians might, but also and especially those features present but not used, and for purposes of elimination those present today but not on the day of battle.

The two final sections attempt to summarize our expectations as filtered through an understanding of "good military practice" derived from military writings (as in the concept of "inherent military probability" discussed by John Keegan).[5] It is, we believe, the *dysfunctional* behavior (that is, the apparent mistakes or omissions) which can give a clue to cultural attitudes and expectations of the battlefield space which differ from our own. In applying this analysis to examples of warfare from various periods, the differences between periods become evident.

In approaching the landscapes that are our object, we use what we have called "the archaeologist's eye," that is, the capacity of a trained landscape archaeologist to interpret space and to identify (especially manufactured) features in landscapes otherwise unfamiliar to them to reach an understanding of the spaces of battle. By approaching such sites with a structured set of questions and by recording data in a standard format, it becomes possible to recognize what such sites have in common and how they differ from one another. This in turn, by tabulating the results, allows the identification of the types of location favored as battle sites in particular periods of history. Overall, it presents an opportunity to gain a direct insight into the ideological factors guiding warfare practice in that period and to compare them with that guiding warfare practice in a different period.

BATTLEFIELD LANDSCAPE AND TERRAIN

The notion of "terrain" most commonly applied in battlefield studies is perhaps something different from the concept of "landscape" which we apply. Battlefield terrain generally consists of those features considered relevant or important to military purposes. Landscape, by contrast, is all those features present regardless of their military usefulness. This includes the general shape of the area as it presents itself, and all those elements that help to define it, separate it from surrounding land, or bind it together as a more-or-less coherent space. The Bloody Meadows Project is concerned not with terrain but with landscape and so takes a view different from that of conventional military history. In so doing, we distinguish coastal or estuarine places from those further inland; and high places from lower. We also concern ourselves with the relation of the space to urban centers: battles may be fought through, just outside of, within sight of, or completely away from towns and cities. One of the things that are interesting is the different types of space that cluster together as choices for battlefields in different periods of history. Here, all our classical Greek battlefields show the same characteristics, as do all our medieval battlefields; the only battlefields not to fit our patterns are those seventeenth- and eighteenth-century fights at Linton, Fontenoy, and Quebec, all of which were fought within or close to towns. We are frankly surprised there isn't more variation in our sample than this, and we know of only a very few more actual battles of the early modern period fought adjacent to or within urban space.

Apart from the general shape of the land on which battles were fought, we are also interested in the specific features that may be scattered across the battlefield space; some of these are also listed. There may be natural features, the products of geology such as ridges or depressions; or biological entities such as woods, forests, or hedges; or made features, such as ancient burial mounds, earthen banks and ditches, or buildings. Some of these play a part in the battlefield action; many do not. Some may have been noticed on the day, and others not. The presence of some may have been one reason why the place was chosen for battle; that it was considered to be "marked" in some way as significant to those who fought there. To give an indication of how we approach these issues, two examples are used of things that may be present on a battlefield: woodlands, and churches and monasteries.

Woodland can offer a place to hide troops, may be an area to avoid, or may simply provide a source of raw material. At Aljubarotta and at Bosworth the woodland areas were avoided by troops and provided a boundary to the battlefield space. The trees themselves at Aljubarotta were a source for the material used to construct a *chevaux de frise* protecting the defenders' position, and their presence on steeply sloping ground served also to protect the flanks of the position. At Northampton trees provided a boundary to the battlefield space along its southern edge but also provided a modicum of protection from the elements to troops encamped there overnight. At Tewkesbury and at Fontenoy the woods were used to hide the presence of troops from the enemy. Spearmen at Tewkesbury were able to catch a contingent of the enemy by surprise, and artillery at Fontenoy was able to enfilade attacking troops by using woodlands to mask movements and positions. The specifics of particular circumstances seem to determine the role of woodland in battle, as an inconvenience or an asset, as a landscape feature or as merely a number of individual trees. The manner in which woodland is treated by soldiers in different periods may indicate how such features are perceived more generally in that period. These few examples may suggest that trees are more likely to be seen as woodland landscape features in more recent periods, and

Battlefield Landscapes and Features by Period

Classical

Landscape:	Low ground *and* visibility from at least one major settlement
Features:	None
Battlefields:	Levktra 371 BC
	Marathon 490 BC
	Philippi 42 BC
	Plataea 479 BC
	Thermopylae 480 BC

Medieval

Landscape:	High ground *or* visible from / within major settlement *or* both
Features:	Near or adjacent to church / monastery
Battlefields:	Stamford Bridge 1066
	Bouvines 1214
	Courtrai 1302
	Aljubarotta 1385
	St. Albans 1455 & 1461
	Northampton 1460
	Tewkesbury 1471
	Bosworth 1485
	Stoke 1487

Seventeenth & Eighteenth centuries

Landscape:	Low ground *and* invisible from major settlement
Features:	None
Battlefields:	Roundway Down 1643
	Cropredy Bridge 1644
	Naseby 1645
	The Dunes 1658
	Sedgemoor 1685
	Oudenaarde 1708

A medieval site: Bouvines 1214 AD. High open ground near settlement and monastery, beside a Roman road.

An early modern site: Oudenaarde 1708 AD. Low open ground away from settlement.

more as sources of material in earlier times. There may be scope for more research here.

Churches and chapels are a significant and common feature in any European landscape; accordingly, their presence in the battlefield space may not be remarkable, and also as what are very often the largest stone structures in their area they may inevitably attract attention. The great churches at Tewkesbury and St. Albans dominate the space of and around those towns. Battlefield action bypassed St. Albans Abbey on both occasions, but at Tewkesbury may have penetrated the church itself and certainly reached as far as the doorway where fleeing soldiers were caught and brutally killed. Fighting took place around Linton church and also the church at Fontenoy. At Linton it was sought as refuge for fleeing combatants, while at Fontenoy it was central to the fortified village at the center of the battlefield. Other church buildings are more ancillary to the battlefield action. Sutton Cheney church was the site of devotions prior to the battle of Bosworth and is visible from the battlefield, and the church at Westonzoyland is a few hundred meters only from the site of the action at Sedgemoor but is not visible from it. Stoke church stands off the battlefield across the road, though it is not visible today from the battlefield because of a stand of trees; these may not have been present in 1487 and the church may have been a dominant feature to combatants. By contrast, the chapel at Sorauren, not the village church which may have been fortified, but a small hillside shrine no longer extant, provided a convenient location for scouting enemy dispositions, but no more.

An ancient site: Plataea 479 BC. Low open ground overlooked by settlements.

A nineteenth-century site: Sorauren 1813 AD. Heavily featured space including two rivers, hills, valleys, and settlements.

Where churches are not evident, monastic establishments sometimes are. Monasteries stood just off the battlefield space at Bouvines and Courtrai, and a nunnery was immediately adjacent at Northampton. Battle avoided these places but they provided rescue and medical aid for the wounded once the fighting was over. At the time of the battles, both Tewkesbury and St. Albans Abbeys were the center of monastic activity, and it is possible other battlefields may also have had monasteries or nunneries nearby. It may be significant therefore that eight out of our sample of nine medieval battlefields are known to be close to or involve churches and monasteries while only four out of eleven more modern sites do. Fighting penetrates only one such structure in the medieval period while three in the modern period are in the center of the fighting. This suggests a change of attitude toward such places over time: that while churches and church foundations are not to be fought in or over in the medieval period, their presence nearby is desired or expected; while in later times they form merely another part of the battlefield space and no longer command special respect.

CONCLUSIONS

As our title suggests, our work can be seen as the construction of battlefield "typologies" as indicators of what features and type of landscape may be expected to constitute the place chosen for battle in any particular period of history. Rather than taking a top-down approach, based upon our expectations of how people in the past ought to be choosing battlefields, we hope we are taking more of a bottom-up approach, letting the kinds of places they have chosen tell us something about them. We believe we have tapped a source of information about how people in the past perceived the landscape around them.

The modern approach to choosing a battlefield, one that takes root in the late eighteenth or early nineteenth century, is to see it as a source of functional utility; as a set of obstacles to movement, as places to hide troops, as good cover, as dead ground. But in earlier periods this emphasis on usefulness seems to be less evident; instead, ground is chosen because it contains other kinds of value. In the classical and medieval periods, high visibility, especially from a population center, seems to be a key factor; and in the medieval period proximity to a religious foundation also seems to be desirable. In the early modern period sites are chosen that are not overlooked and in general avoid population centers. By the early nineteenth century, sites that contain a number of features, settlements, high and low ground, and woodland, are actively sought as places to do battle. These objects have utilitarian value and are actively used as part of a battle plan. In earlier times, such features are actively avoided or simply ignored.

Our particular approach has, we believe, three distinctive values. First, it represents an approach to battlefields grounded not in military history but in archaeology. We think this matters because it allows us to say things that a military historian cannot by virtue of the inevitable limitations of that field of study (please note: archaeology has its limitations, too, but they are different). Second, we believe that our work may have some predictive value where scholars are seeking to locate a battle from the past. By using our typology for that period some places may appear more likely, others less so. Third, because we highlight not functional rationality in decision making but the unstated assumptions that lie behind choice in the past, we also help to undermine the current myth of war as a rational activity and an appropriate response to perceived threat. The way wars are fought is not grounded in rationality but in cultural beliefs, and these vary across time and across space. Our work reveals some of this variation.

NOTES

1. Carman 1999; Carman & Carman 2001; Carman 2002; Carman & Carman 2006.
2. Schofield et al. 2002; Saunders 2002.
3. Tilley 1994:67, 208.
4. Tilley 1994:75.
5. Keegan 1976:33–34.

REFERENCES CITED

Carman, J. 1999. Bloody Meadows: The places of battle. In S. Tarlow and S. West (eds.), *The Familiar Past?: Archaeologies of Later Historical Britain*, 233–245. Routledge, London.

Carman, J. 2002. Paradox in Places: twentieth century battlefield sites in long-term perspective. In J. Schofield, W. G. Johnson, and C. M. Beck (eds.), *Matériel Culture: The Archaeology of 20th Century Conflict*, 9–21. Routledge, London.

Carman, J., and P. Carman. 2001. Beyond Military Archaeology: Battlefields as a research resource. In P. W. M. Freeman and A. Pollard (eds.), *Fields of Conflict: Progress and Prospect in Battlefield Archaeology*, 275–281. Archaeopress, Oxford. BAR International Series 958.

Carman, J., and P. Carman. 2006. *Bloody Meadows: Investigating Landscapes of Battle*. Stroud Publishers, Sutton, UK.

Keegan, J. 1976. *The Face of Battle*. Jonathan Cape, London.

Saunders, N. 2002. Excavating Memories: Archaeology and the Great War. *Antiquity* 76:101–108.

Schofield, J., W. G. Johnson, and C. M. Beck (eds.). 2002. *Matériel Culture: The Archaeology of 20th Century Conflict*. Routledge, London.

Tilley, C. 1994. *A Phenomenology of Landscape*. Berg, Oxford.

Characteristics of Ancient Battlefields: Battle of Varus (9 AD)

Achim Rost

ANCIENT BATTLES AS A SUBJECT OF BATTLEFIELD ARCHAEOLOGY

Investigating an ancient battlefield by archaeology often depends on interpreting artifact find maps, especially when there are traces of a battle in an open field, without fortifications, and far from a fortified camp or settlement. This type of research requires the preservation of a sufficient number of artifacts. With about 5,000 items from Kalkriese, we have the opportunity to examine an open field battle of the Roman era in detail (compare Wilbers-Rost in this volume).

At an early stage of the research, the percentage of metal objects from military equipment, which is high compared to ceramic remains, as well as bones of men, mules, and horses, allowed identification of the site as a battlefield. However, connection of the archaeologically demonstrated battlefield with events described by Roman historians as the "Battle of Varus" (Tacitus, Annales I 59–62; Cassius Dio 56, 18–23) caused difficulties. Until now, some historians[1] have tried to connect Kalkriese with the 15/16 AD campaigns of Germanicus. Attempting to find indications for a reliable identification by archaeological observations was made more difficult because comparable investigations of ancient battlefields that might aid in understanding the archaeological features of Kalkriese do not exist.

Therefore we have to examine information from finds and features at Kalkriese. We have to clarify whether conclusions can be drawn to better understand the course of the fighting or whether later events, such as plundering, may be identified better than the battle itself. It is possible we will find reasons for the lack of comparable sites during such reflection.

METHODICAL ANALYSIS OF ARCHAEOLOGICAL SOURCES AS A THEORETICAL MODEL

To judge the quality of preservation on the site discussed in this paper, it is necessary to analyze those factors that had an effect on the archaeological remains of a battlefield over the centuries. The factors are diverse and only some of them can be dealt with here. Landscape, vegetation, and agriculture, for example, will be ignored for the time being, as this chapter focuses on processes of looting expected on all battlefields. These activities manipulated the remains originally lying on the field, meaning, they destroyed, reduced, or moved artifacts.

The amount of archaeological material on battlefields depends on the size of the military units involved in the action as well as on the proportion of the forces of two fighting armies. Only when large units were involved, and one party was clearly defeated, is there a chance for archaeology to find enough remains of equipment after plundering the battlefield.

Even if these requirements are met, later archaeological proof depends on the fact that the dead and wounded soldiers, of which there should be many, remained on the battlefield. If the losers were able, or the winners wanted, to gather those killed in action—to bury them or just despoil them far off the battlefield—this would probably have caused a nearly complete removal of most equipment and weapons attached to the soldiers. For a modern investigation, this would have negative consequences since the potential finds were taken away.

On a concentrated battlefield, plunderers would probably have noticed the bigger pieces of equipment or weapons that were not connected directly to the dead bodies, such as swords, lances, or shields, and were lying about the site as single objects. Thus, most objects usually left on a battlefield may have been pieces of long-range projectile weapons that were scattered widely and were too small and worthless to expend search time.

There are sites that illustrate those aspects. In Olynthos, Northern Greece, for example, where an ancient town was besieged and stormed, almost exclusively slingshots and arrowheads from the attackers were excavated.[2] Find maps of the battlefield of Palo Alto (U.S.–Mexican War) are first of all based on small-arms ammunition.[3] One can easily imagine what remains of military actions if neither firearms, nor slingshots or arrows with iron heads were brought into action. Under such circumstances, very few objects would be left; they would hardly be taken as undoubted proof of a battlefield. Most favorable for an archaeologist investigating a battlesite would be the complete destruction of a large army, with much metal equipment and a large baggage, left to the arbitrary selection of the victors, with no possibility to recover the wounded or dead.

KALKRIESE AS AN EXAMPLE FOR METHODICAL ANALYSES OF ARCHAEOLOGICAL RESOURCES

Traces of such a battlefield are at Kalkriese. In principle, however, one has to consider that the Germans were not only interested in intact pieces of Roman military equipment for further use. Under the aspect of obtaining raw materials, fragments of gold, silver, bronze, and iron were valuable, and the damage or destruction of objects may have been irrelevant. Bigger pieces might have been destroyed; objects that were less handy, such as long shield edgings, were torn away from the wood and folded several times. Made more compact, they could be more easily carried in baskets or sacks over long distances.

Quite early we noticed artifacts that illustrated the processes of plundering vividly. We often found pieces of military equipment that were once tightly fastened to soldiers, such as buckles and plates from armor, hooks from ring mail shirts, scabbard fittings, belt buckles, and apron fittings. Some might have been lost during the battle; since there are such a large number, most must be interpreted as hints of plundering the dead at the site of their death. These finds can plausibly be explained if we imagine looting as a drastic process. Only a few hours after death, equipment could not be removed except with violence. While collecting booty, the plunderers might fail to notice small pieces and fragments hidden in the grass or under bushes, or that may have been trampled into the earth that preserved them until today.

Roman legionary of Augustan time with equipment (following Horn 1987, Fig. 1). Shading indicates those items that were found in Kalkriese.

In spite of well-developed archaeological fieldwork, no other sites quite like Kalkriese have yet been found. Therefore we have to assume that the battlefield of Kalkriese and the processes of plundering are rather an exceptional case among battle sites of antiquity and not, as we thought in the beginning of the research project, a typical example of a plundered ancient battlefield.

Following these ideas about looting dead soldiers, we also have one reason for the lack of Germanic finds in Kalkriese. The Germans presumably did not have many losses; besides, as victors in their own territory they were able to retrieve their dead, together with their equipment, and bury them according to their cultural rules.

MAPPING ARTIFACTS OF THE BATTLE

Attempts to map artifacts from excavations on the "Oberesch" allow a first check on the above assumptions. Many artifacts were found close to the wall. The reason for this may be destruction of some parts of the wall during the battle or shortly after; therefore the looters may have overlooked the items even when they were the larger objects. This should not be interpreted as an indication of more violent fighting. In the zone near the wall, however, details of some battle activities might be reflected more directly.

More important for methodical reflections about looting is the area a short distance in front of the wall where the Germans had free access to the corpses of the soldiers and the booty. Here we found fragments of military equipment that were not attached to soldiers are rarer than those which were tightly connected.

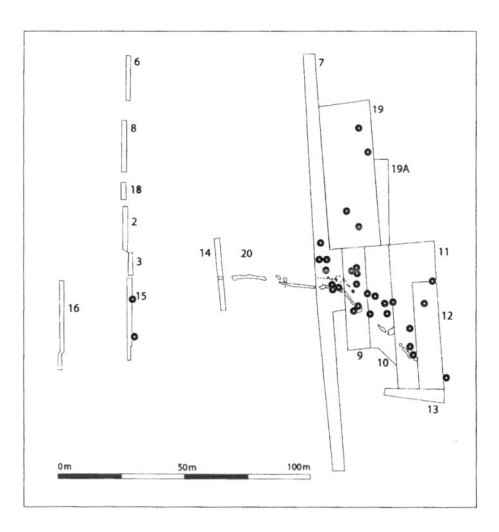

Distribution of pieces of the equipment that were not fixed to the soldier (for example, lances, spears, "pila," blades of swords, shields). (Museum und Park Kalkriese)

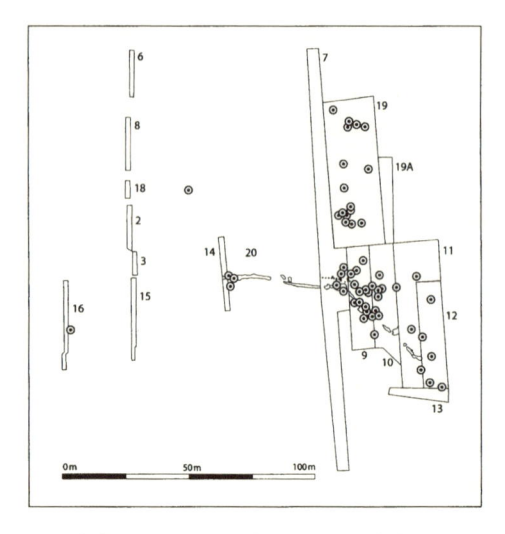

Distribution of pieces of the equipment which was tightly connected to the soldiers. Also shown: drainage ditch and post holes of the wall. The first attempt of mapping such artifacts was made for the trenches No. 1 to 19. (Museum und Park Kalkriese)

A dead legionary lying on the battlefield with his equipment was, as a concentration of objects, easily visible. Only if he were not carried from the battlefield with his equipment but was despoiled at the place where he had been killed would some small objects and fragments be left. In the main activity areas of a battle of annihilation, we should expect many such small pieces of the "fixed" equipment. Places of very violent action must have been strewn with many corpses and equipment. In such concentrations, "not fixed" weapons such as swords, lances, or shields would be noticed, even when lying separated from their owner. Therefore they should be rare in the excavations.

The Kalkriese investigations give the first hints that show the correctness of these theoretical ideas. On the "Oberesch" site, only one fragment of a blade has been found to date that might be part of a sword. Other remnants of this weapon are missing. We found only fragments of the scabbards that were once attached to a soldier's belt. More often, pieces of equipment not fastened to the man, such as lance heads, as well as fragments of pila and shields, were discovered on the "Oberesch" site. One must take into account that some of these artifacts were so badly damaged during the battle, for example when they were run over by baggage carts, that plunderers could not see the small metal points or fittings separated from their wooden parts.

The maps of just a small part of the battlefield at Kalkriese take into consideration only a few groups of Roman finds and cannot give more than a first methodical indication. We have to map the finds over a much larger area. Fragments of equipment carried by legionaries on the march, and of the baggage, including pieces of horse harnesses, carriages, chests, tools, and medical instruments, must be mapped and analyzed in the same way.

Trying to interpret the distribution of finds on a battlefield after considering plundering, it may not be so important to subdivide military equipment fragments according to their original use. Rather, we should think about characteristic criteria that fit those activities and perceptions we expect from battlefield looters. For the different groups of finds, plausible explanations must be developed to help understand why these objects were not taken but, instead, left on the battlefield. Different interpretive models of a group's distribution may exist and must be explained. Only when we are successful in identifying the individual processes of despoiling a battlefield may we have the chance to draw further conclusions about the course of the actions during the battle itself.

For Kalkriese, however, we have to consider that at least the action on the "Oberesch" was a battle in a defilade, fought from on top of the wall. For the relatively restricted area of the "Oberesch," that is the center of the narrow pass between hill and bog, and at the same time the main place of the battle, we have to expect that more and more Roman units reached this place, though no longer in their usual march formation. Therefore we have to assume that many military events continuously overlapped here. Thus, the possibility of reconstructing events of the battle in detail from archaeological observations might be quite restricted.

Mapping artifacts in a larger area, not only on the "Oberesch," may give us even more information. The density and quality of finds in the area of the Battle of Varus (about 50 km^2; see Wilbers-Rost figure in this volume) are in no way uniform. For the "Oberesch," we can infer looting of the dead on the battlefield from the small pieces of the equipment once attached to a soldier. Here we can presume a zone of intensive combat with many dead soldiers. From areas off the main scene, however, we get a different impression. To draw definite conclusions is not yet possible because of the low quantity of finds resulting from field surveys and limited excavations. It is remarkable, however, that a Roman sword scabbard, of which the metal parts were nearly complete and which is a precious silver object ornamented with intaglios, was found at the edge of a bog about 2 km north of the "Oberesch." Concentrations of silver coins are, compared to the "Oberesch," also more often found in this more remote area. Different explanations for this phenomenon have been considered by others including the possibility of war booty sacrifices or that officers might have been involved in the battle here more than at "Oberesch." Those finds, however, were originally connected to a Roman soldier by a belt or they were kept in a leather bag as "pocket money." At sites with many dead soldiers, the plunderers would probably not have failed to notice such pieces. Therefore, I believe that such finds may characterize battle zones with less intensive action that might have left fewer dead soldiers and artifacts. Here, the chance to miss valuable artifacts was much greater because a single object could hardly be seen among grass or bushes by the plunderers. We must now check for further indications that support this assumption. The small fragments of equipment once attached to the soldiers should be fewer in such zones. Someday, maybe, we will be able to distinguish by archaeological methods more intensive, or violent, zones from less important fighting areas or zones of flight.

CONCLUSIONS

The foregoing observations suggest that the distribution of battlefield finds may cause erroneous conclusions if there is no theoretical analysis of the archaeological sources. The retrieval of corpses together with their equipment may cause considerably less finds available on the main sites. In zones on the edges of the battle with fewer casualties, we may expect more striking single objects today, provided that plundering was less thorough on a site with a few bodies and objects. Looting a battlefield usually resulted in a reduction which is not proportionate, but selective, and thus manipulates the later picture of the distribution of artifacts. Archaeological sources may sometimes indicate the opposite of the original proportions.

If these theories are correct, we may also obtain archaeological indications for identifying Kalkriese with the Battle of Varus. The despoiling of many dead Roman soldiers on the battlefield itself, as is highly probable for Kalkriese, can be connected with the complete destruction of three Roman legions in the Battle of Varus known from written tradition. No written Roman sources suggest that during the actions of Germanicus (15/16 AD; Tacitus Annales I, 63–72) Roman units were destroyed to an extent comparable to the Battle of Varus, nor that the remains were left to the arbitrariness of Germanic plunderers so extensively that the victors plundered even the equipment attached to the soldier on a large scale.

The intention of this chapter is to identify the processes of plundering and their effects on the archaeological record by referring to the example of Kalkriese. I also tried to reconstruct patterns of behaviour that might stand behind differing pictures of the distribution of finds on an ancient battlefield. Additional processes that might influence the preservation of finds after the end of the battle, such as religious ceremonies, cannot be discussed in this chapter, nor can the organization of the plundering. A comparison with more recent battlefields, for which more detailed information concerning such postbattle processes might exist, may help to understand events on more ancient battlefields.

NOTES

For helping me with the translation of my text I want to thank Ingrid Recker, Osnabrück, and Lawrence Babits, Greenville, NC.

1. See Wolters 2003; Horn 1987.
2. Lee 2001.
3. Haecker 2001.

REFERENCES CITED

Haecker, Charles M. 2001. The official explanation versus the archaeological record of a US-Mexican War battle. In P. W. M. Freeman and A. Pollard (eds.), *Fields of Conflict: Progress and Prospect in Battlefield Archaeology*, 135–141. Proceedings of a conference held in the Department of Archaeology, University of Glasgow. BAR International Series 958.

Horn, Heinz Günther (ed.). 1987. *Die Römer in Nordrhein-Westfalen*. Theiss, Stuttgart.

Lee, John W. I. 2001. Urban combat at Olynthos, 348 BC. In P. W. M. Freeman and A. Pollard (eds.), *Fields of Conflict: Progress and Prospect in Battlefield Archaeology*, 11–22. Proceedings of a conference held in the Department of Archaeology, University of Glasgow. BAR International Series 958.

Wolters, Reinhard. 2003. Hermeneutik des Hinterhalts: die antiken Berichte zur Varuskatastrophe und der Fundplatz von Kalkriese. *Klio* 85:131–170.

Finding Battery Positions at Wilson's Creek, Missouri

Carl G. Carlson-Drexler

IN NUMEROUS PUBLICATIONS, battlefield archaeologists have likened the archaeological investigation of battlefields to crime scene investigation.[1] As with forensic science, archaeologists consider eyewitness testimony in the form of the historical record as well as the physical evidence (DNA, fingerprints, etc.), a ready analog for archaeologically derived data. The processes of interpretation and reconstruction that are the primary research foci of much of the extant literature on battlefield archaeology are methodologically identical to the reconstruction of a crime based on much fresher evidence. This is fundamentally an apt description of the praxis of historical archaeology, but its sanguinary connotations make it particularly appropriate for battlefields.

Battlefield archaeologists are privileged above almost all other historical archaeologists in that their subjects of interest are much more thoroughly recorded than other kinds of sites. The stress and high excitement of battle make these hours in a soldier's life among the most crisply remembered. Memoirs, letters, diaries, newspaper accounts, and so on, as well as a host of secondary sources, fill innumerable shelves on the history of war. There are numerous sources that we may tap in order to learn the history of any given battle, much more than we may learn about the typical settlement site or privy.

However, this blessing of historical data can be a hindrance as well as an aid to archaeology. If we have so much information on the event in the form of historical data, what more will archaeology tell us? At this point, only a partial answer may be advanced. Archaeology allows us to reconstruct the progress of battle, thereby assessing the veracity of or clearing up ambiguities in historical accounts of the events. The part of the answer that cannot be provided at this time pertains to what archaeology can really tell us about battles. Frequently, battlefield archaeologists cease interpretation at the level of historical reconstruction. This obscures information about not only the battle, but also about the cultures involved in conflict. A number of battlefield archaeologists, notably Scott,[2] Fox,[3] Sterling,[4] Harbison,[5] and Sivilich and

Wheeler-Stone,[6] have attempted analyses of artifacts that go beyond reconstruction to focus on processes encompassing larger subsets of the combatant cultures than only the military.

When we reach the point that we can justly give an answer to the question of what archaeology can tell us about battlefields, we can then create the synthetic, multidisciplinary approach advocated by numerous battlefield archaeologists, though perhaps most explicitly set out by Haecker and Mauck.[7]

This study fits into the development of the epistemological bounds of battlefield archaeology by showing a tiny fraction of the potential that spatial analysis, driven by modern geographic information systems (GIS), holds for the future of this area of research. Using artifacts recovered from the fields around Wilson's Creek, just south of Springfield, Missouri, site of one of the first significant battles of the American Civil War, a GIS is used to identify the locations of certain artillery batteries during several different stages during the battle.

Before we become too thoroughly embroiled in the history and archaeology of Wilson's Creek, a few notes should be made to aid in understanding the complex history of this engagement. The Union army at Wilson's Creek was not pitted solely against the Confederate army. The Missouri State Guard and Arkansas State Troops, those two states' militia units, fought alongside the Louisiana, Texas, and Arkansas men already enrolled in Confederate service. Deeper readings of the history of the battle, particularly the command problems experienced by Southern commanders in attempting to coordinate between these three forces, would find some profit in maintaining this distinction. However, for ease of reading, "Confederate" can be here taken along with "Southern" to denote state militia as well as national units.

HISTORICAL BACKGROUND: THE BATTLE OF WILSON'S CREEK

Wilson's Creek is often referred to as the "second great battle of the Civil War." It was fought a few weeks after First Bull Run, and was the first major battle fought west of the Mississippi River. After a summer of campaigning for control of Missouri, the Union and Confederate armies lay barely a dozen miles apart. After advancing from the rail terminus at Rolla, the Federals had occupied Springfield long enough to deplete the stores they had brought with them.[8] They had to move back to Rolla to stay supplied, but could not do so with the enemy so near to the south. Their commander, General Nathaniel Lyon, had to launch a preemptive attack to stall the Confederates long enough to allow him to withdraw to Rolla.[9]

The Federal army left Springfield on the night of August 13, 1861, in two columns. The larger of the two, a force of 3,300 men under the command of Nathaniel Lyon, was to fall upon the Confederate camps from the north at dawn.[10] Simultaneously, the smaller command, 1,100 men under Franz Sigel, after a march to the east of the Confederate camps, would attack from the south.[11] This pincer move was meant to break up the Confederate force before they could mount an effective resistance, and would allow the Federals to break off and move back to Rolla unmolested.

Initially, the attack proceeded as planned. The Missouri State Guard, who had been joined by a brigade of Arkansas State Troops and a brigade of Confederate Army soldiers and now numbered 12,000 men, was completely shocked by the appearance of the Federals, who opened fire on their camps with artillery as the men were cooking breakfast.[12] Lyon and Sigel both capitalized on this confusion by pushing toward each other, squeezing the Southerners between them.

After overcoming the initial shock, the Confederates began to exert their better than two-to-one numerical superiority, halting Lyon on what is now known as Bloody Hill.[13] To the south, Sigel had inexplicably halted his troops in column barely 40 yards from the ravine cut by Wilson's Creek. Confederate soldiers filed into this cover and, at a rush, descended upon the Federals who were, due to their deployment, virtually unable to defend themselves, and therefore fled in confusion.[14]

With the threat posed by Sigel's men neutralized, the Southerners were free to focus on Lyon's men atop Bloody Hill. Repeated attacks had failed to pry the Iowans, Missourians, and Kansans from this position, despite the loss of Lyon, who was struck in the chest by a musket ball.[15] His successor, Major Samuel Sturgis, realized around noon that Sigel was not going to arrive, and that the army had achieved its goal of damaging the Rebels enough to keep them from pursuing, and therefore deemed it time to withdraw. By early afternoon, the battle was over. It had cost the Federals 1,300 men killed, wounded, and missing; 1,200 Southern soldiers were either killed or wounded in the engagement.[16]

Both sides justly claimed victory at Wilson's Creek (known as Oak Hills by some Confederates). The Confederate Army had managed to maintain the field, achieving a tactical victory. On the other hand, the Federals had achieved a strategic victory, as the Southern commanders chose to tend to their damaged army rather than pursue the Yankees back to Rolla. In the following months, the Arkansans and Confederates returned to Arkansas, and the Missouri State Guard did its best to bring Missouri under their control. The Federals remained at Rolla, reeling from the loss of one-quarter of the army as well as their commanding officer. After receiving reinforcements and a new commander that fall, they launched a campaign in January 1862 that culminated in the March battle of Pea Ridge, where they once again faced the combined forces of the Confederate army and the Missouri State Guard.[17]

PATTERNING, RESEARCH QUESTIONS, AND ISSUES OF SCALE

There are literally hundreds of questions that may be posed to the archaeological record of a battlefield. The most obvious questions focus around particularist (i.e., specific to each battle) reconstruction. In essence, these research questions center on the reconstruction of a single battle, linking discrete historical events into a coherent chain through the use of archaeological data. These questions often create ambiguities between the historical and archaeological records, as exemplified by the archaeological investigations of the Little Bighorn.[18]

Reconstruction of historical events is an important component of battlefield archaeology, particularly in cases where the site of conflict has been memorialized in some form of park, as is Wilson's Creek. One of the great services archaeologists can give to the public and to those involved with interpreting a park to that public (i.e., park rangers, historians, tour guides) is bettering our understanding of the event being commemorated.

In pursuing a more nuanced interpretation of a battle, we may follow the gross and dynamic patterning approach developed by the researchers at the Little Bighorn.[19] Gross patterning involves analyzing densities and scarcities of artifacts to arrive at an understanding of where on the battlefield major actions were fought, what ground was most contested.[20] Dynamic patterning, on the other hand, looks at the progress of the battle, using artifact distributions to understand the movement of troops, either individually or in groups, across the landscape.

Archaeological investigations of a number of Indian Wars sites have yielded datasets well suited to dynamic patterning analysis. These sites, where the standard weapons of both warrior and soldier employed metallic cartridges, and generally involved a few hundred troops at the most, allow archaeologists to track individuals through the battle. By comparing the unique marks imparted on both projectile and casing by the discharge of a firearm, the archaeologist may identify numerous shell casings fired by the same weapon at different parts of a single battlefield.[21] By assuming the weapon was held by a single person, we can presume that the dispersal of casings mirrors the movement of that warrior or soldier through the battle.

Unfortunately, American Civil War battles are not nearly so straightforward. Troop strength could vary from a few hundred to nearly 200,000 soldiers on a field at a given time. These staggering numbers of troops could deposit a phenomenal number of projectiles over the course of a single battle, which could last multiple days. Additionally, since most Civil War small arms employed paper cartridges, not metallic ones, we frequently are left only with the bullet, discovered at the point where it fell to earth, with little or no archaeological reference to where it might have been fired from, outside of a limited number of bullets dropped in the haste of reloading.

How, then, would we approach dynamic patterning on a Civil War battlefield? One way would be to look for spent brass percussion caps, used to ignite the powder in a Civil War paper cartridge. Unfortunately, small copper or brass caps are very seldom found. For instance, during archaeological investigations at Pea Ridge National Military Park, Arkansas, only five percussion caps were collected out of a total artifact count of 2,700. These extant examples may be detritus from Civil War reenactors performing living history displays on the site, and are therefore of modern origin.

A second way of approaching dynamic patterning is to identify the cultural and physical strictures placed on units in battle that affected how they positioned themselves upon the battlefield and how they negotiated it during combat. For instance, Heckman's (this volume) study of the battle of Lookout Mountain, Tennessee, deals not only with the culturally defined limits placed on battlefield behavior (i.e., moving men in long lines, two ranks deep), but also with physical aspects of the battlefield (vegetation, relief, etc.). Her analysis shows quite compellingly that the surprise suffered by Confederate troops at the battle was due largely to the approaching Federal force being masked by local terrain until the Union army had drawn very near to the Confederate entrenchments. The archaeologists investigating the battlefields at the Little Bighorn and Palo Alto have employed this approach.[22]

This chapter is similarly focused on dynamic patterning, but instead of concentrating on the level of the army corps, as does Heckman, two individual artillery batteries have been selected for analysis. Using an analysis of cultural and physical constraints on artillery fire at the Battle of Wilson's Creek, we will show how Backof's Missouri Battery, a Union artillery company, and Reid's Arkansas Battery, a Confederate unit, were positioned on the battlefield during the fight between Sigel's Union troops and Confederates from Louisiana, Arkansas, and Missouri for control of Sharp's Field.

ARCHAEOLOGY AT WILSON'S CREEK

Beginning in 2001, a team of volunteer metal detector operators and Civil War enthusiasts, under the supervision of Dr. Douglas Scott, archaeologist for the National Park Service's Midwest Archaeological Center (MWAC), conducted fieldwork that yielded 1,400 metal artifacts, the bulk of which were deposited during the battle. The location of each artifact was recorded using a global positioning system (GPS), allowing MWAC staff to analyze artifact patterns, of both a gross and dynamic character.[23]

The shell fragments associated with Backof's Battery were recovered in the southern half of Sharp's Cornfield, in the area where the Confederate cavalry camps were located. During the early stages of the battle, Backof shelled these camps, and then moved off the surrounding bluffs to join the rest of Sigel's division as it moved north through Sharp's Field. At no other point in the battle did a different battery, either Confederate or Federal, report firing into this area.

Similarly, the artifacts associated with Reid's and Bledsoe's guns were located along the northern edge of Sharp's Field, in an area where Sigel's division was posted prior to being surprised and routed by the 3rd Louisiana and elements of the Arkansas State Troops. This area is out of range of the nearest Federal position on Bloody Hill, and from any point where Backof's guns might have been posted.

CIVIL WAR ARTILLERY IN THE FIELD

"In range" is a fairly nebulous concept, and must be considered from two angles. The first of these is what the cannons themselves were capable of. Both Backof and the two Confederate batteries studied here employed 6- and 12-pounder guns. These weapons, antiquated by the time of the Civil War, had maximum effective ranges of 1,532 and 1,072 yards, respectively.[24] Second, we must consider what the battery commanders and soldiers were capable of hitting reliably. One of the main manuals for the artillery, John Gibbon's *Artillerist's Manual*, published in 1860, clearly states that targets more than 1,000 yards from the position of the battery are not usually fired upon, as they are too difficult to see and to take aim upon.[25] Binoculars or telescopes, frequently carried by battery commanders, could ameliorate this shortfall, but, due to the inaccuracy of some field pieces, they were discouraged from attempting such long-range fire.

Battery commanders on both sides were similarly discouraged from employing a firing technique called "indirect fire." Indirect fire involves posting a battery behind some obstacle, shielded from the target's view, making it impossible to see the target from the actual gun position. In order to hit the target, a spotter would have to be posted somewhere in view of the target to observe how the shots were falling, then relay adjustments in aim back to the battery. This kind of fire is predominant in the modern military. Its use was exceedingly rare during the Civil War.[26]

Much more common in the mid-nineteenth century was "direct fire." As the name implies, direct fire involves firing on targets that are directly within the line of site of the battery.[27] References made by members of Reid's, Bledsoe's, and Backof's batteries indicate that both sides could see their targets when they opened fire, indicating that they were indeed firing directly.[28]

Artifact deposition, in most instances, is a process that occurs perpendicularly to the earth's surface, by dint of gravity. Dropping an artifact, sweeping it through the crack in a floorboard, or discarding it are all depositional processes that involve little horizontal displacement of the artifact from its point of use/origin. The deposition of the various kinds of projectiles used on a historic period battle, on the other hand, is typified by great horizontal displacement. Here, the point of deposition, and the point of firing (discard) are widely separated. In many instances, both of these points may be inferred, either historically, through the use of documents, or archaeologically, through the location of, for instance, spent shell casings and associated bullets. With these two batteries, however, we only have one of these points established concretely, the point of deposition. Luckily, we do know the conditions that governed the depositional event (direct artillery fire). Knowing this, we can use the point of deposition to infer the point of origin.

We infer the point of origin by identifying those places from which the artillery could be firing. We know that the batteries were able to see their targets; meaning that those points where shell fragments associated with either Backof's or the two Confederate batteries were recovered must have been viewable from the battery position. This means that the battery position and the location of each associated shell fragment must be "intervisible." This allows us to apply cumulative viewshed analysis (CVA) to identify cannon positions.

CUMULATIVE VIEWSHED ANALYSIS: METHOD AND CASE STUDIES

Cumulative viewshed analysis (CVA) is simply a means to identify those parts of a landscape that are visible from a given set of points. Most studies employing this technique, such as Wheatley's[29] discussion of Neolithic long barrows around Avebury and Stonehenge, England, focus on intervisibility between sites as a means to identify culturally distinct suites of sites in prehistory. This study obviously breaks from this tradition by focusing on intrasite dynamics, not intersite relationships.

In order to perform a CVA on a set of artifacts, the researcher must be able to calculate a viewshed. The term "viewshed" means those areas of a landscape visible from a given point on that landscape.[30]

Viewshed analyses, when calculated on the computer, are facilitated by files known as digital elevation models (DEMs). A standard DEM is essentially the same as a digital image, a matrix of cells containing a given color value, with the important exception that a DEM, instead of storing color information, stores elevation data. This grid of cells is known as a raster dataset. For this analysis, each cell or pixel within the DEM represents the elevation of a 30-meter-square plot of land. The elevation data may then be used by the computer to calculate viewsheds from any point or set of points on the landscape.

When calculating a viewshed from a given point, the computer simply tests each cell in the raster to see if a straight line can be interpolated from the cell to the designated point without being obscured by another cell. If a cell representing a higher elevation value lies between the point and the cell being tested, then that cell being tested is considered invisible from the selected point. However, if no such intervening value is present, than the cell being tested is within the viewshed of the selected point.

So, given a single artifact location, using viewshed analysis we can determine from where on the landscape that location may be seen, which, given the arguments presented above, represents in the case of artillery fragments all the possible positions from which that shell could have been fired. When presented with a number of fragments, however, we must rely on cumulative viewshed analysis, which is only a single conceptual step beyond the individual-point-oriented viewshed analysis.

To perform cumulative viewshed analysis, focusing on multiple locations, one must begin by calculating individual viewsheds for each of the loci selected for study. In this case, individual viewsheds were calculated for each of the shell fragments in the groupings for Backof's, Bledsoe's, and Reid's batteries. The viewshed results are displayed as a raster dataset (same as the DEM or a digital photograph) coded "1" and "0." Cells labeled "1" are those areas visible from the selected point, and those marked "0" are not. In order to identify those areas visible from a number of selected points, we must only sum the viewshed rasters. There are various means of performing this operation, such as the "raster calculator" feature in the ArcGIS program suite offered by ESRI. The raster calculator simply adds the values of the viewshed cells, returning a new raster with the cumulative viewshed information.

For instance, if we had a sample of 21 shell fragments, we would calculate individual viewsheds for each, and then sum them using the raster calculator. The resultant cumulative viewshed would contain values from 0, those areas where no fragment could be seen from, to 21. The cells of the raster containing 21 as a value would be those areas where all of the viewsheds overlapped, and are, therefore, those areas where all of the shell fragments in question could have originated. In a situation like Wilson's Creek or most Civil War battles, where direct fire was the only method of artillery fire employed, those areas that overlook all shell fragment locations are the only areas where the batteries could have stood while firing.

Backof's Missouri Battery Opens the Battle

The first case study presented here focuses on Backof's Missouri Battery, an organization formed in St. Louis during the early struggle for that city's arsenal, primarily from the German immigrant population of the city who made up the area's core Unionist element. At the outbreak of hostilities, the battery was composed of six 6-pounder guns led by Major Franz Backof, a veteran of the 1848 revolution in Germany and an artillerist with considerable experience.[31] By Wilson's Creek, however, many of the battery's experienced men had left and were replaced with infantrymen pulled from the 3rd Missouri Infantry with only "a few days instruction," and four of the guns had been replaced with 12-pounder howitzers.[32]

Sigel positioned two sections (four guns) of Backof's battery on a rise overlooking the camps of Confederate as well as Arkansas and Missouri state cavalrymen posted in Joseph D. Sharp's field. The bombardment opening the southern portion of the battle began at 5:30 in the morning,[33] surprising and greatly disrupting the Southerners, who were cooking their breakfast at the time.

Archaeologically, the location of the Southern camps has been identified as a scatter of 6- and 12-pounder artillery ammunition, as well as a scattering of personal equipment that would be consistent with an encampment. It is the aforementioned scatter of shell fragments that will be the focus of this analysis.

Fourteen shell fragments were recovered from the south end of Sharp's Field during the archaeological investigations there. The majority of them (n = 12) are fragments of 12-pounder howitzer case shot, with the rest (n = 2) being 6-pounder gun case shot pieces. These are consistent with the types of cannon being fired by Backof's men during the engagement. For each, a viewshed was calculated and then summed using the raster calculator. The final cumulative viewshed is shown in the following figure.

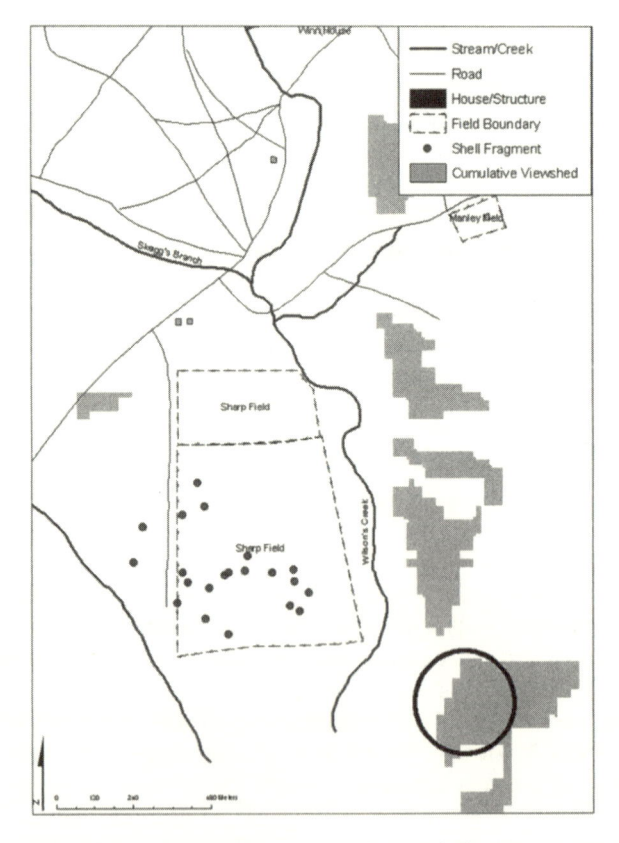

Cumulative viewshed for shell fragments fired by Backof's Missouri Battery (U.S.). Circled area denotes most likely battery position. Courtesy of the National Park Service, Midwest Archeological Center

As the figure shows, based on cumulative viewshed analysis, there are only a few areas along the bluffs overlooking Sharp's Field from which the Federal guns could have fired on the Southern camps.

The history of the early stages of the battle of Wilson's Creek places Backof's battery at the south end of Sharp's Field when they opened fire on the Confederate camps. The figure depicts an area, circled, along the southern margin of the field from which the shell fragments found in the vicinity of the camp could have been fired. This corresponds well with the historical interpretations of the battery's position, and is, based on these two lines of evidence, likely to have been the spot.

In this instance, there is a positive correlation between the position as suggested by historical documents and archaeological data. The next case considered here in part does not enjoy this same correspondence.

Confederate Batteries and the Rout of Sigel's Federals

The rout of Sigel's forces from the north end of Sharp's Field affords us another test of the cumulative viewshed analysis process. In this case, two artillery batteries are known to have shelled Sigel's men in support of Southern troops under the command of General Benjamin McCulloch, who stormed out of a ravine less than 100 yards in front of the Federals, surprising and routing them in a matter of minutes.

The Fort Smith Battery, an Arkansas militia unit under the command of Capt. John B. Reid, fired on Sigel's men from a position in the vicinity of the Ray farmhouse, northeast of the Federals. Simultaneously, Capt. Hiram Bledsoe, commander of a Missouri militia battery placed north of the Federal position, opened fire on Sigel's men.[34] This fire corresponded with the charge of the 3rd Louisiana against Sigel's troops, who believed the onrushing Confederates to be the 1st Iowa, who also wore gray uniforms. Sigel, mistakenly believing that the artillery fire was coming from friendly batteries, was heard to shout, *"Sie haben gegen Uns geschossen!"* (They have fired against us!).[35]

Two viewshed analyses can be performed here. First, both batteries report being able to see the Federal force when they opened fire, so calculating a cumulative viewshed for the shell fragments in the northern portion of Sharp's Field and between the field boundary and the banks of Skegg's Branch should result in a viewshed that suggests possible battery positions for both.

Additionally, archaeological work at Wilson's Creek yielded a number of projectiles that are directly associable with Bledsoe's battery. Prior to Wilson's Creek, the Missouri State Guard, the state militia of whom Bledsoe's unit was a member, found itself woefully short of ammunition. The gunners in the guard were particularly destitute of canister rounds. In order to fill this need, men from the Missouri batteries contracted with local blacksmiths while camped at Cowskin Prairie, near Sarcoxie, to cold cut iron bars and rods into inch-long segments.[36] The use of bar and rod canister by the guard at both Wilson's Creek and later at Pea Ridge has been documented both historically and archaeologically. Three pieces of rod shot were found in the vicinity of the rout of Sigel's forces. These were almost certainly fired by Bledsoe's battery. Not only are such rounds not documented as being used by Arkansas troops (i.e., Reid's battery), the Fort Smith battery was posted at a great enough distance that they had to use long-range shells, the first rounds of which accidentally fell among the Louisianans as they attacked.[37] These three pieces of rod canister can therefore be used as a basis for a cumulative viewshed analysis to identify, in tandem with the analysis of shell fragments, the position of Bledsoe's battery alone.

Rod Canister Viewshed

As stated above, three pieces of rod canister were recovered just south of Skegg's Branch, and can be attributed to Bledsoe's Missouri gunners. Using the locations of these three artifacts, we calculated a cumulative viewshed raster. The next figure shows the raster placed over the Wilson's Creek battlefield. The area of interest in this raster is the region just north of the points of recovery (circled). Canister rounds are only effective at short range, ideally at less than 400 yards. The distance between the nearest area within the viewshed and the points of recovery is greater than that distance, but, since Bledsoe's men were firing downhill at the Federals, the effective range of their projectiles was somewhat greater.

It should be reiterated that outside of the above-mentioned area of interest, no other points on the battlefield are very close to the points of recovery for these canister slugs, meaning that it is unlikely that another battery, such as Reid's Fort Smith unit, fired their own scratch-built ammunition at the Federals. The cumulative viewshed analysis for these canister slugs, then, reliably displays the possible locations of Bledsoe's cannons. The above-mentioned area is, then, the best archaeological guess at where these guns stood during the brief fight for Sharp's Field.

Shell Fragment Viewshed

Calculating a cumulative viewshed for the shell fragments that were found mixed with the rod canister slugs in Sharp's Field, as mentioned above, will provide possible locations for both Bledsoe's and Reid's batteries. In all, four shell fragments were used in conducting this stage of analysis, the results of which appear in the figure below.

Several things should be noted in the outcome of the shell fragment viewshed. First, the area north of Skegg's Branch where the rod canister analysis suggests Bledsoe's battery stood is replicated by the shell fragment

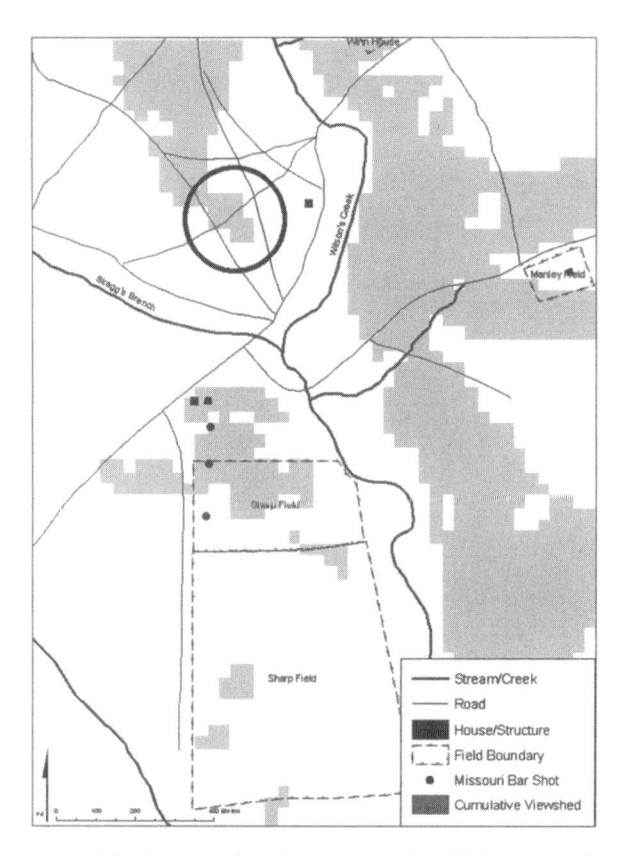

Cumulative viewshed for Missouri bar shot recovered at Wilson's Creek. Circled area denotes possible position of Bledsoe's Missouri Battery (C.S.). Courtesy of the National Park Service, Midwest Archeological Center

analysis. This strengthens the position for Bledsoe's battery suggested by the rod canister viewshed analysis.

Second, the areas west of Wilson's Creek, where many historians have placed Reid's Fort Smith battery during the engagement, are not visible from the sites of the shell fragment finds. This suggests that the actual position of Reid's battery was farther to the north, near the Telegraph Road. The position of this battery is not easily established historically, and, in this case, it may have been positioned too far to the south.

Based on this analysis, then, we can suggest positions for both Bledsoe's battery and Reid's Fort Smith gunners. Bledsoe's men stood roughly where most historical sources document their position as being, but Reid's battery appears to have been placed farther north, closer to the Telegraph Road than was previously believed.

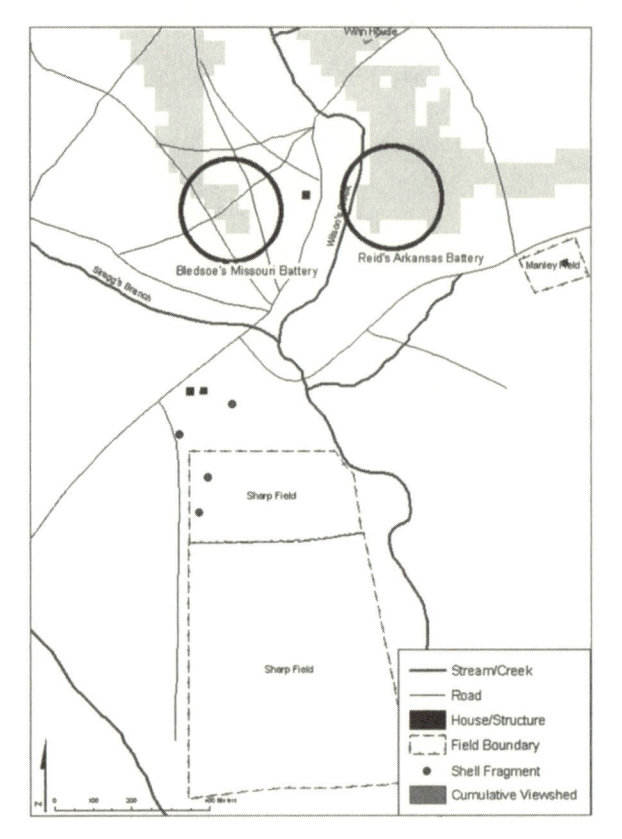

Cumulative viewshed for Confederate shell fragments. Circled areas denote possible positions of Bledsoe's Missouri Battery (C.S.) and Reid's Fort Smith Battery (C.S.). Courtesy of the National Park Service, Midwest Archeological Center

CONCLUSIONS

Using cumulative viewshed analysis has, therefore, allowed us to use archaeologically derived data (artifact locations), coupled with spatial analytical procedures, historical data, and ethnohistoric information (firing methodologies), to construct an interpretation of the locations of some of the units involved in the fighting at Wilson's Creek during different stages of the battle. These suggested locations are approximations only, however, and should not necessarily be considered highly precise, hyper-accurate analyses. There are a few potential confounds that should be noted at this point because of their potential to alter the outcomes of the cumulative viewshed analysis.

The first of these considerations is the actual location of the artifacts. Two factors should be highlighted, one depositional and one taphonomic. The first of these is the fact that shell fragments stem from cannonballs that explode in the air, dispersing fragments over a wide area. This dispersing effect could theoretically deposit a shell fragment in an area not visible from the battery position, thereby creating a measure of error in any attempted cumulative viewshed analysis. The same cannot be said, however, for canister, which was deposited as it fell, within the viewshed of the firing position.

The second consideration, the taphonomic one, is that Sharp's Field was an agricultural field both prior to and subsequent to the battle. Over time, repeated plowing and other land use practices could move artifacts around under the soil. The extent of the effect of this process on artifact locations has not been extensively studied. This source of error is one that needs to be studied more in future.

One final error vector should be mentioned, and this is a flaw inherent to all viewshed analyses. Digital elevation models, the files containing the elevation data for a region, consider only topographic information, neglecting vegetation and cultural elements of the landscape. Stands of trees and housing communities will naturally affect what can be seen from a given location. While suburban sprawl did not begin to encroach on the Wilson's Creek battlefield until recently, ground cover could have an effect on this analysis. Until field and forest areas have been identified through archaeological (soil analysis) and historical methods, an ongoing effort by the University of Arkansas, we cannot gauge the effect on the cumulative viewsheds that vegetation cover poses.

This chapter set out to achieve two tasks. First, it sought to aid the staff and volunteers of the National Park Service in the interpretation of Wilson's Creek to the public who visit the site each year. Through the above-described methods, we have offered an artifact-driven idea of where Backof's, Bledsoe's, and Reid's batteries fired from during salient parts of the engagement. To return to the criminalistic analogy mentioned in the introduction, this analysis has combined the physical evidence (artifact locations) with eyewitness testimony (historical information) to arrive at an interpretation of aspects of the event under study.

The second goal of this chapter is to show how battlefield archaeologists can incorporate spatial analytical procedures into their analyses of battlefield assemblages to refine and expand our historical-archaeological understanding of a past event. Battlefield archaeology possesses great potential for epistemological fluorescence, the bulk of which remains to be fully tapped. There are currently some flaws with this methodology as here presented. None of them are fatal to the effort, however, and can be ameliorated through further, ongoing fieldwork.

It is hoped that by showing how cumulative viewshed analyses can be used to identify battery positions, other archaeologists will explore other ways of asking for more information from their assemblages. Heckman's chapter in this book is another illustration of the suitability of using GIS-based spatial analyses for battlefield interpretation. By exploring a wider range of methods and approaches when studying battlefields archaeologically, not only will battlefield archaeology be able to extend itself beyond the particularist reconstruction focus that currently dominates the field, it will be able to contribute to a growing body of anthropological, sociological, and political science literature focusing on warfare as a cultural process, thereby making battlefield archaeology relevant to historical archaeology as a much-refined approach to interpreting the past and building archaeological theory, and also to understanding processes currently at play in the modern world.

NOTES

1. Gould (2005) reports this analogy as being first published by Collingwood (1946).
2. Scott et al. 1989, Scott and Fox 1987, Scott and Hunt 1998.
3. Fox 1993, Fox and Scott 1991.
4. Sterling 2000.
5. Harbison 2000.
6. Stone and Sivilich 2003.
7. Haecker and Mauck 1997:6.
8. Cutrer 1993:231.
9. Ibid.
10. Piston and Hatcher 2000:185.
11. Ibid., 190.
12. Cutrer 1993:231.
13. Ibid., 236.
14. Ibid., 234.
15. Piston and Hatcher 2000:268.
16. Ibid., 337–338; Confederate casualty totals are estimates due to the lack of existing documentation on the true extent of the losses sustained by the Confederate Army, Missouri State Guard, and Arkansas State Troops.
17. Shea and Hess 1992.
18. Scott et al. 1989, Fox 1993, and other publications on the archaeology of the Little Bighorn deal extensively with the discrepancies between the popular vision of Custer and his men engaged in a valiant "last stand" and the progress of the battle that an analysis of the artifacts suggested.
19. Scott et al. 1989:146.
20. Ibid., 147.
21. Ibid.
22. Scott et al. (1989), and Fox (1993) heavily rely on this approach in their analysis of the Little Bighorn. Haecker and Mauck (1997) employ the same approach in studying Palo Alto.
23. This data is currently being readied for publication by Drexler, Scott, and Roeker.
24. Drury and Gibbons 1993:77–78.

25. Gibbon 1860.
26. Griffith 1989.
27. Haecker and Mauck 1997:77.
28. Piston and Hatcher 2000:222; a private in Backof's battery recalls seeing the Confederates running around in confusion when the battery opened on them. On page 254, Piston and Hatcher clearly note that both Reid and Bledsoe could see Sigel's men from their positions.
29. Wheatley 1995.
30. Wheatley and Gillings 2002.
31. Piston and Hatcher 2000:34.
32. Ibid., 189.
33. Holcombe and Adams 1961[1883]:40.
34. Piston and Hatcher 2000.
35. Holcombe and Adams 1961[1883]:42.
36. Patrick 1997.
37. Piston and Hatcher 2000:254.

REFERENCES CITED

Collingwood, R. G. 1946. *The Idea of History*. Oxford University Press, New York.

Cutrer, Thomas W. 1993. *Ben McCulloch and the Frontier Military Tradition*. University of North Carolina Press, Chapel Hill.

Drury, Ian, and Tony Gibbons. 1993. *The Civil War Military Machine: Weapons and Tactics of the Union and Confederate Armed Forces*. Smithmark Publishers, London.

Fox, Richard A. Jr. 1993. *Archaeology, History, and Custer's Last Battle*. University of Oklahoma Press, Norman.

Fox, Richard A. Jr., and Douglas D. Scott. 1991. The Post-Civil War Battlefield Pattern: An Example from the Custer Battlefield. *Historical Archaeology* 25(2):92–103.

Gibbon, John. 1860. *The Artillerist's Manual*. Morningside Publishers, Dayton.

Gould, Richard. 2005. The Wreck of the Barque *North Carolina*: An Historic Crime Scene? *American Antiquity* 70(1):107–128.

Griffith, Paddy. 1989. *Battle Tactics of the American Civil War*. Yale University Press, New Haven.

Haecker, Charles M., and Jeffrey G. Mauck. 1997. *On the Prairie of Palo Alto: Historical Archaeology of the U.S.-Mexican War Battlefield*. Texas A&M University Press, College Station.

Harbison, Jeffrey. 2000. "Double the Canister and Give 'Em Hell": Artillery at Antietam. In C. R. Geier and S. R. Potter (eds.), *Archaeological Perspectives on the American Civil War*. University Press of Florida, Gainesville.

Holcombe, Return I., and Adams (first name not given). 1961[1883]. *An Account of the Battle of Wilson's Creek or Oak Hills*. Dow & Adams, Springfield.

Patrick, Jeffrey L. 1997. Remembering the Missouri Campaign of 1861: The Memoirs of Lieutenant William P. Barlow, Guibor's Battery, Missouri State Guard. *Civil War Regiments* 5(4):20–60.

Piston, William G., and Richard W. Hatcher III. 2000. *Wilson's Creek: The Second Battle of the Civil War and the Men Who Fought It*. University of North Carolina Press, Chapel Hill.

Scott, Douglas D., and Richard A. Fox. 1987. *Archaeological Insights into the Custer Battle: A Preliminary Assessment*. University of Oklahoma Press, Norman.

Scott, Douglas D., Richard A. Fox, Melissa A. Connor, and Dick Harmon. 1989. *Archaeological Perspectives on the Battle of Little Bighorn*. University of Oklahoma Press, Norman.

Scott, Douglas D., and William J. Hunt Jr. 1998. The Civil War Battle of Monroe's Crossroads, Fort Bragg, North Carolina. Prepared for the U.S. Army, XVIII Airborne Corps and Fort Bragg, Fort Bragg, North Carolina by the U.D. Department of the Interior, National Park Service, Technical Assistance and Partnerships Section, Southeast Archeological Center, Tallahassee, FL.

Shea, William L., and Earl J. Hess. 1992. *Pea Ridge: Civil War Campaign in the West*. University of North Carolina Press, Chapel Hill.

Sterling, Bruce B. 2000. Archaeological Interpretations of the Battle of Antietam through Analysis of Small Arms Projectiles. In C. R. Geier and S. R. Potter (eds.), *Archaeological Perspectives on the American Civil War*. University Press of Florida, Gainesville.

Stone, Gary W. and Daniel M. Sivilich. 2003. The Battle of Monmouth: The Archaeology of Molly Pitcher, the Royal Highlanders, and Colonel Cilly's Light Infantry. Paper presented at the 36th Annual Conference of the Society for Historical Archaeology, Providence, RI.

Wheatley, David S. 1995. Cumulative Viewshed Analysis: A GIS-based Method for Investigating Intervisibility, and Its Archaeological Application. In G. Lock and Z. Stancic (eds.), *Archaeology and Geographic Information Systems: A European Perspective*, 171–186. Taylor and Francis, London.

Wheatley, David, and Mark Gillings. 2002. *Spatial Technology and Archaeology: The Archaeological Applications of GIS*. Taylor and Francis, New York.

Battlefield Viewsheds, or What the General Saw: Lookout Mountain Battlefield, Chattanooga, Tennessee

Elsa Heckman

SOUTHWEST OF DOWNTOWN Chattanooga, Tennessee, Confederate forces occupied Lookout Mountain from September to November 1863; the mountain was considered impregnable by its rebel defenders, who dubbed it "the Gibraltar of America."[1] To their astonishment, it was captured by Federal troops on November 24, 1863. Without closer examination of the terrain and circumstances of the battle, it is difficult to understand how Federal troops were able to overwhelm entrenched Confederate forces on the side of the mountain and effectively rout the startled rebels. By utilizing historic maps and written documents to determine troop placement on the day of the battle and incorporating that data into a series of viewshed displays from key Confederate and Federal positions on the lower slopes of Lookout Mountain, this study draws conclusions about the visibility of attacking and defending forces on the morning of the battle. Given the spotty accounts of the extent of mountainside vegetation at the time of the battle, this is meant only as a cursory evaluation of viewsheds on the battlefield, assuming best possible visibility scenarios.

A viewshed is simply the area that is visible from a particular point of view. It exists in "real space" or three dimensions and is the same in two directions. For example, any point that can be *seen* from point "A" can also *see* point "A". Most post-battle (modern) analyses of troop positions and approach tactics are approached in a two-dimensional context accompanied by written accounts such as historic maps, personal accounts, and official records. With two-dimensional maps it is possible to draw arrows and make inferences about troop locations and paths of movement, but without much discussion of actual visibility and the reality of being a soldier on the ground at these locations.

Once troop placement and movements are established on a three-dimensional map or digital elevation model, advanced analysis can be performed. Computer-generated viewsheds are one of the easiest ways to determine what could be seen by soldiers on the ground. Once generated, these viewsheds can aid in interpretation of troop movements and battlefield positioning based on terrain.

At Lookout Mountain it is easy to assume that attacking Federal troops were marching along the mountainside on a steep slope that rose only to their right and fell to their left. This is the impression that one gets from studying two-dimensional historic maps. In reality, that march was even more difficult than it seems at first glance because the side of Lookout Mountain is undulating and the slope that the soldiers had to contend with was not just to their right and left, but *also* to their front. With this undulating terrain on the Federal approach, it becomes clear from generating multiple viewsheds that their visibility was greatly restricted, as was their detection by Confederates to their front.

BACKGROUND

Although the prospect of taking Lookout Mountain, "... with its high palisaded crest and its steep rugged, rocky, and deeply furrowed slopes" seemed foolish, Union Commander Major General Joseph Hooker was charged with the task of doing just that.[2] With a force of about 15,000 men, the massive body of Federal troops under the leadership of General John White Geary crossed Lookout Creek about two miles upstream from the major Confederate entrenchments and ascended the mountainside. Unexpected aid came in the form of "drifting clouds [that] enveloped the whole ridge of the mountain top and heavy mists and fogs [that] obscured the slope from lengthened vision."[3] General Geary's command stretched from the sandstone cliffs, near the top of Lookout Mountain, to the banks of Lookout Creek. Sweeping northward in formation, perpendicular to the slope of the mountain and crossing large areas of rough terrain, the troops made steady forward progress (see figure).[4]

There are many existing accounts detailing the difficult march by the Federal troops to the northern end of the mountain that day. Lt. John R. Boyle of the Pennsylvania Infantry wrote that "... the mountain sloped downward at an angle of nearly forty-five degrees, and was covered with underbrush and heavy boulders, and broken by yawning ravines from fifty to one hundred feet deep."[5] Private David Mouat, also of the Pennsylvania Infantry, complained of "traveling over the rocks and fallen trees & up and down gullies ..."[6] Based on these accounts, historical photographs, and two paintings by James Walker, it is likely that the lower slopes of Lookout Mountain and the Lookout Creek floodplain were partially wooded at the time of the battle with interspersed areas denuded of vegetation. It is, however, impossible to determine exactly which areas were wooded and which were not in 1863. This is why the viewshed data must be interpreted strictly upon ground relief.

Western slope of Lookout Mountain with highlighted troop positions.

As the main Federal body was working its way north, swiftly encroaching upon the Confederate left and contained earthworks, Major General Edward C. Walthall's 34th Mississippi was contending with a diversionary force across Lookout Creek to their immediate front. At this same time, portions of General Wood's and Grose's Brigade had just successfully forded Lookout Creek approximately 1 kilometer southwest of the 34th's position with full intention of reinforcing Geary's already substantial force on the middle and upper slopes of the mountain. The only obstacle standing between Wood and his goal of linking with Geary's left flank was the battered 34th Mississippi. The Official Records describe this action as follows:

> General Walthall's 34th Mississippi, was cut off, along with the center and right of the picket line, from the rest of the brigade by the swift movement of the Union assault on its flank. As Captain H. J. Bowen of the 34th Mississippi attempted to meet the attack of Wood's brigade head-on, a portion of Grose's Illinois regiments, who were across the burnt out bridge on the west side of the creek, poured enfilading fire into the 34th's ranks.[7]

The Union artillery also effectively raked the ground behind and around the disintegrating Confederate regiment, blocking their only route of retreat. Nearly all of the soldiers in the 34th Mississippi surrendered or were killed.[8]

METHODS AND ANALYSIS

The primary goal was to generate viewsheds along General Geary's route of advance, from Wood's and Grose's river crossing, and from the doomed 34th Mississippi's stationary position on the lower slope of Lookout Mountain. This analysis was conducted using Idrisi raster GIS software but one can achieve similar results with ArcMap spatial analyst. A digital elevation model, or DEM, was obtained from the United States Geological Society (USGS) website in the form of a BIL file. It was necessary to convert the BIL file into ASCII before attempting to import it into Idrisi. Once this was successfully accomplished, a vector contour map was generated from the DEM and the hill shading module was employed. The contour map was created in order to ease identification of details in the landscape. It is from these details that viewpoints could be established. The hill shade module enhanced the visual relief of the landscape.

Next, vector files of both the Tennessee River and Lookout Creek were created for topographical reference purposes. Historic maps of troop placements on the day of the battle as well as historic documents aided in the generation of an approximate Confederate picket line and appropriately placed "points of view." The "viewing" locations were chosen for their strategic value on the battlefield to reconstruct what could actually be seen by soldiers from key positions on the ground.

The southernmost line of three (3) viewsheds (representing Geary's line of sight) was generated from the east bank of Lookout Creek and is representative of the initial Federal line's position immediately after their successful river crossing. The second line of three (3) viewpoints, located approximately one mile north on the mountainside, represents the approximate midpoint between Geary's river crossing and initial contact with Confederate forces. A solitary (1) viewshed was generated from the point where portions of Wood's and Grose's Brigades crossed Lookout Creek and began their thrust toward the 34th Mississippi's entrenched position. And finally, three (3) closely spaced viewshed points were generated from the position held by the 34th Mississippi. Separate viewsheds were generated for each individual viewpoint using a viewer height of 1.6 m, to simulate the height of a man on the ground, and a 4-km viewing distance. To more clearly demonstrate viewsheds from large groups of viewers like Geary's entire line and the 34th Mississippi's stationary position, viewsheds in the same general vicinity were combined to achieve comprehensive views from these more diffuse locations.

Viewshed 1

The combined viewshed from the initial Federal position on the mountain shows the visibility to the north on the western slope of the mountain to be fairly minimal due to the deep furrows running perpendicular to the

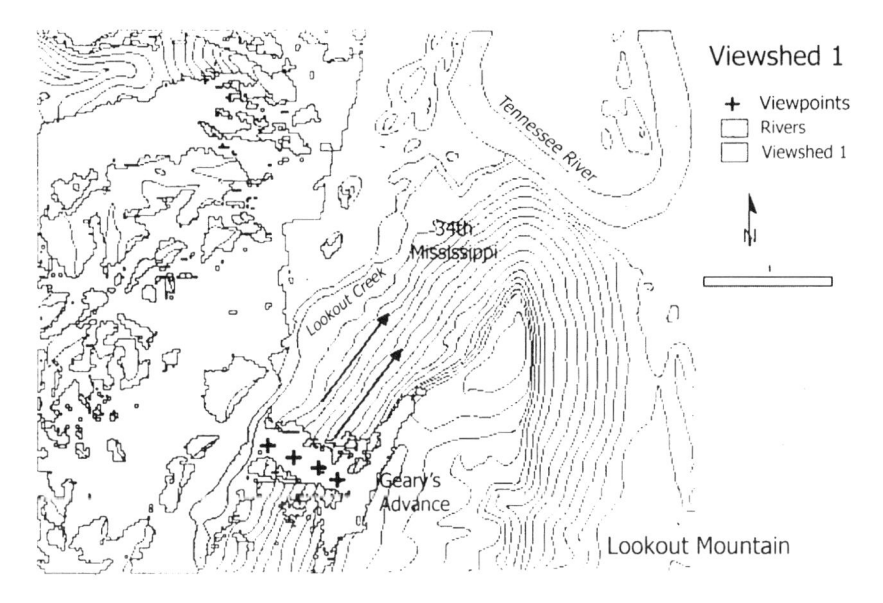

Viewshed from General Geary's initial position on Lookout Mountain.

mountainside (see figure). These gullies are responsible for long linear gaps in visibility to the north, along the entire Federal approach. This somewhat poor visibility could have been further lessened depending on the presence of trees and the dense fog on the upper elevations of the mountain. At this point, the Federal troops would not be in sight of Rebel forces located on the lower slopes of the mountain and due to the reported fog, the Confederates on top of Lookout Mountain would not have been able to detect their presence either.

Viewshed 2

The second viewshed depicts visibility of the advancing Federal forces midway between their Light's Mill river crossing and the Confederate line (see figure). At this point, portions of the Confederate picket line would have been in sight as well as earthworks present at the 34th Mississippi's battlefield position. This suggests that the Federal troops on their northward march would have been in full view of Confederate forces on the lower slopes of Lookout Mountain within approximately 1 km of actual contact. As the bulk of this Federal command became engaged with the Confederate forces higher up on the mountain, the troops of Generals Wood and Grose were pouring across Lookout Creek approximately 700 meters to the rear of the 34th Mississippi.

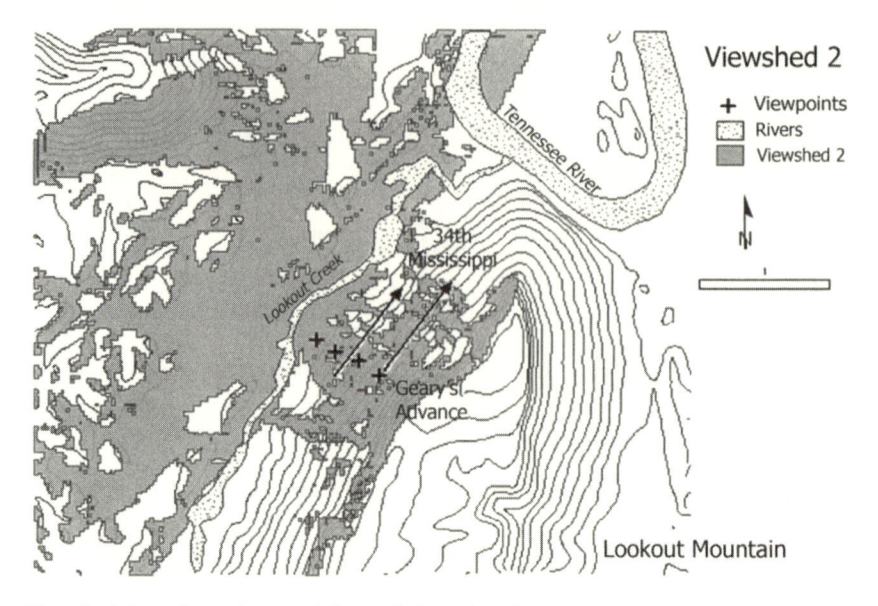

Viewshed from the midpoint of General Geary's advance.

Viewshed 3

This viewshed was generated from Wood's and Grose's river crossing. From this vantage, the soldiers of Wood's and Grose's Brigade had a direct route, with clear line of sight, to close in on the 34th Mississippi (see figure). The attack was a success and the 34th Mississippi's regimental battle flag was captured in this engagement.[9]

Viewshed 4

Finally, the perspective of the 34th Mississippi's position must be examined in light of the previous discussion. This final viewshed was generated from a northward pointing finger ridge at the base of Lookout Mountain which was occupied by troops from the 34th Mississippi (see figure).

A generally circular range of view is apparent around the entrenched 34th Mississippi's battlefield position. Based upon this viewshed, the Federal body of soldiers roaring across the western slope of Lookout Mountain would have been virtually undetectable from their stationary position. By the time that the 34th knew that an enormous body of Federal troops was gaining the Confederate left flank, it would have been too late to request reinforcements. Also, considering that the 34th Mississippi was occupied with fire to its front, its attention would have been diverted away from Wood's and Grose's river crossing. By the time the 34th turned to meet the onslaught of Wood's and Grose's brigades, they were taking fire from their left *and* their front.

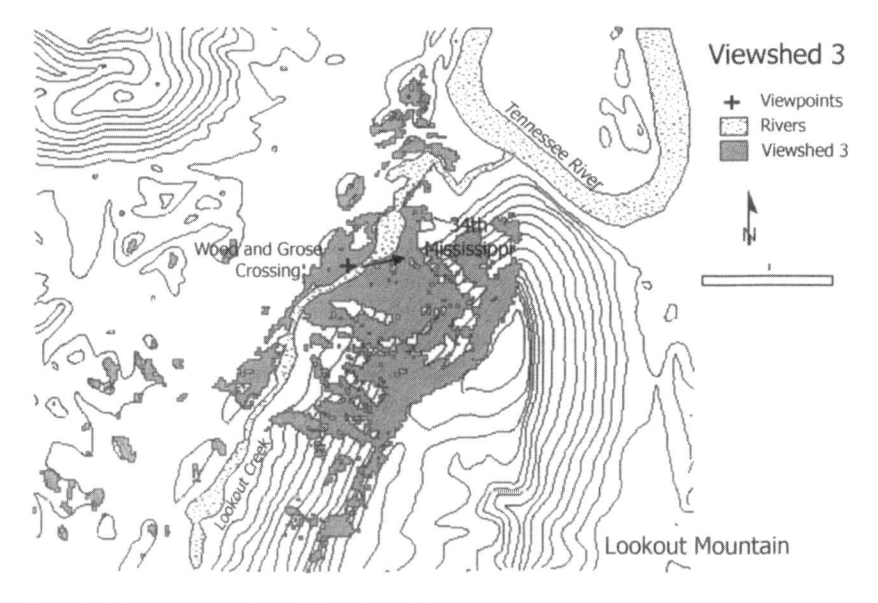

BATTLEFIELD VIEWSHEDS, OR WHAT THE GENERAL SAW   81

Viewshed from perspective of Wood and Grose's troops.

Although in retrospect it is simple to say that this position could not be held, it is obvious, based on this viewshed, why this particular landform was chosen for manning by the Confederate army. This small ridge afforded a prominent view of the railroad bridge spanning Lookout Creek below and

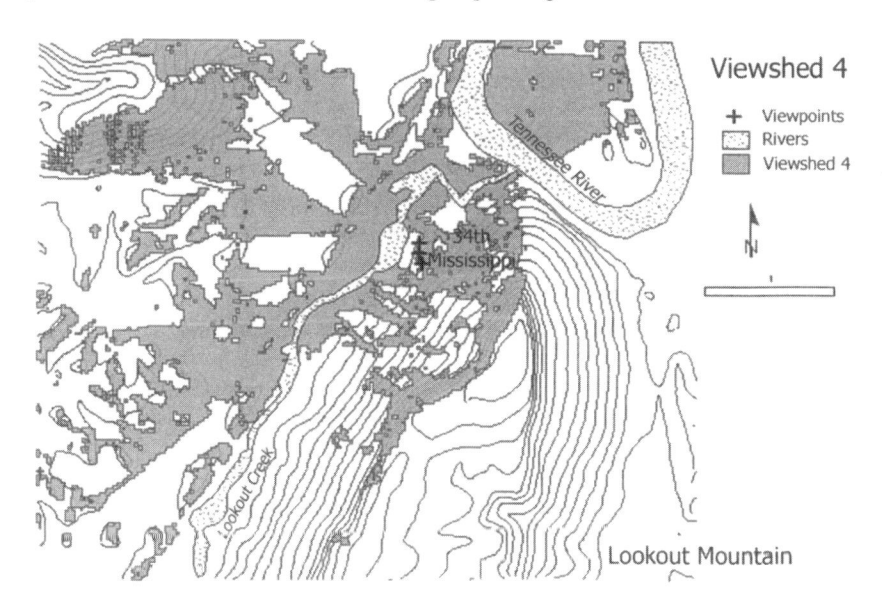

Viewshed from the 34th Mississippi's position.

also provided a good vantage for observing enemy behavior across Lookout Creek.

CONCLUSIONS

By implementing viewshed analysis on the lower slopes of the Lookout Mountain Battlefield, a comprehensive spatial understanding of troop movements and visual reality on the day of the battle can be further explored. An attack from the rear left flank was likely the last place that the Confederates were expecting an advance due to the unbelievably harsh terrain and the Federal demonstration to the Confederate front. This study suggests that the likely way Confederate forces on the lower western slopes of Lookout Mountain could have been alerted to the imminent attack would have been from their own forces on top of the mountain. With the extreme fog hovering over the crest and upper slopes of the hill this was not to be. The extreme furrowing and slight bend in the western slope of Lookout Mountain (apparent in the viewshed analyses) effectively hid the attackers from widespread Confederate observation.

An understanding of the physical environment at Lookout Mountain is best achieved by actually being there, but unfortunately, a trip to the study site is not always practical. Digital landscapes offer the investigator and the curious citizen, alike, a means of exploring the peaks and valleys of the area, without the hike. We have seen here that a first-person perspective in this virtual landscape has much to reveal about the battle of Lookout Mountain, and illustrates how digital technologies can be employed in furthering our understanding of the "reality" of battle situations. Additional research could allow the investigator to approach a complete environmental reconstruction of the site, re-creating field boundaries and forest cover of the landscape as it was in 1863. A three-dimensional representation of troop movements along a landscape, as seen from a soldier's point of view, can also provide visitors with a good and accurate understanding of what this particular engagement may have felt like. Using the Lookout Mountain Battlefield as a test case, this study demonstrates the contribution that viewshed analyses can make in understanding the perspectives of both attacking and defending forces on battlefields.

NOTES

1. Official Records of the War of the Rebellion [O.R], 1890: XXXI, 2: 437.
2. Official Records of the War of the Rebellion [O.R], 1890: XXXI, 2: 315.
3. Official Records of the War of the Rebellion [O.R], 1890: XXXI, 2: 391.
4. Taken from "The Civil War in Lookout Valley" by Harry M. Hays with contributions by Doug Cubbison, found in Alexander and Heckman 2005.

5. Boyle 1903:176.
6. Mouat n.d.
7. Official Records of the War of the Rebellion [O.R], 1890: XXXI, 2: 170, 181.
8. Alexander and Heckman 2005; Official Records of the War of the Rebellion [O.R], 1890: XXXI, 2: 703.
9. Rowland, Dunbar 1978.

REFERENCES CITED

Anonymous. 2001. Muster Roll of the 34th Miss. Infantry. http://www.rootseb.com. Military History of Mississippi by Roland Dunbar was referenced within the site (13 Nov. 2001).

Alexander, L. S., and E. Heckman. 2005. *Archaeological and Historical Survey of the Western Perimeter of the Lookout Mountain Battlefield*. Report submitted to the National Park Service, American Battlefield Protection Association. On file at Alexander Archaeological Consultants, Chattanooga, Tennessee.

Boyle, Lt. J. R. 1903. *Soldiers True, The Story of the 111th Pennsylvania Veteran Volunteer Infantry, 1861–1865*. New York, and Cincinnati, OH.

Mouat, Priv. D. n.d. Unpublished Reminiscences, Historical Society of Pennsylvania, Philadelphia, PA.

Official Records of the War of the Rebellion [O.R]. 1880–1901. War of the Rebellion: a Compilation of the Official Records of the Union and Confederate Armies. 129 Volumes. United States War Department, Washington, D.C.

What the Musket Ball Can Tell: Monmouth Battlefield State Park, New Jersey

Daniel M. Sivilich

A MUSKET BALL is not always a small lead sphere designed to be fired from a musket, pistol, or rifle at a specific target with deadly force. Musket balls were not always made of lead, spherical, or used with small arms. So how does one identify lead artifacts found at early military sites? This chapter will examine that question and develop a typology for spherical balls starting with basic lead balls that did begin as spheres and were designed for use with musket, rifle, or pistol, and then examine variations.

Musket balls are manufactured by pouring molten lead or another alloy into a two-part single or a multiple cavity mold. After the lead cools, the mold is separated and the musket ball removed. The casting sprue is cut close to the ball and any flashing around the mold seam is removed. Usually the musket ball would be put into a paper cartridge with a pre-measured charge of black powder. Eighteenth-century molds were made of iron or brass, but crude molds made of soapstone and brownstone are known.[1] The figure below shows a steatite (soapstone) mold on display at the Monmouth County Historical Association, Freehold, New Jersey. As can be seen, two different musket ball sizes and several sizes of buckshot could be cast with this mold. Seven buckshot cavities are ganged together to maximize the mold's available capacity. The different ball sizes suggest that the owner had two weapons, possibly a Brown Bess smooth bore musket or large bore pistol and a smaller bore rifle. Note the side of the mold is inscribed "1776."

The following terminology (see lower figure on page 85) is used here to describe weapons and musket balls.

> *Mold Seam*: a thin, often raised, line around the ball's circumference. Some molds were crude and the two halves would not match exactly when closed, allowing molten lead to seep out and resulting in musket balls that have two slightly offset or misaligned halves.

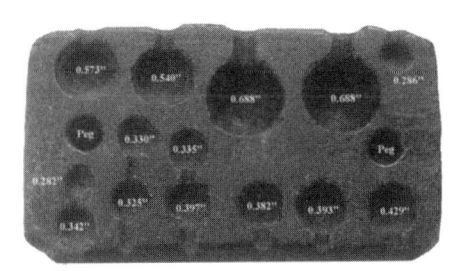

Steatite musket ball and buckshot mold. (Monmouth County Historical Association, Freehold, NJ)

Casting Sprue: a small raised cylinder from the mold's inlet channel. This is usually clipped off close to the surface of the musket ball.

Patina: lead carbonate/oxide. Musket balls buried in the ground for some time develop a white lead carbonate and lead oxide coating.[2] However, iron or other chemicals in the soil can change the color from white to tan to brown. Pine and oak trees produce high levels of tannic acid that can change the color of the patina to a dark reddish-brown.

Diameter: the size of a musket ball (usually measured in inches). This is not the caliber of the gun.

Caliber: the diameter of the gun barrel bore, also known as nominal caliber.

Windage: the difference between the gun caliber and the ball diameter. Typically the windage is approximately 0.05–0.10 inches.[3]

If an excavated musket ball is round, and has a mold seam and a casting sprue, then it probably was dropped and not fired. However, not all dropped musket balls have a mold seam or casting sprue. Some unfired musket balls excavated at Revolutionary War British occupation sites do not have these two features. It is possible that the musket balls were processed by pressing in England to remove surface irregularities. Another possibility is that the musket balls were made in England, packed tightly in crates or barrels, and transported

Musket ball.

by ship and over land by wagons. The rough modes of transportation could cause the balls to bang together many times, causing mold seams or casting sprues to be erased.[4] However, this is most likely not the case for pre-made cartridges. The paper wrapping tends to keep the ball from moving or rotating and also provides protective insulation.

What type of gun was a ball used with? To determine the weapon a ball came from, the diameter of the ball needs to be established (see figure). Diameter can be measured using a good set of calipers. When the diameter is known, the bore of the gun can be estimated. As an example a military British Brown Bess musket has a bore of 0.75 inches or is 75 caliber, but would take a 0.693-inch diameter musket ball. A .69 caliber French Charleville musket usually took a 0.63-inch ball. However, during the seventeenth and eighteenth centuries, musket balls were categorized not by diameter, but as to how many musket balls weighed a pound. For example a service British Brown Bess musket took musket balls that were 29 per two pounds.[5]

Examples of musket balls with different diameters.

If one size of spherical musket balls is found in quantities in areas not known to have a conflict, then this may be an indication of a campsite where musket balls were either cast or cartridges were being rolled. If found in a battle area, unfired balls may indicate a position where soldiers stood and fired. Sometimes during the heat of battle, a soldier would remove more than one cartridge from his cartridge box and inadvertently drop one. Dropped or unfired balls could also indicate where a soldier fell and cartridges spilled from the cartridge box.

By knowing a musket ball's diameter, one can estimate the bore of the gun it came from. However, what if the musket ball was fired, hit something, and is no longer round? The diameter cannot be measured directly. Another method was developed to estimate the diameter of deformed musket balls. Lead has a specific gravity of 11.4. This can be used to calculate the diameter of a musket ball based on its weight in grams. However, eighteenth-century lead contained air and impurities. This can be compensated for by using the Sivilich Formula:

$$\text{Diameter in inches} = 0.223204 \times (\text{Weight in grams})^{1/3}$$

The diameters of 781 musket balls excavated at Monmouth Battlefield State Park and surrounding associated areas were measured and/or calculated. The next figure is a histogram of the distribution of the diameters. There are two very distinct peaks: 0.63- and 0.69-inch diameters. Both the British and Americans were using standardized munitions, and the Brown Bess musket took a 0.693-inch diameter ball. Therefore, musket balls with diameters greater than 0.66 inch were most likely associated with that weapon. The center peak is between 0.60- and 0.66-inch diameter with a peak at 0.63 inch. This size ball was used in a variety of muskets, including two of the most common: the French Charleville, supplied to the Americans prior to Monmouth, and the British fusil.

The Americans used a number of riflemen at Monmouth. Rifles typically took musket balls with diameters less than 0.60 inch. The distribution confirms that the rifles had a wide distribution of calibers rather than being standardized.

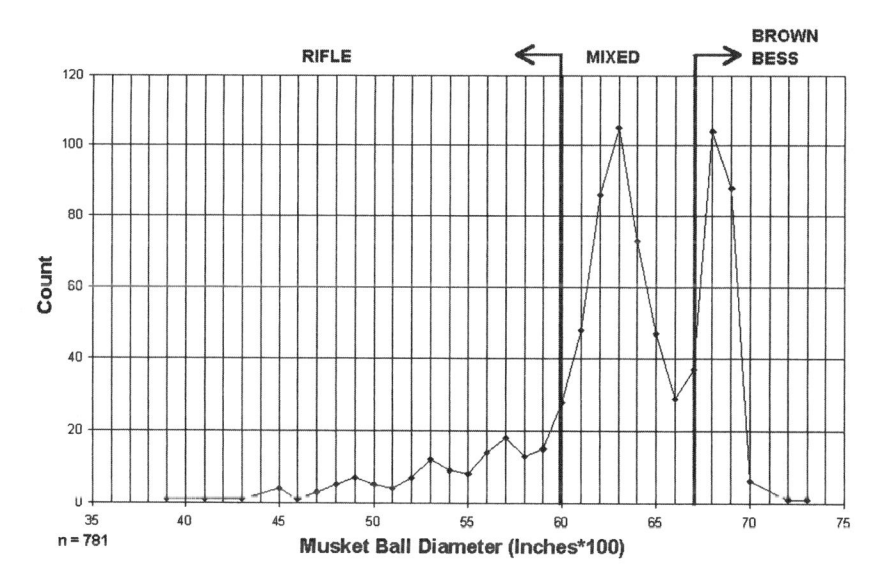

Diameter distribution of musket balls associated with the Battle of Monmouth.

Buck and ball.

A Phase I archaeological survey was conducted as part of the proposed road widening at the site. The archaeologist confirmed that they had found a musket ball. He had not formally measured it but estimated it to be just over a quarter of an inch. It had no visible sprue. This was not a musket ball. Notice that the lowest value on the chart in the above figure was 0.39-inch diameter for a musket ball. Smaller lead projectiles excavated at Monmouth are classified as buckshot. In 1776, George Washington issued a general order that a standard cartridge shall have one musket ball and 3 or 4 buckshot. The figure above shows a typical load and the relative size differences between buckshot and ball. Buckshot has changed little in the past two centuries and standard 00 buckshot today has a diameter of 0.33 inch and 000 buck has a diameter of 0.36 inch. Shot excavated at Monmouth ranges from 0.27- to 0.38-inch diameter. It is very difficult to tell eighteenth-century buckshot from modern buckshot that has been in the ground for only a few years and developed a patina. The most significant difference is that eighteenth-century shot was made in a gang mold and usually has a sprue visible if it is not too flattened from impact.

Some musket balls excavated at Monmouth have shallow circular depressions as shown in the next figure. Based on the author's personal experiences firing black powder flintlock muskets, these appear to be ramrod marks. Even though a ball may sit loosely in the breech of a musket, it is still rammed several times to seat the ball. If the ball is loose, it will rotate slightly with each strike. This ball has three blows from a ramrod.

Impacted musket balls can take many different shapes. One of the most common is a hemisphere. This

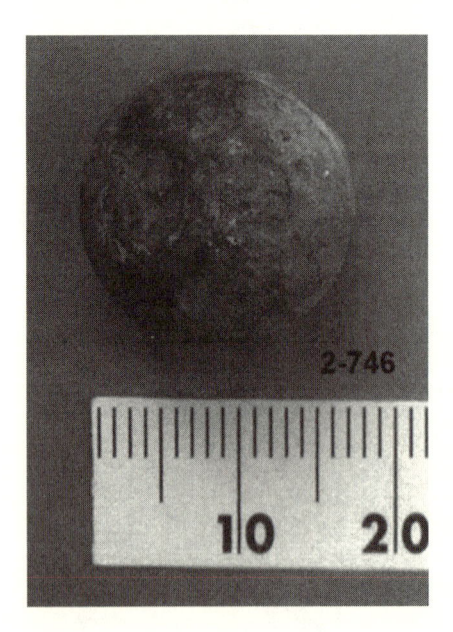

Ramrod marks on a musket ball.

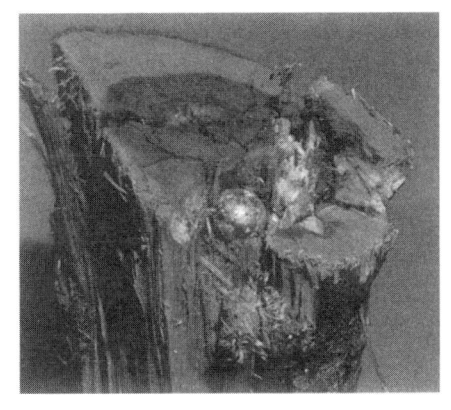

(a) Hemispherical-shaped, impacted musket ball; (b) Reproduction musket ball fired into tree.

form usually occurs when a ball strikes a compressible material such as wood or bone as replicated in the figures above.

Sometimes the shape can be used as a diagnostic tool. The musket ball shown in the figure hit a very smooth, uniformly curved object. The curvature present on this musket ball matches the outside diameter of a Brown Bess musket barrel. It may have hit a Brown Bess musket barrel.

If a musket ball traveling at a relatively high velocity hits a solid object such as a tree, a rock, a fence rail, and so on, at a shallow angle, it can ricochet or glance off. The force of this action will usually deform the musket ball and create a sweeping tail of metal as seen in the first figure on page 90.

After repeated firing, muskets begin to foul, building up a residue of unburnt powder in the barrel. This fouling can cause a musket ball to jam in a barrel. A steel screw commonly called a ball puller can be attached to one end of a ramrod and be drilled into a stuck musket ball to remove it. Distinctive thread marks are left in the musket balls similar to those

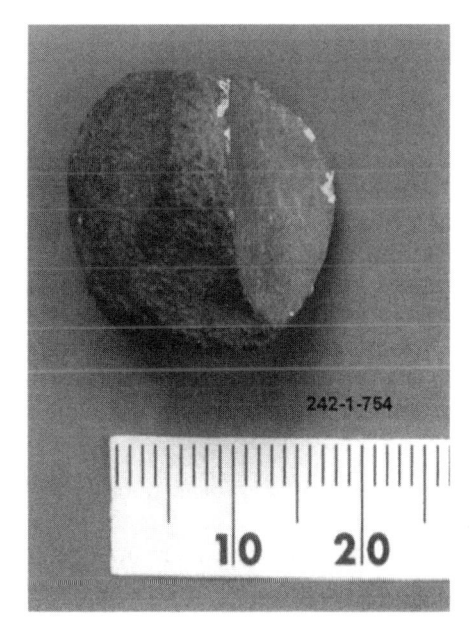

Musket ball that appears to have hit the barrel of another musket.

90   FIELDS OF CONFLICT

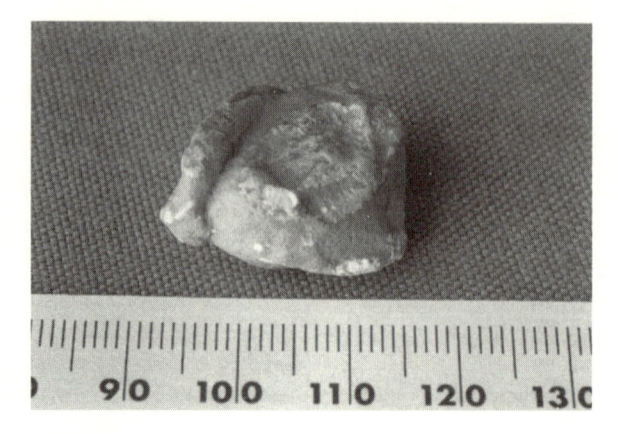

Ricocheted musket ball.

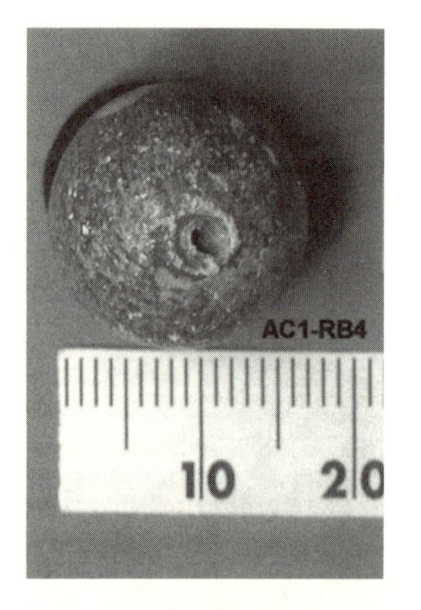

Pulled musket balls with extraction screw marks.

shown in the figure above. These have been excavated both at campsites and on battlefields. The balls were usually discarded after being pulled and are usually still round. Therefore the diameters can be measured.

Occasionally unusual artifacts are excavated that can evoke one's imagination. The musket ball, shown in the top figure on page 91, is hemispherical and probably hit and imbedded in a tree. It appears that it was then hit by two more musket balls. This suggests all three shots were being aimed at a specific target, possibly someone standing behind a tree.

There are the grim realities of war. The musket ball in the lower figure has what appears to be a human front incisor impression in it but is hemispherical in shape. It is hypothesized that this musket ball hit a soldier's front tooth and proceeded through the back of the head.

Anesthetics were not available during the Revolutionary War. If you were an officer and some rum or wine was available, you might dull the pain of surgery a little by getting drunk. However, the average soldier was simply given a stick or a piece of leather or a musket ball to bear down on to keep from biting his tongue or cracking his teeth from the pain of having a limb removed or having a musket ball extracted. This is how the phrase "bite the bullet" may have originated. Chewed musket balls may be an indication where wounded soldiers fell or the location of a field surgery. Thirty-five musket balls excavated at Monmouth have evidence of teeth impressions. These were examined by Henry M. Miller of Historic St. Mary's City, Maryland. A basic question of how much deformation a human can impart to a lead sphere with his teeth was first addressed. The author obtained reagent grade (99.9 percent pure)

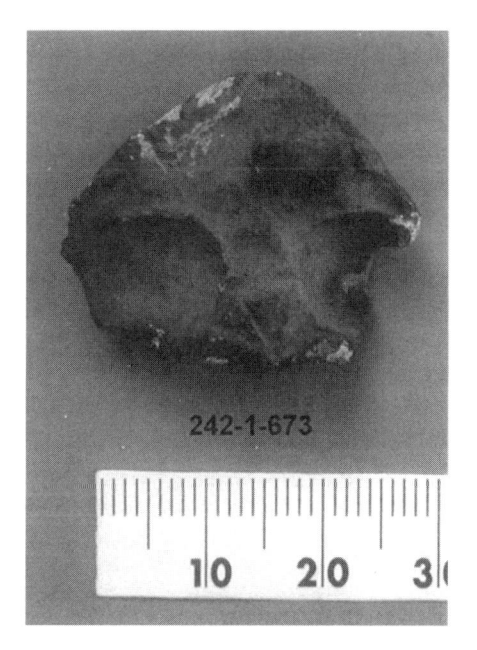

Impacted musket ball that appears to also have been hit by two musket balls.

Musket ball with front incisor impression.

Modern musket balls with human chewing marks.

lead from a chemical supply company and had it cast into 0.69-inch musket balls. The author and Henry Miller proceeded to chew several musket balls using molar and canine teeth with as much force as could be tolerated. The results are shown in the figure above.

This test showed that it was not possible to flatten a spherical musket ball. However, this does not preclude the use of flattened lead as a biting object during surgery. Seven musket balls were identified as being likely human chewed from the Monmouth Battlefield sample.[6]

It is unlikely that all human-chewed musket balls are associated with pain and/or surgery. The musket ball in the figure is a lightly chewed musket ball that has human canine and incisor teeth marks. Incisors are not used as bearing teeth like molars, so these musket balls were probably not chewed to ease pain. These were most likely chewed to promote salivation. The Battle of Monmouth took place on June 28, 1778. It is reported that

Musket ball with human canine and incisor teeth impressions.

temperatures reached 96° in the shade. Many soldiers from both sides fell to heat exhaustion. This has been documented at other battles as well. Thomas Mellen, a soldier at the Battle of Walloomscoik, stated:

> I soon started for a brook I saw a few rods behind, for I had drank nothing all day, and should have died of thirst if I had not chewed a bullet all that time.[7]

One must be careful in analyzing chewed musket balls. Musket balls can also be chewed by animals. Pigs root up objects and chew on them while looking for nuts, edible roots, and tubers. A number of pig-chewed musket balls excavated at Monmouth were identified by Henry Miller. The impressions on these musket balls are usually long deep scrape marks and lack any molar crowns.

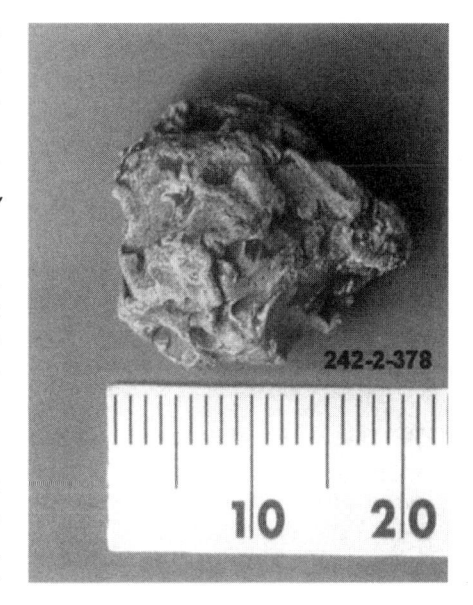

Musket ball chewed by a pig.

However, pigs are not necessarily the only animal to chew musket balls. In his analysis, Dr. Miller also noted a musket ball that a rodent chewed (see figure). It is possible that this musket ball had blood or bits of flesh attached or the sugar of lead (oxidized lead) attracted a rodent.[8]

Artifact 90M16RP4 with possible rodent gnawing marks.

It can be concluded that spherical lead balls can be used as diagnostic tools because:

- Diameters suggest the weapon type used.
- Round, dropped, or pulled balls indicate either a campsite or where soldiers may have stood.
- Impacted musket balls indicate target areas.
- Deformation of impacted musket balls may suggest target types and potentially landscape features of the time period.
- Human molar-chewed musket balls suggest locations of wounded soldiers and possible field surgery sites.
- Lightly chewed (human canine and incisors) musket balls might indicate dry or hot weather.
- Animal-chewed musket balls suggest post-battle farm activities such as hog ranging.

We have reviewed lead musket balls that were originally spherical and used with muskets, rifles, or pistols. Returning to the original question, are musket balls always made of lead? The answer is no. A number of "pewter" musket balls were excavated at Monmouth. Pewter has many different formulae depending on its end use, but it is primarily a tin alloy. "Tin was generally alloyed with small amounts of lead and sometimes also copper to obtain better casting properties. ..."[9]

Some musket balls found at Monmouth have a lower specific gravity than lead and therefore do not exactly fit the diameter formula. These musket balls are rarely flattened from impact, suggesting they are harder than lead. They have a very poor and flaky patina that blisters (see figure). The overall color is grayish. Lead was in short supply in the colonies so other materials may have been used to produce musket balls. There is the story of the gilded leaden statue of King George III that was pulled down in Bowling Green Park, New York City, in 1776 and cast into 42,088 musket balls.[10] Since lead is much too soft for a statue, likely it was hardened with tin and was possibly a pewter statue. Since these "pewter" musket balls do not flatten very much on impact, their approximate diameter can be measured with calipers.

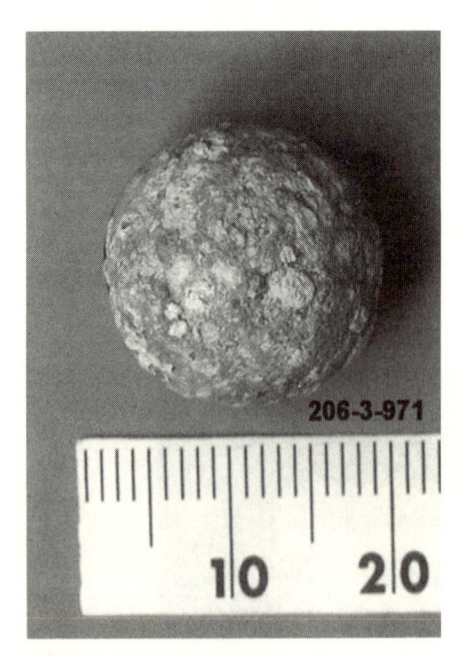

Not all musket balls are spherical (before firing). The musket

"Pewter" musket ball.

balls shown in the next figure were excavated in Zboriv, Ukraine, the site of a 1649 battle between Cossacks and Polish nobility. As can be seen, early musket balls were slightly cylindrical and had a lipped sprue used to secure the musket ball in the paper cartridge by tying the cartridge off with string around the sprue to keep the projectile from separating from the cartridge.

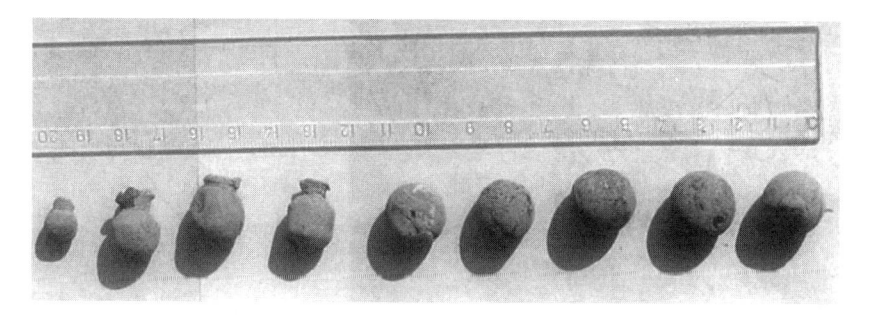

Seventeenth-century musket balls from Zboriv, Ukraine. (Adrian Mandzy, Ph.D., Morehead State University, Morehead, Kentucky)

A variety of cylindrically shaped shot have been excavated at Monmouth and are shown in the figure below. Most of these shot have faceted faces from being hammered.

Cylinder-shaped shot.

Soldiers occasionally altered round balls by hammering them into cylinders or "Sluggs" as they were called in the eighteenth century. This shot type would tumble after firing and rip through human targets, causing massive injury. The use of cylindrical shot is not unique to Monmouth and appears to have a long history. Five specimens recovered from the pirate ship *Whydah* that sank off Cape Cod in 1717 are currently on display in the museum in Provincetown, Rhode Island.

Musket balls were sometimes quartered and halved to fire a spray pattern at the enemy, creating, in effect, a dum-dum bullet. The ball was cut partially through so it would fragment after exiting the muzzle (see figure). Although

Intentionally mutilated musket balls.

not very accurate, one has to wonder if this was done more for psychological purposes. Calver and Bolton reported excavated musket balls with nails driven through them. This was so common a practice that the British General Lord Howe wrote to General Washington in September 1777, complaining about the use of mutilated shot by the Continentals. "My aid-de-camp will present to you a ball cut and fixed to the end of a nail, taken from a number of the same kind, found in the encampment quitted by your troops on the 15th inst. I do not make any comment upon such unwarrantable and malicious practices, being well assured that the contrivance has not come to your knowledge." From his headquarters on Harlem Heights, on September 23, 1776, Washington replied, "Your aid-de-camp delivered to me the ball you mention, which was the first of the kind I ever saw or heard of. You may depend the contrivance is highly abhorred by me and every measure shall be taken to prevent so wicked and infamous a practice being adopted in this Army." It is interesting that Calver and Bolton note that the specimens they found were at the British camp at Inwood. A variety of mutilated musket balls have been excavated at Monmouth, examples of which are shown in the figure (white color). Calculated values of the original diameters suggest that both sides engaged in this practice.

Although we have not found any musket balls with nails in them, a musket ball with a fragment of an iron wire through its axis was found in Burlington County, New Jersey, by metal detectorist Robert Campbell (see figure on page 97).

It is interesting to note that the pair of gang-molded musket balls was found in the same area as the musket ball in the next figure. It is unknown whether they were lost before being separated or were specifically cast as

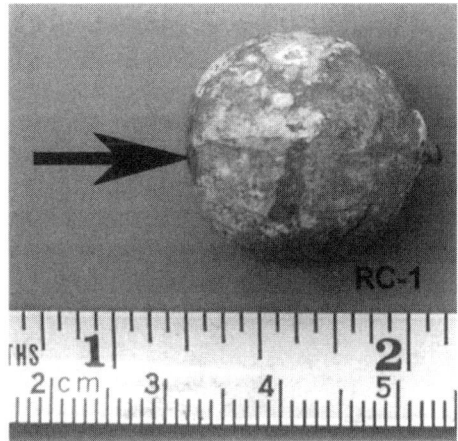

Musket ball with imbedded iron wire.

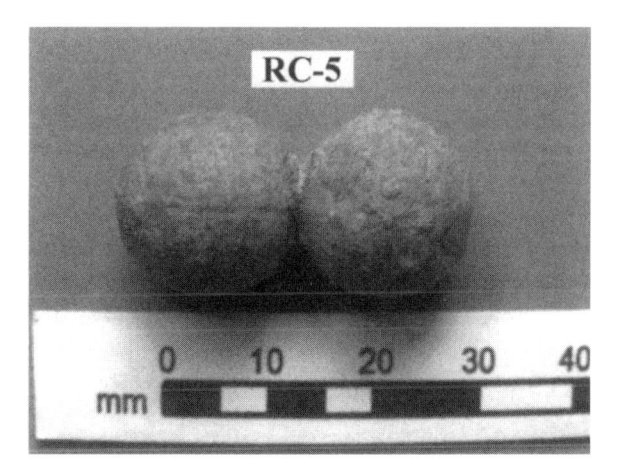

Musket balls molded together.

double shot. I suspect the latter since the joining sprue was so short as to make separation difficult.

Are musket balls always fired from small arms or shoulder arms? The answer is no.

Quantities of wedge-shaped and cubic-shaped "musket balls" were excavated at Monmouth in one specific location. These had multiple concave depressions. Lead will assume the shape of the object it hits upon contact.

(a) Wedge-shaped; (b) Cubic-shaped artillery canister shot.

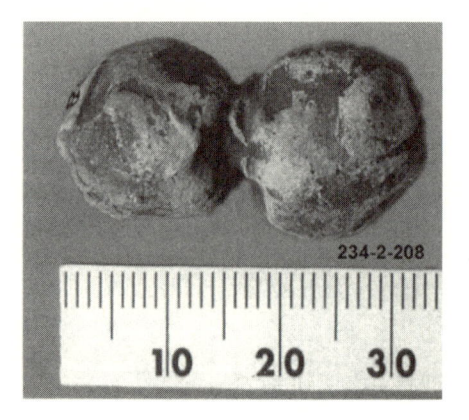

Fused musket balls (canister shot).

A pair of fused "musket balls" were also excavated in the same area. These fused shot also had the same multiple concave depressions.

Numerous fused musket ball pairs were found. All had multiple facets with concave depressions. These were not musket balls, per se, but lead canister shot. Major-General William Alexander, Lord Sterling, wrote about firing grape and canister shot at the British.[11] Canister shot is a tin can filled with lead balls. It is often fired at the ground at a glancing angle about 75 yards in front of the enemy. The can ruptures on firing and the shot skips off the ground and rips through the enemy ranks. Canister is an excellent anti-personnel round. The effect of firing causes the balls in the can to compress. The lead balls get concave depressions from neighboring balls and take on wedge and square shapes. Some shot compresses to the point of fusing together.

Several fused artillery canister shot.

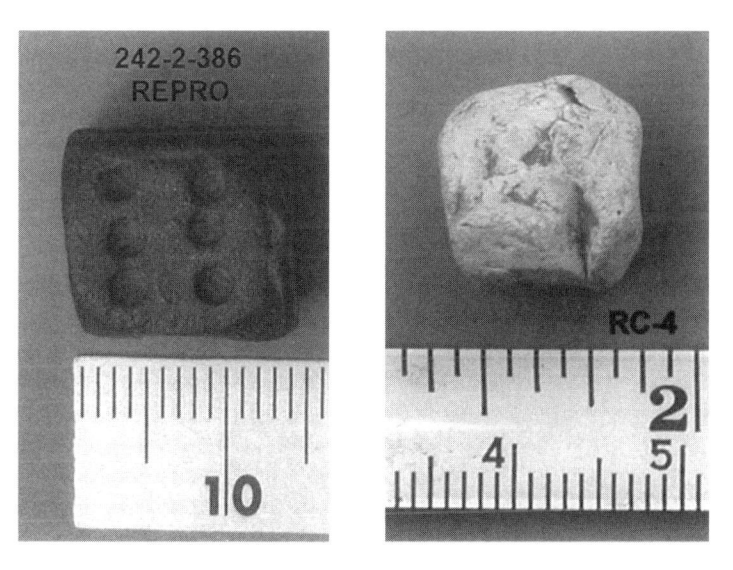

(a) Reproduction lead dice and lead cube; (b) Possible lead dice in the making.

Finally there are the non-projectile uses of musket balls such as gaming pieces. A few examples are shown.

Musket balls were occasionally used to make gun flint wraps. Clamping a gun flint in the steel jaws of a musket hammer without a wrap will either give a poor grip or crack the flint. The flint is wrapped in leather or lead to hold it in place and act as a shock absorber.

Gun flint wrap and "French honey" gun flint.

CONCLUSION

These are but a few examples of musket balls, artillery shot, and other lead artifacts found at Monmouth Battlefield. Next time you excavate a piece of lead at a military site, ask yourself ... was this a musket ball?

ACKNOWLEDGMENTS

The author would like to acknowledge the many people responsible for making this paper possible. Foremost is Garry Wheeler Stone, Ph.D., who had the courage to work with volunteer metal detectorists in a time when many archaeologists had a dim view of metal detecting. His wisdom and knowledge has kept the projects on a professional level. Thanks to the many members of the Battlefield Restoration and Archaeological Volunteer Organization (BRAVO) who spent countless hours excavating in the field and cleaning, measuring, and cataloging artifacts in the lab. Henry Miller, Ph.D., of Historic St. Mary's City in Maryland was kind enough to identify the teeth impressions in a number of "chewed" musket balls as being from pigs. Henry even identified which teeth made the impressions and the approximate ages of the animals. Eric Sivilich and Michael Smith did outstanding work in photographing the re-enactors and the artifacts for this presentation. Monmouth County Historical Association graciously allowed the author to measure and photograph the "1776" steatite musket ball mold. Finally thank you to Russ Balliet and Robert Campbell for allowing the author to photograph artifacts from their collections.

NOTES

1. Neumann and Kravic 1989:190–193.
2. Roberge 2005.
3. Neumann 1967.
4. Sivilich 1996.
5. Muller 1977:14.
6. Miller 2004.
7. Lord 1989.
8. Miller 2004.
9. Petersen 2002.
10. CTSSAR 2002.
11. *Proceedings of the New Jersey Historical Society*, Vol 60, No. 3 (July 1942):173–175.

REFERENCES CITED

(CTSSAR). The Connecticut Society of the Sons of the American Revolution. 2002. *Where is King George's Head*. Internet paper, http://www.ctssar.org/articles/ling_georges_head.htm.

Lord, Phillip. 1989. *War Over Walloomscoick*. New York State Education Department, Albany, NY.

Miller, Henry M. 2004. An Analysis of Marks on Musket Balls Recovered from the Revolutionary War Battlefield of Monmouth, New Jersey. Historic St. Mary's City, St. Mary's City, MD. Not published.

Muller, John. 1977. *A Treatise of Artillery 1780*. Museum Restoration Services, Bloomfield, Ontario, Canada.

Neumann, George C. 1967. *The History of Weapons of the American Revolution*. Bonanza Books, New York.

Neumann, George C., and Frank J. Kravic. 1989. *Collector's Illustrated Encyclopedia of the American Revolution*. Rebel Publishing Company, Texarkana, TX.

Petersen, Karen Steman. 2002. *Preservation of Historical Pewter in Church and Museum Collections*. Internet paper, http://www.natmus.dk/cons/reports/2002/tinbevaring/pewter.htm.

Roberge, Pierre R. 2005. *Lead Corrosion*. Internet paper on the Corrosion Doctors Web Site, http://www.corrosiondoctors.org/MatSelect/corrlead.htm.

Sivilich, Daniel M. 1996. Analyzing Musket Balls to Interpret a Revolutionary War Site. *Historical Archaeology* 30(2):101–109.

"Listen to the Minié Balls": Identifying Firearms in Battlefield Archaeology

Douglas Scott & Lucien Haag

THE IDENTIFICATION OF guns or gun parts found on archaeological sites is a relatively straightforward process. Most archaeologists are aware of expert literature on the subject and can readily use existing references to identify, type, and date guns or gun parts. Archaeologists are also reasonably adept at using available references to identify cartridge case headstamps, allowing them to identify a caliber, and usually a date range, for the use ammunition. However, researchers often overlook a wealth of other information contained in archaeologically recovered ammunition components. Bullets, cartridge cases, cartridges, artillery shot and shell fragments, canister shot, primers, and percussion caps can also provide a range of information on dating, types of firearms present, minimum numbers of firearms, and activities of the site's occupants as they related to the firearms. Our intent is to introduce archaeologists studying sites of conflict, or other sites containing evidence of firearms, to the potential of firearms identification procedures. This chapter is not intended to be a "how to"; rather our purpose is to provide a background to firearms identification and to introduce a variety of analytical firearms identification procedures adapatable to archaeological investigations.

The comparative study of ammunition components is known as firearms identification analysis. Firearms, in their discharge, leave behind telltale signatures or markings on the ammunition components (see figure on page 103). These signatures, more properly termed class and individual characteristics, allow the determination of the firearm type (i.e., model or brand) in which a given cartridge or bullet was fired, including artillery. This identification then allows determination of the number of different gun types at a given site. Further, individualized characteristics allow the identification of individual weapons or grouping of fired bullets or fired cartridge cases as having been fired in a common firearm. This last capability is very important because coupled with precise artifact locations, matching individual characteristics can identify activity loci. With this information, patterns of movement can be established and sequences of activity more precisely interpreted.

FIREARM-GENERATED MARKINGS ON CARTRIDGE CASES
[SEMI-AUTOMATIC PISTOL CARTRIDGE]

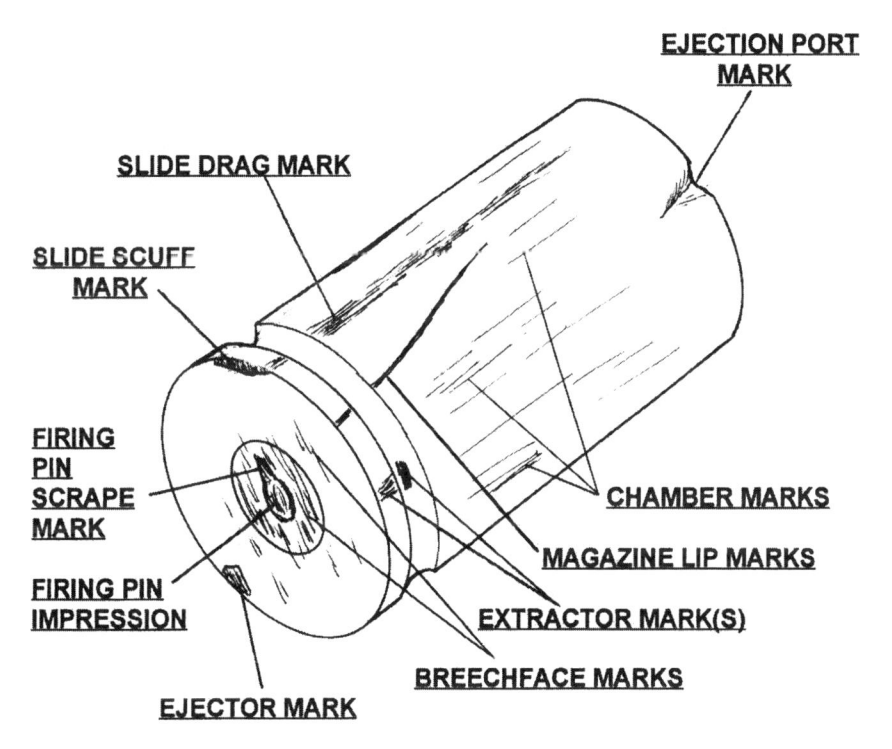

Features that remain on a cartridge case after firing aid in the identification of the firearm type.

The means to this analytical end requires some explanation. When a cartridge weapon is fired the firing pin strikes the cartridge primer, often leaving a distinctive imprint on the case. The primer ignites the powder, thus forcing the bullet out the barrel. Rifling in the barrel imprints the lands and grooves on the bullet in mirror image. The extractor frequently marks the fired case as it is extracted from the gun's chamber. These imprints are called class and individual characteristics. Class and individual characteristics are also present on projectiles fired from muzzle-loading firearms like flintlocks and percussion weapons including some smooth-bore guns.

FIREARMS IDENTIFICATION: HISTORY AND THEORY

Law enforcement agencies have long used firearms identification as an aid in solving crimes. A method commonly used by police departments includes comparison of bullets and cartridge cases to identify weapon types from which they were fired.[1] Law enforcement criminalists and firearms examiners are routinely successful in matching bullets and/or cartridge case characteristics to a crime weapon simply by demonstrating that the firing pin, breechface, ejector, chamber, and extractor marks on fired cartridge cases, or the land and groove marks on fired bullets, could only have been made by a specific weapon. In the event that weapons used in a crime are not recovered, the law enforcement laboratory can say with certainty, on the basis of class and individual characteristics found on recovered bullets and cartridge cases, that specific types and numbers of weapons were used.

Firearms identification procedures, often erroneously called forensic ballistics, are analogous to the archaeological wear pattern analysis. Like wear pattern analysis, firearms identification did not spring up overnight, but has an evolutionary history. Firearms identification had its earliest known beginnings in an 1835 London murder case.[2] A London policeman helped secure a conviction by proving a bullet (ball) with a peculiar flaw could have only been cast in the defendant's mold which had the same flaw. Another case of incipient firearms identification occurred in determining who caused the death of Confederate General Stonewall Jackson on May 2, 1863. An examination of the recovered bullet proved it to be a type and caliber used by the Confederate Army. Jackson was killed by one of his own pickets—a probable friendly fire fatality.

Other cases followed in ensuing years with each building on earlier conclusions. In 1900 Dr. Albert Hall published the first truly scientific treatment on forensic ballistics and began its advancement as a common law enforcement tool. Firearms identification, as it has become known, was used to establish guilt in the 1907 Brownsville, Texas, race riots.[3] The examination resulted in cashiering three entire companies of the all-black 25th U.S. Infantry. By 1925 the field was becoming well established, and in that year the greatest single advancement occurred to ensure a solid footing for its future. The comparison microscope was used for the first time and became the firearm examiner's standard tool. With publication of several textbooks in 1935, the field was firmly established and now nearly every major law enforcement agency has one or more firearms examiners in its laboratory.[4]

THE COMPARISON MICROSCOPE

The comparison microscope is critical to analyzing ammunition components. The microscope is constructed so that two separate microscope tubes are joined by a bridge with prisms mounted over the tubes. Two separate images are transmitted to the center of the bridge, where another set of prisms transmits the images to a central eyepiece. The eyepiece is divided so that each image appears on one-half of the eyepiece. Movable stages allow the object under scrutiny to be manipulated so that it can be directly compared for class and individual characteristics.

CLASS AND INDIVIDUAL CHARACTERISTICS

Class Characteristics[5]

The number of land and groove impressions on a bullet or the size and depth of a firing pin impression are termed "class characteristics." These gross details are common to a type, model, or brand of firearm (see figure). As an example, the Smith & Wesson company designs and builds their revolver barrels with a five land and groove, right-hand twist of specific dimensions. The Colt Company manufactures its barrels with a six land and groove, left-hand twist of slightly different dimensions. An archaeologically recovered fired bullet with five land and groove impressions with a right-hand twist to the rifling was not fired from a Colt. If the bullet's land and groove dimensions are the same as the Smith & Wesson revolver, then it can be assumed the bullet was fired from a Smith & Wesson gun. By knowing caliber and researching the models made by Smith & Wesson in that caliber, it is possible to narrow the bullet down to a specific model and have a firm date for when that model or caliber was introduced on the market, and thus determine an *ante quem* date for the archaeological specimen.

The cartridge case firing pin signature can also be characteristic of the gun type in which it was fired. This is important because many types of ammunition can be fired in a variety of different firearms. By way of example, a .44 caliber Henry cartridge could be fired not only in the Henry repeating rifle (for which the cartridge was designed) but also in the Model 1866 Winchester, the .44 rimfire Colt pistol, and the .44 rimfire Remington revolver, among others. The class characteristics for each weapon type's firing pin are distinctive, and it is possible to identify the weapon type in which a given .44 Henry cartridge was fired. These data allow the archaeologist to determine the *ante quem* date and the number of different firearm types present on a site.

Individual Characteristics

Macroscopically, firing pin impressions often appear identical from weapon to weapon within a single type. However, minute variations, unique to each firing pin, allow identification of individual weapons if they survive the ravages of time in buried contexts. Such features are visible only via the

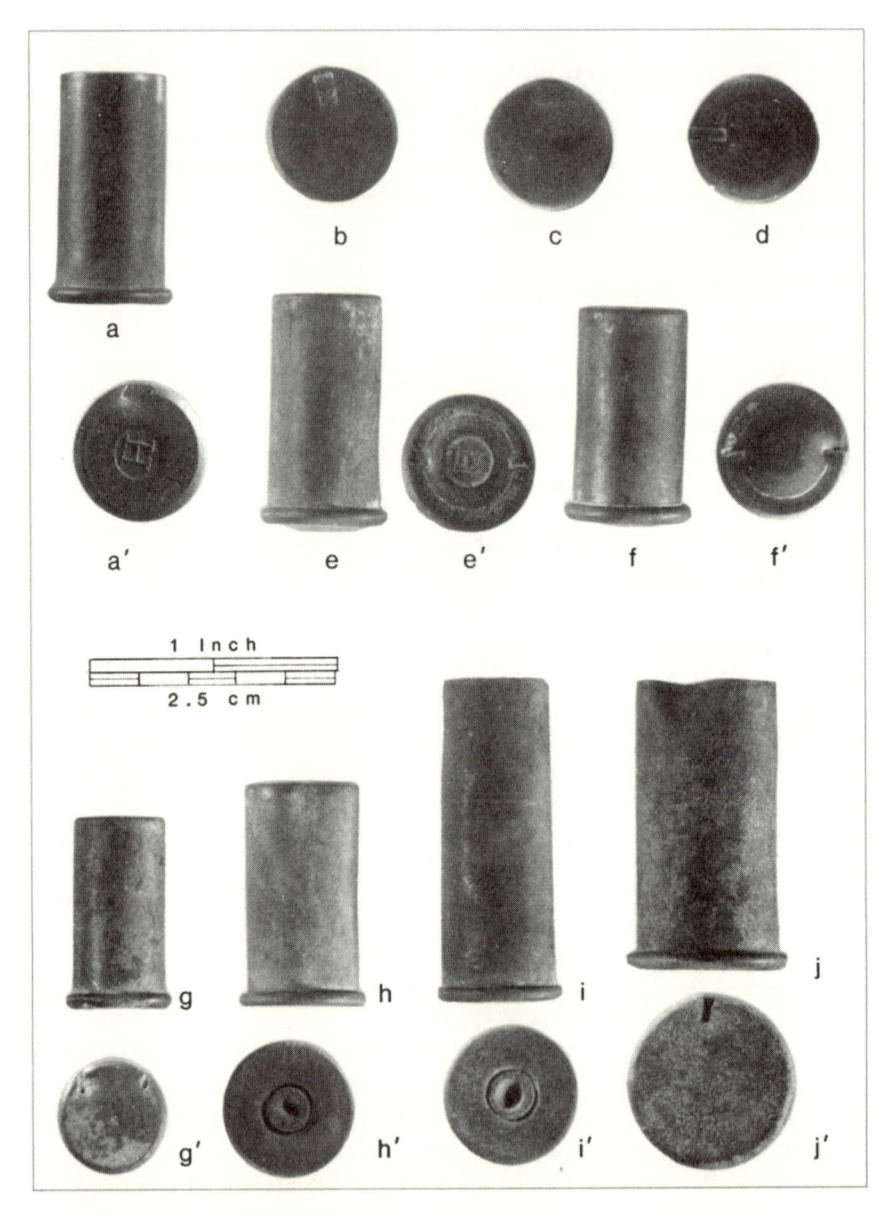

A variety of firing pin imprints shown on .38, .44, and .50 caliber cartridge cases.

microscope. The unique characteristics result from the manufacturing process and subsequent wear, degradation, damage over time, and general use. Because class and individual characteristics are left on the most durable metallic substances—brass, copper, and lead—most ammunition components at archaeological sites are amenable to firearms identification procedures even after a century or more in the ground. In essence, the markings are a metallic fingerprint.

Fired bullets also retain an individual fingerprint. The barrel of rifled guns has a series of lands and grooves that impart spin to the bullet as it travels out the barrel. This spin gives the bullet greater aerodynamic stability and accuracy in its trajectory. The bullet is lead and the barrel is steel. Since the bullet fits tightly in the barrel, the barrel leaves its land and groove impressions, in reverse, on the softer bullet. As with a firing pin, each barrel manufactured for a certain weapon type has individually recognizable characteristics due to wear on the rifling tool during the manufacturing process as well as wear to the weapon during its use. The individual and unique striations left on any given bullet when it is fired will match the striations on any other bullet fired in that same gun. Even though a bullet may be deformed on impact, it may retain sufficient individual and unique striations to permit multiple bullets to be associated with a single firearm or to be matched to a specific firearm in the present-day situation.

ANALYTICAL PROCEDURES

The first step in the analysis is cleaning the artifact. Bullets are made of lead and are sometimes jacketed with copper or other metals. Cartridge cases are made of brass or copper (more properly Bloomfield Gilding Metal), although some are tinned and shotgun hulls usually have a paper or plastic upper body. Lead, brass, and copper oxidize upon prolonged environmental exposure. Oxidation obscures details of the individual characteristics and must be removed before analysis. Very careful sonic cleaning and chemical removal of the oxides mixed with gentle scrubbing are the only satisfactory means to completely clean ammunition components.

Step two of the analysis is identifying class characteristics, and sorting artifacts into like groups. A low power hand lens or microscope (7–40x) is used to identify class characteristics. The process involves handling each bullet to determine the presence or absence of rifling marks, and when present, direction of twist and number of land and groove impressions. Measuring the bullet's diameter and weight as well as the widths of its land and groove marks allows further class segregation.

A similar procedure is followed with cartridge cases or percussion caps. Caliber or size is determined, then the size and depth of firing pin marks, and the location and type of extractor marks. Headstamps are generally not helpful in the class segregation process since many manufacturers loaded cartridges for specific firearms. Percussion caps retain marks, in reverse, of the hammer that fired it. These can also be sorted and identified. At the completion of the class segregation, the investigator will be able to determine the minimum number of weapon types (models, brands, calibers, etc.) present at a site.

Identifying class characteristics is aided by a comparative collection of bore molds and fired cartridge cases from a variety of firearms. Many firearms investigators maintain such collections for firearms manufactured since 1910. Modern firearms investigators have very little experience or reference material on pre-1910 firearm characteristics. Unfortunately most cartridge collectors and antique firearms collectors have little or no knowledge of fired ammunition. At present only a limited number of individuals have direct experience of firing or collecting data on class characteristics of pre-1910 firearms.

Once artifacts are identified as to class the third analytical step begins. The comparison microscope is brought into play. The microscope usually has objectives with a range of 10x to 150x. The analytic procedure is a tedious one, but as yet no means other than comparing each case or bullet against every other case or bullet from the same class has been found satisfactory. Individual characteristics are located and compared under magnification. Striations, flaws, scratches, unusual wear, etc. are the individual characteristics that aid in making a match between two or more cases, bullets, or percussion caps. At the completion of this process the investigator will be able to determine the minimum number of individual firearms represented.

PERCUSSION CAPS

The percussion cap is an external priming device used on a muzzle-loading firearm to ignite and detonate the powder charge and bullet situated in the bore of a gun.[6] Percussion caps were developed in the early nineteenth century and, like other percussion primers, served to improve upon the flintlock system of ignition. Flintlocks were plagued by a high rate of ignition failure due to chronic powder dampness and lack of an adequate spark. Research being conducted on explosive materials around the turn of the nineteenth century soon moved the flintlock system into retirement.

It is generally agreed that the method of using an explosive compound to ignite gun charges can be attributed to the Rev. Alexander Forsyth of Scotland. His experiments and success at using fulminates and chlorate of potash in the early 1800s gave rise to dozens of patents, some of them his own, as inventors experimented with different methods of harnessing this new ignition material. The wave of innovation resulted in the creation of many varieties of percussion primers in the form of tubes, pellets, pills, and caps, as inventors vied for distinction in what was recognized as a significant transition in firearms use and manufacture.[7]

A popular and widely accepted design of that era was the percussion cap, consisting of a small open-ended cup containing a small quantity of igniting compound sealed in place with varnish or another waterproof sealer. The percussion cap was more reliable and easier to use than earlier attempts at percussion primers, and thus began to solidify the movement toward a reliable ignition system. Percussion cap design is most often attributed to British painter Joshua Shaw based on his claims of inventing reloadable iron caps in 1814 or earlier. Shaw received a U.S. patent for his idea in 1822, but claims of percussion cap conception by European inventors around the same period make it difficult to determine who deserves true credit for this innovation.[8]

There was no shortage of patents for variations on percussion cap design. In terms of function, most variations were negligible, focusing mostly on differences in size and material. Caps with ribbed or corrugated sides became popular as a way of lessening the chance of cap fragmentation upon ignition. These primers became known as "common caps," but are also called "pistol caps" due to their smaller size and lighter ignition charge being more suitable for pistol or small rifle operation. Another accepted design was the "top hat" cap, also called the "military" or "musket" cap. This cap was developed with wings or protruding sides for easier handling by soldiers wearing gloves. Top hat caps were not exclusively military-issue, however, as sporting versions were also manufactured and are still in production today.[9]

Manufacture of percussion caps varied slightly depending on individual design, but most required, at a minimum, nine basic steps: (1) rolling copper sheets to a proper thickness, excluding those areas with imperfections; (2) an annealing process to ensure malleability; (3) cleaning to eliminate effects of fire or heat during the annealing process; (4) cutting and/or punching sheets of copper into the proper forms; (5) oiling of cut-outs to promote ease of machining; (6) formation into the desired shape, using a tool and die process; (7) removal of oil by using sawdust; (8) insertion of the ignition compound; and (9) varnishing to seal the ignition compound. By the mid to late nineteenth century, steps 1 through 8 were accomplished at a rate of 31,000 caps per day per machine or workstation, with the finishing touches of varnishing (step 9) accomplished at the rate of 7,000 caps per hour per laborer. A manufacturer's stamp was sometimes included in the formation process, further documenting the company, country, or region of manufacture.[10]

Percussion caps are a well-known artifact type from pre-1870 sites where firearms were used. Many archaeologists mention finding percussion caps, and several provide measurements of the artifacts, but little archaeological study has been made of this artifact type. One exception is an analysis of percussion caps from Fort Union Trading Post National Historic Site, North Dakota.[11] William Hunt used measurements of cap size to predict potential weapon type: pistol, small caliber rifle, or musket.

The Fort Union study notes that there are currently four manufacturers making common or pistol caps today. The modern caps range in diameter from 0.17 to 0.18 inch (0.43–0.46 cm) with lengths of 0.17 to 0.24 inch (0.43–0.61 cm). There are also five manufacturers producing six types of musket or top hat caps that range in diameter from 0.22 to 0.24 inch (0.56–0.61 cm) and in length from 0.22 to 0.25 inch (0.56–0.64 cm). The study found that diameter is a greater predictor of cap/firearm correlation than length. The Fort Union (1829–1868) archaeological percussion caps fell into two size modes similar to modern percussion cap diameters. The smaller or common straight-sided cap from Fort Union ranged in diameter from 0.16 to 0.21 inch (0.42 to 0.53 cm) and the larger top hat or musket cap ranged in diameter from 0.21 to 0.26 inch (0.53 to 0.65 cm).

Baker and Harrison are among the few archaeologists who attempted to identify percussion caps by using measurements. Unfortunately, they equated their measurements to modern percussion caps sizes cited in Barnes[12] without realizing that there is significant variation in cap dimensions through time by manufacturer and even within a manufacturer's lot. Measurements taken from modern and historic percussion caps demonstrate that sizes are not quantifiable by precise measurements, rather that percussion caps can be sorted by measurement into three or four gross types: musket, large rifle/pistol, small rifle/pistol, and shotgun. Individual measurements of percussion caps show statistically significant variation in dimensions by as much as several thousandths of an inch in a single container holding a purported specific cap size, for example, Remington No. 11 caps vary by 3–4 thousandths of an inch in each dimension—length, head diameter, and inside mouth diameter—from a container of 100 caps.

As with modern-day cartridge cases, percussion caps come into contact with parts of the firearm that have both class and individual characteristics due to imperfections and machining techniques used during their manufacturing process coupled with random changes during use. On muzzle-loading firearms, percussion caps come into contact with both the nipple, or cone, and the hammer. The force of the hammer striking the percussion cap, coupled with the explosive force of the igniting compound, cause any imperfections and unique characteristics of the hammer, the nipple, or both, to be imparted to the cap. These markings allow the firearm examiner to make determinations that multiple percussion caps were fired on the same firearm, even without the firearm being present (see figure on page 111). The more unique the markings present, the greater likelihood of being able to single out a specific firearm.

Additional identifying characteristics may be attributed to the black powder shooting process itself. Black powder firearms are easily dirtied or "fouled" during shooting. Fouling can provide additional characteristics for making an identification on percussion caps. Incompletely burned powder and metal particles from the projectile coat the barrel and associated components of the firearm with a sooty residue.[13] The same powder and residue, as well as additional residue and metal particles from the percussion cap, can manifest itself on the firearm's nipple or cone and its hammer. When this occurs, fouling can add to the unique set of impressions and striations created by the hammer and nipple, thus transferring to the percussion cap as well. Fouling

Photomicrograph of two different percussion caps with identical toolmarks indicating they were fired on the same gun.

may remain a part of the hammer and nipple impression for a lengthy period of time as a reproducing mark, or may vanish after the next firing.

Another factor to be considered upon examining percussion caps is the manufacturing process of the caps themselves. At any point during the manufacturing or storage process, it is possible for machined parts, storage receptacles, or even other caps, to impart markings onto a percussion cap. These markings tend to be subtle, but can be confusing if interpreted improperly. Order of placement may need to be determined in order to decide which markings are more critical for examination. One method of determining whether an impression or striation is more recent than another is to look for overlapping or even continuous patterns. If a striation or impression appears to cut off or otherwise obscure another marking, it is probable that the overlapping striation or impression occurred after the interrupted mark. Likewise, if a set of markings are apparent on either side of an impression, and also can be seen throughout the contoured impression, those markings may be a pre-existing set of characteristics incurred during the manufacturing process.

Not all percussion caps retain markings with enough individualization to show that a cap came from a specific firearm. Due to overall consistency in the firearm manufacturing process, individual hammers or nipples installed on a firearm may transfer markings to caps that are similar to other firearms. When markings are not individualized to the extent necessary for identification, it is only possible to say that the cap displays class characteristics consistent with having been fired in a black powder firearm.

In one study, well-preserved percussion caps dating back 150 years were found to yield hammer face and nipple marks that are unique and reproducible, thus expanding our capability to identify minimum numbers of firearms used at an event. Analysis of modern fired percussion caps from 11 different antique and reproduction firearms used as a validation study confirms our ability to identify individual characteristics that define a specific firearm used in an event.[14] Percussion cap analysis demonstrates that these seemingly inconsequential artifacts are a dataset that can be measured, sorted, and studied microscopically and will yield information that can expand our knowledge about an event and the role that firearms played in creating the event under study.

SMALL-ARMS CARTRIDGE CASES

Aside from determining model and brand of firearms at a site, cartridge cases hold other information valuable to the archaeologist. Headstamps on cartridge case bases are the most commonly used temporal indicator.[15] In addition to the headstamp, the primer type, case composition (brass, copper, tinned, rubber, etc.), caliber, and case type (rimmed, semi-rimmed, rimless, rebated, or belted) provide information on the date of that cartridge case's introduction. Each model has a date of introduction, and in most cases, a date for the cessation of manufacture. Combining all this information can provide an archaeologist with some very restricted date ranges for the cartridges.

SMALL-ARMS BULLETS

Likewise bullets can provide some datable information. Like other diagnostic artifacts, some are more temporally sensitive than others. Bullet composition (lead, lead alloy, jacketed, etc.), number and type of cannelures, and shape have date ranges associated with their introduction and, in some situations, last date of manufacture. As was noted, firing pin impressions land and groove marks can identify a firearm type, brand, and model.

Bullets also contain other information depending on their preservation. An analyst can determine if the bullet was cast in a mold or pressed (also sometimes called swaging) in a machine. The introduction of bullet pressing machines is known, occurring in the 1850s with the rise of the industrial revolution. The presence of pressed bullets can serve as a rough dating criteria in some sites.

Lead bullets fired from a black powder firearm usually have one end or side, if a spherical ball, with a rough texture. This stippling effect is the direct result of powder burning behind the bullet during its initial travel down the barrel of the weapon. Likewise the nose of the bullet or other side of the spherical ball, if loaded with the aid of a ramrod, may have distinctive marks that can be associated with a firearm type.[16] For example, the loading mark left by a U.S. Model 1816 "button-tip" ramrod is decidedly different from the mark left by a Model 1855 or 1861 "tulip-shaped" ramrod.

Fired and impacted bullets are often deformed in the process of impact. Conical bullets are more amenable to impact analysis than spherical balls, but the analysis can be applied in some cases to both types. Spin stabilized conical bullets strike their target nose first. Depending on the hardness of the object struck a conical bullet will deform by expanding outward from the nose, the so-called mushroom effect. The amount of nose deformation or mushrooming is a rough indicator of the bullet's velocity on impact, and can be used to aid a rough approximation of range in some situations.

Bullets that were deflected in flight, or are in yaw (not spin stabilized), will strike an object at any number of angles off the bullet centerline. The resulting impact deformation can tell an examiner something of the bullet's stability when it struck and the nature of its yaw. Bullets in yaw can have impact scars ranging from flattened on one side to slight basal deformation, or simple scarring on one side, but all are witness to whether the bullet was tumbling, in slight yaw, or near its terminal velocity. Bullets in yaw reflect an improper sized bullet, a dirty gun barrel, or the fact the bullet hit an intervening object prior to coming to rest.

Bullet impact scars can remain on very hard surfaces such as stone, brick, and other masonry for literally hundreds of years. The direction of impact and thus, the general direction from which the firearm was fired, can be determined using criminalists' shooting scene reconstruction techniques. Even after 100 or more years, it may be possible to lift traces of the lead bullet from an impact scar. The technique requires training to make the lift, but it is possible to do in the field with relatively simple materials.

The trace lead from a lift, or for that matter a bullet, can be analyzed to determine its source and association with other bullets from the site in some cases. Chemical and spectrographic analyses can determine the lead source from any number of mines. A technique used in law enforcement criminal investigations, and employing a variety of spectrographic analyses, identifies trace elements in bullet composition which allow comparisons between bullets to ascertain if they have a different origin or if a common source is indicated. While this level of finite analysis is probably not necessary on many sites, the fact that it can be done is worth knowing as some research questions could be answered using these examination procedures.

ARTILLERY PROJECTILES

Like small-arms bullets and cartridge cases, artillery projectiles and cartridge cases are amenable to firearms identification analysis. Artillery projectiles fired from guns or mortars, whether spherical or conical, are manufactured of iron or steel, and sometimes, in expedient situations, other materials like copper. Standard metallurgical analyses can yield information regarding the iron, steel, or copper, or other base metal and trace element content of a projectile or projectile fragment that may aid in identifying its origin, such as Mexican or American for the Mexican–American War, or Russian or British or Turkish for the Crimean War, and so on. Utilizing fracture mechanics in studying artillery fragments, the physical properties involved in their manufacture and use such as failure analysis can be determined.

Resistance offered by a shell (including case shot) to the force of the powder increases with side thickness. When a shell bursts while stationary, the pieces are dispersed in almost every direction with more or less force according to the resistance of the sides. The number of fragments is directly related to the brittleness of the material.[17] Theoretical and experimental evidence shows that the least amount of resistance and crack initiation propagates through the fuse ring. If the projectile is in motion, the fragments projected forward will continue with an increase in velocity and those in the rear with a decrease in velocity. If the shell is moving very slowly, the fragment velocity may be overcome for the rear parts of the explosion and the pieces may drop to the ground or be thrown backward.

Most artillery projectiles manufactured prior to the beginning of the twentieth century were constructed of gray cast iron. All gray irons fail in a brittle manner. Fracture occurs along the lamellar graphite plates, exhibiting a "gray" fracture surface. The compressive strength of gray cast iron is roughly three to four times its tensile strength. Fracture occurs at the maximum compressive load.[18] Think of a cannon ball as a thick-walled spherical pressure vessel and the failure as an impact overload exceeding the compressive strength. It appears that the mode of failure can be attributed to thermal stress overload wherein the stress from a thermal change (the charge) demands a specific change of dimension. As the gray cast iron cannot expand plastically, the yield strength is exceeded, causing fracture. Spherical shell and case shot fracture in a predictable manner, usually large trapezoidal fragments. Individual fragments can be analyzed to determine if pieces have the same iron and trace element content, thus suggesting they are from either the same projectile or same lot of projectile manufacturing. Gray cast iron conical projectiles exhibit similar fracture patterns and are amenable to similar analyses as are gray cast iron hand grenades.

Steel bodied conical artillery projectiles have more advanced metallurgical theory behind their manufacture. Depending on the era of production, steel artillery projectiles are designed to burst into long, thin splinter-like fragments that may be razor sharp and are intended to make horrific wounds. The transition from gray cast iron projectiles to steel based projectiles occurred during World War I and has seen a number of technological advances since. Steel bodied hand grenades likewise saw similar and concomitant development as to the lethality of the fragments. The presence of iron or iron and steel projectile fragments in a site can aid in dating the site or feature since the introduction of artillery shell types is reasonably well documented.

It is also possible to use spatial attributes to associate fired artillery fragments with specific combatants or even in some cases to specific artillery batteries, by employing the historic record and documentary resources. Another analytical tool uses differences in standardization and formalization to better understand production practices, well developed or exhibiting shortages, among the home cultures that supplied the combatants.[19] In doing so, it provides an example of how battlefield assemblages may be studied in a more anthropological way to assess the logistic and supply networks available to combatant groups, or how stressed the home culture was to provide war materials to the front, such as the greater the diversity in war materials the less able the supply base to provide adequate munitions or greater deviation from the norm in desired quality of artillery projectiles suggesting reliance on dispersed and cottage industries to produce munitions among other possibilities.

ARTILLERY AND MORTAR CRATER ANALYSIS

In some battlefield situations where conical artillery projectiles were fired, there may be impact craters remaining in the archaeological record. If the crater is reasonably well preserved it may be possible to apply a field of military field analysis called crater analysis.[20] A well-preserved impact crater, whether still observable on the surface or a filled-in crater (see figure on page 116), may allow the researcher to determine the approximate bearing from which the projectile originated, determine the type, whether it is an artillery round or a mortar round, potentially determine the caliber of the weapon, and possibly the shell or bomb type.

If shell fragments and/or fuse parts are present in the crater, then it is possible to determine the shell or bomb type and caliber. Measuring the radius of a shell or bomb fragment, compared against a template, will give the approximate caliber. Distinctive body features, such as fins, driving bands, fuse types, and so on may aid in identifying the shell or bomb type.

Crater shape provides some indication of the type of projectile fired (see figure). Shell craters are slightly elliptical in shape, often with two wing-like grooves in the soil on either side of the main crater. The crater often has a smaller and deeper depression, or an undercut within the larger crater. Since a shell strikes the ground at a relatively shallow angle, then bursts, the shell creates a depression. The deeper depression or undercut often found in the

A World War I artillery impact crater at Crossroads near Ieper, Belgium.

center is created by the impact explosion. Shell splinters are thrown to the sides creating the wing-like extension grooves; if the shell was nose fused, then the fuse usually is thrown forward and creates a small trench or track. The wings are usually at a slight acute angle relative to the fuse track. The wings and fuse track define the reverse angle of the gun's orientation.

Mortars are fired at a high angle, are relatively short range devices, and create a high angle trajectory that causes the mortar bomb to strike at a steep angle. The resultant crater usually has the farthest edge away from the weapon undercut and the mortar fuse is often buried in the slightly forward deeper undercut in the crater. The crater edge opposite the fuse usually shows a ragged, almost serrated, series of grooves or trenches. These trenches are a result of splinters from the bomb fragmentation and they point in the direction of the mortar tube's location.

SUMMARY AND CONCLUSIONS

Multidisciplinary studies are not new to archaeology, and the application of firearms identification to archaeology is another example of the utility of multidisciplinary interaction. Archaeologists can expect modern firearms identification techniques to produce additional data for the dating of sites, details

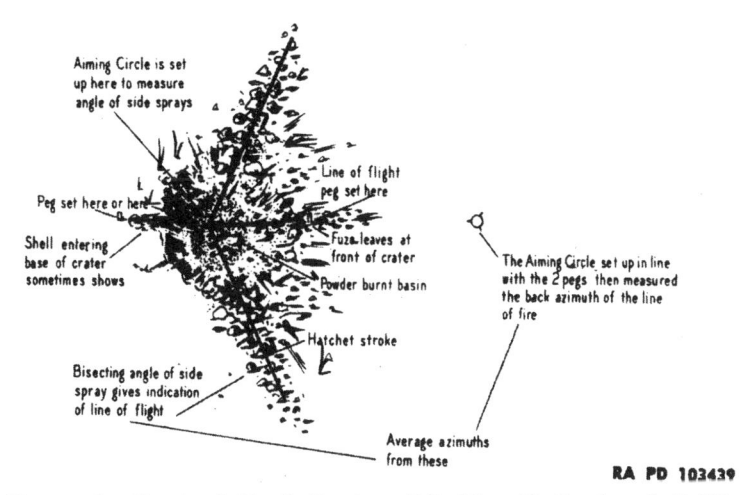

Figure 4—Typical Shell Crater, FQ (Small Angle of Fall)

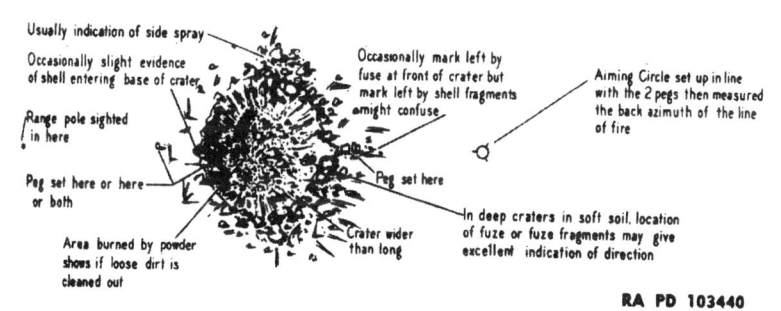

Figure 5—Typical Shell Crater, FQ (Larger Angle of Fall)

Method of artillery crater analysis as portrayed in a World War II manual and still used today. (1945 identification of Japanese shells and shell fragments; location of enemy batteries. War Department Technical Manual TM E9-1901. Washington, DC)

concerning the weapon types utilized and the minimum number of firearms present, and identifying patterns of firearms utilization at a site. One of the more desirable and unique aspects of firearms identification is its ability to pinpoint individual patterns or behavior related to firearms use. There are very few techniques that enable the archaeologist to identify and study the individual in the context of a site. While firearms identification cannot answer all the details of individual idiosyncratic behavior, it does bring us closer to the ability to study specific individual behavioral patterns, and that is an opportunity seldom achieved in most archaeological studies.

NOTES

1. Firearms identification concepts and methods are described by Harris 1980, Hatcher, Jury, and Weller 1977, and Heard 1997.
2. Berg 1977:535–537.
3. Doughtery 1969.
4. Gunther and Gunther 1935.
5. The basic descriptions of class and individual characteristics are taken from Wilhelm 1980:202–215.
6. Lucas 1985.
7. Dickens 2003, Bailey 2003, Gooding 1966a.
8. Gooding 2004, Gooding 1974, Anon. 1869:90, and Coates and Thomas 1990.
9. Gooding 1966b, 1975.
10. Whittemore and Heath 1878:20–22, Benton 1867:350, Gooding 1966a, Thomas 2003.
11. Herskovitz 1978, Hunt 2003, Jensen 1998, Mainfort 1980, Oakes 1990, Reynolds 1983, Ziegler 2001. See also Hunt 1989.
12. Baker and Harrison 1986. See Barnes 1980 for modern percussion cap measurements.
13. Coggins 1990.
14. Weber and Scott, in press.
15. White and Munhall 1977, Datig 1956, 1958, 1967.
16. Bishop 1995:310–313.
17. Gibbon 1860:163, 250.
18. Davis 1996:4, Angus 1976:46.
19. Drexler 2004.
20. War Department 1945, United Nations 2003.

REFERENCES CITED

Angus, H. T. 1976. *Cast Iron: Physical and Engineering Properties*. Butterworths, London.

Anonymous. 1869. Joshua Shaw, Artist and Inventor, The Early History of the Copper Percussion Cap. *Scientific American* 21(6):90.

Bailey, D. W. 2003. Who Invented the Percussion Cap? Joseph Egg, Joseph Manton and the Board of Ordnance Trials of 1820. *Man at Arms* 25(4):41–45.

Baker, T. Lindsey, and Billy R. Harrison. 1986. *Adobe Walls: The History and Archeology of the 1875 Trading Post*. Texas A&M University Press, College Station.

Barnes, Frank C. 1980. *Cartridges of the World 4th Edition*. DBI Books, Northbrook, IL.

Benton, J. G. 1867. *Course of Instruction in Ordnance and Gunnery*. D. Van Nostrand, New York.

Berg, Stanton O. 1977. The Forensic Ballistic Laboratory. In C. G. Tedeschi, William G. Eckert, and Luke G. Tedeschi, *Forensic Medicine Volume I Mechanical Trauma*, 527–569. W. B. Saunders Company, Philadelphia.

Bishop, Eugene E. 1995. Tool Mark Identification on a Black Powder Revolver. *Association of Firearms and Toolmark Examiners Journal* 27(4):310–313.

Coates, Earl J., and Dean S. Thomas. 1990. *An Introduction to Civil War Small Arms.* Thomas Publications, Gettysburg, PA.

Coggins, Jack. 1990. *Arms and Equipment of the Civil War.* Barnes & Noble, New York.

Datig, Fred A. 1956. *Cartridges for Collectors, Volume I.* Borden Publishing, Los Angeles, CA.

Datig, Fred A. 1958. *Cartridges for Collectors, Volume II.* Borden Publishing, Los Angeles, CA.

Datig, Fred A. 1967. *Cartridges for Collectors, Volume III.* Borden Publishing, Los Angeles, CA.

Davis, J. R. (ed.). 1996. *ASM Specialty Handbook: Cast Irons.* ASM International, Materials Park, OH.

Dickens, B. 2003. Forsyth & Co.: An Unrecorded Ignition System. *Man at Arms* 25(6):19–24.

Dougherty, Paul M. 1969. Report on Two Early United States Firearms Identification Cases. *Journal of Forensic Sciences* 14(4):453–59.

Drexler, Carl G. 2004. Identifying Culturally-Based Variability in Artillery Ammunition Fragments Recovered from the Battlefield of Pea Ridge, Arkansas. Master's Thesis, Department of Anthropology and Geography, University of Nebraska, Lincoln.

Gibbon, John. 1860. *The Artillerist's Manual.* Reprint by Benchmark Publishing Company Inc., Glendale.

Gooding, S. James. 1966a. The Top-Hat Cap. *The Canadian Journal of Arms Collecting* 4(1): 26–27.

Gooding, S. James. 1966b. The Percussion Primer. *The Canadian Journal of Arms Collecting* 4(4): 127–149.

Gooding, S. James. 1974. The Development of Percussion Primers. *The Canadian Journal of Arms Collecting* 12(4):283–297.

Gooding, S. James. 1975. Pellets, Tubes, and Caps: The Percussion Primer, Part II. *The Canadian Journal of Arms Collecting* 13(1):107–125.

Gooding, S. James. 2004. Joshua Shaw—Landscape Artist...Con Artist? Or Inventor of the Percussion Cap? *Man at Arms* 26(2):34–43.

Gunther, Jack Disbrow, and Charles O. Gunther. 1935. *The Identification of Firearms.* John Wiley and Sons, London.

Hall, Albert. 1900. The Missile and the Weapon. *Buffalo Medical Journal* (June):37–49.

Harris, C. E. 1980. Sherlock Holmes Would Be Impressed. *American Rifleman* 128(5):36–39, 82.

Hatcher, Julian, Frank J. Jury, and Jac Weller. 1977. *Firearms Investigation, Identification and Evidence.* Stackpole Books, Harrisburg, PA.

Heard, Brian. 1997. *Handbook of Firearms and Ballistics: Examining and Interpreting Forensic Evidence.* John Wiley Sons, New York.

Herskovitz, Robert M. 1978. Fort Bowie Material Culture. *Anthropological Papers of the University of Arizona Number 31.*

Hunt, William J. Jr. 1989. Firearms and the Upper Missouri Fur Trade Frontier: Weapons and Related Materials from Fort Union Trading Post National Historic

Site (23 WI 17), North Dakota. Ph.D. Dissertation, Department of American Civilization, University of Pennsylvania.

Hunt, William J. Jr. 2003. Archaeological Investigations at Fort Clark State Historic Site, North Dakota: 1973–2003, Studies at the Fort Clark and Primeau Trading Posts. PaleoCultural Research Group, Flagstaff, AZ.

Jensen, Richard E. 1998. The Fontenelle & Cabanne Trading Posts: The History and Archeology of Two Missouri River Sites: 1822–1838. Publications in Anthropology, No. 11, Nebraska State Historical Society, Lincoln.

Lucas, A. 1985. Forensic Chemistry and Scientific Criminal Investigation. *Association of Firearms and Tool Mark Examiners Journal* 17(4):57–90.

Mainfort, Robert C., Jr. 1980 Archaeological Investigations at Fort Pillow State Historic Area: 1976–1978. Division of Archaeology, Tennessee Department of Conservation.

Oakes, Yvonne R. 1990. The Glorieta Burials: Report to the Board of Regents Museum of New Mexico. Office of Archaeological Studies, Museum of New Mexico, Santa Fe.

Reynolds, John D. 1983. Archeological Investigations at Old Fort Scott, 14BO302, Fort Scott, Kansas 1968–1972. National Park Service, Midwest Region, Omaha.

Thomas, Dean S. 2003. *Round Ball to Rimfire: A History of Civil War Small Arms Ammunition, Part Three, Federal Pistols, Revolvers, and Miscellaneous Essays.* Thomas Publications, Gettysburg, PA.

United Nations. 2003. Crater Analysis. School for Peace Support Operations Training Manual, New York.

War Department. 1945. Identification of Japanese Shells and Shell Fragments; Location of Enemy Batteries. War Department Technical Manual TM E9-1901. Washington, DC.

Weber, Kent L., and Douglas D. Scott. 2006. Applying Firearms Identification Procedures in the Analysis of Percussion Caps. *Journal of the Association of Firearms and Toolmark Examiners* 37(1):34–44.

White, Henry P., and Burton D. Munhall. 1977. *Cartridge Headstamp Guide.* H. P. White Laboratory, Street, MD.

Whittemore, James M., and F. Heath. 1878. Ordnance Memoranda, No. 21: Ammunition, Fuses, Primers, Military Pyrotechny, etc. Ordnance Board, U.S. Army, Government Printing Office, Washington, DC.

Wilhelm, Russell M. 1980. General Considerations of Firearms Identification and Ballistics. In Werner U. Spitz and Russell S. Fisher, *Medicolegal Investigation of Death*, 202–215. Charles C. Thomas, Springfield, IL.

Ziegler, Robert J. 2001. Historical Archaeology at Locality 6 of Fort Ellsworth Site (14WE26), Kanopolis Lake, Ellsworth County, Kansas. U.S. Corps of Engineers, Kansas City District, Kansas City, MO.

Total Roman Defeat at the Battle of Varus (9 AD)

Susanne Wilbers-Rost

HISTORY OF RESEARCH

Five hundred years ago written accounts by Roman historian Tacitus that told about the so-called "Battle of the Teutoburg Forest," or "Battle of Varus," between Germans and Romans in 9 AD, were found in the northern Germany monastery of Corvey. Since then, many people have tried to find the battlefield where three Roman legions were destroyed by German tribes. Most searchers were unsuccessful because Tacitus (Annales I 59–62), as well as Velleius Paterculus (2, 117–119) or Cassius Dio (56, 18–23), described the situation differently and were not quite exact. Therefore more than 700 theories concerning the battlefield were developed. Theodor Mommsen, a specialist on Roman history, had the right idea as we know today. In the 1880s, Mommsen thought that the hundreds of Roman silver and gold coins found by farmers on their fields north of Osnabrück indicated the battle's site.[1] Since there were no remains of military equipment, not many people believed Mommsen.

It took about 100 years until more details were discovered—not by purposeful research, but by an unexpected discovery. An amateur archaeologist, British Major Tony Clunn, found a hoard of Roman silver coins.[2] During a follow-up metal detector field survey by the Osnabrück Museum, pieces of military equipment were found as well. At that time in 1987/1988, no one thought the battlefield had been discovered; we had the impression that these few Roman equipment fragments had been lost, perhaps by Roman soldiers or merchants, who passed through the area at the time of the battle. In 1989, archaeological excavations started on one interesting site, the field "Oberesch." Apart from many Roman finds, a wall was excavated, and initially it was thought to be part of a Roman fort. After some months, however, we realized that most of the finds lay in front of the wall, not behind it. Together with the nearly complete lack of Roman pottery, the deduction was possible that all the artifacts, coins, military pieces, and the wall itself,

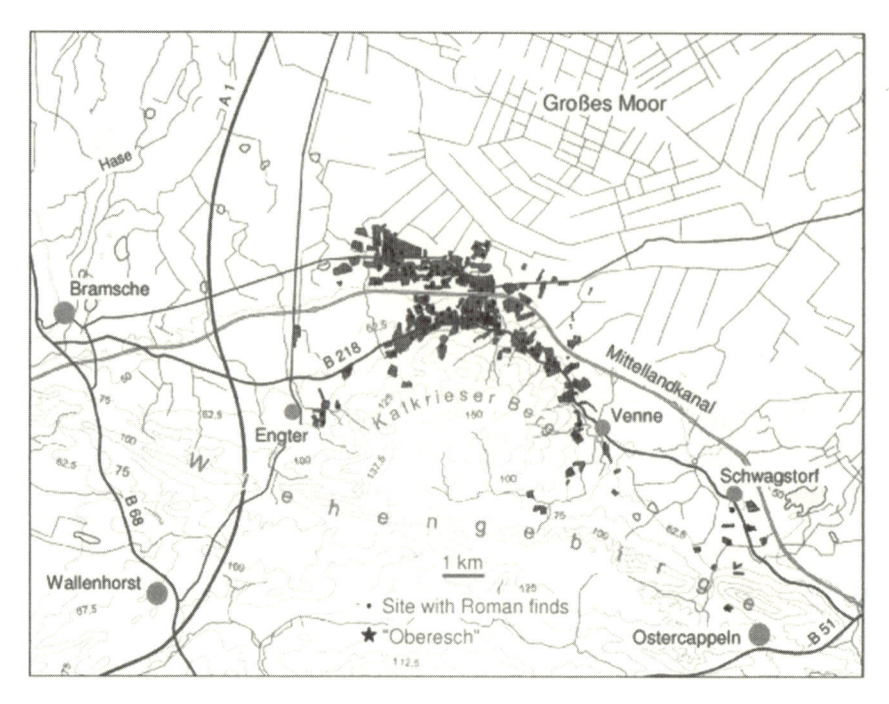

Research area of the "Kalkriese-Project" with surveyed fields, sites with Roman finds, and the field "Oberesch." (Museum und Park Kalkriese)

showed that Romans had been attacked by Germans from on top of the wall and that they had obviously been beaten. In combination with field research in surrounding areas, the idea that the site of the Battle of Varus was now located was one conclusion of these excavations. Other sites with Roman finds indicated that engagements must have taken place in an area of more than 50 km^2 (see figure). Coins of the time before 10 AD and copper coins with countermark VAR of Publius Quinctilius Varus helped date this event to 9 AD.[3]

TOPOGRAPHICAL SITUATION AND HISTORICAL BACKGROUND

The "Oberesch" wall was apparently built by Germans who had obviously planned this ambush perfectly. It was constructed at the narrowest place between the Kalkriese Hill, a part of the Wiehengebirge, and the Great Bog, a few kilometers to the north. Between hill and bog, the land was wet, sandy, and nearly impassable. The topography worked like a fish trap, and when the Romans arrived, coming from the east, perhaps from a summer camp on the Weser as Roman historians reported, they had no chance to fight in a normal formation or to flee once the German attacks began. Two thousand years ago, the land was occupied by Germans in single farmsteads or very small villages.[4] Paleobotanical analysis indicates that there was a wood on the hill, but it was a cultivated forest, not a natural growth.[5] Near the farms, there were fields; small roads connected the settlements. The roads were not comparable to Roman roads, so the legions of Varus would have had difficulties passing through this area even without being attacked.

Until Varus started to integrate northern Germany into the Roman Empire, Romans had not settled east of the Rhine. The nearest Roman camps, at the rivers Lippe and Rhine, were about 100 km to the south and southwest and too far to get help in case of a fight. Therefore, the place for the ambush was tactically well chosen by the Germans. The German leader was Arminius, a young nobleman, who had been educated by the Romans and had led Germanic auxiliaries in the Roman army. He was well prepared because he knew the strong and the weak points of the Roman army as well as the northern German landscape. We do not know how many Germans were involved in preparing the battlefield and the battle itself. The local native population was not enough, and we have to presume that soldiers from other Germanic tribes helped.

THE WALL

Excavations of the last 15 years, together with botanical and soil analyses, revealed many details of the wall construction that were not expected at the beginning of research (see figures on page 124).[6] After two years of excavation, we thought the wall was shaped as a semicircle. Later we saw that the form was much more complex; the wall bent several times, with salient and rentrant angles similar to a fort's bastions. It had a length of about 400 m, parallel to the hillside. This shape was advantageous for the Germans: there was room for more soldiers on top of such a wall than on a straight line. The Germans could attack Roman legionaries from more than one side if the Romans tried to assault the wall.

Among others, these observations led to a conclusion that the Germans had built the wall some time before the Romans arrived. Other details show that the wall was built in a very short time, perhaps only one or two weeks, before the legions came. Different materials were used for the wall: in the western part, grass sods were taken from a deserted pre-Roman Iron Age settlement just in front of the wall. The material of the eastern half consisted of more sand. The archaeological interpretations were proved by soil scientists who analyzed samples collected during excavation. At the western end of the wall, chalk stones stabilized the wall where sand or grass sods were not enough. All the materials were taken from very nearby. It seems as if different groups worked together in a very pragmatic way. The rampart was

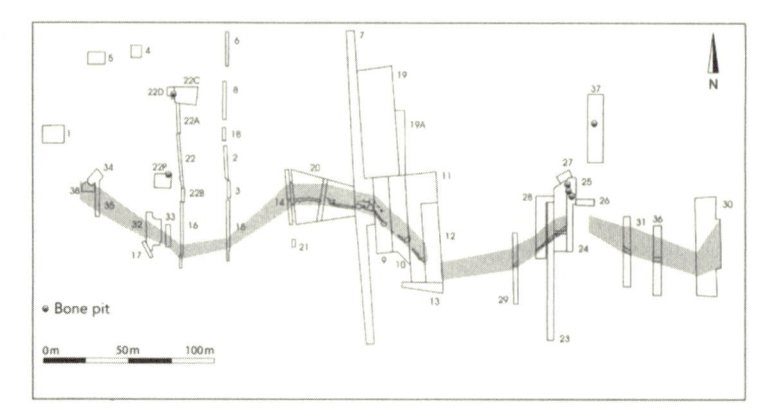

Excavated trenches, wall with drainage ditch, and bone pits at the "Oberesch." (Museum und Park Kalkriese)

probably sufficient for a short time, but was not stable for long-term use. On one side, part of the wall was strengthened by a palisade, probably to protect the most prominent part against the attacks. Many narrow gates through the wall allowed the Germans to sally from cover and engage the Romans in front of the wall, then to retreat into the wall's shelter if pressed too hard. The gates and the shape of the wall demonstrate that the structure is a

Rest of the wall and v-shaped drainage ditch under a thick layer of "Plaggenesch" during the excavation. (Museum und Park Kalkriese)

Germanic construction, not Roman. The Romans would have built a closed fortification to be secure when they were in enemy territory.

Only in one short section was there a ditch in front of the wall. This provided sand for the wall's construction. In different parts, long narrow pits or ditches were discovered behind the wall; they apparently served to prevent water, which could not seep through the impermeable loam, from washing away the wall before the Roman troops arrived. The Germans seemingly realized the necessity of the drainage after they had nearly finished the wall as field observations show; they had to reduce the wall on the inner side to dig the ditch. This caused instability, and during the battle this wall section may have been destroyed, a conclusion drawn from the hundreds of Roman finds concentrated in a small zone in front of the wall. Drainage was restricted to a wall section that was clearly in danger of being destroyed by water, showing that the Germans did only what was absolutely necessary. The Germans also chose a type of flat sandridge to put the wall on with as little expenditure as possible. These details show that the wall could be built in a short time; nevertheless, it was very effective for attacking the Roman legions that went past.

VEGETATION

The investigations and botanical analysis changed our concept of the landscape and vegetation around the wall. The western zone in front of the rampart was open since a former pre-Roman Iron Age settlement may have been used as a pasture. The eastern part, however, must have had different vegetation. The excavation results, soil borings, and analysis by soil scientists provided a picture of the surface, indicating the area in front of the eastern wall had an uneven relief with wet hollows; hints of prehistoric settlement were very rare. Here we suppose were more trees or bushes, but not pasture or open fields. Surface and vegetation must have caused problems for the Romans walking through or trying to fight. Differences in the vegetation also caused different possibilities for the later discovery of objects during post-battle plundering. Dense vegetation might have hidden more objects than open landscape. Therefore, more finds do not necessarily mean more intensive fights.

ARTIFACTS

More than 4,000 iron and bronze artifacts were unearthed on the "Oberesch," in addition to about 400 silver and copper coins. Since these artifact descriptions are published,[7] I will only give a short summary. Most items are only very small fragments, and without a metal detector we would hardly find them; nevertheless, they show the complete equipment of a Roman legion. Besides, we get unique information about Roman legions on the march in Augustan times.

We believe that the large number of objects belonging to fighting units and baggage show that many Roman soldiers must have taken part in the actions. We found fragments of swords, daggers, pila, spears, and lances (see figure), even catapult bolt points, shield bosses, harnesses, medical instruments, tools, personal equipment, pieces of horses equipment. Many items, especially edgings from shields, exhibit damage. They were not only torn from the original artifact's organic material, such as wood or leather, but were then purposely folded, perhaps to carry them away more easily after post-battle plundering.

The distribution of finds on the "Oberesch" is not homogeneous (compare Rost in this volume). Many pieces are from immediately in front of the wall; among them are the bigger finds, including the famous face mask of a Roman helmet, a pioneer's axe, and tools. This concentration resulted from the wall's destruction during the battle and soon after. A few finds lay in the drainage ditch behind the rampart. Some may have been lost there during the fight, but concentrations near the gates may possibly have been caused by Germans plundering the battlefield and trying to hide the booty behind the wall before distributing it.

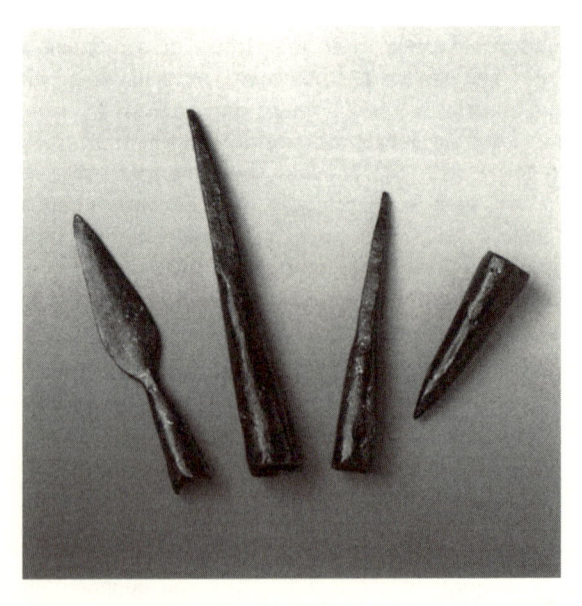

Iron weapons (lance-head, lance shoe, catapult bolts). (Christian Grovermann for Museum und Park Kalkriese)

BONES

Another category of battlefield finds that is important for interpreting what happened during and after the battle are human and animal bones. Because the sand in the subsoil usually does not preserve bones very long, we did not expect many bones when beginning the research. Therefore, we were quite surprised when we found half a skeleton of a Roman mule with many metal harness pieces.[8] It had died just in front of the wall and must have been covered with material from the wall very quickly. If this had not happened, Germans would have taken the metal, including pendants, an iron chain, and a bronze bell, while the bones would not have remained in anatomical position. Preservation of a nearly complete mule skeleton with iron bit and a small bell at the neck can be explained the same way. Wild animals would have torn up the dead mules and scattered the bones over a larger area. This indicates that the wall was partly destroyed during the battle or a short time after. This should not be surprising if one considers the short term and weak construction. These features and single finds of animal bones which zoologists identified as only mules and horses—there are no bones from remains of meals—confirm what metal finds tell us; the Romans were here with their baggage.

Isotope analyses of the mules' teeth may provide another chance to learn some battle details. Archaeozoologists try to determine the time of the death and the region where animals came from. This research is somewhat difficult because comparative material is rare, but we already know that the mules died in late summer or early autumn. The time of death confirms research on plant remains by botanists that demonstrates some plants in the bell worn by a mule were cut in late summer.[9] Another experiment was made by soil scientists; using phosphate analyses, they try finding spots where bodies once lay. It looks as though this may be possible in some places, even when there are no bone fragments left.

During the last years of excavations, we did not only find bones on the old ground surface. We also have six pits where bones of men, mules, and horses were deposed (see figure).[10] The interment was not done immediately after the battle. Since only disarticulated bone fragments were found, one must conclude that some time passed until the bodies were buried. Flesh and sinews had already disappeared completely, and specialists for zoology and anthropology think that the bones had been lying on the surface for 2 to 10 years before burial. These pits are mass graves because all of them contain remains of more than one individual. Human bones, of which some exhibit damage from swords, were mixed with bones of horses and mules; among them were Roman artifacts comparable to those we found on the surface. Some human bones, especially skulls, show careful treatment during the interment. We think that they were buried by Roman troops under the leadership of Germanicus who visited the battlefield six years later (Tacitus Annales I, 62).

Bone pit with fragments of animal and human bones. In the center of the pit is a human skull. (Museum und Park Kalkriese)

Nobody expected such mass graves on the Varus battlefield, because Tacitus described construction of a grave mound. No traces of a mound have been located yet; maybe there was one somewhere in the larger area as a symbol for the whole burial. The bones in the pits, however, clearly show that the bodies of fallen soldiers and animals were left on the battlefield for some time. The Germans plundered them, but they did not bury them. Burial was done some years after most bones were destroyed naturally, by weather and animals, not by burning the bodies as there are no traces of charcoal. For interpreting the battlefield remains, this means that at least two post-battle human activities manipulated the material: plundering and burial.

AGRICULTURE ON THE "OBERESCH" IN EARLIER TIMES

Together with soil scientists we try to get information about the use of the "Oberesch" after the battle. Traces of settlements were not found. More than 1,000 years later, farmers put grass sods as a natural fertilization on the fields.[11] This method, the so-called "Esch" or "Plaggenesch," was used for several hundred years and it probably helped preserve not only the Roman finds but also rampart remnants. Without the "Esch," the plough would have destroyed the remaining wall and many finds would be more fragmentary than they are now. Different kinds of agricultural techniques applied in the area of the battlefield influenced the preservation of finds differently. Though the "Esch" helps archaeological investigations, it causes difficulties because modern survey techniques such as aerial photography or magnetic measurements can seldom be used to support the research.

THE BATTLE AREA

In the beginning, the "Oberesch" was just one place among the sites we discovered during the initial investigation. When excavations started, nobody thought that this place would become the most important site. We did not imagine that the large number of artifacts, the wall, and the mass graves would be the exception in the Battle of Varus area. The field survey continued all the time, and many more sites are now known.[12] None of them, however, compare with the "Oberesch." More than 1,000 coins were found, but the numerous pieces of military equipment, some 400 items, are much less than on the "Oberesch." We have to analyze the differing quality of finds at the different places in the battle zone.

Though excavations were made at other sites, no structures comparable to the wall or other features that might be connected with the battle were found. Besides, there are no other bone fragments or bone pits. This means that the "Oberesch" is not only a very important site, but perhaps the main fighting place. Such a special function is not surprising; the wall was built at the narrowest place where all Romans had to pass when they marched from east to west.

Other sites in the area of more than 50 km^2 demonstrate that the battle did not take place only on the "Oberesch," and that it must have lasted for more than one day. Germans must have attacked the long column of Roman troops at different places and different times. It is possible that they hid in the woods or behind a brush barrier that left no archaeological traces. One aspect, however, seems to be certain after 15 years of research: the number of Romans must have been fewer than was expected earlier. The written sources mention three legions, cavalry, and auxiliaries that were involved in the battle. Theoretically this could mean about 20,000 persons. This large number of people on the Roman side, however, seems too many. Maybe only about 10,000 Romans took part in this engagement. Others may have stayed in the winter camps. Besides, there would have been great logistical problems for the Roman army to get enough rations for men and animals as they moved through this thinly settled Germanic territory.

Finally, it should be mentioned that Roman items with signs of processing and melting drops were found at contemporary native settlements sites in the battle area. They show that the battlefield was plundered and that Germans living nearby used at least a small part of the war booty to make products of their own.

ARCHAEOLOGY AND WRITTEN SOURCES

The information we got from Roman written sources did not really help identify the battle of the Teutoburg Forest site. The results obtained from the archaeological investigations now show a picture which differs in some parts from what one would have expected whilst interpreting the ancient descriptions. Roman historians, for example, did not write that the Germans built a wall to ambush the troops of Varus; they only mention walls of Roman camps, one of them seemingly built by the remaining, diminished Roman legions. Perhaps the new archaeological sources allow us a modified interpretation of the written sources today.

Further reflections are possible if the bone pits can actually be connected with the burial ceremony of Germanicus in 15 AD.[13] Those who buried the dead soldiers six years after the battle must have seen the wall. It is only a short distance from the pits; in 15 AD it was without a doubt visible, though partly demolished. Could this rampart that, according to the archaeological interpretation, was built by Germans, be identical with the fortification which the Roman sources claim, by mistake, was the camp of Varus's legions? Could the wall on the "Oberesch" be the structure described by Tacitus as a flat wall with a shallow ditch, perhaps constructed as a camp for the night by the rest of the three legions of Varus during the battle? Though this is still a thesis, it helps understand how archaeology can augment the interpretation of ancient written sources.

PLANS FOR THE FUTURE

Our plans for the following years are, if we get money to continue our work, to find out more about what happened on the "Oberesch," and on other sites in the surrounding countryside. Excavations, natural sciences, and settlement archaeology will be necessary to get a picture of the battle's landscape, as well as the settlement patterns that were responsible for the Roman march route and the battle's course.

One important approach for understanding the battle's events will be the theoretical analysis of finds and their distribution. The first ideas were described in the chapter by Achim Rost in this volume.

For helping me with the translation of my text I want to thank Ingrid Recker, Osnabrück, and Lawrence Babits, Greenville, NC.

NOTES

1. Mommsen 1885.
2. Clunn 1999, Schlüter 1999.
3. Berger 1996, Chantraine 2002.
4. Rost and Wilbers-Rost 1992.

5. Dieckmann 1998:111–113.
6. Wilbers-Rost 2003.
7. Franzius 1996, Schlüter 1999, Wells 2003.
8. Rost and Wilbers-Rost 1993.
9. Dieckmann 1998:110.
10. Wilbers-Rost 1999.
11. Lienemann and Tolksdorf-Lienemann 1992:335–339.
12. Harnecker and Tolksdorf-Lienemann 2004.
13. Rost 2003.

REFERENCES CITED

Berger, Frank. 1996. *Kalkriese 1. Die römischen Fundmünzen*. Römisch-Germanische Forschungen, Bd. 55, Mainz.
Chantrainc, Heinrich. 2002. Varus oder Germanicus? Zu den Fundmünzen von Kalkriese. *Thetis* 9:81–93.
Clunn, Tony. 1999. *In Quest of the Lost Legions*. Minerva Press, London.
Dieckmann, Ursula. 1998. *Paläoökologische Untersuchungen zur Entwicklung von Natur- und Kulturlandschaft am Nordrand des Wiehengebirges*. Abhandlungen aus dem Westfälischen Museum für Naturkunde 60 (4), Münster.
Franzius, Georgia. 1996. Die Römischen Funde aus Kalkriese 1987–1995 und ihre Bedeutung für die Interpretation und Datierung militärischer Fundplätze der augusteischen Zeit im nordwesteuropäischen Raum. In Carol Van Driel-Murray (ed.), Roman Military Equipment: Experiment and Reality. Proceedings of the IXth International Roman Military Equipment Conference (Leiden, 15th–17th September 1994), Vol. 2. *Journal of Roman Military Equipment Studies* 6, pp. 69–88.
Harnecker, Joachim, and Eva Tolksdorf-Lienemann. 2004. Kalkriese 2 – Sondierungen in der Kalkrieser-Niewedder Senke, Mainz.
Lienemann, Jörg, and Eva Tolksdorf-Lienemann. 1992. Bodenkundliche Untersuchungen im Zusammenhang mit den Ausgrabungen auf dem Oberesch in Kalkriese, Stadt Bramsche, Landkreis Osnabrück. In W. Schlüter, Archäologische Zeugnisse zur Varusschlacht? Die Untersuchungen in der Kalkrieser-Niewedder Senke bei Osnabrück. *Germania*, 70(2):335–344.
Mommsen, Theodor. 1885. *Die Örtlichkeit der Varusschlacht*. Berlin.
Rost, Achim. 2003. Kalkriese – Archäologische Befunde und antike Schriftquellen. – *Archäologie in Niedersachsen*, 25–29.
Rost, Achim, and Susanne Wilbers-Rost. 1992. Die vorgeschichtliche Besiedlung am Kalkrieser Berg zwischen Engter und Schwagstorf. In W. Schlüter, Archäologische Zeugnisse zur Varusschlacht? Die Untersuchungen in der Kalkrieser-Niewedder Senke bei Osnabrück. *Germania* 70(2):344–349.
Rost, Achim, and Susanne Wilbers-Rost. 1993. Fragmente eines römischen Zugtieres mit Resten der Anschirrung. In W. Schlüter (ed.), Kalkriese – Römer im Osnabrücker Land. Archäologische Forschungen zur Varusschlacht, Bramsche, 199–209.
Schlüter, Wolfgang (ed.). 1993. *Kalkriese – Römer im Osnabrücker Land. Archäologische Forschungen zur Varusschlacht*, Bramsche.

Schlüter, Wolfgang. 1999. The Battle of the Teutoburg Forest: Archaeological Research at Kalkriese Near Osnabrück. In John Douglas Creighton and Roder John Anthony Willson (eds.), Roman Germany. Studies in Cultural Interaction. *Journal of Roman Archaeology, Supplementary Series No. 32*:125–159.

Wells, Peter. 2003. *The Battle that Stopped Rome*. W. W. Norton and Co., New York.

Wilbers-Rost, Susanne. 1992. Grabungsbefunde auf dem "Oberesch" in Kalkriese, Stadt Bramsche, Landkreis Osnabrück. In W. Schlüter, Archäologische Zeugnisse zur Varusschlacht? Die Untersuchungen in der Kalkrieser-Niewedder Senke bei Osnabrück. *Germania* 70(2):332–335.

Wilbers-Rost, Susanne. 1999. Die Ausgrabungen auf dem "Oberesch" in Kalkriese: Deponierungen von Menschen- und Tierknochen auf dem Schlachtfeld. In R. Wiegels, W. Schlüter (eds.), *Rom, Germanien und die Ausgrabungen von Kalkriese*. Akten des Internationalen Kongresses vom 2. bis 5. September 1996 an der Universität Osnabrück. Osnabrücker Forschungen zu Altertum und Antikerezeption, Bd. 1, 61–89.

Wilbers-Rost, Susanne. 2002. Kalkriese und die Varusschlacht – Archäologische Nachweise einer militärischen Auseinandersetzung zwischen Römern und Germanen. In P. Freeman (ed.), Limes XVIII. Proceedings of the XVIIIth International Congress of Roman Frontier Studies Held in Amman, Jordan (September 2000). *British Archaeological Reports. International Series 1084* (I):515–526.

Wilbers-Rost, Susanne. 2003. Der Hinterhalt gegen Varus. Zur Konstruktion und Funktion der germanischen Wallanlage auf dem "Oberesch" in Kalkriese. *Die Kunde N.F.* 54, 123–142.

Wilbers-Rost, Susanne. In press. *Kalkriese 3 – Ergebnisse archäologischer und naturwissenschaftlicher Untersuchungen auf dem "Oberesch" in Kalkriese*.

English Battlefields 991–1685: A Review of Problems and Potentials

Glenn Foard

THIS CHAPTER REVIEWS the problems and potentials in the investigation of battles and battlefields across England over the last millennium, from the earliest apparently securely related battle, that of Maldon (Essex, 991), through to the last major field engagement, Sedgemoor (Somerset, 1685).

If one examines the period range of papers given in the past Fields of Conflict conferences, one finds a very heavy bias to the postmedieval and especially to the industrial era. This is mirrored in period distribution of papers at other conferences held in England, such as the battlefields session at the Institute of Field Archaeologists Conference in 2004 and the three National Army Museum conferences on battlefield archaeology in 2001–2003. It demonstrates the way in which the industrial period dominates battlefields research both in England and worldwide. This runs completely contrary to the chronological distribution of battles in England and shows the degree to which especially medieval and earlier battles are being largely ignored, with the notable exception of the late medieval battle of Towton (Yorkshire, 1461).[1] This chapter explores this far wider resource and considers the problems and potentials that we face if we are to deal effectively with the full chronological range of battlefields in England.

The methodology, which must be applicable across the full time span, can be defined under five main headings:

- Locating the battlefield
- Reconstructing its historic terrain on the day of the battle
- Characterizing the armies that fought there
- Using documentary evidence to position their preliminary maneuvers, initial deployments, and subsequent action within the reconstructed terrain
- Validating and refining the interpretation using the wholly independent evidence of battle archaeology

This requires the application of a range of evidence and techniques, each of which bring their own distinctive problems that also vary, sometimes dramatically, depending on where and when the battle was fought.

Location and Chronology

The general location of very few early battles is as clearly and specifically located as Bosworth (Leicestershire, 1485). Christopher Saxton, England's first great national cartographer, depicted the location of the Bosworth battlefield almost within living memory of the battle.[2] The battlefield appeared on his 1576 map of Leicestershire, published in his national Atlas, which was produced specifically for the Tudor government. Bosworth was the only battlefield identified in the Atlas and this was the battle which had brought the Tudors to the throne, so it would be highly unlikely that Saxton would have wrongly placed the action, especially given the consistently high level of accuracy of his work. Despite this and other almost irrefutable evidence, there has recently been a suggestion that the battle was actually fought some six miles to the west, near Atherstone.[3] It is a mark of the difficulty that exists in the location of historic battles that one of the best known and most important of English battles can be open to such dispute by reputable scholars. For lesser battles and especially those of an earlier period the problems are far greater.

Thus the first task of locating the battlefield is for most early battles the hurdle at which we fail. More than 100 documented battles as well as many lesser actions have been fought in England over the last two millennia, from the Roman Conquest of AD 43 through to the skirmishes of the Jacobite Risings and other minor engagements of the eighteenth century. Forty-three of the most securely located, best understood, and best preserved of these battlefields have been identified by English Heritage on their Register of Historic Battlefields.[4] While some were excluded from the Register because they were poorly preserved, many were omitted because their sites were too poorly understood to be able to define reasonable boundaries for conservation purposes. However, the greatest number of battles was excluded because their battlefields are wholly unlocated, with in some cases various alternative sites many miles apart being suggested for the same action. Almost all of the more than 70 battles and other actions from before 1066 are as yet unlocated. The resolution of such major problems of location, if possible at all, must await the effective application of a methodology for the investigation of the battlefields of the last millennium, most of which are at least located in general terms. Perhaps when we understand the archaeology of these battles we will then be able to tackle with more confidence the problem of those from before the Norman Conquest.

In order to effectively manage the resource for its research values it is essential to have a comprehensive record of all fields of conflict, including information on the scale and character of the action. Only then will it be possible to assess, with any confidence, a site's relative potential. Given the rarity of fields of conflict, compared to many other components of the historic environment, the resource can only be effectively assessed at a national scale.[5] The present analysis is based upon the Battlefields Trust's *UK Fields of Conflict* database.[6] Though as yet incomplete, with skirmishes and other lesser actions very inconsistently represented and sieges wholly absent, it provides the best starting point for an assessment of battlefields. In collaboration with Historic Scotland, the database is currently (winter 2004–2005) being enhanced for Scotland from secondary sources and enhancement for England is planned to follow.

Using the current dataset, broad trends can already be discerned. There is a fairly steep decline in the number of actions as one moves back in time from the seventeenth to the twelfth century, when numbers increase once more. The one exception is the sixteenth century where only a handful of battles are recorded. It would appear from the graph (see figure) that the Register provides a relatively representative selection of English battlefields in terms of their chronological spread, that is of course until one gets back to the eleventh century, when the problems of battlefield location really begin to dominate. The Register also gives a relatively good geographical spread in terms of the national distribution of located battles. The Registered battlefields may thus provide a reasonable sample with which to examine many of the problems of investigating battles over the last millennium and across the varied historic landscapes of England. However, the very reason of their Registration, that they are the best documented and located of our battlefields, and as a result the most intensively studied, means that they do not give us a fully representative view of the problems that must be faced in the study of

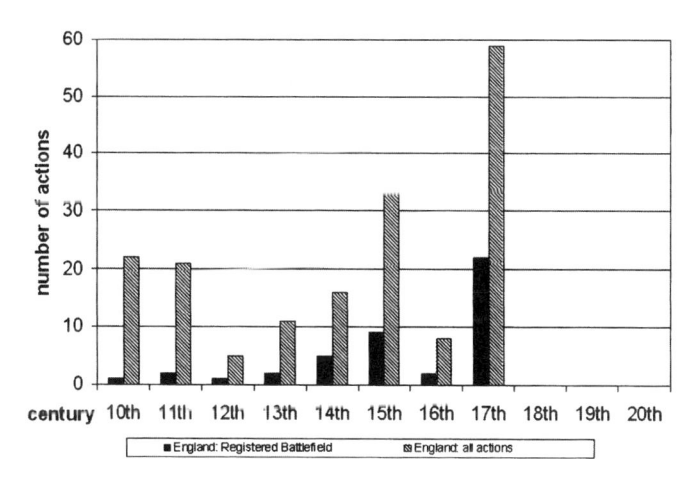

Graph of numbers of registered versus unregistered battlefields in England by century.

battlefields. Therefore it will be essential also to sample from other, poorly preserved and currently poorly located or unlocated battles, to assess their potential.

In any assessment we must also take account of the degree to which our chronological distribution of battles is skewed by the Wars of the Roses in the fifteenth century and the Civil Wars in the mid-seventeenth century. If we are to use battlefields as a major resource for the investigation of warfare in the UK over the last millennium and as an example of a wider tradition of warfare in Europe in that period, then it is important to pay particular attention to those periods where far fewer actions are recorded. Indeed it would be far more effective to sample from the whole of the UK in order to maximize the sample, especially for the less well represented periods, such as the sixteenth century.

Historic Terrain

Understanding the terrain of a battlefield as it was at the time of the action is critical to the understanding of any battle. It has long been known that the English landscape has been transformed a number of times and in very different ways in different regions over the last millennium or so. Despite this one typically finds that, even today, historic battles are discussed and mapped in relation to the modern landscape.

The realization that terrain is a key to the understanding of historic battles can be traced through battlefield studies over the last 300 years, right back to the contemporary military manuals that guided the commanders in the fighting of the actions themselves.[7] Hutton wrote in 1788: "By carefully comparing the writers, the field, and the traditions, I have attempted to remove some absurdities and place truth on firmer ground."[8] In this he was followed by many others, such as Brooke in 1857 in his study of battlefields of the fifteenth century: "the fields of battle, and the positions of the hostile armies, may in several instances, be clearly identified, after a perusal of the statements of the old chroniclers, and a comparison of their descriptions with the present aspect of the localities where the battles were fought."[9] Most students of battlefields in England over the last two centuries have had to independently rediscover this reality rather than follow in a clear tradition of battlefield study. This is because most of the really effective investigations were conducted by people who approached the subject incidentally, not from the subdiscipline of military history. The earliest examples include Scatcherd's study in the 1830s of Adwalton Moor (Yorkshire, 1643) and Fitzgerald's investigation of Naseby (Northamptonshire, 1645) in the 1840s.[10] In the case of Bosworth and Naseby, part of the landscape had only been transformed within living memory from open field to hedged enclosures and thus both Hutton and Fitzgerald were well aware of landscape change. Despite this realization by at least some antiquaries, most battles were largely interpreted in the light of the terrain of the antiquaries' own day.

This is where Twemlow's 1912 study of Blore Heath (Staffordshire, 1459) represents a significant departure, for he attempted to produce a map of the battlefield as it had been in the fifteenth century.[11] Burne, working in the late 1940s and 1950s understood the need for such reconstruction of historic terrain but lacked the expertise to achieve this.[12] Thanks to the work over the last 50 years within the English Landscape tradition, which developed out of the work of Hoskins in the 1940s and 1950s, we are now in a position to reconstruct historic landscapes to a very high standard of accuracy.[13] As a result we can see the inadequacies of Twemlow's work and the degree to which Burne's investigations were undermined by his lack of access to techniques of landscape study that we take for granted today. But we should still acknowledge the pioneering nature of their work.

Some of the shortcomings in battlefield studies can be explained by the way in which the study of the past has evolved over the last century or more. While in the eighteenth and nineteenth centuries antiquaries covered the full range of historical themes, in the later nineteenth and especially twentieth centuries the divergence of the disciplines of archaeology, military history, and historical geography have meant that advances in one field have not effectively fed through into the investigation of the other, at least as far as the study of historic battles is concerned.

Remarkably, the tradition of local historians and historical geographers stumbling upon a valuable application in battlefield studies for their specialist skills in historic landscape reconstruction continued in the second half of the twentieth century. For example, in the 1970s Pannett, while mapping the historic landscape of Warwickshire, realized the implications of his work for the interpretation of the battle of Edgehill (Warwickshire, 1642).[14] It was, however, only with the work of Newman in the late 1970s, in his study of Marston Moor (Yorkshire, 1644), that the next major step was taken.[15] Newman consciously built upon the important base provided by Burne, and wished to extend and develop Burne's method through a coherent approach to the problem of historic terrain. While work such as that by Fitzgerald and Pannett remained unpublished and inaccessible, even the well-known published work of Newman failed to lead to a coherent school of battlefield study.

The failures are best exemplified in the case of Bosworth, where in the 1970s Williams failed to apply the most basic principles of historic landscape reconstruction, with the result that key terrain features were placed where they could never have existed.[16] Again it was only when a local historian, Peter Foss, conducted careful work with key landscape and documentary sources, to establish the basic structure of the terrain as it was in the later fifteenth century, that the difficulties at Bosworth began to be resolved.[17] Yet neither the work of Newman nor Foss has managed to take center stage in the methodology of battlefield study, despite the major advances that it offered.

What seems to lie at the heart of the problem in battlefield studies in the UK is the lack of sufficient critical mass to be able to build, enhance, and sustain a coherent methodology and body of expertise. The problem is compounded by the fact that effective integration of the techniques of different disciplines is essential to battlefield studies, not just in the reconstruction of the historic terrain but in all its other aspects. This remains the most important challenge for the current development of battlefield studies in the UK. What is required is a secure cross-disciplinary base in both an academic and a professional context, and an adequate level of work in battlefield research and conservation to sustain it.

What then of the application of a methodology of historic terrain reconstruction right across the chronological range of our battles? The problem of reconstructing a day in the life of a landscape is far from simple, even given the major advances in the investigation of the English landscape that have been achieved in the last half century. For the earliest battles in particular one may find that even the most basic elements of physical geography have been transformed. This is most clearly exhibited at Maldon (Essex, 991), which is recorded in an epic poem composed within a short time of the battle.[18] The location of the battlefield and the accurate positioning of the events within the landscape are dependent upon the way in which the two armies were initially separated by a tidal stream in the Blackwater Estuary near the burh at Maldon. This was a channel which was impassable at high tide yet was narrow enough to enable a shouted exchange and where there was a causeway which joined the two sides at low tide. This and other related information on the topography of the battlefield led in the 1930s to the identification of the battlefield as lying on the mainland immediately adjacent to Northey Island, less than two miles to the east of the burh at Maldon. But objections were made by various scholars that the channel separating the island from the mainland is too wide at high tide to shout across. Work by Petty and Petty in the 1970s, revised in 1993, demonstrated that the present character of the area and width of the channel had been determined by rises in sea level in this region of England over the last 1,000 years.[19] In the later tenth century the channel had been much narrower than today. Also, while today it is flanked by salt flats, at the time of the battle there had been solid land to the water's edge. Their analysis provides a reconstruction of the physical geography which enables the action to be played out as described in the famous contemporary poem *The Battle of Maldon*. This is a major step forward but, as with all battles, such work on the terrain only provides a context. Whether this was indeed the site of the battle and, if so, how the action fitted within the terrain requires a quite separate study, particularly of our surviving battle archaeology.

For most of the battles of the last millennium it is not naturally induced changes but rather those resulting from exploitation of the landscape that have to be investigated to recover the contemporary battlefield terrain. It might be assumed that in such work there is a simple correlation between the length of time that has passed since the battle and the difficulty of reconstructing the battlefield terrain. In reality this is not the case. It depends to a considerable degree within which historic landscape zone within England the battlefield lay and thus the nature of that historic landscape and the chronology of its evolution. This is best demonstrated in the "central province" of planned open field landscapes and nucleated villages, identified by Roberts.[20] The landscape of the high medieval in the central province was largely an open one which had a high degree of stability for many centuries. In contrast, when enclosure began in earnest in the fifteenth century, gaining pace in the sixteenth century but not completed until the nineteenth century, for a long period it resulted in a continually evolving patchwork landscape, part enclosed and part open. Most of the landscape remained open through the period of the Wars of the Roses, and so for the investigation of those battles the potential for reconstruction of the terrain can be very high. In contrast, for the student of Civil Wars of the seventeenth century it can require considerable effort to establish what remained open field, what was enclosed, and in what form at a particular time.[21] Indeed for some battlefields the fine detail of the landscape as it was on the particular day of the battle may always remain elusive.

However, when one moves out of the central province or, as at Northallerton (Yorkshire, 1135), goes back beyond the period when the open fields had reached their maximum extent, then the problems are multiplied. Determining the character of the terrain for a battlefield as early as 1135, even in the central province, poses great challenges. Yet application of even the most basic of analysis can yield important evidence, as at Northallerton with the identification of areas of former marsh from the evidence of the British Geological Survey 1:50,000 scale mapping of alluvial and peat deposits, together with the mapping of Roman and major medieval roads.[22] The resultant crude reconstruction suggests very clearly why the English commander chose this location at which to try to halt the Scottish advance south. Here he could control the major north–south road where areas of marsh and open water provided a very narrow constriction and also enabled him to anchor his left wing, secure in the knowledge that he could not be outflanked. However, to understand the finer detail of this terrain as it was in 1135, which is so important to the reconstruction of the detail of the action, will require intensive study involving a range of techniques from pollen and soils analysis through to open field mapping, using a combination of both archaeological evidence and documentary sources.

For later battlefields the combination of documentary and archaeological evidence will be far more extensive, yet even in the central province as at Bosworth, the challenge is still a major one, to recover the fine detail necessary to understand the impact of terrain on military action.[23] It must also be recognized that the archaeological evidence for these open field landscapes is under severe threat, being rapidly eroded by intensive arable agriculture. If the necessary recording is not done in the near future, then the potential for terrain reconstruction on many of our battlefields may be severely reduced.

The complexity of the task will vary. Because of the high stability of the open field systems, where a battlefield remained open until the eighteenth or nineteenth century, then the recovery of the broad character of the historic terrain may be relatively simple using later sources. At Naseby, for example, the Ordnance Surveyors' Drawings of circa 1815 show the extent of open field and the pattern of the roads of the southern half of the battlefield, in Naseby township, prior to enclosure.[24] But the northern part of the battlefield, in Sibbertoft township, was enclosed in 1650, just five years after the battle. Though the documentary sources for the latter enclosure are exceptional for the date, it still represents a significant challenge to establish the exact extent of anciently enclosed fields that already existed by 1645. Indeed in our reconstruction of the battlefield the exact position and extent of one small hedged field called Archwrong Close remains a problem, yet it lies in a critical location within the battlefield and probably had great tactical significance in the action.[25] It is this great difference in the chronology of the evolution of the landscape between one township and another, and indeed the vagaries of documentary creation and survival between townships, which makes the study of historic terrain so difficult. In the case of Edgehill for example, Radway has a draft enclosure map of the mid-eighteenth century which shows each furlong and every hedge, whether part of ancient enclosures or not. In contrast Kineton has no enclosure or pre-enclosure map at all and so here we must depend on a written parliamentary enclosure award, yet these never record field closes, only the extent of ancient enclosure.[26] But then in both cases we must, if possible, employ pre-battle documents to confirm that any such enclosures and hedges were not created in the intervening period between the battle and parliamentary enclosure. Thus our knowledge of one part of a battlefield may be exceptionally good while that of another part may always remain far less complete.

Placing the Deployments and the Action within the Historic Terrain

The next step is to characterize the armies involved in the action. For the student of the seventeenth-century Civil Wars there is a wide range of sources. In the case of Naseby for example we have detailed contemporary plans of the deployments, each regiment in the Royalist army being named and its troop numbers specified. There are also many thousands of documents that tell us of the composition and equipping of the New Model Army. In contrast, the earlier in time one goes and the more obscure the battle then the poorer the evidence becomes. Even for the Wars of the Roses of the second half of the fifteenth century there are many uncertainties, while for earlier medieval battles the evidence becomes almost nonexistent in many cases, with the very notable exception of Hastings (Sussex, 1066). But for these earlier battles one can still draw upon more general principles of military practice to guide the interpretation.[27] With such information, however limited, we can begin to consider the problem of placing the troops in the field.

It is now that some of the major limitations of most previous interpretations of our battlefields become apparent. Once one has recovered with reasonable accuracy the historic terrain of the battlefield at the time of the action, it can immediately reveal problems with previous depictions of deployments, which have usually been reconstructed in relation to the modern landscape. This is clearly seen in relation to the various studies over the last 40 years of the initial deployments at Edgehill.[28] Such suggested deployments were viewed in the 1970s by Pannett against the extent of open field and hedged enclosures that he had reconstructed on a small scale in his mapping of the historic landscapes of Warwickshire. He realized immediately that, viewed in this seventeenth-century context, the published deployments by Burne, Young, and others are difficult to accept. On the basis of his limited reconstruction of the historic terrain he suggested a somewhat different alignment for the two opposing armies.[29] Ongoing research on the battlefield tends to support Pannett's conclusions. A more complex pattern of hedgerows has been revealed than that depicted by Pannett and these, together with the broader pattern of ancient enclosures, seem to reveal an even closer correlation between the reconstructed terrain and the topographical clues provided in the accounts of the military events.[30]

It is also necessary to have a detailed knowledge of the military practice of the period. First it enables one to build upon Burne's principle of Inherent Military Probability, in which one explores a problem on an historic battlefield by considering what a modern soldier might do in the same context.[31] A detailed understanding of the relevant historic military practice enables one to better consider what a soldier contemporary with the actual battle would have done, to assess the Inherent *Historic* Military Probability. Second, the evidence contained in the manuals often allows one to calculate the deployment of the armies on the field with a remarkable degree of accuracy, within the limitations of the evidence of troop numbers provided by the historic documents for the battle or for the armies themselves. When dealing with post-medieval battles the manuals specify exactly what space a particular number of infantry or cavalry will take up in both frontage and in depth, depending on whether the commander was using Dutch, Swedish, or German tactics,[32] and the documentary sources often provide clues if not detailed information on the exact formations, while one may also draw conclusions from the military experience of the commanders. Using such evidence, a detailed reconstruction of the initial deployments was prepared for Naseby.[33]

It seems likely that similar principles can be applied, with various important caveats, to the deployment of medieval and earlier armies. This is because there are certain fundamental principles in the deployment of men on a battlefield in pre-industrial warfare that almost inevitably recur for clear practical reasons from century to century. Moreover there are military manuals of the period,[34] mostly drawing heavily upon the manual by Vegetius written around AD 400, which provide the basic rules of deployment. For example Vegetius wrote: "We said that 6 ft. ought to lie between each line in depth from the rear, and in fact each warrior occupies 1 ft. standing still. Therefore, if you draw up six lines, an army of 10,000 men will take up 42 ft. in depth and a mile in breadth."[35] Even for the study of battles as early as the eleventh century we may be able to apply some of these principles and calculations, for the description of a shield wall formation by Vegetius seems, at least at first sight, to bear a striking resemblance to the nature of the shield wall deployments used in Anglo-Saxon and Viking battles. This should not perhaps be considered surprising, for it is known that Vegetius's manual was read by English commanders from at least the time of Alfred up to the late fifteenth century and beyond. Moreover the housecarls of the eleventh century were the highly professional and disciplined core of the English army whose soldiers, in exile after the fall of Anglo-Saxon England, earned a reputation as excellent troops in the service of the Byzantine emperor.[36] But above all where we lack vital evidence for these early periods is in the numbers of troops available on the field in the battles of the period, though many estimates or guesstimates have been made. It is quite clear using such calculations that the troop numbers sometimes suggested for the battle of Towton, on the basis of the evidence in the chronicles, could simply never have been deployed on the field. Only when one reduces the numbers to a figure similar to that of other contemporary battles of the period does deployment become viable in the restricted terrain at Towton, with impassable scarps on one side and lowland marsh on the other.[37] The available frontage is not enough to enable more than perhaps 15,000 men to be deployed 10 deep, the maximum depth recommended by Vegetius, and 6 deep is the more normal depth of deployment he quotes. Moreover this assumes that all the troops are deployed on foot. The more cavalry that actually fought on horseback the more rapidly the numbers possible within a given frontage fall.[38]

Battle Archaeology

While it is true that the analysis described above can enable many impossible and improbable interpretations to be dismissed, up to this point, almost without exception, all that such analysis can produce is a hypothesis or a number of alternative hypotheses. It is with the battle archaeology that the potential exists to apply wholly independent evidence to test these hypotheses.

On only a very few battlefields were defenses constructed or existing structures employed in some way in the action. On a battlefield such as Northampton (Northamptonshire, 1460), where the action took the form of an assault on an embanked and ditched camp, archaeological investigation to identify the ditch may well enable the exact location where the two armies clashed to be pinpointed with high accuracy.[39] Where defenses took the form of upstanding and surviving walls, there may be shot impact scars to indicate the direction and intensity of the firefight, though on battlefields such evidence is exceptionally rare whereas it is more common on siege sites.[40]

On most battlefields there will be mass graves at various locations, the main concentration of burial probably in most cases being, as Burne remarked, at the point where the main engagement began.[41] Other graves may well be scattered far more widely across the landscape, as in the case of Towton where the mass grave excavated in 1996 lay more than a mile from the core of the action.[42] However, such graves are notoriously difficult to locate and, although they can provide dramatic evidence of the nature of the action, may be relatively limited in what they can tell about the distribution of the action.

As has been demonstrated on several seventeenth-century battlefields in the UK and many more eighteenth- and nineteenth-century battlefields in the USA,[43] it is the distribution of projectiles which provides the most valuable evidence as to the extent, intensity, and character of the fighting. The other military equipment and the nonmilitary artifacts lost during the action by the troops can also be of great value in the interpretation. However, there are fundamental problems with the nature of the evidence the earlier one goes. It is particularly at the point of change from lead to iron projectiles in the late fifteenth and earlier sixteenth centuries that the problems really begin. Whereas lead is relatively inert, iron is highly unstable. The work at Towton shows that iron arrowheads exist in the topsoil of at least some battlefields, but it is as yet uncertain if they remain across most of the area in which they were originally deposited on the battlefield. They may only survive where exceptional conditions of preservation occurred.[44] This is why a high proportion of the evidence recovered from the action at Towton has been in the form of artifacts other than projectiles. While Towton, Bosworth, and the other battles of the Wars of the Roses took place just over 500 years ago, Hastings was fought more than 900 and Maldon over 1,000 years ago. The problems of survival on these earlier battlefields may therefore be further compounded by the enormous length of time that the artifacts have lain in the ground.

As with the archaeology of terrain, so with the archaeology of battle there is likely to be great variation both between battlefields and across an individual battlefield, in terms not only of deposition of artifacts during the action but also their survival to the present. In order to establish the nature of the original unstratified deposits before they were depleted through the effects of later agriculture, particularly for the battlefields from before the sixteenth century, it will be essential to identify areas of exceptional preservation, for example beneath alluvial deposits or where waterlogging has occurred. Preservation, particularly of ferrous artifacts, will also vary greatly according to soil pH and the current and past land use, with the mechanical damage occurring during arable cultivation being particularly influential. Hence, for example, where a battlefield has areas of surviving ridge and furrow, as at Bosworth, which have not been cultivated since at least the early seventeenth century, then the preservation of unstratified artifacts may be far better than in surrounding arable land. Burial beneath alluvium or colluvium may even preserve a largely undisturbed area of battlefield surface. Identifying such special conditions will be a key task in assessing the potential of early battlefields. It may provide a crucial guide as to what may once have existed more generally across the battlefield but now no longer survives. A good example of such preservation may exist at Battle, the site of the battle of Hastings, where an abbey was built soon after 1066, in commemoration of the dead, supposedly on the site where the English king fell. It is possible that the terracing for construction of the abbey may have preserved limited areas of battlefield surface from the impact of later activity. In contrast, on battlefields where intensive arable cultivation has continued for long periods, the preservation may be very poor and the continuing rates of destruction of artifacts, through influences such as modern chemical application and mechanical damage, may be exceptionally high. It is therefore particularly urgent that we establish what may survive on battlefields of different dates, types, and locations and how rapidly that battle archaeology is being destroyed by modern agriculture.

Even where the evidence is in the form of highly stable projectiles, particularly the lead shot of seventeenth-century battlefields, major problems still need to be addressed. Our primary objective is to use the projectile distributions to test and refine our hypotheses about the location and nature of the maneuvers, initial deployments, and action that have been based on the evidence of the military history set within the historic terrain. The artifact patterning that exists in the ground relates largely to specific elements of the action and to the effects of battlefield clearance in the hours and days following the battle. The interpretation of the relationship between the events of the battle and the artifact distribution that it left is a complex problem. In order to begin to make effective use of the evidence, the distribution that we recover needs to be as representative a sample as possible of that which actually exists in the ground. Despite having seen, in the 1970s, what were probably the first intensive modern battlefield surveys, England never fully developed the systematic survey and recording techniques for battlefield study that have been applied since the early 1980s in the USA. Almost without exception the work conducted in England has been neither sufficiently systematic nor well recorded to enable the level of analysis that is needed. Neither has most of the work been published. There has thus not been a developing body of work available that could be reviewed, nor has there been until very recently sufficient pooling of expertise to encourage the production of an effective methodology.

This is most clearly seen with the previously unpublished fieldwalking survey of Marston Moor battlefield conducted in the 1970s by Newman and Cammidge, to complement Newman's work on the documentary sources for the battle and the historic terrain.[45] The plan of the distribution of finds from this survey, published here for the first time, has been digitized from an annotated plan and other information provided several years ago to the author for this purpose by the late Peter Newman (see figure). However, we still lack sufficient information to be able to fully understand the methodology and thus the limitations of his pioneering survey of the battle archaeology.

The problems with the 1970s survey become strikingly apparent if one compares the Newman and Cammidge data with that recently published from

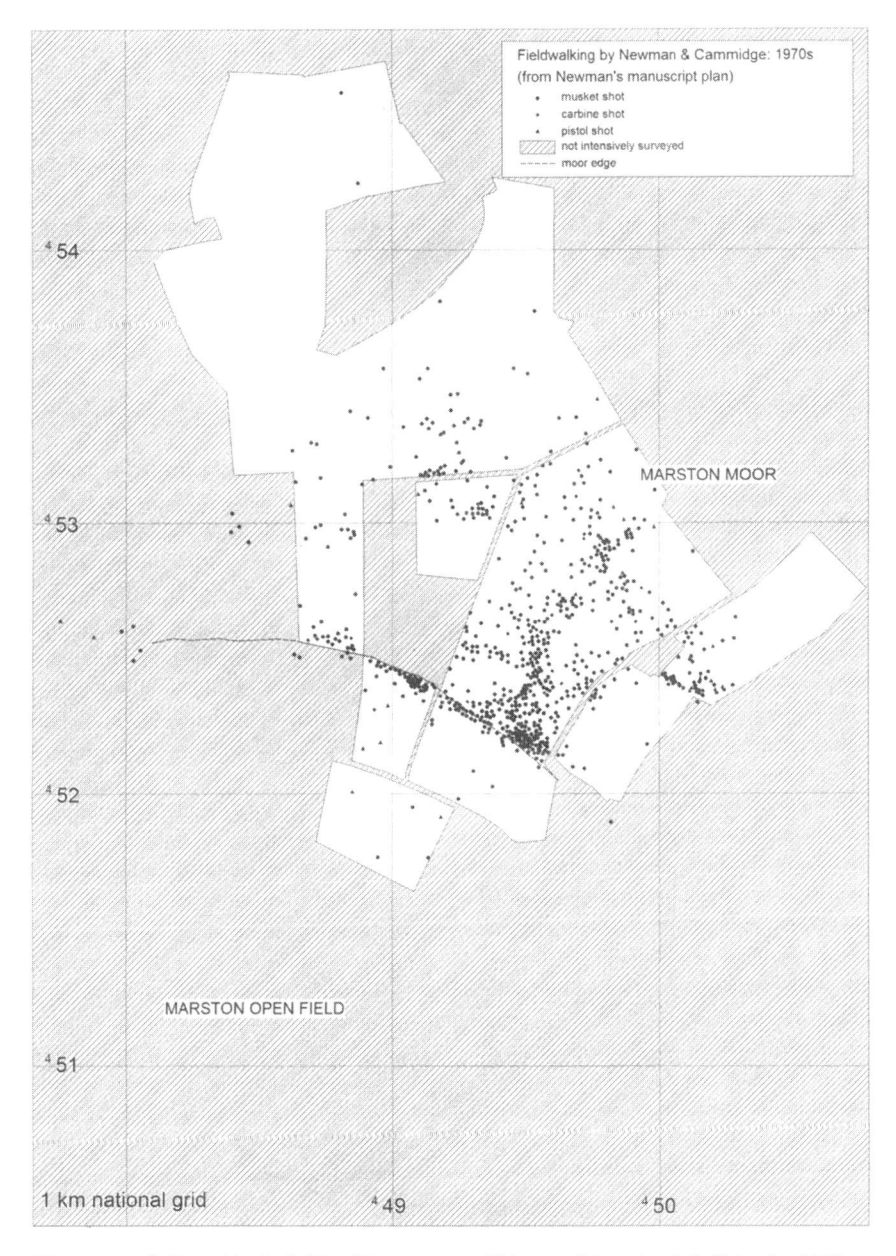

Newman and Cammidge's fieldwalking survey of Marston Moor battlefield in the 1970s.

146 FIELDS OF CONFLICT

Roberts's metal detecting survey of the battlefield in the 1980s and 1990s (see figure).[46] The latter produced a far wider distribution of bullets on the moor itself, while most striking is the extension of the distribution to the south of the moor. A major phase of the battle had been missed by the 1970s survey. To a large degree

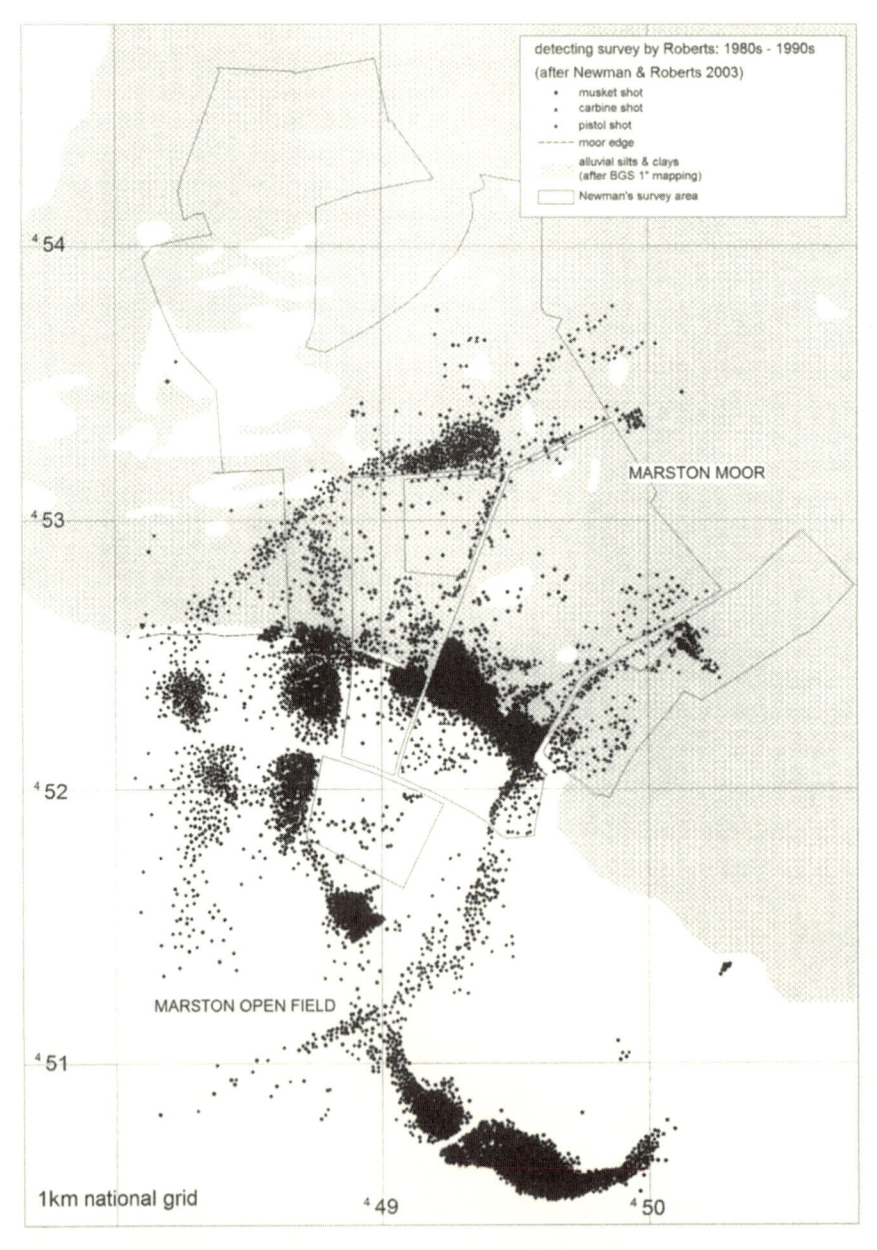

Roberts's metal detecting survey of Marston Moor battlefield in the 1980s.

this difference reflects the limited spatial extent of the Newman and Cammidge survey, while the gross differences on the moor were due to both land use (the pasture being inaccessible to the fieldwalking survey) and land ownership (because Newman was unable to gain access to the western part of the battlefield). However, the pattern to the south of the moor is far more problematic. It is true that Newman and Cammidge carried out very little survey work in this area, but this seems to have been because very little was being recovered as they moved south from the moor. It is possible this was because the dark soils of the moor itself provided an exceptional potential to recover shot from fieldwalking (visual inspection of the field surface, rather than by metal detecting), whereas the higher, sandy ground was far less conducive to the recovery of shot in this way (see figure for the boundary between the major soil types). For the metal detector user such specific biases of land use and soil type were not apparently a significant factor. Yet if one compares the area where both surveys overlap to the south of the moor boundary Newman and Cammidge seem to have sampled an area of relatively light shot distribution and may simply have stopped surveying too soon on the south side, believing they had reached the limit of the scatter.

But other equally important questions must be asked about the patterning right across the battlefield, for in the areas where both surveys were conducted intensively, both on and off the moor, one sees that the two maps often do not coincide in the finer detail of distribution. Yet it is on the analysis of such finer detail that much of the interpretation is likely to rest when analyzing the battle archaeology on this and other battlefields. Marston Moor would appear to be the only battlefield in England where there is extensive comparative data from two completely independent surveys conducted on the same area. The differences revealed in the distribution patterns provide great cause for concern. For example, in the area 4495/4525 Newman's plan shows a broad scatter across the moor, with lesser concentrations within it. In contrast Roberts shows relatively little across the moor but a dramatic density from the moor edge. Similar contradictions between the two datasets are seen elsewhere across the battlefield, as for example at 4492/4532 where the dense concentration on the north side of the track in the Roberts survey is not repeated by Newman. If both plans represent an accurate record of the actual number of bullets recovered, then one can only conclude that there has been dramatic variation in the intensity of surveying or in the effectiveness of recovery. The focusing of survey activity on areas producing the greater number of artifacts is a typical problem with an unsystematic survey. This certainly does appear, from limited personal observation and discussion about it, to be a partial explanation of the variations in the Roberts survey. It is unclear whether similar focusing of attention was a factor in the Newman survey, something that only Cammidge could now answer, for there is no data from either survey indicating the intensity of survey, though unlike Roberts, Newman did, on request, define the extent of intensive survey. The implications of this for the representativeness of the Marston data are substantial and highlight the difficulties of working with unsystematic or poorly recorded surveys from any battlefield.

Despite such limitations of such work it is still essential that we encourage and assist fieldworkers who have done such battlefield surveys in the past to bring the data to publication at as great a level of detail as is possible, as has been done with such good effect in Bonsall's analysis of McGovern's survey of Cheriton.[47] This is not only because such publication provides valuable insights into the nature of the battle archaeology on each site. It also provides key information as to the quantity and distribution of at least some of the material that has been removed from the battlefields. The removal, according to Roberts's published plan, of more than 10,000 bullets from Marston during his survey must have had a significant impact on the in situ pattern of distribution on that battlefield. Knowing approximately from where the bullets have been removed and in what numbers will at least enable the impact of that recovery to be taken into account in analyzing the results of any future systematic survey of that battlefield. With the exception of treasure hunting rallies, of which there was one in 2004 in the general area 4500/4510 at Marston, it is probably intensive but unsystematic and poorly recorded metal detecting surveys of our battlefields that are one of the greatest threats, simply because they remove so many artifacts.

So, while unsystematic surveys have provided a valuable body of evidence for some of our battlefields, one must conclude that such work, as well as simple treasure hunting, should no longer be allowed to continue on nationally important sites. In future only systematic surveys and recording to current standards of best practice ought to be accepted, at least on our Registered battlefields.

The problem can be further considered using the small-scale metal detecting survey conducted on Edgehill battlefield in the late 1970s by Captain Grant, which is analyzed and published here for the first time from data in the Warwickshire Sites and Monuments Record (See Figure). Up to April 1979 Grant recovered 52 musket balls from the battlefield. Given the concerns over the biases in the Marston Moor data the validity of interpretations based on a simple distribution map such as this have to be taken into account. Grant's survey is however exceptional for its time because it includes not only apparently highly accurate mapping of finds at 1:10560 and 1:2500 scale, but also records the amount of survey time spent in each area or on each transect. This enables consideration as to the degree to which absence of evidence may genuinely represent evidence of absence. If the data is processed to indicate the approximate amount of time spent in each hectare of the National Grid across the battlefield, one can begin to draw more secure and detailed interpretations based on the survey (see figure). This method of analysis should enable direct comparison between Grant's dataset and future survey data from the site. However, what has not yet been taken into account are the variable effects of land use on the recovery rates, because unfortunately Grant did not record the land use at the time of his survey. This is important because it would appear, from work undertaken by Kings on one

Captain Grant's survey of Edgehill battlefield in the late 1970s.

small area at Naseby, that on land which has remained under pasture for several hundred years, lead bullets collect at the base of the topsoil and are thus far more difficult to recover than on land which is or has recently been under arable cultivation, where the shot is more broadly distributed through the full depth of the topsoil.[48]

The processed data from Grant's survey seems to support a first stage of re-interpretation of the initial deployments and distribution of the action at Edgehill, based on a re-examination of the primary accounts of the battle in the light of the reconstruction of the historic terrain (see figure above).[49] The major shot concentration probably reflects the Royalist initial advance and the infantry engagement in the center. In contrast the cavalry action on the parliamentarian left wing seems to have produced almost no evidence, as one might expect, because Rupert's Royalist cavalry were instructed to not stand to fire their pistols but to charge home immediately. However, the absence of any evidence of the documented firing by parliamentarian musketeers standing behind the hedgerows on this wing might be considered surprising. But the intensity of survey on this wing can be seen to be considerably lower than in the center of the battlefield, where the main concentrations have been recovered, while the northernmost survey area remains wholly under ridge and furrow and hence has not been plowed since 1757 or 1792. Further analysis is required to reveal the full potential in Grant's dataset, but what has been done so far demonstrates very clearly how essential it is to have a well-recorded

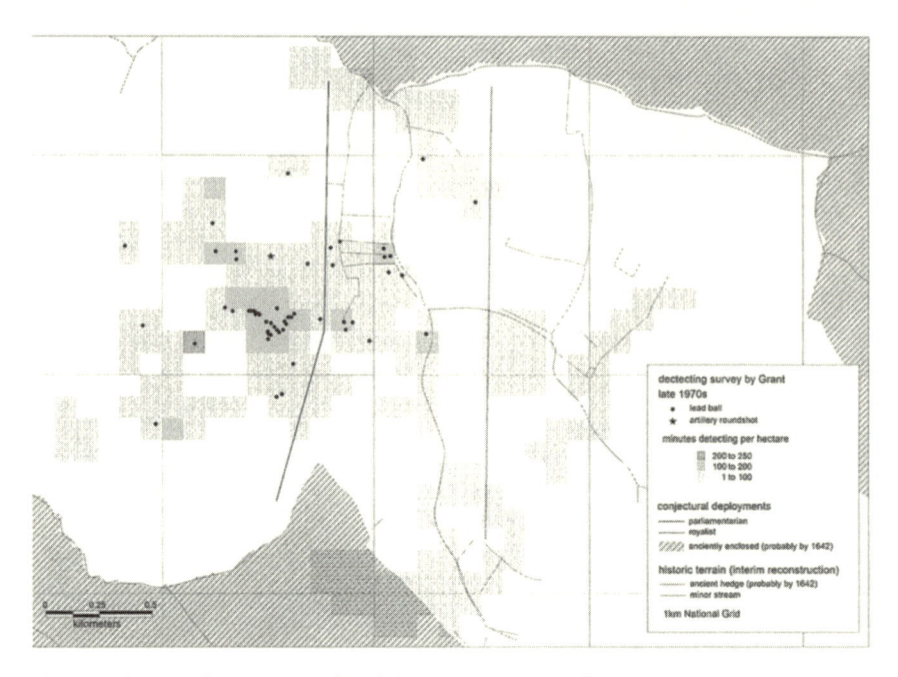

Captain Grant's data integrated with historic terrain evidence.

survey while the limitations it has revealed emphasize the need for comprehensive survey and a systematic survey methodology. In response to these conclusions a new two-year investigation was begun at Edgehill in August 2004, in which a systematic approach is being applied, initially using 10-m spaced transects across the whole of the accessible area in an attempt to recover a consistent dataset across the whole battlefield. Handheld GPS units, fixed to each metal detector, are being used to record individual find locations, to an accuracy of better than 10 m, and to collect track information every 15 seconds to record the exact location and intensity of survey by each detectorist.[50]

There is also the need for comparative study between battlefields, as can be seen from the crude graph comparing the balance of musket versus carbine/pistol bullets from a range of seventeenth-century battlefields and one siege site (see figure on page 151). The Grafton siege assemblage stands out as having a remarkably high percentage of carbine/pistol as opposed to musket (in fact the vast majority appears to be carbine rather than pistol). This graph also reinforces the questions about the nature of the biases in the evidence from Roberts's survey of Marston Moor, for the balance of caliber is quite different in his survey to that from any other battlefield, including the other survey of Marston Moor by Newman and Cammidge. However, it is interesting to note how much closer the interim Edgehill assemblage is to that from Marston than any other assemblage. The Edgehill sample comes from 1.2 sq km

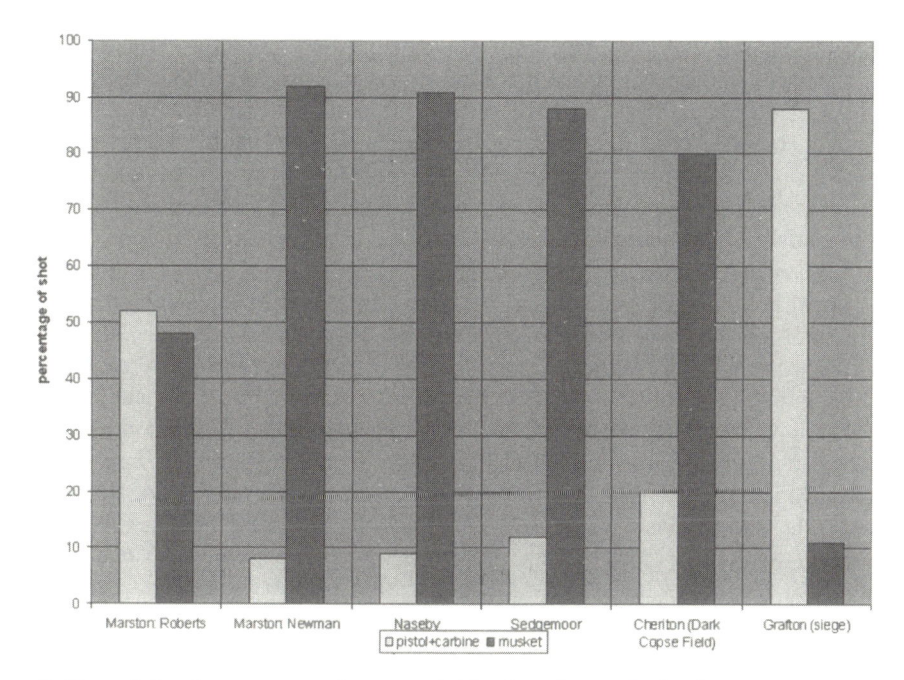

Caliber of shot from seventeenth-century fields of conflict in England.

covering much of the periphery as well as the core to battlefield, though the sample is as yet less than 200 bullets. The reasons for the variations seen in the graph are far from clear and are subject to ongoing research. Among other things this ultimately requires limited systematic sampling to a repeatable standard on each battlefield to attempt some form of calibration. It is possible that in part the differences may reflect sampling biases, with a focusing of attention to particular areas of a battlefield. It could in some cases also reflect a failure to recover the smaller bullets in some surveys, though this seems not to be a significant factor in the variation between Naseby and Edgehill because Burton has made a major contribution to both surveys, providing a degree of comparability between those two.

Such analysis raises many questions that can only begin to be answered by systematic survey on a range of seventeenth-century battlefields and points to the need for accurate recording of the caliber of shot. On most sites the best that has been done is a subjective assessment of caliber (musket, pistol, and sometimes of carbine) being made in the field. As work at Edgehill and Grafton Regis (Northamptonshire, 1643) in England and various battlefields in the USA have shown and are showing,[51] each bullet contains considerable information. The weight and size (caliber) can indicate in many cases the type of weapon it was meant for and thus to some degree the type of troops that probably used it. In the data from Edgehill not only can three very distinct calibers be recognized, there are hints at several possibly lesser subgroupings.[52] But the bullets also have surface evidence for manufacture and use, which shows whether it was dropped or fired and, if the latter, whether it was fired from an artillery piece as case shot rather than from a musket. Thus each bullet recovered from the battlefield needs to be individually bagged, numbered, and accurately located.

When one moves to battlefields of the medieval period, prior to or in the case of the Wars of the Roses at the very first stages of the introduction of firearms on the battlefield, the problems are compounded. As we have seen from the work at Towton, the projectiles in the form of iron arrowheads survive in relatively small numbers and in very restricted areas of the battlefield. Therefore far greater dependence has to be placed on the distribution of nonprojectile military artifacts and especially on nonmilitary artifacts lost in the action. The implications that flow from this are drawn starkly into focus if we take the evidence of a Civil War battlefield, where shot distributions clearly reflect the distribution of key elements of the action. Here one finds that the number of non-shot artifacts that are of military character, and thus almost certainly relate to the battle, represent a tiny percentage of the finds compared with the shot.[53] If one was dependent upon these artifacts alone to determine the distribution of the action, then the investigation would need to be extremely intensive and the potential for interpretation might be very limited. Moreover, the majority of the finds would probably prove, as at Cheriton (Hampshire, 1644), to be of iron and thus very vulnerable to destruction, just as with the iron projectiles. The copper alloy and bronze artifacts are an even smaller percentage of the finds. To further complicate the situation, when one is dealing with artifacts that are not specifically military in character there is the added problem that an unknown percentage of them may have been deposited by agricultural and other activities over a period as long as a century or more. This is likely to be a major problem across large parts of England where intensive manuring has taken place for centuries and is known to have deposited large quantities of artifacts in the plough soil.[54]

So the study of a fifteenth-century battlefield such as Bosworth, where there has been some unsystematic survey across the wider landscape over the last decade, poses major difficulties. There may have been a very few lead shot deposited on the field from hand cannon, but the exact nature and likely quantity remains unknown and none has yet been recovered there. We are therefore dependent, as at Towton, on the other military and especially the nonmilitary artifacts. But finds like horse pendants may or may not actually relate to the battle. In order to address these problems what is needed is systematic survey which includes control samples from areas of nearby landscape that were certainly not affected by the action.[55] Only in this way may we be able to determine the level of "background noise," artifacts probably mainly deposited during manuring carried from village middens contaminated by domestic rubbish, which may be confusing the battle archaeology. These control samples will need to be representative of the different characteristics of the various areas of the battlefield. In the case of Bosworth this means areas historically under marsh and alluvium as well as open field, and areas close to villages as well as distant from them, for manuring patterns are known to have varied dramatically across the landscape.

If one adds to the current lack of such "control" the further confusion provided by surveying without accurate recording of the intensity of survey, as discussed for Civil War battlefields, then some apparent battle-related concentrations may prove to be largely an artifact of the survey method. In reality they might represent objects largely if not wholly deposited by agricultural activities, yet made to appear battle-related because of the concentration of detecting activity. This seems to be fairly clearly exhibited by the Bosworth survey. Where the artifacts are of exclusively military character, as with fragments of armor, or weaponry, then association with the battle may be a reasonable conclusion. However, the vast majority of artifacts recovered at Bosworth were in domestic usage as well as being used by soldiers present on the battlefield. Thus the concentration of finds to the southeast of Sutton Cheney village, which had been interpreted as perhaps representing Richard III's plundered camp, may prove to be largely or wholly the result of intensive survey where there had been intensive manuring in the fifteenth century.[56] After all, we do not yet know whether over a 100-year period the 200 or 300 people in a village might deposit many more nonmilitary artifacts across the landscape than 10,000 troops fighting for a few hours on one day. When systematic work is undertaken, as part of the planned investigation in 2005–2008, the other concentrations already seen at Bosworth, in the area between Shenton and Sutton Cheney, may be shown to reflect the intensity of metal detecting survey rather than concentration of military action.

CONCLUSIONS

To date almost all investigation and conservation of battlefields in England has been restricted to Registered sites. These certainly are the most important and best preserved examples, but there are also many more unregistered sites. Like one or two of the Registered battlefields, such as Newburn (Durham, 1640) or Neville's Cross (Durham, 1346), these unregistered sites often have extremely fragmentary survival of their historic environment and hence of the physical evidence of both battle and terrain. Yet this should not lead us to write them off. Even if there is no extensive, continuous distribution of unstratified projectiles surviving with which to study the course of the action, there is still likely to be limited battle archaeology. On badly preserved battlefields, for example where there has been extensive mineral extraction or urban development, limited areas of artifact scatters could still survive in the undisturbed areas. On other battlefields where the battle artifacts were mostly ferrous but the soil conditions and length of time since the action mean that no substantial unstratified scatters survive, there may still be some projectile preservation in features such as ditches that were open at the time of the battle, or where colluvium and alluvium have protected a battlefield surface, and where waterlogging or other special conditions prevail.

Such limited survival may not, in isolation, warrant a site being considered of national importance for its battle archaeology. However, the battle itself may well be of national importance in historical terms and so it may be particularly important that any surviving battle archaeology is assessed, because it may provide critical validation of hypotheses on the location and nature of initial deployments and action which have been developed from the documentary sources for the battle and the battlefield. Without such testing those interpretations would, almost without exception, remain purely hypothesis. Such potential will be the greater when we have a more detailed understanding of the character, distribution, and meaning of battle archaeology as a result of intensive studies on a few well-preserved "type sites." We may then be far better able to understand how to distinguish and interpret the finer detail of the archaeological signature of different types of action. Neither should it be forgotten that even where the battle archaeology is not well preserved it is still possible for good physical evidence for the earlier landscape to survive, sufficient to enable partial reconstruction of the historic terrain of the battlefield.

So not only must we strengthen the conservation of Registered battlefields and improve the methodology of battlefield study to exploit that resource; but even the poorly preserved battlefields, especially those which do not warrant Registration and have until now been largely ignored, must be considered for they too may prove to have a significant research potential.

NOTES

1. Sutherland and Richardson, in this volume.

2. Glenn Foard, "Bosworth Battlefield: A Reassessment," (Shocklatch: Chris Burnett Associates for Leicestershire County Council, 2004).

3. Michael K. Jones, *Bosworth 1485: Psychology of a Battle* (2002).

4. English Heritage, "Register of Historic Battlefields" (London: English Heritage, 1995).

5. The difficulty of assessment at a lesser scale is revealed in the inadequacy of their treatment in the Research Frameworks process promoted by English Heritage over the last few years. For example, Glenn Foard, "Medieval Northamptonshire" (paper presented at the East Midlands Archaeological Research Framework Seminar Series, 2001). http://www.le.ac.uk/archaeology/east_midlands_research_framework.htm.

6. http://www.battlefieldstrust.com/resource-centre/battlefieldsuk/.

7. For example, Robert Ward, *Animadversions of Warre* (1639). Roman Dyboski and Z. M. Arend, *Knyghthode and Bataile: A Fifteenth Century Verse Paraphrase of Flavius Vegetius Renatus' Treatise 'De re militari'*, Early English Text Society. Original series; no. 201 (London: Published for the Early English Text Society by H Milford Oxford University Press, 1935).

8. William Hutton and J. Nichols, *The Battle of Bosworth Field*, 1999. Alan Sutton, repaginated ed. (London: Nichols, 1813).

9. Richard Brooke, *Visits to Fields of Battle in England of the Fifteenth Century* (London: John Russell Smith, 1857).

10. Dave Johnson, *Adwalton Moor 1643: The Battle that Changed a War* (Pickering: Blackthorn Press, 2003). Glenn Foard, *Naseby: The Decisive Campaign* (Whitsable: Pryor Publications, 1995).

11. Francis Randle Twemlowe, *The Battle of Blore Heath* (Wolverhampton: Whitehead Bros. Printers, 1912).

12. Alfred Higgins Burne, *The Battlefields of England* (London: Methuen & Co., 1950).

13. W. G. Hoskins, *The Making of the English Landscape* (1955). Glenn Foard, "Sedgemoor 1685: Historic Terrain, the 'Archaeology of Battles' and the Revision of Military History," Landscapes 4, no. 2 (2003): 5–15.

14. Unpublished manuscript plan by David Pannett in English Heritage Battlefields Register file for Edgehill battlefield.

15. P. R. Newman, *Marston Moor, 2 July 1644: The Sources and the Site*, Borthwick Papers; no. 53 (York: University of York Borthwick Institute of Historical Research, 1978), P. R. Newman and P. R. Roberts, *Marston Moor 1644: The Battle of the Five Armies* (Pickering: Blackthorn Press, 2003).

16. Daniel Williams, *The Battle of Bosworth, 22 August 1485* (Leicester: Leicester University Press, 1973). D. T. Williams, *The Battle of Bosworth Field* (Leicester: Leicestershire County Council, 2001).

17. Peter Foss, *The Field of Redemore: The Battle of Bosworth, 1485*, first edition. (Headingley: Rosalba Press, 1990), Peter Foss, *The Field of Redmore: The Battle of Bosworth, 1485* (1998).

18. English Heritage, "Battlefield Report: Maldon 991" (London: English Heritage, 1995).

19. G. R. Petty and S. Petty, "Geology and The Battle of Maldon," *Speculum*, 51 (1976): 435–446, George Petty and Susan Petty, "A Geological Reconstruction of the Site of the Battle of Maldon," (1993): 159–169.

20. Brian K. Roberts and Stuart Wrathmell, *An Atlas of Rural Settlement in England* (London: English Heritage, 2000).

21. For example, Foard, *Naseby: The Decisive Campaign*.

22. http://www.battlefieldstrust.com/resource-centre/medieval/battleview.asp?BattleFieldId=32.

23. Foard, "Bosworth Battlefield: A Reassessment." Glenn Foard, "Bosworth Battlefield Investigation: Project Design" (unpublished report for Leicestershire County Council, 2004).

24. Ordnance Surveyors' Drawings, British Library.

25. Foard, *Naseby: The Decisive Campaign*.

26. Glenn Foard, *The Battle of Edgehill Reinterpreted* (in preparation).

27. Flavius Vegetius Renatus, "Vegetius: Epitome of Military Science," ed. N. P. Milner (Liverpool: Liverpool University Press, 1996).

28. Peter Young, *Edgehill 1642: The Campaign and the Battle* (Kineton: Roundwood Press, 1967). Burne, *The Battlefields of England*.

29. Op. cit. in note 13.

30. Individual hedges and field closes were recorded on the draft enclosure map of Radway. Such features were normally omitted by enclosure records because they remained commonable with the rest of the open field, yet such hedges, as much as the ancient enclosures which were held in severalty and thus normally recorded in parliamentary enclosure documentation, seem to be key topographical features which influenced the action on both sides at Edgehill. Without the draft enclosure map their existence may have remained unrecognized.

31. Burne, *The Battlefields of England*.

32. A brief summary is given in Keith Roberts and John Tincey, *Edgehill 1642*, ed. David Chandler, vol. 82, *Campaign Series* (Oxford: Osprey, 2001).

33. Foard, *Naseby: The Decisive Campaign*.

34. Dyboski and Arend, *Knyghthode and Bataile: A Fifteenth Century Verse Paraphrase of Flavius Vegetius Renatus' Treatise 'De re militari.'*

35. Vegetius Renatus, "Vegetius: Epitome of Military Science."

36. Helen Nicholson, *Medieval Warfare* (London: Palgrave Macmillan, 2004).

37. For the terrain see Veronica Fiorato, Anthea Boylston, and Christopher Kunsel, *Blood Red Roses: The Archaeology of a Mass Grave from the Battle of Towton AD 1461* (Oxford: Oxbow, 2000).

38. For general specific information on the Towton battlefield see Sutherland and Richardson in this volume and the works referenced there.

39. English Heritage, "Battlefield Report: Northampton 1460" (London: English Heritage, 1995).

40. Of 25 Civil War battlefields in England examined by the author between 1992–1995, only that at Nantwich (Cheshire, 1644) revealed any extensive evidence of shot impact scars, on Nantwich church which was the focus of action for the royalist baggage train.

41. Burne, *The Battlefields of England*.

42. Fiorato, Boylston, and Kunsel, *Blood Red Roses: The Archaeology of a Mass Grave from the Battle of Towton AD 1461*.

43. For example, various papers in Philip Freeman and Tony Pollard (eds.), *Fields of Conflict: Progress and Prospect in Battlefield Archaeology*, proceedings of a conference held in the Department of Archaeology, University of Glasgow, April 2000, BAR International Series 958 (Oxford, England: Archaeopress, 2001).

44. Most notable in this is the work at Towton. See Sutherland and Richardson in this volume.

45. Newman, op. cit in note 14.

46. Newman and Roberts, *Marston Moor 1644: The Battle of the Five Armies*.

47. James Bonsall, "Archaeological Applications to Dark Coppice Field: A Scene of Retreat from the 1644 Battle of Cheriton" (BA dissertation, King Alfred's College, 2000).

48. Foard, *Naseby: The Decisive Campaign*.

49. Glenn Foard, "Integrating the Physical and Documentary Evidence for Battles and Their Context: A Case Study from 17th Century England" (PhD dissertation, University of East Anglia, in preparation).

50. Ibid. Limited information on the survey is also available online at http://www.battlefieldstrust.com/resource-centre/civil-war/battlepageview.asp?pageid=500.

51. For example, Sivilich in this volume.

52. Foard, "Integrating the Physical and Documentary Evidence for Battles and Their Context: A Case Study from 17th Century England". The Grafton survey is still largely unpublished, but a distribution plan is presented in Glenn Foard, "The Archaeology of Attack: Battles and Sieges of the English Civil War," in *Fields of Conflict: Progress and Prospect in Battlefield Archaeology*, ed. Freeman and Pollard, BAR International Series (2001), 87–103.

53. The best analysis of a Civil War collection in this context is Bonsall, "Archaeological Applications to Dark Coppice Field: A Scene of Retreat from the 1644 Battle of Cheriton."

54. For detailed evidence on manuring patterns in an example landscape of Midland England as revealed by pottery evidence see Steve Parry, *The Raunds Survey* (London: English Heritage, forthcoming).

55. Foard, "Bosworth Battlefield Investigation: Project Design."

56. Foard, "Bosworth Battlefield: A Reassessment."

REFERENCES CITED

Bonsall, James. 2000. Archaeological Applications to Dark Coppice Field: A Scene of Retreat from the 1644 Battle of Cheriton. BA dissertation, King Alfred's College.

Brooke, Richard. 1857. *Visits to Fields of Battle in England of the Fifteenth Century*. John Russell Smith, London.

Burne, Alfred Higgins. 1950. *The Battlefields of England*. Methuen, London.

Dyboski, Roman, and Z. M. Arend. 1935. *Knyghthode and Bataile: A 15th Century Verse Paraphrase of Flavius Vegetius Renatus' Treatise 'De re militari', Early English Text Society. Original series; no. 201*. Published for the Early English Text Society by H Milford Oxford University Press, London.

English Heritage. 1995a. Battlefield Report: Maldon 991. English Heritage, London.

English Heritage. 1995b. Battlefield Report: Northampton 1460. English Heritage, London.

English Heritage. 1995c. Register of Historic Battlefields. English Heritage, London.

Fiorato, Veronica, Anthea Boylston, and Christopher Kunsel. 2000. *Blood Red Roses: The Archaeology of a Mass Grave from the Battle of Towton AD 1461*. Oxbow, Oxford.

Foard, Glenn. 2001. The Archaeology of Attack: Battles and Sieges of the English Civil War. In Phillip Freeman and Tony Pollard (eds.), *Fields of Conflict: Progress and Prospect in Battlefield Archaeology*, 87–103. BAR International Series 958, Oxford.

Foard, Glenn. In preparation. *The Battle of Edgehill Reinterpreted*.

Foard, Glenn. 2004a. Bosworth Battlefield Investigation: Project Design. Unpublished report for Leicestershire County Council, Leicester.

Foard, Glenn. 2004b. Bosworth Battlefield: A Reassessment. Chris Burnett Associates for Leicestershire County Council, Shocklatch.

Foard, Glenn. In preparation. Integrating the Physical and Documentary Evidence for Battles and Their Context: A Case Study from 17th Century England. PhD dissertation, University of East Anglia.

Foard, Glenn. 2001. Medieval Northamptonshire. Paper presented at the East Midlands Archaeological Research Framework Seminar Series.

Foard, Glenn. 1995. *Naseby: The Decisive Campaign*. Pryor Publications, Whitstable.

Foard, Glenn. 2003. Sedgemoor 1685: Historic Terrain, the 'Archaeology of Battles' and the Revision of Military History. *Landscapes* 4(2):5–15.

Foss, Peter. 1990. *The Field of Redemore: The Battle of Bosworth, 1485*. First edition, Rosalba Press, Headingley.

Foss, Peter. 1998. *The Field of Redmore: The Battle of Bosworth, 1485*. Rosalba Press, Headingley.

Freeman, Philip, and Tony Pollard (eds.). 2001. *Fields of Conflict: Progress and Prospect in Battlefield Archaeology*. Proceedings of a conference held in the Department of Archaeology, University of Glasgow, April 2000, BAR International Series 958. Oxford.

Hoskins, W. G. 1955. *The Making of the English Landscape*. Penguin History, London.

Hutton, William, and J. Nichols. 1999. *The Battle of Bosworth Field*. Alan Sutton, London. Reprint of Nichols 1813 edition.

Johnson, Dave. 2003. *Adwalton Moor 1643: The Battle that Changed a War*. Blackthorn Press, Pickering.

Jones, Michael K. 2002. *Bosworth 1485: Psychology of a Battle*. Tempus, Shroud Gloucestershire, UK.

Newman, P. R. 1978. *Marston Moor, 2 July 1644: The Sources and the Site, Borthwick papers; no. 53*. University of York Borthwick Institute of Historical Research.

Newman, P. R., and P. R. Roberts. 2003. *Marston Moor 1644: The Battle of the Five Armies*. Blackthorn Press, Pickering.

Nicholson, Helen. 2004. *Medieval Warfare*. Palgrave Macmillan, London.

Parry, Steve. In press. *The Raunds Survey*: English Heritage, London.

Petty, G. R., and Petty, S. 1976. Geology and The Battle of Maldon. *Speculum* 51:435–446.

Petty, George, and Susan Petty. 1993. A Geological Reconstruction of the Site of the Battle of Maldon. In *The Battle of Maldon: Fiction and Fact*, edited by Janet Cooper, pp. 159–169. Hambledon Press, London.

Roberts, Brian K, and Stuart Wrathmell. 2000. *An Atlas of Rural Settlement in England*. English Heritage, London.

Roberts, Keith, and John Tincey. 2001. *Edgehill 1642*, edited by David Chandler. Vol. 82, *Campaign Series*. Osprey, Oxford.

Twemlowe, Francis Randle. 1912. *The Battle of Blore Heath*. Whitehead Bros., Wolverhampton.

Vegetius Renatus, Flavius. 1996. Vegetius: Epitome of Military Science, edited by N. P., Liverpool Milner. Liverpool University Press.

Ward, Robert. 1639. *Animadversions of Warre*. John Dawson, London.

Williams, D. T. 2001. *The Battle of Bosworth Field*. Leicestershire County Council, Leicester.

Williams, Daniel. 1973. *The Battle of Bosworth, 22 August 1485*. Leicester University Press, Leicester.

Young, Peter. 1967. *Edgehill 1642: The Campaign and the Battle*. Roundwood Press, Kineton.

Arrows Point to Mass Graves: Finding the Dead from the Battle of Towton, 1461 AD

Tim Sutherland & Simon Richardson

THE BATTLE OF Towton took place on Palm Sunday, March 29, 1461, between the armies of King Henry VI of the House of Lancaster and Edward Earl of March, later Duke of York, of the House of York. Preceding the conflict, Edward had been proclaimed the new king in London, which meant that at the time of the battle there were two kings fighting for the English throne. Shortly after his victory at Towton, Edward, Earl of March, was ceremonially crowned King Edward IV.[1]

The small village of Towton is situated four kilometers (two miles) to the south of the market town of Tadcaster and 18 kilometers (10 miles) southwest of the city of York, the medieval secular and ecclesiastical center of northern England. It is perhaps surprising that this tiny medieval hamlet gave its name to what is officially regarded as the largest battle ever fought on British soil,[2] with over 100,000 combatants allegedly taking part, and approximately 28,000 dead.[3]

Archaeological fieldwork on the battlefield at Towton developed as part of the Ph.D. research instigated by the author.[4] This followed the excavation and detailed recording of 37 skeletons from a mass grave, discovered at Towton Hall in 1996, which contained casualties from the battle.[5] The aim of the project was to record additional physical evidence of the conflict, including artifacts, possible earthworks, and the location of other mass graves on the main part of the battlefield, which lies one mile to the south of Towton.[6] This chapter describes the systematic way in which the battlefield was surveyed. This ultimately led to the discovery of a rare and important archaeological site: the mass graves of the combatants from the battle of Towton.

ARTIFACT DENSITY AND PATTERNING

An extensive survey of the Towton battlefield has been carried out using a multidisciplinary array of techniques including desk-based evaluation, geophysical survey, archaeological field walking, and excavation. The most successful survey technique used to identify the general area of the battlefield at Towton proved to be metal detector scanning of the whole battlefield landscape. Because of the considerable contamination of relatively modern ferrous objects, the metal detector search initially had to be limited to the recovery of non-ferrous artifacts. Artifacts that were probably lost during the conflict were generally found to be of a non-military nature, such as clothing fasteners, buttons, buckles, strap ends, and brooches.

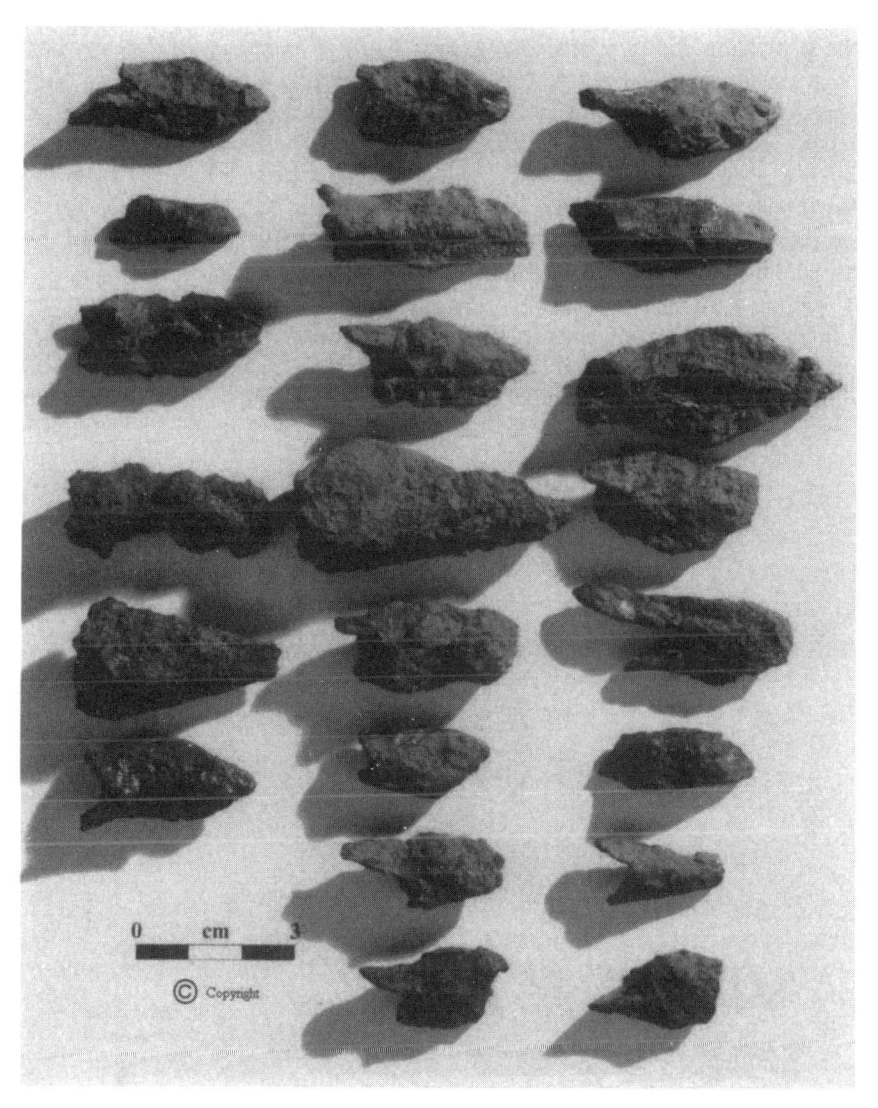

Medieval arrowheads recovered as part of the Towton Battlefield Archaeological Survey Project. (The Trustees of the Royal Armouries)

Using a model based upon the location of over 1,300 of these fifteenth-century artifacts, it has been possible to identify the center of the conflict. This area has now been surveyed using more intensive and detailed survey techniques, targeting both ferrous and non-ferrous artifacts, which has led to the recovery of a substantial quantity of additional artifacts.

Although the ratio of the battle-related artifacts compared to that of the contamination is higher in the non-ferrous category, it has now been possible to locate and recover definite battle-related ferrous artifacts in the center of the battlefield. The proportion of ferrous artifacts identified as "background contamination" compared to that of fifteenth-century military artifacts is still approximately 50:1 within the target area, though the ratio is far greater in other parts of the battlefield, presumably because the fighting there was less intense. Due to logistical constraints, details of ferrous fragments from the background contamination are not usually recorded. The lower proportion of ferrous items from the target areas, however, means that it is now feasible to search for and record ferrous artifacts within intensively studied locations.

During a routine search of one of the target areas, a metal detector was being retuned and accidentally identified the presence of a ferrous artifact, which was identified as a medieval arrowhead. This meant that the signature of medieval arrowheads, which are often barely recognizable as such when

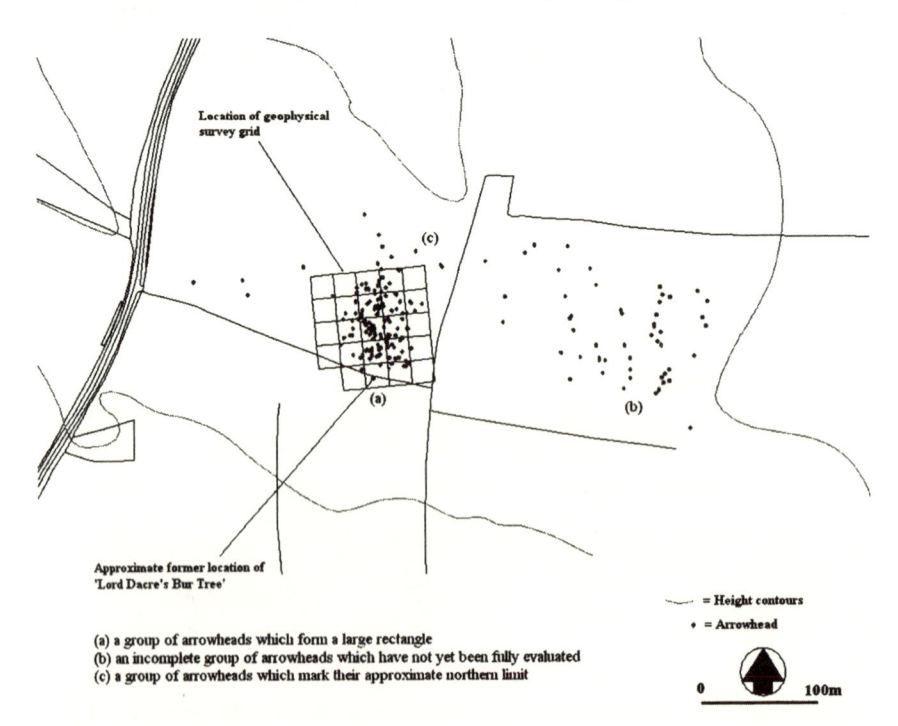

(a) a group of arrowheads which form a large rectangle
(b) an incomplete group of arrowheads which have not yet been fully evaluated
(c) a group of arrowheads which mark their approximate northern limit

Locations of the medieval arrowheads recorded during the survey.

found, could now be positively identified despite their severely corroded nature. This discovery has led to the recording of over 200 arrowheads in areas that have previously been thoroughly searched using both metal detector and magnetometer geophysical survey (see figure).

When plotted, the locations of these arrowheads form three separate anomalies. One concentration forms a large rectangle located in one corner of a field. The second group of arrowheads is situated in the middle of another field, and has not yet been fully evaluated. The third group, which runs in an east-west direction across the center of the battlefield, appears to form an approximate northern limit of the arrowheads.

During metal detecting scanning, the remains of a human distal ulna (lower arm bone) were discovered on the surface of the plough soil. The location of the bone was recorded using a small handheld satellite navigation instrument (GPS).

GEOPHYSICAL SURVEY

Following the identification of the arrowhead concentrations, these areas were more closely investigated using a series of earth resistance and magnetic geophysical surveys. Several distinctive anomalies were identified, the majority of which did not initially appear to be battle-related.

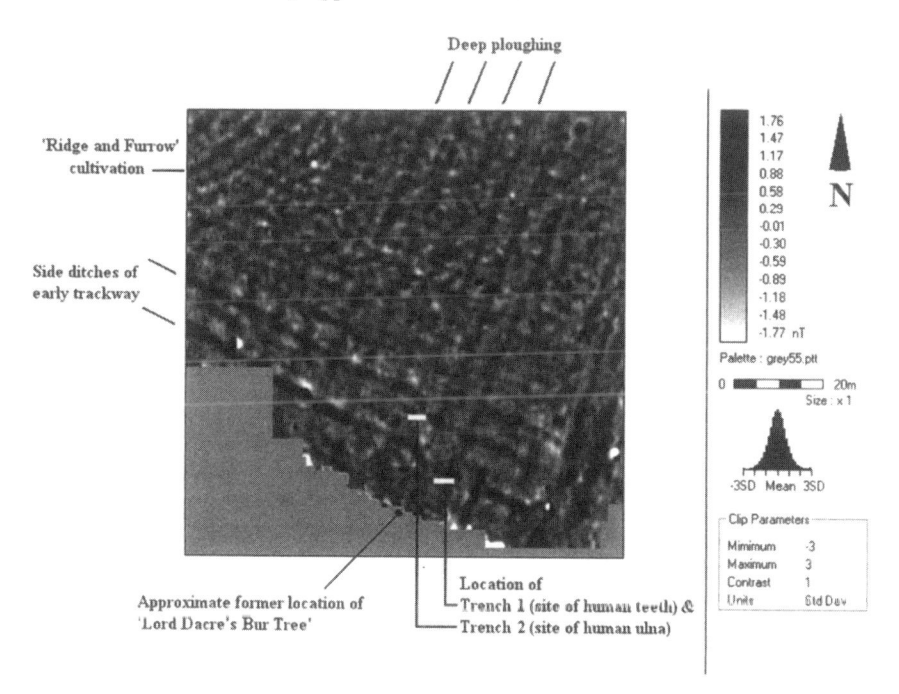

Fluxgate gradiometer (magnetic) survey of part of the Towton battlefield.

164 FIELDS OF CONFLICT

During the earth resistance survey, two human teeth were discovered on the surface of the plough soil within the survey grid and were precisely recorded. When the location of the teeth was superimposed over the magnetic geophysical survey results (see figure), they were found to lie directly over one of two short parallel anomalies which were located in the southeast corner of the survey area. These ran in an almost north-south direction, and consisted of some of the strongest readings recorded from the geophysical surveys. Additionally, when the location of the ulna—found during metal detector scanning—was superimposed over the geophysical survey results, it was observed to be closely associated with another linear anomaly.

EXCAVATION

Following the discovery of the human remains and the corresponding geophysical survey anomalies, it was decided to test their origin using archaeological evaluation. A test trench (Trench 2) was excavated at the location given by the GPS for the ulna, but no associated feature or other distinctive archaeological information could be identified.

Another test trench (Trench 1) was excavated at the location recorded for the teeth, revealing the fragmented remains of an arrowhead and several small

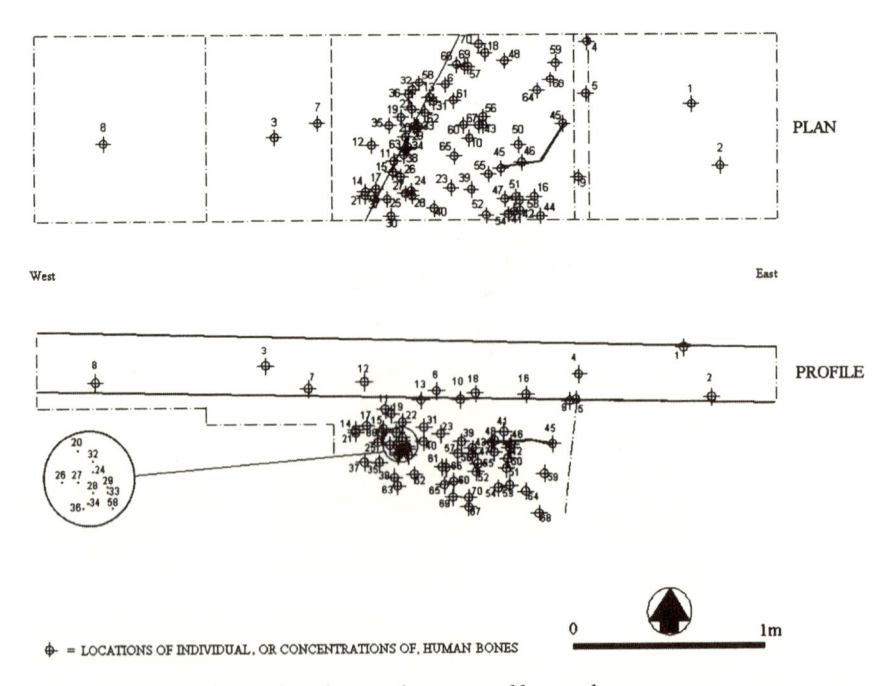

Plan and profile of Trench 1 showing locations of human bones.

human bones and teeth within the topsoil. As the trench was extended further, more human remains were uncovered, including fragments of skull, vertebra, patella, fingers, toes, and additional teeth. The precise location of each find was three-dimensionally recorded and the bones and artifacts removed (see figure). The test pit was excavated until a different soil matrix was encountered, not the expected solid limestone, but gray clay. This material was similar to clay, recorded during another local excavation, which was found to have derived from the silting up of a very large prehistoric ditch.[7] However, the clay in Trench 1 displayed a steeply sloping profile, suggesting that it must have been re-cut. It could also be observed that the feature in Trench 1 continued downward and sideways beyond the limits of the trench, and it was therefore decided not to excavate it further at the time, as the initial purpose of evaluating the feature had been fulfilled. The excavation was then fully recorded and backfilled. The evaluation suggested that the feature might originally have been an earlier ditch that had later been re-cut and re-used for later burial.

INTERPRETATION

The location of the ulna, found prior to the excavation of Trench 2, was not found near any archaeological feature. It might therefore have derived from the feature located in Trench 1 and have been moved, either in antiquity or by recent plowing. Alternatively it could have derived from a separate pit containing additional human remains. Its distance from Trench 1 suggested the latter hypothesis.

The location of the teeth found prior to the excavation of Trench 1 corresponded with an archaeological feature, which appeared to be part of a ditch or pit. The human remains recovered from this feature in Trench 1 were largely disarticulated, although the anatomical position of some bones suggested that the skeletal elements had been partially articulated when they were interred (see figure). It could not be determined, however, whether complete individuals had been interred and subsequently disturbed or whether fragmented parts had been buried in this feature. The distribution of the bones within the pit suggested that the bones had been interred as part of the fill matrix, pointing to the latter hypothesis. It was also observed that all bones and bone fragments recovered were small, and generally no larger than 10 cm in size.

The discovery of human remains in an area where a substantial number of arrowheads has been found suggests that there might be a link between the two. It is therefore possible that the arrowheads might originally have derived from the dead, the remains of which have subsequently been disturbed.

Importantly, it is evident that these arrowheads have deteriorated to such a degree that their ferrous content has largely been depleted and are therefore not immediately visible as "ferrous spikes," the term usually given to fragments of ferrous metal recorded by magnetic geophysical survey.[8] This

Semi-articulated human radius and ulna, recorded in Trench 1.

is important, as a magnetic geophysical survey carried out in 1997 on "The Gastons," a part of the medieval battlefield at Tewkesbury, England (1471), failed to identify evidence from the medieval battle.[9] If it can be shown that the medieval arrowheads, which are known to exist, at Towton cannot be identified on the geophysical survey results of the same area, then it is doubtful whether similar evidence of battle will be identified, using the same methods, on other medieval battlefields. Similar forms of evaluation using fluxgate gradiometer should therefore not solely be used to locate such artifacts.

At Towton, a series of curvilinear anomalies had been identified in the north-western part of the magnetic geophysical survey, which is indicative of a medieval ridge and furrow field system (see figure). Notably, the lack of these features in the rest of the survey grid suggests that only part of the area had been cultivated during the medieval period. The clear lack of medieval cultivation in the corner of this field must have been due to obstructions, such as earlier earthworks, which prevented the plowing of this area. This, together with the discovery of the medieval arrowheads and human remains in concentrated areas, suggests one of the following scenarios: it is possible that burial pits or trenches were excavated coincidentally on the sites of earlier features. The lack of medieval cultivation in this area, however, suggests that these features may still have been recognizable during the medieval period and were therefore re-used following the battle by re-cutting them and using them as burial pits. These burial features might have been filled with the smaller human bones which remained on the battlefield following the clearance of larger skeletal elements. Alternatively, the features might have been used to inter the bodies of casualties following the battle, only to be removed at a later date. The spoil, together with any smaller bones that were overlooked, were then replaced in the burial pits.

Generally speaking, no patterning within the human remains could be observed. However, a linear alignment of several bones within one area of the pit, which ran in an approximate north-south direction across the trench, suggested that some bones had either been arranged in this manner, or that something had disturbed part of the pit fill and aligned some of its contents. The sides of the pit at this point also exhibited traces of a vertical disturbance which ran from the top of the pit fill downward. An on-site visit from the local farmer clarified the reason for this disturbance. Some years prior to the excavation, an external contractor had been employed to plow the field in question. He had come from an area of Britain that required the subsoil to be deep-plowed in order to "break up the iron-pan and release nutrients." The subsoil beneath the field at Towton, however, is Magnesian Limestone rock and should not be deep-plowed—otherwise blocks of limestone are brought to the surface, resulting in the topsoil washing into the newly created ruts and becoming much thinner.[10] This is an important observation as it is therefore apparent that the deep-plowing of the site on a single occasion had caused the arrangement of bones within the feature as well as the linear anomaly in the sides of the test pit. The effects of the same deep-plowing had also caused a number of parallel linear anomalies that had previously been observed running north-south on the magnetic geophysical survey result displays (see figure).

The archaeological evaluation demonstrated that medieval arrowheads and human remains had been brought to the surface by a single episode of deep plowing, causing their identification but also deterioration and degradation through the effects of weather and additional annual plowing.

DISCUSSION

The results of the archaeological excavation of the burial feature are of major importance, as they represent an assemblage of human remains archaeologically recorded in the center of a medieval battlefield.

The current evidence suggests that long before the battle took place, a pre-existing feature, such as a pit or ditch, had been excavated and allowed to silt up. The feature was presumably still evident in the landscape during the medieval period to such an extent that this area was avoided by medieval cultivation. The feature was re-cut and filled with human remains following the Battle of Towton. It could not be determined whether or not the incomplete skeletons represent a primary burial of disarticulated human remains, or the secondary reburial of the human bones which remained after most of the larger bones had been removed.

A historical document dating to February 19, 1484, describes events 23 years after the battle of Towton and appears to confirm this latter hypothesis. It notes that in 1484 King Richard III gave a Royal Grant of Annuity[11] to

Saxton parish church (which lies to the south of the battlefield) so that the human remains from the Battle of Towton could be removed from the battlefield and placed in consecrated ground:

> and the people of this kingdom in a plentiful multitude were taken away from human affairs; and their bodies were notoriously left on the field, aforesaid, and in other places nearby, thoroughly outside the ecclesiastical burial-place, in three hollows. Where upon we, on account of affection, contriving the burial of the deceased men of this sort, caused the bones of these same men to be exhumed and left for an ecclesiastical burial in these coming months, partly in the parish church of Saxton in our said county of York and in the cemetery of the said place, and partly in the chapel of Towton, aforesaid, and the surroundings of this very place.

This grant provides primary documentary evidence for the removal of casualties from the battlefield and may therefore refer to the pit identified in the geophysical survey and excavation.

Areas of graves have been highlighted on most post mid-eighteenth-century maps of the battlefield (e.g., Jeffries's map of Yorkshire)[12] but often in different locations. However, as previous archaeological excavations on such sites have proven,[13] these map locations are generally erroneous, and so it has not been possible to locate the graves using such evidence. However, there is a historical feature that is marked on the early ordnance survey maps, the meaning of which has since been lost or misinterpreted, that might originally have pointed to the location of the graves. As the location of the graves has now been determined by the discovery of the arrowheads and human remains within the pit, it can be shown to lie in close proximity to a position on the 1849 ordnance survey map that is annotated with the words

North Acres: Stump of the Bur Tree from which Lord Dacre was shot.[14]

Although it initially appears that there is little to connect the text and the graves, an understanding of the background relating to this piece of text is enlightening. It refers to Lord Dacre, a leading Lancastrian noble who was killed at the Battle of Towton and whose death is commemorated by a medieval tomb in the nearby graveyard of Saxton church. Large quantities of bones, which were removed from the battlefield, were also allegedly reburied close to his tomb in a large ossuary outside the northern wall of the church.[15] In 1585, Glover recounted the tale of Lord Dacre and the tree thus.

> This Lord Dacres, as the report goeth, was slayne by a boy, at Towton Field, which boy shot him [with an arrow] out of a burtree, when he had unclasped his helmet to drink a cup of wyne, in revenge of his father, whom the said lord had slayne before, which tree hath beene remarkable ever since by the inhabitants, and decayed within this few yeares. The place where he was slayne is called the North Acres, whereupon they have this ryme, "The Lord Dacres, Was slayne in the North Acres."[16]

The tree allegedly marked the site of the death of Lord Dacre. There are therefore several historical and archaeological connections between the area highlighted by the human remains and arrowheads, and this story. Both relate to people killed in the Battle of Towton, both relate to arrows or arrowheads, both potentially have close connections to the dead from the battle that have been reburied in Saxton churchyard, and both relate to exactly the same location (see figure).

It is therefore feasible that the reference to Lord Dacre's tree also refers to the former site of a memorial or marker that might once have been situated near the mass graves of victims of the battle, but which has not been evident since before Glover's visit in 1585. It is also possible that Lord Dacre's remains were removed from the battlefield together with his comrades in 1484, after which a previous marker on the battlefield was allowed to deteriorate. The question must therefore be raised: were Lord Dacre's remains identifiable 23 years after the battle and if so, was this only possible because his grave had been marked? Alternatively, was Lord Dacre really buried inside his tomb in Saxton graveyard or was he interred together with the other bones from the mass grave, in the large ossuary on the northern side of the church?

The hypothesis of a grave marker on the battlefield is important, as it is possible that other sites of former markers on medieval battlefields, or the markers themselves, such as Lord Audley's Cross at Blore Heath, England (1459), might relate to the proximity of graves. A good example of this is the battlefield at Wisby (1361), Sweden, where a large stone cross still dominates the site of the graves of those who died in the battle.[17] It is also possible that other unmarked grave sites might be archaeologically evident by artifact scatters, such as arrowheads, reflecting the disturbed remains of battlefield casualties.

Importantly, it is also evident that deep plowing, even on the one occasion when it was accidentally carried out, has seriously disturbed previously secure archaeological deposits. This action has brought to the surface human remains and large quantities of archaeological artifacts, thereby enabling their discovery. However, unless recorded *in-situ* and collected, they will soon disintegrate due to their current fragile state.

A plan of the arrowhead distribution suggests that they were brought to the surface across a wide area in the approximate shape of a rectangle. It is probable that this concentration of arrowheads represents an area where bodies from the battle were dumped and left exposed, or were partly interred by being placed in shallow graves or pre-existing features. Alternatively, the arrowhead concentrations may reflect areas of an additional mass grave.

The magnetic geophysical survey highlights linear disturbances where the plow has brought deeply buried magnetic material to the surface. The location of arrowheads and human remains within this area of disturbance suggests that other mass graves similar to the two already highlighted might lie deeply buried below the ground. It is therefore possible that other graves, which might not have been emptied of their human remains in 1484, still exist in parts of the field. This hypothesis is strengthened by a reference in Drake[18] who wrote about a visit to the battlefield in the early eighteenth century. He states that

> about a year or two ago, two gentlemen and myself had the curiosity to go and see a fresh grave opened in these fields. Where amongst vast quantities of bones, we found some arrow piles, pieces of broken swords, and five very fresh groat pieces of Henry the fourth, fifth, and sixth's coin. These laid; near all together, close to a thigh bone, which made us conjecture that they had not time to strip the dead before they tossed them into the pit.

This description contains several similarities with the evidence from the test trench—human bones and arrowheads—and is almost certainly describing the same area, although Drake infers that the grave he observed was potentially intact, suggesting that not all of the graves were emptied in 1484.

CONCLUSIONS

The Towton battlefield research has clearly shown that a medieval battlefield can be analyzed and recorded using a multidisciplinary array of archaeological techniques. One such technique is the use of a good quality metal detector by a competent practitioner, with the aim of identifying non-ferrous and non-military artifacts. Once concentrations of these objects have been mapped, they can be specifically targeted using more intensive methods of analysis, including geophysical survey and archaeological excavation. The current investigation has shown that artifacts, which have previously been almost unrecognizable to most forms of prospection, can be located once their archaeological signature has been recognized.

The archaeological investigation at Towton has shown that concentrations of medieval arrowheads can point to areas of body deposition or burial. This suggests that it might not always have been possible to remove every arrowhead from the bodies prior to burial.

Using documentary evidence, as well as archaeological prospection, it has been possible to identify battle-related mass graves in the center of the Towton battlefield. These graves had apparently been inserted into earlier archaeological features, probably to reduce the size and number of new graves required. In 1484, however, only 23 years after the battle, according to Richard III's instructions, at least some of the graves were excavated and the dead reburied in Saxton churchyard and around a chapel in Towton. The recent archaeological excavation demonstrated, however, that not all of the smaller bones were removed from the pits, but that some were backfilled together with the excavated spoil. Partial articulation of some of these bones suggests that the dead were still partially fleshed when the mass graves were re-excavated in 1484.

Research of the battlefield, with the aim of identifying mass graves has also highlighted that archaeological features recorded using geophysical survey should be investigated through archaeological excavation if vital evidence is not to be overlooked.

This research has subsequently led to the first scientific analysis of medieval arrowheads, by the Royal Armouries, from a known conflict. Preliminary results suggest that these weapons were manufactured using previously undocumented technological procedures.[19] The Towton arrowhead collection is therefore, in itself, of great archaeological and scientific importance.

A disturbing outcome of the research is that now, despite the fact that archaeological evidence of a medieval battle has been identified and its location recorded, none of this unique evidence is legally protected. Every day artifacts are being removed from the topsoil by metal detectorists who are not recording where they find them. Such detectorists are destroying the very essence of what they have come to look for tangible evidence of the Battle of Towton.

Other battlefields, such as at Shrewsbury, England, have suffered far worse and have almost been picked clean before their locations have been archaeologically proven.[20] If these nationally important sites cannot be legally protected, it is the duty of the archaeological profession to record them before it is too late. It is therefore necessary for sufficient grant aid and resources for funded projects to be made available to allow those already carrying out this important research, and others who will follow them, to be able to continue at a more efficient and productive rate before this finite resource disappears, unrecorded, forever.

NOTES

1. Myers 1969.
2. English Heritage 1995.
3. Hinds 1912.
4. Sutherland (forthcoming a).
5. Sutherland 2000a.
6. Sutherland 2000b.
7. Sutherland 2002.
8. Clark 1990.
9. Barker 1997.
10. Personal communication between T. L. Sutherland and the farm manager, Paul Saxon of the Hartley Estate, on whose land the excavation in Towton Dale took place, September 25, 2003.
11. Richard III 1484. *Royal Grant of Annuity to Saxton Parish Church, 19 February 1483/84*. From a document of unknown origin handed to the author by Dr. Donald Verity (formerly of Towton Hall; for which the author is duly grateful) from his private collection of works relating to Towton. The document was translated from a facsimile of a later copy written in Latin.

12. Margary 1973.
13. Sutherland (forthcoming b).
14. Ordnance Survey 1849. *The 6 Inch to 1 Mile Map of Towton and Saxton*. Sheet 205 (North Yorkshire County Council Record Office, Ref. MIC3357/191).
15. Brooke 1857.
16. Whitaker 1816.
17. Thordeman 1940.
18. Drake 1978.
19. Starley 2002.
20. Personal communication between T. L. Sutherland and Dr. T. Pollard at the Shrewsbury Museum on July 12, 2003, at a day meeting held by the Finds Research Group.

REFERENCES CITED

Barker, P. P. 1997. *A Report for Cotswold Archaeological Trust on a Geophysical Survey Carried out at The Gastons, Tewkesbury*. Stratascan, Geophysical & Specialist Survey Services Report.

Brooke, R 1857. *Visits to the Fields of Battle in England of the Fifteenth Century*. Russel Smith, London.

Clark, A. 1990. *Seeing Beneath the Soil: Prospecting Methods in Archaeology*. Batsford, London.

Drake, F. 1978. *Eboracum or the History and Antiquities of the City of York from its Original to its Present Time, 1736*. E.P. Publishing, London.

English Heritage. 1995. *The Register of Historic Battlefields*. English Heritage, London.

Hinds, A. B. (ed.). 1912. *Calendar of State Papers and Manuscripts in the Archives and Collections of Milan Vol.1. 1385–1618*. His Majesty's Stationary Office, London.

Margary, H. 1973. *A Survey of the County of York by Thomas Jefferys 1775*. Lymphe Castle, Kent.

Myers, A. R. (ed.). 1969. *English Historical Documents 1327–1485*. Eyre & Spottiswoode, London.

Starley, D. 2002. Unpublished report by Dr. D. Starley of the Royal Armouries, Leeds, for Mr. T. L. Sutherland, on the analysis of arrowheads from the battlefield at Towton.

Sutherland, T. L. (forthcominga). *The Application of an Integrated Prospection Methodology to the Understanding of the Archaeological Landscape of the Towton Battlefield*. PhD Thesis, University of Bradford, Bradford, England.

Sutherland, T. L. (forthcomingb). *Locating and Quantifying the Dead from the Battle of Towton: Analysing the Available Data*. A paper given at the "Fields of Conflict" Conference in Åland, Finland, September 2002.

Sutherland, T. L. 2000a. Recording the Grave. In V. Fiorato, A. Boylston, and C. Knüsel (eds.), *Blood Red Roses: The Archaeology of a Mass Grave from the Battle of Towton AD1461*, 36–44. Oxbow, Oxford.

Sutherland, T. L. 2000b. The Archaeological Investigation of the Towton Battlefield. In V. Fiorato, A. Boylston, and C. Knüsel (eds.), *Blood Red Roses: The Archaeology of a Mass Grave from the Battle of Towton AD1461*, 155–168. Oxbow, Oxford.

Sutherland, T. L. 2002. *An Archaeological Evaluation of an Enclosure Indicated by Crop Marks near Towton, North Yorkshire*. Unpublished report, carried out as part of the Towton Battlefield Archaeological Survey.

Thordeman, B. (ed.). 1940. *Armour from the Battle of Wisby 1361*. Vitterhets Historie Och Antikvitets Akademien, Stockholm.

Whitaker, T. D. 1816. *Loidis and Elmete*. Privately published, Leeds.

Indian Resistance in New Spain: The 1541 AD Battlefield of Peñol de Nochistlán, an Exemplar of Indigenous Resistance

*Charles Haecker, Elizabeth A. Oster,
Angélica Medrano Enríquez, & Michael L. Elliott*

THE MIXTÓN WAR of 1541–1542 AD is a virtually forgotten conflict of early Spanish Colonial Mexico, yet its consequences were far-reaching for both the Spanish victors and the vanquished native peoples of central Mexico. This war of rebellion derived from Spanish policies of forcibly replacing native cultural life ways with an alien European economy, social structure, and religion. Following their conquest of the Caxcan[1] homeland in 1530, the Spanish replaced uncooperative native leaders with those who were willing to accept Spanish rule and culture. At the same time, thousands of Caxcan people were rounded up to work on the newly created agricultural and ranching estates.

Growing resentment found a voice in one charismatic Caxcan leader, Tenamaxtle (var. Tenamaxtli), who planted the seeds of revolt. The opportunity for open rebellion came in the spring of 1541, after hundreds of Spanish had departed from Nueva Galicia with the Coronado and Alarcón expeditions. In the spring of 1541 Tenamaxtle's rebel armies, in a series of coordinated attacks, destroyed Spanish settlements of the province of Nueva Galicia with the goal of driving out the hated enemy from their land.[2] The Spanish viceroy in Mexico City, Antonio de Mendoza, realized that the rebellion had to be quashed as quickly as possible to prevent it from spreading to other regions of Mexico.

Accordingly, the lieutenant governor of Nueva Galicia, Cristóbal de Oñate, requested military assistance from Pedro de Alvarado—an experienced, ambitious, and especially brutal *conquistador*—to destroy the Caxcan centers of resistance within Nueva Galicia. Alvarado scraped together approximately 100 Spanish foot soldiers and cavalry, supported by one artillery piece. The small Spanish force also included a larger body of allied Tlaxcaltecan[3] warriors[4], who were armed with various types of native weaponry. From

Zapotlán Alvarado advanced first northward to the newly established city of Guadalajara to obtain supplies and reinforcements, and then headed north towards Peñol de Nochistlán, a Caxcan urban center situated on a high, rocky hill, or *peñol*. To prepare for the impending Spanish attack thousands of Caxcan warriors at Peñol de Nochistlán manned concentric rings of dry-laid rock walls that encircled the base, slopes, and escarpment of the hill city. Behind these defensive positions the warriors stockpiled an ample supply of sling stones, arrows, and javelins.

Accounts of the battle are sketchy and one-sided. One account states that Alvarado first invested the base of the peñol with a combined force of harquebusiers, crossbowmen, pikemen, and Tlaxcaltecans, "... and stationed squads of horsemen where it seemed fit ...".[5] The one artillery piece, firing solid shot, was intended to breach the concentric rings of rock walls. The Spanish had some initial success, having driven the Caxcan defenders away from two rock wall defensive positions. The cavalry, followed by foot soldiers and Tlaxcaltecan warriors, then chased the retreating Caxcan warriors up slope and toward the heavily defended escarpment. But fierce Caxcan counterattacks pushed the Spaniards and their native allies down slope and onto the rolling plain that surrounded the peñol. Caxcan warriors, now sensing victory, pressed their attacks. Alvarado, "with some recklessness," was in the forefront of a cavalry counterattack when a horse up slope slipped and tumbled on top of him. Unconscious and mortally injured, Alvarado was dragged away from the thick of battle.[6] The demoralized Spanish force, now under constant attack, made its way back to Guadalajara, which the Caxcan army immediately placed under siege. Other tribes, seeing an opportunity to annihilate the hated Spaniards, joined the Caxcan cause. Even Mexico City was in danger of falling.

The Caxcan victory, however, was short-lived. The Spaniards assembled another, even larger army that included over 800 horsemen and foot soldiers along with tens of thousands of allied warriors. They first lifted the siege of Guadalajara, and then methodically destroyed the centers of Caxcan resistance. The Spanish once again arrived at Peñol de Nochistlán. After two days of fierce fighting the overwhelming Spanish force finally reached the top of the peñol and breached its last defensive wall, but "...[the warriors] defended it with many stone weapons and arrows...".[7] Thousands of Caxcan warriors fought to the death; many others committed mass suicide by jumping off a precipice of the peñol. It was reported that "... of the [Caxcan defenders] on the peñol, not even 20 escaped because those who were fleeing encountered the horsemen ...".[8]

By 1542 the Caxcan revolt was stamped out and Spanish authority re-established in Nueva Galicia, although conflicts would continue to the west in the lands of the Nayarita for decades longer. In the process all of the Caxcan urban centers were laid waste, the defenseless Caxcan people either slaughtered or forced to work for the Europeans as virtual slaves.[9] Over the following decades, the region was wracked by Spanish-introduced diseases, which ultimately resulted in the obliteration of the remaining Caxcan peoples and their allies. The region was eventually repopulated by various other indigenous groups as well as Spanish settlers. Although Tenamaxtle's revolt ultimately failed, his memory became immortalized by the native peoples of central and western Mexico. In some of the Indian villages of this region, the Mixtón War is celebrated to this day as a symbol of indigenous resistance.[10]

The identification and recordation of Peñol de Nochistlán, the site of one of the greatest battles of the Mixtón War, would present an opportunity to define a rare event in human history. This is a place wherein soldiers of the Old World, utilizing the technology and tactics reflective of the early modern era, met in pitched battle warriors of the New World who employed a radically different technology with its corresponding appropriate tactics.

There is a respectable body of literature regarding early sixteenth-century Spanish battle tactics as they were applied in the New World. Especially useful are published eyewitness accounts of those who actively participated in the conquest of Mesoamerican peoples, or who fought against the Chichimec tribes of northern Mexico during the latter half of the sixteenth century.[11] Spanish methods of warfare underwent a revolution during the first decades of the sixteenth century, a revolution that aided the transformation of Spain from a regional to a global power. Cohesion, the social force that holds units together in combat and that makes the difference between a unit and a mob of individuals, was a Spanish strong point. The Spaniards fought as integrated units: sword, pike, and shot acted in seemingly automatic concert with horse. John Elliott[12] makes the cogent point that a balanced force of as few as 50 Spaniards, horse and foot, could hold their own against a numerically superior force of Mesoamerican warriors on open and level terrain, unless overcome by exhaustion.

The Spaniards' superior weapons are one of the favorite explanations as to why their soldiers usually could defeat their Mesoamerican counterparts. However, Spanish artillery, harquebus, and crossbows often broke down during battles, while their warrior opponents were known to charge through the hail of harquebus and crossbow bolt fire, and run past the cavalry. Thus, most of the fighting was hand-to-hand. The conquistadors, with their slender blades of steel, had an immense advantage over Mesoamerican warriors since they could strike much more quickly and with far more deadly force, advantages magnified by the warriors' lack of effective armor.

The Spanish invariably fought as a cohesive unit, both fighting well and keeping their ranks. When outnumbered, as they usually were, the Spanish typically formed a box formation that was seldom broken. Crossbowmen and harquebusiers worked as a team, with one set loading weapons while the other set fired, and so on. Swordsmen slashed at the enemy's guts, while the cavalry and pikemen aimed at their faces. Before the enemy warriors could use their slings and bows, Spanish cavalry would charge the group and force them to fight hand-to-hand, and hold them at bay long enough for infantry to come into the fray and effectively end the fight. Pikemen would also form up in lines and present an impenetrable wall of pikes. Cannon and harquebusiers presented firepower sufficient to break up a massed charge of warriors, whereupon swordsmen and cavalry would move in and finish the slaughter. Horses gave the Spaniards crucial advantages in striking power, shock effect, and speed. The well-mounted Spaniard could strike harder and more swiftly and reach farther with his sword than could his companion on foot. He could use the speed and mobility of his mount to drive home the point of his lance, and could do so without coming within reach of his enemy's handheld weapon. Yet even with their unquestioned superiority in weaponry and tactics, conquistador companies owed their amazing victories largely to the support of thousands of native warriors that fought with them.[13]

There are extant codices of the period that suggest the tactics and orders of battle as practiced by the various native military powers encountered by the Spanish.[14] Mesoamerican combat involved an orderly sequence of weapons use and tactics, usually beginning with projectile fire. Although there were specialist archers and slingers, the opening salvo of projectiles was cast by all the combatants, employing whichever projectiles they possessed, and causing considerable harm. Battle descriptions indicate that the initial engagement took place at approximately 150 feet (50 meters) and continued until the projectiles were almost depleted. The armies then closed during the waning moments of the mass barrage to take advantage of the covering fire. Once the armies closed the slingers and archers lost their massed targets and could strike only at individuals. They were also used to counter enemy archers and slingers and to harass reinforcements and prevent encirclement. Sling stones were said to be capable of shattering a horse's thigh, fracturing a skull, or snapping a sword blade in two with a square hit at short range, and the Spanish feared these missiles as they feared no other indigenous weapon. On the whole, however, sling stones usually could only wound whereas crossbow bolts and harquebus balls killed, so the overriding advantage went to the conquistadores.[15]

Codices depicting pre- and post-Hispanic battle scenes indicate that opposing Mesoamerican battle formations favored relatively open ranks in which the combatants were widely dispersed. This spacing was necessary to allow *macuahuitl* or sword-wielding warriors at least a six-foot (two-meter) radius—the length of the extended arm and weapon—to swing these weapons. Thrusting spears were used for jabbing and some restricted lateral movement. Codices frequently depict placement of spearmen between the macuahuitl warriors, with the length of the spear shafts allowing the spearmen to thrust at the enemy without getting in harm's way of a nearby comrade's swinging macuahuitl. The dislodging and breaking of obsidian and chert blades on these and other lithic blade-edged weapons such as spears typically occurred but did not seem to seriously affect the fighting abilities of the warriors who used them.[16] Mesoamerican warfare was highly ritualized in concept, with man-to-man heroic combat between peers of rank considered the ideal match. In contrast, their European enemies were intent on killing and maiming indiscriminately and, whenever possible, at safe distances using long-reaching projectiles. In the eyes of Mesoamerican warriors such fighting behavior was barbaric and cowardly. Unfortunately for them, however, it was also quite effective in getting the job done.

Documents of the period are silent as to how, or even if, Spanish military companies integrated with comparable units of their native allies. Phrased another way, would a Spanish commander mix a company of pikemen with allied warriors armed with javelins and atlatls? Would warriors armed with obsidian-edged hand weapons be supported by crossbowmen? Were companies of Spanish soldiers used as frontline shock troops, with their native allies used solely in a secondary, auxiliary role? Neither do we have a clear idea as to the typical order of battle employed by the various Mexican tribes during the early Colonial periods. As in any other battlefield study, we depend on identifying and interpreting the patterned detritus of battle toward answering these, and other, questions regarding applied tactics.

The findings from Spanish conquistador sites of comparable age suggest the detritus of this battle would include iron and/or copper bolt heads and lead balls, the projectiles fired from crossbow and harquebus, respectively. Other metal objects reflecting a Spanish presence would be fasteners such as buckles, hooks and eyes, buttons, pins, and copper-alloy lace tags, termed "aglets." Aglets, used to prevent fraying of the ends of cords that tied together the doublet and hose, are commonly found on Spanish military sites of this period. These objects would be intermixed with chert and obsidian projectile points, and sling stones of riverine pebbles that were pecked into a more spherical shape. The indigenous counterpoint to fragments of steel-edged swords, daggers, and lance heads would be, for example, obsidian bifaces and blades that once fitted into that classic Mesoamerican hand weapon, the macuahuitl. A nineteenth-century redrawing of the *Lienzo de Tlaxcala* clearly illustrates the wood and metal elements of the macuahuitl carried by native warriors.[17] Metal fittings from crossbows, harquebuses, swords, lances, and pikes might also be present, as well as copper rings used to hold fabric hair braids, and copper bells. We know very little, however, as to what other typical metal objects of indigenous origin might also be present. Contemporary native and Spanish illustrations suggest that non-noble Caxcan warriors wore little more than a breech clout (if even that) and a grim visage.[18] It is possible that badges of rank, and jewelry made of precious metals and semi-precious stones, such as ear spools and lip plugs typically worn by the nobility, will be present on the battlefield.[19]

We have noted that, during both battles at Peñol de Nochistlán, the Spaniards utilized cavalry squads in their attempts to break through the Caxcan defenses, and to chase down any enemies that tried to escape the ensuing slaughter. The recovery of wrought iron horseshoe nails of a type typically used by Europeans during the mid-sixteenth century would be a major component in the determination of battle tactics. Associated artifacts would be horseshoes and horse equipage of the period, such as harness bells. We hypothesize that this location is where one might best attempt an ascent on horseback. Accordingly, we believe Caxcan warriors would have massed behind that segment of breastworks where the Spaniards directed their main attack.

We expect to find an intermixing of European and native-related artifacts along the slopes and base of the peñol. Specific battle locations may be identified by discrete concentrations of lithic projectile points, sling stones, and obsidian blades derived from native hand weapons, intermixed with metallic artifacts that reflect European missile and hand weapons, armor, and apparel. The primary lithic material used by native allies of the Spaniards may well have been obsidian obtained from various sources near Mexico City, located some 240 miles (400 km) to the southeast of Nochistlán. In contrast, the Caxcan had access to West Mexican obsidians[20] and local cherts for making their stone-edged weapons, as well as riverine pebbles as the source material for their sling stones.

Of course, the first issue that must be addressed is simply identifying Peñol de Nochistlán. One might assume that primary documents, complemented by oral tradition and collectors' finds, would make this task simple. However, as is often the case in archaeological investigations of battlefields, this is not so. Decades of historical research conducted prior to this present study has determined only that Peñol de Nochistlán is a steep-sloped hill of respectable height, and located somewhere north of the City of Guadalajara. The hilltop in question should hold archaeological evidence of a Caxcan urban center dating no later than the mid-sixteenth century, and there likely exist remnants of concentric rings of dry-laid rock walls. Recent archaeological reconnaissance suggests that, in fact, there are many hills within the estimated 140 mi^2 (360 km^2) study area that meet these basic qualifications. One must consider that the bellicose Caxcan typically occupied and fortified many habitable peñoles within their domain; therefore, it follows that a considerable number of these peñoles were battlefields during the 1541–1542 war. An archaeological survey that included all of these sites is ideal but hardly practical given the constraints of this present investigation. Instead, we have applied a more thorough research of primary documents that pertain to this specific battle, followed by archaeological reconnaissance of a few of the more promising sites. This approach considerably narrowed the count of hilly contenders for the honor of being identified as Peñol de Nochistlán, the first and arguably the greatest battle of the Mixtón War.

180 FIELDS OF CONFLICT

Nochistlán de Mejía is a town founded by the Spanish prior to the Mixtón War. The name of the town is an obvious clue that Peñol de Nochistlán is likely in its vicinity. According to a document dated 1584, Peñol de Nochistlán was "situated 16 leagues [on average, approximately 50 miles/ 80 km] from the Episcopal cathedral, which is in the city of Guadalajara."[21] Nochistlán de Mejía, in fact, is located approximately 55 miles (90 km) northeast of Guadalajara, and there exist several likely elevations within a 12-mile (20 km) radius of Nochistlán de Mejía.

Documents research includes analyses of three period pictorial representations of the battle of Peñol de Nochistlán. One of the representations (see figure) is by the famous copper plate engraver, Theodor de Bry (1528–1598); the other two were created by anonymous Native Americans (see figures).[22] De Bry did not actually witness the battle; rather, he completed his circa 1596 engraving based on an illustration that was produced prior to 1565 by Giralomo Benzoni (1520–?), an Italian who journeyed to the New World in 1541 and toured the Spanish possessions for some 14 years before returning to Italy.

Woodcut by Theodor de Bry, showing the European version of the 1541 battle of Peñol de Nochistlán. (Courtesy of the Seaver Center for Western History Research, Los Angeles County Museum of Natural History)

Benzoni's *Novae Novi Orbis Historiae*[23] consisted of adaptations of a variety of previously written accounts, which, in turn, described Spanish actions directed against the native inhabitants of the New World. Benzoni included the first battle of Peñol de Nochistlán as an example of such actions. Benzoni never visited Nueva Galicia so his illustration was based on obtaining first- or second-hand accounts from Spanish soldiers who fought at this battle. Thus, one cannot accept at face value this or other scenes that are depicted by De Bry's inflammatory engravings. Nonetheless, it is possible the image depicting the battle of Peñol de Nochistlán presents certain battle events and topographic features that hold a kernel of fact; therefore, these illustrated features should be considered when searching for the battle site.

If taken at face value, the De Bry engraving indicates the battle took place at the base, slopes, and crest of a conically shaped hill. It also places trees on the hilltop, with Caxcan warriors defending a breastwork of felled trees and stacked rocks along the escarpment. There is also a flowing stream at the base of the hill. We see a body of steel-armored horsemen in the foreground and in the process of fording the stream; harquebusiers likewise are advancing up slope, while dead and wounded horsemen and infantry litter the slope of the peñol. Caxcan warriors positioned behind the breastwork appear to be successfully defending their position by rolling logs and boulders down upon their attackers; many of the Caxcan are armed with clubs. Pedro de Alvarado appears as a fallen horseman in the middle of the scene, a contradiction of written documents that indicate Alvarado was mortally injured some distance away from the peñol. There are no indications on the engraving of a troop of native allies that reportedly fought with the Spanish.

Interestingly, De Bry's copper engraving receives some limited corroboration by the Codex Telleriano-Remensis (see figure on page 182). This codex, which describes the major events for the year 1541, supports two features of the De Bry engraving. Besides indicating the importance of Alvarado's death during the battle of Peñol de Nochistlán, it shows a Caxcan warrior shooting an arrow behind defensive rings of rock walls, and a stylized representation of a flowing stream surrounding the defensive position.

Additional detail is provided by the Compostela Map (see figure), thought to have been created in approximately 1550 by a native scribe who had been taught Spanish mapping conventions and orthography. Via text and simple schematic drawings, the map illustrates the various locations of native uprisings during the Mixtón War. One of these drawings depicts a pinnacle ringed by four rock walls, with two warriors firing arrows from the crest (see figure). Adjacent to the pinnacle is a peaked roof structure that symbolizes a pueblo. This drawing is labeled "*P. nochiztlan y pueblo*" ("Peñol Nochistlán and pueblo"). Apparently, at the initiation of the Mixtón War, there existed a close juxtaposition of this Caxcan-occupied peñol and the Spanish-occupied pueblo of Nochistlán.

Detail from the Codex Telleriano-Remensis (Folio 46r), depicting the death of Pedro de Alvarado at the first battle of the Peñol de Nochistlán. (Manuscrit Mexicain 385, Bibliothèque nationale de France)

Cerro San Miguel is a hill within the caldera of an extinct volcano, located approximately 12 miles (20 km) from the present-day town of Nochistlán de Mejía. Local legend holds that this hill is, in fact, Peñol de Nochistlán. In addition, the conical appearance of Cerro San Miguel is evocative of De Bry's engraving of Peñol de Nochistlán. For these two reasons Cerro San Miguel was assigned first priority for a reconnaissance-level survey. The survey crew walked a series of sample transects that traversed the base, slopes, and crest of Cerro San Miguel. The surveyors inspected the ground surface for battle-related lithic artifacts, as well as indicants of the defensive rock

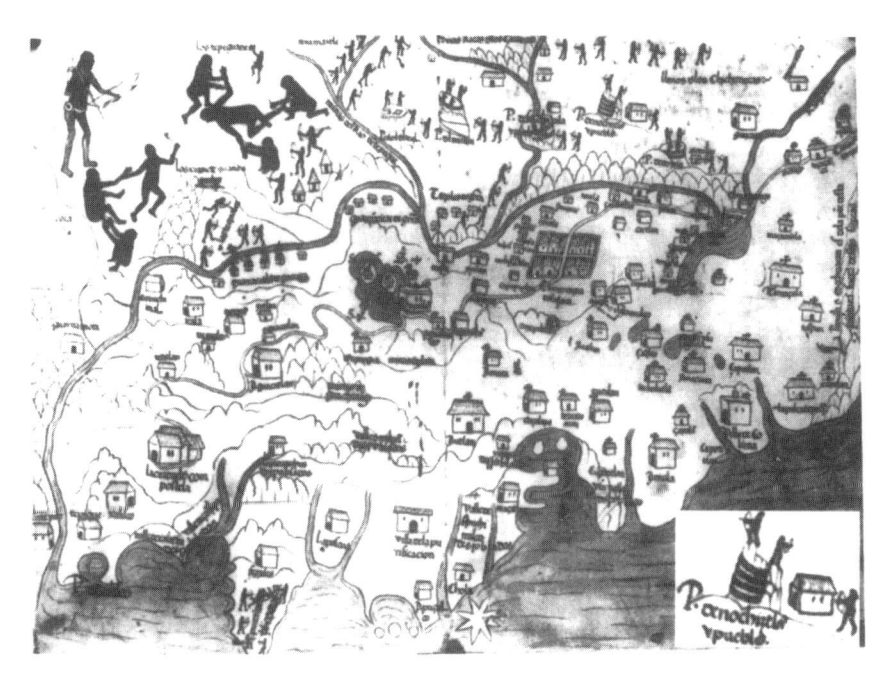

Compostela Map: "Zonas limítrofes entre las Audiencias de Mexico y Guadalajara, ca. AD 1550" (Archivo General de Indias, Mapas y Planos México 560). Probably drawn by a native scribe, this map illustrates the various locations of Mixtón War battle sites, including the Peñol de Nochistlán.

walls reportedly constructed by the Caxcan. In addition, one of the surveyors employed a metal detector. Previous archaeological investigations of a Caxcan urban center[24] indicated that a variety of well-constructed architectural elements typified Caxcan settlements. Residential architecture was represented by structures built from perishable materials, on foundations of vertically laid rock slabs (termed *cimientos*), while elaborate civic-ceremonial precincts—usually built on the hilltops—were characterized by monumental stone masonry structures that were plastered, and probably painted with bright colors when in use. Archaeologists documented small terraces, larger masonry platforms, a variety of stone walls and revetments, and dry-laid masonry constructions that appeared to be more hastily created.

The reconnaissance of Cerro San Miguel yielded some interesting results. The surveyors discovered a segment of vertical slab wall foundation near the base of the hill, substantial remains of a ceremonial platform on its crest, and collapsed remains of two parallel, dry laid stone walls spaced approximately six feet (two meters) apart. These rock walls were likely not intended as a formal ceremonial boundary since they were built by simply stacking tabular rocks directly on top of the ground. In fact, the stones used to construct the walls on the top of the Cerro apparently derived from the nearby ceremonial platform, which is partially stripped of its construction stones. These findings appeared to corroborate an account that Caxcan defenders hastily constructed rings of defensive walls around the peñol.

A battle of the magnitude of Peñol de Nochistlán would have resulted in thousands of bodies of the slain. Many bodies of Caxcan warriors may have been interred in nearby mass burials, as per the custom of the Caxcan peoples.[25] This assumes, of course, there were Caxcan survivors sufficient to exercise this custom. The Spaniards, as victors, would have had some opportunity to collect and bury all or at least some of their own dead, following the custom of their religious beliefs. In contrast, the bodies of those native warriors that were allied with the Spaniards—the Tlaxcaltecans, Mexica, and Otomís—may have remained largely where they fell, unclaimed and undoubtedly unmourned by both Spaniard and Caxcan. Regardless of the numbers of bodies that were removed, the battlefield still would have been a ghastly place of human decomposition for many years following this event. Thus, the chemical signature of bone—calcium phosphate—should be identifiable in elevated total phosphorus readings of battlefield soil.

The researchers applied the "spot test" technique of measuring the total phosphorus content of soil samples. This technique provides a quick means of determining gross measures of the total soil phosphorus, which typically bonds with aluminum, iron, and calcium. Regardless of the wholesale removal of skeletal remains from the battlefield, any dense concentrations of bone will produce elevated levels of calcium phosphate in the soil as the calcium leaching from the decomposing bones chemically bonded with the phosphorus naturally present in the soil. Once formed, soil phosphates are known to be extremely durable and relatively immobile.[26] The expected result of the soil testing was to document if elevated soil phosphorus levels are present within the soils found on the crest of Cerro San Miguel.

The survey team used a commercially available testing kit that provides an accurate, albeit qualitative, measurement of the total phosphorus in the soil samples. Since its relative density is higher than the surrounding background levels, the calcium phosphate comprises the major component of the total phosphorus, which is revealed by the relative degree of color change during soil testing. If present in significant amounts, phosphorus in solution turns "molybdenum blue." Color change was compared to colors in the charts supplied with the test kits, labeled "L," "M," and "H," which indicated low, medium, and high levels of soil phosphorus, respectively. Intensity of the resulting color change in each sample would be an indicator of relative quantity of phosphorus in the sample. For consistency, color changes noted in the soil samples were evaluated by consensus.

The survey team tested relative quantities of soil phosphorus at four locations on the crest of Cerro San Miguel. The team conducted two soil tests at each location: one test at the surface as a control, another at six inches (15 cm) below surface. One of these test locations contained high levels of soil phosphorus; two contained a medium level; and one location contained a low level. These findings give some support to the likelihood that a battle took place at Cerro San Miguel. We realize, however, that the Caxcan employed ceremonial centers as places to conduct human sacrifice, so the presence of significant quantities of soil phosphorus at this location may not be the direct result of a battle.

The reconnaissance survey of San Miguel produced one sling stone recovered near the base of the hill. A metal detection sweep of the crest of the hill yielded a bar of wrought iron having a chisel-shaped end, an object that possibly functioned as the business end of a club. As a whole, these features and artifacts, though scant, represented elements that one might expect from a hilltop defensive position during the Mixtón War. The crest and slopes of Cerro San Miguel were calculated, however, as covering an area of less than 4,000 m^2 (0.4 ha/1.0 acres), an area far too small to contain the reported thousands of Caxcan warriors who defended the urban center of Peñol de Nochistlán. Finally, Cerro San Miguel exhibits very little evidence of habitation architecture, which would be a key identifier for this battle site. The survey team concluded that Cerro San Miguel was a Caxcan ceremonial center worthy of defense during the Mixtón War, and it may even have been attacked by the Spanish army. Yet the fractional acreage of its crest and absence of habitation architecture indicated Cerro San Miguel and Peñol de Nochistlán were not the same hills.

Attention then shifted to the next likely location for the battle, that is, Cerro El Tuiche. This hill is located approximately six miles (10 km) northeast of Nochistlán de Mejía (see figure). Cerro El Tuiche is steep-sided, with a sheer precipice on its northeastern side (see figure). A permanent flowing stream demarcates its northern and eastern approaches. The top of Cerro El Tuiche is flat and encompasses about 7.4 acres (3 hectares), upon which lie the archaeological remains of a Caxcan urban center. Recall the Compostela Map detail (see figure), which implies a close juxtaposition existed between the Caxcan-defended peñol and the contemporaneous pueblo of Nochistlán: one might say the same of Cerro El Tuiche and present-day Nochistlán de Mejía. Finally, one side of Cerro El Tuiche is a sheer-sided precipice. As noted in the history of the battle the last of the Caxcan defenders, when faced with choosing either an ignominious submittal to the hated Spaniards or en masse suicide, chose the latter by jumping off Peñol de Nochistlán.

Utilizing a metal detector, the survey team investigated the base and slopes of Cerro El Tuiche. The surveyors soon discovered artifacts diagnostic of a mid-sixteenth-century battle: iron crossbow bolt heads (see figure on page 187); lead shot of a caliber range appropriate for harquebus; and two undated coins appropriate to the period of the Mixtón War. At Cerro El Tuiche project forensic anthropologist Angélica Medrano Enríquez employed the above-

186 FIELDS OF CONFLICT

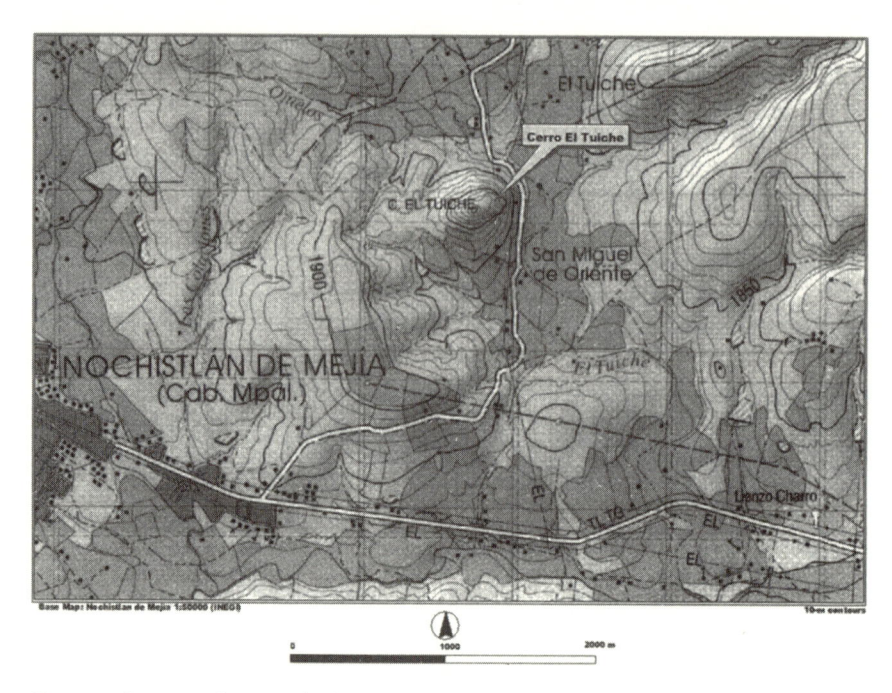

Topographic map showing the locations of Cerro El Tuiche and the present-day town of Nochistlán de Mejía. (from Carta Topográfica, F-13-D-37, INEGI, México)

Cerro El Tuiche, believed by researchers to be synonymous with Peñol de Nochistlán.

described "spot test" method for assessing relative amounts of calcium phosphate at this location. One tested location produced strong evidence that concentrations of subsurface calcium phosphate are present. Medrano Enríquez, who has excavated and analyzed Caxcan mass burials will eventually sample excavate this location.[27] Human skeletal remains, if encountered, will be monitored for battle-related trauma, pathological anomalies due to metabolic and infectious diseases, as well as indicants of the overall health status of the sample population.

These archaeological findings lend strong support to the researchers' present theory that Cerro El Tuiche and Peñol de Nochistlán are one and the same landforms. A comprehensive survey of this archaeological site is now being planned. We believe that, once the physical evidence of this battle is discovered and fully recorded, it will contribute a rarely viewed perspective of past actions and behavior in early Colonial Mexico. All too often, the victors of a war—or, even more frequently, their apologists—recount the events of their day, perhaps believing that they had silenced the vanquished forever. In this instance, we hope to once again give voice to those individuals who took part in a pivotal

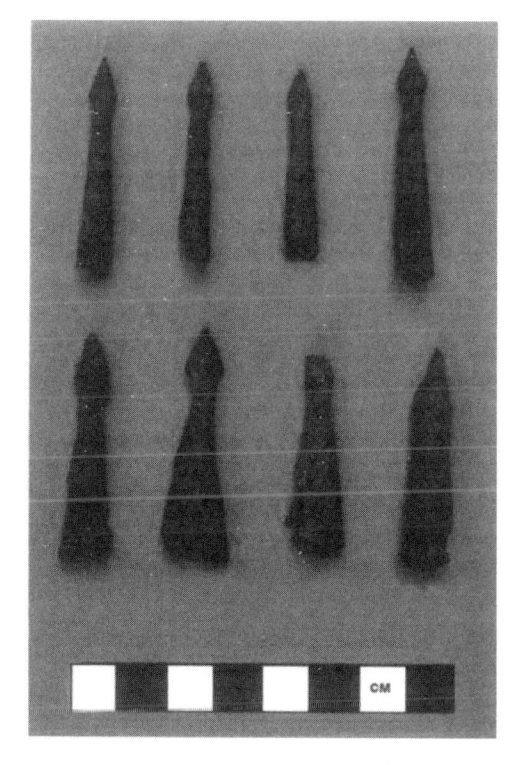

Crossbow bolt heads, recently discovered at Cerro El Tuiche as a result of an archaeological reconnaissance survey.

encounter in the New World, the result of social and political turmoil that marked the end of one era, and ushered in the next.

NOTES

Acknowledgments: The authors wish to acknowledge and thank the pueblo of Nochistlán de Mejía and its presidente for providing us with lodging, hospitality, and information during our stay there. We also are grateful to Richard and Shirley Flint for conducting documentary research related to this topic, and for reviewing and commenting on drafts of this article. ¡Gracias a todos!

1. At the time of the Spanish Conquest, the Caxcan occupied a series of city-states or *cacicazgos independientes* in the region known today as "Los Altos" of Zacatecas and Jalisco. They enjoyed a sophisticated material culture that featured monumental architecture, utility and lapidary stoneworking, and complex ceramics. As was characteristic for their notorious Mexica cousins, Caxcan heads of state were referred to as *tlatoanis* (speakers). Their religious/ceremonial customs were focused on the interlocking intricacies of the *tonalamatl* or annual calendar round and the 52-year calendar cycle observed by most urban or semi-urban Mesoamerican peoples. Caxcan sites feature ballcourts, civic-ceremonial centers, and residential architecture apparently used by occupants belonging to a variety of social statuses, from *macehualtin* to privileged elites. As the Spanish Conquest moved north, the Caxcan settlements were the last outposts of "civilized" peoples participating in the life ways that have come to typify Mesoamerican culture as archaeologists define it. Due north, as depicted on the Compostela map, lay the *tierras de guerra* ocupied by the Chichimeca.

2. Brother Juan Calero, a missionary, was killed near Tequila on June 10, 1541, when he attempted to pacify a group of Caxcan renegades holed up in the mountains. Calero thus attained the dubious honor of becoming the first European martyr in the New World (McCarty 1982:155).

3. Variants of the term "Tlaxcaltecan" that appear in professional and popular literature include "Tlascalan," "Tlaxcalan," "Tlazcalan," and even "Tezcalan." "Tlaxcaltecan" is the closest to the referent in Classical Nahuatl—the language spoken by the Caxcan, the Tlaxcaltecans, the Mexica or Aztec, and a number of other Central Mexican groups—and so is used here. With approximately one and a half million speakers, Nahuatl is spoken today by more people than any other indigenous language in Mexico.

4. Ibarra 1584.
5. Flint and Flint 2005.
6. Tello 1968.
7. Torres 1577.
8. Muñoz 1541.

9. Post-war relations between the Spanish and the vanquished Caxcan rebels are detailed in the *Relación de Agravios*, a petition made to the Royal Council of the Indies in Spain in the 1500s by Don Francisco Tenamaztle, a Caxcan nobleman (believed to be

the brother, and perhaps the betrayer, of the leader of the rebellion) who survived the Mixtón War. According to Reynoso (1959), the petition was written out and probably edited by Fray Bartolomé de las Casas, and incorporates many of las Casas's beliefs about appropriate treatment of indigenous peoples undergoing "Christianization." Don Francisco—or Petecatl, to use his Caxcan name—was believed to have succeeded the *cacique* who ruled at Nochistlán prior to the arrival of Nuño Beltran de Guzmán and his army of adventurers. Unlike his more famous brother who led the Caxcan during the Mixtón War, Don Francisco had behaved in a friendly and accommodating manner toward the Spanish and had even—by his own account—treatied with Don Antonio de Mendoza, leading his own people to suspect his motives (1959:7). At the time that he made his petition, however, he had been declared responsible for the uprisings, arrested, and transported to Spain by Mendoza's successor, Viceroy Don Luis de Velasco (1959:7).

10. The story of the war's end has become ritualized as an important ceremony still celebrated in the Mexican towns and villages located in what was once the Gran Caxcána. The rite celebrates the divine intervention of St. James, patron saint of the conquistadores, in convincing the natives to lay down their arms. The saint's appearance and the capitulation of the native leaders are re-enacted as part of a series of encounters that take place on St. James's feast day. The ritual, referred to as the dance of the "tlastoanis" [sic], features an individual dressed as the saint as well as numerous men garbed in motley costumes topped by elaborate masks, the "tlastoanis."

11. Diaz 1963 [1576], Powell 1975, Sahagún 1978.

12. Elliott 1984:174.

13. Diaz 1963 [1576]: 101–103, Towsend 1993:24, White 1971:171.

14. Davies 1972, Hassig 1995: 95–109.

15. Hassig 1995:98–99, Hemming 1970:192.

16. Diaz 1963 [1576]:103.

17. The *Lienzo de Tlaxcala* is a painted document, created by Tlaxcaltecan scribes around the middle of the sixteenth century. According to Gurría Lacroix (1988:210) two copies were originally painted. Of these, one remained in Tlaxcala while the other was sent to Spain. Both were subsequently lost, although a copy of the version which remained in Mexico had been made by the French Scientific Commission during the Second Empire. A copy was also made in 1773 by Manuel Illañes. This copy is stored today in the National Museum of Anthropology. Copies by Chavero (1892 and 1964) and Cahuantzi (1892) are available for consultation today. The *lienzo* recounts the participation of Tlaxcaltecans in the episodes of conquest directed by Cortés, Alvarado, and Guzmán. The portions of interest with respect to West Mexico are Láminas LVI through LXXI. These pages detail the participation of Tlaxcaltecan allies in the campaigns led by Guzmán and his captains. Lámina LVIII is denominated as "Xuchipila."

18. Note, for example, the contrast in complexity of dress and equipage between the Tlaxcaltecan allies, many of whom were noblemen, with the defenders of "Xochipillan" (Juchipila or Cerro de las Ventanas) illustrated in a fragment from the *Lienzo de Tlaxcala*.

19. Anawalt 1981, Arnold and Weddle 1978, Ewen and Hann 1998:80, Hosler 1988.

20. Darling (1998) reports on sourcing studies for samples of utilized obisidian from Caxcan sites, which point to the Tequila Source Area in Jalisco and the Huitzila-La Lobera Source Area in Durango as important procurement areas for the Caxcan.

21. Calderon 1584.
22. Oster 2006.
23. Don Francisco Tenamaztle 1584:11–20.
24. Oster 2006.
25. Medrano, Enríquez, 1995 a and b, Oster 2006.
26. Bethell and Máté 1989:9, Eidt 1977, Lillios 1992:500, Neff 2002:18–19; Proudfoot 1975:103–104; Sanchez et al. 1996.
27. Medrano Enríquez, 1995a and b.

REFERENCES CITED

Anawalt, Patricia Rieff. 1981. *Indian Clothing Before Cortés, Mesoamerican Costumes From the Codices*. University of Oklahoma Press, Norman.

Arnold, J. Barto III, and Robert Weddle. 1978. *The Nautical Archeology of Padre Island: The Spanish Shipwrecks of 1554*. Academic Press, New York.

Benzoni, Giralomo. 1857. *History of the New World*. Translated by W. H. Smith, originally published in 1578 by the author in Geneva. The Hakluyt Society, London.

Bethell, Philip, and Ian Máté. 1989. The Use of Soil Phosphate Analysis in Archaeology: A Critique. In *Scientific Advances in Archaeology*, edited by Julian Henderson, 1–29. Oxbow Books, Oxford.

Calderón, Juan Gutiérrez. 1584. *Relación geográfica*. Bancroft Library, University of California, Berkeley.

Chavero, Alfredo. 1892. *Antigüdades mexicanas publicadas por la Junta Colombina de Mexico en el cuarto centenario del descubrimiento de América*. México, Oficina Tipográfica de la Secretaria de Fomento.

Darling, J. Andrew. 1998. Obsidian Distribution and Exchange in the North-Central Frontier of Mesoamerica. Ph.D. dissertation, University of Michigan. University Microfilms, Ann Arbor.

Davies, Nigel. 1972. The Military Organization of the Aztec Empire. *Atti del XL Congresso Internazionale degli Americanisti* 4:213–221.

De Bry, Theodor. 1978. *Conquistadores, Azteken en Inca's/Conquistadores, Aztecs and Incas*. A Facsímile Edition of 16th Century Engravings by Theodor De Bry. Van Hoeve, Amsterdam.

de la Torre, Mario. 1983. *El Lienzo de Tlaxcala*. Mario de la Torre, editor. Cartón y Papel de México, México, D. F.

Diaz, Bernal. 1963. *The Conquest of New Spain*. Translated by J. M. Cohen. The Folio Society, London. Originally published in Spain in 1576.

Eidt, Robert C. 1973. A Rapid Chemical Test for Archaeological Site Surveying. *American Antiquity* 38:206–210.

Eidt, Robert C. 1977. Detection and Examination of Anthrosols by Phosphate Analysis. *Science* 197(4311):1327–1333.

Eidt, Robert C. 1985. Theoretical and Practical Considerations in the Analysis of Anthrosols. In *Archaeological Geology*, edited by George R. Rapp and John A. Gifford, 155–189. Yale University Press, New Haven.

Elliott, John H. 1984. The Spanish Conquest and Settlement of America. In *Colonial Latin America*, Vol. I of *Cambridge History of Latin America*. Cambridge University Press, Cambridge.

Ewen, Charles R., and John H. Hann. 1998. *Hernando de Soto Among the Apalachee, The Archaeology of the First Winter Encampment*. University Press of Florida, Gainesville.

Flint, Richard, and Shirley Cushing Flint. 2005. *Documents of the Coronado Expedition, 1539–1542, "They Were Not Familiar with His Majesty nor Did They Wish to Be His Subjects,"* Document 25, Letter to Fernández de Oviedo, October 6, 1541, *from* Segunda Parte, Libro XXXIII, Capitulo LII, *Historia general y natural de las Indias*, 1547, Academia Real de la Historia, Madrid Colección Salazar/Castro 9/555 (H-32), 309–316. Southern Methodist University, Dallas.

Gurría Lacroix, Jorge. 1988. Historiografía de la conquista de Occidente. In *Conquista Hispánica de la Provincias de los Tebles Chichimecas de la America Septentrional*, by José Luis Razo Zaragoza, Apéndice IX, 210–234. Universidad de Guadalajara, Guadalajara, Mexico.

Hassig, Ross. 1995. *Aztec Warfare, Imperial Expansion and Political Control*. University of Oklahoma Press, Norman.

Hemming, J. 1970. *The Conquest of the Incas*. Harvest Books, San Diego, CA

Hosler, Dorothy. 1988. Ancient West Mexican Metallurgy: South and Central American Origins and West Mexican Transformations. *American Anthropologist* 90:832–853.

Ibarra, Diego de. 1584. Testimony, *In* AGI Patronato 78, R1, N1: Informacion de parte en la audiencia de Mexico, año 1584. Ms. on file, Bancroft Library, University of Southern California, Berkeley.

Lillios, Katina T. 1992. Phosphate Fractionation of Soils at Agroal, Portugal. *American Antiquity* 57:495–506.

Lopez Portillo y Weber, José. 1935. *La Conquista de la Nueva Galicia*. Secretaria de Educación Pública, Departamento de Monumentos, Talleres de la Nación.

McCarty, Kieran R. 1982. Los franciscanos en la frontera chichimeca. *Lecturas Históricas de Jalisco antes de la Independencia* Vol. 1, 143–181. Unidad Editorial Guadalajara, Jalisco.

Medrano Enríquez, Angélica. 1995a. *Informe: Rescate Arqueológico: Entierro Múltiple, El Mirador*. Consejo de Arqueológia, Instituto Nacional de Antropología e Historia, México, D.F. Unpublished ms.

Medrano Enríquez, Angelica. 1995b. *Restos Oseos y Malacológicos, Sitio Arqueológico Las Ventanas, Juchipila, Zacatecas*. Tésis profesional de licenciatura, Universidad Autónoma de Guadalajara.

Muñoz, Col. 1541. Document XI, Carta de don Antonio de Mendoza al Obispo de Mexico. De junto al Coyna, October, 1541. Academia de la Historia, t. LXXXII, fol. 223, p. 171. Manuscript on file, Bancroft Library, UCLA, Berkeley.

Neff, Loy C. 2002. Archeological Survey and Soil Testing at Washita Battlefield National Historic Site, Roger Mills County, Oklahoma. National Park Service-Intermountain Region. Western Archeological and Conservation Center, *Publications in Anthropology* 82, Tucson.

Oster, Elizabeth A. 2006. Cerro de las Ventanas: A Northern Mesoamerican Frontier Site in Zacatecas, Mexico. Unpublished Ph.D. dissertation in Anthropology, Tulane University, New Orleans.

Powell, Philip Wayne. 1975. *Soldiers, Indians and Silver*. Center for Latin American Studies, Arizona State University, Tempe.

Proudfoot, B. 1975. The Analysis and Interpretation of Soil Phosphorus in Archaeological Contexts. In *Geoarchaeology: Earth Science and the Past*, edited by D.A. Davidson and M. L. Shackley, 93–113. Yale University Press, New Haven.

Quiñones Keber, Eloise. 1995. *Codex Telleriano-Remensis; Ritual, Divination, and History in a Pictorial Aztec Manuscript*. University of Texas Press, Austin.

Reynoso, Salavador. 1959. Introduccion. In *Colección Siglo XVI*, Ernesto Ramos, ed., 7–9. México, D.F.

Sahagún, Fray Bernardino de. 1978. *The War of Conquest: How It Was Waged in Mexico*. Translated by Arthur J. O. Anderson and Charles E. Dibble. The University of Utah Press, Salt Lake City.

Sanchez, A., M. L. Cañabate, and R. Lizcano. 1996. Phosphorus Analysis at Archaeological Sites: An Optimization of the Method and Interpretation of the Results. *Archaeometry* 38(1):151–164.

Tello, F. Antonio Fray. 1968. *Crónica Miscelania de la Sancta Provincia de Jalisco*. Book Two, Volume One. Universidad de Guadalajara, México. Originally published in 1650.

Tenamaztle, Don Francisco. 1959. [1584]. Relación de Agravios. In *Colección Siglo XVI*, Ernesto Ramos, ed., 11–20. México, D.F.

Torres, Francisco de. 1577. Testimony of Francisco Torres, *In* AGI, Patronato, 75, R3, N1, Servicios de Cristóbal de Oñate en las conquista del nuevo reyno de Galicia. October 31, 1577. Ms. on file, Bancroft Library, University of Southern California, Berkeley.

Townsend, Richard F. 1993. *The Aztecs*. Thames and Hudson, Inc., New York.

White, Jon Manchip. 1971. *Cortes and the Downfall of the Aztec Empire: A Study in a Conflict of Cultures*. St. Martin's Press, New York.

Tatars, Cossacks, and the Polish Army: The Battle of Zboriv

Adrian Mandzy

IN EVERY NATION'S history certain events take on mythological significance. Names like Queenston Heights and Dieppe, Rorke's Drift and Agincourt, Verdun and Dien Bien Phu, Gettysburg and San Juan Hill have taken on almost mythological status. Perception, more than fact, create national myths. Victories and defeats were massaged to serve current political considerations and the identities of the combatants shift in accordance to a regime's ideologies.

Ukrainian history has not been immune to such manipulations. Situated on the crossroads between Berlin, Moscow, Vienna, Istanbul, Stockholm, Warsaw, and Bucharest, each foreign "liberator" rewrote Ukraine's history for its own purpose. Conversely, Ukrainians used their past as a source of identity and modified it to fit their needs. Perhaps no myth is as enduring in Ukraine as that of the events of the late 1640s.

In 1646, a Ukrainian (or, to use the seventeenth-century term, Rutherian) land-owning Cossack[1] by the name of Bohdan Khmelnytsky had his property raided and his youngest son killed by a Polish nobleman. He tried to find redress to his claims in the courts of the Polish-Lithuanian Commonwealth,[2] which then ruled Ukraine. In January 1648 Khmelnytsky fled to the Zaporozhian Sich[3] and persuaded the local Cossacks to seek out justice through the use of force. Unlike other previous Cossack rebellions, which failed due to the lack of cavalry,[4] Khmelnytsky created an alliance with the Muslim Crimean Tatars. Together, these two traditional enemies faced the largest and one of the most powerful states in Europe—the Polish-Lithuanian Commonwealth.

In April 1648, Hetman[5] Khmelnytsky defeated the Polish-Lithuanian army at Zhovti Vody and in May 1648, he was again victorious at Korsun. Ukrainian regiments, who served in the Polish-Lithuanian armies, defected to Khmelnytsky's banner. Invigorated by the success of the Cossacks, serfs, peasants, and urban dwellers also rebelled. In this "Great Revolt," Jews, Catholics, and Polish nobles were killed or driven out from what is today central Ukraine. Polish nobles responded to the massacres in kind and employed their own terror tactics. Following the destruction of a third Polish-Lithuanian army at Pyliavtsi, Khmelnytsky returned to Kiev where the Ukrainian Orthodox hierarchy treated him as a liberator.

Yet in spite of these dramatic victories, the relationship between the rebellious Ukrainians and the Commonwealth remained unclear. The Cossack elite and long-serving rank-and-file had fought to secure the rights and privileges of noblemen. Others within the Orthodox hierarchy fought for parity with Catholics. Serfs, peasants, and the lower urban classes struggled against economic exploitation. Since neither Khmelnytsky nor the monarch could propose a peaceful solution to the ongoing conflict, the war continued into 1649.

Following the initial successes of the previous year's rebellion, Cossacks, Tatars, peasants, and nobles engaged the forces of the Polish-Lithuanian Commonwealth. A Polish-Lithuanian army attacked, but quickly became trapped in the city fortress of Zbarazh. The king personally led a second army to free this trapped army. Khmelnytsky's forces ambushed the monarch's army as it crossed the Strypa River outside the town of Zboriv, less than a day's ride from Zbarazh. Suffering heavy losses, the Polish-Lithuanian forces established a defensive perimeter and as evening fell, the king's army constructed earthworks in preparation for the coming battle. In the morning, Cossacks and Tatars breached the partially completed defensive works. German troops in the service of the crown successfully counterattacked and sealed the breaches in the line, but in doing so the king exhausted his only remaining military reserves. Surrounded, outnumbered, and with no hope for rescue, the crown opened negotiations with the rebels. The resulting Treaty of Zboriv created an autonomous Ukrainian Cossack state.[6]

Although this conflict did not end with the Treaty of Zboriv, the images of the Cossack Wars would be manipulated to further political agendas. With the dismemberment of the Polish-Lithuanian Commonwealth at the end of the eighteenth century, Poles looked to the past for inspiration to build a national Polish state. Despite the Commonwealth's inability to ever suppress the Cossack movement, particular military events, such as the 1649 siege of Zbarazh, were to become important elements in contemporary Polish national consciousness. Although Jan Casimir had made a strong effort to claim the Battle of Zboriv as a major victory for the Polish-Lithuanian Commonwealth, it was the nineteenth-century romantic writer Henryk Sienkiewicz who turned the seventeenth-century Siege of Zbarazh into a call for the restoration of the Polish state. In his work, Poles are noble, civilized, and honorable while the Cossacks are barbarous, petty, and cruel. On the cusp of the twenty-first century, Sienkiewicz's 1884 novel *With Fire and Sword* remained mandatory reading for Polish students. Jerzy Hoffman's recent adaptation of the novel to film strove to address some of the worst excesses of the novel and made the Great Revolt accessible to yet another generation.

Both the Tzarist and Soviet governments have used the Cossacks and Khmelnytsky for their own political purposes. In 1654, Khmelnytsky, unable to secure a lasting peace with the Commonwealth, signed a treaty with Moscow. Russians have traditionally interpreted this 1654 Treaty of Pereiaslav as the natural culmination of the events of 1648. Though early Soviet historians had no purpose for a land-owning "aristocrat," by the late 1930s Khmelnytsky was recast as a national military hero who led his people to unification with the Tsar of Moscow. In October 1943, the Soviets created the Order of Bohdan Khmelnytsky, the only Soviet military order to include a non-Russian hero in Stalin's hagiography of "our great ancestors."[7] In 1954, the Soviet regime celebrated the 300-year anniversary of the Treaty of Pereiaslav to commemorate "the everlasting friendship between two people."[8] Works, such as Kozachenko's, made it clear that the purpose of the 1648 conflict was to bring about Ukrainian unification with Moscow and the liberation to the poor.[9] To this day, many scholars in Ukraine continue to look at Khmelnytsky's action in terms of a "War of National Liberation."

Part of Moscow's long-standing view of Ukrainians and Cossacks was that these people were backward provincials. As early as the eighteenth century, when during the reign of Catherine II the Imperial government sought to modernize by abolishing regionalism, the Cossack elite circulated copies of their own histories which strove to underline their ancient nobility. By the beginning of the nineteenth century, as the Ukrainian Cossack elite became assimilated into Russian society, a new romantic image of Cossack emerged—that of a frontiersman. As the century progressed, new tales of wild and exotic Cossacks riders were popular in the Russian Empire and the world. Although the line between Russian and Ukrainian Cossacks became blurred at the beginning of the twentieth century, Ukrainians during the Revolution of 1917 drew inspiration from the Cossack era. Many Ukrainian military units used the names of Cossack generals and at least one leader, Hetman Skoropatski, based the legitimacy of his rule on the claim of being from the old Cossack elite.

Yet for most of the twentieth century, the terms "Ukrainian" and "Cossack" became synonymous with plebeian. For all the rhetoric of cultural equality, high culture in the Soviet state was Russian. Russian literature, music, ballet, art, and architecture were elevated to the equal of those in the West, while ethnic achievements were considered in the best of times as "rustic." Those who pushed the envelope too far in trying to gain recognition for non-Russian achievements were often branded as "nationalists," a crime which carried the penalty of losing one's job or one's life. Thus, the Soviet pantheon reduced the Cossacks to simple, primitive farmers.

Over the course of generations, the Cossacks, in popular imagery, are often portrayed as simpletons, but an examination of the Battle of Zboriv illustrates the sophistication of the Cossack forces. Although scholars have provided differing analyses of the events at Zboriv, little work has been previously attempted to incorporate the local landscape, the documentary evidence, and the archaeological record into a holistic interpretation.[10] The first endeavor to link the historical accounts of the battle with the topography was undertaken by the Ukrainian historian Ivan Krypiakevych, who in July 1929 created a series of maps of the battle based on his two-day visit to Zboriv.[11] The Soviet regime made a concerted effort to downplay the significance of the events of 1649 and Krypiakevych's initial survey work did not continue. While new information related to the Treaty of Zboriv was published in the West, it was only in the early 1990s that Ukrainian and Polish scholars had the opportunity to focus on the 1649 campaign.[12] Perhaps the most important contribution of the last decade was the publication of two engineering field military maps created during the 1649 campaign (one from Zboriv and one from Zbarazh), which illustrate the disposition of forces and the extended fieldworks.[13]

In Ukraine, battlefield studies have a long tradition, but as elsewhere, it has focused almost exclusively on sites such as camps, castles, and fortresses. The best-known exception to this was Shveshnikov's excavations at the 1651 Battle of Berestechko, where, over the course of multiple field seasons, he excavated numerous graves from a swamp bog.[14] The waters of the swamp prevented the looting of the dead and preserved significant amounts of organic materials. These particular environmental conditions preserved significant quantities of military arms and accoutrements as well as many personal items. By focusing on the swamps to the rear of the actual battlefield, Shvechnikov recovered items such as stocked muskets, arrows with preserved shafts, belts, and leather cartridge boxes. Since he found these artifacts with individual combatants, it is possible to reconstruct how these forces were armed and equipped.[15]

While the Berestechko excavations provide an unparalleled look at the peasants and Cossacks who died while fleeing after their defeat, Shvechnikov's excavations follow the traditional archaeological field methods of digging in a very small area. Since battles occurred over a wide area, sometimes encompassing hundreds of square kilometers, an excavation method that relies on the analysis of a few square meters produces, in most instances, very few results. At Berestechko, researchers did not subject the rest of the battlefield to significant testing.[16] Even with the identification of individual artifacts, no research methodology existed at that time which could document the distribution of artifacts over many square kilometers. Not surprisingly, when in the mid-1990s, archaeologists employed traditional testing methods at Zboriv, they failed to find any material from the seventeenth-century battle.[17]

The study of open warfare, besides a few well-publicized successes such as Berestechko or Wisby,[18] began in earnest only after the work on the Little Bighorn battlefield was published.[19] The use of metal detectors at the Little Bighorn provided a way for archaeologists to deal with the limitations of identifying the distribution of battlefield artifacts over great distances. This data, coupled with extensive primary historical research and topographic information, allowed scholars to deal with the conditions specific to the study of battlefields.

Unlike the area around the Little Bighorn battlefield, where very little human activity had taken place before or after the battle, people farmed the territories around Zboriv and Zbarazh for centuries. Thus scholars recovered artifacts from many periods, including the seventeenth century, during the course of the survey. As on seventeenth-century English Civil War battlefields, generations have used the same areas and many objects were lost or deposited during manuring.[20] On the European continent, military ordnance from later conflicts, especially from the two world wars, is likely to overlay earlier materials.[21]

In 2002, working with Bohdan Strotsen, the regional director in charge of preservation of historical and cultural monuments for the Ternopil Region in Ukraine, the author conducted a joint survey with the purpose of identifying any possible remaining cultural resources associated with the military events of 1649.[22] After integrating the primary accounts of the battle with the historical and geographic topography of the area, we conducted a visual inspection of the territory. Based on this preliminary analysis, we selected areas that appeared to have been least impacted by modern development.[23]

The methodology employed was a variation on the one initially used in the archaeological investigations at the Little Bighorn. After identifying a possible area, students swept the fields with metal detectors. Once a detector registered an object, the artifact was retrieved from the disturbed soil to identify its relevance to the battle. Since locals plowed the areas around Zboriv for generations, all the artifacts lacked stratigraphic provenience and essentially came from the surface. Using a handheld global positioning system (GPS) unit, we recorded the co-ordinates of each find and collected the artifacts from the field. Given the scale of the battlefield and number of square kilometers associated with it, an accuracy of ±5m provided by the GPS was considered to be acceptable. Following the cleaning of the finds, members of the project weighted, measured, drew, and photographed each artifact. At the end of the field season, Bohdan Strotsen presented all of the artifacts to the local regional museum in Zboriv.

Unlike medieval battlefields where very little datable material exists, seventeenth-century battlefields provide quantities of lead shot and iron shot. We recovered quantities of musket balls and iron shot during the survey, but the recovery of hundreds of WWI shrapnel balls, which are only slightly smaller and lighter than the majority of seventeenth-century musket balls, complicated our work. In spite of the contamination of the battlefield with modern lead shrapnel balls, when we plotted out the distribution of musket balls along an X and Y grid, we identified two distinct lines of seventeenth-century ordnance. Based on this preliminary information, we believed that we had discovered the eastern portion of a battle line in an area not yet subject to residential or industrial development (see figure).

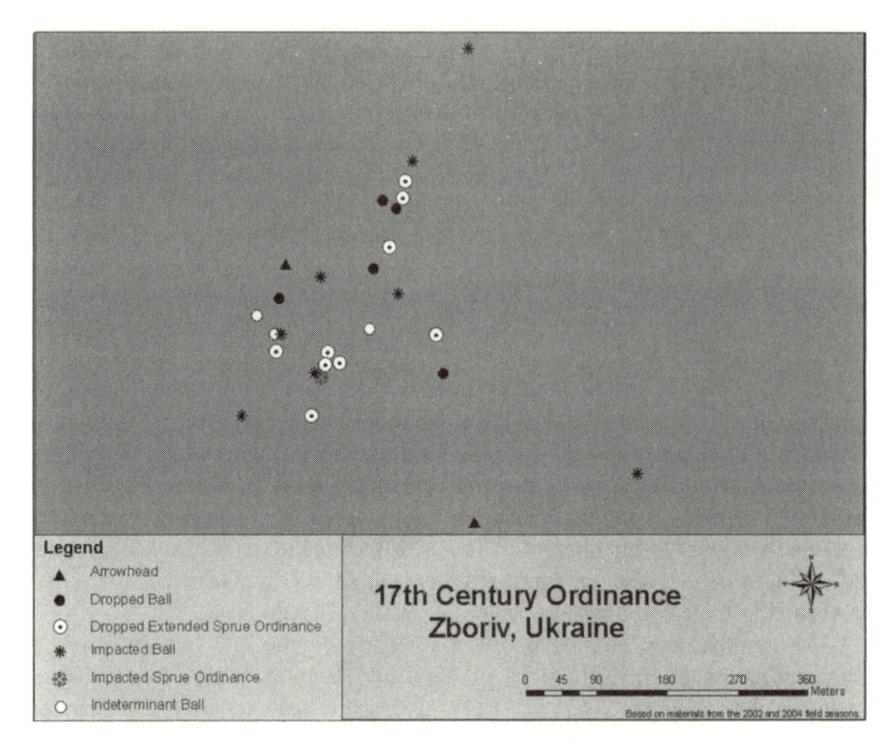

Spatial distribution of seventeenth-century military ordnance at Zboriv.

If we take this distribution of military artifacts and compare them with the local topography, we see that one line of ordnance is on top of a military crest of a small hill. Since the "choice of ground on which to fight and the exact deployment of troops in battalia were based on sound military principles," it is clear that the topographic environment predetermined the establishment of the firing line in this particular location.[24] The fragmentary primary sources provide the historical context in which to further interpret this battle. If we add to our dataset the existing contemporary map of the 1649 battle, which unfortunately is out of scale, we see that these artifacts are all found along what appears to be the eastern defensive line of the Polish camp. The map also shows the disposition of particular units, but it remains unclear to what degree units shifted during the course of the engagement.

To recognize the implications of the distribution patterns of the recovered ordnance, it is essential to understand the way firearms were used in the seventeenth century and how military units functioned. The reorganization of Polish infantry in the 1630s borrowed from both Swedish and Dutch models, which divided regiments into six companies.[25] In the 1640s, musketeers generally represented only two-thirds of a European infantry regiment, as the remaining one-third were pikemen. Within each army this arrangement may have been slightly different. The Swedish armies of King Gustavus Adolphus maintained a theoretical proportion of 216 pikes to 192 musketeers, while slightly larger Dutch battalions strove to maintain a ratio of 250 to 240.[26]

Scholars encounter additional difficulties when trying to link a particular military unit to the recovered ordnance distribution pattern. The general military practice of the period placed pike-armed troops in the center, with musketeers on each flank. Thus when we notice gaps between groups of lead balls it may indicate the space occupied by pikemen, rather than two separate units. Similarly, as throughout the century the number of ranks within particular types of units decreased, the frontage of the same type of unit occupied increased accordingly. Thus, an infantry battle line from the 1630s may have presented a completely different appearance from an infantry battle line of the 1660s. Finally, since most military units were rarely at full strength, the distribution of balls will not necessarily coincide with the theoretical dimensions of a combat unit.

According to a contemporary account of the battle, written shortly after the end of hostilities, the Crown forces built earthen fortifications to strengthen their battle lines.[27] Although the eastern line of these earthen fortifications witnessed no major military engagements, the fragmentary documentary record is quite clear that Tatar troops demonstrated in this area to draw attention of the enemy.[28] The recovery of buttons and metal buckles among dropped musket balls, which we believe troops dropped when they prepared for battle, confirms the location of the eastern section of the Polish defensive earthworks.

The construction of the earthen walls on the night between the first and second day of the battle, while undertaken primarily by attached servants, required the assistance of combat troops. The dire situation in which the Crown army found itself required haste and they would have used any item to build up a barricade. The Commonwealth commonly used heavy military wagons, similar to the fifteenth-century *wagenburg* initially developed by Jan Ziska, the commander of the Hussite Armies of Bohemia, as mobile field defenses. The recovery of so many metal hardware wagon parts found alongside seventeenth-century military ordnance suggests that the army added any broken or damaged wagons to the defensive barriers.

Contemporary descriptions of the Cossack regiments suggest that up to a third of the peasant troops lacked proper armaments during the 1649 campaign. The Cossack army fielded at Zboriv, however, consisted of Khmelnytsky's best troops. Since it was necessary to maintain an active siege of Zbarazh, only a fraction of the army made the march to Zboriv. The majority of these troops, we believe, carried projectile weapons. Cossacks often made use of Tatar-style bows which had a faster rate of fire than a seventeenth-century firearm, could fire in adverse weather, and did not give away the position of the bowman.[29] The recovery of seventeenth-century Tatar style arrowheads from both Zbarazh and Zboriv confirms the continued use of bows in warfare (see figure).

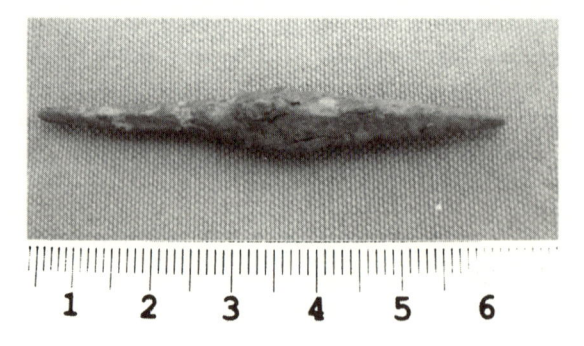

Seventeenth-century Tatar arrowhead recovered at Zboriv.

In the middle of the seventeenth century, there was a great variation in the types of infantry weapons in use. Along the northeastern frontier of the Commonwealth, flintlocks replaced hazardous matchlocks and expensive wheel locks. Excavations at the Berestechko battlefield indicated the overall dominance of flintlock weapons, while the recovery of large quantities of iron spanners suggests the use of wheel locks. The lack of matchlock weapons, however, is surprising. Cheap and somewhat reliable, matchlocks were the dominant firearm during the English Civil War (1642–1648)[30] and remained in use by Austrian military units at least until the 1683 Siege of Vienna.[31] French and English armies retained matchlocks until the turn of the century. Yet among the "poorly armed Cossacks," matchlocks were obsolete by the middle of the seventeenth century.

Another common assumption is the lack of firearm standardization. Rebel armies often have logistical nightmares and given the significant variations in the firearm calibers, one would expect to find a wide range of musket ball calibers. Since all seventeenth-century gunpowder left a residue of unburned soot after only a few shots, the barrel quickly became fouled and increasingly difficult to load. Conventional wisdom is that soldiers usually carried a variety of smaller balls to use as the battle progressed. Yet the recovery of complete bullet pouches and cartridge cases from Berestechko indicates no significant variations of ammunition calibers carried by each combatant. From this information we can make a much stronger argument that the caliber of ball corresponds closely to the weapons used.

A study of collections of seventeenth-century military arms in both the National Army Museum in Warsaw (Poland) and the Historical Arsenal Museum in L'viv (Ukraine) clearly illustrates that seventeenth-century armies standardized their weapon systems. Muskets, usually of Western European design, were predominantly large-caliber weapons with a bore diameter between 24 and 18 mm, with 20 mm being the most common. In 1649 and at the beginning of 1650 the arsenal in Warsaw acquired 1,300 muskets from Holland and 210 Dutch muskets.[32] Most Oriental "Turkish" weapons in the museums of Poland and Ukraine have a much smaller caliber bore, while mid-seventeenth-century Dutch muskets have a barrel bore that approaches 21 mm.[33] Given latitude for windage—that is, the difference between the actual barrel diameter and the size of the ball—the large-caliber musket balls recovered from Zboriv may have come from the Dutch guns imported by the Polish Crown. The battlefield museum at Berestechko identified similar large musket balls as "bullets that killed Cossacks."[34]

Most musket balls recovered from this area of the battlefield of Zboriv are between 11 and 16 mm. Given the close proximity of these finds along a line of battle, it is possible that these rounds all belonged to a particular military unit. In the seventeenth century, dragoons carried a specific type of firearm, called a *bandolet*. This weapon was of a smaller caliber and preserved examples in the museums of Poland and Ukraine have a bore diameter of between 11 and 18 mm, with diameters of 15 to 16 mm most common. At the same time, however, other cavalry units used smaller caliber weapons. In addition, Eastern firearms tended to be of a smaller caliber. While some have suggested that it may be possible in the future to identify certain types of units by the caliber of the shot, the use of small-caliber weapons on both sides of the conflict precludes such an analysis.

During our survey we discovered a great variation in the actual musket balls. Unlike most projectiles that are round or exhibit uncut sprue from their casting, many of those recovered at Zboriv had an added or modified tail along the sprue, which is far more elaborate than a simple by-product of the casting process (see figure). Such additions are unusual, and besides being recovered at Berestechko and Zbarazh, are rarely recognized as such in the archaeological record.[35] Saint Remy, an eighteenth-century French scholar, noted that these tails were previously used to facilitate the construction of paper cartridge.[36] Unlike eighteenth-century cartridges, however, where both the ball and powder were inside a paper tube, makers of these earlier cartridges attached the paper tube to the sprue (see figure on page 202). Sometimes they added a special flange to the ball to help tie the paper cartridge. It is more than likely that the musket balls recovered at Zboriv were modified in such a manner to allow for the production of semi-fixed ammunition. An examination of the Cossack bullet molds recovered at Berestechko indicates that at least some of the molds were specifically modified to create extended sprue musket balls (see lower figure on page 202).

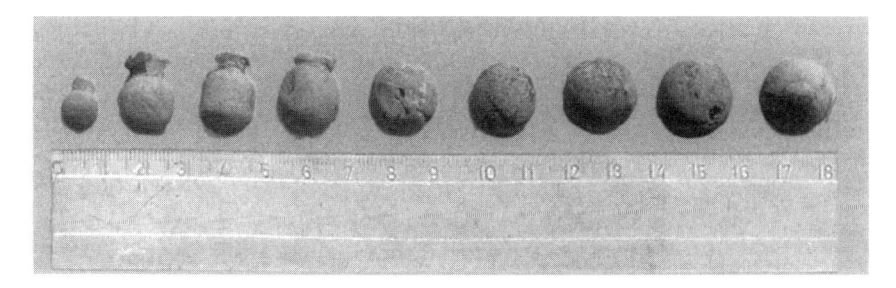

Examples of seventeenth-century bullets recovered at Zboriv.

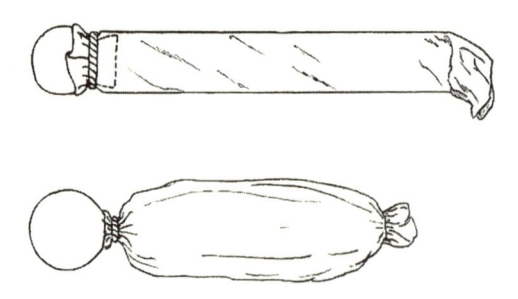

Early type of paper cartridge used with bullets with flanges (after Saint Remy). (Pierre Surirey de St Remy, Memoires d'Atillerir, Paris 1707)

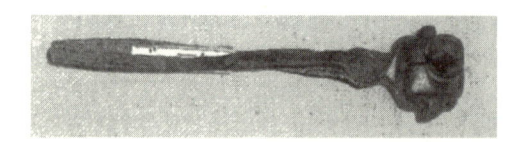

Single cavity bullet mold for the creation of extended sprue ordnance. (Berestechko, Ukraine)

The production of cartridges simplified the loading process. Previously, musketeers relied upon bandoleers of pre-measured powder charges. Lord Orrery, a seventeenth-century military writer, noted that "bandeleers are often apt to take fire, especially if the matchlock musket be used."[37] The results of such accidents could be quite lethal. Although mounted units used small metal cartridge boxes as early as the second half of the sixteenth century,[38] the overwhelming majority of European infantry continued to rely on bandoleers. The numerous leather and wood cartridge boxes recovered at Berestechko are among the earliest known examples of infantry cartridge boxes used in Europe but it is more than likely that the Swedes first developed infantry cartridge boxes. Cartridge boxes quickly became popular and in 1656, 17 cartridge boxes were included in an inventory list of munitions sent to the South River of New Netherlands.[39] Nevertheless, the lack of the recovery of any traces of wooden or metal powder holders from Zboriv, Zbarazh, or Berestechko suggests that these types of containers were no longer used along Europe's eastern frontier. Conversely, the recovery of gunflints from Zbarazh and Berestechko is a good indication that the more modern ignition system, one based on a spark rather than a match, was common along the Pontic Steppe.

While some may argue that the reduced diameter of the barrel reduced the overall effectiveness of "Eastern" firearms (an inherent low muzzle velocity and an increased tendency for the fouling of the barrel), the addition of an extended sprue to the musket ball may have produced a weapon system as effective as Western models. The result of adding an extended sprue to a small-caliber bullet is that when it is fired at a low muzzle velocity, the bullet may not fly symmetrically but rather wobbles through the air. Upon striking its target, the tumbling round bounces through the soft tissue of the body, while large-caliber bullets simply tear through both flesh and bone and exit the body. While such a small-caliber tumbling weapon system does not have the range of a more powerful large-caliber firearm, the wounds inflicted in such a manner can be horrific. Provided that the barrel had not become fouled after repeated firing, such small-caliber weapons could have proved to be just as effective as their larger-caliber counterparts. At this time, ballistic testing of this hypothesis is needed to verify the effectiveness of the "sprue ordnance."

The recovered military ordnance challenges many of the commonly held assumptions of the Cossack armies of the mid-seventeenth century. Most scholars agree that the Cossack rebels wanted to create a new political system that replaced the religious, economic, and cultural elite in the southeastern territories of the Commonwealth, but few also note that the military innovations employed by Cossacks were just as revolutionary. Not only were the rebel armies under the direction of innovative leaders who had significant military talent and expertise in engineering, but the weapon systems used by the rebels were among the most modern and technically developed in both Europe and Asia. Clearly, these armies may have looked rather raggedy, especially when compared to the silver and gold encrusted troops of the Commonwealth, but the Cossack army was a professional force equal to any on two continents.

Without a doubt, the Cossack army was a professional fighting force. The image of a rag-tag mob, although burned in the collective memory, is a stereotype of questionable utility. Rather, while turned out in non-regulated clothing and perhaps intermittently fed, these rebel long-serving Cossacks, former serfs, nobles, and Orthodox clergy adapted new military tactics and weapon systems. This may not be all that unusual, since these same revolutionaries were by their very nature vying to bring about a new social reality. Although existing military establishments are often among the most conservative segments of society, the results of the research from this program suggest that this rebel army, much like earlier and later revolutionary armies, adapted and incorporated the most recent and successful of the new technologies.

The identified section of the Polish defensive earthworks serves as a point of reference for further research. By taking into consideration any minute topographic features in the terrain that contemporary military commanders would have exploited to their advantage, it is possible to correlate the terrain with the features noted on the preserved 1649 map. Using this information, it becomes much easier to see how the actual battle developed. Additional analysis will allow us to identify sections of the battlefield where cultural resources may be present and will let us extrapolate the locations of fieldworks even in areas significantly impacted by modern development.

When compared with other battlefield surveys, our results at Zboriv were not unusual. For 10 years Dan Sivilich and his group of excavators have been returning to the same areas of the American Revolutionary War battlefield of Monmouth (New Jersey) and continue to flesh out the original model. After a decade's worth of research, they are now able to show how and why the battle developed the way it did. Clearly, the results achieved at Zboriv reflect the possibilities offered in studying battlefields and need to be continued. By using new technologies, coupling them with local topography, and comparing this information with the available documentary evidence, it is possible to gain new insights into one of the most important events in the history of Ukraine and East Central Europe.

NOTES

1. The term Cossack has evolved over time. Initially the term was used as a verb to indicate a specific part-time activity that men undertook when in the wild lands of the steppe. Throughout the sixteenth century, as magnates began to place ever increasing restrictions on peasants and subjugate them to ever-increasing servitude, many villagers fled to the steppe frontier. Not all Cossacks, however, were previously farmers—nobles, burghers, and former priests could also be found among this social estate. Though the majority of the Cossacks were ethnic Ukrainians, not all were, as Poles, Germans, Tatars, Russians, and even a few West Europeans joined their number. Over time, as these social outcasts became ever more skilled in the military arts, Cossack year-round fortified camps developed. Royal officials of the Commonwealth, fearful of the growing number of armed Cossacks, began recruiting these freemen as border guards.

2. While the modern-day Polish state considers itself to be the direct successor of the Polish-Lithuanian Commonwealth, it was in fact a multi-ethnic and multi-religious state where class was more important than nationality or religion. During the mid-seventeenth century, many old established Ukrainian nobles held key offices within the Polish-Lithuanian Commonwealth.

3. The Zaporozhian Sich refers to the Cossack armed camp located south of the Dnipro River rapids. Cossacks who chose to live in the Sich did so in stern simplicity without wives or families. The men were organized into military units and worked together for a common good.

4. Although most people think of Cossacks as horse-mounted troops, their earliest renown was as sailors who raided the Ottoman settlements along the Black Sea coast. During the middle of the seventeenth century, most Cossacks fought on foot or served as artillerymen.

5. Originally from the German word *Hauptmann*. Among the Ukrainian Cossacks, the Hetman was the highest military, administrative, and judicial office. This is not to be confused with the use of the title in the Commonwealth, where the term of hetman simply meant commander-in-chief and the highest military authority in the realm.

6. Although the text of the Treaty of Zboriv has survived and the register of Cossacks has been previously published, Ukrainian scholars such as the eminent historian Mykhailo Hrushevsky has interpreted the Zboriv Agreement as "hopeless" (2002: 575–654) or "compromised" (Krypiakevych 1954:165–172). More recently, the Canadian Ukrainian historian Frank Sysyn has indicated that "the guarantee of a forty-thousand-man Cossack army ensured Hetman Khmel'nyts'kyj his place as an almost independent ruler of the Ukraine" (Sysyn 1985:173).

7. As illustrated in a letter from Khrushchev to Stalin, Khmelnytsky was chosen not because he fought for Ukraine's liberation, but because of the union of Ukrainian and Russian peoples (Yekelchyk 2002:69).

8. Basarab 1982.

9. Kozachenko 1954.

10. While many scholars have devoted their attention to the battle of Zboriv, among the earliest and most influential studies remain Kubala 1896 and Fras 1932.

11. I. Krypiakevych published five separate accounts of the battle of Zboriv, but the most detailed description appears in 1929. A later account published by the same author in 1931 includes two maps, one which showed the disposition of forces at the time of the initial ambush and the second map illustrates the attacks of the second day. These two maps were later reprinted by Tyktor (1953).

12. Matskiv 1985.

13. Alexandrowicz 1995:15–23.

14. Sveshinkov 1993.

15. Vasyl'ev and Dzys 1988:2–6.

16. Such a result is not unexpected, since archaeologists who have relied on traditional testing methods of digging in depth rarely have been successful in identifying resources related to military engagements. Using traditional archaeological field methods at the American Civil War First Manassas (Bull Run) battlefield, for example, "only one artifact was found by shovel testing, while several hundred were found using metal detectors" (see Babits 2001:118).

17. Artifacts from these excavations are on display at the local museum in Zboriv.

18. Excavations of a burial pit from the Battle of Wisby, for example, provided a good indication of medieval warfare (Thordeman et al. 1939).

19. Scott and Fox 1987; Scott et al. 1989.

20. Foard 2001:90.

21. The most common artifacts recovered from the 2002 and 2004 survey are from later battles fought at Zboriv. Shrapnel balls, rifle cartridges, bullets, and artillery shell fragments litter the area of the 1649 battlefield. While the majority of these finds are thought to relate to an engagement fought during WWI, the recovery of dated American-manufactured Mosin-Nagaunt rifle cartridges from 1918 indicates that at least some of this early twentieth-century military ordnance relates to an engagement fought during the Chortkivs'ka Offensive in the summer of 1919, almost exactly on the 270th anniversary of the 1649 Battle of Zboriv.

22. The battlefield research at Zboriv was undertaken as a component of Strotsen's 2002 survey of the Zboriv region and was sanctioned by the archaeological license (*vidkrytyj lyst*) No. 216 (Strotsen 2003).

23. As during Scott's (Scott et al. 1989) research at Little Bighorn, where both Native Americans and European Americans took part in uncovering their joint history, the research of the 1649 campaign included both Polish and Ukrainian team members. Since the initial funding for this research project came from a Fulbright-Hays Faculty Research Fellowship, peace building and preservation of historical memory was a critical component of the research and thus it was important that all sides be represented. The students from the departments of history and archaeology who took part in this research came from various institutions, including the University of Warsaw, L'viv Polytechnic University, and Drohobychskyj Pedagogic University.

24. Foard 2001:89.
25. Wimmer 1978:202.
26. Griess 1984:48.
27. Valerij Smolij and Valerij Stepankov, *Bohdan Khmel'nyts'kyj*, Kiev, 2003, 200.
28. Ivan Krypiakevych, "Z Istorii Zborova," 25.
29. Guillaume Le Vasseur, le Sieur de Beauplan, *Description D'Ukranie* [1660], L'viv, 1998.
30. Pollard and Oliver 2002:211.
31. Das Heeresgeschichtliche Museum (Museum of Military History), Vienna, Austria.
32. Górski 1902:121.
33. For a discussion of exported arms from Holland, see Puype 1985.
34. Museum of the "Cossack Mounds," National Historical Memorial Preserve "Field of the Berestechko Battle," Pliasheva Village, Radyvylivs'kyj Region, Rivnens'ka oblast, Ukraine.
35. A sprue is normally created as part of the casting process, but usually it is removed before the ball is fired. As such, unless a scholar is specifically looking for such sprues, they would most likely conclude that these were unfinished balls.
36. Saint Remy 1707.
37. Peterson 1956:63.
38. Krenn and Karcheski 1992:88.
39. O'Callaghan 1855:645.

REFERENCES CITED

Alexandrowicz, Stanislaw. 1995. Plany Obronnych Obozów wojsk Polskich pod Zbarażem i Zborowem z Roku 1649. *Fortyfikacja*, Vol. 1.
Babits, Lawrence E. 2001. Book Archaeology of the Cowpens Battlefield. In P. W. M. Freeman and A. Pollard (eds.), *Fields of Conflict: Progress and Prospect in Battlefield Archaeology*, 117–126. BAR International Series 958.
Basarab, John. 1982. *Pereiaslav 1654: A Historiographic Study*. Edmonton.
Foard, Glenn. 2001. The Archaeology of Attack: Battles and Sieges of the English Civil War. In P. W. M. Freeman and A. Pollard (eds.), *Fields of Conflict: Progress and Prospect in Battlefield Archaeology*, 97–104. BAR International Series 958.
Fras, Ludwick. 1932. Bitwa pod Zborowem w r. 1649. *Kwartalnik Historzcynz* 46.
Górski, Konstanty. 1902. *Historya Artyleryi Polskiej*. Warszawa.
Griess, Thomas E. (ed.). 1984. *The Dawn of Modern Warfare*. West Point Military History Series, Wayne.

Hrushevsky, Mykhailo. 2002. *History of Ukraine-Rus'*. Canadian Institute of Ukrainian Studies Press, Vol. 8. Toronto.
Kozachenko, A. I. 1929. *Zhyttia i Znannia*, No. 10–11, L'viv.
Kozachenko, A. I. 1931. *Litopys Chervonoi Kalyny*, No. 10, L'viv.
Kozachenko, A. I. 1954. *Bor'ba Ukrainskoho naroda za vossoedinenie s Rossiei*. Moscow.
Krenn, Peter, and Walter J. Karcheski Jr. 1992. *Imperial Austria: Treasures of Art, Arms and Armor from the State of Styria*. Munich.
Krypiakevych, I. 1954. *Bohdan Khmelnyts'kyj*. Kiev.
Krypiakevych, Ivan, 1942. Z Istorii Zborova, In Istoriia Ukrainy by Ivan Krypiakevych. Vernyhora, Vienna.
Kubala, L. 1896. *Oblężenie Zbaraża i pokój pod Zborowem, Szkice historyczne*. Krakow.
Le Vasseur, Guillaume le Sieur de Beauplan, 1998. *Description D'Ukranie* [1660], L'viv.
Matskiv, Teodir. 1985. Zborivs'kyj Dohovir u svitli nimets'koi j anhlijs'koi presy z 1649. *Zborivshchyna*, Naukove Tovarystvo im Shevchenka, Ukrains'kyj Arkhiv, Vol. 38. Toronto.
O'Callaghan, Edmund B. (ed.). 1855. *Documents Relative to the Colonial History of New York*, Vol. 1. Albany.
Peterson, Harold L. 1956. *Arms and Armor in Colonial America 1526–1783*. Stackpole, Harrisburg, PA.
Pollard, Tony, and Neil Oliver. 2002. *Two Men in a Trench: Battlefield Archaeology— The Key to Unlocking the Past*. London.
Puype, Jan Piet. 1985. Dutch and Other Flintlocks from Seventeenth Century Iroquois Sites. Proceedings of the 1984 Trade Gun Conference, Research Records, No.18, Vol. 1. Rochester Museum and Science Center, Rochester, NY.
de Saint Remy, Pierre Surirey. 1707. *Memoires d'Artillerie*, second edition, 2 vols. Paris.
Scott, Douglas D., and Richard A. Fox Jr. 1987. *Archaeological Insights into the Custer Battle: An Assessment of the 1984 Field Season*. University of Oklahoma Press, Norman.
Scott, Douglas D., Richard. A. Fox Jr., Melissa A. Connor, and D. Harmon. 1989. *Archaeological Perspectives on the Battle of the Little Bighorn*. University of Oklahoma Press, Norman.
Smolij, Valerij and Valerij Stepankov, 2003. *Bohdan Khmel'nyts'kyj*, Kiev.
Strotsen, B. S. 2003. *Zvit pro arkheolohichni rozvidky v okolytsiakh m. Zborova (Ternopil's'ka obl.) u 2002 r.* Ternopil's'ka oblasna komunal'na inspektsia okhorony pam'iatok istorii ta kul'tury, Ternopil.
Sveshnikov, I. K. 1993. *Bytva pid Berestechkom*. L'viv.
Sysyn, Frank. 1985. *Between Poland and Ukraine: The Dilemma of Adam Kysil 1600–1653*. Cambridge, MA.
Thordeman, Bengt, Poul Noörlund, and Bo E. Ingelmark. 1939. *Armour from the Battle of Wisby, 1361*, Vol. 1, Kungl. Vitterhets Historie OCH Antikvitets Akademien, Stockholm.
Tyktor, Ivan. 1953. *Istoriia Ukrains'koho Vijs'ka*. Winnipeg.
Vasyl'ev, Aleksej, and Igor Dzys. 1988. Bytva pod Berestechkom, *Zeughaus* 8(2)1988:2–6.
Bytva pod Berestechkom", *Zeughaus* No 8. Moscow.
Wimmer, Jan. 1978. *Historia Piechoty Polskiej do 1864*. Warsaw.
Yekelchyk, Serhy. 2002. Stalinist Patriotism as Imperial Discourse: Reconciling the Ukrainian and Russian "Historic Pasts," 1939–45. *Kritika* 3(1):51–80.

Camden: Salvaging Data from a Heavily Collected Battlefield

James B. Legg & Steven D. Smith

THE REVOLUTIONARY WAR Battle of Camden, August 16, 1780, was a disaster for the American cause, destroying the second of three armies sent south to oppose the British occupation of the Carolinas and Georgia.[1] While the fighting spread over an area of some 600 acres, until recently commemoration was limited to a six-acre tract owned by the Daughters of the American Revolution, while the remainder of the battlefield was an expanse of pine plantation. In 2000, Katawba Valley Land Trust and the Palmetto Conservation Foundation (PCF) negotiated a conservation easement for the 310-acre core of the Camden Battlefield, and in 2003 PCF purchased the remaining property rights (see figure). Preservation and interpretation of the battlefield are now the focus of a well-organized consortium of preservationists and historians called the Battle of Camden Project, including archaeologists from the South Carolina Institute of Archaeology and Anthropology. A critical component of this effort is an attempt to define battlefield boundaries and to document battle events across the modern terrain. Controlled metal detector collection, now *de rigueur* in battlefield interpretation, would seem to be the obvious means of addressing these questions archaeologically.

Unfortunately, the battlefield has been very heavily collected by relic hunters for at least three decades. Some collectors consider the site virtually "hunted out," and report having spent entire days detecting there without recovering an artifact. Our approach to this problem has been two-fold. First, in 2001 we initiated the Camden Battlefield Collector Survey, a pragmatic effort to salvage as much information as possible from private collectors. This survey, while not providing the kind of well-controlled data we would prefer, has, at a minimum, assisted in defining battlefield boundaries, and provided new insights into battle events. Interestingly, the synthesis of collector and historical data suggests two very different battle scenarios, each with its camp of supporters. Second, we have defied the predictions of the collector community, and have begun a controlled metal detector sampling regime across the

CAMDEN 209

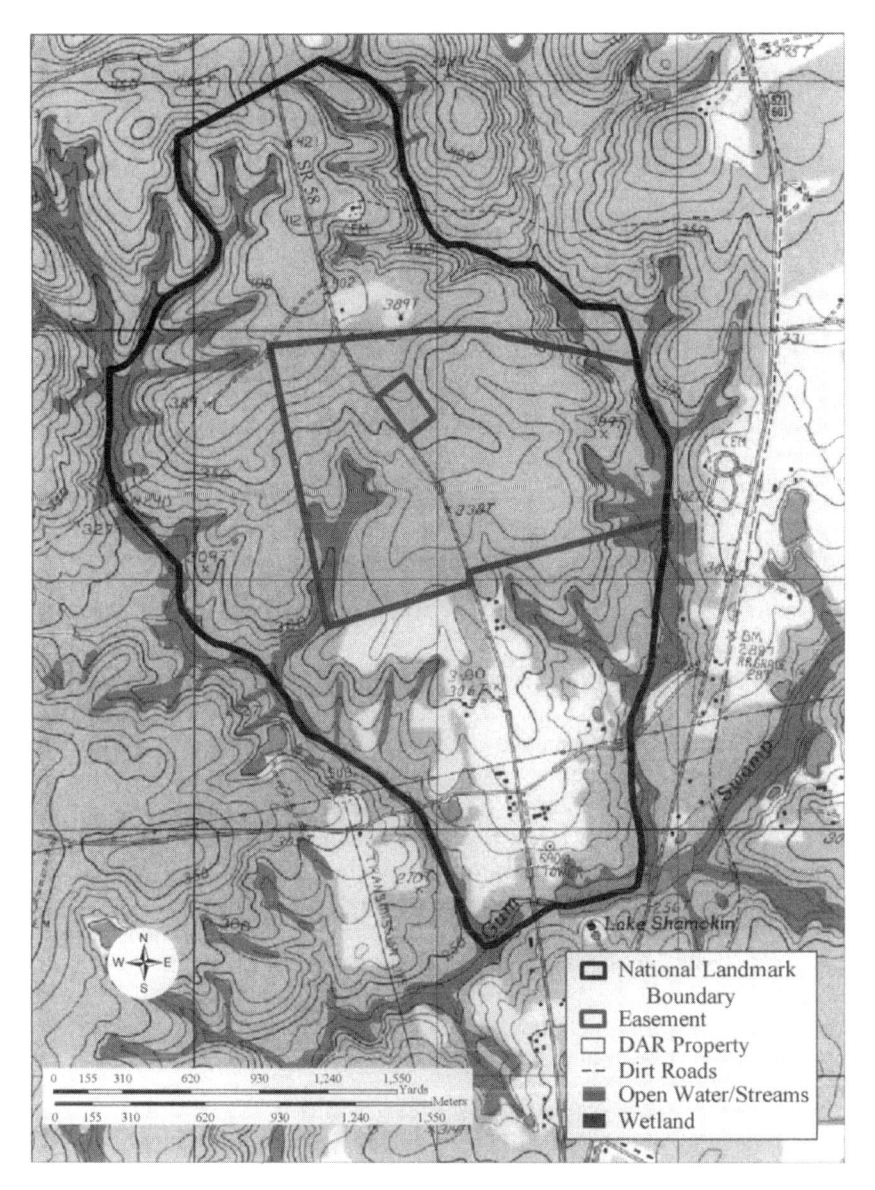

Modern topographic map of battlefield showing boundaries and easements. (South Carolina Institute of Archaeology and Anthropology)

battlefield in the hope of acquiring even a small sample of precise data that would enhance our collector survey data. The metal detecting project is in a preliminary stage, but has already shown surprisingly good results. This chapter describes the first of our two-fold approach, the Camden Battlefield

Collector's Survey, and our struggle to accurately interpret the combined historical and collector evidence.

THE BATTLE OF CAMDEN

The broad outlines of battle chronology are generally agreed upon, if the precise geographic placement of various units and timing are not.[2] When Horatio Gates led his Southern American army from North Carolina into South Carolina in early August of 1780, he was hoping to force the British from their fortified post at Camden, South Carolina. But Lord Cornwallis saw Gates's approach as an opportunity rather than a threat. At 10:00 in the evening of August 15, Cornwallis led his army out of Camden with the intention of attacking the superior force of Americans in their camp at Rugeley's Mill, 13 miles north of Camden. Gates, at that same hour, began a march south from Rugeley's Mill, intending to occupy favorable terrain about six miles north of Camden. At about 2:30 on the moonlit morning of August 16, the two columns collided on a sandy, forested plateau about seven miles north of Camden, and after a brief but fierce skirmish both sides drew off to wait the dawn only two hours away.

Battle participants agreed on certain battlefield terrain features that help in interpreting the battlefield today. Both sides were pleased that they could anchor their flanks on swamps at opposite ends of their lines. The battlefield was wooded, but very unlike the present pine plantation: it was an old-growth longleaf pine forest, the huge trees widely spaced, with their limbs starting 40 feet above the forest floor. No eyewitness indicated any problems maneuvering in the woods. The ground was clear of brush, but covered with pine straw and tall wiregrass. The sandy road from Rugeley's to Camden bisected the battlefield from north to south, perpendicular to the opposing lines, and it was used by both sides to guide the placement of their units. The relative positions of the two armies at the opening of the battle (see figure) are well documented, and while these unit dispositions are not controversial, the placement of the entire array on the present landscape *is*, as we shall see, in dispute.

Gates deployed four small regiments of the 2nd Maryland Brigade, including the Delaware Regiment, with their right flank anchored on a swampy draw. In the center was the North Carolina militia. On the left was Virginia militia, light infantry, and a few cavalry. Two hundred yards to the center rear of the front line, straddling the road, was the 1st Maryland Brigade, in reserve. American artillery included two guns with the 2nd Maryland Brigade, three straddling the road, and two in the reserve line with the 1st Maryland Brigade. Total American strength was about 3,500, but of this number only 900 were Continentals. While the Continentals and North Carolina militia had had a two-day rest before the march, the Virginia militia had arrived at

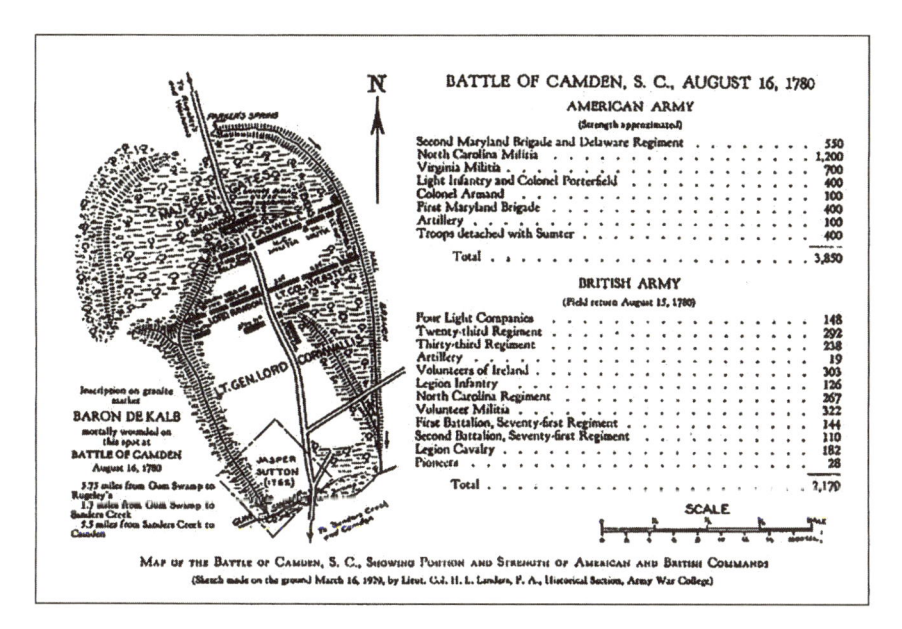

Colonel H. L. Landers map of the Battle of Camden showing combatants. ("The Battle of Camden, South Carolina, August 16, 1780" by Lieutenant Colonel H. L. Landers, F.A.U.S. House of Representatives House Document No. 12, 71st Congress, 1st Session, Washington, DC)

Rugeley's only the day before. They were exhausted. But none of the American soldiers were in much shape for the upcoming fight as they had been fed a full meal of bread, meat, and a gill of molasses that evening before the march, and it was having an obvious effect on their digestive systems.

Cornwallis did not fully deploy his troops until dawn, when they quickly and professionally deployed left and right of the road. East of the road to the British right, Cornwallis deployed a regular brigade including light infantry companies, the 23rd Regiment and the 33rd Regiment. Left of the road, he deployed his Loyalist brigade, under Francis Lord Rawdon, including the Volunteers of Ireland Regiment, the British Legion infantry, and Loyalist militia. Cornwallis's artillery, consisting of two 6-pounders and two 3-pounders, were placed near the center. The 71st Highland Regiment was in reserve, one battalion behind the British right and one behind the left, along with the British Legion dragoons under Banastre Tarleton along the road. Cornwallis's force consisted of 2,179 officers and men.

At dawn, an American artillery captain on the front line announced to Colonel Otho Williams that he could see the British right advancing some 200 yards in front of the American left. Williams ordered the officer to open fire and immediately rode to General Gates who had just placed himself behind the American second line. Williams reported to Gates that the British were displaying to their right and that an advance by the Americans might have a "fortunate effect."[3] With Gates's approval Williams quickly made his way to General Stevens, commander of the Virginia militia, and passed on the order to advance. Williams also saw that a few skirmishers in front of the Americans might blunt the British attack. But his effort was futile since, by that time, the British were closing. The sight of British fixed bayonets was more than the militia wanted and they immediately took flight, most without firing a shot. The effect along the line was devastating, and like dominos, the North Carolina militia followed the Virginians. Within mere seconds, the American left melted away. Only a small body of North Carolinians anchored on the artillery and Continental right held firm. After Williams rode off with orders for the militia to advance, Gates had ordered the 1st Maryland to advance to the left in support of the militia and also ordered the American right to advance. Gun smoke soon mixed with the moist morning air, obscuring the combatants.

The British right quickly moved through the position vacated by the American militia, but were met by the advancing 1st Maryland Brigade who had opened their ranks to let the militia through, reformed, and were attempting to form a new line with the 2nd Maryland. However, two Continental brigades were never able to connect and they remained widely separated throughout the battle—in effect, the American left and right fought different battles. Pressed on their front and left flank, the 1st Maryland Brigade had to refuse their exposed left and eventually their line ended up at a right angle with the 2nd Maryland Brigade. From there the 1st Maryland rallied and fell back as many as three times before eventually being overpowered. Meanwhile, the American right advanced and nearly broke the Loyalists on the British left. Unable to see what was happening to the 1st Maryland Brigade, the 2nd Maryland pushed forward, thinking they were winning the battle. With the two American forces fighting in isolation, Cornwallis ordered Banastre Tarleton's dragoons and the 71st Highlanders into the gap and against the 1st Maryland's left. The American Continentals were out-flanked and overrun. Totally disorganized, many Continentals died on the battlefield, while others fought their way off in small groups.

Gates and much of the senior command on the American left were not around to watch the destruction of the Continentals. They had attempted to rally the militia and been swept away in the panic. Gates had been pushed off the battlefield and on up the road past Rugeley's. He rode on to Charlotte, North Carolina, and eventually reached Hillsboro. American casualty figures for Camden are not exactly known. Cornwallis reported 800 to 900 Americans killed and about 1,000 prisoners taken, but this was certainly an inflated figure. A good number of Continentals dragged into Charlotte over the next few days. But not the General Johann Baron de Kalb, who led the American 2nd Maryland and Delaware Regiments on the American right, and was mortally wounded. As for the British, although it is clear that they won a resounding victory, it was costly. Cornwallis listed 68 killed, 245 wounded, and 11 missing, all veterans that would be difficult to replace.

POST-WAR BATTLEFIELD HISTORY

The land use history of the Camden battlefield since 1780 is essential to understanding the archaeological resource today.[4] In 1786, a visitor reported seeing shattered trees and unburied bones of soldiers and horses, but a visitor in 1830 reported that not a vestige of the battle remained.[5] Historian Benson Lossing examined the Camden battlefield in January 1849, and recorded the first substantial description of the site:

> The hottest of the engagement occurred upon the hill, just before descending to Sander's Creek [Gum Swamp Creek] from the north, now, as then, covered with an open forest of pine-trees. . . . Many of the old trees yet bear marks of the battle, the scars of the bullets being made very distinct by large protuberances. . . . Within half a mile[6] of Sanders Creek [Gum Swamp Creek], on the north side, are some old fields, dotted with shrub pines, where the hottest of the battle was fought. A large concavity near the road, filled with hawthorns, was pointed out to me as the spot where many of the dead were buried.[7]

The Camden battlefield was still wooded at the beginning of the twentieth century, but Camden County historians Thomas Kirkland and Robert Kennedy reported that the character of the forest had changed:

> At the date of the battle the ground was occupied by a close array of tall and stately pines, limbless to a height of forty or fifty feet. These, by the process of turpentining, have been reduced to a scanty few, so that not many of those remain that witnessed the battle. Their thinning has allowed to come up a growth of scrub oaks, which in summer obscure the view much more than did the pines. . . . Those living in that neighborhood have found amongst the leaves of the woods many an old buckle, button, bayonet, bullet, cannon ball, flintlock. . . .[8]

Kirkland and Kennedy found "grape shot and bullets in half-burnt and decayed trees."[9] Their map of the Camden battlefield shows the location of the "Pine where De Kalb lay wounded," which was replaced by the monument to Baron de Kalb erected by the Hobkirk Hill Chapter of the Daughters of the American Revolution in 1909.[10] In March 1929, Lt. Col. H. L. Landers visited the battlefield while researching the battle. His map, prepared for the War Department (see figure), depicts the battlefield south of the present DAR property as fields.

In 1930, the Hobkirk Hill Chapter of the DAR secured an option to buy 425.5 acres of the battlefield for about $6,500, but the land was not purchased. In 1942, the chapter did acquire five additional acres around the de Kalb monument, adding to a single acre acquired there in 1912.[11] An aerial photograph taken in 1949 shows that nearly all of the battlefield south of the DAR property was under cultivation, while the areas to the north and west of the DAR property were in woods, or pine savannah. By 1964, the fields seen in 1949 and the farm site east of Route 58 are in pine plantation, while the formerly wooded areas to the north have been timbered, but are *not* in agricultural fields. The DAR property stands out as a small rectangle of original (if thinned) longleaf pine forest. A massive clear-cutting timber program completed in 1998 stripped any remaining semblance of the battlefield's 1780 appearance.

In summary, it is clear that the local vegetation has gone through several changes since the battle, but importantly the topography is intact and undeveloped. The southern portion of the battlefield was cultivated, while the northern portion was repeatedly timbered but not plowed for agriculture.

THE CAMDEN BATTLEFIELD COLLECTOR SURVEY

The impetus for the present study dates to December 2000, when the first author was asked by the Palmetto Conservation Foundation (PCF) to assess the battlefield's archaeological integrity and potential, and to suggest ways in which archaeology might assist in the battlefield interpretation. He noted that the battlefield was undeveloped and relatively well preserved as a landscape, but as an archaeological resource it had suffered serious damage through decades of relic collecting. He suggested that a concerted effort be made to identify and interview individuals who have collected from the site in an effort to salvage whatever information they could provide and would be helpful in interpretation. PCF contracted with the South Carolina Institute of Archaeology and Anthropology in 2001 to conduct the Camden Battlefield Collector Survey, with funding provided by a grant from the National Park Service's American Battlefield Protection Program (ABPP).[12] The survey is now an ongoing project assisted by a second grant from the ABPP in 2003.

The primary goal was the compilation of a mapped record of artifact distributions from private collector information that might help to tie the Battle of Camden, as understood from the historical record, to the present landscape. Secondary goals included the location of unmarked battlefield burials, and the detailed documentation of artifacts from the battlefield in private collections. While the Collector Survey is by no means complete, it has long since yielded far more information than originally envisioned. There are currently 12 collections fully documented and three partially documented, and at least three additional collectors have been identified. In addition, three important Camden collections have been donated to the project for public ownership, and two more are informally promised.

Data collection methods have been simple and informal, involving on-site visits, phone conversations, and e-mail. Seven collectors were already known to the authors, PCF, or the Camden Battlefield Project, and these collectors introduced others. Initially, not knowing how best to proceed with the collectors, or what level of data to expect, it was hoped at a minimum to accomplish the following tasks for each informant:

1. A meeting on the site, with a walking discussion/interview regarding the collector's finds and impressions, and the individual's collecting history.
2. Recording on a standard base map of the "find spots" of as many particular, described artifacts as possible, together with any general observations.
3. Examination of the collection, if available, and photographic documentation of selected artifacts.

In the end, there was considerable variation among the interviews and the results, largely dictated by the kinds of information offered by the informant. All of the collectors recorded to date have shown great enthusiasm for both the battlefield preservation project and the archaeological project, in spite of the fact that the public effort has put an end to artifact digging. Only two collectors who were contacted ultimately did not follow through with formal recording, and there is still hope for both of those individuals. Two collectors insisted on anonymity, but were otherwise very helpful, and both donated their entire, intact collections to the project. Other collectors expressed willingness to eventually donate their collections if the material goes to a local public facility that will properly curate and exhibit their materials. Once it was clear around the collector community that our goals were to preserve and understand the battlefield, as opposed to confiscating collections or prosecuting the removal of artifacts, more collectors were happy to cooperate with the project. Overall, our informants were pleased with the project, even if some differ with our interpretations.

As noted, the quality of the data recorded varies considerably. No collector provided specific proveniences for ammunition specimens (below), but other battle artifacts of any sort were relatively rare finds, and consequently, their provenience was memorable. In every case, the informants were able to map nearly all of their individual finds *other than lead shot*. The confidence with which artifacts were plotted varied. On the poor end of the scale, a collector might indicate an artifact's location with a wave of a hand in the direction of a clump of weeds – perhaps a 20-meter margin of error. Much of this uncertainty is the result of the unfortunate clear-cutting in 1998, which eliminated the collector's visual frame of reference. On the opposite end of the scale, two collectors used GPS instruments to record their finds, which they cataloged, photographed, and presented on CD-ROM. Still other collectors previously had mapped their finds on their own sketch maps, and their information was readily transferred to a standard base map. Even the most general "plots" of individual items were recorded as points, and all such proveniences were considered adequate for the overall, large-scale distributional information that was sought. While some may question the precision of the provenience data, it is argued that even if every plotted item were reassigned to a random location within 100 meters of its original plot, it would not change any conclusions inferred from the large-scale artifact distributions provided by the data.

All data, from generalized ammunition distribution maps to precise GPS locations, were transferred onto enlarged USGS Camden North quad maps, and each plotted artifact was described in an accompanying catalog. Each artifact was assigned a functional class code, including:

S: Lead shot—musket balls, buckshot, and intermediate shot for pistols, rifles, etc.

A: Arms and accoutrement parts—gun parts, gun tools, bayonets, scabbard and cartridge box hardware, etc.

C: Clothing objects—military and civilian buttons, knee buckles, shoe buckles, neck stock buckles.

G: Iron and lead canister balls.

M: Miscellaneous objects that may or may not be battle artifacts, but which plausibly date to the eighteenth century—eating utensils, wrought iron hardware, iron and brass frame buckles, etc.

N: Miscellaneous objects that are clearly not battle artifacts, but were nevertheless recorded in a private collection or collected during the metal detector survey (e.g., an 1829 dime).

By far the most common artifacts recovered by the collectors were lead shot, chiefly musket balls, and buckshot from musket buck and ball cartridges. These mundane projectiles were ubiquitous, and as a result none of the collectors we have interviewed maintained specific location information for particular ammunition specimens in their collections. More than 2,000 musket balls and buckshot were collected by the informants, but their provenience is remembered only in very general terms. Two collectors had bagged most of their lead shot by various described proveniences (e.g., "west of highway, head of ravine"). Three other collectors maintained sketch maps that indicated quantities of lead shot recovered from different parts of the battlefield, but these notations were not linked to particular specimens. The remaining collectors combined all of their shot into a single collection. The collector ammunition data is rough and incomplete. Nevertheless, the data from the five collections about which something is known, together with observations from several collectors concerning lead shot distribution, have been combined to prepare a generalized lead shot density map (see figure). This distribution necessarily combines fired and unfired shot of all calibers, but it includes no areas that were dominated by unfired ammunition, which would indicate a camp or other non-combat episode. In the private collections as well as in the metal detector survey, the ratio of fired to unfired balls is consistently about three or four to one.

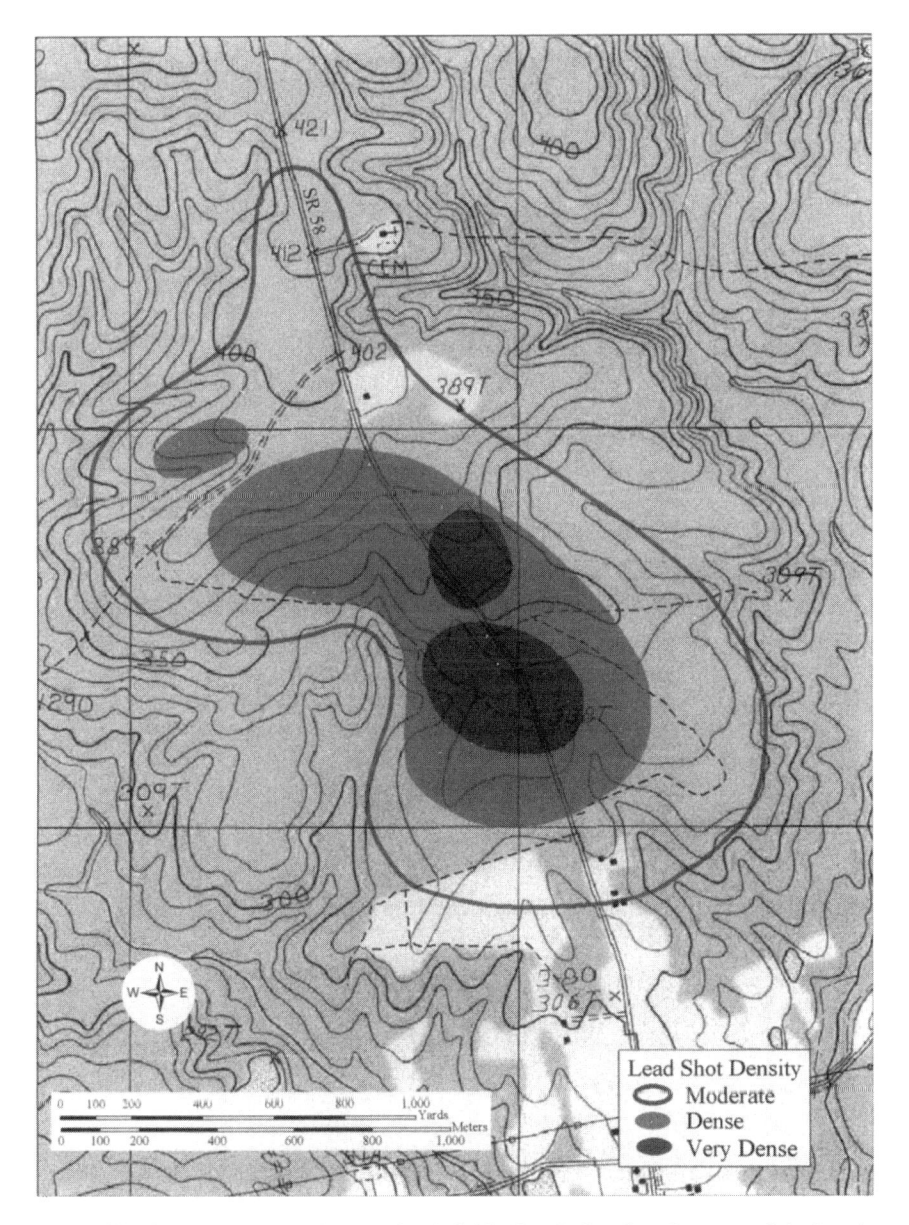

Map of lead shot density at Camden battlefield. (South Carolina Institute of Archaeology and Anthropology)

For artifacts other than lead shot, GIS map layers have been created that illustrate the plotted finds in each collection. The most useful product of the Collector Survey is the next step—maps showing finds, by functional class, of all collections combined. This has yielded distribution maps showing arms and accoutrement artifacts (see figure), clothing artifacts, and artillery canister balls (see figure) from all private collections. Combined with the admittedly less precise data on the ammunition density map (see figure), this information is proving very valuable in reconstructing the battle.

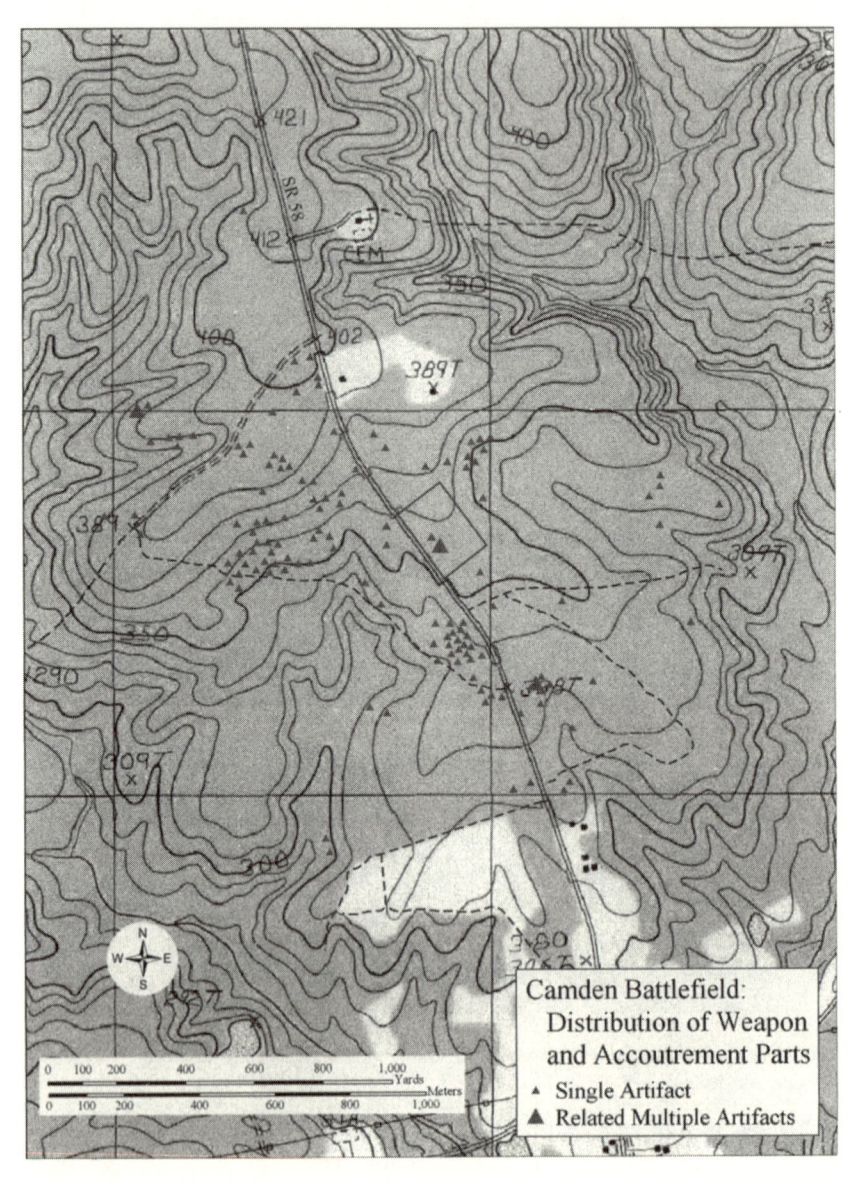

Map of the distribution of weapon and accoutrement parts at Camden battlefield. (South Carolina Institute of Archaeology and Anthropology)

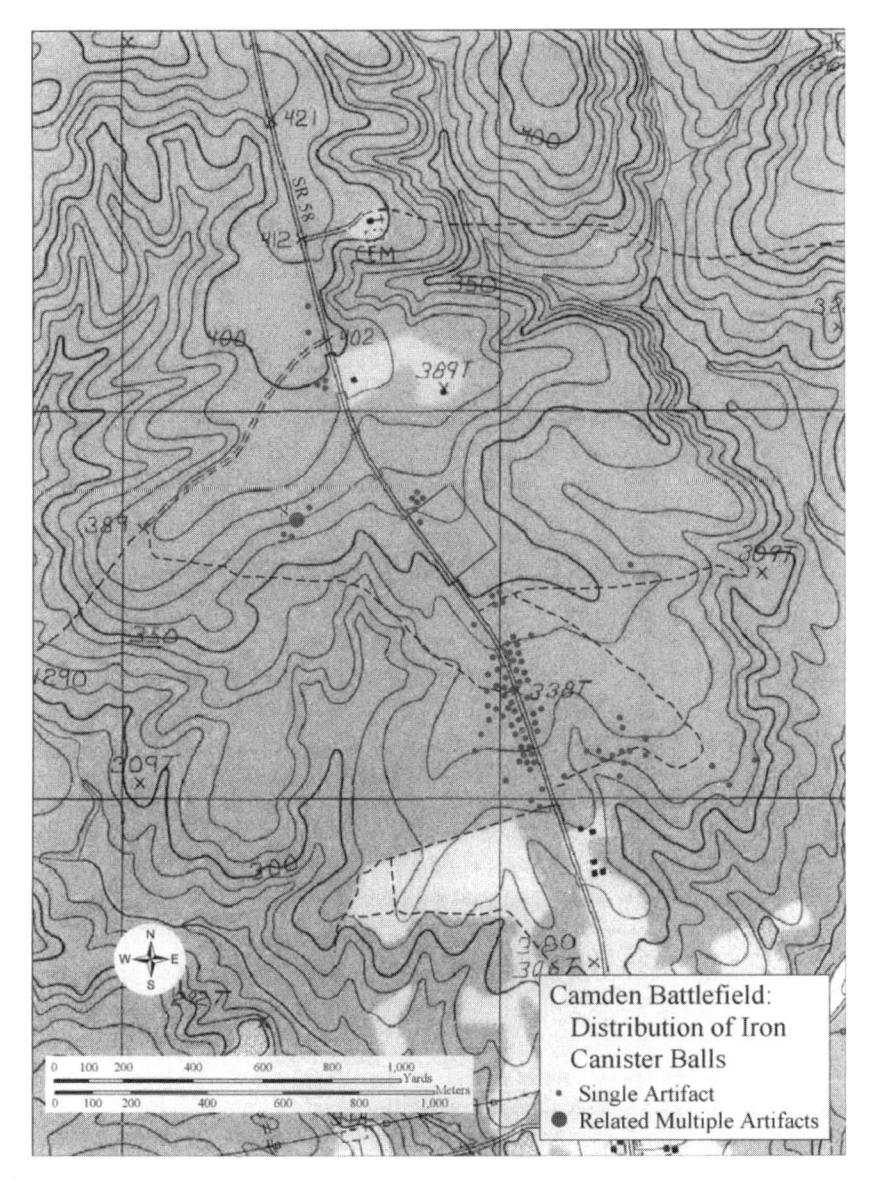

Map of the distribution of canister balls at Camden battlefield. (South Carolina Institute of Archaeology and Anthropology)

An important limitation in the Collector Survey results to date has been the failure to locate any informant who seriously collected from the site prior to 1979 or 1980, when "Anonymous Collector #1" first visited the battlefield. By that time metal detectors had been in use on Civil War battlefields for about 30 years, and indeed the most active and "productive" era of battlefield metal detecting was already over. This is unfortunate because an unprotected site as obvious as the Camden battlefield must have been heavily collected by many different individuals before 1979. Collector #1 reported that by then the entire battlefield as he understood it showed the tell-tale signs of heavy collecting in the past—small, eroded holes, discarded non-battle artifacts on the ground surface, and a scarcity of "easy" artifact readings. Thus, even the present collector data must be considered only a reasonably representative "shadow" of the material originally present, before the advent of metal detectors. The search for earlier informants continues.

One of the stated goals of the Collector Survey was to locate battlefield burials. Some or all of the men killed in action in the Battle of Camden were buried on the field in unmarked graves, and a number of these, confirmed or probable, have been reported by collectors. To date the Collector Survey has recorded the existence of eight burials, six of them certain and two more that are "probable." Of the six certain graves, only three can presently be plotted with any certainty—the others are now only generally located, due to the clear-cutting of 1998. Of the eight burials, one was British, four were Continentals, and three were indeterminate. There are probably between 200 and 300 burials on the field, but the only ones found happened to include metallic artifacts that were shallow enough to detect. Others may be too deep to detect, or the remains may have been stripped of clothing, shoes, and equipment—one of the "indeterminate" individuals bore no artifacts at all other than a musket ball embedded in his chest.

As discussed below, the Collector Survey and other information have indicated an interpretation of the battlefield that the authors believe is essentially correct. That interpretation is not free of controversy, but as the Collector Survey and other research efforts continue, it is hoped that a consensus can be arrived at that all interested parties (not merely the authors) can agree upon. The Camden Collector Survey has already resulted in three important conclusions that are not controversial:

1. Regardless of initial unit placements and subsequent movements, the outermost density boundary encompasses the area of significant action during the Battle of Camden (see figure).
2. A minority, but substantial part of the battlefield is located outside of the present conservation easement, to the north and northwest, on property that is currently unprotected.
3. Unmarked battlefield graves exist both within the conservation easement and on unprotected private property.

CAMDEN BATTLEFIELD INTERPRETATION

The most important goal of both the Collector Survey and the metal detector sampling effort has been to better understand how the Battle of Camden unfolded across the present landscape. Where were the armies initially deployed, and where did they maneuver? In the interpretation below, we synthesize what has been learned into a battle scenario tied to the modern geography. As new data emerges, it is hoped that this scenario will be refined, improving our understanding of the historical events, illuminating factors such as visibility, timing, and duration of movements, and firepower effectiveness. Obviously, this is not the last word about the Battle of Camden, but this scenario is offered as a "line of departure" for future debate.

The significant action in the Battle of Camden can be confidently located within the outermost boundary (see figure on page 217). This area encompasses the traditional battlefield, and while there has been very little battle material found beyond the boundary, thousands of battle artifacts have been recovered from within it. Unfortunately this leaves more than enough terrain for a variety of possible interpretations, and the historical and material evidence is admittedly complex. Two possible interpretations have emerged, which for clarity, are called the Southern and Northern Solutions. The authors strongly favor the Southern Solution, while some other serious students of the battle champion the significantly different Northern Solution. Both interpretations are outlined below, followed by an analysis of why the authors favor the Southern Solution.

The Southern Solution

The initial positions of the opposing forces as championed in the Southern Solution are depicted in the figure on page 222. In this interpretation, the dense concentration of material in the south-central portion of the battlefield (see figures) marks the protracted fight between the American right wing under Baron de Kalb and the British left wing (and 33rd Regiment) under Lord Rawdon. The vicinity of the DAR property is the site of the isolated struggle by the American reserve, the 1st Maryland Brigade, against the British right wing. The heavy scatter of material stretching far to the west of the DAR property probably represents the envelopment and rout, and/or capture of the remnants of both American brigades. The small, isolated concentration in the extreme northwest appears to represent an undocumented "last stand" by some portion of the American army—on this last point both factions agree. This interpretation provides a plausible reading of the artifact densities in the three figures above—the southern artifact concentration represents the intense combat between the British left and the American right, while that in the area of the DAR property represents the struggle of the American left as they advance, fall back, rally and stand again, ultimately ending up entirely behind the American right, where they collapse and many surrender.

The Northern Solution

The alternate interpretation, the Northern Solution, begins the battle with the two armies positioned several hundred yards further north, with the British line crossing the road at about the middle of the DAR property, where the Southern Solution places the American reserve (see figure). In this scenario, the extensive concentration of artifacts running west from the vicinity of the DAR property (see figure) represents the entire day battle, with the artifact

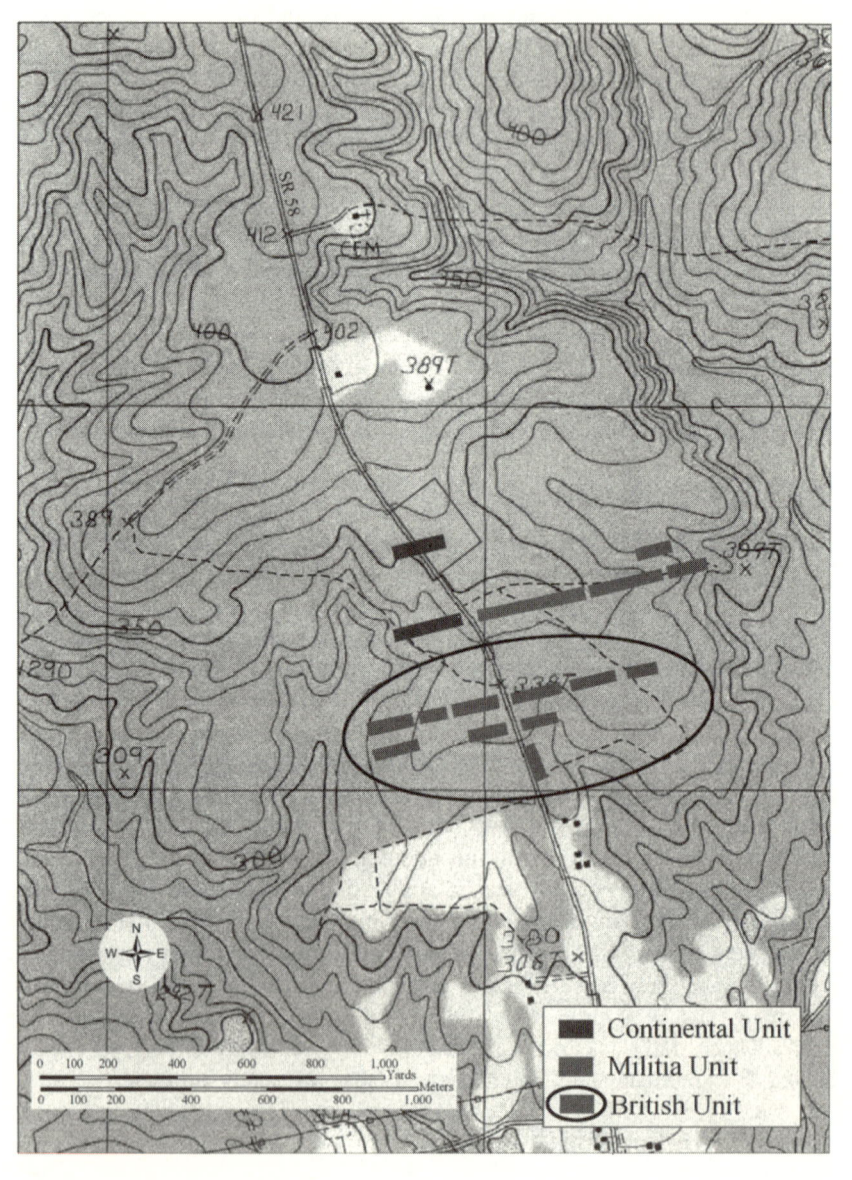

Initial deployment of combatants on modern topographic map at Camden battlefield. (South Carolina Institute of Archaeology and Anthropology)

concentration to the south interpreted as the site of the night meeting engagement only. The Northern Solution is favored by several collectors who found the bulk of their artifacts in the battlefield's northern section.[13]

Resolution

These "Southern" and "Northern" interpretations are so different that one or the other must ultimately be discounted as incorrect if the battle is to be tied to the present landscape. The strongest argument favoring the Northern Solution is the remarkable array of artifacts recovered by several collectors in an area running west from the DAR property for some 500 yards (see figure). This area yielded artifacts which were rare or absent on other portions of the field, including numerous complete shoe buckles (some in matching pairs), large gun parts, bayonets, and clusters of uniform buttons, as well as fired and unfired musket ammunition. In contrast, these same collectors found relatively little to the south, where the Southern Solution places the hardest fighting.[14] In spite of these intriguing findings, a careful study of all of the available evidence, including the artifact distributions, strongly favors the Southern Solution. Four important areas of evidence support the Southern Solution, including: (1) primary historical sources regarding the combatants' initial deployment; (2) artifact distributions in light of land use history; (3) artifact distributions in light of the chronology of relic collecting; and (4) projectile distributions.

There is no single, primary historical source that describes the battlefield in sufficient detail to place the action on the current terrain. Taken as a whole, however, the contemporary sources provide a location for the initial dispositions of the armies that can only match the Southern Solution (see figure). Of the six eighteenth-century maps of the battle known to the authors, one (Finnegan n.d.) is completely incoherent, and the other five all suffer from significant distortions of scale, among various other problems (these include Senf 1780, Barrette 1780, Barron n.d., Vallancy/DesBarres 1780, and Faden 1787).[15] Errors aside, the five usable maps share certain important consistencies, including reasonable agreement in the relative placement of units,[16] and the basic orientation of the two armies astride, and perpendicular to, a north-south road. All five maps show the right flank of the 2nd Maryland Brigade and the left flank (at least) of the British line resting on swamps. Eyewitnesses on both sides consistently state that their flanks were protected by swamps. Otho Williams reported, "It happened that each flank was covered by a marsh, so near as to admit the removing of the First Maryland Brigade to form a second line...."[17] Gates reported that Gist's 2nd Maryland Brigade took position "upon the Right – with His Right close to a Swamp," while Col. Senf recalled "an almost impassable swamp" on the American right.[18] Lord Cornwallis was "well apprized by several intelligent Inhabitants that the ground on which both armies stood, being narrowed by swamps on the right & left, was extremely favorable for my numbers...."[19] Stedman reiterated, "A swamp on each side secured [Cornwallis's] flanks, and narrowed the ground in front...."[20] A nineteenth-century British narrative based on now-unknown primary sources provides an additional, critical detail: "The ground... was a sandy plain with straggling trees, but a part of the ground on the British left was soft and boggy ... the Provincials were on the left, with the marshy ground in their front."[21] This same detail is depicted in the front of the Loyalists on the Faden Map of 1787. An examination of the figure readily reveals that the Southern Solution fits very well with the historical sources cited above, while the Northern Solution does not. The Northern Solution places the American army on a broad ridgeline with their right flank exposed and *not* anchored on any drainage, and places the British left with a swamp *behind* them. This swampy drainage is nearly impenetrable today, and it is unlikely that the British would have maneuvered into or around it during the early morning hours prior to the battle.

The second consideration concerns land use after 1780. The historic land uses detailed above have certainly impacted the available artifact evidence, and have affected the distributions recorded by the Collector Survey. Although more recently wooded, the southern portion of the battlefield is an expanse of old agricultural fields, with a plow zone as much as a foot in depth. A resident of one of the two farms on the site collected "buckets full of musket balls" in the fields, suggesting substantial surface collecting.[22] In contrast, the northern part of the battlefield apparently remained in old-growth turpentine trees through much of the twentieth century, and it generally does not exhibit an old, agricultural plow zone, as distinct from evidence of logging and pine-plowing. This would help to explain why artifacts like bayonets, musket locks, and pairs of shoe buckles survived undamaged as well as undiscovered by farmers and visitors in this northern area.

The history of relic collecting with metal detectors on the Camden battlefield is another important consideration, because the battlefield was not collected uniformly. A site as obvious as the Camden battlefield was almost certainly collected with metal detectors in the 1960s, if not in the 1950s. This is supported by the testimony of our earliest informant who began collecting from the battlefield in 1980. He reported that in 1980, the southern and northeastern parts of the battlefield already had been intensely collected by unknown parties. Although those areas were still quite productive in 1980, the artifacts removed before then are not reflected in the Collector Survey distribution data. Four of the earliest collections currently known, gathered mostly in the early- and mid-1980s, were derived substantially from the southern concentration. These four collectors combed the southern portion of the battlefield for several years, and found a seemingly endless supply of fired and unfired musket ammunition. Other artifacts were generally small objects, or fragments of larger items, contrasting with the larger, well-preserved objects and clusters of related objects later found to the northwest.

While they collected the evidence for the heavy fighting to the south, none of the four earlier collectors wandered far enough to the west and north to discover the artifact concentration that appears to support the Northern Solution. By the time the authors of the Northern Solution arrived on the scene in about 1986, the southern part of the battlefield presented only a weak ammunition scatter, while the as-yet-uncollected northwestern concentration (which they immediately discovered) was still an impressive trove of artifacts. Given their late arrival, their battle interpretation is not unreasonable, but it is not supported by a full understanding of land use and the history of collecting at the site.[23]

Finally, there is archaeological evidence in the form of lead shot and iron canister ball distributions. As discussed above, the musket ball provenience data from the Collector Survey is poor—only five collections include any plotting of musket balls, and no actual specimens are tied to particular locations. In spite of these limitations, an important observation can be made regarding the location of the heaviest small-arms fire during the battle. The concentration of arms artifacts (see figure) and clothing artifacts running west from the DAR property was accompanied by relatively few musket balls in comparison to the musket ball concentration to the south. The ratio of musket balls to other objects is dramatically higher in the southern concentration, where the Southern Solution places the Continentals' protracted struggle. This can be demonstrated in spite of the poor quality of the musket ball provenience data. For example, Collectors #5 and #7, who discovered the northern concentration, recorded finding a total of 212 musket balls in the area.[24] These were accompanied by 99 arms and clothing artifacts, including (for example) 13 shoe buckles and 46 buttons. In the southern concentration, Collectors #1, #2, and #3 together recovered at least 538 musket balls (actually many more), but only 29 arms and clothing artifacts, including no shoe buckles and only five buttons.[25] These are ratios of about 2.1 to 1 and 18.5 to 1, respectively. Furthermore, the ratio of fired to unfired balls appears to have been higher in the southern area, although we have no objective measure of this. The suggestion here is that there was comparatively less firing (suggesting less intense combat) in the northern concentration west of Highway 58. The concentration of arms and accoutrement material found in the northern concentration may be the archaeological expression of headlong flight, slaughter, and surrender, and the subsequent processing of prisoners and the wounded.

In contrast to the far more abundant musket balls, the locations of individual canister balls were more precisely remembered by Collector Survey informants, and their distribution is significant in our battlefield interpretation (see figure). There is a heavy concentration of canister along the road in the southern portion of the battlefield. In either interpretation, most of these balls would be behind the British lines; but in the Northern Solution, many would be 600 to 800 yards behind the British lines.[26] While it is physically possible to fire canister from an elevated six-pounder gun (the heaviest in use at Camden) to these ranges, the effective range of the load was only about 200 to 300 yards, with only a minority of the balls traveling further downrange—this assuming they did not encounter trees, personnel, or other obstacles. It is well documented that American guns were deployed along the road at dawn, and that they caused heavy British losses with their initial fire, apparently at a range of about 200 yards.[27] The southern concentration of canister in the figure fits much better with the Southern Solution, the guns being located in the road on the American front line (see figure).[28] The canister distribution on the battlefield also argues against the Northern Solution interpretation that the southern artifact concentration represents the night meeting engagement. We have found no source that indicates either side used artillery during that action.

CONCLUSIONS

The authors are convinced that the initial positions of the opposing forces in the Battle of Camden are those depicted in the figure on page 222. It is hoped that the arguments marshaled above will sway those individuals who have disagreed thus far, and that this interpretation can be refined in the future with additional historical and archaeological research.

A broader conclusion concerns the use of collector data from battlefields generally. We believe this study has clearly demonstrated the value and utility of collector data in reconstructing battle history on existing topography. Like metal detecting technology, however, the "collector informant" technique may be some time in gaining general acceptance. There was a time, perhaps 25 years ago, when most archaeologists objected to the use of metal detectors in any archaeological context, thanks to the association of the technology with private collectors and a general ignorance of its potential. With the exceptions of a few pioneers like Roy Dickens, and more recently Douglas D. Scott, the archaeological community was slow to recognize the great utility of metal detecting on non-architectural military sites, together with the futility of certain traditional methods such as shovel testing and block excavation. Metal detectors are finally in general use, however, and the literature of successful applications has grown dramatically over the last 20 years.[29]

While metal detectors now appear to be acceptable tools for many archaeological applications, most archaeologists still seem to have a poor understanding of the scope and time depth of nonprofessional metal detecting on military sites and its impact on battlefield interpretation. Questions such as, "Has this battlefield been metal detected?" or, "Will our work encourage pot hunters?" might have been pertinent 30 or 40 years ago, but they are merely naive today. With rare exceptions, all reasonably accessible battlefields, field fortifications, and campsites in North America have been collected for several decades by numerous individuals. Nearly all such sites have lost most of their easily detectable metallic artifacts.[30] This condition extends to even the most obscure skirmishes and bivouacs, thanks to the rigorous historical research conducted by thousands of collectors. The exceptions are those few sites or portions of sites that have both legal protection and 24-hour security, and sites where the use of metal detectors is not practical (e.g., developed areas or trash dumps). While the literature of archaeological metal detecting on military sites is growing, most reports fail to address how previous collecting might affect their interpretations or even mention that there are missing collections that were removed long before any archaeological effort was undertaken.

It is not surprising, then, that few archaeologists have recognized the collector community as a resource that can and should be carefully tapped for information. Certainly we would all prefer that metal detecting at military sites had not happened in the past, and that it was not so popular today. To ignore it, however, is to put one's head in the sand, and to settle for a less informed interpretation of previously detected sites. In many cases, collector data is now the best (or only) distributional evidence available. Thus we feel it is the obligation of archaeologists to salvage what information can be gained from relic collectors and integrate it into their work. While the quality of the provenience data is usually not as precise as we would like, it is unique and very usable information that is otherwise entirely lost. We encourage archaeologists to develop strong relationships with the collectors in their region. We also encourage relic collectors to allow professional archaeologists access to their material, and urge them to make arrangements for their collections to be protected in perpetuity.

NOTES

1. The authors thank the National Park Service, American Battlefield Protection Program, the South Carolina Palmetto Conservation Foundation, and the South Carolina Institute of Archaeology and Anthropology for their financial support of this research. Also supporting this project was the Katawba Valley Land Trust. Special individuals who we want to thank include foremost Brigadier General (Ret.) George D. Fields, Dr. Douglas D. Scott, and Dr. Lawrence E. Babits. We are also most grateful to the members of the Battle of Camden Project and the collectors who offered their knowledge and allowed us to inventory their collections. Ms. Tamara Wilson developed the maps for this project.

2. An essential component of Battle of Camden Project is an effort to compile a definitive archive of primary sources relating to the battle. This task has been undertaken by the project on a large website, *battleofcamden.org*. The website includes numerous participant accounts of the battle from both sides, as well as several eighteenth-century maps. The

following primary sources were used in the development of this battle narrative: Report of Earl Cornwallis to Lord George Germain, Camden, South Carolina, August 21, 1780 in, Walter Clark, editor, *The State Records of North Carolina*, Volume XV 1780–81 (Goldsboro: Nash Brothers, Book and Job Printers, 1898), 268–273; Guilford Dudley, "The Carolina's During the Revolution, A Sketch of the Military Services Performed by Guilford Dudley– Then of the town of Halifax, North Carolina, During the Revolutionary War," in *Southern Literary Messenger*, 1845, Volume XI, March 144–148, April 231–253, May 281–287, June 370–374; Report of General Gates to President of Congress, August 20, 1780, in John Austin Stevens, "The Southern Campaign, 1780, Gates at Camden," *Magazine of American History*, October 1880, V(4):241–301; General Thomas Pinckney, "General Gates's Southern Campaign, July 27th, 1822" in *Historical Magazine* (1866), Volume X (8):244–253; Thomas Pinckney, Letter to Judge James, dated July 31, 1822, Thomas Pinckney Papers, South Caroliniana, University of South Carolina, Columbia, SC; Lieutenant Colonel Banastre Tarleton, *A History of the Campaigns of 1780 and 1781 in the Southern Provinces of North America* (Reprint, North Stratford, NH: Ayer Company Publishers, 1999, original 1787), 103–116; Colonel Otho Williams, "A Narrative of the Campaign of 1780," Appendix A, in William Johnson, *Sketches of the Life and Correspondence of Nathanael Greene, Major General of the Armies of the United States in the War of the Revolution*, Volume 1 (Charleston: A.E. Miller, 1822), 485–503. A good secondary narrative is Lt. Col. H. L. Landers, *The Battle of Camden*, House Document No.12, 71st Congress, 1st Session (Washington, D.C.: U.S. Government Printing Office, 1929).

3. Williams, "Narrative," 495.

4. The most complete history of the battlefield thus far has been R. Bryan Whitfield's 1980 thesis, *The Preservation of the Camden Battlefield* (Department of History, Wake Forest University, Winston Salem, NC).

5. Whitfield, 56.

6. The southern end of the battlefield is actually nearly a mile north of Gum Swamp Creek.

7. Benson Lossing, *The Pictorial Field Book of the Revolution*. Volume II (New York: Harper and Brothers, 1855), 460.

8. Thomas J. Kirkland and Robert M. Kennedy, *Historic Camden, Part One: Colonial and Revolutionary* (Columbia, The State Company, 1905), 169.

9. Kirkland and Kennedy, 162n.

10. Whitfield, 58–61.

11. Whitfield, 64–65.

12. George Fields, Steven D. Smith, and James B. Legg, *Strategic Plan for the Battle of Camden National Historic Landmark* (Columbia: Palmetto Conservation Foundation, 2003).

13. Calvin Keys, "Map of Day Battle Lines," in Charles Baxley, *Camden. American Battlefield Protection Program, Battlefield Survey Form*, National Park Service.

14. The Northern Solution would also seem to be favored by the location of the de Kalb monument, which was erected at the location of a pine tree where tradition held that de Kalb "fell." There is other traditional evidence, however, that de Kalb fell on the west side of the road, "at the head of a little bay, in the deep shades of the forest"

(Kirkland and Kennedy, 188). This would fit de Kalb's position at the climax of the battle in the Southern Solution. A participant account of de Kalb's death is found in the same source indicating that de Kalb was riding away when shot. This might support the contention that the de Kalb monument is indeed the location of his fall.

15. Ed Barron, "Sketch of the disposition and commencement of the action near Camden," Duke of Cumberland Collection, Public Archives, Nova Scotia, Canada; William Faden, "Plan of the Battle fought near Camden, August 16th, 1780," 1787, British Museum, London, and Tarleton's *History*; Lieutenant Finnegan, "Plan of the Batel close Campton in South America between the British under Gen. Lord Cornwallis and the Americans under Command of Gen. Gates," North Carolina Collection, University of North Carolina, Chapel Hill, North Carolina; Lt. Colonel Johann Christian Senf, "Battle of Camden," in Senf, "Journal"; C. Vallancy, "Sketch of the Battle of Camden," Library of Congress, 71000873. These maps can be seen at www.battleofcamden.org.

16. The major exceptions are the Vallancy and DesBarre Maps, which are actually manuscript and engraved versions of the same map. These are the best of the lot cartographically, but the American unit dispositions and identifications are wildly incorrect. Among other problems, they depict half of the American militia west of the drainage on the American right.

17. Williams, 495.

18. Gates, 303; John Senf, "Extract of a Journal Concerning the Action of the 16th of August 1780 Between Major General Gates and General Lord Cornwallis." Ms, Library of Congress.

19. Cornwallis, 270.

20. Charles Stedman, *The History of the Origin, Progress, and Termination of the American War*. Volume II (London: J. Murray, 1794) 208.

21. Col. David Stewart, *Sketches of the Character, Manners, and Present State of the Highlanders of Scotland*. Volume II, 2nd ed., Reprint of 1877 ed. (Edinburgh: John Donald Publishers, 1977), 67.

22. Whitfield, 65n.

23. It has been the experience of the authors that when collectors locate an area abundant with artifacts they will stay in that area until the finds become rare. Only then do they radiate outward from the core area. In fact, we have observed that some military sites may exhibit a reversal of actual historic density. In this phenomenon the central historic location of a camp, battlefield, or skirmish has been collected to the extent that it is nearly devoid of archaeological evidence, while the site's peripheries still retain some artifacts. Archaeologists should be mindful of this manifestation when assessing sites that have been heavily collected.

24. For the purposes of this example the "northern concentration" is the area bounded by Highway 58 on the east, by the dirt roads on the north and west, and on the south by a line running west from the southwest corner of the DAR property; the "southern concentration" is the larger dense contour on figure, page 217.

25. These totals do not include burial artifacts—currently, two burials are recorded from the southern concentration, none from the northern sample discussed here.

26. In our own metal detector sampling survey, a canister ball was found even further south than any recorded on figure, page 219.

27. Pinckney, Letters, July 22 and 31, 1822, Williams, 1130.

28. The question of canister range is critical to the correct interpretation of the Camden Battlefield. According to Brent Nosworthy, "Canister was generally limited to targets within 350 yards, and the absolute range of the heaviest canister was less than 700 yards." Here Nosworthy is discussing Civil War field guns, which were generally heavier than Revolutionary War guns. See his *The Bloody Crucible of Courage: Fighting Methods and Combat Experience of the Civil War* (New York: Carroll and Graf, 2003), 64–65. Lawrence Babits suggests that individual canister balls from an elevated six-pounder gun might conceivably travel 800 yards (personal communication, February 2004), but certainly most would come to rest at much shorter ranges. Firing over nearly level ground at targets 200 yards away would have required little or no elevation of the gun, which would have brought most of the canister balls to ground at minimal ranges. See also Garry Wheeler Stone, Daniel M. Sivilich, and Mark E. Lender, "A Deadly Minuet: The Advance of the New England 'Picked Men' against the Royal Highlanders at the Battle of Monmouth, 28 June 1778," *Brigade Dispatch*, XXVI(2), Summer 1996. They found a few canister balls and "grape shot" more than 600 yards from presumed gun positions, but 500 yards was more typical, and the firing was over open terrain, and from higher to much lower topography.

29. For example, Melissa Connor and Douglas D. Scott, "Metal Detector Use in Archaeology: An Introduction," *Historical Archaeology*, 1998, 32(4):76–85; Christopher T. Espenshade, Robert L. Jolley, and James B. Legg, "The Value and Treatment of Civil War Military Sites," *North American Archaeologist*, 2002, 23(1):39–67; Charles M. Haecker and Jeffrey G. Mauck, *On the Prairie of Palo Alto* (College Station: Texas A&M University Press, 1997); James B. Legg and Steven D. Smith, *"The Best Ever occupied...": Archaeological Investigations of a Civil War Encampment on Folly Island, South Carolina* (Columbia: South Carolina Institute of Archaeology and Anthropology, 1989); Richard A. Fox Jr., *Archaeology, History, and Custer's Last Battle* (Norman: University of Oklahoma Press, 1993); William B. Lees, "When the Shooting Stopped, the War Began," in Clarence R. Geier Jr., and Susan E. Winter, eds., *Look to the Earth: Historical Archaeology and the American Civil War* (Knoxville: University of Tennessee Press, 1994); Douglas D. Scott, "Oral Tradition and Archaeology: Conflict and Concordance from Two Indian War Sites," *Historical Archaeology*, 2003, 37(3):55–65; Douglas D. Scott, Richard A. Fox Jr., Melissa A. Connor, and Dick Harmon, *Archaeological Perspectives on the Battle of the Little Bighorn* (Norman: University of Oklahoma Press, 1989); Douglas D. Scott and William J. Hunt Jr., *The Civil War Battle at Monroe's Crossroads, Fort Bragg, North Carolina: A Historical Archaeological Perspective* (Tallahassee: Southeast Archaeological Center, National Park Service, 1998); Steven D. Smith, "Archaeological Perspectives on the Civil War: The Challenge to Achieve Relevance," in Geier and Winter 1994; Steven D. Smith and James B. Legg, "Archaeological and Historical Analysis of the Camden Battlefield, August 16th, 1780," Southeastern Archaeological Conference, Charlotte, NC, November 13, 2003; Bruce B. Sterling

and Bernard W. Slaughter, "Surveying the Civil War: Methodological Approaches at Antietam Battlefield," in Clarence R. Geier and Stephen R. Potter, eds., *Archaeological Perspectives on the American Civil War* (Gainesville: University of Florida Press, 2000).

30. Roy Dickens, "Archaeological Investigations at Horseshoe Bend National Military Park, Alabama," *Special Publications of the Alabama Archaeological Society*, No. 3, 1979. A remarkable overview of battlefield relic collecting as it was during its peak can be found in Stephen W. Sylvia and Michael J. O'Donnell, *The Illustrated History of American Civil War Relics* (Orange, Virginia: Moss Publications, 1978).

REFERENCES CITED

Barrette, Lt. Col. Thomas George Leonard. 1780. Map of the Battle of Gum Swamp Alias Sutton-Ford. Clements Library, University of Michigan, Ann Arbor. http://battleofcamden.org/barrette.gif.

Barron, Ed. n.d. Sketch of the Disposition and Commencement of the Action Near Camden, South Carolina, 16 August 1780. http://battleofcamden.org/ed_barron_map.jpg.

Baxley, Charles B. 2000. Camden. American Battlefield Protection Program, Battlefield Survey Form, National Park Service.

Connor, Melissa, and Douglas D. Scott. 1998. Metal Detector Use in Archaeology: An Introduction. *Historical Archaeology* 32(4):76–85.

Cornwallis, Lord Earl. 1780. Report of Earl Cornwallis to Lord George Germain, Camden, South Carolina, August 21, 1780. In Walter Clark (ed.), *The State Records of North Carolina*, Volume XV 1780–81, Nash Brothers, Book and Job Printers, Goldsboro, North Carolina, 1898, 268–273.

DesBarres, J. F. W. 1780. Sketch of the Battle of Camden. On file, Library of Congress. http://battleofcamden.org/desbarres.jpg.

Dickens, Roy. 1979. Archaeological Investigations at Horseshoe Bend National Military Park, Alabama. *Special Publications of the Alabama Archaeological Society*, No. 3.

Dudley, Guilford. 1845. The Carolina's During the Revolution, A Sketch of the Military Services Performed by Guilford Dudley–Then of the town of Halifax, North Carolina, During the Revolutionary War. *Southern Literary Messenger* XI(March):144–148, (April):231–253, (May):281–287, (June):370–374.

Espenshade, Christopher T., Robert L. Jolley, and James B. Legg. 2002. The Value and Treatment of Civil War Military Sites. *North American Archaeologist* 23(1):39–67.

Faden, William. 1787. Plan of the Battle fought near Camden, August 16th, 1780. British Museum, London.

Fields, George, Steven D. Smith, and James B. Legg. 2003. *Strategic Plan for the Battle of Camden Historic Landmark*. Palmetto Conservation Foundation, Columbia, South Carolina.

Finnegan, Lieutenant. n.d. Plan of the Batel close Campton in South America between the British under Gen. Lord Cornwallis and the Americans under Command of

Gen. Gates. North Carolina Collection, University of North Carolina, Chapel Hill, NC.
Fox, Richard A. Jr. 1993. *Archaeology, History, and Custer's Last Battle*. University of Oklahoma Press, Norman.
Geier, Clarence R., and Stephen R. Potter (eds.). 2000. *Archaeological Perspectives on the American Civil War*. University Press of Florida, Gainesville.
Geier, Clarence R. Jr., and Susan E. Winter (eds.). 1994. *Look to the Earth: Historical Archaeology and the American Civil War*. University of Tennessee Press, Nashville.
Haecker, Charles M., and Jeffrey G. Mauck. 1997. *On the Prairie of Palo Alto: Historical Archaeology of the U.S.–Mexican War Battlefield*. Texas A&M University Press, College Station.
Keys, Calvin. 2000. Map of Day Battle Lines, in Charles Baxley, *Camden. American Battlefield Protection Program, Battlefield Survey Form*, National Park Service.
Kirkland, Thomas J., and Robert M. Kennedy. 1905. *Historic Camden, Part One, Colonial and Revolutionary*. The State Company, Columbia, SC.
Landers, Lieutenant Colonel H. L. 1929. *The Battle of Camden, South Carolina, August 16, 1780*. House Document No. 12, 71st Congress, 1st Session, U. S. Government Printing Office, Washington, D.C.
Lees, William B. 1994. When the Shooting Stopped, the War Began. In Clarence R. Geier Jr. and Susan E. Winter (eds.), *Look to the Earth: Historical Archaeology and the American Civil War*. University of Tennessee Press, Knoxville.
Legg, James B., and Steven D. Smith. 1989. "The Best Ever Occupied..." Archaeological Investigations of a Civil War Encampment on Folly Island, South Carolina. *Research Manuscript Series* #209, South Carolina Institute of Archaeology and Anthropology, Columbia.
Lossing, Benson. 1855. *The Pictorial Field-Book of the Revolution*. Harper and Brothers, New York.
Nosworthy, Brent. 2003. *The Bloody Crucible of Courage: Fighting Methods and Combat Experience of the Civil War*. Carroll and Graf, Inc., New York.
Pinckney, General Thomas. 1866. General Gates's Southern Campaign, July 31, 1822. *Historical Magazine* X(8):244–253.
Pinckney, General Thomas. 1822. Letter to Judge James, dated July 31, 1822. Thomas Pinckney Papers, South Caroliniana Library, University of South Carolina.
Scott, Douglas D. 2003. Oral Tradition and Archaeology: Conflict and Concordance from Two Indian War Sites. *Historical Archaeology* 37(3):55–65.
Scott, Douglas D., Richard A. Fox Jr., Melissa A. Connor, and Dick Harmon. 1989. *Archaeological Perspectives on the Battle of the Little Bighorn*. University of Oklahoma Press, Norman.
Scott, Douglas D., and William J. Hunt Jr. 1998. *The Civil War Battle at Monroe's Crossroads, Fort Bragg, North Carolina: A Historical Archaeological Perspective*. Southeast Archaeological Center, National Park Service, Tallahassee, FL.
Senf, Colonel John. 1780. "Extract of a Journal Concerning the Action of the 16th of August 1780 Between Major General Gates and General Lord Cornwallis," Library of Congress.
Smith, Steven D. 1994. Archaeological Perspectives on the Civil War: The Challenge to Achieve Relevance. In Clarence R. Geier Jr. and Susan E. Winter (eds.), *Look*

to the Earth: Historical Archaeology and the American Civil War. University of Tennessee Press, Knoxville.

Smith, Steven D., and James B. Legg. 2003. Archaeological and Historical Analysis of the Camden Battlefield, August 16th, 1780. Southeastern Archaeological Conference, Charlotte, NC.

Stedman, C. 1794. *The History of the Origin, Progress, and Termination of the American War*. J. Murray et al., London.

Sterling, Bruce B., and Bernard W. Slaughter. 2000. Surveying the Civil War: Methodological Approaches at Antietam Battlefield. In Clarence R. Geier and Stephen R. Potter (eds.), *Archaeological Perspectives on the American Civil War*. University of Florida Press, Gainesville.

Stevens, John Austin. 1880. The Southern Campaign, 1780, Gates at Camden. *Magazine of American History* October V(4):241–301.

Stewart, Colonel David. 1977. *Sketches of the Character, Manners, and Present State of the Highlanders of Scotland*. Volume II, Second edition, John Donald Publishers, Ltd., Edinburgh, reprint, original 1877.

Stone, Garry Wheeler, Daniel M. Sivilich, and Mark E. Lender. 1996. A Deadly Minuet: The Advance of the New England "Picked Men" against the Royal Highlanders at the Battle of Monmouth, 28 June 1778. *Brigade Dispatch* XXVI(2), (Summer 1996):2–18.

Sylvia, Stephen W., and Michael J. O'Donnell. 1978. *The Illustrated History of American Civil War Relics*. Moss Publications, Orange, VA.

Tarleton, Lieutenant Colonel Banastre. 1787. *A History of the Campaigns of 1780 and 1781 in the Southern Provinces of North America*. Reprint, Ayer Company Publishers, North Stratford, NH, 1999.

Vallancy, Charles. 1780. Sketch of the Battle of Camden. On file, Library of Congress. http://battleofcamden.org/vallancy2.jpg.

Whitfield, R. Bryan. 1980. *The Preservation of Camden Battlefield*. MA Thesis, Department of History, Wake Forest University, Winston-Salem, NC.

Williams, Colonel Otho. 1822. Narrative of the Campaign of 1780, Appendix A. In William Johnson, *Sketches of the Life and Correspondence of Nathanael Greene, Major General of the Armies of the United States in the War of the Revolution*, Volume 1. A.E. Miller, Charleston, SC.

Apache Victory against the U.S. Dragoons, the Battle of Cieneguilla, New Mexico

David M. Johnson

THE BATTLE OF Cieneguilla is located on the Camino Real Ranger District of the Carson National Forest, New Mexico, with a small portion of the advance and retreat routes on Bureau of Land Management and New Mexico State Land.[1] Although the battle has been known about for years[2] and many have searched for the site, only the general location was previously known. On March 29, 1854, 60 men of the First Dragoons under the command of Lieutenant John W. Davidson left Cantonment Burgwin, New Mexico to search for a group of Jicarilla Apache known to be in the vicinity of the Embudo Mountains. Lt. Davidson's instructions were to observe the Apache, and to avoid a confrontation.[3] The Dragoons arrived at the small village of Cieneguilla on the Rio Grande late that night. The next morning they proceeded along the trail to Embudo, rode off into the mountains, and found the Jicarilla Apache camped on a small ridge a few miles above the village of Cieneguilla (see figure). Although it is unclear who initiated the ensuing battle, a fight erupted, ending in a major defeat of the Dragoons. The soldiers retreated, making it back to the fort late that night.[4] Apache casualties are unknown, and may have been as few as two[5] or as many as 50.[6] The troop casualties included 22 dead in the field, and 36 wounded, of which two died later from their wounds.[7] This battle was largely responsible for launching a campaign against the Jicarilla Apache that lasted several years, and led to their eventual defeat and relocation to their present-day reservation.[8]

The news of the battle spread quickly, and questions soon emerged as to how such a defeat of the military could have happened. Two weeks following the battle, Christopher "Kit" Carson wrote that it was his opinion that the Apache were "driven into the war, by the action of the officers & troops."[9] Later that year, Lt. David Bell of the First Cavalry in a letter to Lt. Williams of the First Dragoons wrote, "It is at least doubtful who fired first – but what matters it? – Was not the advance upon the Camp in a hostile attitude a <u>bona fide attack</u>? Nobody would doubt it practically if his position was that of the

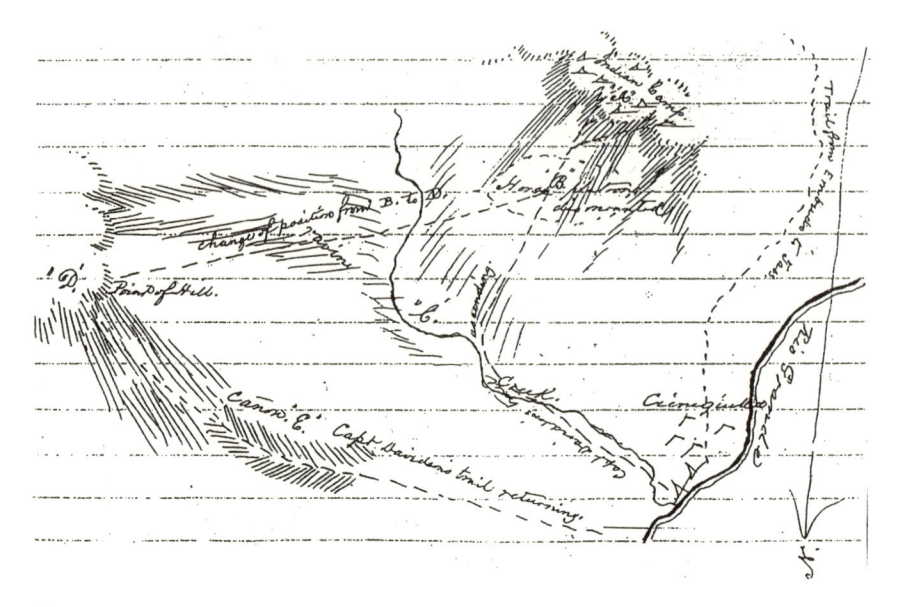

Sketch of the battle from Francisco testimony at Court of Inquiry. (Reproduced from Proceedings of a Court of Inquiry Convened at Santa Fe, New Mexico, February 9, 1856. Judge Advocate General's Office, records group 153, National Archives, Washington D.C.)

Indians and Lt. D. would have been one of the last to do so. If he had been under the command of almost any officer other than Maj. Blake he would have been tried for disobedience of orders."[10] After reading the letter, Lt. Davidson filed a suit against Lt. Bell, but later dropped the charges in favor of a court of inquiry where he could lay the questions to rest.

The court of inquiry convened in March 1856. Over the course of several days, a number of soldiers gave their account of the battle. Witnesses included Kit Carson, Sergeant Bronson (a.k.a. Bennett),[11] and Mr. M. J. Francisco, who helped to retrieve the bodies the day after the fight. Davidson, now a captain, directed the majority of the questioning. The inquiry revolved around the accusations Bell made in his letter. The portion of the letter that most influenced the court proceedings is as follows:

> Lt. Davidson now dismounted his command in a cañon ... The command advanced in two platoons as nearly in line as the nature of the ground and other circumstances would admit. This was the most unmilitary as well as the most exposed order possible – it could not be expected that a display of numbers would intimidate the Indians while a large mark was thus presented to their concentrated fire. This is no labored scientific deduction – A non-commissioned officer who would not have appreciated it upon the ground should have been reduced for incapacity. But if exception is taken to this mode of approaching a crouching and concealed foe what are we to think of the second attempt to go up a steep hill each man leading his horse. The horses alarmed by the noise and confusion of the fight would refuse to

advance and the men would struggle with them unwilling to abandon them and thus instead of using their weapons would fall victims to the fire of a concealed enemy. An attack could not be made mounted and to attempt to lead the horses would expose the men. What was then to be done? To abandon the horses of course. This ill-advised and unfortunate attack finally arrived at the top of the hill, leaving behind those who were killed or wounded, and now the command is given "mount men and save yourselves" – this Lt. does not or at least did not deny. This order was calculated to strike terror to the heart of the bravest soldier, for he would know that nothing but the utmost exertion could prevent his falling a prey to the merciless savage. This order was alone sufficient to ruin a command. The consequence was a disorderly flight over ground of the difficulties of which the Indians knew well how to take advantage. Every other consideration was forgotten in that of personal safety and hence the entire abandonment of arms etc. Every man exerted his energies to save his own life while he abandoned his wounded comrades to the heathens. I have conversed with Major Blake, Maj. Thompson and Mr. Quinn all of whom visited Cieneguilla the next day and the result of their stories is this that 5 men only were found dead upon the side of the hill up which Davidson advanced, and it is by no means certain that they were dead when the retreat was ordered, while 14 men were found on the hill side down which the flight took place, and two or three more in the ravine below. This cannot be denied and it proves that a command of 57 Dragoons retreated without an attempt to presume order when they had lost 5 of their number. Davidson says in his official report, which I have read, that there were 250 or 300 Apache and Utah warriors in the fight that he fought for three hours and has every reason to believe he killed a large number of Indians. In the first place there were no Utahs in the fight & secondly there were not more than 130 warriors (Apache) in it, as Carson or any person who followed them will tell you. If 50 or 60 of these had been killed the rest must have been wounded if any sort of usual proportion between killed and wounded obtained. As to fighting three hours that is the most ridiculously absurd assertion in the whole report. A Cartridge Box (cavalry) holds some 30 to 50 Cartridges. How long would it take a man to fire this number of Cartridges assuming that he fired all of them? But in the excitement of action most men will lose a large portion of their ammunition. I think any reasonable man will agree that Davidsons fight never lasted 30 minutes, his assertion to the contrary notwithstanding. In regard to the probable number killed I forgot to say that it is a remarkable fact that the number of lodges after the fight was the same as before and we were informed in every Mexican settlement through which we passed in the pursuit, that the Indians said they had lost only two men in the battle.[12]

Kit Carson was one of the first to testify. It is interesting that two years after claiming that he felt the Indians were drawn into the battle by the Dragoons,[13] he backed Davidson in his testimony. As each soldier got up to testify, Lt. Davidson asked a series of questions. Time and again, the soldiers testified that Lt. Davidson was in control of the battle and his men, and undoubtedly saved the lives of those who made it out alive. The court declined an invitation to visit the battle site, and ruled on the testimony presented. Lt. Davidson was exonerated, and went on to further his illustrious career in the military.

METHODS

One of the primary objectives of the project was to locate and record the footprint of the battle. The research focused on defining the precise location of the engagement and comparing the archaeological results with the historic records including written accounts by Lt. Davidson and others. An accurate description and comparison with the written accounts would provide a detailed look not only at the battle, but at the mid-nineteenth-century military and Indian war tactics as well. It would also serve as a final chapter to the court of inquiry that took place in 1856, as the exact location of the battle and the positions of the troops and Apache could now be examined. Another goal was to accurately describe the artifacts to provide a description of the diagnostic military and Apache artifacts in New Mexico in the mid-nineteenth century.

In light of the research goals and data needs, it was most appropriate to use a combination of standard pedestrian survey techniques augmented with metal detectors. The use of metal detectors has proven to be an efficient and accurate way to record historic battle sites.[14] For this project, a variety of state-of-the art metal detectors with different frequencies to avoid cross-talk, and double-d coils for greater coverage, were used.[15]

Descriptions from the historical accounts and an 1856 sketch map from the M. J. Francisco testimony[16] helped to refine the search area. Transects were closely spaced, averaging two to three meters apart. As artifacts were located, the positions were marked on the ground with numbered metal tags and pin flags, and the individual artifact locations were initially recorded using handheld GPS units. Artifact locations were delineated on a topographic map generated in ArcView 8.1. Diagnostic artifacts, and those slated for analysis, were collected. The final mapping employed a total station for more precise documentation, and each artifact was accurately re-mapped. Permanent datum points were established using a Trimble 4700 series geodetic GPS with RTK capabilities.

Most of the battle site is located on the Carson National Forest, with a small portion of the access route and retreat route on lands administered by the Bureau of Land Management and the state of New Mexico. The research was conducted by archaeologists from the Carson National Forest, Lincoln National Forest, National Park Service, Bureau of Land Management, Jicarilla Apache Tribe, University of Michigan, and local volunteers. The mapping was completed with land surveyors from the Carson National Forest. This research was funded in part through a grant from the National Park Service Battlefield Protection Program.

SURVEY RESULTS

More than 1,000 artifacts were found during the survey (see figure). As expected from the use of metal detectors, the majority of the artifacts recovered were metallic. The primary exceptions were the micaceous ceramic fragments found in the Apache camp. While this undoubtedly skews the information from the Apache camp in particular, most of the military and battle-related artifacts were expected to be metal, and the results provide an accurate description of the military action.

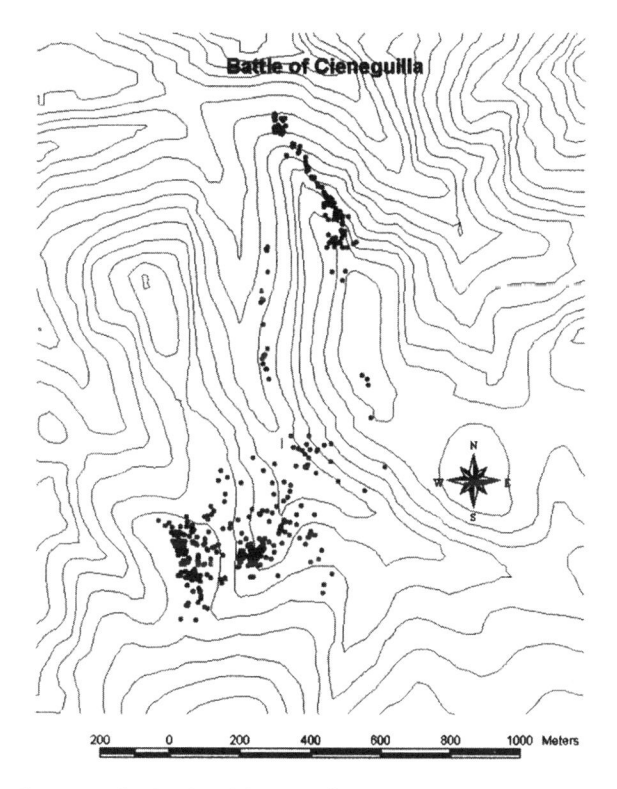

Artifact distribution at the Battle of Cieneguilla.

The artifacts were scattered across a large area, but there were several distinct concentrations of specific artifact types (see figure) that corresponded well with the 1856 sketch map of the battle (see figure). The artifact concentrations identified the access route, horse position, Apache camp, and retreat route. The artifacts are described below.

APACHE ARTIFACTS

The survey recovered hundreds of Apachean micaceous shards from the camp. The Jicarilla Apache manufactured and used pottery for storage and cooking. Typical Jicarilla Apache micaceous pottery is thin, well made, with striations on the exterior surface.[17] Another important identifier for Apache ceramics in northern New Mexico is the presence of a flattened rim. Pottery was a common trade item, however, and some Puebloan ceramics were also present on the site. Twenty-nine locations with micaceous shards were identified in and around the Apache camp. These ranged from small areas with one or two shards, to scatters of dozens of shards from multiple vessels. Two distinct concentrations of ceramics are on the site, located about 60 meters apart. The ceramics in each concentration exhibit differences in the temper, and are associated with different overall artifact assemblages.

The majority of the remaining Apache artifacts were metal. One of the most diagnostic is the arrow point. Europeans introduced metal by the late seventeenth century, and early metal trade points and the materials to manufacture them soon replaced stone arrow points.[18] By the mid to late nineteenth century, scrap metal was readily available for use in arrow point manufacture from wagon parts, trunks, barrel hoops, and utensils. Points were usually chiseled out of a strip of barrel band or other suitable metal and then filed to refine the shape and sharpen the edge. Commercially made trade points were also available, and can often be identified by their uniform shape and thickness, beveled edges, and consistency in size and proportions.[19]

Forty metal points were found on the battle site. Most were cut from barrel bands, but some might have been commercially manufactured trade points. It is remarkable that there is little consistency in the size or shape of the points at this site (see figure). In contrast, the size and shape of metal points from Mescalero Apache sites on the Lincoln National Forest in southern New Mexico are generally consistent. This variation on the Cieneguilla battlefield is likely a result of the Taos trade fairs, where points would have been available from a variety of sources in a variety of styles over a long period of time. It is also possible that a number of different bands of Apache were present at the battle, each with their own point style. Additional research is needed to determine whether this variety of point styles is typical of other Jicarilla Apache sites.

Sample of metal points from the battle site.

Small pieces of metal, cut from a barrel band or other piece of metal, were also found. This scrap metal debitage is primarily the result of point manufacture. The chisel-cut fragments exhibit uneven parallel cuts and the lateral margins of the fragments are also uneven. The iron fragments are often long triangular cut pieces or small square or trapezoidal shapes. The long triangular pieces represent the areas cut out along the point edges and the small square angular pieces represent the tang and stem cuts. These fragments are fairly thick, indicating the use of barrel hoops and metal straps to make arrow points.[20]

Fifteen locations of metal debitage were recorded. The debitage offers firm evidence that the Jicarilla were making their own points on the site. A number of the debitage pieces were trapezoidal in shape. All appear to have been chisel cut. Most of the metal debitage is located around the southern ceramic concentration.

Another common Apache artifact is the small metal "tinkler" or "jingle," a small conical tin or brass ornament made by cutting sheet metal into triangles and curling them into cones. The Apache often obtained tin sheet metal by flattening cans. Brass was obtained through trade or raiding or from cutting up brass kettles and other utensils. The metal cones were attached with cords or buckskin thongs as ornaments on clothing, moccasins, bags, baskets, and quivers. When the clothing or object was in motion, the cones hit each other, producing a tinkling or jingling sound. In the late nineteenth century, brass cartridges flattened on the end and pierced through the base or flattened end were often used as tinklers.[21]

Twelve metal tinklers were found on the battle site (see figure). Three tinklers were brass, and the rest were tin or iron. Seven were found in the Apache camp; one was across the creek near the initial retreat route; and the rest were scattered along the slope below the camp.

Metal tinklers and tinkler manufacturing debris.

The manufacture of tinklers produces diagnostic by-products. Shear and/or chisel-cut can fragments, tin, or brass, either in the form of blanks for manufacturing tinklers or the scraps of metal discarded from the production of tinklers, were also found. These scraps are generally thinner than the point debitage. They consist of irregularly shaped slivers and pieces of metal, and help to identify tinkler manufacturing areas.

No specific Apache firearms were identified. Without a written account detailing which weapons the Apache used against the Dragoons, it is difficult to assign cultural affiliations to these artifacts. Any one of these artifacts found in isolation would be impossible to attribute to Apache, military, or civilian use. Flintlocks were often used by the Apache well after the introduction of percussion caps and metal cartridges because they were easy to maintain, and ammunition for muzzle-loading firearms was easier to obtain or fabricate. It was assumed that gun parts and ammunition of calibers and makes that were not attributable to the Dragoons were from the Jicarillas. One trigger guard from an older flintlock pistol was found near the camp. One possible mainspring from an unidentified firearm was also located.

The Apache often used irregularly shaped pieces of lead cut from a larger piece or from lead rods to use as ammunition. Cut marks, knife marks, and so forth are often visible, and the bullet is not always round. Often, the piece of lead was chewed to get the size and shape to fit the caliber of the firearm, a practice documented on the frontier as early as the 1850s.[22] These chewed lead ball fragments illustrate Apache resourcefulness when proper-sized ammunition was scarce. On this battle site several dozen examples of both chewed balls and cut pieces of lead were found.

Other Apache artifacts, primarily from the Apache camp area, include iron awls, coscojos (horse bridle jingles), brass conchos, scrapers, a curved canvas needle, two knives, and several fragments of a brass kettle. One kettle fragment had a hand-forged iron handle attachment, but the handle was missing (see figure). This particular fragment had numerous chisel marks, and was apparently cut up to make tinklers or other items. Several small cut pieces of brass were found nearby.

MILITARY ARTIFACTS

Military artifacts were found throughout the battle site with the most common being firearms related. The Dragoons were using the .69 caliber 1847 musketoon, the .54 caliber 1842 "horse pistol," and the Colt .44 Dragoon revolver.[23] Ammunition for all three of these guns was found. No firearms were recovered but several gun screws, one from an 1847 musketoon trigger guard, and one brass side plate from a model 1847 musketoon[24] were located (see figure).

1847 musketoon tools and side plate.

One of the most common military artifacts on the battle site was dropped and fired .69 caliber and .54 caliber lead balls. More than 50 dropped/unfired military balls were located. Several of the dropped .69 caliber musketoon balls also had three .31 caliber balls or buckshot associated with them, forming a "buck and ball" load.[25] One .54 caliber buck and ball load was also recovered. Only two .44 caliber conical bullets from the Colt Dragoon revolver were found, and both appear to have been dropped. The largest number of dropped balls was along the final retreat route.

Percussion caps were also common on the site. The typical military percussion cap looks like a small top hat, divided into four segments that flare out when fired. Pistols used a smaller cap without the flared "rim" at the bottom. One hundred and ten percussion caps were found throughout the site. The caps were analyzed to identify toolmarks resulting from firing in an attempt to track troop movements.[26] Four sets of matches were identified, most clustering around the horse position, but one match involved a fired cap in the Apache camp, and another on the narrow ridge of the final retreat, providing further proof that the two areas where artifacts were recovered are related. Approximately 60 percent of the caps were dropped overall, with larger percentages of dropped caps found along the retreat route.

The military issued gun tools specific to their various weapons.[27] Two model 1847 musketoon worms and two model 1847 musketoon combination screwdriver/nipple wrenches were found, all along the retreat route (see figure).

Military buttons are another common artifact from battle-related sites. Two brass Dragoon cuff buttons depicting an eagle with a "D" in the shield and four plain pewter or white metal four-hole trouser buttons of two different sizes were found. Two of the trouser buttons and one spur were found in the Apache camp. The uniform cuff buttons were manufactured by Scovills & Company between 1840 and 1850.[28]

Spurs were issued to the enlisted men and were produced following strict standards. They are generally readily identifiable. The officers would purchase their own spurs, but they purchased them from military suppliers, and they too can often be identified. The military issue spur for the Dragoons for this particular time period is presumed to be the Grimsley Spur, which was designed in 1847 and went into production in 1851, and was the official military spur until the model 1859 spur replaced it.[29] The exact configuration of the 1851 pattern spur, however, is uncertain.

Four military spurs were located on the site (see figure). Two are solid brass military issue spurs, and two are brass-plated iron spurs, presumably purchased by the officers. All four are similar in size and shape.

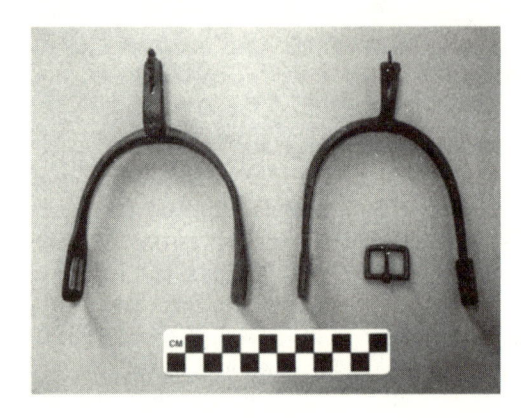

Military spurs.

The two solid brass spurs are more similar to the model 1859 military spur than the ones illustrated in Dorsey[30] and Steffen[31] as the model 1851 spur. They have a curved, almost right-angle shank, instead of straight as shown by Dorsey[32] and Steffen, yet the casting is smooth as opposed to the stippled appearance of the 1859 spur. The strap ends, although basically square, gently diminish in size as it connects to the heelpiece. The rowels on the spurs are different sizes. The inside surface of the spur is smooth, and there is no groove as in the later models of the 1859 spur. The solid brass spurs found on the site are almost identical to a spur drawn by Steffen as a model 1872 military spur,[33] but identified by Dorsey as a commercially produced spur from about 1860 to 1890[34] that is often misidentified as a military spur.

The two plated spurs are similar to the solid brass spurs in form, with a few notable differences; the metal is thinner, the spurs are lighted, and the strap ends are square. The rowels on these spurs are also different sizes. A strap buckle was found with one of these spurs. It is a rectangular brass-plated iron buckle with slightly rounded corners on the outside edge.

Because of the year of the battle, and the lack of any evidence that any other spur was issued between 1847 and 1859, it is possible that this is the model 1851 military spur (which is presumed to be the 1847 Grimsley design), and may have been the model for the commercially produced spurs from the 1860s to 1890s.[35] The plated spurs are examples of the officers' spur styles available from suppliers in New Mexico at the time.

One accoutrement hook from a model 1851 saber belt was found on the retreat route.[36] The hook is bent, and has what appears to be lead residue from a bullet where it may have been shot off a Dragoon's belt. Other military artifacts located include buckles, boot taps, boot nails, horseshoes, horseshoe nails, and a mess kit handle.

THE BATTLE

Davidson's official account of the battle is brief, and focuses on naming the casualties.[37] The distribution of the artifacts located during the survey, however, combined with several other written accounts and the sketch map of the battle,[38] provide a detailed picture of the battle and clarify several questions, many of which were raised during the court of inquiry.

The written accounts seem to suggest that the Dragoons were heading cross-country when they left the trail to Embudo to head up into the mountains, but it is more likely they turned off onto an existing trail that leads from the village of Cieneguilla to Picuris Pueblo. The cañon sides are too steep to have been climbed, and the cañon bottom is blocked by a rock outcrop. Although no archaeological evidence was found near the trail to the village of Embudo, historic artifacts were found on the trail as it neared the Apache camp. This well-established trail has been in place for many years. The earliest written reference to this trail is the account of Roque Madrid, who in 1705 left Picuris toward Cieneguilla along a trail through Agua Caliente Cañon.[39] The footprint of the trail is now fading, but it is still discernible. This is the only reasonable way to get to the area of the battle from Cieneguilla (see figure).

The trail climbs the steep slope of a ridge to the southeast, makes one switchback, and then heads straight up the ridge. The trail crosses a narrow saddle and then passes along the western slopes of a ridge adjacent to a deep cañon. It was in this area that the troops likely picked up the trail of the Apache, who were camped up a small side cañon just ahead. The metal detector survey located numerous artifacts in this area, primarily dating from the nineteenth century, that were associated with travel along the trail and confirm that it was in use for a long time. A few battle-related items were found, apparently representing overshot bullets and points from the actual battle location. Following this trail on horseback, it is unlikely that it took the troops much more than an hour to reach the Apache camp from Cieneguilla.

As the Dragoons entered the "narrow defile," or narrow side canon, they proceeded up the bottom of the cañon until they reached a rock outcrop and steepening slopes that hampered further progress. There they climbed the bank toward their right and dismounted on a more gently sloping area near

Battle layout.

the base of the ridge just above the cañon bottom. Lt. Davidson claimed in the court of inquiry that he did not leave his horses in the bottom of a cañon or next to the stream prior to the advance on the camp, but the artifacts show that he did leave his horses and a handful of troops *near* the cañon bottom, and clearly in a poor location. It is possible that he could have advanced farther up the slope before he dismounted his men, or circled around by going up the adjacent ridge and entering the camp from the south or southeast.

The written accounts state that someone from the Apache camp called out to the troops to come ahead if they wanted a fight. A small group of soldiers under the command of Dr. Magruder was left with the horses. The troops then split into two companies, advanced up the slope, and entered the camp. The archaeological evidence supports that as well. Artifacts are sparse, but there is evidence that one company went up a small draw just to the north. Fired balls and numerous arrow points, with an orientation showing they were fired from the ridge above, were found along its course. The other company apparently went straight up the slope where points, bullets, and caps were found. The dropped balls, caps, and uniform components on the ridge crest support the claim that they had entered the camp. No skirmish lines as reported by Bell[40] could be identified, and if indeed the troops went up the small draw, it is unlikely they formed any sort of line.

The Apache camp occupied the top of the narrow ridge. The artifact scatter is approximately 200 meters long, and 50 meters wide. No conclusive evidence of structures or hearths is present, although there are a few cobbles and rocks that seem out of character with the shale deposits that cover most of the ground within the camp. These rounded cobbles could be the remains of hearths or possibly structures. Evidence for the camp included numerous Apache domestic artifacts including metal cone tinklers, ceramics, metal awls, conchos, scraps of metal from point and cone tinkler manufacture, and dropped lead balls that had been chewed. The ceramics seem to cluster in two distinct areas, perhaps an indication of where the lodges were located. The majority of metal debitage is associated with the lower concentration, and the brass tinklers and brass scraps are associated with the northern concentration. The military artifacts are primarily located in the north section of the camp, around the northern ceramic cluster. It is possible that the southern concentration of ceramics represents an unrelated, earlier occupation of the site and not a separate group or band associated with the battle. If so, the area of the camp would be even smaller.[41] Further research and subsurface excavations may provide clarification regarding camp layout.

It is apparent that the Dragoons were not prepared for the resistance the Apache provided, nor had they considered the fact that the Apache would attack the troops and horses that were left behind. It is possible that the Apache encouraged the soldiers to come into the camp with the intent of drawing them away from their horses. The reports state that not long after the soldiers reached the camp, the Apache withdrew, went around the ridge, and attacked the horse position from several directions, catching them in a crossfire. The soldiers who had been left to guard the horses called for help. The Dragoons had no choice but to leave the Indian camp and move down the slope to reinforce the troops that were with the horses. The accounts say they formed a circle around the horses. This left them on the low ground, surrounded by the Apache firing from positions above. The archaeological evidence supports this scenario. Dropped balls, percussion caps, horseshoes, and horseshoe nails pinpoint the horse position, and it appears that soldiers were stationed in and around the horses just above the cañon bottom. There is also a concentration of fired Apache balls and arrows in this locale. Although only five of the 22 Dragoons who died in battle were killed in this first part of the battle, being pinned down for a long period of time undoubtedly affected the soldiers' ability to effectively continue the fight. Had the Dragoons not positioned their horses and soldiers at this location, they might not have been pinned down at all, and the battle might have had a different outcome.

Davidson is reported to have held this position for several hours, and then led the troops to a small hill about 150–200 meters away that seemed more defensible. This move to a new location appears to be true. Metal points, caps, balls, and two military spurs were found showing a movement of the troops to the adjacent ridge about 175 meters away. The limited density of artifacts suggests that the Dragoons were at this new location briefly, as described in the written accounts,[42] and then proceeded down to the Agua Caliente creek. It is likely that the Apache had blocked the Dragoons' retreat down the trail they came up, or perhaps the troops did not want to go through the narrow cañon where an ambush would have been certain. A move to the right would also have led them back toward more Apache. Davidson instead chose to go straight up the steep slope of the large ridge located across the creek. The mouth of the small side cañon is marked by several spent bullets, metal points, and dropped items along the creek crossing, indicating that this is where at least a portion of the troops crossed to go up the ridge.

It is no wonder that the written accounts state that the troops stopped halfway up the ridge. The long steep slope is difficult to climb without any gear. Despite numerous transects repeated over different times of the year, very little evidence of a fight was found on the slope. A few boot nails and horseshoe nails on the slope above the fired bullets, and a musketoon side plate, a trigger guard screw, and a nearby dropped ball for a horse pistol on top of the ridge were the only artifacts found. This may indicate that the fighting had ceased as the troops climbed the ridge, which would be implied by the fact that they stopped halfway up to catch their breath. It is not likely that they would have taken this time to take a break in the midst of a fight. Also Bell's statement that they abandoned the dead and wounded and eventually their horses while climbing the hill is not true. Again, the near lack of artifacts indicates that they were not under attack at this time.

The Dragoons were reported to have met the Indians as soon as they reached the top of the hill. If this is true, there were essentially no artifacts to support the claim. This may be due to artifact collectors finding this portion of the battle and "cleaning it out," but it is unlikely that they would have recovered every small piece of lead, every percussion cap, and every boot nail. It is possible we did not locate the position where they reached the summit. It seems more plausible that the Dragoons did not encounter the warriors until they reached the "point of the hill" as shown on the sketch map (see figure), and as shown by the artifact distribution. If this is the case, the Dragoons might have been able to retreat down the side of the ridge to the cañon to the north and avoid the second encounter that left 17 men dead. It is likely that the Dragoons were exhausted from the fight at the horse position and the climb up the steep slope, and were lulled into a sense of security upon reaching the top of the ridge. By the time they arrived at the narrow ridge where they were to descend to the trail, however, they found the Apache were there first. The Apache then closed in on the soldiers from the rear, trapping them on the narrow ridge with warriors above and below. At this point, the Apache appear to have lured the soldiers into a trap.

The archaeological evidence seems to confirm that the troops were not scattered, but stayed together during their final retreat from the point of the hill down the narrow ridge. However, the ratio of dropped to fired bullets and caps indicates that the soldiers were likely weary if not frantic during the push down the narrow ridge. A saber belt hook found in this area appears to have been shot off someone's belt, and numerous metal arrow points were found. The position just prior to the final retreat was littered with dropped balls, percussion caps, tools, and equipment, suggesting that the retreat may not have been as controlled and orderly as reported. As they neared the saddle where the trail to Cieneguilla was located, the troops found they could go no further. Taking advantage of a slightly less steep slope, the Dragoons made a final retreat down the side of the ridge to the adjacent cañon. A single fired cap among dozens of dropped balls, tools, and personal items at this location suggests that they discontinued the fight to flee down the hill toward safety. It is likely that many of the fallen soldiers were found here.

Bell, in his letter to Williams, contended that the battle could not have taken several hours: "As to fighting three hours that is the most ridiculously absurd assertion in the whole report. A Cartridge Box (cavalry) holds some 30 to 50 Cartridges. How long would it take a man to fire this number of Cartridges assuming that he fired all of them? But in the excitement of action most men will lose a large portion of their ammunition. I think any reasonable man will agree that Davidsons fight never lasted 30 minutes, his assertion to the contrary notwithstanding."[43] While we were not able to determine the length of the fighting, we were able to confirm that a large percentage of the caps and balls were dropped by the soldiers. The relatively small number of artifacts recovered could indicate that this was not a prolonged battle with constant shooting, but some of the written accounts confirm that there were pauses in between attacks. The overall time the Dragoons were on the battlefield would have been much longer than the amount of time they were actually engaged in firing, and it is likely that several hours had passed from the time they entered the Indian camp to the time they made their final retreat down the side of the narrow ridge.[44]

The claims as to the numbers of Apache in the fight appear to have been exaggerated. The written accounts of the court proceedings claim there were 60 to 90 lodges, and anywhere from 250 to more than 300 warriors. Given the size of the camp, approximately 10,000 square meters, half of which may not even have been occupied at the time of the battle, it is unlikely that there were more than 50 or 60 lodges on the ridge. If there were 250 to 300 Apache engaged in the battle, perhaps another group was camped nearby and joined these Apache in the fight. It is more likely that there were no more than 100 or 130 warriors as claimed by Carson[45] and Bell.[46] This number is consistent with other accounts concerning the number of Jicarilla living in the area at that time.[47]

SUMMARY AND CONCLUSIONS

The archaeological evidence confirms that the Cieneguilla battle site has been found, and provides an opportunity to closely examine the engagement. It also provides an opportunity to compare the written accounts with the actual footprint of the battle, and in essence re-open the court of inquiry of 1856. While the evidence shows that most of the official historic descriptions of the battle written at the time are generally accurate, it also shows some important differences. The research reveals that many of the accusations made by Lt. Bell in his letter of December 27, 1854, which formed the basis of the charges in the court of inquiry, are largely correct.

The court of inquiry, however, found Lt. Davidson innocent of any wrongdoing. Perhaps it is true that in 1854 a soldier could not retreat from an enemy's camp without engaging in a fight once the "war whoop" had commenced, or his honor and reputation would be impugned. In this setting, at this time, Davidson may have done the only thing he could to protect his honor. As noted by Taylor,[48] the higher command was more interested in Davidson's gallantry and bravery than his judgment. The court of inquiry did not look into the tactics or decisions that led to the deaths of 22 men in the field, or delve into the honor of losing a third of one's command. Nor did they deem it necessary to visit the site to see the layout of the battle for themselves. If they had, perhaps Davidson's military career would have taken a decidedly different track. This apparent desire to protect an officer's honor above all else was also reflected in an investigation into the Lt. Grattan massacre in Wyoming in August of 1854.[49] In that incident, Grattan and his entire command were killed, and the court was reluctant to disparage the name of a valiant deceased soldier despite evidence that he had likely caused the massacre. The final word on whether Lt. Davidson made some poor choices that resulted in his defeat rests in the hands of military strategists. We have provided the archaeological evidence, and compared the primary historic accounts to what actually lies on the ground. Whatever the conclusions, this fight has gone down in history as a decisive victory for the Jicarilla Apache against the U.S. government, and stands as a grim tribute to their skill not only as warriors but as military strategists as well.

NOTES

1. David M. Johnson, *A Preliminary Report on the Battle of Cieneguilla, a Jicarilla Apache Victory against the U.S. Dragoons*, paper presented at the 2003 Apache Archaeology Conference, Carlsbad, NM, 2003; David M. Johnson, Chris Adams, and Diane White, *A Research Design for the Investigation of the Battle of Cieneguilla between the First Dragoons and the Jicarilla Apache on March 29, 1854*, unpublished manuscript, Carson National Forest, Taos, 2002.

2. Jack K. Boyer, in *Battle of Cieneguilla*. Ms. on file, Carson National Forest, Taos, 1965, Taos, talks about the battle and its approximate location.

3. Bell to Williams, December 27, 1854. Letters Received, Department of New Mexico, Adjutant General's Office, Record Group 94, National Archives, Washington, D.C.

4. James A. Bennett, *Forts and Forays: A Dragoon in New Mexico 1850–1856*. University of New Mexico Press, Albuquerque, 1948.

5. Bell to Williams, December 27, 1854. LR, DNM, AGO, RG 94, NA.

6. Proceedings of a Court of Inquiry Convened at Santa Fe, New Mexico, February 9, 1856. Judge Advocate General's Office, Records Group 153, National Archives, Washington, D.C.

7. James A. Bennett, *Forts and Forays: A Dragoon in New Mexico 1850–1856*. University of New Mexico Press, Albuquerque, 1948.

8. Proceedings of a Court of Inquiry Convened at Santa Fe, New Mexico, February 9, 1856. JAGO, RG 153, NA.

9. Bell to Williams, December 27, 1854. LR, DNM, AGO, RG 94, NA.

10. Ibid.

11. Bennett apparently enlisted under an alias. See James A. Bennett, *Forts and Forays: A Dragoon in New Mexico 1850–1856*. University of New Mexico Press, Albuquerque, 1948, vii.

12. Bell to Williams, December 27, 1854. LR, DNM, AGO, RG 94, NA.

13. Carson to Messervy, April 12, 1854. New Mexico Superintendency, BIA, Letters Received.

14. Christopher D. Adams, Diane E. White, and David M. Johnson, Last Chance Cañon Apache/Cavalry Battle Site, Lincoln National Forest, New Mexico. United States Department of Agriculture, Forest Service, Southwest Region, Albuquerque, New Mexico, 2000; Christopher D. Adams, Diane E. White, and David M. Johnson, Dark Cañon Apache Rancheria Battle Site. United States Department of Agriculture, Forest Service, Southwest Region, Albuquerque, New Mexico, 2000; Charles M. Haecker and Jeffery G. Mauck, *On the Prairie of Palo Alto*. Texas A & M University Press, College Station, 1997; Larry L. Ludwig and James L. Stute, *The Battle at K-H Butte*. Western Lore Press, Tucson, 1993; D. Scott, R. A. Fox Jr., M. A. Conner, and D. Harmon, *Archaeological Perspectives on the Battle of the Little Bighorn*. University of Oklahoma Press, Norman, 1989.

15. David Johnson, Chris Adams, and Diane White, *A Research Design for the Investigation of the Battle of Cieneguilla between the First Dragoons and the Jicarilla Apache on March 29, 1854*, unpublished manuscript, Carson National Forest, Taos, 2002.

16. Proceedings of a Court of Inquiry Convened at Santa Fe, New Mexico, February 9, 1856. JAGO, RG 153, NA.

17. A. H. Warren, *The Micaceous Pottery of the Rio Grand*. Archaeological Society of New Mexico, Anthropological Papers No. 6, Albuquerque, 1981.

18. Marc Thompson, A Survey of Aboriginal Metal Points from the Apachería. *The Artifact*. The El Paso Archaeological Society 18(1). El Paso, Texas, 1980, 2.

19. Ibid.

20. Christopher D. Adams, Diane E. White, and David M. Johnson, Last Chance Cañon Apache/Cavalry Battle Site, Lincoln National Forest, New Mexico. United States Department of Agriculture, Forest Service, Southwest Region, Albuquerque, New Mexico, 2000; Christopher D. Adams, Diane E. White, and David M. Johnson, Dark Cañon Apache Rancheria Battle Site. United States Department of Agriculture, Forest Service, Southwest Region, Albuquerque, New Mexico, 2000.

21. Ibid.

22. Rudolf Kurz, Journal of Rudolf Friederich Kurz. Translated by Myrtis Jarrell, Edited by J. N. B. Hewitt, Smithsonian Institution, Bureau of American Ethnology, Bulletin 115, Washington, D.C., 1937, 322.

23. Proceedings of a Court of Inquiry Convened at Santa Fe, New Mexico, February 9, 1856. JAGO, RG 153, NA.

24. Major James E. Hicks, *U.S. Military Firearms 1776–1956*. Borden Publishing Company, Alhambra, CA, 1962, 43.

25. James E. Thomas and Dean S. Thomas, *A Handbook of Civil War Bullets and Cartridges*. Thomas Publications, Gettysburg, 1996, 50.

26. Kent Weber and Douglas Scott, Firearms Identification Procedures in the Analysis of Percussion Caps from the Battle of Cieneguilla, New Mexico. Manuscript on file, Carson National Forest, Taos, 2003.

27. James B. Shaffer, Lee A. Rutledge, and R. Stephen Dorsey, *Gun Tools, Their History and Identification*. Collector's Library, Eugene, 1992.

28. Warren K. Tice, *Uniform Buttons of the United States 1776–1865*. Thomas Publications, Gettysburg, 1997, 31.

29. Stephen R. Dorsey, *The American Military Spur*. Collector's Library, Eugene, 2000.

30. Ibid.

31. Randy Steffen, *The Horse Soldier 1776–1943 Vol. II: The Frontier, The Mexican War, the Civil War, the Indian Wars 1851–1880*. University of Oklahoma Press, Norman, 1978.

32. Dorsey notes that the shank was probably not straight as illustrated, but he had no other information to go on to dispute that.

33. Ibid.

34. Stephen R. Dorsey, *The American Military Spur*. Collector's Library, Eugene, 2000, 57–58.

35. It is also possible that these spurs are an earlier example of commercially available spurs, and were not military issue.

36. Frederick P. Todd, *American Military Equipage 1851–1872 Vol. 1*. The Company of Military Historians, Providence, 1974.

37. Davidson to Blake, April 1, 1854. LR, DNM, AGO, RG 94, NA.

38. James A. Bennett, *Forts and Forays: A Dragoon in New Mexico 1850–1856*. University of New Mexico Press, Albuquerque, 1948; Proceedings of a Court of Inquiry Convened at Santa Fe, New Mexico, February 9, 1856. JAGO, RG 153, NA.

39. Rick Hendricks and John P. Wilson, *The Navajos in 1705, Roque Madrid's Campaign Journal*. University of New Mexico Press, Albuquerque, 1996, 13, 66.

40. Bell to Williams, December 27, 1854. LR, DNM, AGO, RG 94, NA.

41. Even if the entire area was used by the Apache, it is too small to have been able to accommodate a large number of lodges.
42. Proceedings of a Court of Inquiry Convened at Santa Fe, New Mexico, February 9, 1856. JAGO, RG 153, NA.
43. Bell to Williams, December 27, 1854. LR, DNM, AGO, RG 94, NA.
44. This is consistent with some of the accounts presented in the Court of Inquiry.
45. Carson to Messervy, April 12, 1854. NMS, BIA, LR.
46. Bell to Williams, December 27, 1854. LR, DNM, AGO, RG 94, NA.
47. Averam Bender, A Study of Jicarilla Apache Indians, 1846–1887. In *Apache Indians IX*, Garland Publishing Inc., New York, 1959, 28, 61, 63, 66, 171.
48. Morris F. Taylor, Campaigns against the Jicarilla Apache. *New Mexico Historical Review*, Vol. XLIV, No 4. 1969, 226.
49. Paul L. Hedren (foreword), *The Massacre of Lieutenant Grattan and His Command by Indians*. The Arthur H. Clark Company, Glendale, CA, 1983.

REFERENCES CITED

Adams, Christopher D., Diane E. White, and David M. Johnson. 2000a. Last Chance Cañon Apache/Cavalry Battle Site, Lincoln National Forest, New Mexico. United States Department of Agriculture, Forest Service, Southwest Region, Albuquerque, NM.
Adams, Christopher D., Diane E. White, and David M. Johnson. 2000b. Dark Cañon Apache Rancheria Battle Site. United States Department of Agriculture, Forest Service, Southwest Region, Albuquerque, NM.
Bennett, James A. 1948. *Forts and Forays: A Dragoon in New Mexico 1850–1856*. University of New Mexico Press, Albuquerque.
Bender, Averam. 1959. A Study of Jicarilla Apache Indians, 1846–1887. In *Apache Indians IX*. Garland Publishing Inc., New York.
Boyer, Jack K. 1965. *Battle of Cieneguilla*. Ms. on file, Carson National Forest, Taos.
Dorsey, Stephen R. 2000. *The American Military Spur*. Collector's Library, Eugene.
Haecker, Charles M., and Jeffery G. Mauck. 1997. *On the Prairie of Palo Alto: Historical Archaeology of the Battlefield*. Texas A & M University Press, College Station.
Hedren, Paul L. 1983. (foreword). *The Massacre of Lieutenant Grattan and His Command by Indians*. The Arthur H. Clark Company, Glendale, CA.
Hendricks, Rick, and John P. Wilson. 1996. *The Navajos in 1705, Roque Madrid's Campaign Journal*. University of New Mexico Press, Albuquerque.
Hicks, Major James E. 1962. *U.S. Military Firearms 1776–1956*. Borden Publishing Company, Alhambra, CA.
Johnson, David M. 2003. *A Preliminary Report on the Battle of Cieneguilla, a Jicarilla Apache Victory against the U.S. Dragoons*. Paper presented at the 2003 Apache Archaeology Conference, Carlsbad, NM.
Johnson, David, Chris Adams, and Diane White. 2002. *A Research Design for the Investigation of the Battle of Cieneguilla between the First Dragoons and the Jicarilla Apache on March 29, 1854*. Unpublished manuscript, Carson National Forest, Taos.

Kurz, Rudolf. 1937. Journal of Rudolf Friederich Kurz. Translated by Myrtis Jarrell, Edited by J. N. B. Hewitt, Smithsonian Institution, Bureau of American Ethnology, Bulletin 115, Washington, D.C.

Ludwig, Larry L., and James L. Stute. 1993. *The Battle at K-H Butte*. Western Lore Press, Tucson.

Scott, D., R. A. Fox Jr., M. A. Conner, and D. Harmon. 1989. *Archaeological Perspectives on the Battle of the Little Bighorn*. University of Oklahoma Press, Norman.

Shaffer, James B., Lee A. Rutledge, and R. Stephen Dorsey. 1992. *Gun Tools, Their History and Identification*. Collector's Library, Eugene.

Steffen, Randy. 1978. *The Horse Soldier 1776–1943 Vol II: The Frontier, The Mexican War, the Civil War, the Indian Wars 1851–1880*. University of Oklahoma Press, Norman.

Taylor, Morris F. 1969. Campaigns against the Jicarilla Apache. *New Mexico Historical Review* XLIV(4).

Thomas, James E., and Dean S. Thomas. 1996. *A Handbook of Civil War Bullets and Cartridges*. Thomas Publications, Gettysburg.

Thompson, Marc. 1980. A Survey of Aboriginal Metal Points from the Apachería. *The Artifact*. The El Paso Archaeological Society 18(1). El Paso, TX.

Tice, Warren K. 1997. *Uniform Buttons of the United States 1776–1865*. Thomas Publications, Gettysburg.

Todd, Frederick P. 1974. *American Military Equipage 1851–1872 Vol. 1*. The Company of Military Historians, Providence.

United States Government. 1854a. Bell to Williams, December 27, 1854. Letters Received, Department of New Mexico, Adjutant General's Office, Record Group 94, National Archives, Washington, D.C.

United States Government. 1854b. Carson to Messervy, April 12, 1854. New Mexico Superintendency, BIA, Letters Received.

United States Government. 1854c. Davidson to Blake, April 1, 1854. Letters Received, Department of New Mexico, Adjutant General's Office, Record Group 94, National Archives, Washington, D.C.

United States Government. 1856. Proceedings of a Court of Inquiry Convened at Santa Fe, New Mexico, February 9, 1856. Judge Advocate General's Office, Record Group 153, National Archives, Washington, D.C.

Warren, A. H. 1981. *The Micaceous Pottery of the Rio Grand*. Archaeological Society of New Mexico, Anthropological Papers No. 6, Albuquerque.

Weber, Kent, and Douglas Scott. 2003. Firearms Identification Procedures in the Analysis of Percussion Caps from the Battle of Cieneguilla, New Mexico. Manuscript on file, Carson National Forest, Taos.

The Confederate Cantonment at Evansport, Virginia

Joseph Balicki

BATTLEFIELDS ARE ONLY part of warfare; other factors are equally important to an examination of conflict. Camp locations, the positioning of troops, strategic goals, and political concerns are essential to understanding strategy, and how responses to hostile fire were formulated. Beginning in October 1861 and continuing until March 9, 1862, Confederate shore batteries shut down most Federal traffic along the Potomac River. The majority of artillery was in the vicinity of Evansport (Marine Base Quantico), Virginia, where approximately 3,500 Confederate troops supported the batteries. Federal troops countered by erecting batteries on the Maryland shore and, using balloon ascensions, spied on the Confederates. The result was a prolonged six-month artillery duel where neither side gained an edge. The Confederates used the landscape to conceal and protect their camps, which were located just out of range of Federal artillery. Archaeological investigations found a well-preserved Civil War landscape that included 697 habitation features clustered into four camps, an artillery magazine, target range, picket posts, paths, an earthwork, and road traces.[1] Military doctrine dictated camp layout, but topography, troop preference, and hostile fire were also influential, while landscape was essential in protecting support troops from hostile fire. Landscapes of conflict are larger than just the battlefield, and the conflict along the river had a profound effect on the nearby camps. This cantonment location is viewed within the local and larger landscape of conflict in northern Virginia.

REGIONAL LANDSCAPE OF CONFLICT

Northern Virginia, encompassing the counties of Fairfax, Alexandria, Arlington, Prince William, Stafford, and Loudoun, was host to extensive military operations during the Civil War. Between May 1861 and March 9, 1862, northern Virginia was a major war front (see figure). In May, the Federal Army established a foothold in Virginia, occupying Alexandria and fortifying the Potomac River bluffs overlooking the capital. By the spring of 1861, the

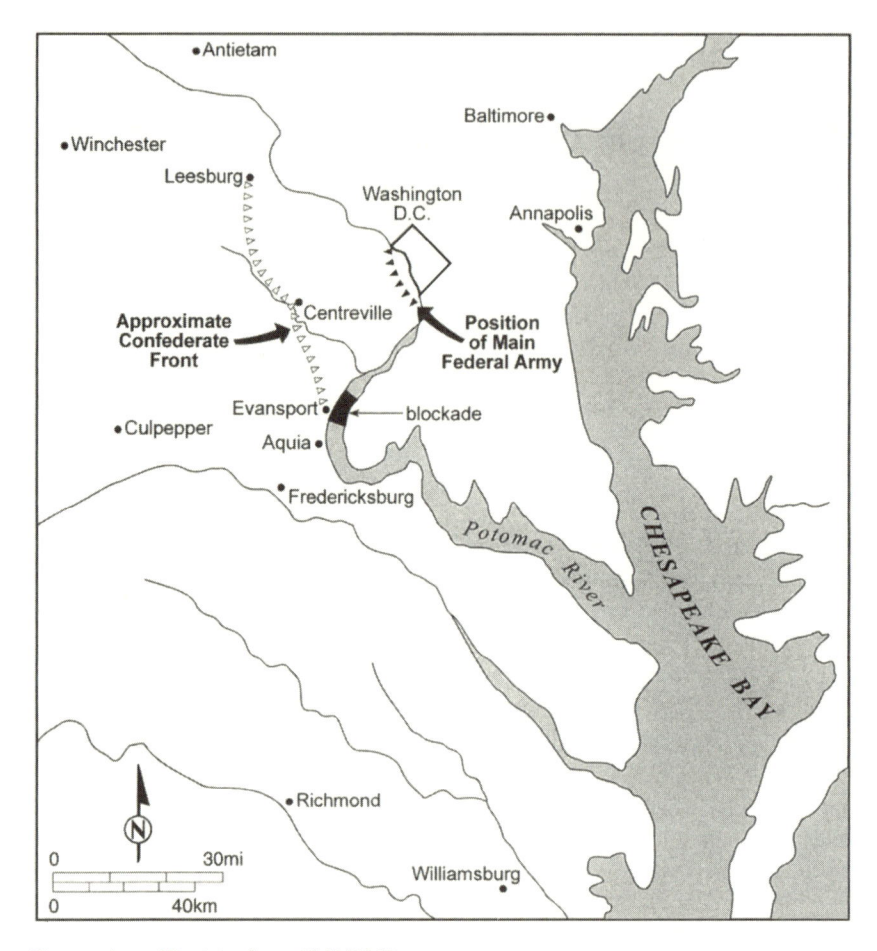

The northern Virginia front 1861/1862.

Confederate Army was thinly spread across northern Virginia. Approximately 20,000 troops occupied positions from Leesburg in the north to Aquia Creek in the south. Most of these forces were within 30 miles (48.3 km) of Washington, D.C.[2]

In July 1861, Federal forces were defeated at the First Battle of Bull Run (First Manassas), 25 miles (40.2 km) from Washington. Confederate forces established their headquarters at Fairfax Courthouse, 15 miles (24.1 km) outside of Washington, D.C. From the White House, Confederate flags could be seen above the advance positions on Munson's and Miner's Hills.[3] After Bull Run the main elements of Federal Army were encamped in three separate locations, in the shadow of the defenses of Washington, to protect the main thoroughfares and railways leading to Alexandria and the Potomac River bridges. From these positions pickets, vedettes, foraging parties, and scouts periodically engaged the Confederates. At this time the capital's only links to the North were the primitive road system, a rail line to Baltimore, and navigation on the Potomac River.[4]

The Potomac River forms the boundary between Maryland and Virginia. Washington, D.C., is located at the western-most point of navigation by ocean-going vessels. Just west of the city is a geological formation known as the Fall Line. This is the point where low rolling hills of the Piedmont meet low-lying coastal plain deposits. At the Fall Line a change in gradient occurs, as evidenced by a series of non-navigable falls along the river. West of the Fall Line the Potomac flows west-to-east, and is approximately 2,000 ft (610 m) wide. Along this stretch of river, the nearest fords to Washington, D.C., are those in the vicinity of Leesburg, Virginia. East of the Fall Line the Potomac widens, is tidal, and begins a sweeping turn toward the southeast. At Evansport, 34 miles (54.7 km) below Washington, D.C., the river is 1.5 miles (2.4 km) wide.

The river was a formidable obstacle for both armies. At Washington, D.C., only three bridges linked Federal forces in Virginia to the relative safety of the Maryland shore. In the general vicinity of the capital, the bluffs on the Virginia side have a commanding view over the capital. From positions on the Arlington and Alexandria heights a military force could command Alexandria, Virginia, and the Federal capital itself. For the Federals the occupation of these heights was essential and likely influenced the May 24, 1861, invasion of Virginia. They promptly fortified an approximately 10-mile-long (16.1 km) section of the Arlington and Alexandria heights, and from this foothold the Federal Army would expand their reach west into Virginia. By December 1861 approximately 108,000 Federal troops were positioned in northern Virginia and the Washington, D.C., environs.[5]

To counter a Confederate advance across the fords west of Washington, the Federals positioned an army, under General Stone, in Maryland.[6] Further, they also deployed troops at Harpers Ferry, Virginia, to counter Confederate forces under Stonewall Jackson operating in the Shenandoah Valley. South and east of the capital the Federal forces began fortifying the Anacostia heights and occupied Fort Washington, a War of 1812–era fortification south of Washington.[7] It was not until September 1861, two months after the defeat at Bull Run, that a large force of Federal troops occupied the Maryland shore opposite the Confederate right flank positions along the Potomac.

Opposing these Federal forces was a Confederate force of approximately 48,000 troops, spread over an approximately 40-mile (64.4 km) front anchored on both sides by the Potomac River.[8] Most of Fairfax County was the "no-man's land" between the two armies. Radiating from the Federal positions west and south were several railroads and roads that could be used as corridors for a Federal westward movement. The Confederates positioned themselves to counter movement along the Orange and Alexandria railroad,

Loudoun and Hampshire railroad, Leesburg Pike, Little River Turnpike, and Telegraph Road.

By fall 1861, the Confederate Army took steps to solidify their positions. The Confederate left flank was anchored at the Potomac River fords near Leesburg. There, approximately 2,500 Confederates under General Shanks Evans constructed several small earthworks to defend the fords, as well as movement along both the Leesburg Pike and the Loudoun and Hampshire railroad.[9] Although small, Evans's garrison could be easily reinforced, since Leesburg was directly linked to the Confederate center by a road. The main Confederate concentration was at Centreville, approximately 18 miles (29 km) west of the Federal positions. Centreville was a small village located on a plateau that commanded the eastward approaches from Washington, including the Warrenton Turnpike, Braddock Road, and the Orange and Alexandria railroad. Here, approximately 36,000 troops under General Joseph Johnston constructed fortifications and built winter quarters.[10] Advance troops briefly occupied Upton's, Mason's, and Munson's Hills and were in direct contact with Federal forces, but were pulled back as winter approached.

On their right flank, along the Potomac, the Confederates began construction of numerous gun batteries in the Evansport area, in hopes of disrupting Federal supply lines (see figure). The right flank was the weak point along the Confederate line. The Confederate center could not directly aid it in case of a Federal attack. In fact, the Confederate right was closer to the main Federal Army at Alexandria than to Centreville, and there was a direct road link, Telegraph Road, between the two opposing armies.

Protecting the Confederate right and the Potomac batteries were approximately 7,600 troops under General Whiting.[11] An additional 6,000 troops were deployed to support the batteries and protect Aquia Landing and the Potomac shore south of Evansport. The Occoquan River formed a natural obstacle between the Federal Army and the Confederate right flank. Strategically, the topography and forests along this river allowed for a defense utilizing only a small number of troops. The Confederates concentrated their defense at the Telegraph Road crossing of the Occoquan. The rough forested terrain lying between the Telegraph Road crossing and Centreville was not protected in force. The deployment of troops along the Confederate right was a concern for the Confederates as they expected a Federal assault along this portion of their line.

The fall of 1861 was a critical time for the Confederates; winter was approaching and they had to determine where and when they would establish winter quarters. They correctly surmised that the Federal Army was not going to advance, so they began establishing winter quarters. In mid-November, however, this perception changed and the Confederates believed that there was a significant threat to their right flank, especially the Potomac batteries. The problem for the Confederates was the separation between the Potomac River batteries and the main Confederate Army at Centreville. Additionally,

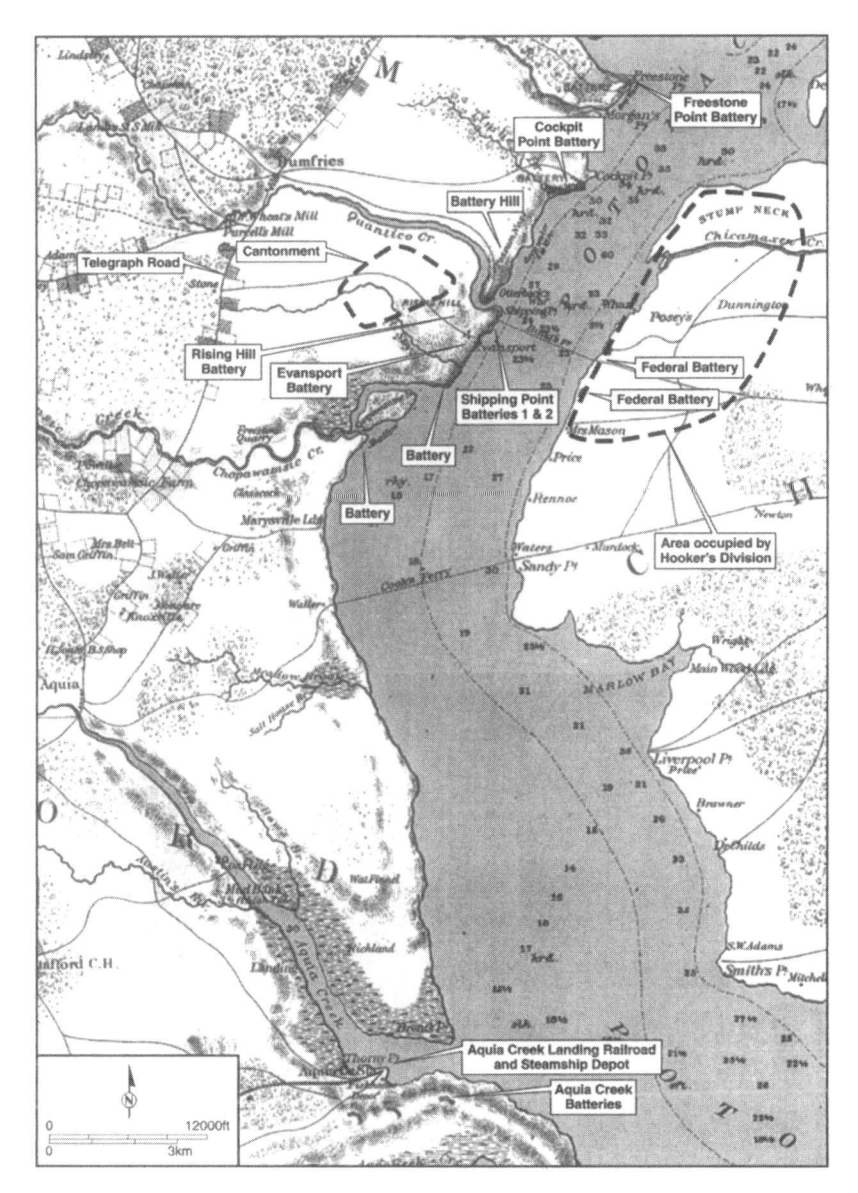

Sketch of Virginia and the Rebel Camps and Batteries, in Front of Gen. Joe Hooker's Division in Charles County, Maryland. (Library of Congress)

while there was a direct road from Alexandria to Evansport, none existed between Evansport and Centreville. Confederate President Davis became involved, suggesting that General Johnston (commander of the Confederate forces in northern Virginia) personally evaluate the blockade and troops in the vicinity.[12] General Johnston's report presents a concise assessment of the Confederate troops, strategy, perceived threats, and conditions of the road network. He believed the Confederate right was threatened, a Federal attack had a chance of succeeding, and that poor road conditions would hamper a defense. Because Civil War armies were restricted to primarily moving along established dirt roadways, weather conditions had a profound effect on the troops and on strategy. Along the Potomac the Federals held the advantage because they could move along the river while any Confederate counter would have to been done over poor roads. The threat of a Federal advance between the Confederates at Centreville and those on the Potomac eventually contributed to the Confederates' decision to withdraw.

The Northern Virginia Front remained static through the fall and into the early winter of 1861; both sides prepared winter quarters and no major offensives were undertaken. The main contact between the armies was the six-month artillery duel between shore batteries on the Potomac. While this conflict did not result in large numbers of battlefield casualties, it had a profound effect on both sides. The Confederates lost hundreds of raw, untrained recruits to camp diseases. For the Federals, the Confederate shore batteries were more a source of embarrassment, a cause for apprehension, and an example of military and naval ineptness, than an obstacle for supplying the capital or the army.

By February 1862, the Confederate leadership concluded that the Northern Virginia Front was becoming unsustainable.[13] On February 20, 1861, the worsening conditions of the roads between the Confederate front and Richmond led Confederate President Jefferson Davis and his cabinet to order General Johnston to withdraw Confederate forces to south of the Rappahannock River. Preparations for the withdrawal took several weeks. Finally, on March 9, 1862, the Confederates abandoned their positions along the Northern Virginia front. Incidentally, on March 8, 1862, President Lincoln ordered "that the Army and Navy cooperate in an immediate effort to capture the enemy's batteries upon the Potomac between Washington and the Chesapeake Bay,"[14] just the type of action the Confederates had feared.

THE POTOMAC BLOCKADE

Before the war, the Potomac River was the main supply route to Washington, D.C., and both sides realized its strategic value. Prior to the war, Richmond and Washington, D.C., were linked by a combined railroad and steam ship route. The Richmond, Fredericksburg, and Potomac Railroad ran between Richmond and Aquia Landing; there steamships plied the Potomac River to and from Washington, D.C. In early May 1861, Virginia State troops established batteries at the railhead at Aquia Landing approximately 9 miles (14.5 km) downriver from Evansport.[15] Adjacent to Aquia, the main navigation channel is nearer the

Maryland shore. Thus, these batteries could not be used to obstruct Federal shipping on the river. Federal gunboats attacked the Aquia Landing batteries several times in the spring of 1861.[16] It is likely that the first shots fired by the United States Navy in the Civil War occurred at Aquia Creek on May 31, 1861.[17]

Initially, Mathias Point in King George County, approximately 24 miles (38.6 km) downriver from Evansport, was chosen by the Confederate leadership as a good location for an offensive shore battery.[18] General Daniel Ruggles, commander of the area's Virginia State forces, understood the offensive limitations of the Aquia batteries and the proposed one at Mathias Point. Ruggles also evaluated the Confederate-held Potomac shore and recommended Evansport. General Theophilus H. Holmes, Ruggles's replacement when Virginia troops were absorbed into the Confederate Army, evaluated the situation and reported: "I respectfully recommend that the neighborhood of Evansport should be preferred to Mathias Point.... If you can send me two 32-pounders (rifled), or two 8-inch columbiads, I believe I could stop the navigation of the river, if the general commanding thinks it a matter of sufficient importance to justify the expense."[19]

General Holmes received orders from Robert E. Lee on June 28, 1861, authorizing him to construct batteries at Evansport.[20] Apparently, the specific placement of the batteries was left to General Holmes, but they were to be erected clandestinely. Elsewhere in northern Virginia, events quickly overshadowed the activities along the Potomac. After the First Battle of Bull Run Confederate authorities renewed their efforts at constructing offensive shore batteries near Evansport.

On August 1, 1861, Confederate President Jefferson Davis wrote General Johnston, informing him that "General Holmes will establish a battery above his present position, near the mouth of the Chopawamsic, where it is reported the channel can be commanded so as to cut off that line of the enemy's communication with their arsenals and main depots of troops. This measure will, no doubt, lead to an attack, and hence the preference for a position between his column and yours, rather than one lower down the river, as that of Mathias Point."[21]

In August 1861, Johnston wrote the Confederate president that he was surprised that the batteries had not yet been built; that General Holmes had taken five captured guns for positioning in the batteries; and that there should be a unified command structure with him (Johnston) as commander.[22]

There was a rift between Johnston and the Confederate command in Richmond concerning the overall conduct of the war in northern Virginia. Johnston's correspondence was an attempt to consolidate his power along the front. President Davis tried to explain Holmes's situation and the batteries to General Johnston in a September 5, 1861, correspondence.

> In relation to the command of Brigadier-General Holmes I will only say that it is in easy communication with this place by railroad and telegraph, but has little and

tedious connection with Manassas; wherefore it has been kept in direct correspondence with Richmond. The battery [Evansport] above Aquia Creek was located with reference to width of channel of river and defensibility against attack from Alexandria. The lower side of the Quantico commands the upper. The upper side of the Occoquan is reported to command the lower. The long and circuitous march from Alexandria to Quantico would enable you to strike the column in the flank and reverse. The direct and short march to Occoquan offers no such advantage. If we drive off the vessels from that part of the Potomac, the Marylanders can come safely to us and we may cross to that part of Maryland where our friends are to be found.[23]

The fact that the Confederate president knew the tactical, logistical, and topographic reasons for positioning the batteries at Evansport indicates the importance the authorities were placing on this endeavor. The authorities in Richmond would not consolidate the commands along the Potomac until October 1861.

General Holmes was in need of a competent field engineer who could design the Evansport batteries which included Evansport, Shipping Point Battery 1, Shipping Point Battery 2, Rising Hill, and South Point. The authorities in Richmond indicated that General Johnston should furnish an officer, an order he was slow in carrying out.[24] On September 3, 1861, Johnston received the command that "the President desires that you will order Brigadier-General Trimble to Evansport, on the Potomac, to command the battery and troops at that point."[25]

Upon arriving at Evansport, General Isaac Trimble, with troops under the jurisdiction of Department of Fredericksburg Commander General Holmes, constructed the batteries with assistance from Confederate Naval Officer Commander Frederick Chatard.[26] In early September eight "guns of heaviest caliber," including the rifled gun taken at Manassas, and three 32-pounders, one rifled, were sent to Evansport. On September 15, Trimble reported: "Our enterprise here is scarcely less important than any now being executed anywhere in the South. [sic] and no efforts or risks should be wanted to insure success. I have begun the work, and in a week shall want the guns. I have 3,000 men to support the batteries and hope to erect them unnoticed by the enemy, who keep a daily watch on us from the river, $1\frac{1}{2}$ miles [2.4 km] distant from our position."[27] Work on the batteries was done clandestinely. A screen of trees was kept between the earthworks and the river.

The first Evansport battery was completed by September 29.[28] Trimble's batteries at Evansport were not the only offensive Confederate batteries on the Potomac, but they were the only ones within General Holmes's Fredericksburg department. Concurrent with the building of the Evansport batteries, work was under way to the north at Freestone and Cockpit points by Potomac District troops under General Johnston. The chain of command for the batteries was muddled. It appears that the battery at Freestone Point was constructed by troops under Johnston with little, if any, knowledge of the

Richmond authorities. Further complicating the command structure was the presence of Confederate Navy officers who had direct command of the Evansport batteries, but do not appear to have been assigned to the Potomac District batteries.

By September 1861 the Federal authorities knew that the Confederates were constructing offensive batteries between Freestone Point and Aquia Creek. The Potomac flotilla and observers on the Maryland shore noted the increased activity along the river. By late September, a battery had been established at Freestone Point. Federal authorities knew the presence of this battery, but considered this battery to have little potential to disrupt traffic upon the river, and was either defensive in nature or a ruse.[29]

On September 25, a small engagement between the Freestone battery and Federal ships occurred, confirmation that the Confederates were building offensive batteries on the river. Although the Evansport batteries were finished by late September, they did not reveal themselves. General Johnston exerted his overall control and insisted that the batteries remain concealed. For some reason, General Johnston did not want the Evansport batteries to fire. Possibly he wanted to wait until all the batteries along the shoreline had been constructed and not revealing the batteries piecemeal would have a psychological effect on the Federal forces when one impressive display of firepower was released on Federal shipping. It is also possible that the delay in showing the batteries was due, in part, to the pending restructuring of the Confederate command. On October 22, 1861, the Potomac Valley and Aquia districts were combined into the Department of Northern Virginia under the command of General Johnston.[30] However, General Holmes retained his command and, apparently, a degree of autonomy.

On October 15, 1861, the United States Navy forced the Confederates to reveal the presence of their batteries when a brief exchange occurred between the batteries and Federal ships.[31] On October 25, 1861, Captain John Dahlgren, commander of the Washington Navy Yard, informed the Secretary of the Navy that "the Potomac is now so far obstructed that it is no longer used by the army for transportation of supplies and the sole dependence for that purpose and for the supplies of the inhabitants of this city is limited to railroads alone."[32] Federal traffic on the Potomac was brought to a standstill; the Confederates now had control of approximately 15 miles (24.1 km) of the river. Shortly after the batteries revealed themselves, over 40 vessels were on the lower Potomac, waiting to make passage.[33]

Once the Confederate batteries were revealed, the Potomac flotilla was thought to be no match for the Confederates. Commander Craven, head of the flotilla, did not believe he could stop the batteries from closing the river and as a result never challenged them.[34] Things only got worse for Craven and his small flotilla. On October 18, 1861, the Confederates cleared away the trees from their battery at Cockpit Point, just north of Evansport. Upon being notified of this, Craven detained all ships bound downriver from

Washington.³⁵ The Confederates had the small steamer, *George Page*, at Aquia Creek, which they fearlessly sailed to Quantico Creek. The steamer found sanctuary near the Evansport and Shipping Point batteries and was able to conduct limited operations on the river. The *George Page* was routinely used to ferry goods and men across the Potomac.³⁶

The Federal response was to stop river traffic and send 8,000 troops, under General Hooker, to establish counter-batteries across from Evansport, in Budd's Ferry, Charles County, Maryland.³⁷ From these positions Federal guns exchanged fire with the Confederate batteries almost constantly. Both sides could reach the opposite shore, but with the exception of a small number of rifled-guns, the artillery fire was wildly inaccurate. The Federal batteries included several Whitworth rifled artillery pieces. The Federal Army tested these guns but never widely adopted them after the spring of 1862; on the other hand, later in the war the Confederates found these guns worth the effort it took to run them through the Federal blockade. The Whitworth guns that Federal troops used fired a solid hexagonal iron bolt approximately 2 miles (3.2 km) with great accuracy. Since the distance between the Shipping Point and Evansport batteries and the Federal batteries at Budd's Creek was approximately 1.8 miles (2.8 km), the Whitworth guns could be fired upon the Confederates with a degree of accuracy. It is interesting to note that the Confederate camps are about 2-to-2.5 miles (3.2-to-4 km) from the Federal batteries, or just out of range.

The Federals relied on balloon observations to determine the scope of the batteries and the size of the supporting forces (see figure). Through January and February, constant observation of the Confederate positions was kept from balloons.³⁸ In addition to ascensions done from land, a balloon and its supporting gas apparatus were placed on a barge and floated.³⁹

There is no record of the Confederate batteries ever sinking or seriously damaging a Federal ship, but just the threat was enough to close the river. Although they had no success firing on ships, the Confederates did manage to inflict additional fear on October 19, 1861, when they captured the schooners *Fairfax* and *Mary Virginia*.⁴⁰ These vessels were taken to Quantico Creek and were subsequently scuttled when the Confederates withdrew.

On November 7, 1861, General Samuel French replaced General Trimble as commander of the Confederate batteries.⁴¹ Despite some misgivings, French felt that the blockade was accomplishing its goals. On January 14, 1862, he noted his dissatisfaction with his troops' efforts but added, "As regards the blockade of the river, not a sail has passed for weeks. The river would be lifeless and desolate except for the eight or ten steamers always in sight above and below."⁴²

Hooker's view from the Maryland shore was somewhat different.

> This afternoon the rebels have discharged no less than seventy or eighty guns at a solitary steamer passing down the river without effect. The batteries used were

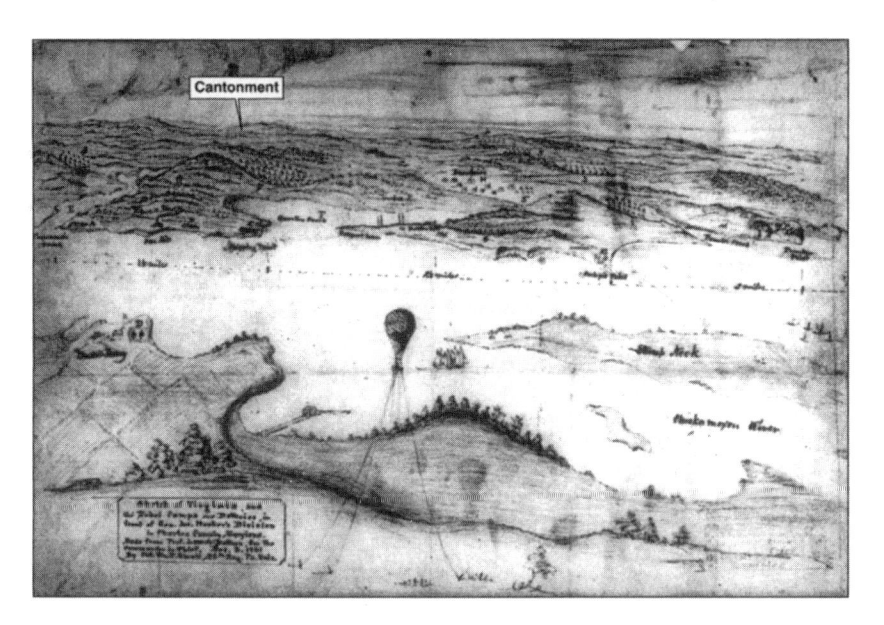

Detail of Map of Northern Eastern Virginia and Vicinity of Washington. (Library of Congress)

those in the immediate vicinity of Evansport. It cannot be possible that they will persevere much longer in their fruitless efforts to close the navigation of the river. The result of their labors to-day confirms me in the opinion I have entertained for ten days past that it is not in their power to present any formidable barrier to the almost uninterrupted passage of vessels up and down the Potomac. I am aware that a different opinion prevails among those whose experience should entitle their opinion to more consideration than my own, and for that reason it is with some reluctance that I advance it; nevertheless it is my conviction. For instance, today the vessel descended the river soon after midday with a three or four knot breeze and was not struck. Of all the rebel firing since I have been on the river, and it has been immense, but two of their shot have taken effect, and that was the wood schooner anchored in the middle of the river. She was hit twice, once in her hull and once in her main-sail, if that may be called hit. With a light breeze or a favorable current, a seventy-four line of battleship can ascend or descend the river at night with impunity.[43]

General Hooker was continually amused at the lack of skill of the Confederate gunners, commenting, "They do fire wretchedly. Whether it is owing to the projectiles or the guns I am not informed. From what was witnessed today and on previous occasions, I am forced to the conclusion that the rebel batteries in this vicinity should not be a terror to anyone."[44] Hooker correctly inferred the failings and weaknesses of the batteries.[45] He then developed a plan for a combined naval and army attack against the Confederates. Essentially, Hooker proposed the plan that the Confederates, in their analysis of the situation, feared the most. The Federal commander of all troops in the region, General McClellan, would not approve the operation.

During the six months the batteries operated it is estimated the Confederates shot over 5,000 rounds. Inexperienced gunners were one reason the Confederates had little success actually hitting targets. The Confederates assigned experienced naval officers to oversee the batteries, but the troops manning the batteries were inexperienced infantry troops. In this case, troops from 22nd North Carolina Infantry, Company I, in the military for only four months, manned one of the batteries. Low quality gunpowder was also a concern. General French commented that "the ammunition found in the magazine for the large guns was very indifferent. The powder was a mixture of blasting with rifle powder. Sometimes the Armstrong gun, at the same elevation, would not throw a shell more than halfway across the river; then again far over the river."[46] The inexperience of the troops and poor powder caused Confederate casualties. On December 9, 1861, while firing at passing schooners and at the Federal batteries across the river, Privates William J. Staley and Everett W. Wallace, both of Company I, were wounded when the 42-pound gun they were firing burst.[47]

Although not especially lethal, the bombardment from the Federal counterbatteries also had its effect on the Confederates, and they resorted to only working on the batteries at night. At one point the Confederates reported that they were under fire 28 straight days. Captain J. G. Anderson of the 2nd Tennessee Infantry Regiment reported that in "three months of the time they were on continual engagement with the enemy. They fired from forty to 100 shells a day. During December they fired 1,000 to 2,000 shells at us, during which time I never lost a man or had one hurt in any way. My men had to fight the guns from one to five times a day or night."[48]

General French reported: "For the last three weeks they have daily opened more or less fire on us from small rifled guns in position on the Maryland shore. On Sunday last 2 men were severely wounded by a shell, and to-day 2 more were slightly wounded. Eighty-three shells were thrown at the battery to-day. Under this fire teams cannot safely cross the plain to the batteries, and much labor has to be done at night. We could easily silence their fire, but have not ammunition to spare."[49]

Still, the blockade was viewed as a serious threat by the Federal government. One of the principal effects of the blockade was a reduction in the amount of forage being supplied to the capital. In the nineteenth century, armies relied on draft animals for the movement of troops, equipment, and foodstuffs. Forage for these animals was a necessity. As the forage supply dwindled, the number of animals available decreased, and, accordingly, the viability of the army was reduced. Federal General Wadsworth questioned whether the army could have successfully undertaken a move because of the insufficient forage for the horses.[50] The want of forage led to several Federal forays into Fairfax County, the no-man's-land between the armies. Troops were dispatched to obtain forage from local farmers. The Confederates contested some of these Federal moves and this led to engagements at Lewinsville, Doolan's Farm, Gunnells, and Dranesville.[51]

During the six months the batteries operated, the Confederates shot over 5,000 rounds from at least 37 heavy guns and an unknown number of field guns.[52] The primary achievements of the blockade were the psychological effect it had on the Federal leadership and as a propaganda tool for the Confederates. The fact that the Federal government and army could not dislodge the Confederate forces approximately 25 miles (40 km) downriver from the capital was a source of embarrassment. Lord Lyons, British ambassador at Washington, reportedly sent a dispatch stating, "Washington is the only city in the United States that is really blockaded."[53] The Federal leadership feared European intervention on the side of the Confederates and the Potomac blockade was a weakness that would provide the Europeans a reason to openly support the Confederates.

The March 1, 1862, *New York Tribune* reported:

> There has been no safe communication by water between this city and the capital of the nation during all this time—a period of six months. This is one of the most humiliating of all the national disgraces to which we have been compelled to submit. It has been most damaging to us in the eyes of the world. No one circumstance has been used more to our disadvantage with foreign nations than this. And it has helped the Confederates just in proportion as it has injured us. It has been their haughty boast that they had maintained steady and effectual sway over the great channel of commerce between this city and Washington, through which the immense supplies of our grand army of the Potomac would naturally have passed.[54]

The Confederate presence in northern Virginia, including the blockade, contributed to Federal strategic planning for the rest of the war. The Federal leadership demanded that the army protect Washington with a sizable garrison and that protection of the capital city was paramount to any other military activities in the eastern theater of the war.

LOCAL LANDSCAPE AND CANTONMENT AT EVANSPORT

The Confederates concentrated their effort to blockade the river at Evansport. Here, inland from the Shipping Point and Evansport shore batteries, the majority of support troops were bivouacked in a large cantonment (see figure). The Confederates established their winter camps approximately 1 mile (1.6 km) inland from the batteries, just out of range of Federal artillery. Prior to the Federals establishing counter-batteries, the Confederates camped in the open and closer to the batteries, with some camps on the shore of the Potomac. The layout of the cantonment uses elements of the landscape for protection

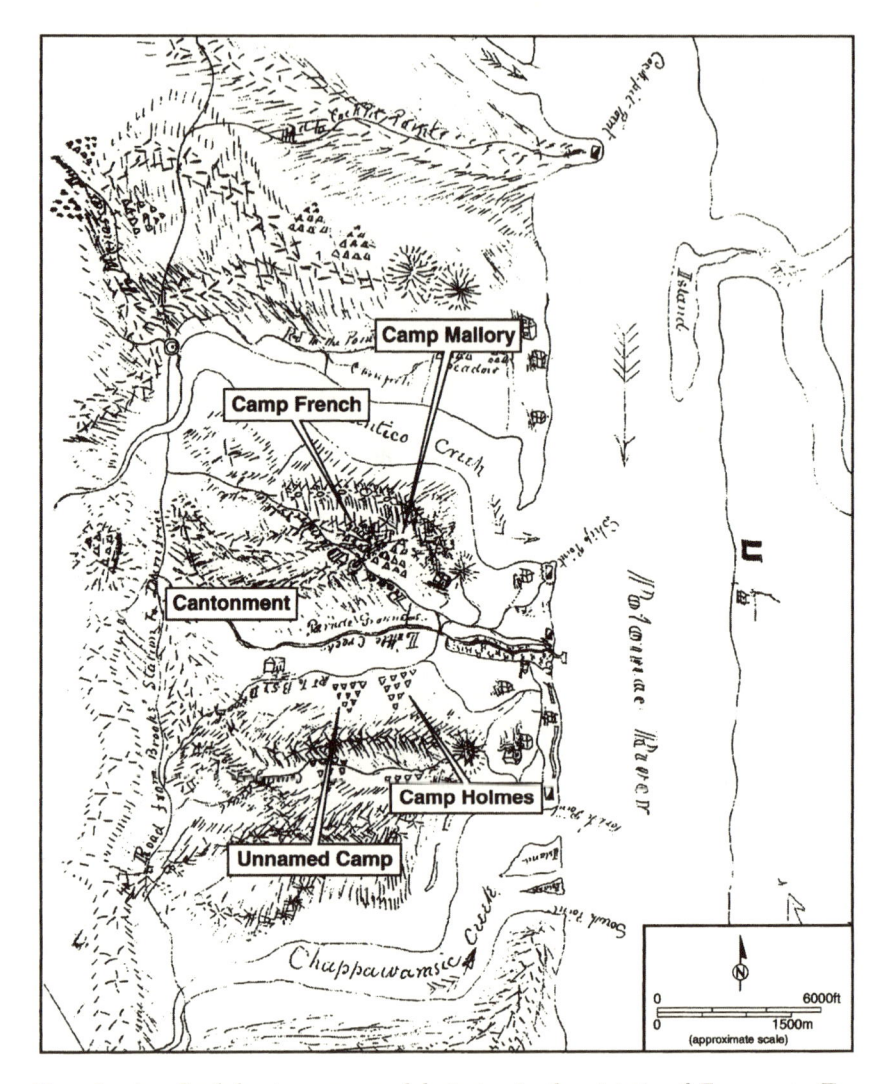

Map showing Confederate camps and batteries in the vicinity of Evansport. (Tennessee State Library and Archives)

from the direct bombardment occurring along the river, but this was not the sole factor affecting camp locations or layout.

In November 1861, General Hooker gave a brief report on the position of Confederate troops, based on his balloon ascensions:

> The main body of the enemy's forces visible are stationed in rear of the batteries between Quantico and Chopawamsic Creeks. Two regiments appear to be posted

near each other on the bank of the Quantico, and one regiment is about one-third of a mile [0.5 km] to the south of them. In the rear of the former, in the valley extending towards Dumfries, are a long line of encampments, and a valley making off from that at Quantico at nearly right angles in a southerly direction is also occupied with camps. To the observer on this side of the Potomac all hills covered with forests that conceal a line of smoke rising above them. Farther to the south other camps can be seen at intervals of a mile [1.6 km] or more.[55]

General Hooker was, in part, describing the Confederate cantonment at Evansport.

In the four months General French was in charge of the Evansport batteries starting in November, he commanded the 47th Virginia, 22nd North Carolina, 2nd Tennessee, 14th Alabama, 35th Georgia, 1st Arkansas, 2nd Battalion Arkansas Infantry, as well as the Maryland Flying Artillery and a company of cavalry.[56] The cantonment area was home to troops from several of these regiments. In letters home, soldiers referred to the regimental camps by various names including Camp French, Camp Holmes, and Camp Mallory. Troops under direct naval command were also present, but records on these men have proven difficult to locate.

The Confederates chose the Little Creek Valley for their cantonment. The Little Creek runs perpendicular to the Potomac River, and enters the Potomac River near Shipping Point battery number 1 (see figure). The Confederates occupied this valley and the smaller stream valleys that branch off the main stream. The main valley, in view of the Potomac, was only used as a parade ground. Camps were positioned in the side valleys and on side slopes, hidden from view. Archaeological investigations at the cantonment investigated a landscape that contained 697 winter huts clustered into four regimental camps, a magazine, an earthwork, picket posts, a target range, and the road network.[57] These investigations and the historical record allow a reconstruction of the cantonment.

The engineering journal of Major Samuel Sidney Gause contains several drawings of the Evansport area including a detailed map of the Little Creek valley that can be used to examine the 1861 landscape.[58] The main stream valley contained the road to Evansport. A marsh extended approximately 5,000 ft (1,525 m) from the mouth of Little Creek up the valley. Where cultivatable land was present, small plots of corn, sedge, and pasturage were grown. The valley sides were all forested. Approximately 1 mile (1.6 km) from the river, an officers' quarters is situated in the Little Creek valley. To the west of this quarters was a large area of pasturage used as the cantonment's parade ground. North of the officers' quarters, sheltered within a steep-sided valley, is a large ammunition magazine and regimental camp. The 22nd North Carolina Infantry Regiments winter quarters is located on the wooded slopes of the Little Creek valley along the main road. Two more regimental camps are located in side valleys approximately 1 mile (1.6 km) west

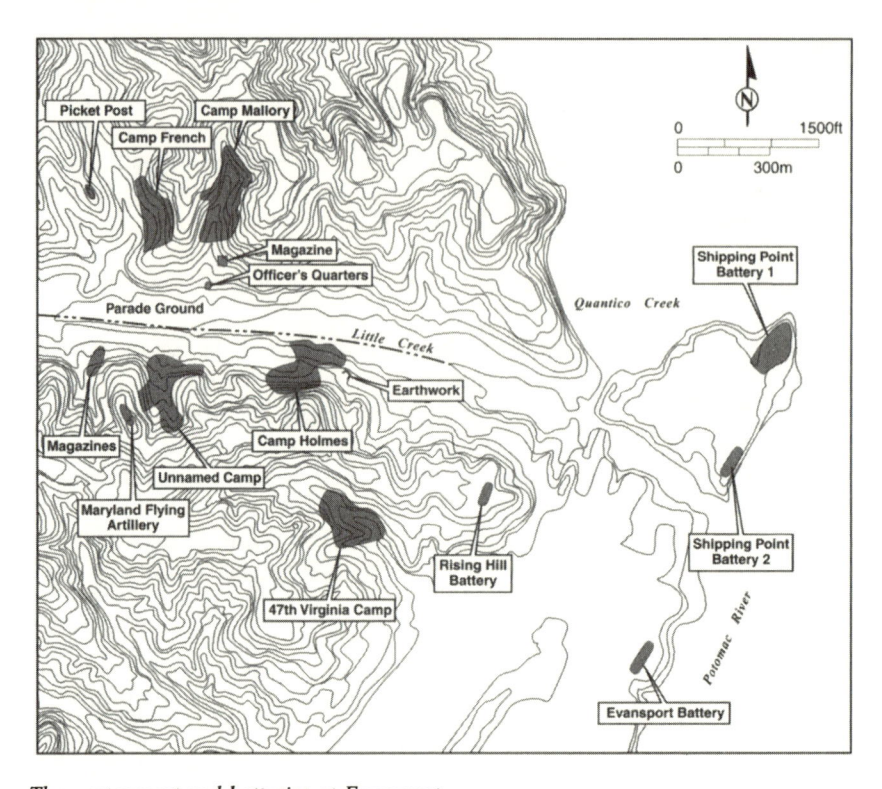

The cantonment and batteries at Evansport.

of the river. One of these camps is the winter quarters of the 35th Georgia Infantry regiment, the occupants of the other are unknown. A target range is associated with this camp. Three more ammunition magazines were located along the main road, approximately 1.25 miles (2 km) from the Shipping Point battery, but these have not been located archaeologically.

The Confederates set up a defensive perimeter to protect the cantonment. Picket posts were established along the Potomac and on the hills adjacent to the camps. Two companies of cavalry (Company A, the Stafford Rangers, and Company B, the Carolina Light Dragoons) detached from the 9th Virginia Calvary Regiment provided a cavalry screen, west of Evansport. The Maryland Flying Artillery was stationed at Evansport, and manned field guns in positions protecting the camps. At least one of these defensive earthworks has survived, east of Camp Holmes.

The cantonment at Evansport contained four regimental-size camps: Camp French, Camp Holmes, Camp Mallory, and an unnamed camp. Initially the troops lived in tents, but as winter approached, huts were built. The terrain was considered when the cantonment was laid out. Protection from Federal artillery and shelter from the prying eyes of aeronauts were the major concerns while livability was secondary. A southern exposure, to maximize winter sunlight, did not factor into the positioning of winter quarters. One camp faces west, one north, and two are in north to south running stream valleys.

While the cantonment was the largest concentration of troops in the area, there were several other regimental camps between Quantico and Aquia creeks. Notably, the 47th Virginia Infantry regiment occupied winter quarters within a secluded steep-sided valley on the opposite side of the ridge from the cantonment. This camp supported the Evansport batteries, and like the cantonment camps was situated with protection and stealth as the pervading factors determining location.

At the cantonment, adherence to the military regulations varied and this can be seen in the archaeological record pertaining to camp layout.[59] The reason was the experience of the officers and their familiarity with regulations. The infantry officers were seasoned veterans who participated in the traditions and regulations of the army. They were able to transfer these ideas to their men, who were new recruits. On the other hand, naval officers had no experience organizing infantry camps and were not familiar with the regulations; their camps were organized on different principles or even on an ad hoc basis.

Once Federal counter-batteries were established, and with balloon ascensions occurring daily, the Confederates made an effort to conceal their camps. Camps behind the batteries that were visible from balloons in early December were moved by the end of January.[60] Clearly, the Confederates were aware they were under observation and took countermeasures. In this case, these measures included situating camps in secluded locations which did not have the best living conditions.

Battlefields are locations of intense, short-term, violent fighting; on the other hand, the conflict affecting the cantonment is less obvious. Attrition caused by factors secondary to the continual bombardment seriously weakened the force at Evansport. Poor camp conditions, infectious disease, close quarters, cold weather, picket duty, and un-acclimated troops led to the deaths of hundreds of men and severely limited fighting capability of the force. For the Confederates, the Potomac blockade resulted in great loss of life, but the deaths were caused by factors more subtle than an exploding shell. It appears that direct enemy fire killed no one; accounts report only four injuries due to hostile fire. However, the harsh duty, stress, and poor living conditions that the Confederate troops had to endure to make the blockade a success resulted in the death or temporary incapacitation of a large percentage of the troops. For the troops in the Evansport vicinity, returns for August, September, October, November, and February 1861 have survived.[61] In August the Confederates had only about 75 officers and men in the Evansport vicinity. Once they committed to building the batteries, in September total troop strength grew to 3,160. By October the number was 3,422. After the October reorganization of the Confederate command in northern Virginia monthly returns only provide summaries for the whole Aquia district and do not provide detail on the Evansport garrison. The approximately 3,000 troops reported in the Evansport vicinity for September and October is the total troop strength. In actuality, the number of officers and men present for duty was about a third less. Absenteeism caused by disease got worse after the troops established winter quarters. Sickness was rampant in the Confederate winter camps and the troops at Evansport suffered greatly due to contagious diseases (e.g., measles) and camp diseases (e.g., dysentery). The available troops reporting present in October is less than that reported for September. On December 30, 1861, General French reported his troop strength; he could only field approximately 772 men for duty. With this complement of men the Confederates had to picket the Potomac shore, man the batteries, maintain the roads, and perform regular camp duties. General French stated, "You will further perceive that for the labor to be performed in strengthening the works by shelters and ditches, and the large guards at night required on the river front, the force is inadequate, and, considering the constant annoyance day and night from the enemy, no troops in this Confederacy are as unpleasantly situated."[62]

Through the fall and into the winter of 1861/1862, diseases, especially measles and dysentery, were rampant all along the entire Confederate front. The troops that appear to have been the most devastated by disease were from rural populations. These troops, who previously had led isolated civilian lives, were congregated into large groups living in close quarters. Many had not been exposed to contagious diseases. The cold winter of 1861/1862 contributed to the problem. A member of the 5th Alabama stationed at nearby Cockpit Point related as to how this winter was the coldest he or any of his fellow soldiers had ever experienced.[63] Duty along the Potomac was harsh. Each regimental company was expected to undertake regular camp duties such as fatigue (work parties) and policing (camp cleanup); work constructing and repairing the batteries and other fortifications; assistance in maintaining the roads; and every fifth day undertaking night picket duty along the Potomac River.[64] Once the epidemics began, fewer and fewer men performed these activities. At Evansport, the 14th Alabama was hard hit; 200 men, approximately 43 percent of the regiment, died of measles and the regiment was withdrawn to Richmond.[65] The 35th Georgia lost about 20 percent, approximately 145 men.[66] The 22nd North Carolina Regiment also lost several dozen soldiers, but due to their commander's efforts at sanitation and discipline, death from disease was lessened.[67] In contrast, during this same period, the 47th Virginia, made up of local men, lost only four men to disease.[68]

At Evansport aggregate troop strength at the end of October was 3,160 men; by the end of December only 772 (less than 25 percent) were reporting for duty. The majority of men (2,388) were not reporting present. In two months, the Confederate force had been reduced by 75 percent. In actuality, the force was probably somewhat larger because a number of troops, under direct command of naval officers, are not accounted for in the returns for the Aquia District. As French explained, the small number of troops had difficult duty. The small size of the effective force must have contributed to Confederate fears of an attack by Federal troops.

On March 9, 1862, the Confederate blockade was lifted, camps were abandoned, guns spiked, magazines blown up, and Confederate positions occupied by the Federals. The cantonment was ransacked by Federal troops who removed a large amount of goods the Confederates had to abandon due to poor roads and manpower and wagon shortages.[69] The depleted Confederate force was not able to move all the accumulated materials, and several large artillery guns and large amounts of equipment were abandoned.

DISCUSSION

The cantonment was not only examined in regard to its placement within the local landscape of conflict, but as part of the larger northern Virginia front. The Potomac batteries were isolated from the main Confederate forces concentrated at Centreville, and there were no direct transportation links. In contrast, the main Federal Army at Alexandria was closer to the batteries and there was a main road connecting the locations of the opposing armies. Faced with the Federal presence across the river and to the north, the Confederates perceived a strategic weakness along their right flank. The Confederates believed the Federal balloon ascensions from Hooker's camp were a prelude to an imminent invasion, and they were becoming convinced, as winter wore on, that they could not adequately respond to a Federal move on the batteries. In October 1861, General Hooker had devised an assault combining naval and land forces, just what the Confederates feared most. But, the overall Federal commander, General McClellan, would not approve the operation. However, President Lincoln overrode McClellan and ordered an attack, but before such an attack could be made the Confederates withdrew.

In northern Virginia, during the fall and winter of 1861/1862 the landscape of conflict went beyond the battlefield and was not marked by a large clash between the armies. The conflict was more a war of attrition and response to perceived threats. The cantonment supporting the winter of 1861/1862 Confederate blockade of the Potomac is an example of how numerous factors including landscape, military doctrine, perception, stealth, new technologies (balloon ascensions), regional strategy, and political considerations contribute to how troops are deployed during a regional conflict.

The cantonment at Evansport is located to take advantage of local topography. Initially, the Confederates were not concerned with secrecy when they located their camps. However, once the Federal bombardment and balloon ascensions began, the Confederates at Evansport responded by shifting their camps away from exposed locations to secluded side valleys. These locations hid them from view and were just out of range of Federal artillery. These factors were more important than the comfort of troops. The poor conditions caused, in part, by choices made in locating camps are reflected in the decreasing numbers of available troops, increased deaths, and the viability of the command.

The archaeological record reflects responses to the above factors, and it is only when these factors are taken into consideration that these sites can be understood. The locations of the Evansport camps reflect choices other than factors which would have normally been a priority to troops setting up a winter camp. Such factors as optimizing exposure to winter sunlight and being out of the wind became secondary considerations. An understanding of the conflict and the strategic decision-making process in which both armies were engaging offers insight into the location of these camps.

Conflict is emerging as a popular area of research. As more researchers focus on the repercussions conflict causes on groups, attention will expand beyond battlefields and into areas where conflict produces subtle, but just as deadly, results.

NOTES

1. Balicki et al. 2002a, Balicki et al. 2004.
2. Cooling 1975:41. Reprinted 1991.
3. Leech 1986:112, Cooling 1975:66.
4. Balicki et al. 2002b.
5. Cooling 1975:71. Reprinted 1991.
6. Beatie 2002:466.
7. Cooling 1975. Reprinted 1991.
8. Hanson 1953, Govan and Livengood 1956.
9. Silverman et al. 2002:75–92, Kundahl 2000.
10. Hanson 1953:36–41.
11. Govan and Livengood 1956:96.
12. Official Records of the Union and Confederate Armies [O.R.] Series I, Vol. 108:1072–1073.
13. O.R. Series I, Vol. 108:481, Hanson 1953:67.
14. O.R. Series I, Vol. 5:50.
15. Wills 1975:19–32.
16. Wills 1975:19–32, Hanson 1953:43, O.R. Series I, Vol. 2:55–59.
17. Hanson 1953:43.
18. O.R. Series I, Vol. 2:57.
19. O.R. Series I, Vol. 2:133–134.
20. O.R. Series I, Vol. 2:959.
21. O.R. Series I, Vol. 5:767.
22. O.R. Series I, Vol. 5:797–798.
23. O.R. Series I, Vol. 5:830.

24. O.R. Series I, Vol. 5:801–802.
25. O.R. Series I, Vol. 5:828.
26. Scharf 1877:99.
27. O.R. Series I, Vol. 5:853.
28. O.R. Series I, Vol. 5:883.
29. Wills 1975:69.
30. O.R. Series I, Vol. 5:913–914.
31. Hanson 1953:48, Wills 1975:78.
32. Official Records Navy Series [O.R.N.] Series I, Vol. 4:735.
33. O.R.N. Series I, Vol 4:729.
34. O.R.N., Series I, Vol. 4:733.
35. O.R.N., Series I, Vol. 4:726.
36. Wills 1975: 106–108.
37. Wills 1975:89.
38. O.R. Series I, Vol. 124:269.
39. O.R. Series I, Vol. 124:265–266.
40. Hewett 1998, Vol. 66, Series 78:444–445
41. O.R. Series I, Vol. 5 108:372.
42. O.R. Series I, Vol. 5:1032–1033.
43. O.R. Series I, Vol. 5:652–653.
44. O.R. Series I, Vol. 5:649.
45. Wills 1975:133–135.
46. French 1999:143.
47. Clark 1991:167, Daves 1991:167, Hewett 1994–2001, Vol. 48:762.
48. Hewett 1994–2001, Vol. 66, Series 78:444–445.
49. O.R. Series I, Vol. 5:469–470
50. Wills 1975:99.
51. Balicki et al. 2002b.
52. Wills 1975:66, 110, and 112.
53. Quoted in French 1999:143.
54. Quoted in Scharf 1877:102.
55. O.R. Series I, Vol. 5:655.
56. Balicki et al. 2002a, Balicki et al. 2004, Balicki 2005.
57. Balicki et al. 2002a, Balicki et al. 2004.
58. Gause 1861.
59. Balicki et al. 2002a, Balicki et al. 2004, Balicki 2005.
60. Small 1861, O.R. Series I, Vol. 5:711.
61. O.R. Series I, Vol. 5:824, 884, 933, 974, 1086.
62. O.R. Series I, Vol. 5:1012–1013.
63. Fulton 1924:427.
64. Thomas 1862.
65. Hurst 2002.
66. Irvine 1891.
67. Wilson 2002:155.
68. Musselman 1991:12–13.
69. Wills 1975:158–159, O.R.N., Series I, Vol. 5:23.

REFERENCES CITED

Balicki, Joseph. 2005. "Masterly Inactivity": The Confederate Cantonment Supporting the 1861–1862 Potomac River Blockade, Evansport, Virginia. In Clarence Geier, David Orr, and Mathew Reeves (eds.), *Huts and History*. University Press of Florida, Gainesville, FL.

Balicki, Joseph, Bryan Corle, and Sarah Goode. 2004. Multiple Cultural Resources Investigations at Eight Locations and Along Five Tank Trails, Marine Corps Base Quantico, Prince William, Stafford, and Fauquier Counties, Virginia. Report to EDAW, Inc. Alexandria, VA, from John Milner Associates, Inc., Alexandria, VA.

Balicki, Joseph, Kerri Culhane, Walton H. Owen II, and Donna J. Seifert. 2002a. Fairfax County Civil War Sites Inventory. Report to the Fairfax County Park Authority, Fairfax, VA, from John Milner Associates, Inc., Alexandria, VA.

Balicki, Joseph, Katherine L. Farnham, Bryan Corle, and Stuart J. Fiedel. 2002b. Multiple Cultural Resources Investigations, Marine Corps Base Quantico, Prince William and Stafford Counties, Virginia. Report to EDAW, Inc. Alexandria, VA, from John Milner Associates, Inc., Alexandria, VA.

Beatie, Russel H. 2002. *Army of the Potomac: Birth of Command November 1860–September 1861*. Da Capo Press, Cambridge, MA.

Clark, Walter (editor). 1991. *Histories of the Several Regiments and Battalions from North Carolina in the Great War 1861–65. Volume II*. Reprinted by Broadfoot Publishing Company, Wilmington, NC.

Cooling, Benjamin Franklin. 1975. *Symbol, Sword, and Shield: Defending Washington during the Civil War*. White Mane Publishing Company, Inc., Shippensburg, PA. Reprinted 1991.

Daves, Graham. 1991. *History of the Twenty-second Regiment of North Carolina Troops in the late War Between the States*. http://members.aol.com/jweaver301/nc/22ncinf.htm.

French, Samuel G. 1999. *Two Wars: An Autobiography of Gen. Samuel G. French*. Blue Acorn Press, Huntington, WV.

Fulton, William F. 1924. War Reminiscences of William F. Fulton, 5th Alabama Battalion, Archer's Brigade, AP Hill's Light Division. Reprinted 1986, Butternut Press, Charlestown, MA.

Gause, Samuel S. 1861. Confederate Engineering Journal of Major Samuel Sidney Gause, 1861–1865. Manuscript on file at the Tennessee State Library and Archives, Nashville, TN.

Govan, Gilbert E., and James W. Livengood. 1956. *A Different Valor: The Story of General Joseph E. Johnston C.S.A.* The Bobbs-Merrill Company, Inc., NY.

Hanson, Joseph M. 1953. *Bull Run Remembers: The History, Traditions, and Landmarks of the Manassas (Bull Run) Campaigns*. National Capital Publishing, Manassas, VA.

Hewett, Janet B. (editor). 1994–2001. *Supplement to the Official Records of the Union and Confederate Armies*. Broadfoot Publishing Company, Wilmington, NC.

Hurst, M. B. 2002. *History of the Fourteenth Regiment Alabama Volunteers*. Paint Rock River Press, Paint Rock, AL.

Irvine, W. T. 1891. Old 35th Georgia: A Brief History of the 35th Regiment of Georgia Volunteers from its Organization to its Surrender at Appomattox Court House, April 9, 1865. In *The Sunny South*, May 2, 1891. Atlanta, GA.

Kundahl, George G. 2000. *Confederate Engineer: Training and Campaigning with John Morris Wampler*. The University of Tennessee Press, Knoxville, TN.

Leech, Margaret. 1986. *Reveille in Washington*. Carroll and Graf Publishers, Inc., New York.

Musselman, Homer. 1991. *47th Virginia Infantry*. H. E. Howard, Inc., Lynchburg, VA.

Official Records of the Union and Confederate Armies (O.R.). 1997. *The War of the Rebellion: A Compilation of the Official Records of the Union and Confederate Armies*. CD-ROM version, originally published 1880–1901. Guild Press of Indiana, Carmel, IN.

Official Records of the Union and Confederate Navies (O.R.N.). 1999. *Official Records of the Union and Confederate Navies in The War of the Rebellion*. CD-ROM version, originally published 1894. H-Bar Enterprises, Oakman, AL.

Scharf, J. Thomas. 1877. *History of the Confederate States Navy from its Organization to the Surrender of its Last Vessel*. The Fairfax Press, Virginia.

Silverman, Jason H., Samuel N. Thomas Jr., and Beverly D. Evans IV. 2002. *Shanks: The Life and Wars of General Nathan George Evans, C.S.A.* Da Capo Press, Cambridge, MA.

Small, W. F. 1861. *Sketch of Virginia and the Rebel Camps and Batteries, in Front of Gen. Joe Hooker's Division in Charles County, Maryland*. Made from Prof. Lowe's Balloon, for the Commander in Chief, Dec. 8, 1861. By Col. Wm. F. Small, 26th Reg. Pa. Vols. National Archives and Records Administration, College Park, MD.

Thomas, Edward L. 1862. Letter to Honorable J. P. Benjamin, Confederate Secretary of War. Letters received by the Confederate Secretary of War 10430-1862 (January 21, 1862). Manuscript on file, National Archives and Records Administration, Washington, D.C.

United States Topographic Engineers. 1862. *Map of Northern Eastern Virginia and Vicinity of Washington*. Compiled in Topographical Engineers Office at Division Headquarters of General Irvin McDowell, Arlington, VA. National Archives and Records Administration, College Park, MD.

Wills, Mary A. 1975. *The Confederate Blockade of Washington, D.C. 1861–1862*. McClain Printing Company, Parsons, WV.

Wilson, Clyde N. 2002. *Carolina Cavalier: The Life and Mind of James Johnston Pettigrew*. Chronicles Press, Rockford, IL.

Fort Davidson Battlefield, Missouri

Steve Dasovich & Walter Busch

HOW CAN PUBLICLY managed historic sites continue significant, meaningful research with reduced or often drastically cut budgets? Across the United States, many such sites have been experiencing significantly lower operating budgets. Support staff, that may include such positions as historians, public education specialists, curators, and other collections specialists, are now rare commodities for many of these historic preserves. The staff positions that still exist are barely enough to keep the facilities functioning and the grounds kept. Hours of operation are being reduced, seasonal tour guides are not being hired, and, in some cases, whole parks are being closed to the public. All of this is occurring in a time when research techniques and technologies make available more avenues for addressing research questions. Even when finances allowed more staffing, most public historic sites did not have the luxury of full-time researchers in any discipline. Site managers may have relied upon grants to be able to bring in outside help from archaeologists and historians. While this is still a viable option, finding time for the staff to write grants is difficult when so many other duties have been added to the job descriptions of the remaining staff.

This chapter discusses a project involving a public-private partnership, with the principals being the Fort Davidson State Historic Site, a historic site managed by the state of Missouri, USA, and SCI Engineering, Inc., a private consulting engineering company (see figure). These two parties, as well as other ancillary groups with a direct or vested interest in the results of the project, both profited from the research conducted, and the resulting public exposure. Originally conceived as a result of a repair project to an historic property, the Immanuel Lutheran Church, located off the park grounds but with a direct link to the interpretation of the park and the Battle of Fort Davidson, the project morphed into an effort to answer one primary and one secondary research question. These questions were: did the church serve as a battlefield hospital, and was the church property actually a part of the contested area of the battlefield? The research conducted by the partnership

Fort Davidson showing current-day entrance (not original) near the northwest corner of the fort. (Courtesy of Missouri Department of Natural Resources, Division of State Parks, Fort Davidson State Historic Site Collection)

provided significant data that allowed both of these questions to be positively addressed. These results show that a public-private partnership is a viable option for public historic sites to help them to continue to pursue research on their historic properties. Before this is discussed though, the historical framework should be set.

THE BATTLE OF FORT DAVIDSON, 1864

With a primary goal of capturing St. Louis, Missouri, and secondarily capturing Jefferson City, Missouri, as well as conscripting men and gaining supplies, Confederate Major General Sterling Price invaded Missouri from Arkansas, leading an army of over 12,000 men in the fall of 1864. Short of supplies and hopeful of new recruits, Price chose a path which would take him through areas of Missouri thought to be sympathetic to his cause. His army followed several different paths as they entered southeast Missouri around the area of Doniphan, sweeping the countryside for forage and new soldiers. After arriving at Fredericktown, his spies informed him that 5,000 troops under General A. J. Smith were between him and St. Louis. Rather than risk a significant battle, Price opted to move toward his secondary objective, the state capital of Jefferson City, and along the way gather supplies, especially weapons.

The largest supply of military goods and weapons outside the major cities was at Pilot Knob, Missouri. Price moved from Fredericktown along the old military road toward Pilot Knob. He hoped to quickly capture the fort and garrison as he had reports indicating less than 1,000 men were stationed in the area.

Pilot Knob and the Arcadia Valley were protected by Fort Davidson. The fort was constructed in 1863 with the primary purpose of protecting the terminus of the Iron Mountain Railroad line that shipped iron ore mined at Pilot Knob, Sheppard, and Iron Mountains to St. Louis. Because iron ore was a vital war resource, and because of the fort's proximity to the railroad, the fort was garrisoned by the 3rd Missouri State Militia Cavalry, a company of the 47th Missouri Infantry, and some companies of home guard units. Normally commanded by Major James S. Wilson of the 3rd Missouri, Brigadier General Thomas Ewing Jr., the brother-in-law of then Major General William Tecumseh Sherman, arrived at the fort from St. Louis on September 25 to ascertain Price's intentions. At the time of Ewing's arrival, he commanded roughly 1,350 men.

The fort's armament consisted of four, 32-pounder rifled, pivoting cannon that formed the nucleus of the defense of this earthen-berm fortification. Three, 24-pounder smooth-bore howitzers commanded the valley approaches. The earthen-berm was roughly hexagonal, measuring approximately 129 feet (39 meters) in diameter at its longest to 86 feet (26 meters) at its shortest. The earthen-berm was surrounded by a deep, dry moat, making any climb up the outside of the walls a very long 13 feet (3.9 meters), according to the current height of the wall's tallest point. The artillery rested on wooden artillery pads, apparently partially enclosed. One sally port faced the southwest and allowed entrance to the south rifle pit from underneath the walls. The north and south rifle pits extended out from the fort 150 yards (137 meters) each. These pits were probably more of a shallow trench. The main gate faced to the east toward the railroad terminus and mining areas. The powder magazine rested, mostly buried, in the center of the fort. While a formidable obstacle to any small cavalry raiding party, it was defiled on three sides by mountains and never meant to withstand an artillery barrage.

The battle started on September 26, 1864, as the outpost pickets from the fort's garrison first made contact with the advanced guard of the Confederate forces approximately two miles (3.2 kilometers) south, around the southwest entrance to the Arcadia Valley at Shut-Ins Gap (for an overview of the progression of the battle, see figure on page 280). The Confederate forces drove the Union troops, consisting of both cavalry and infantry, back into Arcadia and Ironton, only to be driven back in a see-saw battle. By nightfall, the Confederates recaptured the two towns. As the Union forces held a line along Stout's Creek east of Ironton, they watched as over 10,000 soldiers poured into the valley and set up camps.

By morning, the overwhelming Confederate forces caused the Union defenders to conduct a fighting withdrawal back into the fort. Ewing's tactics involved forcing the Confederates to fight for every inch of ground so that he could delay an attack on the fort. Although he had orders to evacuate if necessary, he believed his troops could withstand only one major assault, and he would try to limit it to just that. As the Confederates overran positions on

THE BATTLE OF PILOT KNOB AS DRAWN BY SGT. H.C. WILKINSON, 47TH MO INFANTRY

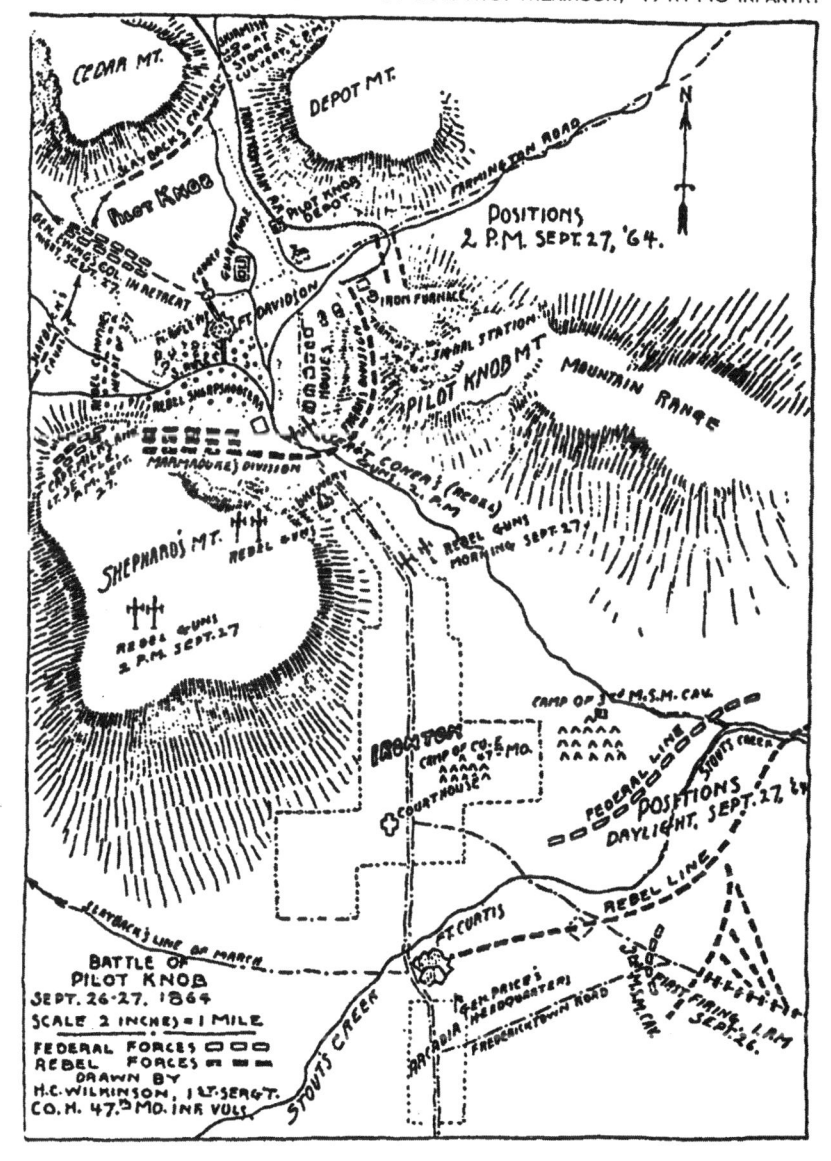

Map drawn by Sergeant H. C. Wilkinson, 47th Missouri Volunteer Infantry, participant of the Battle of Fort Davidson. (Courtesy of Missouri Department of Natural Resources, Division of State Parks, Fort Davidson State Historic Site Collection)

Sheppard Mountain, immediately to the west of the fort, they moved two cannons up the heavily wooded mountain to positions that defiled the small fort. When they opened fire on the fort, the accurate, deadly returning fire crippled one cannon and forced the other's crew to move the cannon out of harm's way. The only effective fire the fort took was from a small cannon set up on the sloping west side of Knob Creek.

With the artillery bombardment failing to take the fort and Union skirmishers fighting for every inch of ground, Price made a fatal decision to attack with cavalry and infantry unsupported by artillery. Ultimately, he failed to utilize his now fully consolidated forces and the assaults came off as piecemeal efforts. One after another, charges were made across a field which was several hundred yards long and sloped up to the fort. Only once did the Confederate forces gain the dry moat, where they were halted by Ketchum grenades and short-fused cannon balls. An attack on the north rifle pit by cavalry which had circled around Sheppard's Mountain on the opposite side of the fort was briskly fought off with the infantry rising out of the pit and charging at the horses. As daylight waned, Price's attack caused Ewing to order his men from the north rifle pit to more fully support the fort. Price's efforts cost him approximately 300 killed and around 900 wounded.

That night, Price ordered General Jo Shelby to come to Knob from Potosi to help with the next day's assault. He also had his men preparing scaling ladders for the attack. Inside the fort, Ewing decided that he should retreat. Knowing he couldn't withstand another day of attack, Ewing waited for late night, covered the horses' hooves and the wheels on his artillery to muffle the sound, and marched his entire command out of the fort up the north rifle pit. As he did so, the eerie glow from a Confederate bonfire caused by 50 tons (45.4 tonnes) of burning coal lit the battlefield. Leaving town by way of the Potosi-Caledonia road, Ewing's men marched past several Confederate camps without being challenged. A few hours after the garrison had escaped, the magazine inside the fort was detonated. The 20,000 pounds of powder caused an explosion that could be heard as far away as Ste. Genevieve, Missouri, approximately 50 miles (80 kilometers) to the northeast.

The explosion denied Price the military supplies he needed. Enraged, he ordered a contingent of his army under General Marmaduke to give chase. As the Union forces neared Caledonia, they met and fought off an advance guard of Shelby's men moving in from Potosi. Surprised, Shelby believed he had somehow been encircled by A. J. Smith's 5,000 men from St. Louis because he did not know that Ewing had escaped Price at Pilot Knob. He formed lines for battle. Ewing realized he was in the middle of a possible trap between Shelby and Marmaduke, and so veered off to the west along a ridge line running from Caledonia to the Huzzah Valley. Thirty-nine hours, several skirmishes, and one sharp fight at the Huzzah later, Ewing's tired forces barricaded themselves in a railroad cut near Leasburg. After holding off Shelby and Marmaduke for another day, relief arrived. The small Union garrison from Fort Davidson had made good their escape.

Price's decisions cost him any chance to capture Pilot Knob's supplies, which went up with the magazine in the fort. His delay in forcefully chasing

Ewing eventually cost him a chance of capturing Jefferson City. The fact that he was allowed to remain in Missouri for almost another month is not necessarily testimony to his skill as a raider so much as the ineptness of the Union forces to coordinate an attack until the Battle of Westport, Missouri, near Kansas City. After the disastrous loss at Westport, Price's army finally collapsed at the Battle of Mine Creek in Kansas and the remnants quickly retreated to Arkansas.

Price's Raid prolonged the war by several months. He drew almost 24,000 troops needed to attack Mobile, Alabama, and protect Sherman's supply line in Tennessee. The Confederacy failed to decisively act in those theaters. Price did manage to obtain some men and supplies, but he squandered them. While historians can look to some strategic successes of the raid, it was largely a tactical and strategic failure.

The two-day battle in the Arcadia Valley saw a wide variety of military maneuvers. Portions of the battlefield saw running cavalry action, while others saw infantry fighting infantry in line of battle. Large and small caliber artillery was used liberally, especially on and around Sheppard Mountain where Price's artillery was effectively silenced by the extremely well practiced and deadly fire from the fort's 32-pounder pieces. The end result, from an archaeological perspective, is that the signature of battle in the form of artifacts left behind, from several different types of military units and their associated modes of operation, may still be possible to discern.

BATTLEFIELD DESCRIPTION

Our definition of the battlefield includes not just the locations of fighting and maneuvering, but also the associated ancillary components related to the military presence in the Pilot Knob area. As is the case with most battlefields of the American Civil War, this battlefield has many ancillary activity locations such as field hospitals, supply depots, and campsites. Also, being a garrison town, other military facilities such as a military telegraph office, railroad depot, barracks, stables, picket posts, freedman's barracks, and even a prisoner-of-war camp are in the immediate vicinity. Further, a significant iron ore mining operation including the mine and ore processing facilities provided a target with military significance. When viewing the battlefield area as an archaeological site, the site formation/destruction processes must be considered. Given the large area in which military activity occurred relative to the battle, the following local affecting issues should be reviewed to assess their impact on the battlefield.

The Battle of Pilot Knob took place in the Arcadia Valley, a north-south trending valley in Iron County, Missouri. This area is located in the St. Francois Mountain Range. The battle raged along an approximately two mile long by one-half mile wide area of the valley and the surrounding low mountains. Soils in the area play a critical role in the preservation of archaeological materials. The soils on the mountains are thin and rocky while the soils in the valley are deep but interspersed by relict, gravelly stream channels. The main water body that ran through the main portion of the battlefield area is Knob Creek. It is a usually slow moving waterway with the typical Ozark region gravelly stream bed. The tributary drainages are typically U-shaped but can change course rapidly. The mountains were and are still heavily forested with several hardwood species. Coniferous species are rare except in areas where recent clear-cutting has allowed them access. The valley is essentially clear of significant wooded areas.

Starting just before the Civil War, mining became the dominant way to make a living for the residents who later found themselves involved in the battle. Iron ore was so rich in the surrounding mountains that the county was named for this resource. The peak of Pilot Knob Mountain was the main source of iron ore in the 1860s and immediately after the end of the war. The peak was an open quarry site for the ore and is now defunct. Significant areas of the valley around Pilot Knob are covered in fill from the mining spoil from the local processing facilities. Mining stopped in the area during the late 1970s. Today, the dominant industry is tourism. The valley contains several popular outdoor parks offering a variety of outdoor activities. It also has well-known antique shops and other associated cottage tourist industries. The valley draws tourists and visitors from a 150 mile (241 kilometer) radius nearly year round.

At the time of the battle, there was a separation of approximately two miles (3.2 kilometers) between the towns of Ironton and Pilot Knob. Today, the separation is barely noticeable with perhaps one-quarter mile of lightly developed land between the two. Since the battle, the towns have expanded mostly through the addition of single-family residential areas and some light industrial zones, disturbing or destroying much of the actual battlefield. The growth of the towns has also destroyed many of the ancillary military-related buildings and period structures. The town of Pilot Knob, for instance, has only three buildings left that stood silent witness to the battle.

Starting after the Confederates left the area, the battlefield, from an historic preservation stance, became endangered. As the towns of Ironton and Pilot Knob changed and grew, more areas of the battlefield were disturbed or destroyed. The issues affecting the battlefield, as described above, all play a part in the changes to the battlefield over time. The lack of protective soil accumulation on the mountains, scenes of some of the more important actions of the battle, is a hindrance to preservation. Historical materials did not become covered quickly, allowing much to be lost to the elements. Treasure hunters have an easier time finding artifacts as well. The mining industry has greatly affected the battlefield. For instance, most of the historic site property had been covered with fill from mining spoil before the state of Missouri acquired the property. Fill depths are estimated to range up to 3 feet in depth with fill being placed within 100 yards (91 meters) of Fort Davidson. But perhaps the largest threat to the battlefield has always been the normal growth of the two towns. The authors estimate that only approximately 20 percent of the battlefield is essentially untouched by significant human activity since the battle. This battlefield is now listed as a Priority I property by the National Park Service, making it one of the United States' most endangered battlefields. Fortunately, Fort Davidson itself is protected by the Missouri Division of State Parks and resides in the Fort Davidson State Historic Site in Pilot Knob.

RESEARCH PROBLEMS

The Battle of Pilot Knob included approximately 13,500 combat soldiers. This number does not rank very high in the ranking of large-scale battles of the Civil War. This can mean that relatively little about this battle is documented. The Official Records barely mention the battle, and while there are books and articles written about the battle, all are written with a broad brush and none have bothered to research the garrison structures and soldier lives in the Arcadia Valley.[1] Interest generated by these smaller scale battles is often only at the local level. The staff of the Fort Davidson State Historic Site consists of local residents, many of whom have lived most of their lives in the valley. This has resulted in an excellent compilation of battle-related data, historical accounts, and an excellent collection of battle-related artifacts. Unfortunately, much of this data is disjointed and unprovenienced. This problem, coupled with the significant loss of actual battlefield, leaves much about the battle currently lost or unanswered. Many significant questions about the prosecution and execution of the battle are unresolved. Locations of significant events as well as many battlefield landmarks are unknown. If information does exist, it is often so general in nature or fragmentary as to be unhelpful. Another important issue is the lack of archaeological research on any part of the battlefield. This leads us to a basic problem when trying to answer questions about the battle using historical archaeology. There are few historical sources and no archaeological data.

Even with well-documented battles where there is a plethora of historical sources, the locations of ancillary activity such as field hospitals, campsites, and troop formation are often unknown. The focus on the actual progression of the battle leaves these important support areas unstudied. Archaeological excavations have typically focused on forts or on the progression of battle. More recently, archaeological techniques have been developed to study the progression of battle as evidenced by interpreted behavioral patterns based upon artifact types and locations. Studies by Scott and Connor,[2] Scott and Fox,[3] and Scott et al.[4] have tested this approach and found that it is possible to learn a great deal more about a battle through archaeological techniques and analysis than, for example, just locating artillery positions. These mentioned studies, though, took place on the Little Bighorn battlefield that has minimal ground disturbance and offered the researchers a comparably unobstructed field of battle in which to pursue their fieldwork. The Fort Davidson battlefield does not offer a similar situation.

Another problem encountered when developing research questions is that the battle's constituent cultural features are often prime targets for local treasure hunters. Dating back to the 1870s, artifact hunting has been and continues to be a popular hobby as a result of the battle. Certain areas of the battlefield have seen extreme disturbance and loss of archaeological data due to the hobby. The park's staff occasionally receives information from local treasure hunters who use metal detectors off the park property. These individuals have located many campsites and troop formation areas. However, because of the "competitive" nature of their hobby, these locations are not always made known so no confirmation of their assumptions by professionals has been made. Through the years, park staff members have been able to record suspected locations of these battle-related sites on their maps.

Archaeologists have learned that building relationships with local treasure hunters can be beneficial. Learning about their particular "find" locations is brought about first by gaining their trust, but is often more directly related to whether or not they feel the locale has been thoroughly picked clean, or if the suspected location is considered to be so disturbed, even by the treasure hunter's standards, that the reward for time spent on site is thought to be low. Even at locations considered unworthy of further effort on the part of the hobbyists, archaeological investigation can still yield useful information. Dasovich[5] successfully utilized local hobbyists for a small survey on two earthen work outposts along the military road between Ellington, Missouri, and Pilot Knob, Missouri. Scott and Fox[6] also found this relationship to be beneficial. The hobbyists are often highly skilled in the use of their metal detectors and this experience can be valuable when applied in a scientific approach.

RESEARCH QUESTIONS AND ARCHAEOLOGY AT THE IMMANUEL LUTHERAN CHURCH

In 2001, the church needed to undergo renovation work on the limestone foundation to repair failing mortar and pointing. In order to properly complete the job, the general contractor had to excavate the soil away from the foundation along the back of the church. Steve Dasovich of SCI Engineering, Inc., out of St. Louis, Missouri, volunteered to conduct test excavations before the pointing project in order to see if significant intact archaeological deposits still existed in this area. The pointing work necessitated this simple research question and research design. The plan was approved by the church elders. Dasovich met with Walter Busch, site administrator of the Fort Davidson State Historic Site and also one of the elders of the church, to develop a research plan, and this public-private partnership was born. Tasked with not just the preservation and interpretation of the actual fort, but also the collection and archiving of data about and related to the battle, the staff of the Fort Davidson State Historic Site has a vested interest in any research anywhere on the battlefield. The historic site offered their services in the form of helping with local arrangements and allowing access to their research collections.

The church is located on the northern end of the battlefield at the foot of Cedar Mountain. Stories have persisted through the years that the church served as an impromptu Union field hospital during the battle. There was also some question as to whether or not this was the church that the Union garrison congregated by after exiting the rifle pits during their nighttime escape. Finally, it is possible that the church served as a backdrop to a small Union artillery battery position during much of the September 27th battle activity.

German immigrants constructed the Immanuel Lutheran Church in Pilot Knob, Missouri, in 1863 (see figure). The church consists of a sanctuary, two rooms on the ground floor, and a single room on the second floor in the rear of the church. The church is a front gabled wood frame building with clapboard siding and a tall steeple on the front of the church. The building rests on a limestone foundation excavated several feet into the ground. There is no basement or cellar, though a trapdoor was installed in one of the back rooms presumably for storage purposes in the crawlspace and for access to the interior of the foundation. The ground floor ante-rooms served as the living quarters for the various pastors and their families. The second floor room, built after the end of the Civil War, served as a schoolroom. The church still has its original floors, pews, light fixtures, school desks, schoolbooks (from the 1880s with German text), rugs, kneeling pillows, various religious accoutrements, and pastor's robes. An air pump organ built in 1871 is still in use today, but it is not the original church organ. The original, built in 1831 and shipped from Europe to the United States, is in storage in a back room and is still in working order. The church is a wonderful time capsule.

Photograph of the Immanuel Lutheran Church, taken in the early 1900s. Even today, the church has not changed in appearance since its construction in 1863. (Courtesy of Immanuel Lutheran Church)

Dasovich excavated a total of 13 square meters over two weekends in 2001, and one weekend each in 2003 and 2004, using all volunteer labor (see figure). SCI Engineering, Inc., provided all field equipment and other logistical support. Eight test units measured one by one meter and two units measured one by two meters. Only unit 4, placed just 50 centimeters from the rear wall of the church, and the trapdoor unit under the church, yielded undisturbed Civil War–period levels. Personal items such as bone comb fragments and a hand-carved bone die or domino half (in the normal number "5" pattern of dots, see figure) and items of clothing such as a paperbacked button often used on military issue pant flies, survived intact along with fragments of 1850s period, salt glazed ceramics. All other units showed either significant disturbance, or had little or no artifact content.

In 2001, Dasovich excavated approximately two square meters underneath the church for the trapdoor unit. The trapdoor exists in the back, ground floor room of the church. The idea to excavate under the church resulted from a second research question meant to try to determine if the church was used as a field hospital. If the rooms were used to perform operations, it was reasonable to suspect that debris from this medical activity may have been deposited in the trapdoor opening just as the pastor's families deposited certain types of household garbage later. The excavation in 2001 revealed a debris pile made up of discarded coal stove material and household trash dating back to the construction of the church and through the mid-1900s. Dasovich excavated approximately one-quarter of the debris pile in 2001. The stratigraphic sequence remained completely intact. This proved vital to understanding the disposition of artifacts within the pile, specifically the location of a spent Minié ball (see figure). Dasovich located the Minié ball near the south foot

Test unit along the south side of Immanuel Lutheran Church, 2001.

Left: Minié ball from the trap door unit; Right: Die fragment from test unit 4.

of the debris pile, on the northern side of a piece of limestone displaced from the foundation. Excavation of the remainder of the debris pile was postponed to a later field session.

The Minié ball yielded vital information, supporting the story that the church had been used as a field hospital. During the initial laboratory analysis at SCI's archaeological laboratory, marks on the bullet seemed similar to forceps marks seen on other lead projectiles as discussed by Doug Scott[7] in a paper presented at the American Battlefield Protection Program National Conference in Nashville, Tennessee, in 2004. After initial discussions, Scott graciously offered to analyze the bullet to determine if the marks may have been made by forceps. The significance of the forceps marks lies in the reason for their existence. Surgeons used forceps to pull projectiles from the soft tissues of the wounded. Muscle tissue tends to wrap around such foreign objects, often causing the surgeon to use significant pressure and force to extract the object. In lead objects, this leaves impressions unique to the instrument. Scott's analysis of the bullet confirmed that the marks came from the use of forceps.[8]

Locals have hypothesized that the room with the trapdoor was used during and after the battle as an operating room for the wounded. One purported bloodstain still exists on the original floor, now fully exposed in this room (this stain has never been tested). Probably originally intended for storage for the pastor's family who lived in the church until sometime around 1900, stories have persisted that the trapdoor was also used to hide James Farrar, an African American man, wounded during the battle while fighting for the Union. His wound was a severe belly wound, and the surgeons could do little for him except hide him from the Confederates. Supposedly, they hid him under the church, just under the trapdoor as the Confederates controlled the town. Unfortunately, the man is reported to have died under the trapdoor.

While this is an interesting anecdote to the story of the battle, there is no documentation that such an event took place. Further, outside of oral tradition, there is no documentation that the church was used as a hospital for the battle's wounded. The location of the Minié ball under the church precluded it from having arrived there by being fired through the church's wood walls or the limestone foundation. Had the bullet struck the walls or foundation, it would have been flattened. Dasovich located the bullet in a position that was 63 centimeters south of the south edge of the trapdoor opening. Its location, resting against a large piece of limestone at the bottom of the slope of the debris pile, suggests that the bullet was dropped or thrown into the trapdoor opening and it then rolled down the pile, coming to rest against the stone. This information coupled with the forceps marks suggests that the room with the trapdoor was indeed used as a surgical room for the battle's wounded. Scott further suggests that the bullet was fired from either a Hall's carbine or a British Kerry rifle. As both of these weapons were predominantly used by Confederate forces in the western theater of war, the wounded person from whom the bullet was extracted was probably a Union soldier.

During the field sessions in 2003 and 2004, the purpose of the excavations shifted from one of identification of intact deposits to that of determining whether or not the church was used as a hospital during and/or after the battle. The Minié ball recovered under the church determined the shift in focus. One key to making this determination archaeologically was the continued excavation under the trapdoor. As discussed earlier, the authors hypothesized that the trapdoor would have made an ideal place for depositing non-human waste material generated from the operations in the room. Blood and surgically removed body parts would most likely have been deposited at a location outside the church. However, with the trapdoor open, other items could have easily been deposited as garbage under the church. Due to structural support issues with the joists of the church, the excavation under the trapdoor was delayed until 2004.

In 2003, the volunteer crew continued excavations outside the church. They also conducted a metal detector survey of the entire backyard of the church with the help of local hobbyists. This property has been somewhat protected from metal detecting by the church itself. So, this type of a survey should have had the opportunity to locate any other battle-related materials in the churchyard. The metal detectors identified 101 anomalies in the yard. The crew excavated 47 of the anomalies. Besides six cut nails that could possibly date to the Civil War period, the crew only found two other Civil War period artifacts in the form of a .54 caliber Minié ball and a round musket ball. Both of these items are undamaged and appear to be "drops" as they were never fired from a gun. The other excavations that year did not locate any further Civil War–related artifacts.

An ancillary goal of the fieldwork included the search for direct evidence of the battle in this location. If the artillery battery fired from this area, or if this area had been directly fired upon, the authors hoped to locate such evidence through the metal detector survey by locating fired rounds or shrapnel, among other items. However, the vast majority of artifacts recovered from the metal detector survey belonged to the metal fastener or farm implement categories.

In 2004, Dasovich excavated the remainder of the trapdoor debris pile. He did not locate any other military artifacts. Unfortunately, structural work on the church had removed approximately one-third of the remainder of the debris pile in the area where the Minié ball was located in 2001. This fill material was lost during construction activity.

Public participation was very important during the first two field sessions of this project. Staff from the Fort Davidson Historic Site put out a call for volunteers, and the authors announced the excavations as an event of Archaeology Month in Missouri during each of the three field sessions. During the first two sessions, approximately 25 volunteers participated, including graduate students from the University of Missouri, U.S. Forest Service employees from Mark Twain National Forest, members of three chapters of the Missouri Archaeological Society, archaeologists and employees from SCI Engineering, Inc., local residents, members of the Friends of Fort Davidson, Immanuel Lutheran Church members, and off-duty staff from the Fort Davidson State Historic Site. For the metal detector survey, the authors solicited help from several local metal detector enthusiasts who are highly skilled in the location of Civil War–period items. Three people, along with the authors, provided essentially 100 percent coverage of the backyard of the church.

The authors are currently discussing the possibility of further archaeological reconnaissance in other areas of the battlefield where questions as to the conduct and/or position of the battle still remain. Battlefields are and probably will forever be enshrouded in mystery. Questions will always remain unanswered. Due to the constant endangerment of the remaining undeveloped areas of this battlefield off of the state historic site boundaries, the authors hope to be able to conduct field investigations in areas highly threatened or in areas that will maximize the small amount of time available for volunteer fieldwork.

THE PUBLIC-PRIVATE PARTNERSHIP

The public-private partnership realized between SCI Engineering, Inc., the Fort Davidson State Historic Site, local residents, and church members, while a small-scale project, is an excellent example of how well such an arrangement can work to the benefit of all parties. SCI, while not being paid for the work, realized other important benefits in the form of a better working relationship with a state agency, and in the form of positive public relations for the company through media coverage of the field sessions as a result of participation in Archaeology Month. For-profit companies can benefit from the positive exposure of conducting pure research projects such as these, especially when conducted on high-profile sites such as battlefields where there is usually a significant level of public interest. The Fort Davidson State Historic Site gained further awareness of the site from the general public through media coverage and the advertising of the excavation sessions as a part of Archaeology Month. They also gained more exposure to their site amongst the professional archaeological community by working with professionals and by having the project announced in professional archaeological newsletters. The small town of Pilot Knob gained a small amount of tourist income and tourist exposure from the crew, volunteers, and other out-of-town visitors to the excavations. Finally, the church gained visibility from the valuable exposure of their historic property. Donations to aid in the continued restoration and preservation efforts of the building increased during the final weekend when the session was part of the activities during the tri-annual re-enactment of the battle. Ultimately, this partnership resulted in a successful effort for all parties. The authors were able to address the research questions generated for the work at the Immanuel Lutheran Church. A hospital function for the church was successfully determined and the relative lack of battle-related debris on the church property suggests that the battle was not fought in the immediate vicinity. Eventually, the work successfully completed by the partnership at the Immanuel Lutheran Church should serve as a springboard for further research on this battlefield.

Non-profit entities should consider searching for such partnerships as the financial burden for conducting important research projects might be borne by their wealthier partner. Strategic partnerships with private companies, such as that discussed in this chapter, may offer new research avenues to publicly managed historic sites or other non-profit entities with meager annual budgets, in any part of the world.

NOTES

1. Official Records, Series I, Vol. 41/1 (S#83) page 446 Ewing's Report; Official Records, Series I, Vol. 41/1 (S#83) page 701 Price's Court of Inquiry; Official Records, Series I, Vol. 41/1 (S#83) page 678 Brig. Gen. John B. Clark's Report; Official Records, Series I, Vol. 41/1 (S#83) page 652 Shelby's Report; Official Records, Series I, Vol. 41/1 (S#83) page 625 Price's Report.

2. 1986 Post-Mortem at the Little Bighorn. *Natural History* 95(6):46–55.

3. 1987 *Archaeological Insights into the Custer Battle*. University of Oklahoma Press, Norman.

4. 1989 *Archaeological Perspectives on the Battle of the Little Bighorn*. University of Oklahoma Press, Norman.

5. 2003 Phase One Cultural Resource Survey: Two Possible Civil War Forts, Reynolds County, Missouri. Ms. on file, Missouri State Historic Preservation Office, Jefferson City, Missouri.

6. 1987 *Archaeological Insights into the Custer Battle.* University of Oklahoma Press, Norman.

7. 2004 "Listen to the Minié Balls": Using Firearms Identification Techniques in Battlefield Archeology. Paper presented at the American Battlefield Protection Program, 7th National Conference on Battlefield Preservation, Nashville, TN.

8. 2004 Analysis of a .54-caliber Minié Ball from the Immanuel Church, Pilot Knob, Missouri. Ms. on file, Fort Davidson State Historic Site, Pilot Knob, Missouri.

REFERENCES CITED

Scott, Douglas, and Melissa Connor. 1986. Post-Mortem at the Little Bighorn. *Natural History* 95(6):46–55.

Scott, Douglas, and Richard Fox Jr. 1987. *Archeological Insights into the Custer Battle: A Preliminary Assessment.* University of Oklahoma Press, Norman.

Scott, Douglas D., Richard A. Fox Jr., Melissa A. Connor, and Dick Harmon. 1989. *Archaeological Perspectives on the Battle of the Little Bighorn.* University of Oklahoma Press, Norman.

The Confederate Forward Line, Battle of Nashville, Tennessee

Carl Kuttruff

AMERICAN ARCHAEOLOGICAL STUDIES of warfare and battlefields have become a legitimate archaeological research interest in the past decade or two.[1] Within the field of American archaeology there is an expanding body of research and publications on excavations, surveys, and documentary studies of battlefields, fortifications, and other military constructions. This interest is also illustrated by numerous sessions on the topic at recent national and international archaeological meetings, such as the 2003 Fifth World Archaeological Congress, and the American Battlefield Protection Program 7th National Conference on Battlefield Preservation in 2004 and earlier meetings of that conference. In the United States, archaeological military studies range from the early Spanish forts[2]; to ones like Jamestown in the American colonies[3]; numerous French and Indian War, Revolutionary War–period military sites, and fortifications of the late eighteenth and early nineteenth centuries[4]; Civil War–period battlefields, forts, and field fortifications[5]; and military posts and battlefields of the American Western frontier.[6] Much more recently there has been a growing interest among some archaeologists in the archaeological remains and documentary resources of twentieth-century American military installations and battlefields.[7]

In 1989, I noted, that despite the constant interest in this country in the Civil War and particularly the revival of that interest in the last two and a half or three decades, there does not seem to have been an equivalent increase in interest in the field of archaeology. It certainly does not approach the zeal of historians, re-enactors, and perhaps the obsession of collectors and relic hunters. Ironically, most archaeologists working with Civil War materials and artifacts are almost totally dependent on studies of Civil War artifacts that have been done by serious collectors, who in many cases have produced quite scholarly works on the various classes of artifactual materials that have been gotten from Civil War battlefields, encampments, and other related sites.[8]

Since then, professional archaeological research on Civil War–period battlefields and installations has, of course, been increasingly carried out, much of it under cultural resource management programs. A notable recent publication is *Archaeological Perspectives on the American Civil War*.[9] However, even within the area of research on military-related sites in this country, and although the number of projects is growing, Civil War battlefield studies still seem to be in the minority. For example, Tennessee, which is the context for this report, has perhaps hundreds of existing earthworks, campsites, and other related Civil War sites. Despite that, there have been, to my knowledge, only a few professional archaeological excavations in that state which have been done on the fortifications or battlefields of that period. These include test excavations at Fort Rosecrans near Murfreesboro[10]; Fort Granger in Franklin and near the Carter House in the same town, which was near the center of fighting in the Battle of Franklin that immediately preceded the Battle of Nashville[11]; Fort Pillow in West Tennessee north of Memphis[12]; and the excavations on the Confederate entrenchments in Nashville which are discussed in this chapter. A statewide survey of Civil War sites in Tennessee has been done to identify, locate, and record many of the existing Civil War sites in Tennessee[13], and a detailed survey of the Lookout Mountain Battlefield at Chattanooga has recently been carried out.[14] Important for comparative purposes for this study of the Nashville entrenchment is the extensive excavations done on a long section of a Confederate entrenchment at Gilgal Church near Marietta, Georgia.[15]

With that brief introduction, the following sections of this chapter will present a brief summary of the development and major events of the Battle of Nashville to provide the historical context for the excavations that were done on a portion of the Confederate forward line in Nashville. Following that, the chapter then focuses on the archaeological research that was done to mitigate the effects of the planned interstate construction. The historical and archaeological research methodology that was used to determine the location of the Confederate entrenchment, and to excavate large portions of that defensive line, is outlined. The results of the excavations are then presented and illustrated with plans of the excavations and selected features that were found during the course of that work.

THE BATTLE OF NASHVILLE

In February 1862, Nashville, Tennessee, was occupied by the Federal Army under the command of General George H. Thomas after the Confederates retreated from Middle Tennessee.[16] Nashville soon became a major quartermaster supply depot for funneling supplies and troops from the North to the Southern theaters, from Mississippi to Georgia. To protect the city an extensive series of earthworks were constructed with redoubts and forts at key points in the defensive line (see figure). There was an inner line of defensive works encircling Nashville from the Cumberland River on the west to Granny White Pike (or Middle Franklin Turnpike) near the south side of town where its left flank was anchored at Fort Morton, situated on a hill between Granny White Pike and the Franklin Pike. The main defensive line also began near the Cumberland River on the west, but about 1.7 miles (2.7 km) from the edge of the city. It encircled the city, and extended to the Cumberland River on the eastern edge of town, connecting a series of low hills and ridges that formed an arc that surrounded the city on the south. The Federal main salient, and southernmost point of the defenses, was anchored on Montgomery Hill located between Granny White Pike and Hillsboro Pike. Two forts were along the eastern part of this line, northeast from Montgomery Hill. Fort Casino was just east of Franklin Pike, and Fort Negley was situated on a hill between Franklin Pike and Nolensville Pike. In this position, Fort Negley commanded approaches to the city from those two roads, and was also in a position to protect the intersection of two railroad lines from the south and east just before they entered the city. In addition to the fortifications at Nashville, the approaches to the city were also guarded by Fort Rosecrans in Murfreesboro at a distance of about 30 miles to the southeast, and Ft. Granger in Franklin, about 20 miles south of Nashville. Smaller earthworks and redoubts at river crossings on the roads and railroads away from the city provided additional protection from approaches along the major routes of transportation into and out of Nashville.

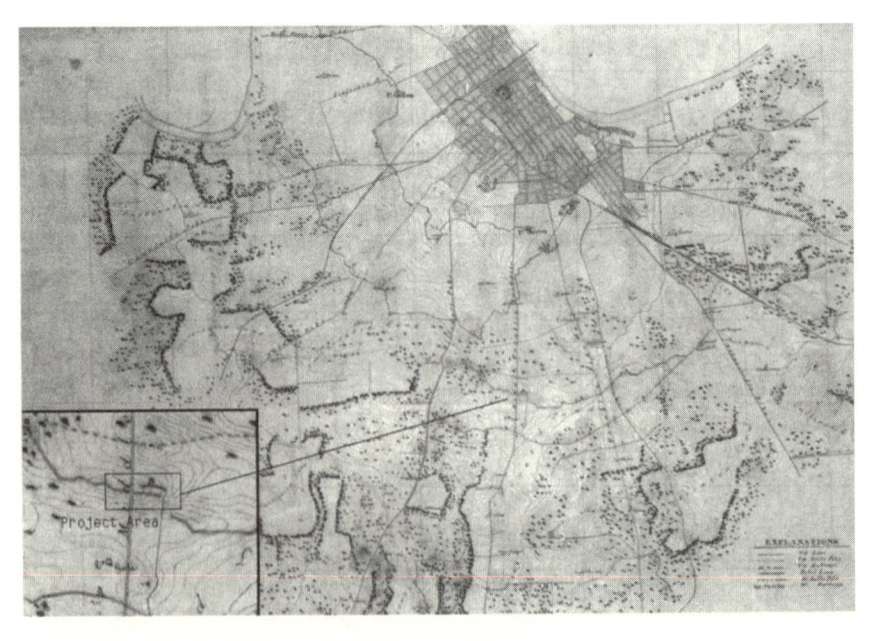

A portion of the 1864 map of the Battle of Nashville.

In July of 1864, General John Bell Hood assumed command of the Confederate Army of Tennessee. In the early fall of that year, Hood sustained heavy losses fighting Sherman's army in battles near Atlanta, Georgia. Hood evacuated Atlanta and moved his troops to northeastern Alabama. Sherman subsequently occupied and burned Atlanta, and began his march to the sea across Georgia. Regrouping his army, Hood developed a plan to recapture Nashville, in order to sever the Federal supply lines to Sherman and other Federal units operating in the South. His tactics were to move quickly into Middle Tennessee, and regain possession of Nashville. After the capture of Nashville, he planned an advance into Kentucky toward Louisville and Cincinnati.

General Hood sent his army across the Tennessee River in northern Alabama in November of 1864, and marched to Pulaski, Tennessee, engaging the Federal troops there under the command of General Schofield. Schofield withdrew north from Pulaski and deployed his troops at Columbia, Tennessee, on November 27. Hood and his army reached Columbia two days later, established battle positions, and demonstrated against the Federals who retreated to Spring Hill. There the Federals established a strong defensive position. Hood had hoped to encircle Schofield at Spring Hill late on the 29th, but because of confusion in communications and oncoming darkness the Confederate movement was halted. Schofield used the night of November 29th to remove his troops to Franklin, Tennessee, where on the morning of November 30th his troops entrenched themselves in a defensive line on the southern outskirts of Franklin. Realizing that the Federals had evacuated Spring Hill, Hood quickly took up pursuit on the morning of November 30th, arriving south of Franklin about mid-afternoon. The Confederates began an immediate assault on the Federal lines. Although they were persistent in their attack, they were unsuccessful in overrunning the Federal entrenchments, and by about 9:00 P.M. the firing ceased, with the Confederates having suffered some 6,000 casualties.

Once again, Schofield disengaged his troops and used the night of November 30th to move his troops into the defenses of Nashville. The morning of December 1st found General Hood and his Confederate army in possession of the Franklin battlefield with no opponent. That day he began marching his troops toward Nashville and by the next day, December 2nd, they were deployed below Nashville on the hills and ridges from about a half mile to two miles south of the main Federal defenses. Hood's strategy was to entrench his troops in a defensive line, invest the city from a threatening position, and wait for General Thomas to attack.

At the time that the Confederates approached Nashville and formed their lines south of the city, the weather was fair and mild. Since the Federals did not launch an immediate counterattack, the Confederates had ample time to spend preparing field entrenchments, breastworks, and other defenses fronting the Federal positions. A defensive stance was often better than attacking a defensive works in terms of losses during the Civil War. Confederates had become adept at hastily constructing field entrenchments, as reported by a Federal, Colonel Theodore Lyman:

> It is a rule that, when the Rebels halt, the first day gives them a good rifle pit; the second, a regular infantry parapet with artillery in position; and the third with a parapet with abattis in front and entrenched batteries behind. Sometimes they put this three days' work into the first twenty four hours....[17]

The in-depth defenses that the Confederate Army of Tennessee constructed consisted of a main defensive line of entrenchments, earthworks, and redoubts, a forward line of entrenchments, and in front of that a line of rifle pits (see figure). Numerous gun batteries were emplaced at strategic points along both the main and forward lines. The Confederate forward line was anchored at its left on a small hill just east of Hillsboro Pike and about 1,500 feet (467 m) south of the Federal main salient on Montgomery Hill. From there it extended eastward approximately three miles (4.8 km), crossing Granny White Pike and Franklin Pike, then joined the main Confederate line just west of Rains Hill on the west side of Nolensville Pike. Along this line were located seven gun batteries. North of the forward line was a line of rifle pits stretching from about 1,000 feet (300 m) east of Hillsboro Pike to some 2,000 feet (600 m) east of Franklin Pike. The main Confederate line was also anchored near Hillsboro Pike. It began at a hill with a redoubt on the east side of Hillsboro Pike, about 3,000 feet (900 m) south of the forward line. It ran eastward to Nolensville Pike on the east where it was anchored with a redoubt at Rains Hill. Additional segments of this line extended northward to the Nashville and Chattanooga Railroad to the east, giving it a length of about 4.1 miles (6.7 km). Some 10 gun batteries were along this line, in addition to the redoubts. Yet another defensive line about 7,500 feet (2,286 m) in length was present behind, and centered on the main defensive line. This was perhaps a line for troops held in reserve. In apparent anticipation of the flank attack that came from the west during the battle, an additional entrenchment began at the left end of the Confederate forward line and extended southward along the east side of Hillsboro Pike past the left end of the main Confederate line, for a total distance of nearly 8,500 feet (2,590 m).

On December 8th the weather took a sudden change, the temperature dropped rapidly, and cold rain mixed with snow began to fall. On December 9th the ground was frozen and covered with sleet and snow. The freezing rain continued for a week, making life difficult for the poorly supplied Confederates. The Federal forces suffered less physical discomforts from the weather, but it made an attack against the Confederate positions an impossibility. General Thomas, in command of the Federal Army of the Cumberland, was forced to postpone his battle plans, much to the dismay of his superiors in Washington. During the week of inclement weather, Thomas received several orders to take the initiative and attack, even after trying to convince his superiors that the condition of the terrain rendered maneuvers impossible.

General Thomas called a conference of his corps commanders on December 10th, and on the next day they were making final preparations necessary for the attack. It took an entire day to get the troops into position because of the frozen and icy terrain; the troops remained in position for two days waiting for the weather to break. On December 14th, the temperature began to rise and thaw the frozen ground, and General Thomas called his corps commanders to a council of war to discuss the battle operations to begin the next day. On December 15th the attack was launched in a heavy fog at 6:30 A.M. The Federal assault started with a feint to the Confederate right, followed by the main Federal force of two corps making a flanking attack against the Confederate left. The advanced lines gave little resistance and were quickly overrun, with the defenders withdrawing to the main line of defense. By about 12:30 P.M., the Confederate left was under sustained assault along the main line of defense. Late afternoon attacks by the Federals overran the five redoubts along the Confederate left, exposing the remainder of the Confederate main line to flanking attack and enfilading fire. By nightfall, the two opposing armies were scattered in disarray. The Confederate center had held, but the left had collapsed, and had regrouped somewhat along a line roughly parallel to Granny White Pike. The Federal troops ended the day's engagement occupying the captured earthworks, and in position in front of the Confederate left.

Hood's plan for the next day was to again take another strong defensive position and await attack by the Federal troops. On the night of the 15th Hood's troops established a new defensive line about three miles south of their original one, and spent the rest of the night preparing what defenses they could. On the morning of the 16th the Federals began moving toward the Confederate line, and their artillery was concentrated on the strong points at either end of the Confederate line. A cold rain began to fall about noon, but the Confederates, weak from battle and retreat, with no rest during the night, were repelling the Federals successfully on their right flank. However, the left of their line was gradually being turned and was approaching collapse. About 3:00 P.M., the Federals made a successful assault on the Confederate right, with that segment of the line rapidly collapsing. Within an hour of the collapse of the right flank the Confederates began a general retreat to the south. The Federal troops pursued the Confederates, with several resulting skirmishes in southern Middle Tennessee. On Christmas day the Confederates crossed the Tennessee River, then began their march to a winter encampment at Tupelo, Mississippi. The Federal troops halted their operations on December 29th.

ARCHAEOLOGICAL WORK

During the summer of 1982, this writer directed an archaeological survey of a portion of the proposed right-of-way for Interstate 440 that now goes through the middle of south Nashville.[18] That survey consisted of a shovel testing program of units dug at 50-foot (15-m) intervals and selected test units excavated at potential historic sites and one prehistoric site. During the course of that research it was realized that a portion of the Confederate forward line of the Battle of Nashville would have been located within a section of the proposed right-of-way. Parenthetically, a methodological consideration must be inserted here. The systematic shovel testing program, which included the area of the Confederate entrenchment that was subsequently excavated, failed to produce a single soil profile or artifact that would have suggested a Civil War–period occupation or usage of any of the right-of-way.

Research efforts were altered to determine whether any evidence of that battle line still existed, if in fact it originally consisted of an entrenchment. However, the underlying assumption, of which the author was reasonably confident, was that there would have been an entrenchment. The specific area that held the potential for remains of these entrenchments was located in a portion of the right-of-way that had been developed in the 1930s and later and was centered on the intersection of Granny White Pike and Gale Lane. A large interchange was planned for this location, and the state had purchased a rather large block of land. The 1930s development consisted of residential streets and tract houses (most with basements) on adjacent lots, with relatively large front and back yards. The right-of-way had been acquired about 10 years prior to the archaeological work, and all the houses had been moved or demolished, and the basements filled. The next figure shows a portion of the project area, the intersection of Granny White Pike and Gale Lane, the locations of the previous houses, and the proposed interstate construction. The Confederate forward line is also shown. Its location within the limits of the right-of-way was determined by the excavations, and that beyond the project area was extrapolated from the 1864 map of the Battle of Nashville.

There was a close correspondence between the contours shown on the 1864 map of the Battle of Nashville and those on the present-day topographic maps. A careful examination of the topography of the project area and other parts of the surrounding neighborhood revealed that there had been apparently little alteration done to the original terrain prior to the residential development, excepting some cutting and filling for the streets. Going on the confidence that the estimate of the location of the Confederate forward line was relatively precise, and the assumption that the relatively unaltered large yards would still contain evidence of an entrenchment, a simple research plan was then developed that would determine whether remains for the entrenchment were still present.

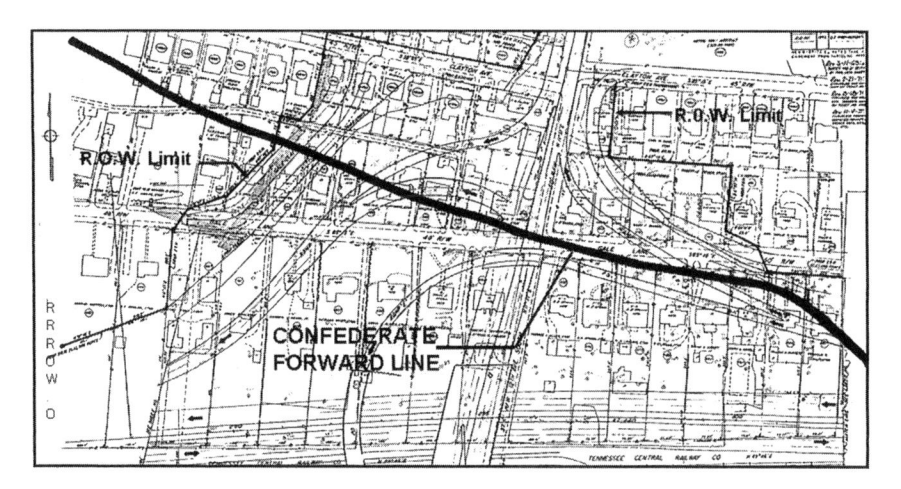

A portion of the project area showing the intersection of Granny White Pike and Gale Lane.

The potential existed to accomplish several important goals. The first was simply to locate and verify the existence of any archaeological remains of the Confederate works in that area. This would, in turn, confirm the accuracy of the maps of the Battle of Nashville from the 1860s and allow for more accurate location of other sections of this line, and other defensive lines in Nashville. The second possibility was either the actual excavation of a large portion of a Civil War field entrenchment, which had not been done previously, and/or the possibility of being able to preserve large sections of one of these entrenchments. Because of construction design changes which removed the interchange from this location, only a part of the right-of-way where the Confederate entrenchment was located would be subject to direct impact, leaving large areas of that part of the right-of-way unaffected by construction. The third possibility was that in the event that sections of the entrenchment existed, and were excavated, it would be possible to recover information and materials which would provide some insight into life in the trenches and the activities that took place there. In this case, it would only be a quick glimpse though, limited to a period of only 13 days. But those proverbial archaeological slices of time are often more revealing (and certainly much easier to interpret) than occupations of longer duration. Lastly, the excavations would provide information with which to make an assessment of the potential for additional archaeological remains of the Battle of Nashville in the suburban residential areas of the city. This urban area now covers nearly all of the area of the battlefield, and where there are only a few examples of above-ground features remaining from the 1864 earthwork construction. It was possible that this information might also be applicable to similarly developed battlefields in other cities and towns.

By comparing the 1864 map of the Battle of Nashville with modern topographic maps of the same area, it became apparent that a portion of the Confederate forward line and one gun battery would have been located within the interstate right-of-way. This was established with reasonable confidence due to the close correspondence of the nineteenth- and twentieth-century maps, and the presence of Granny White Pike which bisected the area of interest and which had not changed location since the 1860s. Several nearby houses shown on the Civil War maps were still standing, providing additional landmarks. An examination of the topography within the right-of-way along with the maps suggested the probable placement of the Confederate entrenchment for military advantage (e.g., the military crest of a ridge).

The survey project of 1982 was then expanded to include some backhoe trenching across the probable line of the Confederate entrenchment to determine whether any remains existed, and if so to determine the location of that entrenchment across the right-of-way. The plan was to machine excavate a series of trenches perpendicular to the assumed Confederate line until it was located, then follow its trace with similar trenches as required. A metal detector survey was ruled out because of expected metal clutter resulting from twentieth-century occupations and structure demolitions. The excavation work was done with a backhoe equipped with a three-foot-wide bucket. A total of 18 trenches varying in length from 2 to 10 meters were eventually excavated. The locations of those trenches are shown in the figure below.

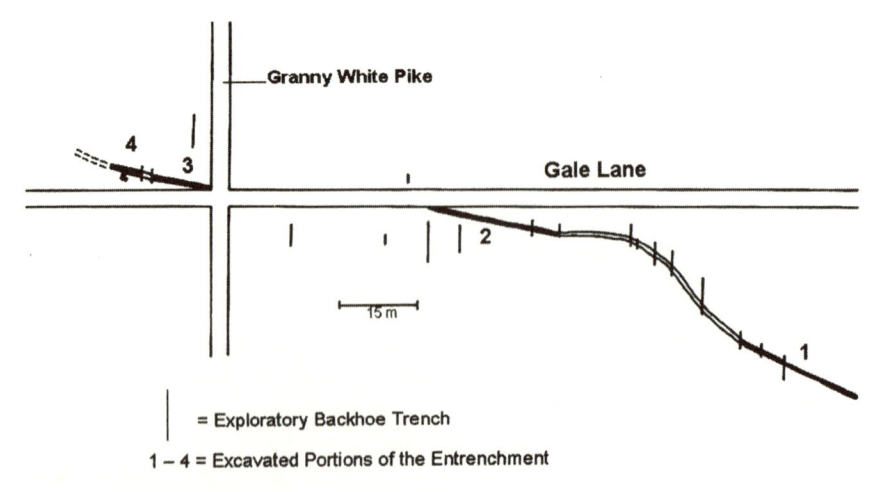

| = Exploratory Backhoe Trench
1 – 4 = Excavated Portions of the Entrenchment

Plan of the excavations showing the exploratory backhoe trenches and the four sections of the Confederate entrenchment that were excavated.

The first two trenches were excavated well into the subsoil, and the profiles were examined for evidence of a filled-in ditch or entrenchment. With good fortune, a 1.25-meter-wide trench, with a depth of 45 cm from the top of the subsoil was noted in the profile walls of the second backhoe cut. The original top of the trench was buried beneath approximately 50 cm of humus and/or old plowzone. This stratum was capped with more recent fill from the 1930s, most likely with soils removed from a nearby basement excavation and spread over the front yard. A third backhoe cut was made close to the second one, but excavated only to the depth necessary to define the upper outline of the trench. The trench fill was excavated by hand, recovering a Minié ball and a couple of other artifacts on the base of the trench, verifying that it dated to the time of the Battle of Nashville. A subsequent backhoe trench was done in the same manner and hand excavations revealed a fired hearth area on the floor of the trench.

With a confirmed fix on a portion of the entrenchment, and the topographic map of the battlefield, it was relatively easy then to approximate the location of the remainder of this entrenchment within the right-of-way. A series of spaced backhoe trenches was then excavated to determine the extent of the entrenchment within the right-of-way and its precise location. All the subsequent exploratory machine trenches were excavated only to the top of the subsoil where the trench could be defined. In these, the trench fill was not excavated, but left intact. The locations were then accurately mapped in relation to the nearby streets. The results were that the entrenchment was found to be remarkably well preserved, and that at least 365 meters (1,200 feet or nearly a quarter of a mile) of it was within the right-of-way. Approximately 50 meters of the entrenchment was assumed to have been destroyed by the construction of Gale Lane and its intersection with Granny White Pike. Only one former house basement was clearly intrusive to the Confederate trench.

The final plans for the interstate had changed from the original. The interchange was removed, but the actual route of the interstate remained the same and would impact part of the area. The only other construction that would be done in the area north of the interstate was the widening and lowering of the intersection of Granny White Pike and Gale Lane. Based on the results of that work, recommendations were then made for the excavation of those portions of the entrenchment that would be destroyed by that construction, and for the preservation of the remainder of the line that existed in the right-of-way. The portions of the Confederate entrenchment that were expected to be impacted by construction (plus a little extra) are shaded in the figure. These were the portions later excavated. Section 1 was to be impacted by the interstate; and Sections 2–4 were to be affected by the cutting and grading work necessary to lower the street intersection.

In the fall of 1982, once it was clear that construction of the interstate would actually begin, additional funds were provided by the Tennessee

Department of Transportation for the excavation of those portions of the entrenchment that would be affected by the construction. The areas that were not going to be directly impacted by construction activities (i.e., grading or other similar earth-moving alterations) were to be left intact and preserved. The excavation of the four sections of the entrenchment that were subject to impact began in November and continued until late December. Ironically, during these excavations the December weather approximated that of the time of the battle, providing us with some sense of what it was like to be in those trenches in 1864.

The four segments of the entrenchment that were excavated had a total length of 114 meters or just less than one-third of the entrenchment line that was within the right-of-way (see figures). These excavations were carried out using a backhoe (operated by this writer) to clear the topsoil and overburden above the trench to a depth where the trench outline and its fill could be defined as before. Then working along the length of the trench with the backhoe, the trench fill was excavated to within about 20 cm of the sides and bottom of the original excavation. The remaining fill was then hand excavated with shovels and trowels to expose the original walls and bottom of the entrenchment. All artifacts located in the base of the trench were plotted on large-scale maps of the excavations. Features within the entrenchment (namely hearths and fired areas) were drawn, photographed, and excavated.

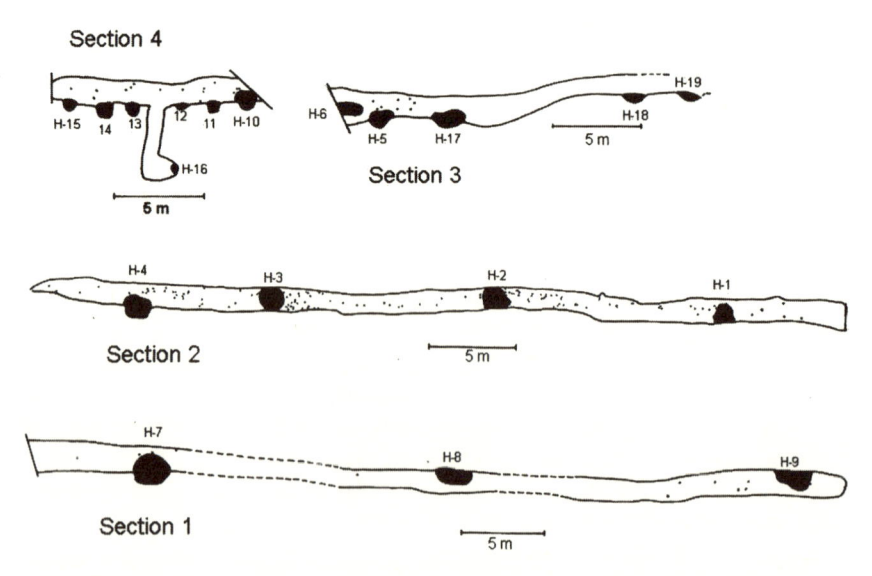

Plans of the four excavated sections of the Confederate entrenchment showing the hearth locations and the artifact scatter in the base of those trenches.

Those segments of the trench that had been hand excavated after being defined in the first exploratory backhoe trenches showed that the initial after-battle fill of the trench consisted of a distinct layer of sheet wash (2 cm to 10 cm thick) that covered the base of the trench. This zone of silt at the base of the trench was certainly the result of rains during the time the trenches remained open after the battle. In the hand excavated segments, all of the artifactual materials that were recovered were either located on the base of the trench or within this zone of wash. Above the sheet wash, the remainder of the fill within the original trench consisted of apparently sterile soil, which was believed to have been the soil that had originally been excavated to create the trench and form a paralleling parapet or breastwork, and then subsequently used to refill the trench. It was assumed and later determined that this stratigraphy was relatively consistent in all the excavated sections.

Several factors suggested that the trench was filled a relatively short time after the battle. The relatively thin layer of silt did not suggest long exposure to numerous rains, particularly since the earth removed from the trench (the breastwork), lacking any vegetative cover during the winter, would have been readily eroded by rainfall. Similarly, there was no evidence of any erosional features in the sides of the trench that would have suggested much weathering. This was especially clear in the hearth features that had been excavated into the rear wall of the trench where the fired walls of those features remained intact almost to the top of the original trench (see figure). Additionally, the intact appearance of the hearth features that were revealed in the entrenchment, their associated artifacts, and the artifact scatters around them belied any suggestion of long-term exposure.

Undoubtedly there may have been some scavenging after the battle, especially since this portion of the entrenchment was bisected by Granny White Pike, one of the main roads leading to the south from Nashville to Franklin. However, the impact of that may have been lessened by the winter season, and the fact that these earthworks were on privately held farms and at a distance of about two miles from the southern edge of Nashville. Since the trenches ran across areas that were cleared, and what were probably cultivated fields at the time, based on the map of the Battle of Nashville (see first figure), it is assumed that they were refilled soon after the battle, or at the latest, prior to spring plowing. The zone of fill above the zone of silt in the base of the trench, and which completely filled the trench, was homogeneous throughout the trench, and lacked any zones of wash or internal stratigraphy that would have been expected had the trench been open for a long time or just gradually filled. This suggested that the trench had been filled in essentially one episode.

In general, the 114 meters of trench that were excavated (see figures) revealed that the entrenchment appeared to have been a continuous excavation varying in width from one to one-and-a-half meters. It had a defined depth (from the top of the subsoil) ranging from 50 cm to about one meter.

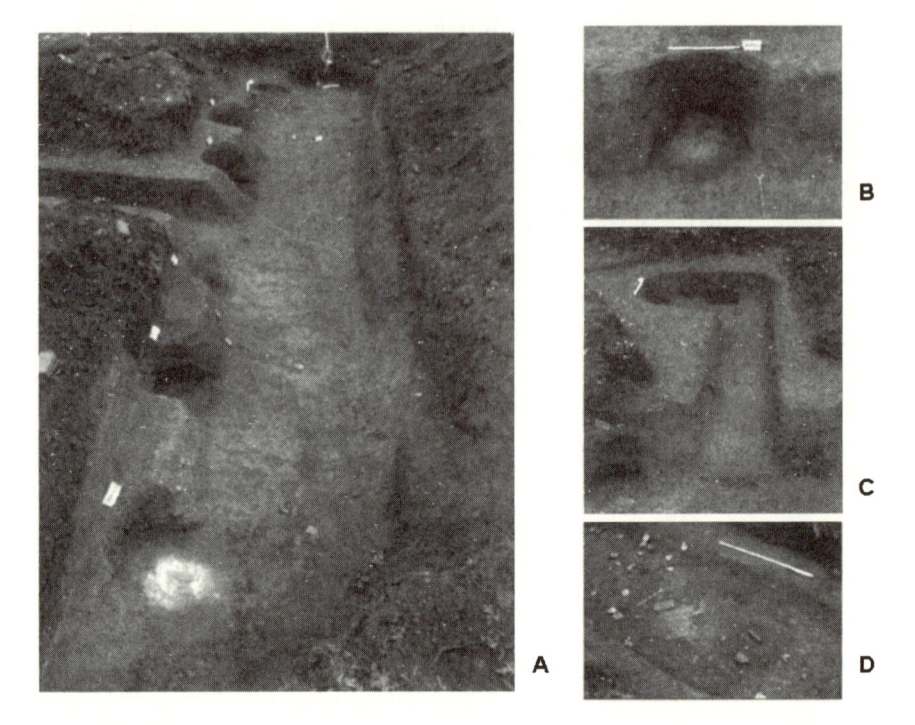

Trench sections.

Along the length of the excavated portions of the trench some 19 hearths or fired areas were located, either on the base of the trench, or in the rear side wall of the trench. These were spaced at distances of up to 13 meters, but one 14 meter segment of the trench had 6 hearths spaced at distances varying from only 1.5 to 2 meters apart. The same segment of the trench also had an L-shaped (and perhaps covered) extension to the rear with another hearth. Stratigraphy within the hearths consisted of alternating layers of ash and earth, indicating that the fires had been started and extinguished on several occasions.

All artifacts from the hearths and the base of the trench between the hearths were plotted on large-scale plans of the trench. It was hoped that they might provide some information on use patterns within the entrenchment. Of particular interest was the possibility of determining the disposition of troops in the trench during the battle, based on the distribution of fired percussion caps. This was inconclusive, since many of the fired caps were located within and around the hearths. Most of the other artifactual remains were located in the vicinity of the hearths, although there was a light to moderate scatter of artifacts in the base of the trench in all sections excavated. Numerous nails in all of the hearths suggested the scavenging of wood from nearby buildings for firewood.

Section 1 was a 49-meter (161-ft) segment in the eastern part of the project area (see figures). Three hearths were present (Hearths 7–9). The easternmost two were spaced 20 meters (66 ft) apart and the third had a spacing of 18 meters (59 ft). Two of these were just repeatedly fired areas in the trench base adjacent to the north wall. The third (Hearth 7) was a somewhat more formal feature, having been excavated into the south wall of the entrenchment. The back wall of this feature was heavily fired, and that firing preserved the cut marks resulting from a flat spade used for excavation. A light scatter of artifacts was present in the base of the trench, primarily in close association with the hearths. Approximately 15 meters of the upper part of this trench had been disturbed (see dashed lines on figure, section 1), with only about a third of that disturbance impacting the base of the entrenchment. The entrenchment terminated at the eastern end of this section. This corresponds to the short gap in the forward line shown on the first figure, where the forward line was discontinuous across an area of low ground and a small creek.

Section 2 was a 47-meter-long section of the entrenchment nearly parallel to Gale Lane. The excavations began at the eastern end at a point that was somewhat beyond the area that would be affected by construction, and continued westward to where the trench had been removed by the original construction of Gale Lane and a shallow drainage ditch at the edge of the street. Four hearths (Hearths 1–4) were present in this section. Three of them were simply repeatedly fired areas in the base of the trench (see figure), while Hearth 4 had been cut into the south wall of the trench. Three were spaced at 13 meters (43 ft), while the westernmost one (Hearth 4) was only 8 meters (26 ft) from the adjoining one. The artifacts that were recovered were concentrated in the hearths, but there was a moderate scatter in the base of the trench along its entire length.

During this phase of the work only the western five meters of Section 3 was excavated. The trench was well defined and two hearths (Hearths 5 and 6) were exposed. The excavation began as close as possible to a large oak tree and extended eastward to a sidewalk paralleling Gale Lane, which could not be removed at that time, since this was not yet a construction area. However, based on the depth of the entrenchment that was excavated north of Gale Lane, it was suspected that perhaps 50 meters of the Confederate entrenchment may have still been preserved beneath the sidewalk and asphalt of Gale Lane. However, after construction had begun, it was possible to monitor the earth-moving for the modification of the intersection. While this monitoring was not ideal, it was possible to define and map an additional 17 meters of this part of the entrenchment and excavate three additional hearths (Hearths 17–19) that were present in that segment. This resulted in the definition of a total of 22 meters (72 ft) of entrenchment and five hearths. Four of those hearths had been excavated to some extent into the south wall of the trench, while Hearth 6 was only a fired area of the floor of the trench. Artifactual materials were present in the hearths, and in the western five meters of this section where the base had been hand excavated there was a moderate scatter of artifacts present. No information on artifact distribution was obtained during the monitoring operations.

Section 4 was an 11.5-meter-(38-ft) long part of the trench. It was separated from Trench 3 because of the presence of a large previously noted tree. In the south wall of the trench were six rather formal hearths or fireplaces that had been excavated into the south wall (see figures). Spacing was very close, being only 1.5 to 2.0 meters between centers. Floors and walls of these features were very heavily fired (see figure), and like other hearths had been repeatedly used for fires and extinguished on several occasions. From the central part of this trench, another trench one meter in width extended to the rear of the line four meters, and then expanded into a chamber 1.5 meters wide and extended eastward the same amount (see figure). On the base of the chamber and against the east wall was yet another hearth (Hearth 16). Although there was no remaining evidence, it is assumed that this was perhaps a covered shelter for someone of a higher rank than the soldiers in the main trench. Or maybe it was a bomb-proof of sorts used by several individuals during a possible artillery attack.

The excavation work also included the excavation of some 19 two-meter squares immediately behind Section 2 of the Confederate entrenchment. The original shovel testing program had produced some early- to mid-nineteenth-century ceramics in that area. It was not known whether these were the result of troop occupations or not. Although the excavations recovered moderate quantities of artifacts from that period, no features were defined to indicate whether this occupation was related to a former house site, or a Civil War encampment immediately behind the line. Since most of the artifacts, such as the ceramics, could be associated with a domestic occupation, it is assumed that this was the location of a former house site, although no structural remains were defined.

ARTIFACT ASSEMBLAGE

The artifact assemblage that was recovered from the entrenchment was modest, but clearly reflected the military occupation of the forward line. A total of 27 Minié balls, including .58 caliber, as well as Williams Cleaner type bullets, were recovered, approximately half of them having been fired. The only artillery shell fragment found was from a Hotchkiss shell. Percussion caps were relatively numerous, both fired and unfired. These clustered in and around the hearth areas. It is perhaps reasonable to assume that the hearths may have represented the firing positions of one or more soldiers, but the presence of expended caps within the ash in the hearths could perhaps represent some sort of entertainment, rather than battle activities.

One axe head was found in a hearth. A total of 190 cut and wrought nails were recovered from the hearths within the entrenchment, reflecting scavenging of wood from nearby buildings for firewood. Foodstuff remains were scant. A few animal bones, primarily cow and pig, were recovered from the hearths and base of the entrenchment. Carbonized corn kernels were present in several of the hearths. These most likely resulted from being burned while being parched, or grains that did not pop while being parched and were discarded. A few pieces of tin found in the entrenchment may be from ration cans.

Accoutrements included a brass belt buckle, the brass finial from a scabbard, pieces of probable canteens, an iron harness ring, and iron harness buckles. Several slate pencils and a slate writing board from one of the hearths in Section 2 may have derived from an artillery battery that was stationed immediately forward of this section of line.

Items of a more domestic nature included 320 ceramics including annular wares, hand-painted pearlwares, porcelain, blue and green shell edge, spatterware, and blue transfer ware. Only a few of the shards were recovered within the trench itself, most coming from the excavation units behind the defensive line. Four coins—an 1849 large cent, 1838 Liberty dime, 1827 Liberty dime, and a probable Spanish $1/2$ Real—were also found. These and the ceramics suggest an earlier occupation than the 1864 trench, and are most likely from an earlier house site. One mill crank was recovered. Also, 244 pieces of glass representing pharmaceutical vials, beverage bottles, and flasks were recovered, but the majority of these were from the area of the probable house site, and not the entrenchment.

CONCLUSIONS

These excavations, although limited, clearly show the potential for excavations on military sites of the Civil War era, as have other excavations that have been done on Civil War sites since this one. This example at the Battle of Nashville indicates that the nineteenth-century topographic maps are quite accurate and useful for determining rather precisely the locations of battle lines and entrenchments, even though there may be no above-ground features remaining. More exciting, however, is that these excavations demonstrated that there may be more potential than one would have believed for remaining evidence of these types of remains in urban and suburban residential areas, which now cover many of the Civil War battlefields, or portions of them. It is assumed that these trenches would have been scavenged after the battle, resulting in the loss of information, but it appears that the filling of the trenches within a short time of the battle was instrumental in preserving the remaining artifact scatter, and particularly the hearths that were present. Subsequent use of the fields for plowing possibly cut into the upper part of the entrenchment somewhat but not enough to effectively minimize the information potential.

While the development of the area into residential streets and housing clearly destroyed portions of this entrenchment, the long-term use as family homes basically served to protect the remaining archaeological features. In some instances where soil from basement was placed in the yards over the entrenchment line, it served to add another layer of protection to the trench below. The archaeological excavations that were done along some 140 meters (459 ft) of this Confederate forward line demonstrated that about 95 meters (312 ft) of the entrenchment (or 68 percent) remained in an intact enough condition to provide excellent archaeological information. Much of the remainder of the Confederate forward line (as well as large portions of the main Confederate line) runs through similar neighborhoods. If in fact the percentage that was intact in the excavation area is any indicator, there should be large portions of the Confederate lines that still remain. If one would assume a somewhat lesser figure of 50 percent (possibly high) of the defensive entrenchments was still intact, there could still be nearly two miles (3.3 km) of archaeological potential remaining for providing information on the Confederate defenses of the Battle of Nashville.

NOTES

1. Earlier versions of this paper were read at the 1989 Joint Archaeological Congress, Baltimore, Maryland (Kuttruff 1989a), and at the American Battlefield Protection Program 7th National Conference on Battlefield Preservation, April 2004, Nashville, Tennessee (Kuttruff 2004).
2. See for example "The Presidios of the North American Spanish Borderlands" (Bense 2000).
3. Kelso et al. 2000.
4. For example see McBride et al. 2003; Kuttruff 1989b, 1990; Hanson and Hsu 1975; Grimm 1970; Smith 1993; Smith and Nance 2000; Polhemus 1979.
5. See Geier and Potter (2000) for a sampling of recent Civil War archaeological studies; Mainfort 1980; Dilliplane 1974, 1975.
6. For example Scott and Fox 1987.
7. See Kuttruff 1991, 1996; Christiansen 1994.
8. Geier and Potter made a much more recent, but quite similar comment in their recent *Archaeological Perspectives on the American Civil War* (2000:xxxi–xxxii).
9. Geier and Potter 2000.
10. Fox 1978.
11. Dilliplane 1974, 1975.
12. Mainfort 1980.
13. Prouty and Barker 1996; Smith and Nance 2003; Smith et al. 1990.
14. Personal communication 2003 Lawrence S. Alexander, and Alexander 2004.
15. Braley 1987.
16. The following summary of the Battle of Nashville is based on Brown 1964; Horn 1964, 1978; Crownover 1955; Lindsley 1886; and Walker 1964. The description of the defenses is based on Beasley and Gotto 1964, Horn 1978, and various maps including Topographical Map of the Battlefield of Nashville, Tenn., 15th and

16th Dec. 1864 (National Archives N.D.a); Battlefields in Front of Nashville Where the United States Forces Commanded by Major General Geo. H. Thomas Defeated and Routed the Rebel Army under General Hood December 15th and 16th 1864 (National Archives N.D.b); Davis et al. 1891–1895:Plate LXXIII-1.

17. McWhiney and Jamieson 1982:75.

18. The project was funded by the Tennessee Department of Transportation. The fieldwork was carried out by Tennessee Division of Archaeology personnel under the direction of this writer.

REFERENCES CITED

Alexander, Lawrence. 2004. The Process of Preservation of Chattanooga's Battlefields. Paper presented at the American Battlefield Protection Program 7th National Conference on Battlefield Preservation, April 2004, Nashville, TN.

Beasley, Paul H., and C. Buford Gotto. 1964. Fortress Nashville: How the Federals Fortified the City. In *Hood's Nashville Campaign*, Special Nashville Campaign Edition, Civil War Times Illustrated, 25–26.

Bense, Judith A. 2004. Presidios of the North American Spanish Borderlands. *Historical Archaeology* 38(3).

Braley, Chad O. 1987. *The Battle of Gilgal Church: An Archaeological and Historical Study of Mid-Nineteenth Century Warfare in Georgia*. Report prepared for Oglethorpe Power Corporation. Southeastern Archaeological Services, Inc., Athens, GA.

Brown, Col. Campbell H. 1964. To Rescue the Confederacy—Why and How Hood Invaded Tennessee. In *Hood's Nashville Campaign*, Special Nashville Campaign Edition, Civil War Times Illustrated, 12–15, 44–48.

Christiansen, Heinrich. 1994. *The Archaeology of World War II in the Marshall Islands* (Volumes 1–5). Historic Preservation Office, Ministry of the Interior, Majuro, Republic of the Marshall Islands.

Crownover, Sims. 1955. The Battle of Franklin. *Tennessee Historical Quarterly* XIV(4).

Davis, Major George B., Leslie J. Perry, and Joseph W. Kirkley. 1891–1895. *Atlas to Accompany the Official Records of the Union and Confederate Armies*. Government Publishing Office, Washington, D.C. Reprinted 1978 by Arno Press and Crown Publishers, New York.

Dilliplane, Timothy L. 1974. *Fort Granger (Franklin, TN): A Study of Its Past and Proposal for Its Future*. Report submitted to the Tennessee Historical Commission, National Park Service, and on file at the Tennessee Division of Archaeology.

Dilliplane, Timothy L. 1975. *Exploratory Excavations at Fort Granger*. Report submitted to the Tennessee Historical Commission, National Park Service, and on file at the Tennessee Division of Archaeology.

Fox, Steven J. 1978. *Archaeology of Fortress Rosecrans: A Civil War Garrison in Middle Tennessee*. Report submitted to the National Park Service, Tennessee Historical Commission, and the City of Murfreesboro, TN.

Geier, Clarence R., and Stephen R. Potter. 2000. *Archaeological Perspectives on the American Civil War*. University Press of Florida, Gainesville, FL.

Grimm, Jacob L. 1970. *Archaeological Investigations of Fort Ligonier, 1960–1965.* Annals of the Carnegie Museum, Volume 42. Pittsburg, PA.

Hanson, Lee, and Dick Ping Hsu. 1975. *Casemates and Cannonballs: Archaeological Investigations at Fort Stanwix, Rome, New York.* U.S. Department of the Interior National Park Service, Publications in Archaeology 14. U.S. Government Printing Office, Washington, D.C.

Horn, Stanley F. 1964. The Most Decisive Battle of the Civil War. In *Hood's Nashville Campaign*, Special Nashville Campaign Edition, Civil War Times Illustrated, 5–11, 31–36.

Horn, Stanley F. 1978. *The Decisive Battle of Nashville.* University of Tennessee Press, Knoxville, TN.

Kelso, William M., Nicholas M. Luccketti, and Beverly A. Straub. 2000. *Jamestown Rediscovery V.* Association for the Preservation of Virginia Antiquities, Jamestown, VA.

Kuttruff, Carl. 1989a. Excavations on Confederate Entrenchments, Nashville, Tennessee. Paper presented at the Joint Archaeological Congress, January 1989, Baltimore, MD.

Kuttruff, Carl. 1989b. Fort Loudoun Tennessee. Manuscript on file at the Tennessee Division of Archaeology, Fort Loudoun State Historic Area and in possession of the author.

Kuttruff, Carl. 1990. Fort Loudoun, Tennessee, a Mid-18th Century British Fortification: A Case Study in Research Archaeology, Reconstruction, and Interpretive Exhibits. In Peter Gathercole and David Lowenthall (eds.), *The Politics of the Past*, 265–283. Unwin Hyman, London.

Kuttruff, Carl. 1991. Corregidor and the Defenses of Manila Bay. In W. Raymond Wood (ed.), *Anthropological Studies of World War II*, 29–47. Museum of Anthropology Monograph Number 10, Department of Anthropology, University of Missouri, Columbia.

Kuttruff, Carl. 1996. *World War Phase II Archaeological Survey and Subsurface Testing at Kwajalein and Roi-Namur Islands, United States Army Kwajalein Atoll, Republic of the Marshall Islands.* Report prepared for United States Army Space and Strategic Defense Command, Environmental and Engineering office, Huntsville, Alabama, by Earth Technology, Inc. and EDAW, Inc., Huntsville, AL.

Kuttruff, Carl. 2004. Excavations Along the Confederate Line, Battle of Nashville, Tennessee. Paper presented at the American Battlefield Protection Program 7th National Conference on Battlefield Preservation, April 2004, Nashville, TN.

Lindsley, John Berries (ed.). 1886. *The Military Annals of Tennessee. Confederate, 1st Series.* J. M. Lindsley and Company, Nashville, TN.

Mainfort, Robert C., Jr. 1980. *Archaeological Investigations at Ft. Pillow State Historic Area: 1976–1978.* Research Series 4, Tennessee Division of Archaeology, Nashville, TN.

McBride, W. Stephen, Kim Arbogast McBride, and Greg Adamson. 2003. *Frontier Forts in West Virginia: Historical and Archaeological Explorations.* The West Virginia Division of Culture and History, Charleston, WV.

McWhiney, Grady, and Perry D. Jamieson. 1982. *Attack and Die: Civil War Military Tactics and the Southern Heritage.* The University of Alabama Press, University of Alabama, Tuscaloosa, AL.

National Archives. n.d.a. *Topographical Map of the Battle Field of Nashville, Tenn., 15th and 16th Dec. 1864.* Record Group 77: Z76 1/2.

National Archives. n.d.b. *Battlefields in Front of Nashville Where the United States Forces Commanded by Major General Geo. H. Thomas Defeated and Routed the Rebel Army under General Hood December 15th and 16th 1864.* Record Group 77: T 86-5.

Polhemus, Richard R. 1979. *Archaeological Investigation of the Tellico Blockhouse Site 40MR50: A Federal and Military Trade Complex.* Report of Investigations 26. Department of Anthropology, University of Tennessee, and Tennessee Valley Authority Reports in Anthropology 16, Knoxville, TN.

Prouty, Fred M., and Gary L. Barker. 1996. *A Survey of Civil War Period Military Sites in West Tennessee.* Report of Investigations 11, Tennessee Division of Archaeology, Nashville, TN.

Scott, Douglas D., and Richard A. Fox Jr. 1987. *Archaeological Insights into the Custer Battle: An Assessment of the 1984 Field Season.* University of Oklahoma Press, Norman, OK.

Smith, Samuel D. (ed.). 1993. *Fort Southwest Point Archaeological Site, Kingston, Tennessee: A Multidisciplinary Interpretation.* Research Series 9, Tennessee Division of Archaeology, Nashville, TN.

Smith, Samuel D., Fred M. Prouty, and Benjamin C. Nance. 1990. *A Survey of Civil War Period Military Sites in Middle Tennessee.* Report of Investigations 7, Tennessee Division of Archaeology, Nashville, TN.

Smith, Samuel D., and Benjamin C. Nance (eds.). 2000. *An Archaeological Interpretation of the Site of Fort Blount, a 1790s Territorial Militia and Federal Military Post, Jackson County, Tennessee.* Research Series 12, Tennessee Division of Archaeology, Nashville, TN.

Smith, Samuel D., and Benjamin C. Nance. 2003. *A Survey of Civil War Era Military Sites in Tennessee.* Research Series 14, Tennessee. Division of Archaeology, Nashville, TN.

Walker, Hugh F. 1964. Bloody Franklin: Where 6,000 Confederates Fell in Vain. In *Hood's Nashville Campaign.* Special Nashville Campaign Edition, Civil War Times Illustrated, 16–24.

Seven Eventful Days in Paraguay: Reconnoitering the Archaeology of the War of the Triple Alliance

Tony Pollard

OUTBREAK

ALTHOUGH PARAGUAY HAD a history of conflict with Argentina dating back to the independence of Argentina from Spain in 1810 and Paraguay from Argentina in 1811, it was her disputes with Brazil that drew her in to the War of the Triple Alliance. In truth, Argentina did not have her troubles to seek, with internal bickering between the provinces, essentially Federalist Buenos Aries against those of the Unitarian interior, regularly leading to outbreaks of civil war. As it happened though, it was Uruguay, a small country uncomfortably sandwiched between her larger neighbors, which really detonated the bloodiest war ever to be fought in the Southern Americas.

In October 1864, the Brazilian army crossed into Uruguay and began a campaign in support of Brazilian landowners and the Colorado party against the ruling Blancos. By the end of the month Blanco resistance was focused on the defense of Payasandú, the garrison surrendering after a brutal artillery bombardment on January 2, 1865. The capital, Montevideo, fell in early February and Venancio Flores became provisional president at the head of the victorious Colorado party. Paraguay, fueled by the Brazilian intervention in Uruguay to the south and continued border strife with the Brazilian Mato Grosso in the north, went on the offensive. A naval squadron carrying 3,000 troops was sent up the River Paraguay into the Mato Grasso, while a land force of 2,500 cavalry and infantry supported the amphibious assault. The poorly manned Brazilian outposts were quickly captured, and only shallow, impassable rivers saved the province's capital at Cuiaba from occupation.

THE CORRIENTES CAMPAIGN

The Paraguayan leader, Mariscal President Francisco Solano López, had chosen not to support the Blancos in their hour of need but once they had been overthrown he ordered his army to take on the new Uruguayan government and the Brazilian force that put it in power. Paraguayan troops mobilized on the borders of the Misiones region in the southeast. López then made a mistake in asking President Mitre of Argentina for permission for his troops to pass through the Argentinean province of Corrientes in a move on Uruguay. Mitre turned down the request and this response was received in Asunción, the Paraguayan capital, to the sound of rattling sabres. Corrientes was governed by General Urquiza, a political opponent of Mitre's Buenos Aires. He also despised the Brazilians and was a sympathizer of the López regime, but a threatened incursion by the Paraguayans left him with no choice but to stand in support of Mitre. Thus a potential ally of Paraguay was alienated and Argentina inadvertently pushed into its strongest ever state of unification.

In response to this rebuff López convinced the Paraguayan General Congress to declare war against Argentina. Now all the players were at the table, but López took his time to inform the Argentinean government that the game was under way, delaying delivery of the formal declaration in Buenos Aires until May 3, after having already seized the provincial capital and port of Corrientes on April 14. The Argentineans, however, needed no official declaration of war to show their hand, and the Treaty of the Triple Alliance, which united Argentina, Brazil, and Uruguay in a war against Paraguay, was signed on May 1, 1865. The treaty included the statement that the war was not waged against the people of Paraguay but their leader, a war aim which was to have a profound effect on the longevity of the war and perhaps has a particular resonance with more recent events elsewhere in the world. The most immediate result, however, was to galvanize the Paraguayan population in support of their president and defense of their country.

ALLIED COUNTERATTACK

On May 25 an Allied force 2,000 strong, largely made up from Argentinean troops, counterattacked at Corrientes (see figure), landing from Brazilian vessels on the River Paraguay. A fierce battle broke out with the defending 1,600 Paraguayans, resulting in the death of 900 of the latter and the first victory for the Allies. The importance of the rivers had shown itself and in response López resolved to neutralize the Brazilian fleet. The resulting river battle, at Riachuelo to the south of the port of Corrientes, was another painful defeat for the Paraguayans. Efforts by their fleet, led by the flagship *Taquari*, to maintain the element of surprise were woefully inept as they steamed past the enemy flotilla in daylight before returning upstream for the attack. In the ensuing four-hour struggle the Paraguayans lost four steamers, one sunk and three disabled, while the surviving four, including the *Taquari*, suffered heavy damage and limped back upstream.

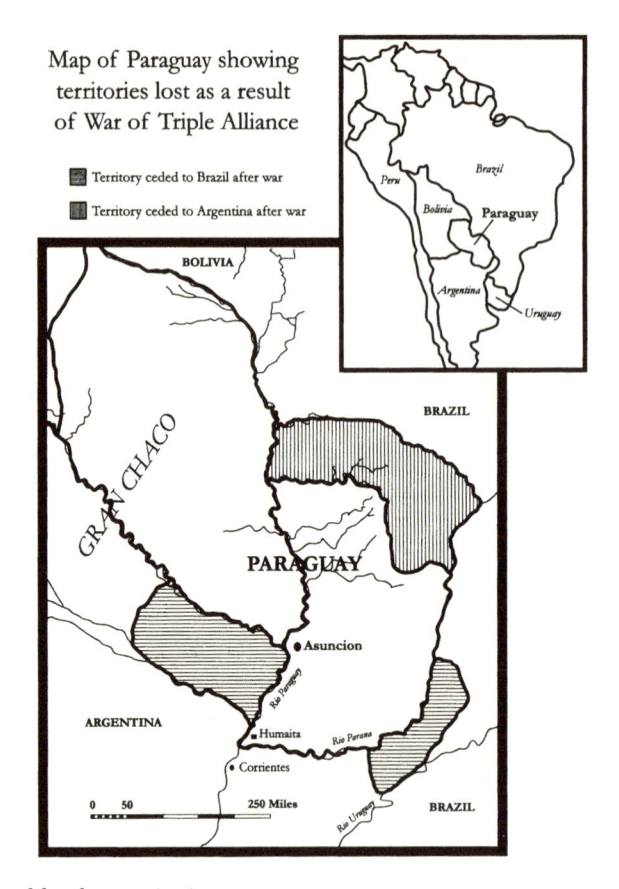

Map of Paraguay showing territories lost as a result of War of Triple Alliance

▨ Territory ceded to Brazil after war
▩ Territory ceded to Argentina after war

Paraguay and her lost territories.

PARAGUAYAN FAILURE IN BRAZIL

At the same time as the battle of Riachuelo the Paraguayans crossed into Brazilian territory in the Rio Grande do Sul, north of the Uruguayan border. Things went from bad to worse for the Paraguayans. At Yatai on August 17 a Paraguayan force of 2,500 under Major Duarte was wiped out almost to the last man, an early example of Paraguayan tenacity against heavy odds. The remainder of the expeditionary force, numbering just over 4,000, was besieged at Uruguaiana by a Brazilian force of 17,000. On September 18, the garrison, under General Estigarriba surrendered to generous terms. López, distressed by this string of defeats, which had thus far cost his forces around 20,000 men in combat in addition to at least the same number to disease, realized that Paraguay could not sustain an offensive campaign in enemy territory and so pulled his forces back into Paraguay, where they would fight a defensive war on home soil. The army now numbered some 30,000 souls. As 1865 drew to a close they faced the prospect of invasion by an Allied force of some 50,000 now well established in Corrientes under General Mitre, president of Argentina.

ALLIED INVASION

Despite the retreat behind its own borders the Paraguayan army was far from cowed and regularly harassed the Allies with raids carried out with lightning speed across the River Paraná. The Paraguayans established defensive positions near the confluence of the rivers Paraguay and the Paraná at Paso de la Patria and further north on the eastern banks of the Paraguay at the small town of Humaitá, where a heavy shore battery and a chain barrier stretched across the river protected the approaches to the capital from incursions by the Brazilian fleet.

The inevitable Allied invasion began on April 16, 1866, in the face of which the Paraguayans withdrew northward to consolidate their defenses in the marshlands of the Estero Bellaco. It was here, on May 2, that around 5,000 Paraguayans launched a surprise attack against Allied positions under the command of Flores, the Uruguayan president (later to be assassinated). The attack was an initial success, but in spite of the loss of several guns was turned into an Allied victory by an effective counterattack. This relatively small action was followed on May 24 by the biggest and one of the bloodiest battles of the war at Tuyuti, the first of two fought over the same ground.

Since the middle of April the Allies had built up their force in southern Paraguay and by May around 35,000 troops had crossed the river at Paso de la Patria. The Paraguayans were now established behind strongly defended positions to the north of Tuyuti, where trenches were strategically placed between areas of impenetrable marshland. López had wisely decided to fight a defensive battle and let the Allies come on to his well-protected guns. But in a move that now seems rash in the extreme, he changed his mind and opted for a massive assault on the Allied positions, in which he hoped to deploy 22,000 men in a surprise attack. The sting of surprise was removed by delays caused while deploying the troops, who were to attempt a complex enveloping maneuver with frontal and flanking attacks. The Brazilians had also had the foresight to dig their artillery into a defensive trench, thus giving them the same advantage the Paraguayans had chosen to discard. The fighting raged for hours with the Paraguayans throwing themselves against the enemy guns, but despite taking ground on some parts of the front the envelopment failed. By late afternoon the Paraguayans had lost between 10,000 and 12,000 men and the Allies around 3,000 and 4,000.

DIGGING IN (CURUPAITY)

The few months following the first battle of Tuyuti saw the cessation of major engagements, in part at least due to the severe shock the battle had caused to both sides. The Paraguayans spent much of this time constructing entrenchments and fortifications in front of Humaitá. These were especially strong on the line stretching to the east from the bank of the River Paraguay at Curupaity. As the year progressed the Allies built up their forces and brought in large numbers of reserves, many of them Brazilians from the 2nd Army Corps based in the Rio Grande.

On September 3 these troops were pushed into an assault on the Paraguayan defenses at Curuzu, which despite stiff opposition were successfully stormed. Unfortunately for the Allies they failed to follow through with this success, which may have enabled them to go on and take the defenses at Curupaity before they were completed. It is said that an impromptu peace conference between López and Mitre on September 12, 1866, and attendant cease-fire was a deliberate attempt by the former to buy time for the completion of defense construction.[1] If there is any truth in this then the ploy worked, for when full hostilities resumed with an Allied assault on September 22 the invaders were to suffer their biggest setback of the war.

Following a heavy naval bombardment from the river, 18,000 Allied infantry set out on a frontal assault across marshy ground and were mown down in their thousands by well-covered Paraguayans largely unaffected by the bombardment (see figure). This time, however, it was the Paraguayans who failed to seize an opportunity and in the absence of an immediate counterattack the Allies were allowed to recover and regroup. Once again the shockwave of battle brought a temporary halt to major engagements, this time lasting for 14 months. But it was not just shock that brought a respite in heavy hostilities. Serious outbreaks of malaria and cholera caused thousands of deaths on both sides. Military activities were again limited to strengthening positions, skirmishing, and artillery bombardments. This period also saw a change in the Allied leadership with the Brazilian Marques de Caxias replacing the Argentinean President General Mitre. The Argentinean leader had to return south of the border to quell a domestic uprising—things were still far from settled within the Argentinean confederation and the country's involvement in the war was to become an increasing focus for dissent and would lead to Brazil playing the dominant role on the Allied side.

The stalemate could not last forever—despite massive losses to disease the Allies had a seemingly limitless supply of manpower and by July 1867 there were about 45,000 men under arms that included 40,000 Brazilians and 5,000 Argentineans. The Paraguayans on the other hand were beginning to scrape the bottom of the barrel and were down to around 20,000 all told. The second battle of Tuyuti was fought on November 3 and was a Paraguayan initiative in response to increased pressure from the Allies on their left flank, which included heavy artillery bombardment. One of the aims of the attack by 8,000 men was to capture pieces of Allied artillery and this time they managed to maintain the element of surprise. The Brazilian trenches were overrun. The Paraguayans then set about looting the rich Allied camp and were entirely unprepared when the Allies mounted a counterattack, many of them weighed down with booty, including a much-prized 32-pounder Whitworth gun.

Detail of Argentinean assault on Curupaity from an 1893 painting by Candido López.

THE TIDE TURNS (THE FALL OF HUMAITÁ)

Second Tuyuti was a relative success for the Paraguayans but an inconclusive battle, and the tide was about to turn irrevocably in favor of the Allies with the isolation and capture of Humaitá, the last defensive backstop before Asunción. This turning point came to pass on February 18, 1868, when the Brazilian fleet, after much dawdling, finally forced a way past the shore batteries as a ground assault stormed the Paraguayan defenses to the north of Humaitá. On February 22 the fleet bombarded Asunción, which was already partially abandoned—Allied troops were not to enter the city until January 1, 1869. Humaitá, although entirely surrounded, continued to be a thorn in the side of the Allies until it was abandoned, women and children first, by its garrison under cover of darkness on July 23–24, 1868 (the surreptitious evacuation was so effective that it was not discovered by the Allies for almost a full day but it did not impress López and he had the garrison commander's wife flogged and executed).

On March 19 López had taken his army, by then down to around 10,000 troops, across the River Paraguay into the inhospitable Chaco country. He then made his way north and over the next two years continued to confound the Allies. At this time López became increasingly paranoid and ordered the execution of hundreds, if not thousands, of supposed plotters, including members of his own family. Two new capitals were established and abandoned as the Allies pursued López and his bedraggled army.

RETREAT

Some of the most vicious fighting of the war was still to come, at Ytororó on December 6, 1868; Avay on December 11; and Itá-Ibaty on December 21. Despite heavier Allied casualties these battles all but destroyed the Paraguayan army, which by the end of the year had been reduced to around 1,000 troops. But López was still at large and, having refused an offer to surrender on December 24, was about to accomplish what many historians have seen as nothing short of miraculous.[2] Instead of admitting defeat he set about building another army and by April, after scraping together between 6,000 and 13,000 poorly armed men and boys, felt strong enough to go on the offensive.

His forays against the Allies included the use of light guns on railway carriages, undoubtedly the first use of an armored train in South America. Despite the incredible tenacity and audacity of the Paraguayans the end of the story had been written five years earlier in the treaty of the Triple Alliance. It has been suggested by some historians[3] that after December 1868 the capture of López could have been achieved with relative ease had Caxias committed his troops to the task, but he chose to procrastinate. Various reasons for this perceived deliberate prolonging of the war have been offered, including that the continued state of war allowed the extermination of the Paraguayan people to proceed on a legitimate basis. This rather extreme motive does not marry with Caxias prematurely declaring the end of the war on January 1, 1869, the same day he resigned his command. Nor should it be forgotten that delay and indecision had to a degree characterized the Allied approach to the war from the very beginning.

ENDGAME

Eventually, on August 12, 1869, the Allies, which by then essentially meant the Brazilians, under the command of the Conde d'Eu, the emperor's son-in-law, attacked the third and final Paraguayan "capital" at Peribibuy, not long vacated by López and the main part of his army. Despite a stiff defense by the Paraguayan troops left behind the town fell and according to some authors the victorious troops proceeded to put many civilians and wounded to the sword, while others have credited López with equally harsh treatment of the Paraguayan people in the retreat from Peribibuy.[4] The following day the Allies caught up with the entrenched rear guard of the Paraguayan army at Campo Grande (called Acosta Nu by the Paraguayans). The last major action of the war saw the final destruction of the stubborn Paraguayan army as an effective fighting force. By now many of the troops were invalids, old men, or young boys (some of the latter are said to have worn false beards to fool the enemy into believing they were facing men). This holding action enabled López and his remaining followers, around 1,000 to 2,000 exhausted troops and hundreds of civilians, to slip away.

Now hounded like an outlaw with a posse on his trail, López managed to evade Allied patrols for another seven months, and a provisional civil government in Asunción declared him a common outlaw. López certainly didn't cover himself with glory during those final months. Despite his reduced numbers and circumstances he found time to have his soldiers execute 86 suspected traitors and deserters, but due to a lack of ammunition the accused were stabbed to death with lances. On March 1, 1870, his camp was attacked and he was lanced and then shot dead by Brazilian troops as he tried to flee across a stream.

With López dead, the war was at last over. It had cost Paraguay almost everything. Around 220,000 Paraguayans were killed by war, famine, or execution, while the Allies lost well in excess of 100,000 men (but see below). The war also cost the country over a third of its territory. The area of the Chaco, on the west bank of the River Paraguay as far north as the River Pilcomayo, and the Misiones to the east of the River Parana went to Argentina, while the Mato Grasso to the north of the River Apa was lost to Brazil (see previous map)

DOCUMENTING THE WAR OF THE TRIPLE ALLIANCE

Written Histories

The War of the Triple Alliance has produced a body of documentary literature, of both primary and secondary sources, which is notable for its level of internal contradictions, variations, inconsistencies, and plain inaccuracies. Nowhere else in the annals of military history has the present author come across such diversity of opinion and belief. It is undoubtedly an exaggeration, but it sometimes seems that no two books agree on anything, from the correct spelling of names through to the dates of events and the death tolls of battles (for instance, the death toll for the whole of the war ranges from around 300,000 up to well over a million, depending on which source one reads).

This interesting situation is obviously not just the result of poor research, though there is a measure of that on display. It has been exacerbated and to a degree caused by the partisan nature of many of the early accounts.

Outside South America, the earliest accounts are those by the foreigners who, for whatever reason, were in Paraguay during the war, and so could be described as eyewitnesses. Notable here are the British technicians employed by the Paraguayan government who later published their memoirs. They include the former Apothecary General George Masterman, whose book *Seven Eventful Years In Paraguay* provided a prompt for the title for the present chapter. He published his memoir in 1869, not long after escaping from the country, where he had fallen foul of the totalitarian regime. The vengeful Masterman set a trend for salacious written portraits of López and the war.

These early accounts, perhaps not surprisingly, painted López as an evil dictator who drove his country to destruction, the very model of a despot and a prototype for many to follow in Paraguay and her South American neighbors. This simplistic picture certainly found few detractors in a country that was to suffer the devastation of the war at least into the early years of the twentieth century. It was in fact the small cadre of twentieth-century dictators, who periodically came to rule Paraguay right up to the overthrow of Stroessner in 1989, that was largely responsible for giving the Mariscal a dramatic image makeover. There is after all nothing the modern despot likes more than to hark back to the golden days of an even more brutal dictator, setting a precedent for a president so to speak.

The first real about-face was O'Leary's very flattering *El Mariscal López*, which appeared in 1905, but perhaps the most enthusiastic rehabilitator of López was Colonel Rafael Franco, who having seized power in 1936 in the wake of the disastrous Chaco war with Bolivia, took a cue from his Spanish namesake and turned Paraguay into South America's first Fascist state. López became a national hero who sacrificed himself in the fight against those who would turn Paraguay into a pariah dependency. Today statues of the Mariscal can be seen in every town, usually in a plaza off the main street, which likely as not is itself named after him. His portrait also appears on the 1,000 Guaranies bank note, which although the lowest denomination of the nation's paper currency has by far the widest circulation. Even the main shopping mall in Asunción, which would not be out of place in London or Madrid, is named after him.

López is, however, not alone in appearing as a central character in a drama which involved no less a cast than a country's entire population. Just as many words have been expended on Elisa Lynch, the Irish-born courtesan who returned with him from Paris in 1854. At least half a dozen Lynch biographies appeared between 1870 and 1987. She has shared the ups and downs of vilification and rehabilitation, which have characterized the Mariscal's literary legacy. At times she has been portrayed as the evil puppet master behind the throne—a Lady Macbeth driving López to greater and greater excess in her ambition to establish him as the Napoleon of South America.[5] Her admirers, on the other hand, have painted her as a tragic Eva Perón type character that sacrificed everything for the man she loved and the people she came to regard as her extended family.[6]

The enduring appeal of this strong female character is clearly reflected in the appearance of two new biographies in 2003: *Empress of South America* by Nigel Cawthorne and the better informed *The Shadows of Elisa Lynch* by Siân Rees, which incidentally is only slightly more forgiving of its subject than the former. Cawthorne's book in a way epitomizes the problematic nature of some of the literature. It is essentially tabloid history, which revels in the more fantastic earlier accounts. This certainly makes for an entertaining read but does so at the cost of good history. In his retelling, the battle of Curupaity is reduced to a night attack by Brazilian troops who lost 5,000 men because they forgot to take along their scaling ladders. Cawthorne has apparently confused the battle of Curupaity, fought on September 22, 1866, with a Brazilian attack on a much beleaguered and under-manned Humaitá on July 16, 1868.[7] To a degree, it would appear the history of the war is a history written through "Chinese whispers."

Although thinner on the ground than these memoirs and biographically driven accounts, studies of the war itself have provided a somewhat more balanced view, removed as they are from the strong emotions engendered by the concentration on individual figureheads—though it is obviously impossible to ignore the role played by López given his position of absolute power. An exception among the memoirs is undoubtedly George Thompson's *The War in Paraguay*, 1896, which is based on his own experiences during the war as the chief military engineer in the Paraguayan army and provides a quite unique insight into the course of the war written by one who was actually in the thick of the fighting.

Numerous Argentinean and Brazilian accounts of the war appeared during the later nineteenth and first half of the twentieth century, but these are generally regarded to be somewhat biased (being a poor reader of Spanish and entirely illiterate in Portuguese the present author must obviously accept the general view of those writing in English). Perhaps the most extensive of these rather partisan works is the five-volume *Historia da Guerr Entre a Triplice Aliance o Paraguai*, by A. O. Fraggaso, 1934, who was for a time a member of the Brazilian military junta. Despite its pro-Brazilian stance this work does contain a very impressive collection of campaign and battle maps (though preliminary use in the field suggests that in parts at least these are of questionable accuracy).

The first and most influential attempt by a non–South American writer to place war in its historical and political context was Pelham Box's *The Origins of the Paraguayan War* published in 1930 and based on his doctoral thesis. This work's sympathies lie if anywhere with the Allies as Box sees the totalitarian Paraguay of López posing a threat to the spread of liberalism through the region. As the title suggests *The Rise and Fall of the Paraguayan Republic 1800-1870* by J. H. Williams, written in 1979, Williams sees the war as the disastrous, if avoidable, climax to 50 years of Paraguayan independence. Like Box's work it provides a detailed survey of the build-up to the conflict, which is then dealt with in a single chapter.

The 1960s and 1970s saw the publication of a very few more specific military histories, including Kolinski's *Independence or Death!*, 1965, which despite its rather melodramatic title provides a fairly balanced overview of the conflict and displays wide reading of the Latin American sources. A reasonably well-informed and accessible narrative of the war also appears in *Tragedy of Paraguay* by Gilbert Phelps, 1975. There is certainly a need for a thorough, up-to-date military history, which deals with the individual engagements in a more detailed fashion than previous studies and it is hoped that an archaeological project geared toward the battlefields will provide the opportunity to provide such a work, integrating history and archaeology to produce a fresh perspective.

As a postscript to the above, it should be reported that two recently published books on the subject[8] have lately come to the attention of the author and although recently reviewed could not be read in time for the completion of this chapter.[9]

The Visual Record

The hostilities that were to escalate into the War of the Triple Alliance broke out in late 1864 just as the American Civil War was entering its last bloody phase. Given this chronological overlap it is not surprising that both wars have certain similarities, including weaponry, technology such as the telegraph, use of trench fortifications, and even styles of uniform. One striking technological contrast lies in the richness of the photographic archive of the American Civil War when compared to the very sparse collection available for the War of the Triple Alliance. There was no equivalent of Mathew Brady working in Paraguay at the time of the war and our knowledge of the conflict is much the poorer for this. Photographs do exist, but they are few and far between. The most famous examples are probably those showing Brazilian officers, looking for all the world like soldiers in the Union army, standing among the ruins of the church in Humaitá (see figure); troops massed in a trench just before the battle of Tuyuti; and most tragically a pile of putrefying corpses photographed after the battle.

The closest thing the war had to a Mathew Brady was not a photographer but a painter. The works of Candido López provide a unique visual narrative of the war through the eyes of an Argentinean soldier. Candido López fought his way through the entire war making sketches of everything he saw. Even the loss of his right hand at the battle of Tuyuti didn't distract him from his task. In the years following the war he spent most of his time turning his sketches into a cycle of around 50 striking paintings, all of them characterized by an incredible eye for detail. Candido López was a common soldier, and so were many of his subjects. In his paintings armies are represented as

Allied officers pose in the ruins of the church at Humaitá. (see also fig., page 331)

crowds of individuals not just as vast anonymous masses. The artist bequeathed his paintings to the Argentinean nation but outside of temporary exhibitions they spend most of their time in storage. This is a shame, as he deserves to be recognized as one of the most important war artists of the nineteenth century. It is hoped that a documentary film currently being produced by my colleague José Luis Garcia will help to bring him to the attention of a wider audience.

Museums and Treasure Hunting

The Paraguayan government has recently made some advances in establishing historic sites as museums and visitor attractions. These include the iron foundry at Ybycuy and the ship museum at Vapor Cué. Museums are, however, still thin on the ground. The largest collection of war-related material is to be seen in the Ministry of Defence Museum in Asunción, which is largely devoted to the War of the Triple Alliance and the Chaco War. The museum is run by the military and accordingly is rather old-fashioned and pantheon-like, even having a dress code. At present, the most interesting museums take the form of private collections of battlefield relics displayed in their owners' houses, with some of them turning entire rooms into small museums. The author visited two private museums in Paso de Patria and one in Humaitá.

The museums in Paso de Patria exhibited a wide array of finds, including bullets, buttons, badges, spurs, bayonets, lance tips, clay pipes, musical instruments, and shell fragments. One of the museums takes up what appears to be a family bedroom, but the bed is said to have been used by the Mariscal while his headquarters was in Paso de Patria—the house in which he lived is currently being reconstructed after its demolition some years ago. The most striking museum visited was located in Humaitá (see figure) and is curated by a widow in memory of her late husband who built up the collection over many years. The collection includes several wooden crates filled to the brim with thousands of bullets and musket balls. In the backyard rusting shell fragments are piled in a heap bigger than the average family car—a reflection of the heavy bombardment the place suffered during the war.

The sight of all these de-contextualized artifacts may bring tears to a sensitive battlefield archaeologist's eye but we should not forget that Paraguay is one of the poorest countries in South America, and a handful of objects picked up from a maize field may bring a peasant farmer a few hard-to-come-by Guaranies. The objects also remain in the hands of local people who have an interest in them and are delighted to show them off to visitors. The same cannot be said for other impoverished countries with historic battlefields. In South Africa, for instance, relics from the Anglo–Zulu war of 1879 fetch high prices among collectors in the UK and USA. This financial

Private museum in Humaitá displaying the wide variety of artifacts commonly picked up from the battlefields and related sites. (T. Pollard)

incentive in tandem with terrible poverty has done much to promote illegal looting using metal detectors and poses a serious threat to already denuded sites. At present there appear to be very few metal detectors in Paraguay, though at least one homemade device is being used by an avid collector of battlefield relics, and more efficient machines may be used by collectors travelling from Argentina.

Although not many people in Paraguay have access to a metal detector, another legacy of the war is digging for treasure buried by Paraguayans in the face of the Allied advance through the south of the country. There is a strong oral tradition of gold and silver, furniture, paintings, and other valuable personal possessions hidden in deep pits, usually in side chambers. There is some evidence that on occasion this did happen[10] but its prevalence has undoubtedly been exaggerated over time. Poverty once again is the motivation behind the search for what in most cases will obviously be mythical treasures. Just before the author's arrival in Paraguay two treasure hunters died when the pit they were digging in while searching for treasure collapsed on them. Treasure hunting is clearly dangerous to those who partake in it, but as it involves the hand digging of deep shafts of limited diameter it actually presents a very limited threat to archaeological deposits on sites covering extensive areas. Why people dig where they do is a bit of a puzzle, and may be guided as much by access to land as by local tradition and the identification of a specific location with stories of buried treasure. The only example seen by the author was in Humaitá, where a backfilled pit was still visible in the garden of the man who had dug it to find nothing.

THE BATTLEFIELD RECONNAISSANCE

The area visited occupies the eastern bank of the River Paraguay in the southernmost corner of the country, bordered by Argentina on the west bank of the Paraguay and on the southern bank of the River Paraná. Although largely confined to the region of Ñeembucá, the area is commonly referred to as the Quadrilátero, after the roughly trapezoidal shape traced by Paraguayan trench systems shown on maps drawn up during and after the war. Travel by land is for the most part limited to dirt tracks, which can become impassable even by four-wheeled-drive vehicles during the rainy season. These same roads existed at the time of the war and were used by troops from both sides.

The terrain is low-lying and generally flat, corresponding to the floodplains of the two major rivers (the area has suffered several catastrophic floods over the last 10 years). Open grasslands, which maintain cattle ranches and subsistence-level farms, and a patchwork of palms and other forests are punctuated by lakes and marshes. Islands of slightly higher ground and low ridges rise above the plain at places like Tuyuti and Curupaity. This terrain played a vital role in determining the nature of fighting during the war, with the Paraguayans incorporating impenetrable wetlands into their field fortifications dug into the higher ground and using forests as cover.

South of Pilar the only two settlements of any size are Humaitá, on the shore of the River Paraguay and Paso de Patria, some 20 miles further south on the shore of the River Paraná. It was in the latter of these two small towns that the Allies established their beachhead after crossing into Paraguay in April 1866, while the former was to become the focus for Paraguayan efforts to stave off the Allied advance on Asunción. The country between these two places was to see some of the heaviest fighting of the war and a number of these sites were visited during the reconnaissance.

At several sites a rapid, small-scale metal detector sweep was carried out in order to get some idea of the amount of cultural material present and these sites are discussed below. The locations of all finds were mapped and a small selection of artifacts brought back to the UK for closer examination. Although it represents the biggest battle of the Qaudrilátero campaign, no metal detecting of the Tuyuti site was carried out as the landowner had previously experienced difficulties with treasure hunters.

BOQUERÓN-SAUCE

It is widely held that the three months following the battle of Tuyuti saw no major battles, as both sides struggled to recover and consolidate their positions. During this lull the Paraguayans were especially busy, constructing and embellishing the series of field fortifications that would give the Qaudrilátero its name.

This is, however, a less than accurate picture. On July 16 and 18, 1866, heavy fighting took place at Boquerón-Sauce (which roughly translates as "the wide mouth through the willows"). This place is not to be confused with Boquerón, which is much further to the northwest and in September 1932 was the scene of a much celebrated Paraguayan victory against Bolivia during the Chaco War. In 1866 the area was heavily wooded and "the wide mouth" place name refers to a gap between the trees. With typical audacity the Paraguayans crept close to the Allied lines under cover of darkness and overnight dug themselves into a series of trenches before bringing up their artillery.

As dawn broke on the morning of the 16th the battle began with heavy artillery fire from both sides, with the Paraguayans benefiting from their dug-in positions and the shelter of the trees. The Allies advanced and in heavy fighting that lasted for around 16 hours lost upwards of 2,000 men.[11] After a respite on the 17th the Allies opened up a heavy bombardment on the morning of the 18th, which caused the Paraguayans to retire from parts of their forward trenches. The Allied infantry were met by murderous musketry as they advanced, while an attempt by Allied cavalry to flank the Paraguayan positions also came to naught. The fighting ebbed and flowed with trenches lost and regained. By the time the fighting came to an end on the 18th the Paraguayans succeeded in holding their positions, but at a cost of around 2,000 men, while the Allied dead and wounded numbered upwards of 5,000. A number of senior officers on both sides were also killed, including Colonel Aquino, the Paraguayan commander during the battle, and the Brazilian General, Victorino.

The site of the battle has changed little since 1866. The Paraguayan trenches can still be traced through the trees and at least one opening through the woodland could be interpreted as the "wide mouth." The area to the east of the trees, across which the Allies advanced, is still open ground, today occupied by fields grazed by cattle. A number of monuments have been erected on the site, including one to Colonel Aquino. An area close to the monuments was selected for a metal detector sweep. Half an hour's work in an area measuring no more than 15 × 15 meters revealed a Minié ball fired from an Allied rifle and three musket balls from less-sophisticated Paraguayan weapons. A number of shell fragments, probably from Paraguayan artillery, were also recovered. The close proximity of the Paraguayan and Allied bullets fits well with a battle ebbing and flowing with heavy close-quarter fighting. The musket balls possibly mark a volley fired from the Paraguayan positions into the advancing Allies.

CURUPAITY

The rapidly dug trenches at Boquerón-Sauce were nothing when compared to the heavily fortified line anchored on the River Paraguay at Curupaity, from where they follow a ridge of high ground for at least 2,000 yards. The trenches were constructed under the supervision of the British Colonel George Thompson, chief military engineer for the Paraguayan army. Thompson had also been responsible for the trenches at Boquerón-Sauce and served the Paraguayans extremely well during the war until his surrender in the face of overwhelming odds at the fortress of Angostura on December 30, 1868.

The impressive defenses were fronted by *abatis*, sharpened stakes created from trees felled to create a clear field of fire (the name Curupaity means "tree plantation"). The main trench line incorporated gabions for artillery and platforms for Congreve rockets. Forty-nine artillery pieces, including eight 8-inch 68-pounders, were emplaced along the main trench line. Watch towers also provided important vantage points from which enemy movements could be observed over tree lines. On September 2, 1866 the Brazilian Ironclad, *Rio de Janeiro*, was struck by a torpedo (mine) while shelling the Paraguayan batteries and sank with much loss of life (the twin masts of the sunken ship appear in a painting by Candido López).

The Allied assault began with a prolonged bombardment from the Brazilian fleet on the River Paraguay and was followed at noon by a wide frontal advance by 7,000 Argentinean and 11,000 Brazilian troops. In a move presaging the disastrous British advance on German trenches on the Somme 50 years later, the Allies firmly believed that the bombardment had done most of the hard work for them. They were badly mistaken, as the Paraguayan defenders had survived the shelling, and the overconfident Allies were mown down in their thousands by cannon fire and concentrated musketry. Lakes and marshes in front of the trenches also served to break up the attack, especially toward the right of the line where the Argentineans were positioned. As many as 9,000 Allied troops were reported by Thompson[12] to have been killed or wounded in the aborted assault, while the Paraguayans lost just 54 men.

Today, the trenches at Curupaity still survive as impressive earthworks, but most are now obscured by woodland (see figure). While exploring the trench it soon became obvious that a system of interlinking trenches had been constructed. The open killing zone in front of the trenches, to the south, has also been re-colonized by dense brush. The area immediately behind the trenches is more open and accommodates a number of memorials, including one to General Diaz, the Paraguayan commander at Curupaity who was later to be mortally wounded during a canoe reconnaissance. This was the area of the Paraguayan camp and a contained metal detector sweep picked up various pieces of camp debris including a large iron staple probably used to hold the revetments and gun platforms together, along with several fragments of Brazilian shells fired from the river.

Shell fragments were also found in the side of the trench interior, clearly demonstrating the accuracy of the bombardment if not its effectiveness. The most telling vignette was provided by a scan across the front bank of the

A surviving trench at Curupaity. (T. Pollard)

trench at a point where it would have overlooked the Allied assault close to the river. Here, a fired Paraguayan musket ball was recovered close to a shell fragment. The musket ball, obviously fired at very close range, adds some forensic credence to the claims that Allied troops, in this case Brazilians, actually made it up onto the parapet before they were forced back by the defenders. An attempt was made to examine the ground over which the Allies advanced, but in the sector visited the scrub was too thick to allow effective metal detecting.

HUMAITÁ

Humaitá is today a sleepy little town far removed from the overcrowded garrison and besieged fortress it became during the war. The most obvious reminder of the conflict is the shell-scarred facade of the church (see figure), which is probably the most recognizable relic of the war anywhere in Paraguay (there is a replica on the outskirts of Asunción). Other reminders can be found, including the length of heavy chain hanging across a storefront. This had once been part of the defensive barrier stretched across the river. The Brazilian fleet took a long time to negotiate the Paraguayan defenses and the heavy guns in the nearby Batterie Londres were particularly feared (the use of the name Londres reflecting both the importance of British military engineering and the Mariscal's fondness of all things French). This fortified emplacement stretched along the bank of the river to the west of the town and was subject to prolonged periods of shelling from the Brazilian fleet, which stayed at a respectable distance until the Allied land forces tightened their grip on the town in early 1868.

The ruined church at Humaitá with bust of Lopéz. (T. Pollard)

The site of the battery has suffered from erosion of the riverbank and is also obscured by dense, monkey-inhabited jungle. Despite these constraints several large shell fragments were recovered and numerous un-investigated detector signals suggested a very dense concentration of material. One very big shell fragment came from a hollow in the trees, which probably represents a large shell crater.

THE *TAQUARI*

The imminent fall of the defenses of Humaitá heralded the loss of an important symbol of Paraguayan military power. The *Taquari*, named after a Paraguayan victory over Argentina in 1811, was the flagship of the Paraguayan fleet. The vessel was built at Limehouse on the River Thames by J. and A. Blyth, under commission from the Paraguayan government. Blyth also acted as a procurement agent for Paraguay, recruiting engineers and technicians and supplying equipment, including weapons.

The ship (see figure) was a twin-engine paddle steamer and is listed in Lloyd's Register as weighing 428 tons, with her engines producing 140 horsepower. Only two pictures of the ship are known to exist and these differ in that one image shows a single funnel and the other two.

While the ship was under construction the young General Francisco López was enjoying the high life in Paris, where he met Elisa Lynch. In 1854 López and a small army of British engineers and technicians sailed from Bordeaux to Paraguay aboard the *Taquari*, her hold packed with the finest luxuries from Paris, several steam engines, and crates of the latest rifles

A rare contemporary illustration of the Taquari.

(issued to his elite troop of bodyguards). Elisa sailed on the regular packet steamer and, by the time she arrived in the capital, Asunción, had given birth to López's son.

Once in Paraguay, the British engineers and technicians set about the mammoth task of industrializing a country, which for most of its history had adopted a deliberate policy of isolationism. The British contingent grew steadily and included surgeons, soldiers, and sailors. They were to play central roles in establishing and running the shipyard, arsenal, foundry, and railway; building fortifications; and overhauling the medical system. Some of them would live out the war in the service of López, while others were destined to fall foul of him and died on his orders.

Accounts of the *Taquari*'s last hours are sketchy. On March 23, 1868, she fled north up the River Paraguay as Brazilian ships finally found the nerve to defy the Paraguayan defenses and began to take full control of the river. She then turned into the River Guaycuru, a much smaller tributary of the Paraguay on the Chaco side, which after the war became and still is Argentinean territory. She apparently foundered in the shallow waters, and after having her deck guns thrown overboard the vessel's wooden hull was set alight by her crew. She then sank in the shallow waters. Over the years, this watercourse gradually silted up and today no longer exists. Whatever remains of the *Taquari* is now buried on dry land.

The *Taquari* is not the only ship now buried on land. The Brazilian Ironclad *Rio de Janeiro* was torpedoed in a sheltered lagoon in the river south of Curupaity, with the loss of most of her crew. Over time the lagoon silted up and today the upper parts of the ship's superstructure can be seen protruding from the ground in a forest clearing.

ARCHAEOLOGICAL POTENTIAL

As far as archaeological potential is concerned the War of the Triple Alliance has a number of key factors in its favor:

- The war was characterized by intense, large-scale battles involving vast numbers of troops, so maximizing the amount of material entering the archaeological record.
- Both sides constructed substantial field fortifications and camps occupied over long periods, which represent an obvious focus for investigation.
- For the most part the landscape of rural Paraguay has undergone very little change since the time of the war, thus enhancing levels of archaeological survival.
- Although low-impact treasure hunting does take place Paraguay does not have the same culture of hobbyist metal detecting which has done much to denude historic battlefield sites in the UK and USA.
- Due to the technologically impoverished nature of much Paraguayan weaponry it is possible to distinguish the ammunition fired by both sides (the Paraguayans using muskets and the Allies using more up-to-date rifles).
- The wealth of literature on the conflict, much of it Latin American, provides conflicting accounts which can be tested archaeologically.
- No archaeological work has previously been carried out on the battlefields of Paraguay, a country which as yet lacks an archaeological infrastructure.
- Despite the above there is a growing interest in the war within Paraguay and the other combatant nations coupled with a desire to see archaeological investigation take place. The motives for this interest include the desire for reconciliation and understanding through education and increased historical awareness, along with the potential for tourism.

CONCLUSION

The foregoing summary has hopefully demonstrated the rich archaeological potential of sites associated with the War of the Triple Alliance. The visit has laid the foundations for a collaborative project involving Britain, Argentina, and Paraguay.

The first phase of the project will involve the search for the wreck of the *Taquari*, involving the use of satellite imaging and the latest generation ground radar. Although much of the ship's wooden hull presumably burned away, total destruction by fire in water seems unlikely. The ship also contained huge amounts of iron, not least in the form of her funnels, boilers, and engines. These will probably be the best preserved and most readily found elements of the ship. It is also hoped that the guns, which sank in muddy water alongside her, will also be present on the site.

This initial phase will also involve the mapping and survey of battlefield sites, which in many cases have changed very little since the soldiers of four young nations fought upon them.

ACKNOWLEDGMENTS

I would first and foremost like to thank Ana Aizenberg and José Luis Garcia for inviting me to Paraguay. The trip would not have been possible without the support and hospitality of Anthony Cantor, the British ambassador in Asunción, and Félix Córdova, the Argentinean ambassador in Asunción. Renaté Costa made a great job of ensuring everything ran smoothly and saved me from the clutches of Paraguayan customs. Jorgé Rubiana was a wonderful guide and shared his unique knowledge of the War of the Triple Alliance. Sian Rees very kindly shared her experiences of this wonderful country prior to my visit. Once again thanks to Minerals International for the use of their splendid Sovereign metal detector. I continue to appreciate the support of the University of Glasgow and GUARD.

NOTES

1. Kolinski 1965:128.
2. Kolinski 1965:175.
3. Phelps 1975:242.
4. Cawthorne 2003:265.
5. Cunningham Graham 1933, Box 1930:181.
6. Chaves 1957.
7. Thompson 1869.
8. Leuchars 2002, Whigham 2002.
9. Wilson 2005.
10. Williams 1979:219.
11. Thompson 1869.
12. Thompson 1869.

REFERENCES CITED

Box, P. 1930. *The Origins of the Paraguayan War*. Russell and Russell, New York.
Cawthorne, N. 2003. *The Empress of South America*. Heinemann, London.
Chaves, M. C. L. de. 1957. *Madame Lynch, Evocación*. Livraria Freitas Bastos, Buenos Aires.
Cunningham Graham, R. B. 1933. *Portrait of a Dictator*. William Heinemann, London.
Fraggaso, A. O. 1934. *Historia da Guerr Entre a Triplice Aliance o Paraguai*. Estado-Maior do Exército, Rio de Janeiro.
Kolinski, C. J. 1965. *Independence or Death! The Story of the Paraguayan War*. University of Florida Press, Gainesville.

Leuchars, C. 2002. *To the Bitter End: Paraguay and the War of the Triple Alliance*. Greenwood, Westport, CT.
Masterman, G. F. 1869. *Seven Eventful Years in Paraguay: A Narrative of Personal Experiences amongst the Paraguayans*. Samson Low, Son, and Marston, London.
O'Leary, J. E. 1925. *El Mariscal Solano López*. Reprint 1970 Editorial Paraguaya, Madrid.
Phelps, G. 1975. *The Tragedy of Paraguay*. Charles Knight and Co., London.
Rees, S. 2003. *The Shadows of Elisa Lynch*. Headline, London.
Thompson, G. 1869. *The War in Paraguay*. Longmans Green, London.
Whigham, T. L. 2002. *The Paraguayan War: Volume I; Causes and Early Conduct*. University of Nebraska Press, Lincoln and London.
Williams, J. H. 1979. *The Rise and Fall of the Paraguayan Republic, 1800–1870*. Institute of Latin American Studies, The University of Texas at Austin.
Wilson, P. H. 2005. Review of Leuchars and Whigham. *War in History* 12(1): 102–105.

Buffalo Soldiers versus the Apache: The Battle in Hembrillo Basin, New Mexico

Karl W. Laumbach

THE VICTORIO WAR of 1879 and 1880 was the culmination of a 10-year struggle by the Warm Springs Apache to maintain a reservation at Ojo Caliente or Warm Springs, located 30 miles northwest of modern-day Truth or Consequences, New Mexico.[1] After years of negotiation, Ulysses S. Grant had approved the Southern Apache Reservation in 1874. Only three years later, San Carlos Agent John Clum, on a mission to capture an errant Geronimo, decided to take the Warm Springs Apache back to the San Carlos Reservation as well. Due to conflict with the resident White Mountain Apache, the Warm Springs Apache quickly decamped San Carlos and surrendered to Col. Edward Hatch. Hatch, Commander of the Military Department of New Mexico consisting of the 9th Cavalry "Buffalo Soldiers" and the white 15th Infantry, quickly took Victorio back to Ojo Caliente. Despite Hatch's efforts, the Interior Department soon insisted that Victorio's people return to San Carlos. When the escort arrived, Victorio and his people were gone. Victorio eluded troops for several months before surrendering to the Indian Agent at Mescalero. Within two months that relationship went sour and Victorio led his band off the reservation, vowing to never surrender again.[2] With him went an unknown number of Mescalero Apache. Outfighting and outrunning the army, Victorio went into Mexico in October 1879 only to reenter the United States in January 1880.[3] For the early months of 1880, Victorio's non-combatants were ensconced in well-hidden camps as his men raided the countryside and gathered supplies.

In the fall of 1879, Col. Hatch reassigned several companies of the 9th to Colorado to quell a Ute uprising. Returning to New Mexico in 1880, Hatch quickly organized a sizable campaign.[4] Knowing that Apache Scouts would be the only effective way to pursue Victorio, Hatch borrowed two companies of Apache Scouts and recruited a third from the Department of Arizona. Accompanying the scouts was Company L, 6th Cavalry consisting of about 60 men. Captain Curwen B. McLellan commanded the Arizona contingent.

From west Texas, Hatch requested assistance from his old Civil War colleague Col. Benjamin Grierson, who commanded the 10th Cavalry Buffalo Soldiers. The cavalry units converged at the Mescalero Apache Reservation to disarm and discourage those Apaches who were supporting Victorio.

THE HEMBRILLO CAMPAIGN

The Hembrillo (em-bree-o) Basin is a classic stronghold, averaging two miles in diameter and encircled by an 800-foot-high rim of limestone.[5] Other than climbing over the rim into the basin the only entrance is the Hembrillo Canyon that exits the eastern side of the San Andres Mountains and flows toward Lake Lucero and the White Sands in the Tularosa Basin. Known and probably named by the early Spanish military expeditions against the Apache, the basin contains three small springs that provided reasonably permanent water. The San Andres range, shaped by a seemingly unending north-south series of bedded limestone uplifts, is a rugged labyrinth protecting the basin's location. Lower ridges within the basin also present a series of uplifts, each providing a defensible location. The most famous of these internal uplifts is the 400-foot-high Victorio Peak, named for the Apache leader and allegedly the location of a fabled treasure.[6] When Victorio brought his people out of Mexico early in 1880, it is likely that he brought them almost immediately to the Hembrillo Basin in the San Andres Mountains. The Hembrillo Basin was a safe place, a stronghold with permanent water.

With the women and children safe in Hembrillo, the men went out for supplies and ammunition. Several engagements were fought in the Black Range and in the San Andres Mountains in January and February of 1880. On at least two occasions, Victorio made contact with non-military personnel, attempting to negotiate a peace agreement.[7]

In the meantime, from the combined forces of the 9th Cavalry and the borrowed elements of the 6th Cavalry, Hatch had organized three battalions for the campaign.[8] One battalion commanded by Captain Henry Carroll consisted of four companies of the 9th Cavalry positioned at Ft. Stanton east of the San Andres Mountains. The other two battalions were located west of the Rio Grande and, besides several companies of 9th Cavalry Buffalo soldiers, included the company of 6th Cavalry commanded by Captain Curwen McLellan and the three companies of predominantly White Mountain Apache Scouts from Arizona.

Hatch's first objective was to go to the Mescalero Reservation and disarm the Mescalero Apache, many of whom were aiding Victorio. As the battalions gathered, it became known that Victorio was camped in the San Andres Mountains. In his report to the Commissioner of Indian Affairs, the agent at Mescalero reported that approximately 250 Mescalero had left the reservation to join Victorio, 50 or 60 of whom were fighting men.[9] Victorio's camp now contained over 400 Apaches and up to 150 fighters.

In late March 1880, Captain Carroll was ordered to leave Ft. Stanton, cross the Tularosa Basin, and patrol the east side of the San Andres Mountains.[10] At the same time, Hatch and another battalion would move from Palomas, south of present-day Truth or Consequences, across the Jornada del Muerto to attack Victorio's camp (see figure). Carroll's troops were intended to act as the anvil to Hatch's hammer and prevent Victorio from retreating to the east.

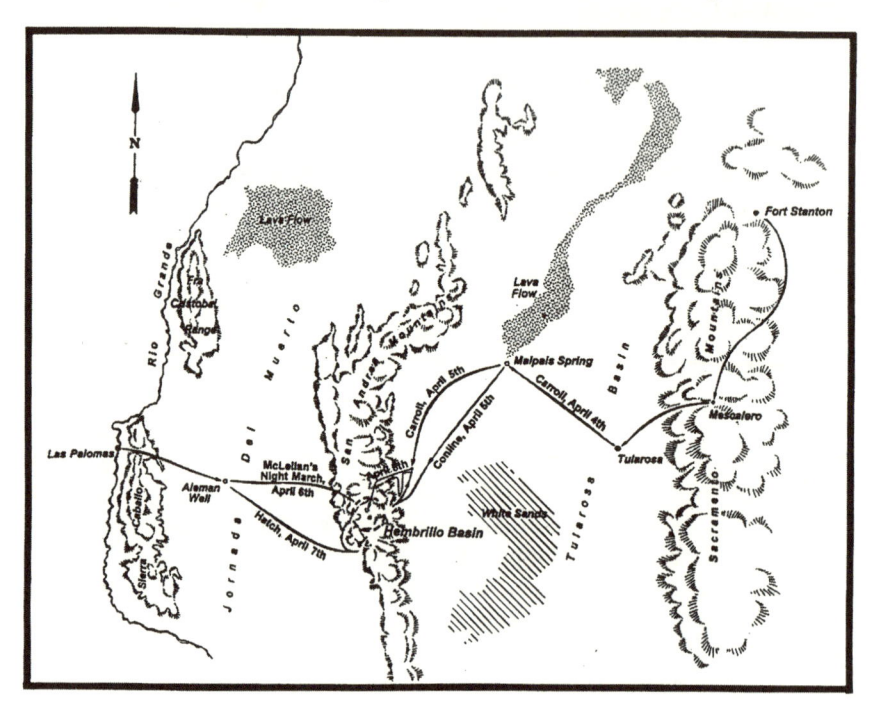

Troop movements relating to the Victorio campaign. (Department of Defense, U.S. Army, White Sands Missile Range)

THE HISTORY AS WRITTEN

In 1890, ten years after the campaign, several officers from the 9th and 6th United States Cavalry received brevet promotions for action in the San Andres Mountains of southern New Mexico on April 7, 1880. The details of the battle were by then a hazy memory and it was not until the memoirs of then 2nd Lt. Thomas Cruse were published in 1941[11] that the story of the battle was generally available to either historians or the general public. By the time Dan Thrapp produced his seminal work on Victorio, Cruse's account, supplemented by a post return submitted by Captain Curwen McLellan,[12] had become the accepted story of the battle.[13] Both Cruse and McLellan were officers in the 6th Cavalry when they participated in the fight. The story, as told by Cruse and McLellan, augmented by newspaper accounts, and then retold by historians went as follows.

In late March 1880, Captain Henry Carroll, commanding four companies of 9th Cavalry Buffalo Soldiers, marched from Fort Stanton, as ordered. He overnighted on April 5 at Malpais Spring to the northeast of the San Andres Mountains. Lieutenant John Conline, scouting independently with Company A, skirmished for two hours with an Apache group he was pursuing before returning to Carroll and the main body of troops that night. During the skirmish he suffered one soldier wounded (Corporal Hawkins) and lost two horses killed, while his own horse was wounded.[14]

Carroll's men and animals drank the clear, cool water at Malpais Spring, unaware that it contained gypsum in sufficient quantity to make man and beast ill.[15] By the next morning, Carroll's command was partially incapacitated, but he pressed on toward an unnamed spring in the San Andres known from a scout the previous fall. However, this was a drought year, and the second spring was dry.[16] At this point, finding water became more important than locating Victorio.

Cruse states that Carroll arrived at Hembrillo Canyon by 6:00 P.M. on April 6.[17] Desperately searching for water, he had split his battalion, possibly sending Companies A and G, under Lieutenant Patrick Cusack, to a sure water source at San Nicolas Spring some 20 miles further south. Carroll personally led Companies D and F toward another sure source of water at the head of Hembrillo Canyon.[18] According to Thrapp,[19] Carroll may or may not have known that Victorio was at Hembrillo. If so, the need for water outweighed the risks. Once there, the risks were soon obvious. Victorio's Apache turned on the thirsty troopers. The next morning found them at the mercy of the Apache.

As the dawn broke over the Hembrillo Basin, Curwen McLellan's company of 6th Cavalry and three companies of Apache Scouts arrived dramatically on the western rim. Hearing shots, McLellan ordered his Apache Scouts to the rescue.[20] Following them into the basin, the combined force drove the Apaches away from Carroll and, by the end of the day, out of the basin. The newspapers reported that "it is universally admitted that but for the arrival of McLellan, Carroll would have been badly whipped and most of his men killed."[21] Colonel Eugene Carr, Arizona Commander of the 6th Cavalry units loaned to Hatch, had the following scathing remarks to make about the role of the Buffalo Soldiers in the fight:

> It appears from this report that the only fights during the last campaign in New Mexico, at least the only ones I have heard of, were principally carried on by Arizona Troops; and the one on which Col. Hatch, according to the Newspapers, reported that Victorio was so badly punished that he must surrender, and for which he received the congratulations of the General of the Army was commanded by Capt. McLellan of my Regiment, who, besides our troops, had only the one scout company of Lt. Maney, and Capt. Carroll's Company which latter he found in a condition of "helplessness."[22]

Thus the oft-repeated history has credited the 6th Cavalry and the Apache Scouts with the heroic rescue of the Buffalo Soldiers, who, allegedly weak from bad water, were "in a condition of helplessness."

THE ARCHAEOLOGY

In 1988, archaeologists working for Human Systems Research, Inc., a contractor on White Sands Missile Range, came across several panels of rare Apache rock art near the spring at the head of Hembrillo Canyon.[23] The rock art included depictions of the Apache Mountain Spirits and a warrior on horseback. When White Sands Missile Range funded the recordation of the rock art, interest in the area led to a review of the literature, including the memoirs of Thomas Cruse. Cruse's memoirs described the battle at "Memtrillo" and precipitated a search for the battlefield. At first it was thought that the battle was around the Rock Art Spring, but no evidence could be found on the surface. Then Harold Mounce came forward, who, years before, had accompanied his father in a search for the alleged treasure in Victorio Peak and who remembered finding cartridges. Simultaneously, Robert Burton, White Sands Missile Range archaeologist, located cartridges within the basin. On Harold Mounce's first trip back in almost 50 years, archaeologists located breastworks and cartridges on a ridge in the center of the basin.[24] It turned out that the primary spring over which the battle had been fought had been destroyed by dynamite intended to eradicate a den of rattlesnakes in the 1950s.

The second trip to the battlefield included a cadre of metal detector–wielding volunteers, a group that would ultimately total 59 in all. Over the course of six years and supported by additional funding from White Sands Missile Range, the battlefield boundaries expanded with discovery as archaeologists conducted a metal detecting reconnaissance of over 900 acres of rugged terrain.[25] The reconnaissance covered the 900 acres in 5-meter intervals. More intense coverage was given to areas that produced artifacts. Fieldwork was made more complex by the dense shrub cover in many areas of the battlefield. While mesquite and creosote prevented standardized coverage in many areas, it was the cat claw with its hooked thorns that created the most difficulty. As much of the battle was fought from positions on rocky ridge tops, the artifacts were rarely more than 10 centimeters deep and occasionally could be seen on the surface. It should be noted that the intervening arroyos and low areas would also have been strategic positions during the fight but due to erosion and refilling, artifacts in those areas have either been washed away or buried too deeply for detection.

Jim Wakeman of Las Cruces directed the mapping of the battlefield. Initially using the code-phase global positioning system (GPS) to outline ridges and drainages and then filling in the gaps with a combination of conventional surveying and precision GPS units, a detailed map of the uplifted ridges and major and minor drainages was produced using TerraModel software. The resulting contour map was then placed on an ArcView geographic information system (GIS).

Over 800 cartridges, 48 pieces of spent lead, and almost 250 other artifacts were collected and their locations mapped with a total station and marked on the ground with numbered aluminum tags anchored by 7-inch nails. Other battle-related artifacts[26] included military and handmade buttons, crossed saber insignias, a chin snap to a dress helmet, lead rein snaps, curry combs, buckles, tack fragments, a spur, and broken bridle bit. Apache artifacts included an incised brass bracelet, a metal arrow point, modified cartridges, and a modified tip to an infantry bayonet scabbard.

Dr. Douglas Scott, an archaeologist with the Midwest Archaeological Center, National Park Service, performed a firing pin/extractor mark analysis on the cartridges.[27] This police-style forensic analysis determined which cartridges were fired from the same weapon and what type of weapon it was (e.g., Sharps, 1866 Springfield, Remington, etc.). Dr. Scott's analysis revealed that the 801 cartridges had been fired from 146 different rifles and carbines and 37 separate pistols. Of the 48 specimens of spent lead, only 22 could be identified by caliber and only a fraction of those by gun type. Bullets that might have been preserved in place on a less rocky battlefield had instead fragmented, glancing off of the limestone to ultimately land far from the original target area.

When Dr. Scott's forensic database from the cartridges was entered into the GIS system and could be viewed on the topographical map, the virtual battlefield became positively dynamic. The troopers had been armed with army issue .45 caliber carbines and .45 caliber Colt pistols. Two linear concentrations of .45–55 carbine and .45 Colt cartridges on an uplift of the central ridgeline marked the location of Carroll's beleaguered forces. While the Apaches had a fair number of the same .45–55 Springfield carbines that the troops carried, the Apache positions also contained cartridges from the nonmilitary weapons listed in the table. Apache-related cartridges were found on each of the surrounding ridges as well as on uplifts and in arroyos located above and below Carroll's position. Curiously, others were found on the upper part of the same ridge but far to the west and too far away to have been part of the attack on Carroll's final location. Another line of Apache cartridges was found along the drainage bottom below the now dry spring.

Col. Hatch had reported that McLellan had "discovered Captain Carroll, surrounded by Indians, within a semi-circle upon hills of higher range. Carroll was then fighting. The hostiles had thrown up rifle pits on the crest of this range, covering three-fourths of a circle around Carroll's command, where nature had not furnished them with shelter."[28]

The distribution of artifacts found on the battlefield was a perfect match for Hatch's description. The remaining unknown was how Carroll's troops

Cartridge Cases and Guns Represented by Gun Type and Caliber

Gun Type	Caliber	No. of Guns	No. of Cases
Rifles and Carbines			
Ballard	.44 Extra Long	1	1
Sharps	.50–70	3	7
Sharps	.45–70	1	1
Winchester	.44–40	15	27
Remington	.50–70	3	8
Wesson	.44 Extra Long	1	1
Henry/1866 Winchester	.44 rimfire	3	27
Springfield	.45–55	80	529
Springfield 1866	.50–70	31	104
Springfield 1868	.50–70	8	22
Subtotal		**146**	**728**
Pistols			
Colt Cloverleaf/1871	.41 rimfire	1	4
Colt 1873 Army	.45 centerfire	30	63
Colt	.38 rimfire	2	2
Colt 1872	.32 rimfire	1	1
Royal Irish Constabulary	.44 centerfire	1	1
Smith and Wesson	.44 centerfire	1	1
Unidentified	.38 rimfire	1	1
Subtotal		**37**	**73**

had ended up in that position. As neither Carroll nor his embattled officers had left accounts of the fight, we assumed that the companies had entered the basin through the Hembrillo Canyon. If that were so, then the Apache positions found on the western side of the basin did not make sense.

CONLINE'S REPORT: THE MISSING LINK

The officers and men of the 9th Cavalry wrote very little about the Hembrillo Campaign in their official summaries. Captain Carroll, severely wounded in the main battle, apparently wrote nothing at all. Until Lt. John Conline's account of the events preceding the Battle of Hembrillo were discovered, researchers were dependent on contemporary newspaper articles and secondhand accounts made by the officers of the 6th Cavalry. The following summary encapsulates the information available in the newspapers:

> In late March 1880, Captain Henry Carroll marched from Fort Stanton, as ordered. He overnighted on April 5th at Malpais Spring to the northeast of the San Andres

Mountains. Lieutenant John Conline, scouting independently with Company A, skirmished for two hours with an Apache group he was pursuing before returning to Carroll and the main body of troops that night.[29]

Dr. Charles Kenner, who became an unofficial and incredibly helpful consultant for the project, provided the first of two accounts by Conline. This account, written by Conline for the *Order of Palestine Newsletter* in 1903,[30] turned out to be almost verbatim from Conline's muster roll account for March through April 1880.[31] This unusually long muster roll account was written a scant three weeks after the action. Conline related the events of April 4th, 5th, 6th, and 7th in his article:

> On April 4th, 1880, the Second Battalion New Mexico Troops, composed of Companies A, D, F and G, 9th U.S. Cavalry, comprising seven officers and 148 enlisted men commanded by Capt. Henry Carroll, 9th U.S. Cavalry, moved from Tularosa, N.M., to Mal Pais Springs, N.M., a distance of 28 miles, to take the field against Victorio's band of hostile Indians, then supposed to be located in the San Andres Mountains, a range running parallel to and about 25 miles east of the Rio Grande in Southern New Mexico, and only a few miles westward from Mal Pais Springs. Arriving at the Springs two hours before dark, we went into camp for the night. The next morning, April 5th, my troop A, 9th Cavalry, was ordered in advance to ascertain the location of Victorio's Band in the San Andres range, and communicate with and assist Major Monoio's [Morrow's] command, a part of the force operating against Victorio from the west. I made a rapid march of about 37 miles nearly due south to Mimbrillo Canon, San Andres Mountains, and at 4:20 P.M. I struck a fresh trail of about 50 horses and 10 or more head of cattle, heading up the canon a short distance from its mouth. I followed the trail about $1^1/_2$ miles, to a point where the canon became much narrower, or boxed up. Here the Troop was halted and dismounted; and, owing to the strong impression gained that the Indians were not far away, a small guard was placed over the horses in rear, and the company on foot, was immediately formed in a concave line of battle, in open order, with right and left flanks resting against the steep sides of the canon and facing toward the head.[32]

Within a short time, Apaches appeared in the canyon and a sharp fight ensued. Conline's troopers were forced to repel flank attacks and two of their horses were killed. During the fray, José Carillo, an interpreter from Mescalero who was serving as a scout, positively identified Victorio directing the Apache attack.[33] At dark, the Apache disengaged and Conline led his troopers out of the canyon.

Thus, the Apache were located and late that night Conline's troops rejoined Carroll's Second Battalion, which was most likely coming south on the Salt Trail. The Salt Trail was a long-established road for wheeled vehicles that connected the Rio Grande communities of Mesilla, Las Cruces, Doña Ana, and El Paso with the salinas or salt lakes located just west of Malpais Spring in the Tularosa Basin. The Salt Trail skirted the west side of the White Sands and followed the eastern slope of the San Andres Mountains.[34]

At this point, Carroll must have decided that the Apache were alerted to the troop movement and that aggressive action was called for to prevent Victorio from escaping once again. Conline's account alone tells the tale. On the morning of April 6, the command marched west to the mouth of San José Canyon (possibly modern-day Sulphur Canyon), where Carroll split the command. Companies D and F went into the mountains with Carroll, while Companies A and G, under the command of Lieutenant Patrick Cusack, were sent south with the intent of ascending the mountain slopes to gain access to the interior. Unable to accomplish this, Companies A and G proceeded south to the mouth of Hembrillo Canyon when couriers sent by Carroll instructed them to return and follow his trail into the mountains.[35] That afternoon Carroll and his two companies rode into the Hembrillo Basin from the north only to be attacked and encircled by Victorio's Apache. Early on the following morning of April 7th, the timely arrival of Conline and Cusack at about the same time as the 6th Cavalry and the Apache Scouts prevented Victorio from achieving a major victory.

Conline's accounts are mute on the subject of bad water. Instead they reflect aggressive action on the part of Carroll and his troops, who, having located and engaged the Apache, were moving to maintain the pressure and give the troops arriving from the west an opportunity to surround and capture Victorio. The bad water story, told only by Cruse and repeated by all subsequent historians of the Victorio War, is also undone by the discovery of a letter from 2nd Lt. Walter Finley, 9th Cavalry, which was written to his mother after the battle. In the letter Finley reveals: "The reason that I was not in the last fight was that I had been appointed Asst. Quartermaster for the Battalion and had to stay with the train. I had two water wagons loaded with water barrels and I camped out on the plain."[36]

ARCHAEOLOGY AND HISTORY MERGE

Conline's long-ignored account contained the revelation that Carroll's approach to Hembrillo was from the north. Suddenly, the distribution of Apache cartridges far to the west of Carroll's position began to make sense. A search of the archives revealed additional accounts from the 6th Cavalry participants including muster roll accounts from the Apache Scout Companies led by Gatewood and Mills, Surgeon McPherson's version of the night march to Hembrillo from the west, and additional details in the letters and notes of Thomas Cruse.[37] The historic accounts combined with the GIS study of gun association and movement yielded a detailed interpretation of the battle. The maps on pages 345, 347, 350, and 351 track the stages of the battle.

Carroll's Troops Enter the Basin

Late in the afternoon of April 6, 1880, Carroll and two companies (D and F) of the 9th Cavalry rode off of the north rim of the Hembrillo Basin toward the location of the Apache camp, which was hidden by the limestone ridges that criss-cross the center of the Basin (see figure). Victorio, a recognized master of defensible camp locations, had prepared defensive stone breastworks at strategic points on the limestone ridges. One such breastwork is located on a promontory ridge that rises almost 600 feet above the valley floor and, while too distant to be a factor in the battle, would have made an excellent vantage for a lookout. A single expended .45–55 carbine cartridge was found in association.

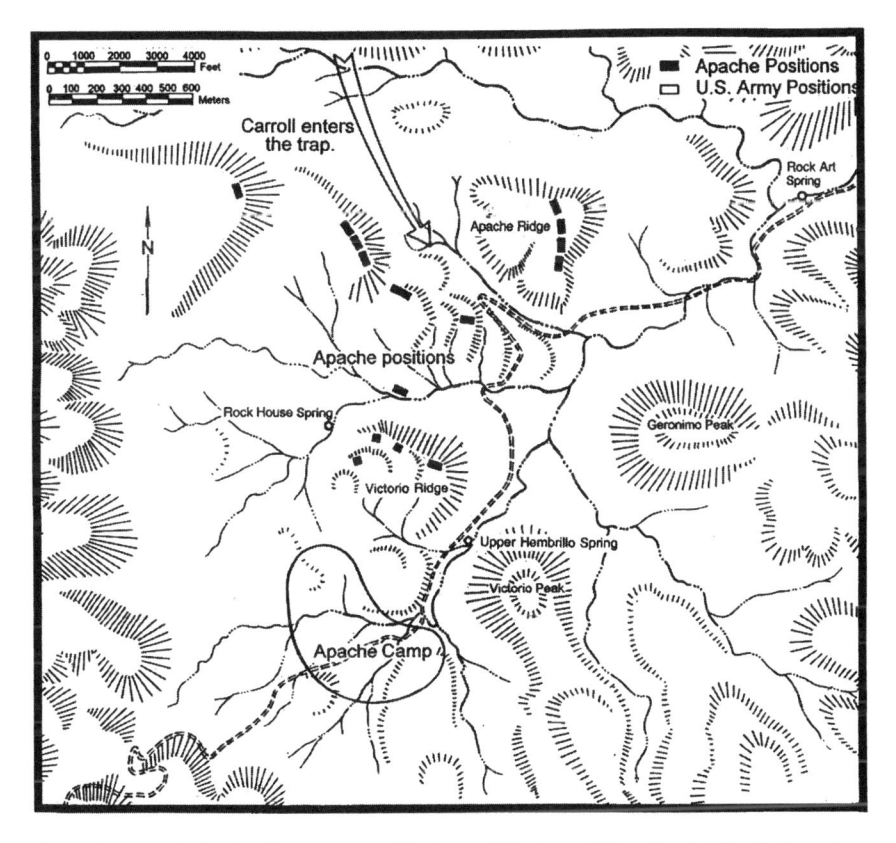

Carroll enters the basin. (Department of Defense, U.S. Army, White Sands Missile Range)

Apache lookouts quickly spotted Carroll's approach and Victorio prepared to defend the camp, which contained more than 200 women and children. Cartridge locations indicate that the Apache positions on the bluffs of limestone ridges formed a natural V-shaped trap (see figure). Carroll was allowed to cross the flat ground until the troops were well into the trap and when the first volley of Apache fire hit, the only place left for them to go was forward. Charging the lowest section of the ridge in front of them, the troops forced the Apache in that area to abandon their position. That the Apache had the advantage of surprise is reflected in the muster roll account of Lt. Martin Hughes (Company F), whose sole comment was "On April 6, 1880, the company was attacked in Membrillo Canyon."[38] The only known Apache account came from James Kaywaykla who quoted his stepfather, Kaytennae: "We had lain in hiding when the cavalry came in from Ft. Stanton and attempted to reach the spring. On a ledge above it, Victorio had stationed warriors to command the approach."[39]

The spring in question was only 300 more yards in front of Carroll's thirsty troops, who had had no source for water since leaving the water wagons early that morning. Victorio's strategic positioning of men near the spring made it difficult to access. Cartridge distributions indicate that almost all of the .44–40 Winchesters employed by the Apache were involved in the defense of the water. Other Apaches held the high ground of Victorio Ridge above the spring location. As soon as Carroll reached the top of the ridge, his troops faced the intensive firepower of the Winchesters. An attempt to reach the water resulted in Carroll and two men being seriously wounded.[40]

Carroll's Long Night

Carroll's command arrived only an hour or two before sunset. Apache fire poured into his command until it was too dark to see, with the horses and mules taking the bulk of the punishment. The concentration of over 50 Apache guns represented on the right (eastern) wing of the trap, known as Apache Ridge, was likely due to reinforcements arriving from down canyon where Apache had no doubt waited for another approach by Conline's troops. By nightfall Carroll's 71 troopers were outnumbered almost two to one. It was the darkness of night that saved Carroll's troops from even greater losses. According to calculations on the U.S. Naval Observatory's website the sun went down at 6:30 P.M. and the moon did not come up until 4:30 A.M. and then it was only an eight percent sliver. It was a very dark night.

Carroll's companies were arranged in two skirmish lines, one along the higher northeast side of the ridge and another along the lower southwestern slope (see figure). One hundred and fifty-five .45 cal. carbine cartridges and forty .45 cal. pistol cartridges define the troopers' defensive perimeter. The distribution and forensic analysis of the cartridges reveal the movement of Apache weapons to positions closer to Carroll's command. Apache guns, including three Henrys or 1866 Winchesters that had been fired from the eastern wing of the trap at the beginning of the battle, were also fired from a low uplift only 160 yards below Carroll's position. Cartridges from these weapons also provided an unusual perspective on the length of time that the Apaches held these positions. These early lever action weapons were rim fires that utilized a double firing pin. Subject to dirty mechanisms, the firing pin strike was often too light to detonate the primer. The cartridge would then have to be manually removed from the chamber, turned slightly to rotate the cartridge away from the previous firing pin marks and replaced to attempt a second, and hopefully, more successful firing. Twenty-one of the .44 Henry cartridges from the battlefield had been struck from 2 to 27 times before they had fired. As Dr. Scott succinctly put it, "this all takes time."[41] Apache cartridges discovered only 50 yards from Carroll's northeast skirmish line may reflect a night attack that stampeded a number of horses as alluded to in the regimental returns.[42]

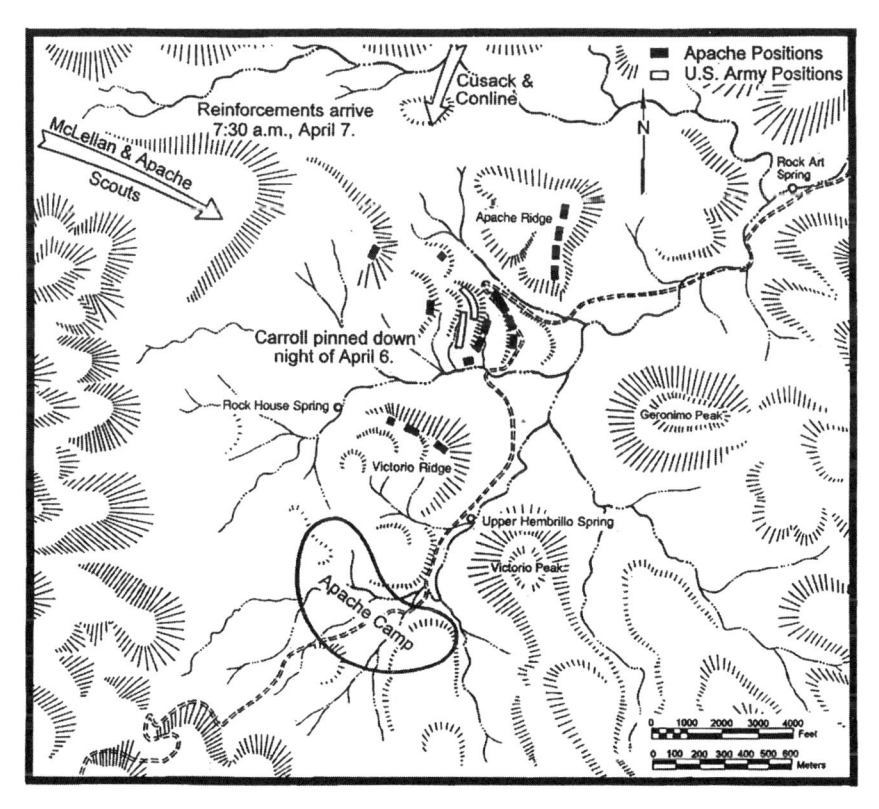

Carroll pinned down overnight. (Department of Defense, U.S. Army, White Sands Missile Range)

The intensity of the fighting was most clearly reflected by the distribution of .45 caliber pistol cartridges representing 20 individual weapons in Carroll's northeast skirmish line. At some point during the fight, possibly when the horses were stampeded, the Buffalo Soldiers in that company were forced to drop their carbines and fight with pistols at close range. By 7 A.M. on April 7th, numerous horses and mules were down and seven troopers, including Carroll, were wounded, two mortally.

The "Rescue"

While Carroll's companies approached the basin on April 6th, Hatch's combined forces had gathered at Aleman Well located west of Hembrillo in the Jornada del Muerto basin (see figure). The well was not producing water at a sufficient rate to supply the entire command. In desperation, Hatch sent Captain Curwen McLellan with his company of 6th Cavalry and the three companies of Apache Scouts ahead. Hatch's three companies of the 9th and a contingent of the 15th Infantry with a Hotchkiss gun would not follow until 1 P.M. the next day.[43] Leaving in the evening, McLellan's command struggled through the dark night (the Apache Scout companies were on foot), reaching the rim of the Hembrillo Basin as the sun rose on the morning of April 7th (see figure).[44] McLellan reports:

> On the morning of the 7th I reached the point designated and found that the Indians were there in force. Occasional shots were being fired but it was some time before I could discover to whom this fire was directed as my command had not yet been discovered by the Indians.
>
> I at once proceeded to put my pack train and animals into a secure position and ordered the Indian scouts to the attack and gallantly they went into action. In less than half an hour we discovered Captain Carroll with his company in a helpless condition, he being wounded twice and eight of his men also wounded through some misapprehension of orders given he got into the pass one day too soon and was when discovered completely at the mercy of the Indians. The enemy was strongly posted and had full control of what little water was in the pass. At 7:30 every available man of my command was engaged....[45]

It is from this report that the company of 6th Cavalry and three companies of Apache Scouts have been credited with the rescue of Carroll's beleaguered troopers. Conline's 9th Cavalry account of the action provides a much needed reality check to the "rescue":

> In the morning at daylight, on the 7th, having found the lost trail, we moved forward and joined Capt. Carroll's command near the head of Mimbrillo canon [sic], at 8:30 A.M. While marching up the hillside to the position occupied by Capt. Carroll, the Indians opened fire upon us from the opposite hills [Victorio Ridge] but did no damage in Troop A. While the officers were consulting as to the best course to drive the Indians from positions covering the water, their deliberations were interrupted by two or three volleys fired into the group of officers by the Indian scouts of Major McClellan's [sic] command, who mistook us for Victorio's band. These volleys were fired from the crest of a high hill in rear of and commanding our position; and although about 150 or 200 shots were fired at 400 yards range into the four troops of the Second Battalion, including horses, no damage was done except the wounding of one mule in the knee, showing very poor shooting on the part of the friendly Indians.[46]

So, instead of a rescue, the Apache Scouts poured "friendly fire" into Carroll's position. McLellan's forces were not aware that Carroll had split his command or that only two companies had been pinned down. Obviously, they had not made contact with Carroll before Cusack's arrival and it was the two companies of 9th Cavalry commanded by Cusack and Conline, not the Apache Scouts, that made the first contact and relieved Carroll. Even the one Apache account by James Kaywaykla gave the Buffalo Soldiers credit for the rescue: "The troops were easily beaten back until more cavalry came in from the <u>Tularosa Basin.</u>"[47] The different times of arrival respectively recorded by McLellan (7:30 A.M.) and Conline (8:30 A.M.) are due to the difference in standard times used by Arizona versus New Mexico based troops.[48]

Harvey Nash-kin, a White Mountain Apache Scout, remembered their arrival this way: "Next morning they [we] heard the Negro soldiers fighting with the Chiricahuas in a canyon there. Pretty soon [they] could hear the bugles blowing and then the scouts started into the fight."[49] Perhaps he heard an exchange of bugle calls between the wounded trumpeter Zach Guddy of Carroll's Company D and Cusack's approaching command.[50]

The Standoff

The Apache reaction to the arrival of fresh troops is clearly reflected by the distribution of cartridges. Retreating from the positions surrounding Carroll, the Apache moved to protect the camp. Realizing that his forces were now outnumbered, Victorio directed men with the longer ranged .45 and .50 caliber rifles to defend Victorio Ridge (see figure) and fight a rear-guard action while the rest of his people left the basin. This they did, holding the combined force of 300 men at bay for almost six hours as they fought a disciplined, organized retreat out of the basin, holding the high ground with each movement to rear. Cartridges from Victorio Ridge indicate that there were at least 40 defenders, all armed with the long-range single shot weapons rather than Winchesters.

Cartridge distributions on Victorio Ridge also reflect an Apache shift to the westernmost uplift to respond to the deployment of the 6th Cavalry and Apache Scouts on the western side of Carroll's position (see figure). As Carroll's position cannot be seen from that vantage, it is obvious that fire from the uplift was focused further west. One focus of that fire was 2nd Lt. Thomas Cruse who remembered: "I am sure that I did not kill any Indians, because I did not see a single thing to shoot at; in fact I saw nothing except a long ridge from which came smoke and bullets. After it was over I met Taylor of our class and he told me how the Indians had put it to them."[51]

The Assault and Flanking Action

The Apache position on Victorio Ridge was finally broken by a well-executed flanking action by Lieutenants Charles Gatewood and Stephen Mills and their companies of Apache Scouts around the extreme right flank (see figure).[52] A simultaneous leapfrog assault or assault by rushes by the combined forces of

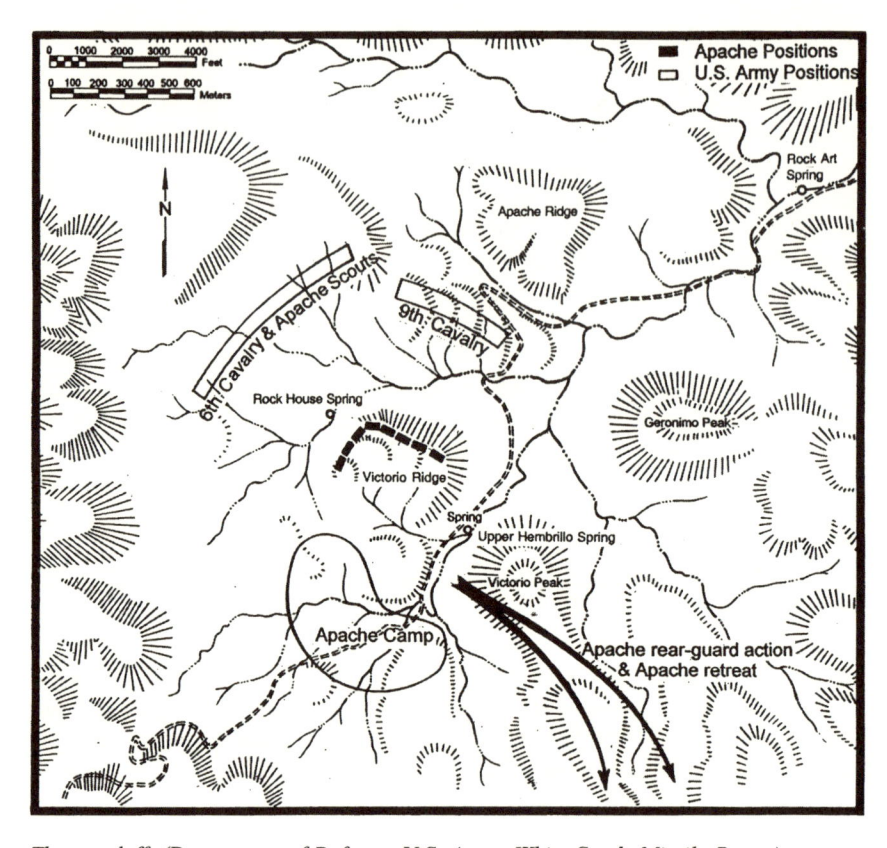

The standoff. (Department of Defense, U.S. Army, White Sands Missile Range)

the 6th and 9th Cavalry took Victorio Ridge but found no Apache there on their arrival.[53] The distribution of Apache cartridges tracks the Apache retreat from Victorio Ridge in response to Gatewood and Mills's attack on the camp location. At least three Apache fighting men gave their lives to ensure that the others escaped.[54] Most continued to fight a rear-guard action, first from Victorio Peak and then from each of the successive ridgelines that lead out of the Hembrillo Basin to the south. Conline described the retreating Apache front as over two and one-half miles wide.[55] One party boldly rode their horses down the canyon giving Carroll and his men a fleeting target (see figure).[56]

Aftermath

By late afternoon, the exhausted scouts and troopers abandoned the pursuit and returned to the spring locations, digging holes in an attempt to obtain sufficient water for the 400 troops and over 300 horses and mules.[57] Hatch and three additional companies of Buffalo Soldiers and a contingent of 15th

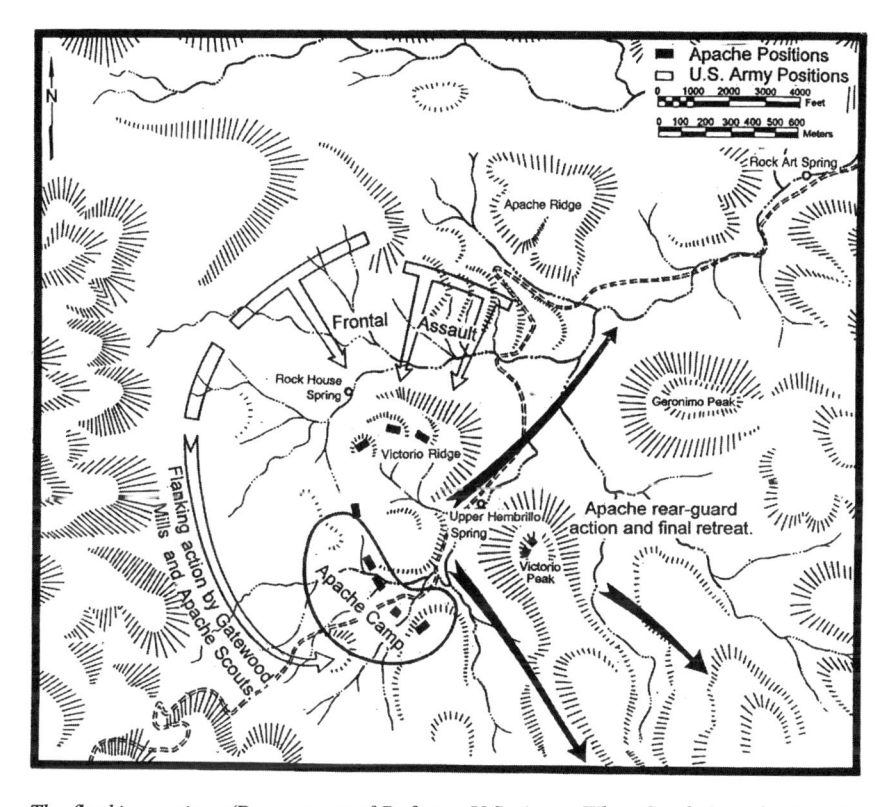

The flanking action. (Department of Defense, U.S. Army, White Sands Missile Range)

Infantry with a Hotchkiss gun arrived after the fighting was over. At least some of the military artifacts can be attributed to the overnight bivouac of April 7th. The next morning, Hatch led a contingent to the south rim of the basin. He reported that the Apache were waiting in force but after a brief skirmish, they again retreated.[58] Tracks showed that Victorio's people had divided into smaller parties and crossed the Jornada del Muerto to refuge in the Black Range west of the Rio Grande.[59] James Kaywaykla recalled an anxious moment as the Apache women and children hid in an arroyo while Hatch's column passed them on its way to the battlefield.[60]

The Battle of Hembrillo was over. Other than the three dead reported on the battlefield, Apache casualties are not known. Of the seven troopers wounded during the battle, two died of their wounds. Captain Carroll, wounded twice early in the fight, was convalescent for a year before rejoining the 9th.[61]

In need of water, Hatch marched his troops down canyon and into the Tularosa Basin on the night of April 8th.[62] Resting in Tularosa for a few days, the Buffalo Soldiers reflected on their experience. George Sligh, a young boy at the time, remembered hearing them talk as they rested under the trees near the acequia: "I ain't never going up no canyon again for no officer. If they let us fight the Indians the Indian way, I fight them, but I ain't going up no more canyons."[63]

Carroll's combined command met Grierson's 10th Cavalry at Mescalero where, on April 15th, they rounded up and disarmed all the Mescaleros on the reservation. Over 50 Mescalero fighting men escaped this dragnet and at least some of those eventually rejoined Victorio's band.[64]

From that point on, the troops and scouts hounded Victorio, finally forcing him into Mexico by early summer.[65] An attempt to cross the border in west Texas was thwarted by Grierson's strategy of defending the available water.[66] Victorio's people were soon tired, starving, and out of ammunition. Finally, on October 14, 1880, Mexican troops commanded by Lt. Colonel Joaquin Terrazas caught the majority of Victorio's band at Tres Castillos.[67] Victorio with 60 men and 18 women and children were killed and the remaining 68 women and children were marched to Chihuahua as prisoners. Only the men out on a raiding party for ammunition and a few women and children escaped.

SUMMATION

The archaeological study yielded a number of significant insights on Apache warfare in general and the action at the Battle of Hembrillo in particular. The historical research associated with the archaeological project has in turn produced a revisionist history of the battle that complements and supports the archaeological interpretation.

Victorio's habit of selecting defensible positions and augmenting the natural landscape with fortification is clearly evident in the use of terrain and breastwork placement at Hembrillo. James Gillett, a Texas Ranger who pursued Victorio in Texas and Mexico commented that "in following this wily old Apache I examined twenty-five or more of his camps. He was very particular about locating them strategically, and his breastworks were most skillfully arranged and built. If he remained only an hour in camp he had these defenses thrown up."[68]

The distribution of cartridges clearly reflects the fact that Victorio had firm control over his forces. The rapid-fire Winchesters were placed to defend the spring. The longer-ranged weapons of heavier caliber were chosen to fight the rear-guard action from Victorio Ridge. The three Apaches armed with .44 Henrys (or 1866 Winchesters) moved as a team during the fight, perhaps sharing ammunition. Other "teams" could be discerned as cartridges from specific weapons were consistently found together in a variety of locations on the battlefield.

The distribution of cartridges also allowed the analyst to follow the flow of the battle. Apache weapons moved closer to Carroll's position following their initial attack from the V-shaped trap. The pistol cartridges in Carroll's northeast skirmish line provide a dramatic insight into Carroll's long night, an experience that none of the combatants chose to record on paper. Victorio's redeployment of forces upon the arrival of the army reinforcements is clear. The rifles that surrounded Carroll's position reappear on the imposing Victorio Ridge to hold back the troops as the women and children leave the basin. Likewise, clusters and lines of cartridges from the same weapons mark the Apache shift to the westernmost uplift and ultimate retreat from Victorio Ridge.

That the Apache "liked to fight with a mountain at their backs" as succinctly noted by James Kaywaykla[69] is another aspect of Apache strategy that is classically reflected by the data from Hembrillo. The disciplined Apache rear-guard action was required to protect the women and children in the camp. That action, in the face of a numerically superior force, utilized first Victorio Ridge, then Victorio Peak, and finally a series of ridges leading higher and higher until the south rim of the basin was reached. The entire retreat was accomplished while continually maintaining the high ground. After an earlier fight in January 1880, 2nd Lt. Walter Finley noted that "the Indians choose their own position on almost inaccessible peaks and when we have driven them out by hard fighting they have just as good positions two or three hundred yards behind."[70]

Conline's muster roll account and subsequent article provided the key to understanding the initial defensive position held by the Apache and to interpreting the archaeological data. When combined with the archaeological evidence, the result is a very different picture of the role of the Buffalo Soldiers than was presented by the officers of the 6th Cavalry. Instead of being weak from bad water and stumbling into Hembrillo looking for the spring, Carroll's troops had carried two wagons filled with water on the campaign. They had found and engaged the Apache on April 5th and had identified Victorio as the commander. In order to prevent his escape, they moved aggressively to hold Victorio in place until the rest of Hatch's plan could be implemented. Carroll, knowing that approaching the camp with only two companies was a dangerous endeavor, had arranged for his own rescue by ordering Cusack and Conline to follow his route into Hembrillo. Captain Carroll's concerns were real and his 71 troopers were placed in a difficult position but the cartridge data reflects a disciplined defense punctuated by fighting at close range with drawn pistols. And, finally, it was Cusack and Conline's companies of Buffalo Soldiers who made first contact and forced Victorio to abandon his positions surrounding Carroll's troops.

C. L. Sonnichsen, when discussing the Battle of Hembrillo in his history of the Mescalero Apache observed: "They [the participants] found themselves involved in an unusual bit of military action which has never been described in detail by historians of the Indian Wars."[71] Archaeology and history have now been combined to shed belated light on this episode from the Victorio War.

NOTES

1. Dan L. Thrapp, *Victorio and the Mimbres Apaches.* University of Oklahoma Press, Norman (1980), 133–217.
2. "Indian Warfare—General Hatch's Opinion," Army and Navy Journal (1882, 7 January), 496.
3. Dan L. Thrapp, *Victorio and the Mimbres Apaches.* University of Oklahoma Press, Norman (1980), 260
4. Ibid., 265.
5. Karl W. Laumbach, *Hembrillo: An Apache Battlefield of the Victorio War.* Human Systems Research, Inc. Report No. 9730, White Sands Missile Range Archaeological Research Report No. 00-06, Las Cruces, New Mexico (2000), 3.
6. David Leon Chandler, *One Hundred Tons of Gold.* Doubleday and Company, Garden City, New York (1978).
7. Karl W. Laumbach, *Hembrillo: An Apache Battlefield of the Victorio War.* Human Systems Research, Inc. Report No. 9730, White Sands Missile Range Archaeological Research Report No. 00-06, Las Cruces, New Mexico (2000), 121–125.
8. Dan L. Thrapp, *Victorio and the Mimbres Apaches.* University of Oklahoma Press, Norman (1980), 265.
9. S. A. Russell, Report to Commissioner of Indian Affairs, 16 August 1880, Sonnichsen Papers, University of Texas at El Paso Library, El Paso, Texas.
10. Colonel Edward Hatch to Secretary of Interior, 15 June 1880. Victorio Papers File 6058, RAGO, National Archives, Washington, D.C.
11. Thomas Cruse, *Apache Days and After.* University of Nebraska Press, Lincoln (1987), 70–77.
12. McLellan to Post Adjutant, 16 May 1880 In Letters Received by the Office of the Adjutant-General, 1871–1880, [Letters Received] Main Series. Papers Relating to Military Operations against Chief Victorio's Band of Mescalero Apaches in Southern New Mexico, 1879–1881 [Victorio Papers], Records of the Adjutant-General's Office [RAGO], 1780s–1917, National Archives Record Group 94, Microfilm Publication 666, Rolls 526, 527, Washington, D.C.
13. Dan L. Thrapp, *Victorio and the Mimbres Apaches.* University of Oklahoma Press, Norman (1980), 268–270.
14. *Las Cruces 34*, 21 April 1880:1.
15. Thomas Cruse, *Apache Days and After.* University of Nebraska Press, Lincoln (1987), 72.
16. Thomas Cruse, *Apache Days and After.* University of Nebraska Press, Lincoln (1987), 71; John Pope to AAG, Report to the Secretary of War (1880–1881), 89.
17. Thomas Cruse, *Apache Days and After.* University of Nebraska Press, Lincoln (1987), 72.
18. *Las Cruces 34*, 11 April 1880:2.
19. Dan L. Thrapp, *Victorio and the Mimbres Apaches.* University of Oklahoma Press, Norman (1980), 269.
20. McLellan to Post Adjutant, Second Endorsement, 16 May 1880 In Letters Received by the Office of the Adjutant-General, 1871–1880, [Letters Received] Main

Series. Papers Relating to Military Operations against Chief Victorio's Band of Mescalero Apaches in Southern New Mexico, 1879–1881 [Victorio Papers], Records of the Adjutant-General's Office [RAGO], 1780s–1917, National Archives Record Group 94, Microfilm Publication 666, Rolls 526, 527, Washington, D.C.

21. *Las Cruces 34*, 11 April 1880:2

22. McLellan to Post Adjutant, Second Endorsement, 16 May 1880, Letters Received.

23. Sale, Mark and Karl Laumbach, 1989.

24. Karl W. Laumbach, *Hembrillo: An Apache Battlefield of the Victorio War*. Human Systems Research, Inc. Report No. 9730, White Sands Missile Range Archaeological Research Report No. 00-06, Las Cruces, New Mexico (2000), 20.

25. Karl W. Laumbach, *Hembrillo: An Apache Battlefield of the Victorio War*. Human Systems Research, Inc. Report No. 9730, White Sands Missile Range Archaeological Research Report No. 00-06, Las Cruces, New Mexico (2000), 19–27.

26. Ibid., 41–52.

27. Douglas Scott, "Forensic Analysis of Cartridges." In *Hembrillo: An Apache Battlefield of the Victorio War* by Human Systems Research, Inc. Report No. 9730, White Sands Missile Range Archaeological Research Report No. 00-06, Las Cruces, New Mexico (2000), 33–37.

28. Hatch to AAG, Report to the Secretary of War (1880–1881), 95.

29. *Las Cruces 34*, 21 April 1880:1.

30. John Conline, The Campaign of 1880 Against Victorio. *The Order of Palestine Bulletin* 1:81. In John Conline Personal file (V-1), Order of Indian Wars Archives, U.S. Military History Institute, Carlisle Barracks, Pennsylvania (1903), 80–81.

31. Muster Roll, Company A, 9th Cavalry, March–April 1880. National Archives, Washington, D.C.

32. John Conline, The Campaign of 1880 Against Victorio. *The Order of Palestine Bulletin* 1:81. In John Conline Personal file (V-1), Order of Indian Wars Archives, U.S. Military History Institute, Carlisle Barracks, Pennsylvania (1903), 80–81.

33. Muster Roll, Company A, 9th Cavalry, March–April 1880. National Archives, Washington, D.C.

34. Richard Wessel and Christy Comer, Historic Properties of the Salina de Andres Trail, National Register of Historic Places Multiple Properties Documentation Form, on file at White Sands Missile Range, Directorate of Environment and Safety, White Sands Missile Range, New Mexico (1998), 7–11.

35. John Conline, The Campaign of 1880 Against Victorio. *The Order of Palestine Bulletin* 1:81. In John Conline Personal file (V-1), Order of Indian Wars Archives, U.S. Military History Institute, Carlisle Barracks, Pennsylvania (1903), 81.

36. Walter Lowrie Finley, 9th U.S. Cavalry, April 14, 1880, in extracts from letters to his mother from New Mexico Territory, 1879–1881. Adjutant-General Collection, Fort Stanton, State Records Center and Archives, Santa Fe, New Mexico.

37. Thomas Cruse, Necrology, Prepared for West Point personnel file, West Point Military Academy, West Point, New York (1918); Thomas Cruse to Frederich Abbot, letter, 25 May 1883. Gatewood Papers, Arizona Historical Society, Tucson; Dorsey McPherson, Acting Assistant Surgeon, account of a campaign against Victoria,

2 January–September 1880. Order of Indian Wars Archive File A-8, U.S. Army Military History Institute Archives, Carlisle Barracks, Pennsylvania; Dorsey McPherson, to fiancée, letter, 10 April 1880. Letters of a Tenderfoot in Arizona, partial copy of ms. on file in the Lee Myers Collection, Rio Grande Historical Collections, New Mexico State University Library, Las Cruces; Muster Roll, Company A Apache Scouts, Sixth Cavalry, March–April 1880. National Archives, Washington, D.C.; Muster Roll, Company D Apache Scouts, Twelfth Infantry, March–April 1880. National Archives, Washington, D.C.

38. Muster Roll, Company F, 9th Cavalry, March–April 1880. National Archives, Washington, D.C.

39. Eve Ball, *In the Days of Victorio: Recollections of a Warm Springs Apache.* University of Arizona Press, Tucson (1972), 85.

40. Thomas Cruse, *Apache Days and After.* University of Nebraska Press, Lincoln (1987), 72.

41. Douglas Scott, "Firearms Identification of the Cartridge Cases from the Hembrillo Battlefield." In *Hembrillo: An Apache Battlefield of the Victorio War*, by Human Systems Research, Inc. Report No. 9730, White Sands Missile Range Archaeological Research Report No. 00-06, Appendix A, Las Cruces, New Mexico (2000), A-6.

42. Regimental Return, 9th U.S. Cavalry, April 1880. Department of New Mexico Regimental Returns, National Archives, Washington, D.C.

43. Morrow to AAG, 27 June 1880, Letters Received.

44. Dorsey McPherson, Acting Assistant Surgeon, account of a campaign against Victoria, 2 January–September 1880. Order of Indian Wars Archive File A-8, U.S. Army Military History Institute Archives, Carlisle Barracks, Pennsylvania.

45. McLellan to Adjutant, 16 May 1880, Letters Received.

46. John Conline, The Campaign of 1880 Against Victorio. *The Order of Palestine Bulletin* 1:81. In John Conline Personal file (V-1), Order of Indian Wars Archives, U.S. Military History Institute, Carlisle Barracks, Pennsylvania (1903), 81.

47. Eve Ball, *In the Days of Victorio: Recollections of a Warm Springs Apache.* University of Arizona Press, Tucson (1972), 85.

48. Karl W. Laumbach, *Hembrillo: An Apache Battlefield of the Victorio War.* Human Systems Research, Inc. Report No. 9730, White Sands Missile Range Archaeological Research Report No. 00-06, Las Cruces, New Mexico (2000), 184.

49. Harvey Nash-kin, interview with Grenville Goodwin, Goodwin Papers, MS 17, Folder 32, Museum Archives, Arizona State Museum, Tucson (1932), 5.

50. Fort Stanton Post Returns, April 1880. Returns from U.S. Military Posts, 1800s-1916, Records of the U.S. Army Continental Commands, 1821–1920, National Archives Records Group 393, Microcopy 617, Roll 1218, Washington, D.C.

51. Thomas Cruse to Frederich Abbot, letter, 25 May 1883. Gatewood Papers, Arizona Historical Society, Tucson.

52. Thomas Cruse, Necrology, Prepared for West Point personnel file, West Point Military Academy, West Point, New York (1918), 8.

53. Thomas Cruse, *Apache Days and After.* University of Nebraska Press, Lincoln (1987), 75; John Conline, The Campaign of 1880 Against Victorio. *The Order of Palestine Bulletin* 1:81. In John Conline Personal file (V-1), Order of Indian Wars Archives, U.S. Military History Institute, Carlisle Barracks, Pennsylvania (1903), 81.

54. Thomas Cruse, *Apache Days and After.* University of Nebraska Press, Lincoln (1987), 75; Muster Roll, Company A Apache Scouts, Sixth Cavalry, March–April 1880. National Archives, Washington, D.C.; Muster Roll, Company D Apache Scouts, Twelfth Infantry, March–April 1880. National Archives, Washington, D.C.

55. John Conline, The Campaign of 1880 Against Victorio. *The Order of Palestine Bulletin* 1:81. In John Conline Personal file (V-1), Order of Indian Wars Archives, U.S. Military History Institute, Carlisle Barracks, Pennsylvania (1903), 81.

56. Thomas Cruse, *Apache Days and After.* University of Nebraska Press, Lincoln (1987), 75.

57. Hatch to AAG, Report to the Secretary of War (1880–1881), 95.

58. Ibid., 95.

59. Thomas Cruse, *Apache Days and After.* University of Nebraska Press, Lincoln (1987), 76.

60. Eve Ball, *In the Days of Victorio: Recollections of a Warm Springs Apache.* University of Arizona Press, Tucson (1972), 85.

61. Karl W. Laumbach, *Hembrillo: An Apache Battlefield of the Victorio War.* Human Systems Research, Inc. Report No. 9730, White Sands Missile Range Archaeological Research Report No. 00-06, Las Cruces, New Mexico (2000), 245–246.

62. McLellan to Adjutant, 16 May 1880, Letters Received.

63. George Sligh, Interview with Leland Sonnichen, 1948, Sonnichen Files, University of Texas at El Paso Library, El Paso, Texas.

64. Dan L. Thrapp, *Victorio and the Mimbres Apaches.* University of Oklahoma Press, Norman (1980), 271–273.

65. Ibid., 282.

66. Ibid., 285–289; Jack Crawford, "Pursuit of Victorio." *Socorro County Historical Society Publications in History Volume 1*, edited by Paige W. Christiansen. Socorro County Historical Society, Socorro, New Mexico (1965), 7.

67. Hatch to AAG, 22 October 1880, Letters Received.

68. James B. Gillett, *Six Years with the Texas Rangers: 1875–1881.* University of Nebraska Press, Lincoln (1976), 187.

69. Eve Ball, *In the Days of Victorio: Recollections of a Warm Springs Apache.* University of Arizona Press, Tucson (1972), 75.

70. Walter Lowrie Finley, 9th U.S. Cavalry, January 20, 1880, in extracts from letters to his mother from New Mexico Territory, 1879–1881. Adjutant-General Collection, Fort Stanton, State Records Center and Archives, Santa Fe, New Mexico.

71. C. L. Sonnichsen, *The Mescalero Apaches.* University of Oklahoma Press, Norman (1958), 175.

REFERENCES CITED

Anon. 1882 Indian Warfare–General Hatch's Opinion, *Army and Navy Journal*, 7 January, 496.

Ball, Eve. 1972. *In the Days of Victorio: Recollections of a Warm Springs Apache.* University of Arizona Press, Tucson.

Chandler, David Leon. 1978. *One Hundred Tons of Gold*. Doubleday and Company, Garden City, NY.

Crawford, Jack. 1965. Pursuit of Victorio. In *Socorro County Historical Society Publications in History Volume 1,* edited by Paige W. Christiansen, 285–289. Socorro County Historical Society, Socorro, NM.

Cruse, Thomas. 1987. *Apache Days and After*. University of Nebraska Press, Lincoln.

Gillett, James B. 1976. *Six Years with the Texas Rangers: 1875–1881*. University of Nebraska Press, Lincoln.

Laumbach, Karl W. 2000. *Hembrillo: An Apache Battlefield of the Victorio War*. Human Systems Research, Inc. Report No. 9730, White Sands Missile Range Archaeological Research Report No. 00-06, Las Cruces, NM.

Sale, Mark and Karl Laumbach, 1989. Reconnaissance in the Upper Jornada del Muerto and Hembrillo Canyon and Other Special Projects, White Sands Missile Range, New Mexico. Human Systems Research Report No. 8721. Tularosa, New Mexico.

Scott, Douglas. 2000. Forensic Analysis of Cartridges. In *Hembrillo: An Apache Battlefield of the Victorio War*, by Human Systems Research, Inc. Report No. 9730, 33–37. White Sands Missile Range Archaeological Research Report No. 00-06, Las Cruces, NM.

Sonnichsen, C. L. 1958. *The Mescalero Apaches*. University of Oklahoma Press, Norman.

Thrapp, Dan L. 1980. *Victorio and the Mimbres Apaches*. University of Oklahoma Press, Norman.

Scars of the Great War (Western Flanders, Belgium)

Mathieu de Meyer & Pedro Pype

THE PROVINCE OF Western Flanders in Belgium contains a particular kind of heritage and archaeological resources: the extensive remains of military activity during World War I (1914–1918). Of the long portion of the famous Western Front, crossing Western Flanders from Nieuwpoort (Nieuport) to Mesen (Messines), the so-called Ypres Salient is one of the better known parts in which German and Allied forces faced each other in a stalemate of trench warfare. Until recently, however, systematic archaeological excavations of World War remains have been highly localized. Now conditions have enabled us to conduct more thorough surveys and undertake more extensive excavations.

In 2002, new plans were announced for the extension of the A19 motorway connecting Kortrijk (Courtrai) with Ieper (Ypres). The projected path of this highway would run through the battlefield (see figure). In April of that same year, the Flemish Heritage Institute (Vlaams Instituut voor het Onroerend Erfgoed, VIOE) received a special commission from the Minister of Interior Affairs, Culture, Youth, and Civil Administration for the Flemish Community, Paul van Grembergen, to undertake a detailed archaeological evaluation of the area. What was still preserved beneath the surface? Which remains of the First World War and other periods could be localized? Could the area of the future A19 be considered for protection? On the one hand the minister wished to have a number of carefully selected areas excavated. On the other hand he asked for an international commission of experts[1] to be appointed whose task it would be to compile a report on the significance of the region during the First World War.

From Wieltje on, near Sint-Jan (Saint Jean, Ypres), the road would be extended over a distance of seven kilometers to Steenstraete in Bikschote (Bixschote, Langemark-Poelkapelle). The route crosses the northern half of the Ypres Salient (see figure). In order to complete our preliminary research we consulted a wide range of sources. The oral sources consist of testimonies

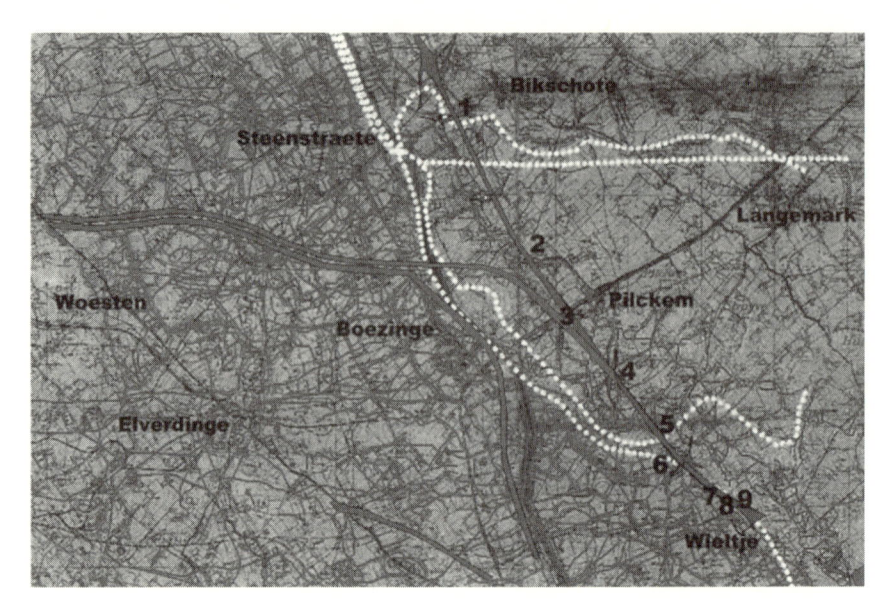

The possible A19-extension and three alternative routes projected on top of a German trench map from July 1917. (Flemish Heritage Institute/In Flanders Fields Museum/ Mathieu de Meyer)

of people who were directly involved, or their children,[2] and of information from the contemporary inhabitants of the region. Besides these, there were also many written sources (e.g., literature, archival documents, regimental books), aerial photographs, and trench maps used for the research.

Both World Wars left substantial archaeological traces in Western Flanders. The Ypres Salient (WWI) and the Yser Front (WWI) are of course the most famous features, but there were also defensive lines along the Belgian coast during both wars (WWII: the Atlantic Wall). Less known but at least as well preserved is the Hollandstellung, which is a World War I defensive line along the Belgian-Dutch border. All these "battlefields" were the subject of earlier research carried out by the VIOE. Parts of Belgian concrete shelters along the Yser Front have been localized and mapped. A deep dugout[3] was discovered during the excavations of a medieval abbey in Zonnebeke. Several other examples in the Ypres Salient were drawn in co-operation with the Diggers, an association of amateur archaeologists. On the industrial estate of Boesinghe (Boezinge, Ypres) several trenches and a deep dugout were excavated. Several human remains were recovered during this campaign. A part of a cleared German cemetery was excavated at Leffinge, near Oostende (Ostend). In 2004, new excavations were started in Boezinge, covering the German frontline. Very recently the VIOE also excavated the remains of two parts of the WWII Atlantic Wall (Knokke-Heist and Zeebrugge). In 2004, the

Institute excavated and documented several bunkers under threat of destruction: two Atlantic Wall bunkers (in Oostduinkerke and Westende), a bunker at Roeselare, and a unique Belgian WWI bunker in Oostvleteren.

Meanwhile parts of the Hollandstellung and remains of WWI heritage in several villages along the frontline have been the subject of an extensive inventory, the CAI (Centrale Archeologische Inventaris).[4] Taking inventory of this heritage (consisting of trenches, meter gauge railways, [deep] dugouts, concrete shelters, etc.) and placing it in proper archaeological and historical context was not an easy task. Therefore the study of the so-called trench maps[5] and aerial photography from the Great War were an important source of information with which to begin the fieldwork itself.

In 2001 a first attempt was made to overview the archaeological World War I heritage in the villages of Houthulst, Klerken, Jonkershove, and Merkem. This region is not a part of the Ypres Salient, but the German frontline follows the border from Merkem along the Yser River and the Ieperlee Canal (this stream runs from the Yser to Ypres). Klerken, Jonkershove, and Houthulst were part of the German hinterland. The forest of Houthulst was used as the headquarters of the Germans for both the Yser Front and the Ypres Salient. The region clearly was an important area during the Great War.

At first an inventory was made of the "normal" archaeological heritage (e.g., prehistoric, Roman, medieval remains). In a next phase trench maps and aerial photographs were used to locate the World War I remains.

Locating the huge amount of structures on modern maps proved to be time-consuming but enlightening, but this study gave us a great deal of information and filled in some important gaps in the inventory.[6]

Because there is a huge amount of World War I remains in Flanders, the CAI decided to prioritize its work and make an initial inventory of the most seriously threatened areas. Several techniques had to be tried out and a unique opportunity came with the A19 project, the first big-scale battlefield archaeology project in Flanders. 2004 saw the beginning of a new important project: the inventory of all the World War I remains in Western Flanders.

This chapter is a summary of the work done by the Institute in the framework of the A19 project up to the end of 2004, combining GIS research[7] (inventory), historical research, and excavation.[8] Here the combination of trench maps, field walking techniques, and aerial photography was crucial in researching the archaeological value of the area and for planning and achieving excavations of nine different sites. These excavations started in November 2002. The combination of an intensive GIS study and fieldwork proved to be very successful.

The future A19 section crosses the frontlines of the First Battle of Ypres (October 19–November 22, 1914), the Second Battle of Ypres (April 22, 1915–May 25–27, 1915), and the Third Battle of Ypres (July 31, 1917–November 10, 1917).

Summary of the Results in the Nine Selected Areas

Priority	Site	Significance	Means of research
1	Turco	British trench network: May 1915–July 1917.	Excavations
2	High Command Redoubt	British and German trenches, *deep dug-outs*, the remains of concrete shelters, No-Man's-Land: 1915–1918.	Excavations
3	Battle of Bixschote	German and French front line (1914–1915) (First Battle of Ypres, Battle of Bixschote), gas attacks (Second Battle of Ypres).	Excavations and geophysical research
4	Cross Roads	British trenches (1915–1917).	Excavations
5	Canadian Dugouts	Canadian dugouts (1915), No-Man's-Land.	Excavations
6	Forward Cottage	A forwarded position in British front lines, deep dugout.	Excavations and geophysical research
7	't Verzet	German trenches, numerous casualties in 1915.	Geophysical research
8	German Hinterland	German trenches and positions.	Excavations and geophysical research
9	Wood 15	German trenches, location of a Welsh company under fire on 31 July 1917.	Geophysical research

SUMMARY OF THE BATTLES AND CONFLICT AREAS

The assassination of Archduke Franz Ferdinand in Sarajevo on June 28, 1914, was the start of a series of events, in which several countries were involved. This culminated in the First World War. When France announced the war against Germany on the 3rd of August, the Germans invaded neutral Belgium on the 4th of August, seeking to reach Paris by the shortest possible route. Britain declared war against Germany on that same day. The British were obligated to defend neutral Belgium by the terms of a 75-year-old treaty. With Britain's entry into the war, her colonies and dominions abroad variously offered military and financial assistance, and included Australia, Canada, India, New Zealand, and the Union of South Africa. The United States entered the war on April 6, 1917. All these countries became active in and around the Ypres Salient.

In August 1914 the Belgian Army occupied the stronghold of Antwerp after the Battle of Liège. Nevertheless the enemy forces proved too numerous and on October 10, 1914, the Belgian Army had to retreat toward the coast. On the 7th of October German troops had already crossed the river Leie (Lys) from the south (Wallonia) and moved forward toward northern France. The army of King Albert I took up position behind the river IJzer (Yser) and the Ieperlee channel. Between this line and the river Lys there is a gap of approximately 20 km. The French, British, and Germans brought as many troops as possible to this region, where later on that year the ill-reputed Ypres Salient came into being.[9] During the preliminary research it became clear that the planned A19 would cross many important areas of this particular frontline.

The First Battle of Ypres (First Ypres) took place between the 19th of October and the 22nd of November 1914. French, British, and Belgian troops took their positions around Ypres to defend a well-defined salient. The Germans began an offensive to break through the allied line and to capture the ports of Dunkirk, Calais, and Boulogne. Before the attack against Ypres, the Belgian defenses on the Yser River (Battle of the Yser) had already stopped the German advance. The fighting around Ypres lasted until November 22, when winter forced a break in hostilities. Both armies suffered many casualties. From 1914 onward, the Germans began to dig trenches on high ground, particularly the low ridges that surround Ypres to defend themselves from fire by the Allied forces. When the Allies realized that a breakthrough was impossible, they also started to dig themselves in. They were at a disadvantage, however, because they had to use the topographically lower areas, closer to the city and beneath the surrounding ridges. After only a few months German and Allied trenches were dug all along the Western Front, from the North Sea Canal to the Swiss border.

The portion of the frontlines of the First Battle of Ypres that would be crossed by the proposed A19 highway extension is near Campagne (Bixschote) where, among others, the Battle for Bixschote took place between French and German units. This first German attempt to capture Ypres left significant archaeological traces between Campagne and Steenstraete (Bikschote). On the eve of the Second Ypres both the Allied forces and the Germans took heavy losses near 't Verzet.

In April 1915 the Second Battle of Ypres (Second Ypres) commenced (April 22–May 25, 1915). This second attempt by the Germans to conquer

Ypres is remembered for the first large-scale use of poisonous chlorine gas. Within only a couple of hours the German advance reached nearly as far as the Ieperlee channel, pushing forward in a southwestern direction. Within the gained territory the Germans built an extensive and heavily fortified system of trenches of which the High Command Redoubt[10] section (also known as Mauser Ridge) is of importance to the A19 archaeological survey. The opposing Allied forces were located down the slope in the Turco Farm–Forward Cottage–Cross Roads area, places which were also threatened by the A19 extension plan. Contemporary military records indicate that once again vast numbers of soldiers died between Steenstraete and Mauser Ridge (French, Algerian, Canadian, Indian, British, German, and Belgian), the estimated total reaching as high as 105,000.

After this heavy combat the position of the frontline stabilized and remained very much the same from May 24, 1915, for the next two years to come. The soldiers entrenched themselves and fortified their positions. From there both sides continuously attempted to win ground but failed to consolidate the gained territory, leaving the situation more or less unchanged. The future A19 extension partially overlaps a section of the British lines (over 1 km up to Turco Farm) and then continues toward the German forward trenches (High Command Redoubt) and the German occupied hinterland.

On July 31, 1917, the first day of the Third Battle of Ypres (Third Ypres/ July 31–November 10, 1917), the British broke through the enemy lines and advanced toward Paschendaele (Passendale). That day the renowned Battle of Pilckem Ridge took place, with Allied forces beginning a large-scale offensive to push back German lines. Between Turco Farm and Wieltje, Third Ypres began on the precise location where the A19 extension is planned. The Third Battle of Ypres cost approximately 450,000 victims, of which a lot of individuals are still registered as missing in action. On the first day alone 12,000 to 13,000 soldiers died. On that day the biggest advance was made near Pilckem, giving the site its great symbolic value. On July 31, 1917, heavy fighting took place to the north, near Wood 15 and Hey Wood, where the A19 extension is planned.

A large amount of ground won in Third Ypres was later again lost but the British kept ground at Pilckem (and the region through which the A19 would be extended) because of the strategic importance of the hilltop location. Trenches and other infrastructure were maintained until October 1918; some trenches were even enlarged. On August 8 that same year the Allied forces broke permanently through the German lines. The war ended on the November 11, 1918.[11]

In summary, the proposed route of the A19 extension crosses the frontlines of the three major battles around Ypres and threatens to cut through many military structures (see figure). This area was the fighting ground for Belgian, Indian, British, Moroccan, German, French, and soldiers of other nationalities, hence its international importance. According to the calculations of Prof. Chasseaud, the

Ypres soil still contains around 200,000 human remains. Indeed, many casualties remained in no-man's-land. When possible the deceased were buried in temporary graveyards near the front.[12] The research plan for the present project, however, encompasses far more than just battlefield search and recovery.

PRELIMINARY RESEARCH AND FIELD WALKING

In a primary phase of field research, the most important sectors of the frontlines were mapped using French, Belgian, British, and German trench maps and aerial photographs. Surface indications such as trenches, barbed wire entanglements, meter gauge railways, bunkers, and shelters were drawn in a GIS. Another map was generated indicating altitude, clearly showing the tactical advantage the Germans had at Pilckem Ridge.

These collected and analyzed data were used as a guide for the subsequent field-walking campaign (total length of 7 km and 100 m wide). The majority of farmland was checked for the presence of material rising to the surface from continuous sloughing. Enthusiastic volunteers frequently joined our team. This study revealed clear concentrations dating from the First World War and provided us with a great variety of finds. These include various types of ammunition (shrapnel, shells, lead and iron shrapnel balls, bullets, explosives, and scrap metal), barbed wire entanglements (rolls of barbed wire, fragments of barbed wire), trenches (duckboards, petrified sandbags), meter gauge railways, telephone lines, bunkers (complete examples and remains of destroyed structures that indicate their presence in the past), weaponry, supplies (potshards and pieces of glass from bottles of rum), and the personal gear of the soldiers (fragmentary helmets, a harness, spades, etc.).[13] Later on, during the excavations, it became clear that underneath concentrations of surface finds noted during the field walking, well-preserved trenches remained.

Farmers working land located along the proposed A19 route were interviewed to gain additional information on the presence of remains from the First World War. More than 70 farmers cooperated and several oral witnesses proved to be of great value. In addition, agricultural drainage ditches emptied in winter were checked and integrated in the research results. In this way several traces of trenches and meter gauge railways were located. Also the existing depressions in farmlands and meadows were mapped since these might indicate the presence of deep dugouts.

On several places along the A19 route the ditches were cleaned while doing the field walking and excavating, revealing some important features. Two trenches could be identified near the Turco excavation area and further on the track the remains of a meter gauge railway were uncovered. Those structures have been registered and mapped. Near the Turco site one of these trenches consisted of three levels of duckboards. Close to that structure, the remains of a small concrete shelter were uncovered.

It is hardly necessary to explain that in the course of this work, we were forced to deal with a great deal of potentially hazardous or explosive material.[14] Remains of all kinds of ammunition can be found on every farm in the immediate vicinity and make up the majority of the collected finds. In handling these explosives there was intensive cooperation between archaeologists and DOVO (Service for the Disposal and Demolition of Explosives—Dienst voor opruiming en vernietiging van ontploffingstuigen), a unit of the Belgian army specializing in the dismantling of explosives. With the help of these specialists a safe methodology for excavation and handling of the dangerous finds was determined. They gave the excavating personnel a briefing about the possible hazards.

The results of the field-walking campaign were processed in a GIS database and all collected finds were closely studied. The concentrations on the surface were compared with the first maps already compiled using literary sources, photographs, and trench maps. The different sources showed clear convergences.

NINE ZONES SELECTED FOR FURTHER RESEARCH

Based on this gathered information and a report compiled by Prof. Chasseaud, nine zones were selected in the autumn of 2002, on which extensive archaeological fieldwork would take place (see figure). Some sites were to be excavated partially, while other areas were to be investigated by geophysical means.[15] Of each of these nine zones, a more detailed inventory was to be made based upon aerial photography.

Up until now six excavation zones have been partially dug: Turco, High Command Redoubt, Cross Roads, Battle of Bixschote, Forward Cottage, and the Canadian dugouts. In the area of the Battle of Bixschote, High Command Redoubt, and Forward Cottage a geophysical survey was undertaken. Meanwhile, many trenches and other remains have already been studied and mapped using aerial photographs.

THE EXCAVATIONS

This summary focuses on four excavations, part of the A19 project: Turco, High Command Redoubt, Canadian dugouts, and Cross Roads. The Battle of Bixschote and Forward Cottage sites are not included, because the excavations were not finished at the time of writing.[16]

Turco

The first excavations took place near the Moortelweg, a road called "Admiral's Road" by the British soldiers. During the war, the nearby farm was named Turco, thus providing the archaeological site there with its current name. Reaching agreement with the current landowner[17] the VIOE excavated three long test pits to evaluate the site. They were dug over a distance of 100 meters and a width of 4 meters, transversing the planned A19 trajectory.

The Allied Turco frontline system was set up after the Second Ypres (April 22–May 27, 1915), when the Germans pushed back the Allies to this area with poisonous gas.[18] No-man's-land was just across Admiral's Road and the German front was a hundred meters further back. The orientation of the trenches changed several times up to the summer of 1916. These trenches also served as one of the jumping-off points for the third battle of Ypres, which started on the 31st of July 1917. After that historic event, the area was used as rear supporting lines until the end of the war.

The most remarkable structures found during the excavations were the remains of trenches and the traces of large and small shell holes. Sometimes it was possible to detect which type of ammunition was used to cause the explosion, and the direction from where the shell was fired could be reconstructed by investigating the shape of the crater. Some archaeological features were disturbed severely by the intensity of the shelling. In one of the test pits only a fragment of an A-frame could be recorded.[19] Nevertheless, another test pit contained two well-preserved segments of trenches. In one of them, wooden duckboards were placed in perpendicular fashion, exemplifying the typical "zigzag" pattern of the trench system (see figure). The deep sloughing carried out in the field after the war made it impossible to study the walls of the trenches, although some remains of parapet sandbags were found in the filling. An interesting discovery was the remains of a dump of ignition material from a Livens projector. This is an early type of mortar, consisting of a launching tube and a supporting plate to launch chlorine-gas grenades. They were placed in an angle of 45 degrees in batteries consisting of 20 to 25 pieces. It proved to be a very effective weapon.[20] We learned from the owner of the field that he had found three launching tubes while plowing a couple of years before.[21]

A third test pit also contained some remains of trenches, of which one segment was reinforced by corrugated iron. In the filling, the remains of sandbags, used for the parapet, were also found. Near another trench the remains of a collapsed shelter could be studied. It was constructed alongside the trench. The structure found was probably the wooden roof, covered with corrugated iron plates. Some sandbags that served as part of the walls of the shelter were preserved *in situ*. Though the textile covering was gone, the shape of the bags and the marks of the textile could still be recognized.

Numerous objects were found during the dig, which had to be differentiated between those used in the trenches during the fighting and those that were deposited there during the cleaning at the end of the war. Three categories of material could be distinguished: standard equipment, other articles of use, and ammunition.[22]

Duckboards at the Turco excavation site. (Flemish Heritage Institute/Mathieu de Meyer)

Most of the finds are part of the standard equipment used by the British soldiers.[23] Several buttons from uniforms were found in different structures. A well-preserved woolen stocking was also recovered from one of the trenches. A standard red copper spoon was lying in the collapsed shelter. Two blue standard water bottles were retrieved in a trench. Every soldier carried one of these with him. In another trench an aniline pencil was found. These were used by the soldiers to write messages or letters to their homes. Finally, it's worth mentioning a standard hair comb was found.

Besides those, there were many objects used in everyday life on the front. Especially numerous were the fragments from ceramic rum jars, found in almost every concentration of war-related artifacts. Rum was used to reinforce the morale of the troops during the war. It was also consumed in cold periods. The letters SRD were written on each jar, meaning Supply Reserve Depot. Another important category of objects is glass containers, including bottles used for beer, wine, water, other drinks, and medicines. Several examples were found on the Turco site. On some of them the marks from the production factories were still visible. From time to time screw caps from iron petrol tins were retrieved. Two pickaxes were also collected from the site.

Near the collapsed shelter the remains of a wader (a jackboot) were found, which was made in New York by the brand Goodyear. Fireballs from a flare pistol were also spotted on the site.

Of course, the single largest class of finds consists of ammunition: 0.303-inch bullets, shells, shrapnel-balls, grenades, and so forth. Hand grenades are very common, and several types have been collected (Mills N° 5, Jam Tin grenades, N° 3 Hale). On the Turco site there was a dump of Mills hand grenades, and two Mills rifle-grenades (N° 23 and 36 Pattern). A lot of the shells and shell fragments found on the excavation site were filled with a conventional High Explosive payload, with a toxic payload, or with lead "shrapnel" balls.[24] Very interesting are two self-made improvised grenades, made with the remains of 18-pounder shells.

At this first site the remains of two soldiers were recovered and examined. One of them could be identified as British, based on the uniform buttons which were preserved, and a pair of standard gloves. The physical anthropologist of the VIOE[25] could determine that the person had to be 25 to 30 years old. The remains of another soldier were found in a ditch near the site. The French nationality was determined on the basis of the buttons and the manufacturing marks on the soles of his shoes. The skeleton was almost complete, and he was about 30 years old at the time of death.

High Command Redoubt (Mauser Ridge)

The second excavation area was a site which was located on the German frontline between the end of April 1915 and the 31st of July 1917. This site was an important German observation post, protected by many small concrete shelters. All but one of these was destroyed after the war. Their remains can still be seen scattered in the fields. After that period the British probably re-used the German frontline system as their own rear support trenches. We had the authorization from the owner[26] to dig two test pits here, similar to those at the Turco site (100 × 4 m).

At this site, the traces of shell holes seemed to be dominant. In the northern half four rectangular wooden platforms were uncovered (see figure). They were probably used as floors for heavy field artillery (Howitzers). One of them was linked with a solidly built trench system, in which large wooden planks were placed on top of heavy inverted A-frames. A remarkable feature was an iron pipeline underneath the trench. It could be an illumination pipeline for a deep dugout, since it leads in the direction of a depression in the field, which is an indication for such an underground structure. The walls of another trench were built from branches and twigs. Another large wooden structure could also be identified as a field artillery platform. Some traces of concrete shelters could also be found, but no real structures.

Two rectangular wooden platforms excavated at High Command Redoubt. (Flemish Heritage Institute/Mathieu de Meyer)

It was remarkable that there were almost no artifacts on this site, indicating the high probability that it had been "cleaned" when the Germans left. The only objects found were a bayonet (used for a Mauser Gewehr 98), the poorly preserved remains of a shovel, and some ammunition (German *Stielhandgranate* [stick bombs] and remains of British shrapnel).

The "Canadian Dugouts" (Buff's Road)

The third selected zone was a place where Canadian soldiers built some "dugouts" before the Second Battle of Ypres. They show up very clearly on several aerial photographs taken during the war. Although we gained permission from the owner[27] to excavate the area, there were unfortunately very few results.

Meanwhile we found the reason why: a historical document[28] proved that British soldiers destroyed the dugouts in May 1917 for tactical reasons. They were probably used by the Germans as forward observation posts. On the World War I aerial photographs we can clearly see several paths leading from the German lines to the dugouts.

The only traces found during the excavation were shell holes and some remains of ammunition (grenades and shell-cases from 13- and 18-pounder artillery and 4.5-inch Howitzer). The most important discovery on this site was a cap badge from the Royal Irish Fusiliers.

We hoped to find the remains of a sap leading to a jumping-off trench,[29] which was used to start the Third Battle of Ypres, but unfortunately we were unable to locate it.

CROSS ROADS

Cross Roads is named after the nearby farm, which used to be called "Cross Roads Farm" by the Commonwealth soldiers. The excavations of this part of the British frontline are the most extensive so far undertaken. Here we were allowed to excavate quite a large area. The land was hired from the same owner of the "Canadian dugouts" site. The nearby road is Admiral's Road (which continues to the Turco site). Next to the site, there is a small Commonwealth cemetery: Track × Cemetery.

This place became important during Second Ypres when the Allied troops conducted counterattacks against the Germans. The first trenches were dug at the end of April 1915. After the Second Ypres the British frontline was dug in another orientation and stayed there for two years until the Third Ypres began on the 31st of July 1917. Indeed, Cross Roads is one of the places where this famous battle began.

Excavating here enables us to study the various periods and the evolution of trench-building techniques throughout the entire course of the war. Most trenches dug in this area were rediscovered and on the basis of archival documents gave us detailed information about the dates in which some structures were built. Aerial photographs are now being used to date some structures more precisely. It was even possible to identify one of the soldiers who was in action on the Cross Roads site; his story could be reconstructed with some pictures, several letters, and a self-drawn map that were kept in archives. Lt. Robin Skeggs was a member of the Rifle Brigade, arriving just a few weeks after the start of the Second Ypres.[30] Both Belgian and foreign specialists offered us a great deal of scientific information and archival pieces about the Ypres Salient which are of great importance to the investigation.

Traces of sandbags were found in several places on the site and many duckboards were discovered at the bottom of the trenches. At some places these were "repaired" using bricks, stones, and even stable doors. Sometimes, three layers of duckboards were found on top of each other. There seemed to be a difference in shape between the older duckboards and the more recent ones: three different models could be determined. Several structures, depots, and artillery platforms were linked up with the trenches. In an ammunition depot a case was found filled with 0.303-inch cartridges for a standard Lee-Enfield rifle (SMLE). A short communication trench connected the frontline trench with a pit containing metal cans of food. Another wooden platform was probably used for a Stokes trench mortar. The remains of a "dugout frame" were also found. It used to be 2 × 2 m and could have been used as a store. The floor and walls were made of wood, and some traces prove that sandbags were used. The remains of a small rectangular shelter were along another part of the trenches and survived only as a collapsed wooden wall and a dump of 25 empty glass water bottles. Nearby was a dump of 35 unused Stokes 3-inch high explosive mortar bombs, suggesting that a Stokes-trench mortar had been placed here.

The movement between the frontline trenches was ensured by the presence of thin communication trenches, five of which have been excavated. Their floors were generally made from duckboards although in one of the excavated examples, the soldiers had placed a layer of bricks.

One major trench, broader and deeper than the others and reinforced with corrugated iron and A-frames, could be followed through the entire excavation site (see figure). Large fragments of natural stone were used to replace some duckboards. At several places where it crosses older trench segments, it represents the actual frontline between the Second Ypres and the Third Ypres. The remains of a shelter found at the rear of the trench are of particular interest. At its front side a similar, yet larger structure was excavated, probably a machine-gun post.

Starting from this important trench, a sap leading to a jumping-off trench was dug toward Admiral's Road to prepare for Third Ypres. The trench was dug quite deep and was reinforced with expanded metal, inverted A-frames (Short Revetting Frames; Second army pattern, May 1917), vertical planks, and horizontal posts. Along the trench the entrance to a well-preserved underground wooden room (1.60 m × 0.95 m/height: 1.50 m) was discovered which could be reached with a staircase. A brass pump was found at the entrance with a rubber tube leading to the room (see figure). It's not clear yet what the function was of that room; it could be a sump, but it is more likely to be a store (possibly for ammunition). On top of the staircase two well-preserved Mills N° 5 grenades were found. One of them had a base plug with the following markings: N° 5 Mk I Mills Patents 8/16 (September 1916) M M C° B' Ham (Birmingham).

Another interesting feature was a brick floor connected by some duckboards to the previously mentioned trench. This could have been a platform for an 18-pounder field artillery gun, as suggested by depressions in the surface of the

A view at a part of the frontline (Cross Roads). (Flemish Heritage Institute/Mathieu de Meyer)

The entrance and the room of the shallow dugout, probably an ammunition store. The pump was found at the entrance of the dugout. (Flemish Heritage Institute/Mathieu de Meyer)

bricks, which seem to match the positions of the wheels and tail of such an artillery piece. Traces of sandbags were noted in front of the platform and unused N° 101 Mk II (1917) 18-pounder shells were collected nearby.

Numerous artifacts were collected, most being parts of standard combat equipment. These included uniform buttons, several copper buckles, and other fragments of the leather webbing. The remains of two peaked caps were retrieved, one of them with a cap badge which was not very well preserved. Four regimental insignia were collected from the trenches: one from the Buffs (East Kent Regiment), a second one from the Royal King's Rifle Corps, a third one of the Royal Horse Artillery Brigade, and a fourth one from the Dorsetshire Regiment. Several yellow copper standard spoons from different production factories were also present. A fragment of one of them is very interesting because it contains the personal number of a soldier (3SK 28403: 3rd Battalion Suffolk Regiment). The staff of the In Flanders Fields Museum attempted to identify the individual but failed to find any information about the person in the casualty lists, suggesting that this soldier probably survived the war.

Also noteworthy were the rectangular mica eye lenses from gas respirators, which are the remains of the oldest type (Hypo gas hood). Soldiers started to use these in July 1915. Several round eyepieces from the later "P" and

"PH" gas respirators were also collected. Only a few typical blue water bottles were uncovered, close to a concentration of leather webbing used to carry water bottles. Pocket-knives and razors were also part of the standard equipment of the soldiers, and a couple of these were also found on the site. Some fragments of toothbrushes and the handle of a shaving brush were also retrieved. Some entrenching tools and the webbing of one of them was also found. Only three remains of standard Lee-Enfield rifles were collected. Standard 0.303-inch cartridges were found in large quantities in every trench, two full cases were found in a dump. Brass oil containers which were used to maintain the rifles were also retrieved in several places, one of them still filled with oil. Four complete shovels were found in the trenches and the underground structure. The remains of several aniline pencils were also present at this site. Another find was a small glass ampoule (phial) which used to be filled with iodine to disinfect wounds.

In addition to the standard equipment, a complete French "Vermorel" sprinkler was found. Such objects were used at the end of the nineteenth century to destroy the weeds, but during the First World War the British soldiers used them against the poisonous chlorine gas from the Germans. By sprinkling a certain chemical solution the gas dissolved. On this site a well-preserved sniping plate was also found.[31]

In terms of glassware, numerous remains of rum jars and glass bottles were collected on the site, some of them complete. Large and small bottles were found, together with small glass jars used for meat. Some of them still contained marks offering indications about the contents and the place of manufacture. Copper screw caps of petrol tins were also found here. Besides those common objects, there were also some rare finds including small ceramic medicine jars, remains of candles used as lights during nighttime, a completely preserved iron hammer, pincers, nails, and several pickaxes. Two different types of cartridges from flare pistols were recovered (Eley London: 4.5 cm and "J.P.&S. IV [Joseph Parkes & Sons: 1.2 cm]).

The standard types of ammunition were also present: several dumps and loose examples of hand grenades (Battye- or Bethune grenade [1915], Jam Tin [1915], Mills [1915–1917]), rifle grenades (No. 3 Hale [1915], No. 22 Newton Pippin [1915], French Viven Bessiére [1916]), mortar bombs (Stokes 3-inch high explosive), and remains of shells (German HZ 14, 150 mm, British 18-pounders). It was remarkable to see how the shell holes caused by German attacks were all very close to the British trenches.

The last category of artifacts are the personal objects: some fragments of ceramic pipes, well-preserved matches, parts of mouth organs, and two copper coins.

Five remains of soldiers were recovered from Cross Roads. Three of them were piled on top of each other; they probably died during an attack (see figure). The equipment from two of these soldiers was very well preserved: the uniform, the Pattern 1914 leather webbing, the Royal Sussex Regiment insignia, and the ankle boots were in astonishingly good shape. One of them carried a Webley 0.45-inch pistol, which means he could have been a machine-gunner. The equipment was investigated by several specialists: L. Milner (Imperial War Museum, London [UK]), A. Robertshaw (National Army Museum, London [UK]), and Peter Doyle (University of Greenwich [UK]). The men probably died in the spring of 1917. One of the soldiers carried a small box respirator with him.

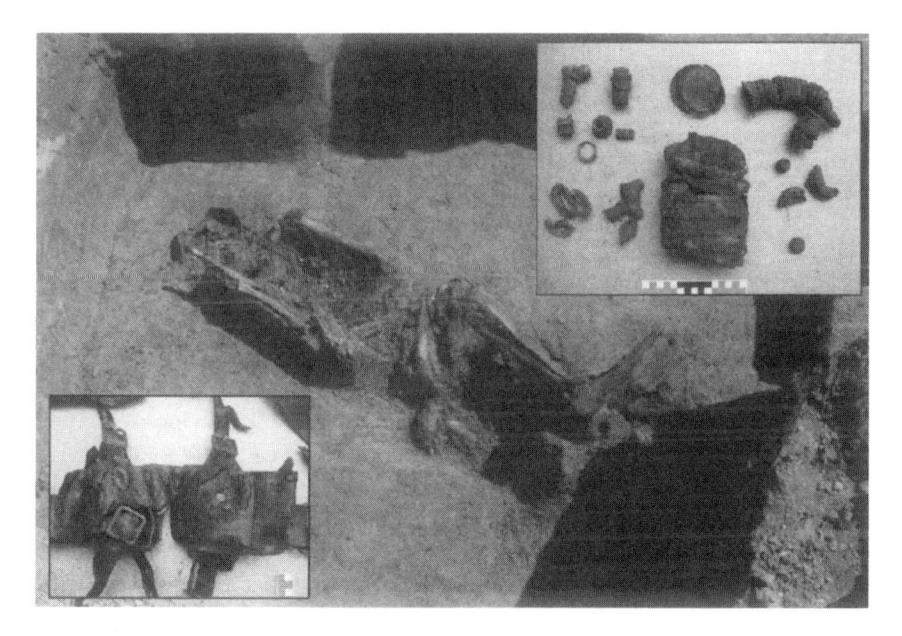

The remains from one of the three Royal Sussex soldiers. (Flemish Heritage Institute/ Mathieu de Meyer/Franky Wyffels)

A fourth human's remains were found completely scattered in a shell hole. An insignia shows that he belonged to the 5th Battalion of the Nothumberland Fusiliers.

The fifth individual was also found in a shell hole, only two parts of his legs and a part of his skull were recovered. Some buttons, two shoes, the remains of a bicycle-lamp, and a rare ink-pen with inscription "The Military Stylo DVC" were found together with the body. But this was not enough to identify the specific regiment for which he served.

BURIAL OF SOLDIERS AND REMEMBRANCE

Throughout the work, there was a strict procedure to be followed when human remains were found. After the examination of the bodies and the accompanying artifacts, the recovered remains of British soldiers are re-buried in one of the many British cemeteries around Ypres. The French remains are deposited in a mass grave at one of the major French cemeteries in the area.

The British soldiers found during the excavations at the Turco and Cross Roads sites have been buried next to each other at Track × Cemetery near the Cross Roads excavation site. Each burial was accompanied by a short ceremony led by an Anglican priest and organized by the CWGC (Commonwealth War Graves Commission). The first burial, which was the British soldier found at the Turco site, was attended by Lord Faulkner (House of Lords [UK]), Ivor Caplin MP (British Minister of Veteran Affairs [UK]°) and his military assistant, Commander Nigel Amphlett (UK).

Many tourists and visitors to the Cross Roads excavation site expressed their respect for the retrieved bodies of these soldiers. At the several places where soldiers were found, makeshift memorials of poppies and remembrance crosses were made, thus indicating that the excavation site itself became some sort of place of pilgrimage and a focus of great interest for the public.[32]

GEOPHYSICAL SURVEY AT FORWARD COTTAGE AND "THE BATTLE OF BIXSCHOTE"

Three sites have been the subject of a geophysical survey. The first one was a resistivity survey carried out at "The Battle of Bixschote" site. It was undertaken by the VIOE together with British colleague Martin Brown (East Sussex County Council [UK]). The first application of the technique unfortunately did not yield many results. In a second attempt, the private firm BAC-TEC[33] performed a magnetometry search of the Forward Cottage site. This time, the results were positive: trenches showed up very clearly and other anomalies became clear. Recently, a magnetometry survey was carried out at the High Command Redoubt site.

INVENTORY OF AERIAL PHOTOGRAPHS

The nine previously mentioned selected zones have also been more closely investigated using aerial photographs, documents, and maps.

The focus of our attention lies on the processing of aerial photographs taken during the war. All warring parties built up a collection of aerial photographs taken above the Western Front, in advance of, during, and after the different attacks. Millions of these photos can be examined in Great Britain, Belgium, Germany, and France. The Imperial War Museum (London, UK) and the In Flanders Fields Museum (Ypres, Belgium), supplied us with photographs which have been processed in a GIS using the "image warping" technique: the computer recalculates the photo to fit on a contemporary map according to a number of indicated points, e.g., crossroads or structures (see figure).

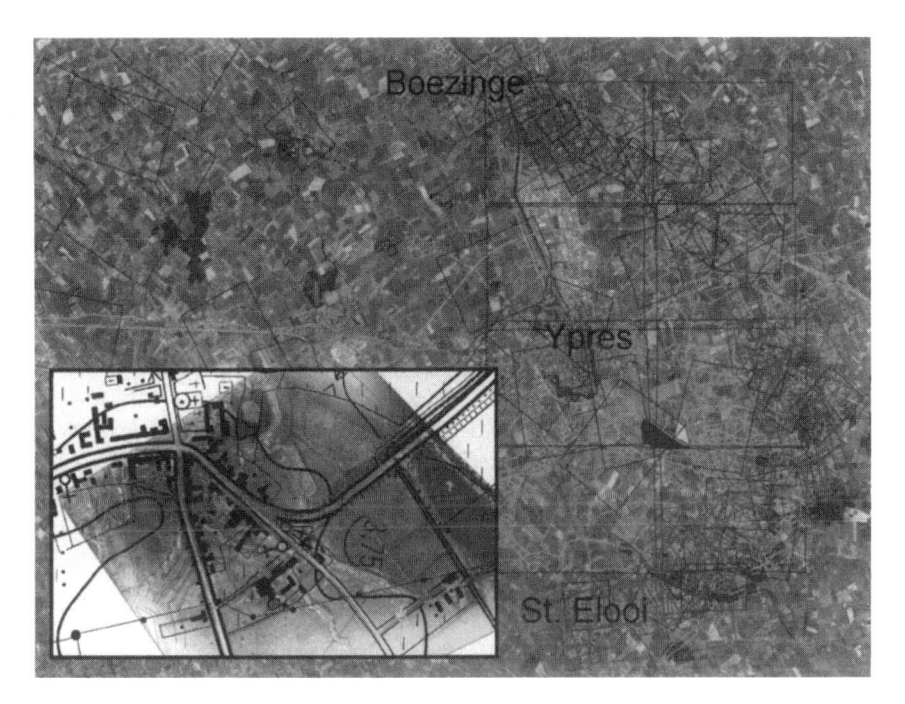

An overview of the wartime aerial photographs and trenches which have been put into the inventory up to January 2005 in the area around Ypres. (Flanders Fields Museum/ Mathieu de Meyer)

Next, polygons, lines, or dots can be drawn on the modern map; they indicate the structures visible on the aerial photograph (see figure). Trenches, barbed wire, tracks, old field boundaries, battery positions, and other structures could be located exactly. This technique is applied on aerial photos of different periods; the results can be placed in overlay. In this way the evolution of the terrain can be thoroughly studied. Furthermore it offers a convenient way to accurately date the trenches found within the excavations. The large number of contemporary photographs available for such a small area can help greatly in tracing the history and evolution of the war in its geographical (and archaeological!) context. Of course, it is also an indication of the complexity of the research, given the continuing change of structures. To apply this technique one requires vertical photographs, though other images can provide us with a great deal of important information.

Aerial photographs offer us a much more reliable image than the trench maps. The aerial photographs show us a clear evolution in the appearance of the trenches, while the same trench is sometimes depicted in a totally different manner on different trench maps of the same period.

In February 2004, a new inventory project was started. All World War I remains in Western Flanders, which could have an archaeological value, are added to the CAI inventory using several kinds of documents, trench maps, and—last but not least—aerial photographs. In a GIS system these are processed using the "image warping" technique, in the same manner they were used in Houthulst and on the A19 Project. At this moment the aerial photographs collection of the In Flanders Fields Museum is put in the inventory, completed with aerial photographs from the Imperial War Museum, private archives, and publications.

Our attention now focuses on the Ypres Salient as it was established after the Second Battle of Ypres (see figure). Aerial photography was pretty common in the armies at conflict from 1915 onward. The trenches dating from before 1915 are sometimes visible on the photographs, but the information has to be completed with other kinds of sources: maps and archival documents. Such documents are also used for the localization of certain specific types of sites, such as deep dugouts. A special database was developed in order to make the World War inventory. By the end of 2004, 887 aerial photographs were put in the database and over 2,000 traces had been drawn (see figure).

CONCLUSION

Archaeology of World War I poses unique challenges and resources that are not usually encountered in "conventional" archaeology. The excavated structures were only used for a very short period of time. Yet the availability of archival information, aerial photographs, trench maps, witness testimony, and innumerable contemporary accounts and war literature offer invaluable information in locating and identifying features found in the excavation.

What special role can archaeology play in the study? Historians have long studied this period quite intensively and theories about some aspects still change every year. Typologies exist for most of the objects which are found. Nevertheless, archaeology can uncover a sometimes forgotten material reality. Even some of the best known battles are not completely clear to scholars studying the First World War. The archaeological excavations make the horror of soldiers' existence during the First World War more real and immediate than paper relics. Living in trenches, waiting for the next charge in a shelter: the entire picture becomes clearer as the archaeologist reveals more remains. In addition, trench maps and contemporary aerial photographs offer a snapshot of the terrain, but these are narrowly restricted in time. Excavations often reveal a constantly and swiftly changing terrain where trenches and fortifications were continually adapted to new threats and needs. Given this situation, archaeological research provides another dimension to the available information and helps to locate unknown structures and remains.

In terms of physical conservation, the most important threats to the remains are erosion, construction activities, illicit excavations by collectors, and the natural processes of corrosion and decay. It is therefore necessary to recover and collect for conservation exposed remains as quickly as possible. It is to be hoped that eventually the combination of comprehensive research and a constantly updated database will encourage public awareness and support for archaeological protection. With possible future technical developments in mind the present research in all its aspects can give a decisive direction for the approach to specific terrain or circumstances. Perhaps it will even be possible to produce a 3D model of some part of the trenches, based on aerial photographs.

The international attention received by the VIOE for the project highlights its importance to a wide community of scholars. We would like to thank the following people for their help and expertise: Peter Barton (co-secretary of the All Party War Graves and Battlefields Heritage Group/Parapet Archives [UK]), Lauri Milner (Imperial War Museum London [UK]), Nigel Steel (Imperial War Museum London [UK]), Peter Chasseaud (University of Greenwich, Department of Military Cartography [UK]), Peter Doyle (University of Greenwich [UK]), Nicholas Saunders (University College of London [UK]), Piet Chielens (In Flanders Fields Museum Ypres [Belgium]), Andrew Robertshaw (National Army Museum London [UK]), and last but not least Martin Brown (Assistant County Archaeologist, East Sussex County Council [UK]). All of them, together with many volunteers (archaeology students and others) have been crucial to the success of the project. Networking with foreign specialists, among others, has helped the VIOE-team gain familiarity with archival resources and artifact types.

On November 10, 2003, the creation of a special World War I archaeology department was formerly announced to the press and the public in Ypres's Cloth Hall. Its objectives are clear and can be expanded when required. Archaeological research, study, documenting inventories, and management of First World War heritage make up a first clear goal. A detailed database will provide immediate access to this unique heritage, and can be used to support or supplement a wide range of related cultural and tourist initiatives.

At the same time, the department of First World War archaeology will seek to direct the abundant but very diverse private initiatives undertaken by museums, amateur excavators, historians, and so forth, by getting a clear picture of the expertise and different specialities of the different participants. In this way a forum can be created for the vast amount of dispersed knowledge that most certainly will result in greater cooperation. In addition, international projects, for example the French collaboration on the joint project on the First World War in Arras, can lead to an interesting refinement of the research agenda at Ypres itself.[34] In November 2004 the new department was transformed into the A.W.A. (Association for World War Archaeology).[35]

In February 2004 a new CAI project started with the goal of making an inventory of all World War I remains in Western Flanders. At first, a basic inventory is made of all the frontlines and defensive lines. The inventory of threatened areas will continue in a very detailed manner using aerial photographs. Until now, we have only conducted research on one of the possible

A19 trajectories. There are also some alternative routes which should be examined. The extension of the industrial estate of Ypres is also an important challenge. An inventory has been made from the area, and excavations started in May/June 2004. The inventory already proved to be an important tool for the management and protection of certain sites, and of course, the excavations. In sum, there is still a lot to be done!

NOTES

1. The international commission of experts consists of Yves Buffetaut [historian (F)], Prof. Peter Chasseaud [FRGS School of Earth & Environmental Science, University of Greenwich: Department Of Military Cartography (UK)] and Nigel Steel [Imperial War Museum (UK)]. The foreign historians were asked to compile a report illustrating the historical and cultural significance of the region in all its facets.

2. Every year they grow fewer in number, but in the United Kingdom, vast archives of audiovisual testimonies can be accessed.

3. A *deep dugout* is a type of underground shelter for soldiers. Some of these were turned into field hospitals.

4. The Central Archaeological Inventory (CAI—Centrale Archeologische Inventaris) is an inventory of all the archaeological sites in Flanders. Prehistoric, Roman, medieval, and more recent remains are mapped in a GIS-system; information about the sites can be found in a database. The project started in 2000.

5. Trench maps are maps which were made during the war with trenches, meter gauge railways, wire entanglement, etc. drawn on them.

6. de Meyer, M. and Demeyere, F. 2004.

7. GIS: Geographic Information System.

8. An unpublished extensive report about the project and its results has been written by the archaeologists involved in the project: Mathieu de Meyer, Pedro Pype, Marc Dewilde, Janiek De Gryse, and Frederik Demeyere.

9. This was called the "Race to the Sea." This so-called race ended at the North Sea coast after each army attempted to outflank the other by moving north and west to reach the Channel ports.

10. British, German, and French troops used names in their own language for streets, villages, farms and other important features in the landscape. In this way soldiers could better understand where they were and where they had to head for.

11. More information about the Battles of Ypres can be found in Giles 1979.

12. Some of these cemeteries have already been destroyed during the First World War.

13. More information about these categories of finds can be found further in this article, in the sections dealing with the excavations.

14. Pype and Wittouck 2005.

15. Resistivity survey, radar, or magnetic survey.

16. More information about the excavations can be found in these publications: Raemen et al. 2004; Silberman 2004; de Meyer and Pyep 2004.

17. Mr. G. Verhaeghe.

18. The gas-attack and the story behind it is explained in Keech 2001:30–56.

19. An inverted A-frame was a wooden structure, in an upside down A-shape, within a trench to support the duckboards, standardized wooden platforms on which soldiers could walk without sinking away in the mud.

20. Saunders 2000a:152–156.

21. The tubes are preserved by the owner, G. Verhaeghe. We were allowed to examine them.

22. Good reference collections of these objects can be found at the In Flanders Fields Museum, Museum Hooge Crater, the Hill 60 Museum and the Hill 62 Museum, all of them in or near Ypres.

23. More information about the standard equipment can be found in Beraffato 1995:36–47 and Pyep 2005.

24. More information about the shrapnel can be found in Hamilton 1915:251–259.

25. M. Vandenbruaene.

26. Mr. P. Debaillic.

27. Mr. P. Descamps.

28. The document was found by Peter Barton of the All Party War Graves and Battlefields Heritage Group and the Parapet Archives.

29. These jumping-off trenches were dug to narrow the distance which the troops had to cover to cross no-man's-land on the 31st of July (Third Battle of Ypres).

30. The Lt. Skeggs research was carried out by Peter Barton.

31. More information about sniping plates can be found in Saunders 2000b:13–14.

32. Every year the region receives 300,000 to 350,000 battlefield tourists.

33. BACTEC International Ltd; Explosive Ordnance Disposal & Landmine Clearance.

34. More information is found in Dewilde et al. 2004.

35. The website of the A.W.A. is http://www.a-w-a.be; it contains a lot of information and pictures about several World War archaeology projects in Flanders.

REFERENCES CITED

Berrafato, L. 1995. Le Fantasin De La Grande Guerre 1914/1918 (2ème partie). Gazette des uniformes, n° 4.

De Meyer, M. 2004. Het A19 Project. Deel 2: Historisch Onderzoek en inventarisatie, Woumen (not published).

De Meyer, M., and F. Demeyere. 2004. De inventarisatie van de gemeente Houthulst (prov. West-Vlaanderen), CAI I—De opbouw van een archeologisch beleidsinstrument CAI, IAP-rapporten 14, Brussel.

De Meyer, M., and P. Pyep. 2004. The A19 Project. Archaeological Research at Cross Roads, Zarren. Association for World War Archaeology, Zarren, Belgium.

De Wilde, M., M. De Meyer, P. Pyep, and F. De Meyere. 2004. Het A19 Project. Deel 1: Synthese en evaluatie, Woumen (not published).

De Wilde, M., P. Pycp, M. De Meyer, F. De Meyere, W. Lamens, J. Degryse, F. Wyffels, and N. J. Saunders. 2004. Belgium's New Department of First World War

Archaeology. *Antiquity* 78:301, September 2004 (Project Gallery: http://antiquity.ac.uk:ProjGall/saunders/).
Giles, J. 1979. *The Ypres Salient: Flanders Then and Now*. After the Battle, London.
Hamilton, D. T. 1915. *Shrapnel Shell Manufacture*. Industrial Press, New York.
Keech, G. 2001. *St Julien*. Casemate Publications, South Yorkshire.
Pype, P. 2005. De standaarduitrusting van de Britse infanterist 1914-1918 (not published).
Pype, P., and J. De Gryse. 2004. Het A19 Project. Deel 3: De opgravingen, Woumen (not published).
Pype, P., and T. Wittouck. 2005. Aangetroffen Britse munitie uit de Eerste Wereldoorlog tijdens het archeologisch onderzoek langs het A19-traject (not published).
Raemen, E., V. Hendriks, P. Pype, M. de Meyer, R. Renr, A. Peelaerts, A. Dierickx-Visschers, A. Van Balen, S. Boyen, C. Boffin, L. Janssens, and J. Van Looveren. 2004. Loop!Graven. Een archeologische zoektocht naar de Eerste Wereldoorlog, Katholieke Universiteit Leuven.
Saunders, A. 2000a. *Weapons of the Trench War 1914–1918*. Saunders Publishing, Cornwall.
Saunders, A. 2000b. *Dominating the Enemy: War in the Trenches* 1914–1918. Sutton Publishing, Somerset.
Silberman, N.A. 2004. In Flanders Fields: Uncovering the Carnage of Word War I. *Archaeology* 57(3):24–29.

Pointe-du-Hoc Battlefield, Normandy, France

*Richard Burt, James Bradford, Bruce Dickson,
Mark E. Everett, Robert Warden, & David Woodcock*

POINTE-DU-HOC HISTORIC SITE in Normandy, France, is one of the most iconic of the D-Day battlefields that still retains many of the cultural resources from June 6, 1944. The site is under the perpetual care and maintenance of the American Battle Monuments Commission. This chapter explains how the Historic Resources Imaging Laboratory at Texas A&M University is attempting to survey and document the battlefield using topographic survey data, aerial reconnaissance photographs, subsurface geophysical investigation, and other documentary evidence. The chapter addresses the following topics: battlefield significance, project objectives, and the results of two reconnaissance visits to identify cultural resources and evaluate the scope of the project, the availability of supporting documentary evidence such as bombing reports and aerial reconnaissance photographs to support development of the site plan, and the results of the first season of fieldwork.

SIGNIFICANCE OF THE SITE

Pointe-du-Hoc is the most culturally important historic site of the Normandy invasion in terms of site preservation. Celebrating the 40th anniversary of D-Day, President Ronald Reagan, from top of the command post remarked that "their mission was one of the most difficult and daring of the invasion: to climb these sheer and desolate cliffs and take out the enemy guns." Ten years later, at the same site, President Bill Clinton stated, "We stand on sacred soil. Fifty years ago at this place a miracle of liberation began. On that morning, democracy's forces landed to end the enslavement of Europe." Both presidents were referring to the early morning of June 6, 1944, when Lt. Col. James Earl Rudder led elements of the 2nd Ranger Battalion in one of the most famous and heroic actions of D-Day.[1] Their mission was to destroy 155 mm cannon capable of firing on troops and ships landing on Utah and Omaha beaches. The story of the battle has been recounted many times using narrative supported by large-scale maps that unfortunately do not show all the battlefield elements necessary to fully appreciate the intricacies of the battle. Rather, the accounts concentrate mainly on the preparation of the Rangers prior to D-Day and their action on D-Day and D-Day plus one. Although research has been done on the construction of German coastal fortifications in general, there has been remarkably little research on the Pointe-du-Hoc fortifications, both above and below ground level, or the damage that was inflicted to them by bombing and shelling conducted prior to H-Hour on D-Day.

The Pointe-du-Hoc battle site was designated a Class A Historic Site by the French government on February 28, 1955. On January 11, 1979, the site was formally transferred to the American Battle Monuments Commission, a small independent agency of the executive branch of the federal government, for perpetual care and maintenance. Unfortunately, even up to today, the historic site has very little site interpretation and individual buildings and structures are not even identified. The command post, which was a critically important point of the battle, has been inaccessible to the public since 2001, primarily due to erosion of the cliff. It contains a memorial to the Rangers, is one of the iconic sites of D-Day, and is an important part of our nation's cultural heritage. The historic site, situated close to eroding sea cliffs, is subject to rapid, destructive geological processes including landslides, atmospheric corrosion of steel reinforcements, and spalling and cracking of the concrete structures. The project team believed that on-site research was a *critical need* to locate and identity all buildings and structures, as well as all key bomb and shell craters. Unless prompt action was taken to preserve the key elements of this historic site, information regarding its importance to the success of the military actions on D-Day will be irretrievably lost to historians and future generations, and particularly to the memory of the brave soldiers who gave their lives upon the site.

The project's *objective* is to comprehensively document, using Historic American Building Survey (HABS) standards, the specific layout of the Pointe-du-Hoc Historic Site using various surveying techniques to locate the three-dimensional position of all the buildings, structures, and craters, including all key elements important to the strategic military significance of this site to the success of the D-Day invasion. The production of a detailed site plan will allow for better interpretation of historic records and photographs that will accurately tell the true events that transpired during the battle. High-resolution geophysical signatures of buried steel and concrete structures, zones of disturbed earth, and hidden metal artifacts shall also be included in the site plan.

This project is innovative in that, to date, no WWII battlefield has been documented to HABS standards. The historical significance, the completeness of the major buildings, the incorporation of subsurface geophysical information, and the amount of supporting documentary evidence add to the uniqueness of this project. At the completion of this project we expect to have produced a detailed site plan showing the location of the 155 mm gun emplacements, gun casements, bunkers, command post, anti-aircraft batteries, tobruks, trenches and tunnels, bomb and shell craters, and additional significant items. This will serve as a basis for the future production of a conservation master plan for the site, which will address the interpretation, and the care, management, and maintenance of the site. Detailed drawings of the command post will also be produced. These will include plans, elevations, and sections. The site plan, drawings, and geophysical maps will be deposited with the Library of Congress and other institutions such as the D-Day Museum in New Orleans, where they will become a valuable resource for military historians. The ultimate outcome will be a fitting tribute to Lt. Col. James Earl Rudder and his 2nd Ranger battalion, and especially to the soldiers who gave their lives so that the D-Day invasion would be successful.

PROJECT OBJECTIVES

Our interest in Pointe-du-Hoc is multifaceted. As members of the Texas A&M University (TAMU) faculty we feel a special connection with Pointe-du-Hoc through James Earl Rudder's brave and important involvement with Pointe-du-Hoc and his significant tenure as president of TAMU. But Pointe-du-Hoc doesn't derive its significance as a WWII site solely from James Earl Rudder. Long before James Earl Rudder was famous for his leadership on D-Day and his presidency at TAMU, Pointe-du-Hoc was understood by the Germans as one of the most strategically important sites of the Atlantic Wall. The value the Germans placed in the strategic advantage of Pointe-du-Hoc fueled the drive to provide the labor and resources to construct a modern fortified city, impenetrable from the land and sea.

It is this strategic value and its subsequent realization through the construction of bunkers, gun emplacements, trenches, and tunnels that forced an Allied counter-strategy bordering on the impossible. Each of these ideals—the German Fortress and the Allied "Impossible Mission"—were the products of real human tales. Though significant points of the overall story are well known—the creation of the "city," the movement of the guns, the difficult ascent of the cliffs, and the eventual Allied success—many of the important details that contributed to the development of the well-known story remain hidden.

The truth in these details can be queried through a series of questions:

1. What was built on the site of Pointe-du-Hoc, above and below ground, and for what purposes?
2. Was Pointe-du-Hoc unique in its fortification strategy? What does it share with other German fortification strategies?
3. Which constructed objects are no longer present?

4. How accurate was the Allied intelligence about the German defenses constructed on the site?
5. What was the effect of the Allied bombing and shelling strategy on both the German defenses and the Ranger attack?
6. Exactly how did D-day unfold for the Rangers, the Allied support, and the Germans?
7. To where exactly were the 155 mm guns relocated?
8. What is the present state of the constructions on site, both above and below ground?
9. What is the present state of the artillery and bomb craters and how have they changed since D-Day?
10. What is the present state of visitation on the site and how should the experience be strengthened?
11. What is the history of erosion and present-day mass movement susceptibility of the cliffs?

These questions require information in many forms. To gather that information and analyze it properly a diverse team composed of many disciplines must work closely together.

Mark Everett from the department of geology and geophysics is using non-invasive geophysical techniques such as 3D interpretation of ground-penetrating radar (GPR), magnetics, and electromagnetic induction signatures to test our suppositions about the existence and nature of subsurface structures. The information gathered by his team will be closely integrated with Bruce Dickson from the department of anthropology to provide definitive answers to many of our questions regarding archaeological issues. Pointe-du-Hoc provides an excellent natural laboratory for investigating new techniques with high-resolution geophysical imaging due to the abundance, complexity, variety, and cultural importance of the buried prospection targets.

Bruce Dickson will take information from Mark's team together with personal observation and determine the best places for future archaeological trenches. These trenches will bring firsthand observation to our suppositions about the intentions and operations of these structures, provide information about the state of the structure on D-Day, and yield possible valuable information about how the battle unfolded. Archaeology is necessary not only for testing hypotheses but also for generating new discoveries for questions yet to be asked.

Richard Burt from the department of construction science will gather information about the construction of the "city" from archive aerial photographs and photogrammetry. The aerial photographs taken prior to D-Day will aid in the determination of stages and processes of construction and the state of construction when Allied bombing commenced in the spring of 1944. Aerial photographs taken after D-Day will help determine the effects of the bombing and shelling on the site and its structures. Photogrammetry will aid in determining details of construction and details of the battle by revealing the nature of artillery damage to various structures.

Robert Warden from the department of architecture will oversee both the detailed measurements of individual buildings and the overall documentation of all site elements. The relationships between buildings on the site will aid in understanding the unfolding of the story on D-Day, the effects of the bombing and shelling on the Germans and the Rangers, and the understanding of the role each building played. The detailed documentation of each structure will be linked with aerial photos and archaeological data to help tell the story of each structure from construction to destruction.

James Bradford from the department of history will play a significant role by tying together the field data, our research questions, and existing histories of the site. Burt and Bradford have been continually collecting archival material from a variety of sources. Initial searches have focused on the Public Record Office at Kew in London which holds many of the wartime records of the Allies. Copies of documents detailing the bombing missions carried out on Pointe-du-Hoc have been obtained and a narrative of the bombing activities is being prepared. Future archival research will focus on obtaining copies of aerial reconnaissance photographs from Keele University in England.

As a consequence of these investigations but no less important is the fact that the information gathered and presented through 3D models and drawings will create an accurate record of the state of the buildings and the terrain as they existed in 2004. Later generations will be able to see how the site has changed over the years but more importantly this information will be invaluable for fashioning a preservation plan to ensure that the memory of Pointe-du-Hoc remains alive.

THE RECONNAISSANCE VISIT (SEPTEMBER 2003)

The team identified the following cultural resources during the visit:

- The Command Post or Fire Control Post—this building contains the Rangers Memorial
- 6 – 155 mm Open Gun Emplacements
- 2 – Anti-Aircraft or Flak Emplacements
- 2 – Covered Gun Casements
- 7 – Covered Bunkers
- 1 – Machine Gun Tobruk
- Trenches
- Tunnels
- Bomb Debris—large pieces of concrete from destroyed buildings
- A Gun Wheel from one of the Open Gun Emplacements
- Numerous Bomb and Shell Craters

The reconnaissance visit revealed that many cultural resources are at significant risk due to large-scale mass movement triggered by intense physical and chemical weathering at the cliff face. The command post and the eastern anti-aircraft battery are now only several meters from the cliff's edge.

During the reconnaissance visit we visited the Ranger Museum in Grandcamp and were able to photograph the original map that Lieutenant George Kerchner carried with him on D-Day. The map was reproduced using Auto-CAD and is shown in the figure below. It would appear that this map was derived from the *Neptune Monograph* which was produced in April 1944 as part of Operation Neptune, the landing phase of Operation Overlord.

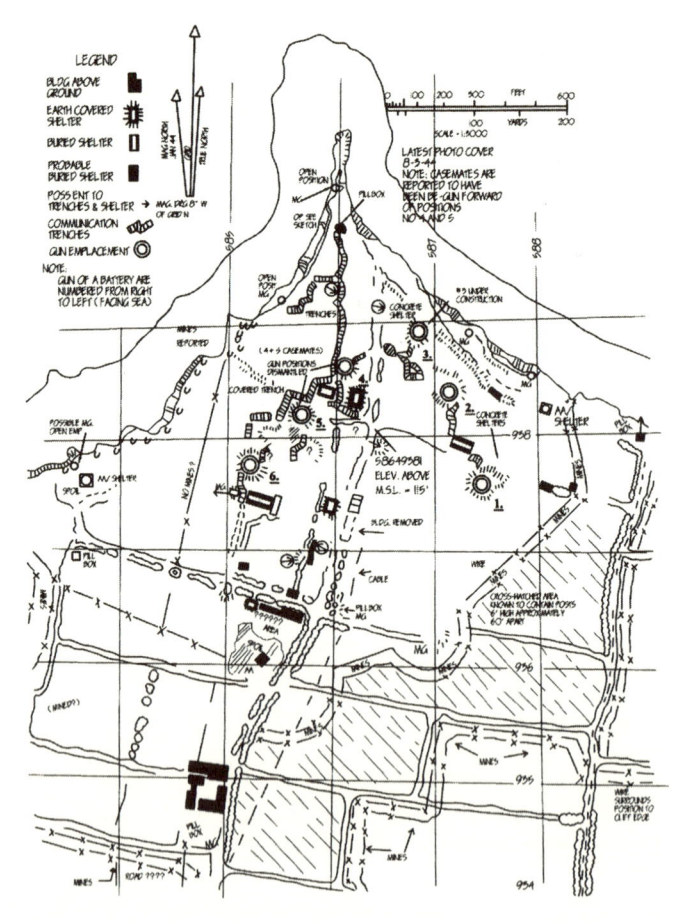

AutoCAD drawing of Lieutenant George Kerchner's map based on the Neptune Monograph.

POINTE-DU-HOC BATTLEFIELD, NORMANDY, FRANCE   389

SUPPORTING DOCUMENTARY EVIDENCE

Various sources of documentary evidence will be used together with the results of the topographic survey to develop a series of site plans that will more accurately tell the story of the battle. It is proposed to create a series of site plans showing the development and destruction of the site prior to D-Day. Examples of some of the documentary sources include:

1. Aerial Photography. The site was extensively photographed from the air before and after D-Day. The Aerial Reconnaissance Archive (TARA) at Keele University in the United Kingdom provides online access to 5.5 million photographs taken over occupied Western Europe, by the Allies during World War II. Searches are conducted using a geographical reference for the site (W492005). Limited access to the website revealed that the site was photographed extensively from May 1942 to the end of the war. When these images become available for analysis, they should allow us to establish how the site was developed and to establish a history of the bombing of the site which may help to explain why two gun casements had been constructed to replace some of the open gun emplacements
2. Topographic Reports. The Public Records Office (PRO) at Kew in London houses the majority of documents relating to the Allies' activities during the Second World War. In order to review the suitability of the occupied countries' coastline for an amphibious assault, topographic surveys were conducted by the Inter-Services Topographical Department. The report covering Pointe et Raz de la Percée to Pointe-du-Hoc (Hoe) is dated May 1, 1943 (W0 252/163). The report describes the topography of the site and appraises its suitability for assault. The report considers the cliffs "unscalable over the length of the report" due to the fragile nature of the cliffs. The report also mentions that "a considerable amount of excavation has occurred" and it is suggested that it is of a military nature. This report along with its accompanying map will allow us to develop a plan of the site in its early development phase.
3. Interpretation Reports. The Central Interpretation Unit produced reports after each bombing mission based on analysis of aerial photographs. The reports give information on the number of aircraft, the command conducting the bombing, the time of the attack, and the number, type, and weight of the bombs dropped. The reports also give details of the attack including identifying when bombs hit the intended target. We have identified that bombing missions were carried out against Pointe-du-Hoc on April 25, 1944, May 13 & 22, 1944, and June 4, 5, & 6, 1944. For example on the morning of June 5, 1944, the report (AIR 34/373 – SA 1963) states that the U.S. 8th Air Force attacked tactical targets in the Caen area with 98 aircraft and dropped over 1,200 500-lb bombs on several targets. The attack on the medium coastal battery describes more than 50 bursts on the target area and probable hits on two of the gun emplacements. These reports, together with the aerial photographs, will help us develop a history of the bombing of the site.

4. *USS Texas* Action Reports. Prior to the Rangers landing at Pointe-du-Hoc, the site was shelled by *Battleship Texas* among others. The Action Report dated June 28, 1944, covers the period from June 3–17 when *Texas* was operating as part of Task Force 124 in support of the Normandy landings. Part IV of the report covers battle damage. The report states that the uncompleted casemate and the three open emplacements were destroyed as were the command post and pill poxes.

SUMMER 2004 DOCUMENTATION

For three weeks in June 2004 four members of the team of investigators and 12 graduate students from the departments of architecture, geology and geophysics, construction science, and archaeology began the task of gathering the information necessary to answer the questions mentioned above.

Much of the student work was focused on getting very accurate measurements of some of the important buildings. These measurements are the basis for creating 2D drawings of the buildings in the present condition. We focused on six structures for this brief period of time, which amounts to about 24 drawings. The six structures recorded during this period were the Command Post, the East and West Anti-Aircraft Emplacements, Open Gun Emplacements No. 3 and 6, and Casemate No. 4. To illustrate the methods we used to gather data we will focus on the methods used to record the Command Post.

THE COMMAND POST

Our intent is to create both 2D and 3D products for this structure since its existence is in peril due to erosion of the cliff. We gathered enough information both by hand and through photogrammetry to complete these products. The next figure indicates an example of the field drawings created to organize the dimensional information for the plan. These drawings are produced by hand initially to provide a platform for recording measurements but also as an aid to students' engagement with the building. The more they "see" the building the better decisions they make concerning its documentation.

For the command post we took measurements for both longitudinal and transverse sections. Many more sections could be taken to show every part of the building but we believe a 3D model will serve these purposes better. This figure shows some of the modeling that has resulted from the photogrammetric data gathered. This is done by marking the same point on the building on at least three digital images taken from different positions, and then when a sufficient number of points have been marked on the images, computer software is able to locate the three-dimensional position of the cameras. Once the

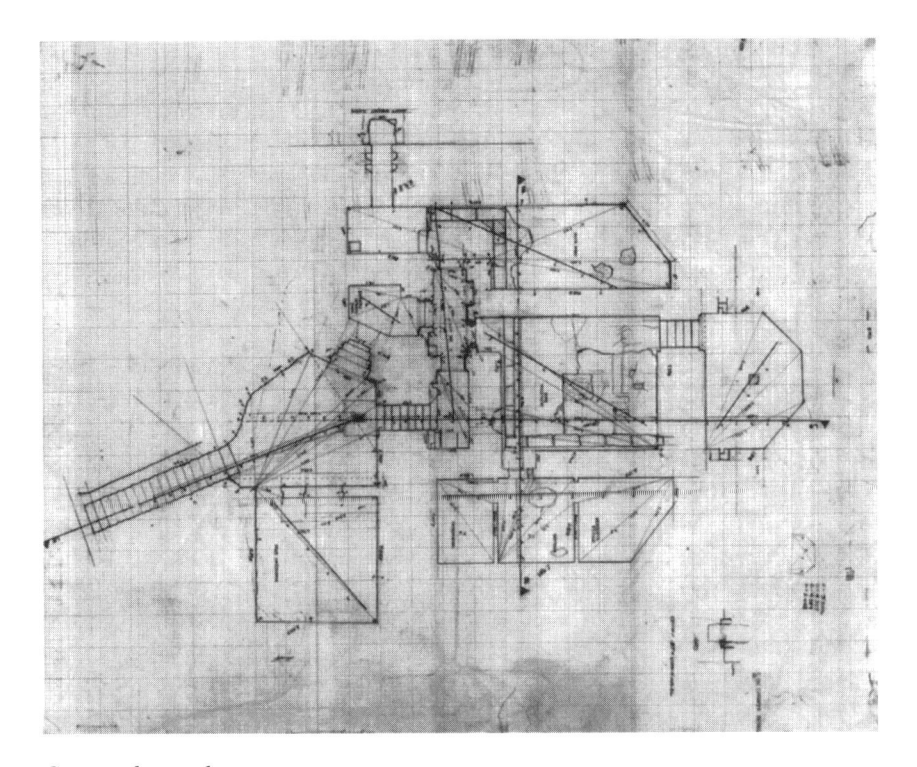

Command post plan.

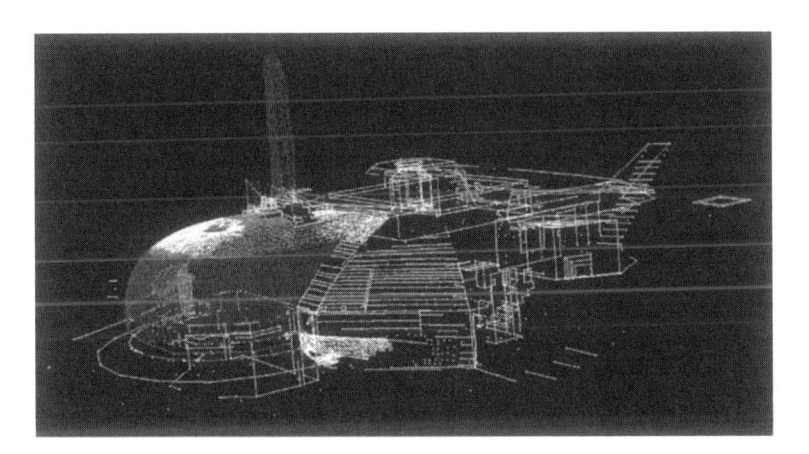

Partially complete 3D model of command post.

camera positions are located, a series of mathematical calculations locates the position of all marked points. These points are used to create a virtual model of the building that appears as a three-dimensional image on a computer screen.

GEOPHYSICAL AND ARCHAEOLOGICAL EXPLORATIONS

Archaeological work was primarily observation and coordination with the other disciplines in preparation for future efforts. A significant goal is to locate and verify through physical and visual evidence the trench system established by the Germans and the location to where the 155 mm guns were moved. The method used was to perform archaeological site observation in order to narrow the scope of investigation for the geophysical investigation. The results of the geophysical information will help determine locations for proposed physical archaeology for later investigations.

The types of geophysical data acquired at the site are indicative of certain subsurface physical properties. The ground-penetrating radar (GPR) signals respond most strongly to spatial variations in moisture content, which in the context of the Pointe-du-Hoc site reflects mainly buried concrete and hidden void spaces. The magnetometer data responds to iron, or natural soil magnetite content, and will indicate, for example, concrete reinforcing bars, ordnance fragments, or soil in-fill. The electromagnetic induction (EMI) measurements are diagnostic of subsurface electrical conductivity, which is very high in the presence of both ferrous and non-ferrous metal.

The GPR, magnetometer, and EMI systems were used for both lateral reconnaissance mapping and for sounding of the subsurface to depths of 0.0–3.0 meters below the surface. Co-registered GPR and magnetics data have revealed buried voids and reinforced concrete structures. Generally, the GPR and magnetics work synergistically as reinforced concrete possesses both a radar and a magnetic signature. The EMI measurements have revealed unambiguous signs of metal fragments in the bomb craters and complex buried metal structures.

The Pointe-du-Hoc site is challenging from a geophysical perspective due to the fact that the current landscape is the integration of various human disturbances that have modified the geological subsurface over time: pre–World War II farming; the German fortification construction; the Allied bombing campaign; the battle itself; the site modification associated with cleanup and recovery from the battle; the tourist impact; and 60 years of soil weathering, consolidation, and corrosion.

LOCATION OF THE GERMAN TRENCH SYSTEM

The command post, gun emplacements, and bunkers at Pointe-du-Hoc were evidently connected to one another by a series of open trenches and concrete-covered passageways. In order to locate surface evidence of the covered and open German trenches, it was necessary to undertake a preliminary surface examination of site topography. Such surface examination, called "pedestrian site reconnaissance" in archaeology, is standard field practice in the discipline.

The first step in our surface reconnaissance was to examine the maps and aerial photographs of the site. Copies of these original maps and photographs were then taken into the field to aid in the location of the trenches. Unfortunately, for two reasons, these data proved to be of only limited utility. First, the Germans had evidently been successful in obscuring the location of many of their concrete-covered trenches from aerial reconnaissance simply by covering them with thick layers of earth. Second, the extraordinary aerial and naval bombardment that the site received on D-Day and before appears to have obliterated many of the trenches and altered the original topography and structure of the site beyond immediate recognition. We therefore employed the following strategy for locating the German trenches at Pointe-du-Hoc by means of the following pedestrian site survey procedures.

- Walking a series of more formally oriented pedestrian transects along east-to-west and north-to-south axes across the site searching for linear depressions in the earth or other suggestions of subsurface features. Of course, the numerous shell craters, concrete slabs, and damaged structures on the site made strict maintenance of the orientation of these transect lines difficult.
- Locating and examining all the points of covered ingress and egress in the concrete structures such as bunkers and gun emplacements. In doing so, we sought at the same time to determine how these entranceways were connected to the overall trench system.
- Assigning numbers to all of the surface features and covered entranceways found in this manner, photographing them, and having their locations plotted on the project topographic map using the Total Station.
- Generating a series of hypotheses about the morphology of the German trench system based on the nature and locations of the surface features and covered entranceways we had located.

Following these procedures four locations were selected for exploration with geophysical subsurface prospecting tools:

1. BK1: an area of exposed cement paving that may represent the roof of a covered trench;
2. CT5-CT6: a low flat area that may house a second covered trench that runs approximately west to east across the middle of the site just north of and parallel to a low earthen ridge (see figure);
3. C14: a U-shaped pattern of exposed earth and stunted vegetation that may be part of a narrow gauge track system used for moving ammunition at the site (see figure);
4. CT9-CT10: a long, linear mound that runs north to south from the middle to the southern end of the site and may contain a steel conduit and telephone line.

The data obtained from these four locations by means of 100 MHz ground-penetrating radar, Cs-vapor magnetometry, and time-domain electromagnetic induction (metal detection) are suggestive. However, "ground truth" needs to be obtained for these results by archaeological means.

In sum, the archaeological and geophysical data gathered in the Phase II surface reconnaissance will allow us to assemble a preliminary reconstruction of the German trench system. At the current stage of our knowledge, the

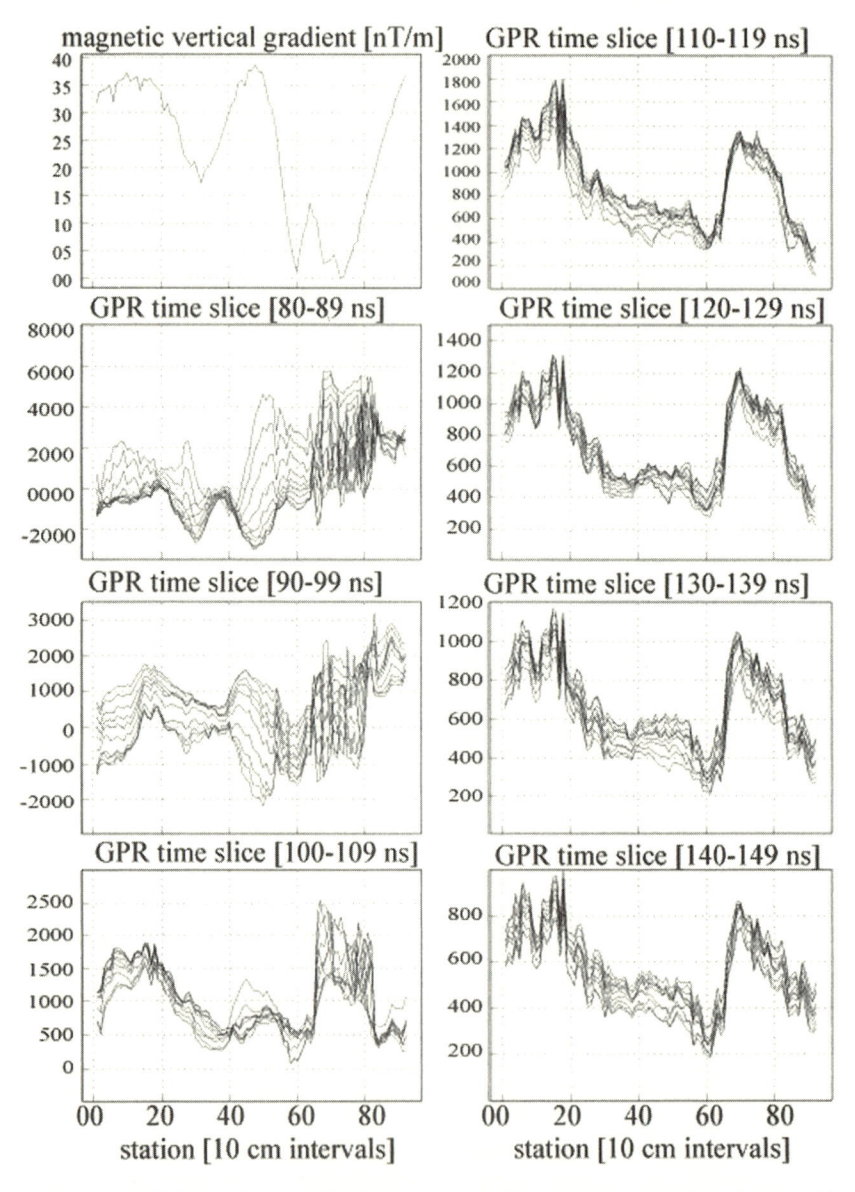

Magnetic (top left panel) and GPR horizontal profiles across the strike of a possible buried concrete trench. (Mark Everett, Carl Pierce, Neelambari Save, Robert Warden, and Bruce Dickson, Geophysical Investigation of the June 6, 1944 D-Day Invasion Site at Point du Hoc, Normandy, France, Near-Surface Geophysics, *EAGE, Netherlands)*

location and orientation of the various covered entranceways should prove to be key to this reconstruction. After these entranceways are plotted on the master topographic map of the site, we can begin to generate hypotheses

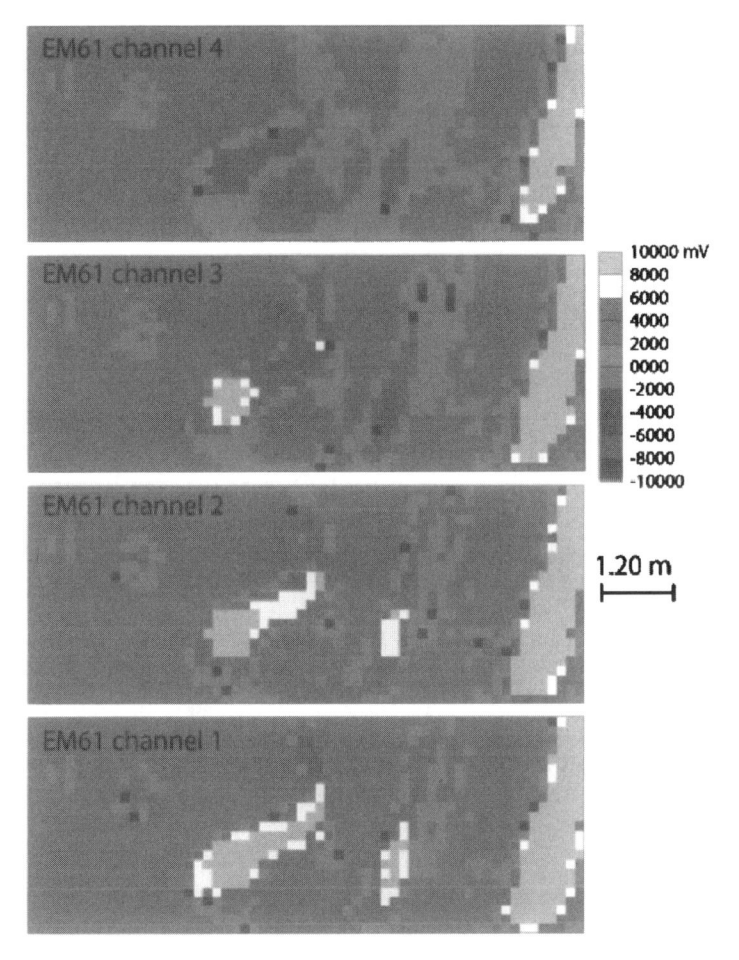

EMI signature of U-shaped target C14. (Mark Everett, Carl Pierce, Neelambari Save, Robert Warden, and Bruce Dickson, Geophysical Investigation of the June 6, 1944 D-Day Invasion Site at Point du Hoc, Normandy, France, Near-Surface Geophysics, *EAGE, Netherlands)*

about the location and orientation of the covered trenches that were connected to them. We can then test these hypotheses in Phase III through a combination of geophysical prospecting and archaeological excavation. This work should allow us to complete the reconstruction of the trench system.

LOCATION OF THE HIDDEN ARTILLERY PARK

Finding the precise location of the place where the 155 mm guns from Pointe-du-Hoc had been moved before D-Day turned out to be both a technical problem and a problem of human memory. The people of the tiny village of Cricqueville just south of Pointe-du-Hoc know the former location of these guns in a general way. This location is not on property under the management of American Battle Monuments Commission. However, Mr. Gene Dellinger, director of Normandy American National Cemetery and Memorial at St. Laurent, arranged for our team to meet the mayor of Cricqueville, Mr. LeDevin. Mayor LeDevin very kindly allowed us to copy an old aerial photograph of the coastal region from Pointe-du-Hoc to Cricqueville in the town's possession and arranged for our access to the farm of the Pain family where local memory places the guns on D-Day. Using the aerial photograph as our template, we assigned numbers to the fields encompassing the location of the hidden German battery.

Mayor LeDevin accompanied us to the Pain farm in order to show us the presumed location of the guns firsthand. It was the mayor's opinion that the guns were situated near the corner of the field. Two potential locations for the guns were identified for metal detection. Metal detectors are the geophysical tool of choice since historical accounts say the Rangers disabled the guns through the use of thermite grenades which would have left molten metal on the ground. Also the location of the battle in the field would be marked with rifle shell casings which would make an attractive target for the detectors.

The results of this metal detection work is encouraging in one sense as some of these metal objects may allow us to conclude that this field was indeed formerly used as an artillery park, was the scene of a battle, or was, at least, a German military encampment. However, the large number of anomalies that we encountered also makes it likely that, in the course of excavating them, we will encounter a large number of false alarms.

In sum, our brief reconnaissance work on the Pain farm indicates that the use of a metal detector there will make it possible for us to locate patterns of artifacts that might mark the location of the artillery that were moved from Pointe-du-Hoc before D-Day. However, in the absence of the excavation of these EMI anomalies, we can make no claim that we have at this time collected material evidence as to the location of these elusive guns.

PROPOSALS FOR FURTHER STUDY

In light of the results of work accomplished during 2004, we have set six goals for this third phase of our project. These goals include:

- To continue the measurement and documentation of the German structures on the site. This would include measurement of the Gun Casements 1 and 2 and several of the underground Bunkers.
- To conduct controlled archaeological excavations to determine the depth and nature of the footings beneath each of the major types of German buildings recognized at the site.

- To continue the geophysical mapping of the site using ground-penetrating radar, magnetometry, and metal detection while paying particular attention to the location of possible unexploded ordnance on site.
- To excavate at least four key locations in the German covered trench system identified by archaeological and geophysical means during Phase II. The four locations include: BK1, CT5-CT6, CT9-CT10, and CT14. We intend to accomplish this excavation work using hand archaeological techniques supplemented by limited earth moving equipment.
- To test additional hypotheses about the location of the German trenches generated from the analysis of data collected in 2004.
- To conduct a systematic metal detector survey of fields on the Pain farm, to map the located anomalies with a Total Station and excavate each one. Metal objects of the relevant age and function plotted and excavated in this manner would be collected and recorded. These materials would then be taken to Texas A&M University where they would be cleaned and preserved in the Conservation Laboratory of the TAMU department of anthropology. Following their conservation, these materials would be analyzed, dated, photographed, and recorded. They would then be returned to France for ultimate disposition and display.

NOTE

1. See Ambrose 1994; Historical Division, War Department 1946; Lane 1994; McDonald 2000.

REFERENCES CITED

Ambrose, Stephen E. 1994. *D-Day June 6, 1944: The Climatic Battle of World War II.* Simon & Schuster Inc., New York.

Historical Division, U.S. War Department. 1946. *Small Unit Actions: Pointe du Hoe, 2nd Ranger Battalion, 6 June 1944,* Washington, D.C.

Lane, Ronald. 1994. *Rudder's Rangers.* Ranger Associates, Inc., Altamonte Springs, FL.

McDonald, JoAnna M. 2000. *The Liberation of Pointe du Hoc: The 2nd Rangers at Normandy: June 6–8, 1944.* Rank & File Publications, Redondo Beach, CA.

"For You the War Is Over": Finding the Great Escape Tunnel at Stalag Luft III

Peter Doyle, Lawrence Babits, & Jamie Pringle

STALAG LUFT III was a German POW camp for Allied aviators during WWII. Situated at Zagan, Poland, in what was once eastern Germany, the site is famous for repeated escape attempts, particularly the mass escape of 79 POWs in March 1944. Although made famous by the film *The Great Escape*, little attention has focused on the site. Three tunnels were dug associated with The Great Escape: two ("Tom" and "Harry"—the eventual escape tunnel) were discovered by the Germans; the third ("Dick") was never found. This chapter reports on a one-week investigation of tunnel Dick, its entrance, and present conditions at its location within Hut 122 at the former camp.

Fieldwork consisted of a site survey, geophysical and geological investigations, surface collection, inspection of hut washroom sumps, excavation to reach Dick, and an inspection of the vertical entrance shaft. Despite widespread damage due to post-war looting and recent relic hunting, the site retains significant integrity. Considerable variation was found throughout the site, which has not been surveyed before the current research, and distinct hut types that have not been documented previously were encountered.

Surface collecting in Hut 122's southern end provided evidence of stratigraphy as well as indicating what relic hunters did not take. Significant artifacts associated with the period of POW occupation were noted. Study of the stratigraphy revealed the gray, humic surface soils commented on by the POWs, below which yellow alluvial sands display remarkable uniformity to tens of meters' depth. The shaft and gallery of tunnel Dick were examined during excavation, although the work chamber at the base of the shaft was not entered. Examination of the tunnel showed that it was not backfilled, although most shoring was removed. It has since been refilled naturally. The vertical shaft was filled with rubble but evidence of construction, collapse, shoring, and looting is still present. These finds associated with prisoner activity give valuable insights into POW efforts to continue the war, even after being captured.

The aim of the project was to examine, for the first time archaeologically, the site of the WWII POW camp for Allied aircrew, Stalag Luft III at Sagan, Silesia, now Zagan in Poland. This POW camp is famous for a number of escape attempts that have been described in contemporary and modern accounts[1] and particularly that of Paul Brickhill[2] which was to be the basis for the 1965 film of the same name. The investigation intended to examine the camp, and in particular to trace the remains of an undiscovered tunnel, Dick, which formed part of the planning for The Great Escape, commencing on April 4, 1943.

The project began with a site inspection in May 2003. This involved a simple tape and compass survey, as more detailed surveying techniques were hampered by the density of the forest that has grown back over the site since 1945. Hut locations were keyed to air photographs taken during wartime reconnaissance missions over the site (see figure), and hut remains were identified, comprising mostly the brick and concrete piers that supported the huts, and the foundations and concrete floors of the washrooms; critical, as the entrance to Dick was through the drainage sump in just such a washroom floor. The initial investigation was complicated by the identification of at least two hut configurations; one, with the washroom at the north of the hut; one, with the washroom at the south of the hut. Hut 122 was of the first type; Hut 104, the location of Harry (the actual escape tunnel), was of the second.

Contemporary air photograph, taken in 1944, showing the location of Hut 122 in the North Compound, Stalag Luft III. (Keele University)

The target was Hut 122, the location of tunnel Dick, which was found using the methods described above. The condition of the hut was assessed, and a range of geophysical techniques employed, including a magnetometer and ground-penetrating radar survey to establish that anomalies existed in the vicinity of Hut 122. Based on the May 2003 information, the project was continued with a larger team in September 2003.

Prior to assembling, the team discussed in considerable detail what was likely to be found and why. There were questions relating to whether or not the tunnel, chamber, and access shaft had been backfilled, collapsed, or might still be open. Other questions centered on the movie, *The Great Escape*, and its version of reality versus what we would encounter on the site.

Once on site, it was clear that major alterations had occurred since 1944. The huts were represented only by brick and concrete piers and scattered foundations in a young pine forest. There were numerous post-war fighting positions associated with post-war Polish maneuvers, linear ditches from post-war looting of reusable materials, and extensive relic hunting evidence. Trenches dug by looters were already overgrown but the relic hunting excavations were open, with numerous artifacts scattered about. The ground cover also confused the three former prisoners (self-styled "kriegies"—after the German *Kriegsgenfangener*, or POW) who were brought to see the work. These men included one "manufacturer," Lt. Col. Charles Huppert, one "penguin" (and Great Escaper) Squadron Leader "Jimmy" James, and one digger (who had worked on Dick) General David "Tokyo" Jones. Their presence compounded the eeriness of the project because they created the features we were uncovering.

SITE HISTORY

"For you the war is over." All three former kriegies reported being told this on capture or shortly afterward, but they didn't quit. While the escape attempts had something of a lark about them, they had a strategic and tactical purpose:

> When we arrived, we were marched from town and taken into the camp's headquarters where we were given showers and de-loused. We had our pictures taken, issued dog tags and given a lecture on the camp rules. Then we were marched into the Center Camp. Here the Germans counted us. We were marched to the camp theater and told to sit down.... Col. Spivey welcomed us to the Center Camp and informed us we were still in the Air Force and now we had another mission. ESCAPE - ESCAPE - ESCAPE and do everything to cause our captors hell. Harass the enemy and let them know they had a very large and active bear by the tail. By carrying out our duties, if we could do them with a vicious ribald sense of humor, it became more that [sic] a duty; it became a very dangerous game entered with fiendish glee.[3]

> There was more to it than just tweaking the German's nose: Wings [Wing Commander Day, Senior British Officer] said, "it's an operational war. Don't forget that. It isn't just a question of getting a few people home. It's just as important to mess the Goons about. Most of the boys will be caught anyway, but if we get a good team out there'll be a flap all over Germany, and we'll have done something useful ... more useful than getting a few back home."[4]

The official view was that escape was a matter of duty. Escaped POWs could bring back useful information. More importantly, escapes tied up soldiers as guards, and where more escapes occurred, there were more guards. "When any major escape took place tens of thousands of extra troops were turned out all over the country."[5] Brickhill claimed that over 5,000,000 Germans were mobilized to capture the Great Escape POWs.[6]

The entire tunneling exercises were directed toward winning the war, even if they had no weapons and were under guard. What the kriegies did was remarkable and that might be why their story is so interesting and still being told.

By December 1939, the Germans differentiated between air force prisoners and other arms. The Luftwaffe ran their own POW camps for captured airmen. Between May 1942 and March 1943, at least 60 tunnels were begun in the various camps.[7] Eventually, a great many escapers ended up at Sagan, where they were placed in the East Compound—itself a hotbed of escaping activity.[8]

The first prisoners were moved into a new compound of Stalag Luft III— North Compound—on March 23, 1943. By then, over 200 tunnels had been attempted from air force POW camps all over Germany, and this new compound was meant to be secure.[9] In order to expedite North Compound construction, POWs were allowed to clear some of the area of tree stumps; the time was also spent measuring distances, inspecting plans, and preparing escape equipment for the move. A similar expansion occurred during the late fall of 1944 when the South Compound and later West Compound was erected, the first to hold largely American POWs. Stalag Luft III was evacuated largely in January 1945 with the advance of the Red Army, but some POWs were too weak or sick to move.

Escape attempts began as soon as the first POWs arrived. Once North Compound was occupied, all attempts came under the control of the X organization—a finely tuned escape organization run by the resourceful Roger Bushell.[10] Efforts were made to coordinate escapes, provide false documents, civilian clothing, and survival gear.[11] During 1944, while small-scale attempts did occur, the major effort was devoted to simultaneously digging three tunnels—code-named Tom, Dick, and Harry (see table)—for a major breakout.

The "Great Escape" Tunnels (After James 1983: Appendix C; and Flockhart n.d)

Tunnel	Depth/ length (approx.)	Bed boards for shoring (approx. no)	"Klim" tins for air line (approx. no)	Tons of sand removed (approx.)	Fate
"Tom"	25ft/220ft	1500	500	70 tons	Discovered Sept. 8, 1944
"Dick"	25ft/60ft, 42ft unfilled	500	150	30 tons	Undiscovered/ storage and sand dispersal tunnel
"Harry"	25ft/365ft	2000	750	130 tons	Operated March 24/25, 1944

One tunnel, Tom, dug westward, was discovered and blown up. Dick, which was also dug westward, was terminated when West Compound construction began. Continuing the tunnel would have added much too long a distance. Harry, the third tunnel, was used for The Great Escape on March 24/25, 1944. Although 200 POWs were prepared to go out, only 79 actually escaped. Fifty were captured and executed. Another 26 were put back into various camps, including Stalag Luft III, and Sachsenhausen Concentration Camp. Three men made it "home" to Allied territory.[12]

After the camp was evacuated in January 1945, Soviet troops apparently utilized the camp as a holding area for German POWs prior to shipping them further east. After May 1945, looting occurred after the last German prisoners were removed to the east. This recycling of building materials was extensive. None of the huts, except their piers and washroom floors, survive. Stoves were apparently broken down into constituent elements and removed, although many tiles and some occasional iron fittings are still present within hut parameters. Electrical materials are totally gone. The wooden fabric of the huts appears to have been removed as well since very few fasteners were noted. It is probable that all doors, shutters, and any other usable and/or salable materials were taken.

SITE CONDITION

The huts have vanished but their broken piers and washroom floors remained. Given the German propensity for order, it was possible to relocate most features described in the literature. A map view of the surveyed camp is shown in the figure—the first time the camp had been surveyed since German engineers laid it out during WW II. Now, the entire camp is covered with young fir trees, pockmarked with trenches, fox holes, tank emplacements, and relic hunter excavations.

Looting after the camp was abandoned has left its mark as well. There are shallow, linear depressions running across the site. These trenches are the trace of wastewater drainage pipes from the huts to a central collecting point, the abort, from which wastes were collected by the Germans in trucks the prisoners called "honey wagons." Post-war looters followed the terra cotta drainpipes, removed them, and put them to use elsewhere. The sump area in Hut 122 was damaged in this way and was poorly preserved. A possible "crown-hole" was sited in the washroom's center and eastern half, suggesting void collapse.

Relic hunting has severely impacted the archaeological context of cultural material in the North Compound. There are so many holes that they form, in many cases, virtually continuous excavations inside the line of hut piers. While this activity disturbs in situ context, artifacts are removed and, more importantly, much material is exposed but left to rust and decay on the

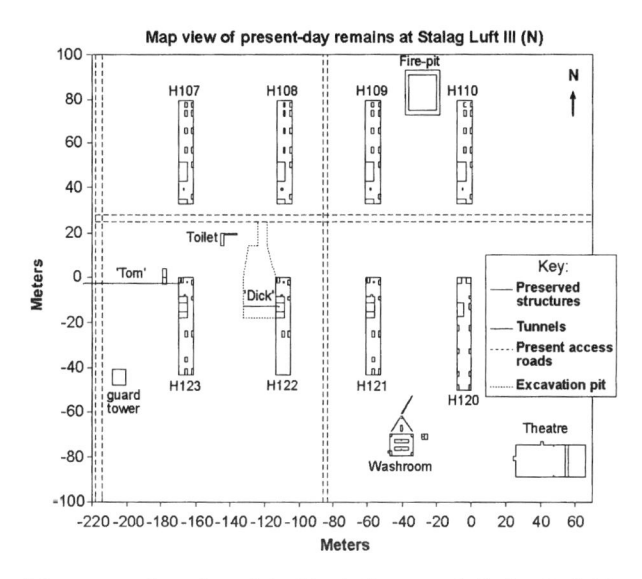

Map view of the surveyed section of the North Compound, Stalag Luft III.

surface. None of this material has been recorded except for the artifacts immediately south of Hut 122's washroom. An assessment of the material remaining suggests that only militaria (buttons, badges, identification tags, and military-marked china) are being kept by the relic hunters. The rest is disturbed and left behind, with others periodically finding their way into the nearby POW museum. Interviews with relic hunters on site suggest that a large amount of military uniforms and other material was gathered together and burnt in pits on site.

About midway in Hut 122's long axis, heavy disturbance by relic hunters suggested that secondary excavation to identify depths and what was left behind might prove fruitful. Among the recovered items was a possible "escape kit." This consists of the rotted, broken remains of an attaché case, bound with wire, which was uncovered in disturbed soil. Among the contents noted were: a toothbrush (marked "US Army") and part of a toothbrush case, a blue glass marble, a mess tin pan, a broken tureen, book fragments (in German), a blue (possibly civilian) coat, with cloth-covered blue civilian buttons, a skein of thread, and a watercolor paint set. Other artifacts from this excavation included: firebricks—from the Saxon town of Colditz, also site of a famous "escaping" POW camp; Luftwaffe marked china; and miscellaneous domestic items, most probably associated with the post-evacuation scavenging of the site. Fragments of phonograph records were also found, items important to the escapers.

Each compass started as a piece of Bakelite phonograph record. The records were cracked into small pieces about 3 inches across, and the pieces were heated over a candle until they became malleable. The Bakelite was

404   FIELDS OF CONFLICT

then placed over an 1¼-inch hole in a board and pushed into the hole with a wooden peg. A metal disk at the bottom of the hole imprinted the inscription "Made in Stalag Luft III–Pat. Pend" neatly on the bottom.[13]

Five hundred compasses, using magnetized needles, had been completed by March 1944.[14]

GEOPHYSICAL INVESTIGATIONS

Prior to disturbing the site, geophysical investigations were carried out around Hut 122 and the projected tunnel area (see figure). A magnetometer was used even though POWs had limited access to metallic objects,[15] as it was thought

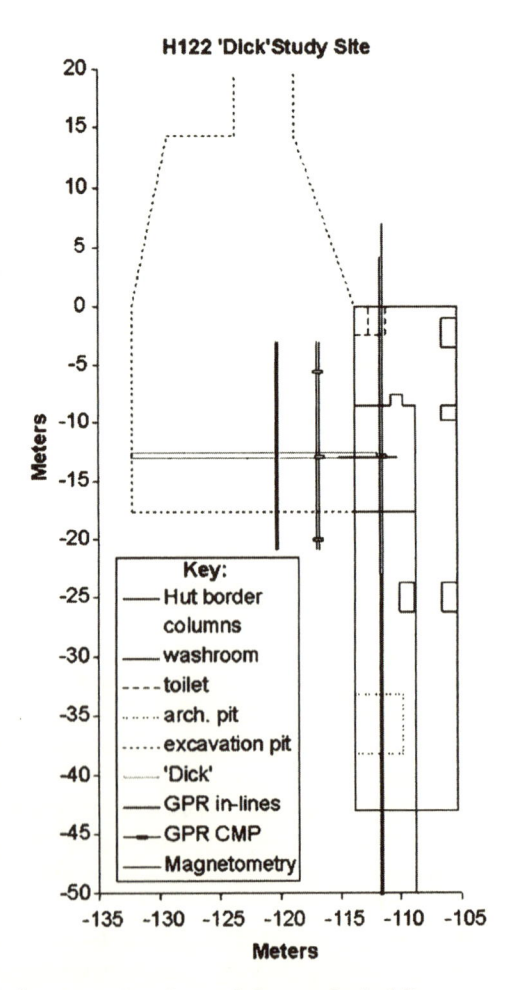

Plan of Hut 122, the excavation site, and the geophysical lines.

that, if any escape or tunnelling gear were still located in the tunnel or storage chamber, there might be enough metal to show up in a magnetometer survey. A proton precession magnetometer was used to acquire magnetic anomaly data by measuring the total earth's magnetic field at a specified sampling point. Variations, or anomalies, in magnetic intensity, can be due to buried ferrous material such as iron objects, pipes, and the like.

Magnetic data were collected along four north-south lines (see figure). One east-west cross-line dataset was also obtained over the supposed entrance shaft. After results were corrected for time and drift, they were plotted and contoured over the study area. Little variation observed around the entrance shaft, but a significant bi-polar anomaly was observed 33 m south of Hut 122's northern end at a depth of 45 meters. The anomaly's depth and character suggested a metallic object approximately 0.5 m in diameter. This was not further investigated by excavation but may have triggered the widespread and deep excavations by relic hunters in Hut 122's middle section.

During excavation of the access track to reach the tunnel, at least one iron fuel drum was encountered at a depth of circa 3 meters. Its size, 0.6 m × 1.3 m, is fairly close to the anomaly's projected size, although other potential targets could have been a stove, or unexploded ordnance.

Ground-penetrating radar (GPR) was used because the tunnels temporarily created a break in the subsurface soils that might be detected. GPR uses very high frequency (MHz) electromagnetic waves to record high-resolution subsurface imagery. GPR is increasingly used for archaeological investigations (Baker et al. 1997), as it rapidly produces high-resolution, 2D subsurface profiles that can be viewed directly during acquisition.

It was hoped that angular wooden supports used for shoring the tunnel might still be intact, and therefore imaged by the GPR. However, Brickhill[16] stated that "Dick was full now to the base of the shaft" with sand removed from "Tom," and that tunnelers were "also taking out the box frames and rails" when Dick's excavation was terminated. Alternatively, estimates by Flockhart,[17] himself a kriegie in Stalag Luft III, suggest that the tunnel may have been filled to at least 40 of its 60-feet length. If this were true, then it could be difficult to differentiate refilled tunnel sand from the background sand.

One GPR profile in-line is shown in the next figure. Note that sedimentary features were observed on the profile, particularly the strong, coherent planar reflectors and inclined sets of related reflectors. These can be correlated to observed features in the excavated pit, interpreted as planar, iron-rich hard pans, and inclined, fluvial sand deposits, respectively. An interpreted disturbance that corresponds to pre-survey estimates of the tunnel's location is also visible. Assuming the tunnel was aligned due west from the entrance shaft, the target reflection events should occur at ~10 m on the in-lines where a bright anomaly is seen at the correct depth.

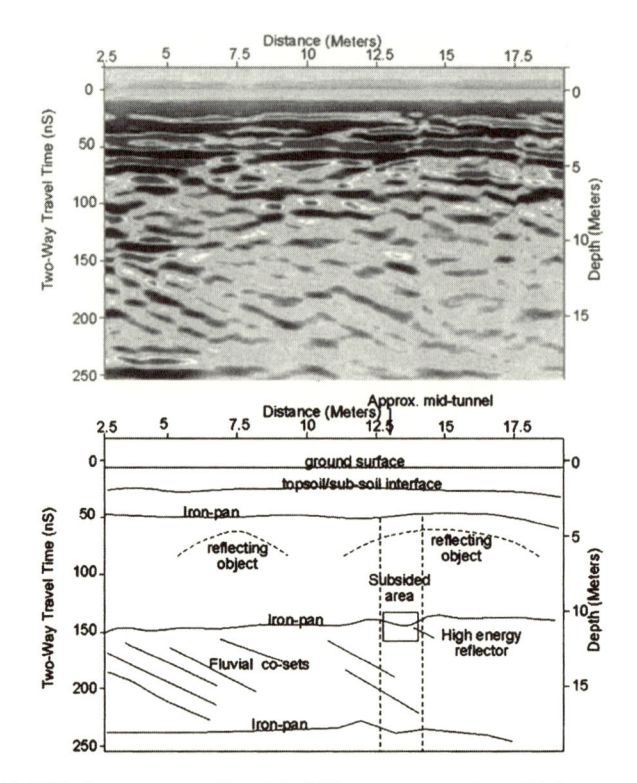

(a) GPR 50 MHz frequency profile with 0.25-m trace spacing; (b) Interpretation from in-line 2, 6.5 m west of Hut 122 perimeter

ENTRANCE SHAFT

The entrance to Dick was through a drain sump in Hut 122's washroom floor (see figure). Less was known about Dick's entrance than the other two tunnels, perhaps because it was never found.[18] Manuscript accounts are closer to the truth.

"In the floor of the washroom there was an iron grating covering a concrete drain 18 inches square and two feet deep. Water ran into this from the north and south sides, and the drainpipe was on the west side. The grating was taken updra, the water baled out, and the east side chipped away and replaced with a concrete slab which could be slid up and down."[19]

Hut 122's sump was damaged by pipe removal sometime after the German evacuation of the camp in January 1945. Based on the complete example in Hut 123 each sump was situated approximately center of the washroom floor, and had a 47-cm-square section, 80 cm deep, and was concrete-rendered over brick. North and south faces of the sump had open-draining 10-cm-diameter terra cotta pipes, while the east face had a non-return pipe. The west face of

View of entrance shaft through sump, showing the concrete "sill" (under the left hand of J. Pringle, who is standing on the undisturbed sand of the shaft wall).

the sump was blank. Excavation of the well-preserved sump in Hut 123 revealed a number of artifacts, including underwear/pyjama buttons, a nail brush, comb, small bones, and other miscellaneous items consistent with its use.

In Hut 122 the square section of the sump was largely destroyed, with an immature tree growing in its place, and the possibility of subsurface collapse into the shaft of Dick was indicated by a conical crown-hole. The site of the sump in Hut 122 was filled with brick, concrete, and terra cotta pipe debris. Given the debris still in the mottled soil, the shaft was probably open when the terra cotta drainpipes were removed. If this were the case, then it is likely that the robbers filled part of the shaft, perhaps not knowing it was there. It is also possible that they entered the shaft and the chamber. Given the unstable nature of the soil, it is more likely that rubble and surrounding matrix soil fell down the shaft while the drainpipes were salvaged and that more collapsed into the shaft later.

A north-south oriented "sill" of concrete was found below the bottom of the sump on the east side that had been constructed by the kriegies (see figure). Between the sump floor and the sill's rounded top, there was a groove at least 4 cm wide to accept the door slab. There was gray clay in the groove, especially at the northern end. The sill sits on two narrow red bricks placed below the level of the sump floor. General Jones—himself a digger on Dick—mentioned that the rounded concrete cast of the sump was a "slipping sill" that the diggers slid over when entering the shaft.

At about 84 cm below datum, an east-west break between darker and lighter soils appeared perpendicular to the southern edge of the sump. There was slightly mottled yellow sand south of the darker disturbed soil. At 90 cm below datum, the shaft was still disturbed soil.

The "door slab" was found in the upper reaches of the pipe robbing fill. This is constructed of cast concrete, the cement stolen by the POWs from material "left lying around the compound by workmen, and examination of it showed admixture of sand/fine gravel aggregate—of which there is an abundant amount in the camp. The concrete work was done by Polish POWs: Gotowski, Kozlowski and Minckiewicz, all Flight Lieutenants with the RAF."[20] The nature of the casting is indicated by impressions of the timber used to make the mould. The slab measures 47.5 cm, and 65.5 cm long, and 4 cm thick. There are two 4-cm-long, and irregular notches on one face (see figure). These are 1 cm wide and 3 cm deep and 10 cm from one end, and 10 cm in from the edge. There is a slight abrasion on the slab's end. On the width edge, there are two round depressions 5 mm in diameter, possibly a result of the casting.

The entrance slab to "Dick" and its lifting hook.

An iron hook with an eye at one end was found in the disturbed fill. This corroded object was about 5 mm thick and 26 cm long. The diameter of the eye was 4.5 cm by 4 cm. The hook end fit into the notches on the slab and the hook's angle fit into a hole in the slab's notch (see figure). It was probably used to pull up the slab door allowing access to the shaft, the implication being that there was a matching hook for the other hole, and abrasion marks on the slab are consistent with this interpretation.

During the archaeological investigation, the shaft was excavated by hand. Removal of brick, concrete, and pipe debris was followed by shovel excavation to a depth of 70 cm below a datum established on the side of the sump. Below 70 cm, trowel excavation was used because the southern third of the excavation was light-colored soil. There was a mottled zone between apparently sterile yellow sand and the darker fill. What was first interpreted as sterile sand was not. It had been backfilled.

> Crump left 'Harry' to help Floody dig the workshops at the base of 'Dick.' They were down there one day with Canton shoring the pumping chamber when they heard a crack in the shaft and Canton looked up and saw a broken bed board sticking out of the frame about twenty-five feet up. Sand was pouring through the gaps, and, as he shielded his eyes from the cascade, there was a rending sound up there; a frame burst out with the pressure behind it, and as the sand crashed down, the shaft framework began to twist and break up.
>
> By some miracle the ladder held, and Canton was going up it like a rocket with the other two rights behind. Canton and Crump shot out of the top and turned to grab Floody just in time. The sand had reached his waist and he was pinned and couldn't heave himself any higher while the sand mounted.... 'Dick's' shaft was full to just below the top.[21]

These two paragraphs help explain some of what we found while excavating Dick's shaft. The soil staining marking the shoring had light-colored, disturbed sand outside it. Inside the wooden soil stain, there was much darker, gray soil with rubble that filled the shaft. The sand outside the wood stain was somewhat disturbed, apparently as a result of the collapse described above. When excavation terminated, the shaft's soil stain was 22 × 25.5 inches. Both Jimmy James and Davy Jones said it was too narrow. This agrees with our findings because we have not yet found the northern, or eastern, edge of the shaft. These edges do not appear in the wall profiles of our excavation.

The southeastern sump corner was detached from the in situ sump wall. Concrete lining indicated where the southern terra cotta drain tile passed through the sump wall. The grooves and ridges in the concrete matched between the loose brick segment with the groove and the intact segment still forming part of the sump. The bricks had been rabbetted out to create a vertical groove about 4 cm wide. The door slab slid into this slot. It now appears that the entire eastern wall of the sump was altered by removing it, then extending the cut into the inner faces of both the north and south walls of the sump. In the northern edge at the bottom, we found gray clay ("putty") that may have been used to seal off the slab and keep it from leaking.

Several artifacts were recovered while excavating the shaft fill, back fill, and the Hut 122 sump, which included a mutton fat lamp, composed of a 6-cm-diameter by 4-cm-deep tin with a 4 mm-thick wire handle. Jimmy James and Charles Huppert believed it to be a cheese tin from a Red Cross parcel, and evidence of its use was a charred wick, probably made from pyjama cord, which would have been dipped in fat skimmed from the ration soup.

This was found associated with a candle 1.2 cm diameter and about 8 cm long. Charles Huppert noted that it was unlikely any kriegie made it; it had to have been obtained from the Germans. Aluminium-jacketed electrical cable was also found, along with a porcelain lamp holder—again Charles Huppert confirmed that this was of the type used in the huts, and both the lamp and the wire had been stolen (800 feet of wire was eventually taken by the prisoners,[22] and reused by the kriegies in the tunnel). Opal lamp glass fragments were also found, some suggesting that the lamp had been partly painted black—presumably to prevent too much light from shining out of the shaft. Together the association of lighting equipment suggests the need to illuminate the top of the shaft. The electrical lights obviously tapped into the camp's supply; the fat lamp and candle were there to provide light during periodic blackouts.

Three rubber artifacts were found that included two fragments from an unworn boot heel, which had been cut to provide a square that could be trimmed further. Former Stalag Luft III Kriegie Alan Bryent recalls having to surrender his boot heels to the X organization on first arriving at the camp, so that they could be used in the manufacturing of "official" stamps for escape papers. Not directly associated with the cut boot heel was a thinner, circular rubber fragment. The rubber disk was smooth and a Wehrmacht eagle had been carefully incised into one side in the negative.

> All the phony documents were endorsed by official Nazi stamps, bearing the eagle and swastika and the titles and signatures of various police branches. Tim [Walenn] used to paint the designs on rubber boot heels, and Al Hake, the compass maker, carved them out with bits of razor blade.[23]

The presence of these two elements directly associated with forging activity in Dick relates in all probability to its use as a store, particularly for the stamps themselves, a most valuable commodity,[24] and this was to continue even after The Great Escape.

TUNNEL GALLERY

Excavation to reach the tunnel gallery itself commenced with tree removal, then mechanical excavation west of Hut 122. This area was known to contain only gardens cultivated by the prisoners, and visible on the contemporary air photos. Ultimately over 2,000 cubic meters of sand was removed to reach the tunnel, which was piled and used to backfill the excavation after the project terminated.

Shovel schnitting uncovered tunnel remains after mechanical excavation was halted, when timbers and uniform fragments were raised by the excavator at a depth of around 30 feet, in line with expectations (see table on page 401). There were two parallel dark stains, each with a slightly mottled interface on the outside and a slightly different soil color between them with less mottling (see figure). The darker soil/wood stains were 23 inches apart and each was about one inch thick. This approximates the thickness of the bed board shoring. There was a distinct contrast with the undisturbed geology outside the wood stains, which show cross-laminations to the north of the stain consistent with the original deposition, which are interrupted by the wood stain. As was to be expected from all accounts, the sands were bright in color (Munsell 2.5Y8/4) in contrast with the surface, gray humic layer. The tunnel sand showed upwardly fining, coarse to medium sand, with some coarser pebbles, mostly quartz, that would have impeded the diggers.

The tunnel gallery, showing the wood stains and "Klim" tin air line.

The wood stains (Munsell 10YR2/1) were clearly the remnants of the tunnel framing that locked in the shoring. We uncovered a number of frames that extended higher than the wall shoring. These were spaced at 2 feet intervals. At one of these, we found clear evidence of a mortise on the lower portions. This would have taken the tenon from the vertical side support, and which matched perfectly a mock-up frame pre-prepared from dimensions given by Flockhart.[25] The spacing suggests that these are the remnants of the square frames against which the bed boards were braced. The mortise and tenon locked the boards together against the pressure of the sand.

Excavation at various frames cut into the tunnel floor to a depth of ca. 20 cm. The profile shows that the horizontal (floor) board rests over a "Klim" tin (powdered milk cans from Red Cross parcels) on its southern end (see figure). Above the floorboard, the overhead frame has collapsed down toward the floorboard without breaking, but rather bending to the pressure of the overburden. This suggests that there was nothing between top and bottom frames. As they bent under pressure, sand spilled down between top and bottom frames.

Shoring was represented irregularly by a few remaining bottom side boards on the northern tunnel edge. These were horizontal and ran parallel to the tunnel axis. The boards were 4 inches wide (high, as it was vertically oriented). The upper shoring boards were missing. Further east, about 20–25 feet (16–18 meters) from the shaft, the northern shoring extended at least three boards high.

Rusty soil stains (Munsell 10YR8/7) were encountered in the tunnel. These were Klim cans modified to serve as air pipes and lamps. From 40 feet (13 meters) west of the shaft, all pipe tins were on the south side. East of that point, few tins were noted, but at 30 feet (9 meters) west of the shaft the Klim can pipes were in the tunnel center. Five meters closer to the hut, they were on the north side. The Klim can piping seemed intact from the chamber westward to about 15–20 feet beyond the hut edge. Brickhill precisely described the piping we found in rusted condition:

> The tins were about four inches in diameter, and the engineers peeled off the bottoms, leaving a clean metal cylinder. Where the lids had fitted, the tins were a shade smaller in circumference, and this section fitted very neatly into the base of the next tin. The joint was wrapped tightly with paper and was strong and airtight enough because once the pipe lines were laid they were never touched. They made yards and yards of the piping and smuggled it down the shafts.[26]

Other accounts explained why these cans were not removed:

> "I guess there's a blockage in the air line somewhere," Floody said gloomily. There was nothing to do but unearth the line till they found the damage—the stickiest job possible because it meant reefing up the floor boards with the risk of the frames above sinking and starting dangerous falls.[27]

The differences in pipe location from north side to center tunnel seem to coincide with structural changes at the 30 foot mark.

> When each tunnel was about thirty feet long, Floody changed the shoring system to conserve wood. Instead of solid framing all the way, they spaced the frames about a foot apart and laid boards over the tops.[28]

Aside from the decayed wood frames and shoring, few artifacts were encountered except recycled Klim cans. These other artifacts included a grommet, some hair in one can, fragmentary lamps, and a little piece of cellophane. The cellophane was probably a cigarette package pull tab. Charles Huppert said its color suggested Chesterfield or Camel brands. This little fragment was found in the tunnel's floor. One man reported that men smoked in Harry's halfway houses,[29] and it is possible that this pull tab was moved along during tunnelling. The lamp fragments were about 12 feet apart.

The scale of the POW effort can be seen in the amount of work it took to reach the tunnel. About 2,000 cubic meters, equalling 13,000 tons, were removed by mechanical excavation in three days. The POWs' effort, operating with more time and much smaller equipment, was calculated during escape activities.

> The amount of work done by the dispersal organization can best be given in figures. Sand which came out of the tunnels was frequently weighed on an accurate

set of German scales, and it was found that twenty cubic feet weighed one ton. Up to the time that "Tom" was discovered 166 tons of sand was disposed of in four and a half months. Since the average load carried was approximately sixteen pounds, this meant in round figures some eighteen thousand individual journeys on the part of the carriers and corresponded to rather more than three feet of tunnel per day. The record rate of dispersal was 3,600 pounds of sand—a ton and a half—in one hour.[30]

CONCLUSIONS

A great deal was accomplished in a week. We found the tunnel Dick and recorded details about its construction that differ from documentary materials. We found the Klim can air pipe, three types of lamp, hair, a grommet, and a cellophane pull strip from a cigarette packet. We found the shaft and learned it was much bigger than thought. We worked out how the shaft was accessed through the sump because we found the slab door, the hook that pulled the slab up, cut bricks that provided a rabbet for the slab, and the sill over which tunnellers entered the shaft. Associated with the shaft were boot heel fragments, a rubber stamp, lamp, and candle. I am not convinced that the lightbulb socket and the glass globe were actually used as part of the escape effort.

The prisoners tested how far sounds from digging carried. At 25 feet, they could hear the noise. At 28–29 feet, they could no longer hear any noise, so they stopped going deeper at 30 feet. While backfillng the vertical shaft excavation, we heard the bricks and stones hitting the shaft fill. This was a vertical distance of about 20 feet and a horizontal distance of over 15 feet.

The site needs protection from relic hunters, tourists, and the Polish Army. Relic hunters have had free access to the site for several years and the resultant damage to structural (housing) features was readily apparent. More damaging is the disturbance to in situ material that might shed light on the huts' internal divisions and POW activities in the various rooms. Some artifact concentrations suggested rather specific manufacturing activity. The distribution of stove tiles suggests different styles of stoves in certain rooms.

Tourists also pick up materials, in particular Luftwaffe ceramics. While not used by the Allied POWs, the ceramics apparently do relate to the camp activity, and were probably removed from the German quarters and scattered in the post-liberation phase. Other materials are collected, moved around, and some kept by tourists, without recording precisely where these artifacts came from.

Finally, the Polish Army runs training exercises over the site. As part of this activity, fighting positions, hull-down tank pits, and trenches are dug. These excavations have, in some places, adversely impacted the hut remains. However, the Poles have little historical context for the prison camp's remains because they were not participants. The camp was built in German

Silesia, garrisoned by Germans, and then by Soviets, to hold Allied prisoners of war captured by the Germans, and then Germans captured by the Soviets. The present-day local population has little interest in the site because it helps few Poles. However, knowledge of the Polish contribution to the Great Escape may change this attitude.

Excavations were designed to avoid disturbing in situ materials. In Hut 122's southern end, surface collection, followed by limited excavation, was conducted in disturbed areas. The tunnel's vertical shaft was heavily impacted by looters who dug through the concrete floor to recover terra cotta drainpipes. The horizontal tunnel excavation took place away from the hut piers, in an open area reported to have been prisoners' gardens.

Additional excavation was halted after much discussion. We did it for safety reasons, but those included the archaeology. If we encountered the chamber, there would be no time to record it. We were not there to destroy the site but to document it. Whether it was full or empty, it made no difference, we'd damage the archaeological context trying to find, observe, and record the chamber.

ACKNOWLEDGMENTS

The work conducted in September 2003 was supported by Windfall Films, a production company that made a documentary screened in the U.S. and UK about the site and our archaeological work. The authors would like to thank the producer/director Mark Radice, for his support and understanding of the work, as well as David Dugan (executive producer), Jamie Lockhead (assistant producer), and Konrad Jankowski (interpreter). We also recognize the fieldwork of Daniel Phillips and Gabriel Moshenska, undergraduates at UCL, who recorded the profiles and artifacts on site. Nigel Cassidy at Keel helped with the geophysical interpretations. At East Carolina University, Matthew DeFilice inked drawings and scanned slides into the computer to help make this presentation possible. Many of the artifacts recovered, the property of the Museum of Allied Prisoners of War and Martyrology at Zagan, have been on loan display at the *Great Escapes* exhibit at the Imperial War Museum, London, during 2004–2005.

NOTES

1. Williams 1945, 1949; Crawley 1956; James 1983; Durand 1988; Vance 2000; Gill 2002.
2. Brickhill 1950.
3. Brown n.d.:145.
4. Brickhill 1950:142.

5. Crawley 1956:8–9.
6. Brickhill 1950:196.
7. Crawley 1956:126.
8. Flockhart n.d., Williams 1945, 1949.
9. Crawley 1956:148 and 156.
10. Brickhill 1950:29–33.
11. Flockhart n.d.:13–20.
12. James 1983, Brickhill 1950.
13. Vance 2000:165.
14. Flockhart n.d.:19.
15. Flockhart n.d., Brickhill 1950.
16. Brickhill 1950:104.
17. Flockhart n.d.:35.
18. Brickhill 1950:39–42, Crawley 1956:159–16.
19. Flockhart n.d.: 28, see also Nelson n.d.:2.
20. Flockhart n.d.: 28 and 37.
21. Flockhart n.d.: 28, Brickhill 1950.
22. Flockhart n.d.:37.
23. Brickhill 1950:106.
24. Vance 2002:206.
25. Flockhart n.d.: 29.
26. Brickhill 1950:54.
27. Brickhill 1950:123–24.
28. Brickhill 1950:81.
29. Crawley 1956:177.
30. Crawley 1956:174.

REFERENCES CITED

Baker, J. A., N. L. Anderson, and P. J. Pilles. 1997. Ground Penetrating Radar Investigations in Support of Archaeological Investigations. *Computers & Geosciences* 23:1093–1099.

Brickhill, Paul. 1950. *The Great Escape.* Fawcett Publications, Greenwich, CT.

Brown, Walter Sheirl. n.d. Recollection of Walter Sheirl Brown. In Arnold Wright, *From Out of the Blue.* Privately published, printed by Palmer Binding Systems, Tulsa, OK.

Crawley, Aidan. 1956. *Escape from Germany A History of R.A.F. Escapes During the War.* Simon & Schuster, New York.

Durand, Arthur A. 1988. *Stalag Luft III.* Louisiana State University Press, Baton Rouge, LA.

Flockhart, C. B. n.d. *A Typescript History of Stalag Luft III (Sagan), Air Force Personnel, April 1942–January 1945.* Unpublished manuscript, RAF Museum Archives, RAF Museum, London. (RAFM B37992).

Gill, Anton. 2002. *The Great Escape.* Review, London.

Harsh, George. 1950. Introduction. In Paul Brickhill, *The Great Escape.* Fawcett Publications, Greenwich, CT.

James, B. A. "Jimmy." 1983. *Moonless Night.* William Kimber, London.

Nelson, Bob. n.d. *Tom, Dick and Harry of Stalag Luft III*. Unpublished typescript, Imperial War Museum, London (IWM 84/45/1).
Nelson, Craig. 2002. *The First Heroes*. Corgi Books, London.
Vance, Jonathan F. 2000. *A Gallant Company. The True Story of* the Great Escape. Ibooks, New York.
Williams, Eric. 1945. *Goon in the Block*. Jonathan Cape, London.
Williams, Eric. 1949. *The Wooden Horse*. Collins, London.
Wright, Arnold. n.d. *From Out of the Blue*. Privately published, printed by Palmer Binding Systems, Tulsa, OK.

Hill 209: The Last Stand of Operation Manchu, Korea

Jay Silverstein, John Byrd, & Lyle Otineru

TO THE WORLD, battlefields represent focal points of international conflict where the course of history was decided. On a national level, battlefields take on meaning as places of pride and communal identity, where the sacrifice and courage of those who fought become symbols of duty to the state and of cultural solidarity. Our job at the Joint POW/MIA Accounting Command (JPAC) stems from the latter rather than the former. Our interest in the Korean War battlefield of Hill 209 comes not from an effort to identify and preserve a battlefield but to search for the remains of soldiers lost during the engagement; an investigation aimed at recovery rather than reconstruction. Although ancillary to our primary purpose, the techniques of topographical analysis, historical research, forensic anthropology, and archaeological excavation provide significant data related to fields of battle. In finding the missing in action, we inevitably reconstruct the course of a skirmish and fill in the blind spots of history, one soldier at a time.

In this chapter we outline the process surrounding the recovery and identification of Second Lieutenant Edmund J. Lilly III, one of the more than 8,000 American MIAs in Korea. We start by describing the known details of the battle, followed by the history of recovery efforts on the hill and our plan for future archaeological work.

THE BATTLE OF HILL 209

The Korean War began on Sunday, June 25th, 1950, at 0400. By the 28th of June, Seoul had fallen and the army of the Republic of Korea (ROK) was shattered. For the next month UN forces, consisting of the hastily assembled and deployed U.S. Eighth Army, along with determined ROK soldiers fought a delaying action against the onslaught of the North Korean People's Army (NKPA). Spearheaded by 150 Soviet-built T-34 tanks, backed by concentrations of artillery, the NKPA drove through the demoralized defenders, inflicting 76,000 casualties, the vast majority of which were ROK. United Nations Command (UNC) forces were rapidly herded back some 300 km toward the southeast corner of Korean Peninsula where the UNC faced the prospect of a Dunkirk-like evacuation from the port of Pusan (see figure).

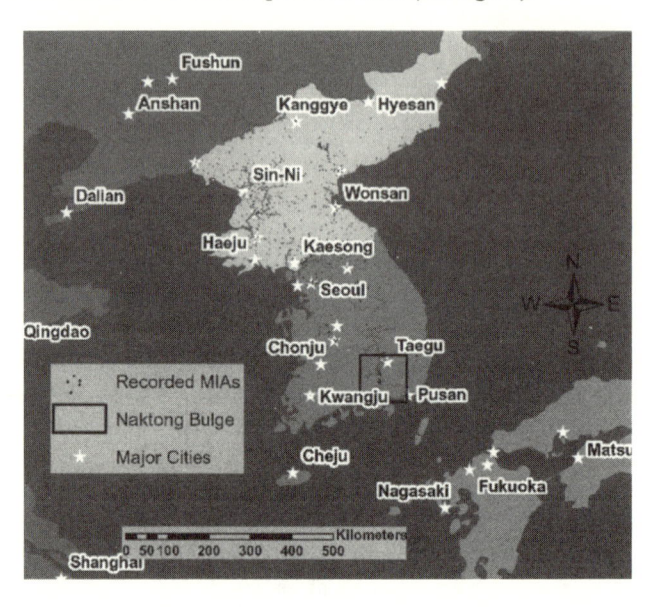

Map of North and South Korea, showing MIA locations and Naktong Bulge.

The UN, however, had made good use of July, throwing reinforcements into the peninsula at an impressive rate. On August 4, 1950, the UN drew a line that had to be held at all costs. The Pusan Perimeter, defined in the west by the Naktong River and by rugged mountains to the north, was the last best defense before retreating to the coast. The front was now small enough that a continuous line with flanks anchored on the sea and internal lines of communication could be formed. The bulwark of the perimeter was the city of Taegu, but some of the most intense fighting would be south of there. The Pusan Perimeter finally offered a chance to negate the NKPA proclivity to flow around strong points, infiltrating lines, ambushing reinforcements, and wreaking havoc among support operations.[1]

By the end of August the NKPA, although now outnumbered by the UNC, still held the strategic initiative and the option of choosing the time and place of attack. The defensive perimeter had a few vulnerable points, one being a westward bulge in the Naktong River just west of the town of Yeong San. If the NKPA could take Yeong San they would cut the vital road and rail network that supported the perimeter. The best approach to Yeong San was across the Naktong River, and the best places for an assault across the river were two large bulges in the river that offered a chance to flank the defenders. This area became known as the Naktong Bulge.

UNC reconnaissance patrols across the river reported exceptional troop and armor movement and eventually confirmed the presence of the North Korean 9th Infantry Division HQ, approximately 2 miles west of the river. The 2nd Infantry Division assembled a company-sized raid of about 200 men for the night of August 31. The majority of the raiding force was made up of elements of the 9th Infantry Regiment. The 9th Infantry, who carried the *nom de guerre* of the Manchu Raiders from their service during the Boxer Rebellion, lent their name to the ill-fated Operation Manchu. Their objective was to disrupt NKPA communications, and to take prisoners for interrogation. Company B formed the guard on their southern flank, setting up on Hill 311, southeast of Hill 209. The assault force consisted of E Company along with light machine guns from H Company; the 2nd Engineer Combat Battalion would take Task Force Manchu across the river at the Pakjin Ferry. Heavy weapons companies D and H furnished heavy machine guns, 81-mm mortars, and 75-mm recoilless rifles for support fire (see figure).

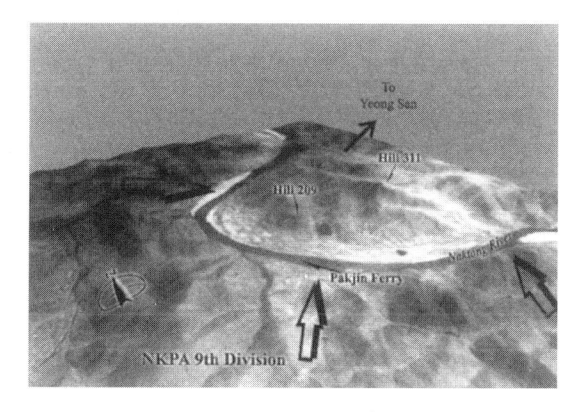

Operation Manchu.

Sometime after dark on August 31st, 1st Lieutenants Charles I. Caldwell and Edward Schmitt, in command of D and H Company respectively, brought their heavy weapons to the base of the southwestern spur of Pakjin Hill, which carried the military designation of Hill 209. The Regimental Commander, Colonel Hill, moved up with 4.2-inch mortars, and his men began preparing positions at the base of the hill while Caldwell and Schmitt took their section leaders up the hill to search out locations for weapons emplacements. E Company was preparing to move out from the rear near Yeong San when, at 2100, the North Korean 9th Infantry Division launched a major offensive. From 2300 to 0100 a heavy artillery barrage along the 9th Infantry's sector of the Naktong River covered the North Korean river crossing. NKPA advanced units waded across, catching the mortars and most of D and H

Company by surprise. At about midnight, as the Division HQ called off Operation Manchu, Colonel Hill fell back.

Sometime around 0200 the enemy stormed Hill 311, driving B Company off and effectively isolating the surviving elements of Task Force Manchu on Hill 209. Through the night stragglers from Companies D, H, B, and the mortar companies gathered on the hill, bringing the total complement of defenders to 65 to 75 soldiers, including five officers. First Lieutenant Schmitt took command and organized a perimeter defense using staggered foxholes to form a skirmish line around the hill with a command and aid post in the center.

Schmitt, a veteran of World War II and with extensive service in Korea, had a reputation as a no-nonsense and effective leader. Two weeks prior, Schmitt had come among some of his men who sat staring at a disabled T-34 tank stymied by recalcitrant NKPA holed up inside. When told that the crew would not surrender, Schmitt hopped up, banged on the hatch, and, in Korean, commanded the crew to come out. The hatch cracked open and the barrel of a pistol slipped out and began to fire. Unharmed, Schmitt returned with a white phosphorous grenade, which he strategically placed in the rear air intake of the tank, killing the crew.[2]

Schmitt continued to display aggressive leadership on Hill 209. Taking inventory, the small group had one SCR-300 radio, two heavy machine guns of which only one was functional, two light machine guns, one Browning Automatic Rifle, and assorted rifles, carbines, and small arms. Lieutenant Schmitt used the radio to notify the command of their situation and receive the obligatory promise that help was on the way.

An American who had been captured by the NKPA during the initial assault was sent up the hill to tell Schmitt and his men that they must surrender or be blown to pieces. Schmitt, after a brief consultation with those around him, refused. After 45 minutes the North Koreans opened fire with a constant barrage from an anti-tank gun, mortars, including those captured the day before, and machine guns stationed higher up on the hill. At dark the firing stopped and a flare lit the sky signaling the NKPA infantry to begin their "banzai" attack. Three determined NKPA assaults were repulsed that night. The defense of Hill 209, even in the early stages, was taking on heroic proportions.

By the morning of September 2, Schmitt's group was running low on grenades. In response, Master Sergeant Travis Watkins of H Company left the perimeter to retrieve the grenades of two enemies he had killed about 50 yards away. He killed three more North Koreans on his way to gather the arms of the first two and managed to return with the weapons and insignia of all five. An hour later, at about 1000, Watkins killed another six NKPA who had worked their way into a position where they could throw grenades into the perimeter. Watkins killed all six, although he was paralyzed from the waist down in the exchange.[3]

That afternoon, requests for an airdrop were answered; unfortunately, most of the supplies landed outside the perimeter. Private First Class Joseph Ouellette made a habit of leaving the perimeter to retrieve weapons and supplies, killing one enemy in hand-to-hand combat.[4] Likewise, Lieutenant Schmitt was wounded while retrieving supplies.[5]

This pattern of attacks continued through September 2nd, with numerous attacks repulsed. By Sunday, September 3rd, out of water and low on food and ammunition, the men were weakening. With the last of the battery on the radio failing, Task Force Manchu provided a last intelligence report and received a promise that a Marine relief column was due to arrive at 0600. The Marines never showed, but relief came in the way of rain in the late afternoon. At this point the enemy had begun to close in, lobbing grenades into foxholes and laying down suppressing fire with machine guns. Ouellette, who had distinguished himself earlier, was forced to jump from his hole six times to avoid grenades before he was killed. Lt. Schmitt was killed by a direct hit in his hole from a mortar round. No airdrops came.[6]

On Monday the enemy fire continued. The NKPA soldiers, after having been repelled as many as 20 times, made only a half-hearted effort at assault, closing, tossing some grenades, and then retreating.[7] That night, after the barrage let up and the attack faltered, the surviving two officers, Lt. Raymond McDoniel,[8] Platoon Leader from D Company, and Lt. Caldwell of H Company, with 27 men broke into groups of four and escaped the hill. Caldwell, captured the next morning by two enemy soldiers, was struck in the head with a rock and tossed off a cliff into the river where they left him for dead.[9] Caldwell, McDoniel, and 20 of their men eventually met up with an advancing UNC armor column. Lt. McDoniel, who became MIA less than two months later in North Korea, provided the most thorough account of the events that befell Task Force Manchu.[7] On September 3, 1950, the 5th Marine Regiment, attached to the 2nd Infantry Division, commenced a three-day offensive that retook all of the lost territory.

INITIAL RECOVERY

Recovery efforts began almost immediately after the NKPA 9th Division was pushed back across the Naktong River. Col. Charles C. Sloane Jr., who took command of the 9th Infantry from Colonel Hill, reported that 9th Infantry personnel who returned to the Hill 209 battlefield found that most of the bodies had been blown to pieces and that it was difficult to tell how many had been in each of the defensive positions. They estimated approximately 30 dead on the hill with 15 identifiable.[7]

On or about September 8, just after Hill 209 was recaptured, a member of B Company went up on the hill to begin identifying bodies. By October 6, 1950, the American Graves Registration Service (AGRS) unit was on the scene (see figure). A total of 34 sets of remains were found, two of which were determined to be ROK soldiers and repatriated to the ROK. Of the 32 remains believed to be American, 31 were eventually identified.[10] Throughout the rest of the Korean War and in the years immediately following, the AGRS conducted surface sweeps in the Naktong Bulge area, interviewed local witnesses, and excavated foxholes in search of the missing. No further recoveries were made from the Schmitt Group's position on Hill 209. Based on the records in the Field Search Case, it appears that after the initial visit by the survivors and the AGRS, the precise location of the battlefield was lost due to confusion or the erroneous recording of map coordinates.[11]

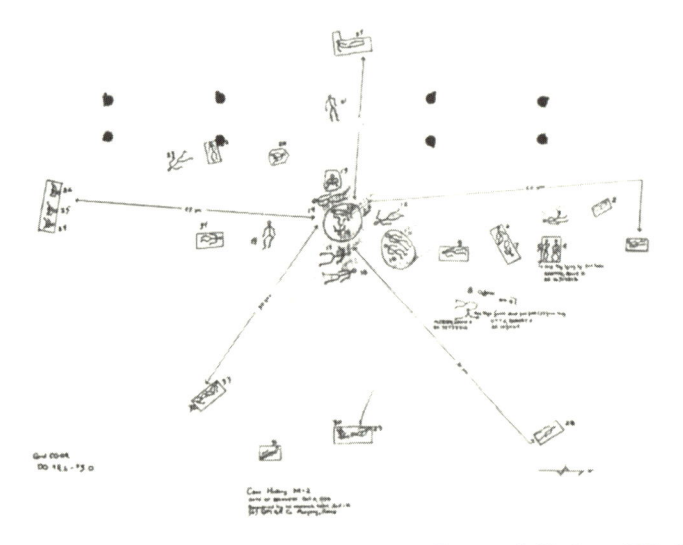

The AGRS sketch map. Joint POW/MIA Accounting Command, Hickam AFB, HI.

At this point we shift the focus of this study to the fate of one of the officers lost on the hill, Second Lieutenant Edmund J. Lilly III.[12] The search for Lt. Lilly ended for the first time in 1956 when he was declared "nonrecoverable."[13] The last report of the whereabouts of Lt. Lilly came from a survivor, SFC William Pistulka, who recalled that Lilly was in charge of rationing water and that the lieutenant had given him a drink during the battle.[14] After that, Pistulka and Lilly were separated on opposite sides of the hill and the sergeant did not see Lt. Lilly again. In his letter, SFC Pistulka described the battle, "The mortars were landing so heavy they were falling in fox holes, which took the lives of many men and blew their bodies apart."

The next report of Lilly came from Master Sergeant Seeger, who climbed up Hill 209 on or about September 8, 1950, just after the hill was retaken.[15] Seeger reported that "Lieutenant Lilly's body was intact, the right side of [his] head had been wounded laying face up.... The remains of Lieutenant

Lilly were approximately five feet from the remains of Louis A. Merino." The body of Louis Merino had been recovered and identified with the original 32 recovered remains. Merino had been located adjacent to the central command position at the apex of the hill.[16] Two men known to have been on the Hill, Lt. Lilly and SFC George Musick, remained missing and one set of recovered remains remained unidentified,[17] although known not to be the remains of Lilly or Musick.

The search for the MIAs waned with the end of the 1950s, and nothing more was learned about the fate of Lt. Lilly until 2002. In commemoration of the 50th anniversary of the Korean War, the ROK army embarked on a three-year plan of archaeological work to find missing South Korean soldiers. On September 6, 2002, the ROK Army Search and Recovery Group excavated remains on Pakjin Hill, also known as Hill 209.[18]

The ROK group recovered one set of remains associated with an identification tag belonging to B Company's Lieutenant Lilly. In addition to the identification tag, other artifacts found with the remains were consistent with equipment carried by U.S. forces (see figure). Subsequent analysis at our Central Identification Laboratory confirmed the remains by correlating the material evidence, dental records, and mtDNA references from family members.

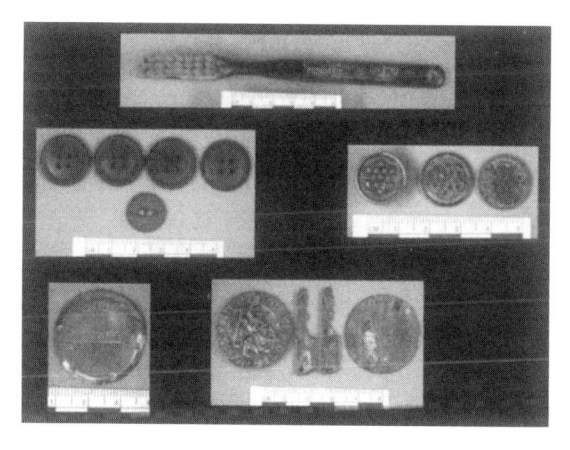

Artifacts from Hill 209.

Some questions exist, however, regarding the post-depositional history of Lt. Lilly's body. Immediately after the battle, a Master Sergeant Seeger saw Lt. Lilly's remains on the surface, blown out of a foxhole, yet a few weeks later, when the AGRS arrived, Lt. Lilly's body was somehow passed over.

Based on the historical research and the archaeology completed thus far, two questions pertinent to our mission arise: (1) what post-depositional disturbances might have occurred during the interval between Master Sergeant's return to the hill and the arrival of the AGRS unit; and (2) how many individuals might remain unrecovered on the hill?

RECENT AND FUTURE WORK

In May 2003, while conducting a reconnaissance in the area, a small team from the Central Identification Laboratory, Hawaii,[19] visited Hill 209. The high point of the hill is marked with an impressive monument to the battle which includes a paved parking lot that covers much of the hilltop (See Figure); however, this was an observation point that was overrun early in the battle and not the location where the Schmitt Group held out. Schmitt's group held the southern spur of the hill, which aside from a more recent burial mound and a small antenna, is still relatively intact. The site is pitted with eroded foxholes and littered with artifacts from the war (see figure). During this reconnaissance we were able to gather some new information related to the post-depositional variables that led to the AGRS passing over of at least one soldier.

On a battlefield there are numerous variables that might have affected the disposition of the remains, including continued combat in the area, bioturbations, particularly dogs, and rain and erosion; however, the one that seems to be the most significant is the intervention of the local population. In the town of Wolsang-Ri, just below Hill 209, our 2003 team encountered an elderly man who was able to add to our knowledge of events. Shortly after the battle, he and a few other young men who had remained in their village, climbed to the top of the mountain where they found numerous dead, both American and North Korean. They proceeded to bury the dead in foxholes, placing one to five individuals in each hole. The holes were reported to range from 30 cm to one meter in depth. This witness identified one area in particular where he recalled burying approximately 25 American soldiers. He knew that, over the decades, American and ROK soldiers had come and searched on the hill but he had never spoken to anyone about it before.[20] The burial activities of the local populace in the period between the battle and the arrival of the AGRS team may account for why some bodies were not recovered.

The ROK monument to the Battle of the Naktong Bulge.

Further compounding the difficulties with the recovery were inaccuracies in map reading. Part of this may have been due to a transition in maps from an old Japanese series to a more current series, and part, undoubtedly, was due to human error. Searches made in 1952 and 1953 appear to have been far from the actual battle location.[21]

The second question is more difficult to answer. There are dozens of MIAs in this area, both from the 9th Infantry and from other units. Considering the chaos involved, it is difficult to know how many soldiers might have ended up on Pakjin Hill with Schmitt's group. The estimates given by survivors range from 60 to 75; however, none of the accounts mention any South Korean soldiers on the hill, yet two were found.

At least one soldier, SFC George Musick, was reportedly KIA on the hill and never recovered. Also, one set of remains was never identified, although it was confirmed that the remains were not those of Musick. With the 29 soldiers who left the hill on the night of September 4, and the 34 originally recovered on the hill, plus the one recently recovered, a total of 64 men have been accounted for. If the high estimate of 75 soldiers present on the hill is correct, the remains of as many as 11 soldiers could still be on the battlefield.

In an effort to plan for future excavations aimed at recovering whatever remains may be left behind on Hill 209, a compass, tape, and GPS sketch map made during last year's reconnaissance was rendered into a 3D model of the southern spur of the hill. The original AGRS map was then digitized, scaled, and rotated to match the 3D model. Many of the original foxholes are still visible, and the central command hole described in various accounts is prominent. These features serve as landmarks facilitating the alignment of the two maps (see figure). Not surprisingly, considering the rough nature of the AGRS map, the foxhole locations identified in the recent survey do not precisely match up with those recorded on the AGRS map. Surprisingly, considering the rough nature of both maps and the amount of time involved, they appear to correlate quite well.

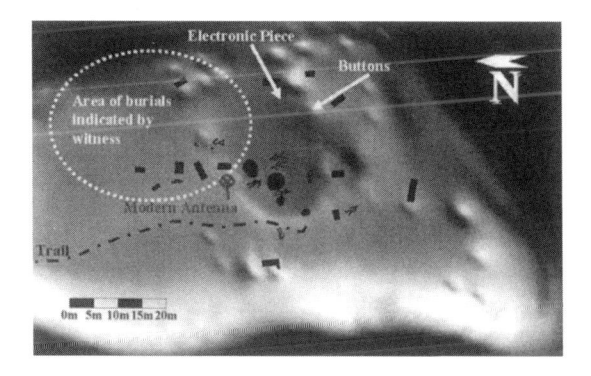

Model of Pakjin Hill, showing the relation of foxholes and recovered remains.

Of particular interest is the area where the witness from the local town reported burying 20 or more Americans and comparing that to the 13 remains recovered by the AGRS in that sector. If the witness is correct, the northern portion of the site may provide some more answers to the fate of the men of Task Force Manchu. Because of the possibility that the remains of U.S. soldiers may still be located on Hill 209, we are proposing this site for recovery excavations in the near future.

CONCLUSION

The United States Army prides itself on leaving no person behind. Because of this commitment, it has dedicated itself to giving a full accounting of all missing soldiers. As researchers working on this effort, we are given the opportunity to investigate and discover not only lost soldiers, but also the events that surround their loss. The battle on Hill 209 is significant, not only because of the heroic action, as demonstrated by the Medals of Honor awarded to Sgt. Watkins and Pfc. Ouellette, the Distinguished Service Cross for Lt. Schmitt, and various other medals earned during the fight, but because their stand on this hill helped slow the last major offensive by the North Korean army in the south. Unfortunately, the battlefields of the Korean War are distant, both physically and psychologically, from the minds of the American public. Ironically, our own mission has neglected South Korea in favor of North Korea. On one hand, this has been a logical choice considering there are over 6,000 unaccounted-for U.S. soldiers in the North and less than 2,000 in the South. However, in the South we are able to work side-by-side with the ROK and without the significant fetters imposed by the North Korean government. One of the possible dividends of our investigation at Hill 209, which complemented the 2002 fieldwork completed by the ROK, is that it may promote a more systematic search and recovery program and establish a precedent for future joint operations.

NOTES

1. See Appleman 2000, Ferrenbach 1963, and Tolland 1991 for histories of the opening and course of the Korean War.
2. Appleman 2000.
3. Medal of Honor Citation for Travis E. Watkins. Note that, after he was paralyzed, Watkins refused food and water so that the men who were still combat able could have his rations. When the survivors escaped from Hill 209, Travis Watkins is reported to have stayed behind with a rifle and one bullet. His body was recovered (see JPAC, FSC 115-F). See also Appleman 2000:459.
4. Medal of Honor Citation for Joseph R. Ouellette. Ouellette's body was recovered (see JPAC, FSC 115-F).

5. Distinguished Service Cross Citation for Edward Schmitt.
6. Appleman 2000:455–459.
7. 9th Infantry Regiment Unit Diary/War Journal Aug.–Sept. 1950.
8. Appleman 2000:458. Initial reports misspelled McDoniel as McDaniel. See McDoniel's account in 9th Infantry Regiment, 2nd Infantry Regiment, Unit Journal/War Diary. Also see Lt. McDoniel's account in the *New York Times*, Sept. 9, 1950:3.
9. Note that a *New York Times* article dateline Sept. 9, 1950, states that only Lt. McDoniel survived since Lt. Caldwell was presumed dead at the time the article was written.
10. FSC-115-F. A Field Search Case (FSC) is the AGRS file that contains a battle narrative of a specific incident, the names and status of those missing from that incident, and data collected relevant to the recovery of MIAs.
11. JPAC, Field Search Report (with maps/diagrams) dated April 17, 1953, and Memo dated April 21, 1953.
12. Appleman 2000:456. 2d Lt. Edmund J. Lilly III was assigned as a platoon leader in B Company. See Lilly's 293 file, JPAC records room. The 293 file (Individual Deceased Personnel File—IDPF) is a file containing personal medical and dental information of an unaccounted individual. Appleman specifically names Lt. Lilly in his footnote as one of the five officers on Hill 209 following notations in the 9th Infantry Regiment War Diary entry dated 0001-2400 1 Sept. 1950 w/ statement by Lt. Raymond McDaniel [McDoniel] listed as Incl. # 4 (1 Sept. 50), entry dated 0001-2400 3 Sept. 1950, entry dated 0001-2400 4 Sept. 1950. See statement by MSgt. Seeger dated 7 Aug. 1951, and statement by William J. Pistulka dated 7 Aug. 1952.
13. JPAC, Lilly's 293 file, record dated 16 Jan. 1956.
14. William J. Pistulka, Letter to the Department of the Army, dated Aug. 7, 1952.
15. Herbert J. Seeger Jr., statement written 7 Aug. 1951.
16. Louis Merino was numbered individual 17 on the sketch map of remains recovered made by the 1st Research Team, 2nd Platoon, 565th Quartermaster Graves Registration Company, dated Oct. 6, 1950.
17. JPAC, Unknown X-243; Otinero 2003.
18. Park 2002.
19. CILHI, as of Oct. 2003, is now called the Joint POW/MIA Accounting Command (JPAC) and the Central Identification Laboratory (CIL) is the scientific division of the command.
20. Silverstein 2003.
21. JPAC, Field Search Report, 1953.

REFERENCES CITED

9th Infantry Regiment Unit Journal/War Diary. 1950, 1 September to 5 September. Box 2470, RG 470, National Archives.
Appleman, R. F. 2000. *United States Army in the Korean War: South to the Naktong, North to the Yalu (June–November 1950)*. Center of Military History United States Army, Washington, D.C.

Ferrenbach, T. R. 1963. *This Kind of War.* Brassey's, Washington, D.C.

Joint POW/MIA Accountng Command (JPAC) n.d. Field Search Case-115-F, JPAC Records Room.

Joint POW/MIA. n.d. Lilly, Edmund J. III, Individual Deceased Personnel File 293, JPAC Records Room.

Joint POW/MIA. n.d. Unknown X-243 file, JPAC Records Room.

New York Times. 1950. U.S. 'Lost Platoon' Outfights Reds, but Only 27 of 60 in Unit Survive. (Sep. 9, 1950):3.

Otinero, L. 2003. Casualty data report for FSC-115-F, 2d Lt Edmund J. LILLY III, B Company, 1st Battalion, 9th Infantry Regiment, 2nd Infantry Division, Republic of Korea. JPAC, Hawaii.

Park, S. J. 2002. *The 2002 Year Excavation Report on Casualties from the Korean War.* Chungbuk University, Korea.

Silvertein, J. 2003. Report of Investigation During the 03-1KS (South Korea), 2003/CIL/039, 1 May to 4 June 2003. Central Identification Laboratory, Hawaii.

Toland, J. 1991. *In Mortal Combat, Korea, 1950–1953.* Quill, William Morrow, New York.

Conclusions: Toward a Unified View of the Archaeology of Fields of Conflict

BATTLEFIELD ARCHAEOLOGY HAS emerged over the last two decades as a legitimate field of inquiry in the fields of archaeology, anthropology, and history. From its earliest manifestations as a method to find relics or gun emplacements, to its present form where the archaeological record is viewed as an independent dataset that can be compared to historical documents, participant accounts, maps, and other sources to build a more complete and accurate picture of an event or develop new views of strategy and tactics—we believe this evolution reflects the growth and maturity of the field. The first battlefield archaeology conference in Glasgow in 2000 and the subsequent publication of the papers from that conference were a true milestone in the field of battlefield archaeology.[1] As the discipline of conflict studies has grown and gained acceptance among scholars of the different disciplines, the field has also captured the public's imagination through various television documentaries and two television series featuring battlefield archaeology as a means to study and learn about the past. The Fourth World Archaeology Congress featured a session on contemporary conflict archaeology which was subsequently published, and there is a growing interest in the physical landscapes of war and warfare;[2] and a new journal, the *Journal of Conflict Archaeology*, began publication in 2005. This awareness and growth of interest in studies of historic and contemporary fields of conflict have given rise to a larger number of scholars conducting field investigations and recovering the physical evidence of battles and conflicts.

One element often discounted in the literature of war, because there is no ready means to study it, is the allure of the warrior life, although the role and function of the warrior is readily documented in the historic literature and in the archaeological record. The allure of the warrior life is part and parcel of the culture of the military and intuitively is suited to some more than others. Those that best adapt to the structure and discipline of the military are often those that require order in their lives. They define the military culture and they refine it for themselves. Often they do their job of war and taking risks whether they are touted by the society as a whole or not. They do it because it is their job and the awards and rewards are not important—extrinsic reward is of only minor interest. There is fulfillment of a personal nature in the sharing of risk and hardship that is purely symbolic and personal, but is satisfying to the group members.

Obviously booty, desire for control, power, new lands, structure, and order are also goals implicit in war making, but they are narrow and limited explanations to the allure of the warrior. These are often national or societal goals established and pushed by the power elite either implicitly or explicitly. These goals are often reflected in the warrior class, but do not explain the willingness to continue taking risks and enduring hardship.[3]

Anthropologists and sociologists use as their basic premise in studying people the tenet that human behavior is patterned. The basic concept is that human behavior is constrained by norms, values, morals, and sanctions of society, all combining to govern a group. Individual behavior may deviate from the expected to a certain degree, but in order to maintain a membership in a group, society, or culture an individual must generally conform to the group standards.

Archaeologists extend this premise to the physical remains of a society. Group and individual beliefs and behavior are reflected in the material culture of that society, and thus can be studied by archaeological means. One aspect of battlefield studies is the level of detail about individual weapon use and weapon movement, particularly with firearms components, that can be teased from the archaeological data. This level of precise knowledge gives the researcher not only the big picture of strategy and tactics carried out on a field of battle, but allows a look at the role of the individual, which is almost unique in most archaeological investigations. While we may never find the physical evidence to address the issue of the allure of the warrior life, archaeologists can recover artifacts of that lifestyle. They can study, analyze, and interpret the context in which they are found, and perhaps gain an increased understanding of the role of the warrior in warfare, even the warrior lifestyle through time and space, if not the allure of war itself.

Regardless of the level of precision that can be garnered from the artifacts and context there is still the matter of how best to study these violent episodes of the past. Although we advocate the use of sound scientific methods, the underlying theory driving the research can be diverse as seen in the chapters of these volumes. Most of the research presented here has, as its basic approach, one of understanding processes and events. Among those advocating a processualist approach to the study of military sites is Kenneth Lewis,[4] who placed the military as a settlement pattern within the American frontier. Lewis was influenced by historian Jerome Steffen's cosmopolitan frontier theory,[5] which espouses the concept that cosmopolitan frontiers are regions of specialized economic activity which exhibit minimal cultural diversity as colonization occurs. Donald Hardesty[6] as well as Steffen has stressed the structural similarity and cultural continuity of these frontiers within the colonization process.

Within this economic model military sites are seen as a slight deviant to the cultural norm in that they are not developed for direct economic exploitation. Instead they stand as bastions of protection and symbols of power that are meant to ensure that the parent culture can exploit those resources without undue interference from native cultures or other competing cultural groups. Lewis stresses that military frontiers are not found in all areas of colonization, but only where threats to the peaceful extraction of resources are seen, and a structured pacifying force is required. The cosmopolitan frontier concept is an excellent umbrella theory in which to view the military establishment. The economic thrust of the concept appears to be valid, and is one which can be subject to archaeological and historical investigation particularly in light of today's Marxist and Post Processualist theoretical paradigms.

Battlefields may seem to be a simple type of archaeological site. Like any other level of archaeological endeavor the site is often more complex below the surface. Ivor Noel Hume[7] once considered battlefield sites to be a poor place for archaeological investigations. He considered them to be good places to find cannon positions and war relics for museum displays, but not sites worthy of serious archaeological investigation. Recent battlefield archaeology at Olynthos, Greece; Naseby and Flodden Field in the United Kingdom; American Revolutionary War sites of Saratoga, New York, and Monmouth, New Jersey; the Mexican–American War site at Palo Alto Battlefield, Texas; Crimean War sites in Finland; an early American Indian Wars site at Fallen Timbers, Ohio; the American Civil War battlefield of Mine Creek, Kansas; and the late Indian Wars sites of Little Bighorn battlefield, Montana; Zulu war sites in South Africa; and the Apache campaign site of K-H butte; as well as sites relating to World War I have shed an entirely different light on the viability of battlefield archaeological studies.[8]

A battlefield might be expected to be the least likely place to find archaeologically definable behavioral patterns. But, those who engage in combat fight in the established manners and patterns in which they have been trained, and it is precisely this training in proper battlefield behavior that results in the deposition of artifacts which can be recovered by archaeological methods and interpreted in an anthropological perspective.[9] One archaeologist has pointed out that shipwreck sites are documents of behavior, and as warfare-related wrecks are documents,[10] then land battlefields are also archaeological documents of past behavior. Battlefields are no less an expression of culture, albeit a violent one, than are architectural elements.

Clearly battlefield studies can yield information on combatant positions during the course of the battle. They can also provide details of dress, equipage, and in some cases individual movements. Archaeological data can retrieve information on troop deployment, firing positions, fields of fire, and weapon types present. Studies of artifact patterning can also reveal unit or individual movement during the battle, weapon trajectory, and range of firing by determining forces of impact. Battlefields viewed in an anthropological context should be seen as the physical and violent expression of a culture or cultures in conflict.[11]

Wars are not fought by any party without some explicit or implicit goal. Different cultures have different goals. Military entities around the world use one form or another of theory of war and operationalize these as tenets of operations and tactics, and these provide a fertile ground for archaeological inquiry. The basic tenets of modern warfare are simply stated in the operations manuals—whenever army forces are called to fight, they fight to win. Army forces in combat seek to impose their will on the enemy. Victory is the objective; no matter the mission. Nothing short of victory is acceptable. The fundamental tenets of any army operational doctrine describe the characteristics of successful operations. In and of themselves they do not guarantee victory, but their absence makes it difficult and costly to achieve. The tenets of modern military operation provide a ready-made set of testable hypotheses for anthropological and archaeological inquiry.[12]

Whatever the underlying theory used to study a battlefield, there are essentially two types of battlefields—siege and transitory—as exemplified throughout these volumes. The archaeological evidence will be similar in some respects; that is, the evidence of warfare and conflict. The siege site can be expected to be associated with towns or fortifications where one of the combatant parties fortified themselves and where the other party was attempting to acquire that locale. The defensive side of a siege battlefield should be associated with some type of relatively permanent fortification or a town with defenses thrown up around it. English Civil War sites and American Civil War sites are among many types of siege sites that have archaeological expressions. The archaeological features associated with a siege site would be the fortifications, artillery positions, long-term camps for both combatants, and extensive trash deposits. Normally large bodies of men were employed in a siege so the camp and trash-related artifacts should be extensive. The possibility of a formal burial ground should not be overlooked in a siege situation.

The transitory battlefield, which is probably the most common, is more ephemeral in nature. Normally these involve a limited engagement of opposing forces both in time and space. This battlefield type should not be associated with permanent fortifications, but temporary breastworks may be found as exemplified in the Anglo-Zulu fort at Eshowe or the Thirty Years War site in the Czech Republic.[13] Camps and burial areas may be found near the battle site. Even the route of retreat or movement can sometimes carry an archaeology signature.[14] The primary archaeological deposits associated with a transitory battlefield are parts of uniforms, equipage, and especially spent cartridges, bullets, artillery shells, and other weapons, such as arrows or spears.

Where similar cultural groups or a cultural group in conflict have fought a battle the artifact patterns may be more difficult to identify. Yet, combatant pattern differences should be discernible. Civil wars pit elements of the same culture against one another, but opposing combatant camps and positions can be fairly easily identified through the material culture remains.[15] The same can be said for military forts and encampments. The material culture remains can often be associated with specific occupations, even though they may have been cultural groups.[16]

Battlefields of the American Indian Wars have yielded artifact patterns that are interpretable. The cultural differences in the manner and practice of warfare by U.S. Army trained personnel versus various Native American groups is clearly delineated in the artifact dispersal patterns at Indian–Soldier battle sites. This concept of the archaeological recognition of the physical evidence of cultural differences in war material and manner of fighting is amply evident in many of the chapters in these volumes. Indigenous peoples may use the war material of their enemy, but the manner in which they fought is left behind as physical evidence that is recoverable and interpretable using archaeological theory and methods.

CONCLUSIONS

The focus of these volumes is on human behavior in conflict situations as seen from the archaeological evidence of warfare and conflict. It is clear from the chapters in these volumes that conflicts leave behind an interpretable archaeological record through time and space. The various chapters have demonstrated that archaeological evidence of warfare, battles, and conflict can be recovered and interpreted from many different contexts. The work of the various authors shows that the archaeological evidence of clothing and equipment will reflect the site's military nature and will, again, show the stratified and ranked nature of the military.

Sites exhibiting evidence of conflict do have patterns of artifact deposition coincident with the training provided to the participants. Combatants fight as they are trained and under the rules of that culture's perception of warfare behavior. Opposing combatant positions, movement, armament, and method of warfare should be discernible in the artifact deposition pattern.

In essence military sites will be revealed in the archaeological record as military sites by their institutionalized architecture, equipment, and patterns of artifact deposition. They will also be seen to reflect the tenets of the parent culture in the artifactual record. Personal goods will reflect social and economic status within the military community and the culture at large. Artifacts and patterns of deposition will also reflect the role of the military in society—the making of or prevention of war.

One important point that is noted over and over again within these chapters is not just how rich the archaeological or physical evidence record is, but that it is an independent line of evidence that tells a different story from the documentary or literary record, and from oral tradition. The value of archaeological research and the recovery and documentation of physical evidence of past conflict lies not in the artifacts alone, but in the context in which they are found. Archaeology can enhance the oral testimonial and documentary record, but that is not its real power. That power lies in the pure fact that archaeological evidence, properly recorded and documented, is a truly independent data source. Historical documents and oral testimony are accounts derived from human memory and can contain intentional or unintentional bias. The archaeological record has its own bias, one of preservation, not one of intent. The archaeological record of a conflict is not dependent on human memory to record it; rather it is the debris and evidence left behind by violent events. It is there and it is recoverable using the best possible data collection methods available. The archaeological record cannot speak for itself, but it is interpretable. This independent line of evidence can be found, recovered, recorded, and interpreted. Its real power lies in the fact that it can be used to correlate, corroborate, or contrast documentary sources or oral testimony to determine the best fit or the accuracy of various information sources. It may be trite, but a crime scene analogy does explain the value of archaeology best. The historical sources and oral tradition are akin to witness, victim, and alleged perpetrator statements in a criminal investigation. The archaeological record is analogous to the physical and trace evidence gathered by forensic scientists. Compared and contrasted, the physical evidence shows who is a reliable witness and sometimes leads to new lines of inquiry in an investigation. The archaeological evidence of conflict and warfare has this power, to test the reliability of various sources, to find new information about the past, and, as a partner to history, to build a more complete and accurate story of past events.

NOTES

1. Freeman and Pollard 2001.
2. Legendre 2001, Hill and Wileman 2002.
3. Keegan 1993:226.
4. Lewis 1984.
5. Steffen 1980.
6. Hardesty 1981.
7. Noel Hume 1968.
8. See Lee 2001; Parsons 2001; Foard 1995; Snow 1981; Sivilich 1995; Haecker 1994; Pratt 1995 and this volume; Lees 1994; Londahl et al. 2001; Scott and Connor 1986; Scott and Fox 1987; Scott et al. 1989; Fox 1993; Pollard 2001; Ludwig and Stute 1993; Doyle 2001; Bulgrin 2005; Harrington 2005; Stichelbaut 2005.
9. Fox and Scott 1991, Dyer 1985.

10. Gould 1983.
11. Fox and Scott 1991.
12. Scott 2001.
13. See Pollard and Banks 2005, Matoušek 2005.
14. See Dimmick 2004.
15. See Harrington 2005, Doyle et al. 2005, Ripley 1970.
16. Miller and Stone 1970, Moreau and Binford 1961, Saunders 2004.

REFERENCES CITED

Bulgrin, Lon E. 2005. The Tudela Site: Fire and Steel Over Saipan, 15 June 1944. *Journal of Conflict Archaeology* 1:1–18.

Dimmick, Gregg J. 2004. *Sea of Mud: The Retreat of the Mexican Army after San Jacinto, An Archeological Investigation*. Texas State Historical Association, Austin.

Doyle, Peter. 2001. Geology as an Interpreter of Great War Battle Sites. In P. W. M. Freeman and A. Pollard (eds.), *Fields of Conflict: Progress and Prospect in Battlefield Archaeology*, 237–252. BAR International Series 958.

Doyle, Peter, Peter Barton, and Johan Vandewalle. 2005. Archaeology of a Great War Dugout: Beecham Farm, Passchendaele, Belgium. *Journal of Conflict Archaeology* 1:45–66.

Dyer, Gwynne. 1985. *War*. Crown Publishers, New York.

Ellis, John. 1986. *The Social History of the Machine Gun*. John Hopkins University Press, Baltimore (reprint of 1975 edition).

Foard, Glenn. 1995. *Nasbey: The Decisive Campaign*. Pryor Publications, Yorklettes, Whitstable, Kent, England.

Fox, Richard A. Jr. 1993. *Archaeology, History, and Custer's Last Battle*. University of Oklahoma Press, Norman.

Fox, Richard A. Jr., and Douglas D. Scott. 1991. The Post-Civil War Battlefield Pattern: An Example from the Custer Battlefield. *Historical Archaeology* 95(2):92–103.

Freeman, P. W. M., and A. Pollard. 2001. *Fields of Conflict: Progress and Prospect in Battlefield Archaeology*. BAR International Series 958.

Gould, Richard A. 1983. The Archaeology of War. In Richard A. Gould (ed.), *Shipwreck Anthropology*. University of New Mexico Press, Albuquerque.

Haecker, Charles. 1994. A Thunder of Cannon: Archeology of the Mexican-American War Battlefield of Palo Alto. Southwest Cultural Resources Center Professional Papers No. 52, Division of Anthropology and History, Southwest Regional Office, National Park Service, Santa Fe, NM.

Hardesty, Donald. 1981. Historical Archaeology at Fort Churchill. *Nevada Historical Society Quarterly* 24(4):283–297.

Harrington, Peter. 2005. Siegefields: An Archaeological Assessment of English Civil War 'Small' Sieges. *Journal of Conflict Archaeology* 1:93–114.

Hill, Paul, and Julie Wileman. 2002. *Landscapes of War: The Archaeology of Aggression and Defense*. Stroud, Gloucestershire.

Keegan, John. 1993. *A History of Warfare*. Vintage Books, New York.

Lee, John W I. 2001. Urban Combat at Olynthos, 348 BC. In P. W. M. Freeman and A. Pollard (eds.), *Fields of Conflict: Progress and Prospect in Battlefield Archaeology*, 11–22. BAR International Series 958.

Lees, William. 1994. When the Shooting Stopped the War Began. In Clarence R. Geier Jr. and Susan E. Winter (eds.), *Look to the Earth: Historical Archaeology and the American Civil War*, 39–59. University of Tennessee Press, Knoxville.

Legendre, Jean-Pierre. 2001. Archaeology of World War 2: The Lancaster Bomber of Fleville (Meurthe-et-Moselle, France). In Victor Buchli and Gavin Lucas (eds.), *Archaeologies of the Contemporary Past*, 126–137. Routledge, London.

Lewis, Kenneth E. 1980. Pattern and Layout on the South Carolina Frontier. *North American Archaeologist* 1(2):177–200.

Lewis, Kenneth E. 1984. *The American Frontier: An Archaeological Study of Settlement Pattern and Process*. Academic Press, New York.

Londahl, Viveka, Neil Price, and Graham Robbins. 2001. Bomarsund: Archaeology and Heritage Management at the Site of a Crimean War Siege. In P. W. M. Freeman and A. Pollard (eds.), *Fields of Conflict: Progress and Prospect in Battlefield Archaeology*, 207–228. BAR International Series 958.

Ludwig, Larry L., and James L. Stute. 1993. *The Battle at K-H Butte: Apache Outbreak-1881: Arizona Territory*. Western Lore Press, Tucson.

Matoušek, Václav. 2005. Building a Model of a Field Fortification of the 'Thirty Years War' Near Olbramov, Czech Republic. *Journal of Conflict Archaeology* 1:115–132.

Maxwell, Moreau S., and Lewis Binford. 1961. Excavation at Fort Michlimacinac, Mackinac City, Michigan 1959 Season. Publication of the Museum Michigan State University 1(1).

Miller, J. Jefferson and Lyle M. Stone. 1970. Eighteenth Century Ceramics from Fort Michilimackinac. *Smithsonian Studies in History and Technology* 4. Washington, D.C., Smithsonian Institution Press.

Noel Hume, Ivor. 1968. *Historical Archaeology*. Alfred A. Knopf, New York.

Parsons, Patrick J. F. 2001. Flodden Field: The Sources and Archaeology of "a marveelouse greate conflicte." In P. W. M. Freeman and A. Pollard (eds.), *Fields of Conflict: Progress and Prospect in Battlefield Archaeology*, 51–60. BAR International Series 958.

Pollard, Tony. 2001. "Place Ekowe in a state of defense": The Archaeological Investigation of the British Fort at KwaMondi, Eshowe, Zululand. In P. W. M. Freeman and A. Pollard (eds.), *Fields of Conflict: Progress and Prospect in Battlefield Archaeology*, 229–236. BAR International Series 958.

Pollard, Tony, and Iain Banks. 2005. Survey and Excavation of an Anglo-Zulu War Fort at Eshowe, KwaZulu-Natal, South Africa. *Journal of Conflict Archaeology* 1:133–180.

Pratt, G. Michael. 1995. The Archaeology of the Fallen Timbers Battlefield: A Report of the 1995 Survey. Heidelberg College, Tiffin, OH.

Ripley, Warren. 1970. *Artillery and Ammunition of the Civil War*. Nostrand Reinhold, New York.

Saunders, Nicholas J. 2004. Material Culture and Conflict: The Great War 1914–2003. In Nicholas J. Saunders (ed.), *Matters of Conflict: Material Culture, Memory, and the First World War*, 5–25. Routledge, New York.

Scott, Douglas D. 1994. A Sharp Little Affair: The Archeology of the Big Hole Battlefield. Reprints in Anthropology, Volume 45, J and L Reprint Company, Lincoln.

Scott, Douglas D. 2001. Archeological Reconnaissance of Bear Paw Battlefield, Blaine County, Montana. Midwest Archeological Center Technical Report No. 73, National Park Service, Lincoln, NE.

Scott, Douglas D., and Melissa A. Connor. 1986. Postmortem at the Little Bighorn. *Natural History* 95(6):46–55.

Scott, Douglas D., and Richard A. Fox Jr. 1987. *Archaeological Insights into the Custer Battlefield.* University of Oklahoma Press, Norman.

Scott, Douglas D., Richard A. Fox Jr., Melissa A. Connor, and Dick Harmon. 1989. *Archaeological Perspectives on the Battle of the Little Bighorn.* University of Oklahoma Press, Norman.

Sivilich, Daniel M. 1995. Analyzing Musket Balls to Interpret a Revolutionary War Site. *Historical Archaeology* 30(2):101–109.

Snow, Dean R. 1981. Battlefield Archaeology. *Early Man* 3(1):18–21.

Steffen, Jerome O. 1980. *Comparative Frontiers: A Proposal for Studying the American West.* University of Oklahoma Press, Norman.

Stichelbaut, Birger. 2005. The Application of Great War Aerial Photography to Battlefield Archaeology, The Example of Flanders. *Journal of Conflict Archaeology* 1:235–244

Index

Albert I, King of the Belgians, 363
Alexander, Maj. Gen. William, 98
Aljubarotta, battle of, 43
Alvarado, Pedro de, 174–75
Anderson, Lt. J. G., 266
Animal-caused artifact damage, 26 (Kalkriese), 93, 100 (Monmouth)
Animal remains, 50, 128 (Kalkriese)
Arminius, 123
Artifact analysis. *See* Pattern analysis
Artifact collecting, 214, 223, 224, 231 (Camden); post-battle plundering, 128 (Kalkriese)
Artillery: ammunition, 66 (U.S. Civil War); field, 10 (Fallen Timbers), 16, 20, 21, 28, 29 (Mackinac Island), 32, 33 (Buffington Island), 43 (Fontenoy), 59, 60, 62, 63–65, 67 (U.S. Civil War); naval, 20 (Buffington Island)

Battlefield casualties, 11–13, 31, 34 (Fallen Timbers), 56 (Kalkriese), 421–27 (Hill 409)
Battlefield degradations: agriculture, 30 (Fallen Timbers), 51 (Kalkriese), 139, 143–44, 152 (English battlefields), 163, 166–67 (Towton), 197 (Zboriv), 224 (Camden), 392 (Pointe-du-Hoc); animal activity, 93–94, 100 (Monmouth), 126–27 (Kalkriese), 424 (Hill 209); post-event relic collecting, 51–56, 127–28 (Kalkriese), 153 (Bosworth), 164–71 (Towton), 196 (Berestechko), 214, 223–24 (Camden), 319 (Curupaity), 399–402 (Stalag Luft III); present-day relic collecting, 148 (English battlefields), 164–71 (Towton, Shrewsbury), 284 (Fort Davidson), 294, 305 (Nashville), 325–26 (Paraguayan battlefields), 378 (Flanders), 399 (Stalag Luft III); soil weathering, 71 (Wilson's Creek), 85 (Monmouth), 154 (English battlefields), 284 (Fort Davidson), 392 (Pointe-du-Hoc), 424 (Hill 209)
Battlefield features: animal bone pits, 128 (Kalkriese); breastworks, 179 (Peñol de Nochistlán), 297, 306 (Nashville), 340, 345, 352 (Hembrillo), 432 (Eshowe); buildings, 284–85 (Pilot Knob), 384, 387 (Pointe-du-Hoc), 399 (Stalag Luft III); earthworks, 43, 46 (Bloody Meadows), 77, 79 (Lookout Mountain), 142 (Northamptonshire), 160, 166 (Towton), 194, 199, 203 (Zboriv), 258, 262,

270 (Evansport), 280 (Fort Davidson), 295, 298, 300–301 (Nashville), 317 (Tuyirti), 320 (Campo Grande), 328 (Curupaity, Boquerón-Sauce), 365–75 (Flanders), 387–90, 392–93 (Pointe-du-Hoc); encampments, 255–74 (Evansport); foxholes, 420–24 (Hill 209); graves and burial pits, 127–28, 130 (Kalkriese), 143 (English battlefields), 164–71 (Towton), 184, 187 (Peñol de Nochistlán), 374–76 (Flanders), 420–24 (Hill 209); tunnels, 406–13 (Stalag Luft III)
Bell, Lt. David, 235–36, 247, 249–50
Bledsoe, Capt. Hiram, 67–69
Bloody Meadows, 39–40, 42
Bosworth, battle of, 43, 46, 134, 136–37, 139, 143, 152–53
Boyle, Lt. John R., 76
Brickhill, Paul, 399–400
Buffington Island, 5; archaeology of, 20–26, 31–33

Cadaver dogs. *See* Survey methods, tools, and techniques
Caldwell, Lt. Charles I., 419, 421
Camden, 208–12; archaeological investigations of, 208–27
Carr, Col. Eugene, 339
Carroll, Capt. Henry, 337–39, 341–53
Carson, Christopher "Kit," 235–37, 249
Caxias, Marques de, 318, 320
Chatard, Cdr. Frederick, 262
Chattanooga, battle of. *See* Lookout Mountain, battle of
Cieneguilla, battle of, 235–50
Clinton, Bill, 383
Clum, John, 336
Clunn, Maj. Tony, 121
Conline, Lt. John, 342–44, 346, 353
Cornwallis, Gen. Lord, 204–5, 211–13, 223
Cotgreaves, Col. William, 16
Croghan, Lt. Col. George, 16, 17, 28–29
Cruse, Lt. Thomas, 338–40, 349

Davidson, Lt. John W., 235–38, 245–48, 250
Duke, Col. Basil, 20–21, 23, 33

Edgehill, battle of, 137, 140–41, 150–51
Edward IV, King of England, 160
Ewing, Brig. Gen. Thomas, Jr., 280, 282

Fallen Timbers, 5–6; archaeological investigations of, 9–16, 26, 30–31
Ferdinand, Archduke Franz, 362
Finley, Lt. Walter, 344, 353
Firearm identification. *See* Specialized studies: firearm and ammunition analysis
Flanders, battles of, 359–80
Fontenoy, battle of, 43
Forsyth, Rev. Alexander, 108
Fort Davidson, battle of, 278–92
Francisco, M. J., 238
Franco, Col. Rafael, 322
French, Gen. Samuel, 264, 266, 272–73

Gates, Gen. Horatio, 210–12, 223
Gatewood, Lt. Charles, 349–50
Gause, Maj. Samuel Sidney, 269
Geary, Gen. John White, 76–78
Germanicus, 50, 150
Gibbon, John, 63
Grant, Ulysses S., 336
Grierson, Col. Benjamin, 337, 352

Hastings, battle of, 144
Hatch, Col. Edward, 336–39, 341, 351
Hembrillo Basin, battle of, 336–53
Henry VI, King of England, 160
Hill 209, battle of, 417–28
Holmes, Gen. Theophilus H., 261–62
Hood, Gen. John Bell, 297, 299
Hooker, Maj. Gen. Joseph, 76, 264–65, 268, 273
Hughes, Lt. Martin, 346
Human remains recovery. *See* Battlefield features: graves and burial pits
Huppert, Lt. Col. Charles, 400, 409–10

INDEX   441

Jackson, Lt. Gen. Thomas "Stonewall," 104, 257
James, Jimmy, 400, 409
Jones, Gen. David "Tokyo," 400, 409
Judah, Gen. Henry, 21, 23

Kalb, Baron Gen. Johann de, 212–13
Kautz, Col. August, 21, 32–33
Khmelnytsky, Bohdan, 193–95
Korean War, 417–26

Landscape analysis. *See* Battlefield features; Pattern analysis; Specialized studies: cumulative viewshed analysis; Specialized studies: topographic analysis
Lee, Gen. Robert E., 261
Lilley, Lt. Edmund J., 417, 422–23
Linton, battle of, 43, 46
Little Bighorn, battle of, 61–62, 196–97
Lookout Mountain, battle of, 62, 75–82
López, Candido, 325
López, Mariscal President Francisco Solano, 314–15, 317–22, 332
Lyman, Col. Theodore, 298
Lynch, Elisa, 322, 332
Lyon, Brig. Gen. Nathaniel, 59–60

Mackinac Island, 5; archaeological investigations of, 16–19, 26–30
Maldon, battle of, 138
Marston Moor, battle of, 137, 144–48, 150
Masterman, Gen. George, 321
McClellan, Gen. George, 265, 273
McDoniel, Lt. Raymond, 421
McLellan, Capt. Curwen B., 336–37, 339, 341, 348–49
Megiddo (Syria), battle of, 39
Mellon, Thomas, 93
Merino, Louis A., body of, 423
Metal detecting. *See* Survey methods, tools, and techniques: metal detection
Mills, Lt. Stephen, 349–50
MisCampbell, Capt. Robert, 10, 13
Mommsen, Theodor, 121
Monmouth, battle of, 87–88, 92–97, 100, 204

Morgan, Gen. John Hunt, 5, 20
Mouat, Pvt. David, 76
Musick, SFC George, body of, 423, 425

Naseby, battle of, 136, 140, 149
Nash-kin, Harvey, 349
Nashville, battle of, 294–310

Oak Hill, battle of. *See* Wilson's Creek, battle of
Olynthos, battle of, 51
Ouellette, PFC Joseph, 421

Palo Alto, battle of, 51, 62
Pattern analysis: artifact wear pattern, 104; battlefield landscape, 43, 387–89 (Pointe-du-Hoc), intra-battlefield artifact patterning, 13–14 (Fallen Timbers), 53 (Kalkriese), 247 (Cieneguilla)
Pilot Knob, battle of. *See* Fort Davidson, battle of
Pointe-du-Hoc, battle of, 383–96
Price, Maj. Gen. Sterling, 279, 282–83
Prisoner of war camps, 389–414

Quebec, battle of, 43

Rawdon, Francis Lord, 211
Reagan, Ronald, 383
Reid, Capt. John B., 67–69
Relic collecting. *See* Battlefield degradations
Remote sensing techniques. *See individual types under* Survey methods, tools, and techniques
Richard III, King of England, 167
Rudder, Lt. Col. James Earl, 383, 385
Ruggles, Gen. Daniel, 261

Sampling techniques, 9–13, 19 (Fallen Timbers), 22 (Buffington Island), 43 (Bloody Meadows), 65 (Wilson's Creek), 92 (Monmouth), 122–23, 130 (Kalkriese), 291 (Fort Davidson), 327–29 (Paraguayan battles), 340 (Hembrillo), 383, 387, 393–96 (Pointe-du-Hoc), 399 (Stalag Luft III), 424 (Hill 209)

Sanders, Col. William, 21, 32–33
Schmitt, Lt. Edward, 419–21, 424–26
Schofield, Gen. John, 297
Sedgemoor, battle of, 46
Shaw, Joshua, 109
Shelby, Gen. Jo, 282
Sherman, Maj. Gen. William Tecumseh, 280, 283, 297
Sigel, Col. Franz, 59–60, 67–68
Skeggs, Lt. Robin, 371
Sloane, Col. Charles C., Jr., 421
Smith, Gen. A. J., 279
Specialized studies: artifact chemical analysis, 91 (Monmouth); calcium phosphate analysis, 127 (Kalkriese), 184 (Peñol de Nochistlán); cumulative viewshed analysis, 64–66, 71; firearm and ammunition analysis, 84–100, 102, 116–17, 289 (Fort Davidson), 308–9 (Nashville), 341; isotope analysis, 127 (Kalkriese); paleobotanical analysis, 123 (Kalkriese); soil analysis, 123 (Kalkriese); topographic analysis, 136–41 (English battlefields), 198 (Zboriv), 268–73 (Evansport), 300 (Nashville), 376 (Flanders), 389 (Pointe-du-Hoc)
Sturgis, Maj. Samuel, 60
Survey methods, tools, and techniques: aerial photogrammetry, 129 (Kalkriese), 376 (Flanders), 386 (Pointe-du-Hoc); cadaver dogs, 18; electromagnetic conductivity, 6, 13, 18, 34; geographic information system (GIS), 341 (Cieneguilla), 365, 376 (Flanders); global positioning system (GPS), 6 (Fallen Timbers), 62 (Wilson's Creek), 150 (English battlefields), 164 (Towton), 216 (Camden), 238 (Cieneguilla), 340 (Hembrillo), 365 (Flanders), 425 (Hill 209); ground-penetrating radar (GPR), 386, 395 (Pointe-du-Hoc), 399, 405 (Stalag Luft III); historic American buildings survey (HABS), 384 (Pointe-du-Hoc);

magnetometer, 6, 13, 18, 34, 392 (Pointe-du-Hoc), 399, 404 (Stalag Luft III); metal detection, 6–14 (Fallen Timbers), 15–22 (Buffington Island), 121 (Kalkriese), 147 (English battlefields), 161–63, 170 (Towton), 183, 191 (Peñol de Nochistlán), 208, 216, 220 (Camden), 290–91 (Fort Davidson), 302 (Nashville), 327–29 (Paraguayan battlefields), 340 (Hembrillo), 396 (Pointe-du-Hoc)

Tarleton, Banastre, 211
Tenamaxtle, 174, 176
Terrain analysis. See Specialized studies: cumulative viewshed analysis; Specialized studies: topographic analysis
Terrazas, Lt. Col. Joaquin, 352
Teutonburg Forest, battle of. See Varus, battle of
Tewkesbury, battle of, 43, 46, 166
Thomas, Gen. George H., 295, 299
Tilley, Christopher, 39–40
Towton, battle of, 133, 143, 160–71
Trimble, Gen. Isaac, 262, 264
Triple Alliance, War of the, 316–33

Varus, battle of, 51–56, 121–30
Vegetius, 142
Victorio, 336–38, 343–45, 352–53
Viewshed analysis. See Specialized studies: cumulative viewshed analysis; Specialized studies: topographic analysis

Walloomsac, battle of, 93
Walthall, Maj. Gen. Edward C., 78
Washington, George, 88, 96
Watkins, Mst. Sgt. Travis, 420
Wayne, Maj. Gen. Anthony, 9, 10
Williams, Col. Otho, 211–12
Wilson's Creek, battle of, 59–72

Ypres, battles of. See Flanders, battles of

Zboriv, battle of, 95, 193–204

About the Contributors

Lawrence Babits, Ph.D., is director of the Program in Maritime Studies at East Carolina University. A battlefield historian, underwater archaeologist, and long-time reenactor, he also coaches ECU's rugby teams and shoots black powder weapons in competition.

Joseph Balicki is a principal archaeologist with John Milner Associates, Inc. He has directed several Civil War archaeological projects in northern Virginia, including a survey of over 750 Civil War sites; earthwork documentation; investigations at Fort C.F. Smith, Arlington County; and investigations at a Confederate cantonment at Marine Base Quantico. He has contributed chapters to *Archaeological Perspectives on the American Civil War* and *Huts and History*.

James Bradford earned his Ph.D. at the University of Virginia and taught at the U.S. Naval Academy before moving to Texas A&M University where he teaches courses in naval and maritime history, early American history, and the history of World War II. He has also taught maritime history and the history of World War II in study abroad programs in Normandy in France, Tuscany in Italy, and the Saarland in Germany.

Richard Burt is an assistant professor in the department of construction science and a faculty fellow of the Center for Heritage Conservation at Texas A&M University. He earned his Ph.D. at Texas A&M in architecture where his focus was on the use of digital photogrammetry for heritage conservation. His main research interest is in cultural heritage documentation, particularly military heritage. He has worked on a number of documentation projects including Fort Davis in West Texas and the Pointe-du-Hoc Battlefield, Normandy, France.

Walter Busch is the site administrator for Fort Davidson State Historic Site and Elephant Rocks State Park. A 21-year veteran of the Missouri Division of State Parks, he received his master's in history at California State University–Dominguez Hills, with his thesis on the life of General Thomas Ewing. He currently lives in Arcadia, Missouri, with his wife, Sandy.

John Byrd is a laboratory manager and forensic anthropologist at the Central Identification Laboratory, Joint POW/MIA Accounting Command. His field excavations have included twentieth-century battlefield sites in North and South Korea, Southeast Asia, New Guinea, Europe, and North Africa, as well as sites of the Civil War and Tuscarora War in North Carolina. Dr. Byrd is board certified by the ABFA and serves on the editorial board of the *Journal of Forensic Sciences*.

Carl G. Carlson-Drexler is a Ph.D. student at the College of William and Mary. He has worked at Pea Ridge and Little Bighorn battlefields, and is preparing a dissertation focusing on El Caney, in eastern Cuba. He is interested in the methodology of conflict archaeology (particularly spatial analysis), differential narrative analysis, variations in heritage management regarding sites of conflict, and exploring connections between conflict archaeology, sociocultural anthropology, and political anthropology.

John Carman, Ph.D., is research fellow and senior lecturer in heritage valuation at the University of Birmingham, England. His previous authored publications include *Valuing Ancient Things: Archaeology and law* (Leicester University Press, 1996), *Archaeology and Heritage* (Continuum, 2002), and *Against Cultural Property* (Duckworth, 2005) together with several edited and co-edited books on heritage and others on archaeologies of warfare.

Patricia Carman is a historian, archaeologist, and teacher. With her husband, John, they are the co-directors of the Bloody Meadows Project on historic battlefields, the first co-authored full-length treatment of which has been recently published as *Bloody Meadows: Investigating landscapes of battle* (Sutton, 2006).

Steve Dasovich, Ph.D., is the head of Cultural Resource Services for SCI Engineering in St. Louis, Missouri. He has long had an interest in American Civil War battlefield archaeology and is now busy compiling information on Missouri's few remaining Civil War earthworks.

Bruce Dickson, a professor of archaeology at Texas A&M University, has undertaken extensive archaeological fieldwork in Central America, the North

American South and Southwest, East Africa, and, most recently, at Pointe-du-Hoc, France. Dickson has published four books and 55 other professional publications. He has served as president of the Council of Texas Archaeologists, as trustee of the Brazos Valley Museum of Natural History, and, since 1984, as a director of the Human Relations Area Files, Inc.

Peter Doyle is a military geologist and battlefield archaeologist. He is a visiting professor at the Universities of London and Greenwich. Peter's work includes assessment of the role of terrain in warfare, which has taken him across Europe to the ill-fated beaches of Gallipoli, and has involved the excavation and exploration of First World War trenches and tunnels.

Michael L. Elliott works as an archaeologist for the SRI Foundation of New Mexico. He has also worked as an archaeologist and as a cultural resources management program manager for the National Park Service and for the National Forest Service, and owns a consulting business, the Jemez Mountains Research Center. He completed a master's degree in anthropology at the University of New Mexico. His current research interests include the archaeology of the Jemez Mountains of New Mexico, Native American–Spanish battle sites of the Americas, and GIS.

Angélica Medrano Enríquez serves as a professor within the Unidad Académica de Antropología at the Universidad Autónoma de Zacatecas in Zacatecas, Mexico. She completed a master's degree in physical anthropology at Mexico's Escuela Nacional de Antropología e Historia, writing a thesis that compared osteological indices of ancient and modern *chinamperos* at the site of Xochimilco, near Mexico City. Her *licenciatura* degree at the Universidad Autónoma de Guadalajara involved study of human and faunal remains and shell recovered from Cerro de las Ventanas. She is currently completing a doctorate at the Universidad Autónoma de México, writing a dissertation that focuses on the identification of human remains recovered from Conquest-era battle sites, including Nochistlán.

Mark E. Everett is professor of geology and geophysics at Texas A&M University specializing in the interaction of electromagnetic fields with geological media and subsurface targets. He is interested in developing near-surface geophysical methods for archaeological, engineering, and environmental site investigations. He received his Ph.D. in geophysics from the University of Toronto in 1991 and subsequently worked as a postdoc at Scripps Institution of Oceanography and the University of Cambridge, UK. He has been on the faculty of Texas A&M since 1995 and is on the editorial board of *Geophysics* and *Geophysical Journal International*.

Glenn Foard, a fellow of the Society of Antiquaries, is a freelance specialist in battlefield studies and landscape archaeology working in the UK. Formerly county archaeologist for Northamptonshire, he is currently leading major survey projects on Edgehill and Bosworth battlefields for the Battlefields Trust; conducting national reviews of battlefields for Historic Scotland and English Heritage; and is a visiting lecturer at Leeds University.

Lucien Haag is a former criminalist and technical director of the Phoenix Crime Laboratory with over 40 years' experience in the field of criminalistics and forensic firearm examinations. He is an independent forensic consultant with his own company, Forensic Science Services, Inc. He is a distinguished member and past president of the Association of Firearm and Tool Mark Examiners, a distinguished member of the California Association of Criminalists, a member of the Southwest Association of Forensic Scientists, a fellow in the American Academy of Forensic Sciences, and a past board member of the International Wound Ballistics Association. He has received numerous awards over the years for his work in the field of forensic ballistics and shooting incident reconstruction. He is also the author of the book *Shooting Incident Reconstruction* (Elsevier/Academic Press, 2006).

Charles Haecker is an archaeologist with the National Park Service–Heritage Partnerships Program, based in Santa Fe, New Mexico. For the past 14 years he has both directed and assisted in the archaeological investigations of historic battlefields throughout the United States including Alaska, as well as in Mexico and Great Britain. He is presently investigating Apache War ambush locations and Apache encampment sites located in the American Southwest and northern Mexico. He is a co-author of *On the Prairie of Palo Alto: Historical Archaeology of the Battlefield* (Texas A&M Press, 1997).

Elsa Heckman, M.A., after intense archaeological research on the battlefields of Chattanooga, wrote a master's thesis designed to expand the geophysical tool kit for conducting battlefield archaeology. She recently moved from her beloved South (but not without battle scars!) and is working as a cultural resources consultant for a private firm in Boise, Idaho.

David M. Johnson, M.A., is an archaeologist with the Taos National Forest, New Mexico. He has worked on many prehistoric and historic sites in the area for the U.S. Forest Service. He is interested in human adaptation in high mountain environments.

Carl Kuttruff is adjunct assistant professor of human ecology; adjunct assistant professor of geography and anthropology; and archaeologist, Louisiana Geological Survey. He received his Ph.D. from Southern Illinois University.

ABOUT THE CONTRIBUTORS   447

Karl W. Laumbach, a native of New Mexico, has been pursuing the state's archaeology and history since graduating from New Mexico State University in 1974. As principal investigator and associate director for Human Systems Research, Inc., a nonprofit corporation dedicated to the preservation and interpretation of New Mexico's past, he has directed hundreds of projects in southern New Mexico. Other than Apache history, his interests include land grants, Hispanic/Anglo assimilation, and the pueblo archaeology of southern New Mexico.

James B. Legg is an archaeologist with the South Carolina Institute of Archaeology and Anthropology, University of South Carolina, and specializes in the archaeology of military sites and military material culture.

Adrian Mandzy was born in Rochester, New York. He received his master's in anthropology from Michigan State University (USA) and his doctorate in history from York University (Canada). He has been conducting research in Ukraine since 1989. He also has a long-standing interest in European expansion during the seventeenth century and continues to work in East Europe and North America.

Mathieu de Meyer was involved in excavations on several Great War and World War II sites in Flanders (Belgium). He also mapped and analyzed the Ypres Salient with contemporary aerial photographs. He worked for the Flemish Heritage Institute (VIOE) before joining the In Flanders Fields Museum (IFFM). He's also a founding member of the Association for World War Archaeology (AWA). He coordinates a European project for the Provincie West-Vlaanderen (Belgium) and Provincie Zeeland (The Netherlands) to conserve and reassess town defenses and Dutch and Spanish forts constructed in the seventeenth and eighteenth century along the Belgian–Dutch border.

Elizabeth A. Oster serves as an archaeologist for the New Mexico Historic Preservation Division. She has also worked as a cultural resources program manager and as a ranger for the National Park Service. Her dissertation research at Tulane University encompassed the first systematic archaeological investigation of another Caxcan center that featured prominently in the Mixtón War, the site of Cerro de las Ventanas in Juchipila, Zacatecas. Her current research interests include the Caxcans and other Nahautl-speaking peoples of Mesoamerica, and battlefield archaeology of the Americas.

Lyle Otineru is a retired U.S. Army Command Sergeant Major with 28 years active duty who has served in Vietnam, Korea, Germany, and Bosnia. He currently works in the Joint POW/MIA Accounting Command's Intelligence Directorate, Korea Section, as a Korean War analyst. He has assisted with investigations in the People's Republic of China, Democratic People's Republic of Korea, and Republic of Korea in support of the JPAC mission.

G. Michael Pratt, Ph.D., is associate vice president for adult programs, dean of graduate studies, and professor of anthropology at Heidelberg College, Tiffin, Ohio. He received his B.A. in anthropology from Miami University of Ohio and his M.A. and Ph.D. in anthropology from Case Western Reserve University. He has conducted archaeological research on prehistoric and historic sites in the Ohio Valley–Great Lakes for over 30 years. He has carried out projects at forts and battlefields associated with the American Revolution, the Fallen Timbers campaign of 1794, the War of 1812, and the American Civil War via Heidelberg's Center for Historic and Military Archaeology. He is active in the efforts to develop both the Fallen Timbers Battlefield (1794) and the River Raisin Battlefield (1813) as units within the National Park System.

Tony Pollard is director of the Centre for Battlefield Archaeology, University of Glasgow. He was co-organizer of the first Fields of Conflict conference which was held in Glasgow in 2000. He has carried out numerous archaeological projects on battlefields in the UK and elsewhere and is co-editor of the *Journal of Conflict Archaeology*.

Jamie Pringle has a Ph.D. in petroleum engineering from Heriot-Watt University and has held positions in applied geophysics, sedimentology/stratigraphy, reservoir modeling and visualization. He currently holds a lectureship in applied geophysics and data visualization at Keele University.

Pedro Pype received his master's degree in archaeology in 1999. In 2000 he started to work for the Flemish Heritage Institute as a scientific employee. Between 2002 and 2003 he was responsible for the daily management of the excavations on the A19 project. At the moment he is working for the municipality of Maldegem within the framework of the ROMA project. This contains the historical and archaeological research and presentation of the heritage of Middelburg. In his spare time he is still active within WWI heritage studies, more specifically the study of British structures and equipment.

Simon Richardson is a professional metal detectorist with 30 years experience. For the last 20 years he has been studying the battlefield at Towton, England (1461) where he has recovered and recorded over 1,400 artifacts. He has also worked on the English battlefields at Blore Heath, Shrewsbury, Marston Moor, and Bosworth. He was involved with the Granada Television production *Blood Red Roses* and the *Battlefield Detectives* programs on Agincourt and Balaclava.

Achim Rost is a prehistoric archaeologist; his former studies dealt with settlement archaeology of mountainous regions in northern Germany. In the

1990s he organized exhibitions about the Kalkriese project. During the past years he has been working methodically on processes on battlefields like looting and treatment of the dead.

Douglas Scott, Ph.D., is retired from the U.S. National Park Service. He is currently an adjunct professor, department of anthropology and geography, University of Nebraska, Lincoln, and an adjunct professor, master's of forensic science program, Nebraska Wesleyan University, Lincoln. He specializes in nineteenth-century military and battlefield sites archaeology and forensics. He was awarded the Department of the Interior's Distinguished Service Award in 2002 for his innovative research in battlefield archaeology that started with his work at the Little Bighorn Battlefield National Monument.

Jay Silverstein is a forensic archaeologist with the Joint POW/MIA Accounting Command–Central Identification Laboratory, Hawaii. His expertise is in military and Mesoamerican archaeology. His fieldwork has included sites in Mexico, Guatemala, England, New Guinea, South Korea, North Korea, Vietnam, and Laos.

Daniel M. Sivilich has a B.S. in chemical engineering from New Jersey Institute of Technology with postgraduate studies in computer science. He has been conducting electronic archaeological surveys at the Battle of Monmouth since 1987. He has worked on numerous battlefield sites in the United States and abroad and has been featured on the History Channel's *Battlefield Detectives* series.

Steven D. Smith is the associate director for applied research at the South Carolina Institute of Archaeology and Anthropology, University of South Carolina, and also directs the Military Sites Program at the institute.

Tim Sutherland, PIFA, M.Sc., B.Sc., is an honorary research fellow in battlefield archaeology at the University of Bradford, England, and is currently writing up his Ph.D. thesis on the archaeological evidence of the Battle of Towton (1461 AD). He has co-written a book entitled *Blood Red Roses: The archaeology of a mass grave from the Battle of Towton AD 1461* and has written several papers on, given numerous conference papers relating to, and has assisted in the production of several television documentaries also relating to the archaeology of battle. He has carried out archaeological fieldwork on the historic battlefields of Agincourt, France (1415 AD) and Marston Moor, England (1644 AD). He is the founder of the Conflict Archaeology International Research Network (CAIRN), a group of individuals from around the world who research the archaeological remains of conflict, both ancient and modern.

Robert Warden is an associate professor in the department of architecture and associate director of the Center for Heritage Conservation. He has been a member of the faculty at Texas A&M for 11 years after coming from Drexel University's Architectural Engineering Program in Philadelphia, Pennsylvania. His primary research focus concerns techniques for documenting and interpreting historic buildings and sites with projects such as: Cathedral St. Just in Narbonne, France; Abbey Valmagne, Meze, France; Fort Pulaski National Monument, Savannah, Georgia; Montezuma Castle National Monument, Camp Verde, Arizona; and Pointe-du-Hoc Battlefield, Normandy, France.

Susanne Wilbers-Rost is a prehistoric archaeologist and specialist for Roman Iron Age in Northern Germany. From the beginning of the project in 1990 she has been responsible for archaeological excavations in Kalkriese; in 2000 she became head of the archaeological department in Museum and Park Kalkriese.

David Woodcock, FAIA, FSA, FAPT, is professor of architecture and director of the Center for Heritage Conservation at Texas A&M University, where he coordinates the cross-disciplinary graduate certificate in historic preservation. He is a past president of the Association for Preservation Technology International (APT) and serves on the advisory group of the American Institute of Architects Historic Resources Committee.